BY THE SAME AUTHOR

The Encyclopedia of Planning Law and Practice (4 Vols.)
The Land and Development; or, the Turmoil and The Torment (1975 Hamlyn Lectures)

AUSTRALIA AND NEW ZEALAND
The Law Book Company Ltd.
Sydney : Melbourne : Perth

CANADA AND U.S.A.
The Carswell Company Ltd.
Agincourt, Ontario

INDIA
N. M. Tripathi Private Ltd.
Bombay
and
Eastern Law House (Private) Ltd.
Calcutta and Delhi
M.P.P. House
Bangalore

ISRAEL
Steimatzky's Agency Ltd.
Jerusalem : Tel Aviv : Haifa

MALAYSIA : SINGAPORE : BRUNEI
Malayan Law Journal (Pte.) Ltd.
Singapore and Kuala Lumpur

PAKISTAN
Pakistan Law House
Karachi

Photograph—Jon Whitbourne, 1986.

An Outline of Planning Law

By

Sir Desmond Heap, LL.M., HON.LL.D.

Comptroller and City Solicitor to the Corporation of London 1947–1973
President of the Law Society 1972–1973
Master of the Worshipful Company of Solicitors of the City of London 1965–1966
Associate Member of the Royal Institution of Chartered Surveyors
President of the Royal Town Planning Institute 1955–56
Honorary Assistant, Worshipful Company of Chartered Surveyors
Honorary Member of the Incorporated Society of Valuers and Auctioneers
Honorary Member of the American Bar Foundation
Gold Medallist, the Royal Town Planning Institute, 1983
Gold Medallist, the Lincoln Institute of Land Policy, U.S.A., 1983
Honorary Life Member, Council of the International Bar Association
Honorary Life President, the International Bar Association, Section on General Practice
General Editor: Encyclopedia of Planning Law and Practice
Member: Editorial Board, Journal of Planning and Environmental Law

NINTH EDITION

LONDON
SWEET & MAXWELL
1987

First Edition	1949
Second Edition	1955
Third Edition	1960
Fourth Edition	1963
Fifth Edition	1969
Second Impression	1971
Sixth Edition	1973
Seventh Edition	1978
Eighth Edition	1982
Ninth Edition	1987

Published by
Sweet & Maxwell Ltd. of
11 New Fetter Lane, London
Computerset by Promenade Graphics Ltd., Cheltenham
and printed in Great Britain by
Butler and Tanner, Frome, Somerset

British Library Cataloguing in Publication Data

Heap, *Sir* Desmond
An outline of planning law.—9th ed.
1. City planning and redevelopment law—England 2. Regional planning—Law and legislation—England
I. Title
344.2064'5 KD1125

ISBN 0–421–35440–2
ISBN 0–421–35450–X Pbk

PREFACE

"Five years have past; five Summers, with the length
Of five long Winters! and again I hear
These waters, rolling from their mountain springs
With a soft inland murmur . . . ."

Lines composed above Tintern Abbey, on
revisiting the Banks of the Wye, 1798
—W. Wordsworth

Part 1—Today

1. Bearing in mind his outburst (by pamphleteering sonnet) in 1844 on the plans for the projected Kendal and Windermere Railway, I wonder what Mr. William Wordsworth would have had to say today about the seething cauldron of planning Acts, Rules, Regulations, Orders and Circulars which has bubbled so energetically during the five years—the "five Summers" with that length of "five long Winters"—which have elapsed since the publication of the last edition of this *Outline*, spilling out, during that time, no less than 9 Acts of Parliament, 26 Statutory Instruments and some 23 Departmental Circulars, all strictly relevant to the "story" which this book is seeking to tell. Yes, I wonder what the Reverberating Poetic Environmentalist (his fashionable styling today) would have had to say? Indeed, what would he *not* have had to say, for he was a great talker and an even greater writer?

2. The need for this Ninth Edition has become increasingly pressing. Because of this I should explain that its publication has twice been deliberately delayed by me so that, when eventually published the book would bring the long running, on-going saga of planning control over the land and its development *bang* up to date—or, at least, as up to date as it is possible to make it in a kaleidoscopic system.

3. Thus, this edition has picked up *all* the aforementioned 9 Acts of Parliament passed since 1981, namely:

(1) The Planning Inquiries (Attendance of Public) Act 1982;
(2) The Local Government (Miscellaneous Provisions) Act 1982;
(3) The National Heritage Act 1983;
(4) The Town and Country Planning Act 1984;
(5) The Town and Country Planning (Compensation) Act 1985;
(6) The Town and Country Planning (Amendment) Act 1985;
(7) The Local Government (Access to Information) Act 1985;
(8) The Local Government Act 1985; and
(9) The Housing and Planning Act 1986.

In addition nearly every one of the aforesaid 26 Statutory Instruments and 23 Departmental Circulars from the Department of the Environment is commented upon in this edition, while a host of new planning cases from the Courts has been included.

4. All this has called for much re-writing of earlier material and the inclusion of several new chapters consequent upon not only the abolition of the Metropolitan County Councils (and the Greater London Council) but also the heralded emergence of Unitary Development Plans (in Metropolitan Districts and in Greater London) and Simplified Planning Zones in those areas agreed by the Secretary of State for the Environment.

5. The vexed questions of planning gain and the use and misuse of planning conditions have, today, so developed in influence and importance that they now claim a chapter to themselves—Chapter 11—as do the associated sensitive matters of conservation areas, National Parks and areas of outstanding natural beauty—Chapter 9—matters into which a strongly based environmental lobby has now got its teeth firmly fixed—to the chagrin of property development companies, entrepreneurial activists and all who would have doings with the land.

6. May I draw attention to the Diagrams (all five of them) appearing at pages 50 *et seq*. They are intended to show (at something like a stroke—or is it "a glance"—as I fondly venture to hope) the "lay-out" of local government and the machinery of planning control as these things have recently functioned, as they function today (February 1987) and as they *will* function in the future when the new and important planning provisions of the Housing and Planning Act 1986 (which received the Royal Assent on November 7, 1986 in the very nick of time before Parliament was prorogued) come into operation as, in due course, they will come into operation, from time to time and place to place, as appropriate Commencement Orders are made under that Act by the Secretary of State for the Environment.

7. I would also mention that the extended detail of the Table of Contents (at page xi *et seq.*) is, again, meant to give a quick overview of what this book is all about. I suggest that, in order to get the full "background to be broadcast," it will be no bad thing to read the Table of Contents straight through—*for its own sake*, as it were.

8. An earlier edition of this book was translated, by a professional linguist and planner at the University of Tokyo, into Japanese. This was encouraging to me and brought along invitations to lecture at the University of Tokyo which I did (in English!) on two occasions. But I found myself most deeply moved of all when presented with a request, some years ago, for permission to put the book into Braille so that blind students could read it. Last year came a further request

to translate portions of the then current edition into Braille. I need hardly say that these requests were readily and freely agreed by me. I felt honoured and humbled—all at the same time. I fervently hope that these esoteric translations are doing good for those whose "light is spent" and who wonderously contrive to read books by the touch of sensitive and dexterous fingers.

* * * * * *

Part II—The Future

9. As to the future I must warn my readers (in all boldness I use the plural) that the Town and Country Planning (Use Classes) Order 1972 (S.I. 1972 No. 1385) and the Town and Country Planning General Development Order 1977 (S.I. 1977 No. 289)—as heavily amended—are now ripe for reform, revision and refinement. Both are currently going the rounds of local government authorities and professional organisations for comments on proposed alterations. This has been the case for months (nay, years) and I decided that this Ninth Edition of the *Outline* could no longer wait upon events. My guess is that within the next few months a new Use Classes Order and maybe a new General Development Order will be with us and my readers will be good enough to bear this in mind particularly when reading Chapters 8 and 10 of this book.

10. But more dramatic things are promised. Mr. Nicholas Ridley, the Secretary of State for the Environment, has it in mind (he broke the news in a keynote speech at the Town and Country Planning Summer School of the Royal Town Planning Institute at Nottingham on September 15, 1986) to replace the present two-tier system of structure plans and local plans in non-metropolitan counties (*i.e.* shire counties) by a single-tier system of development plans as is the forthcoming routine for metropolitan districts which lost their county councils on April 1, 1986—see Chapter 6. In short, the shire counties, in the business of plan-making, are to follow in the wake of the metropolitan counties. But the metropolitan counties lost (as mentioned) their county councils *in toto*. When this occurred there were those of us who trembled for the local government future of the shire county councils. We could have been wrong to do this. Today it looks as though we were right. With the metropolitan county councils gone, what is the betting on the continued existence of the shire county councils? And if *they* go, what follows? Regional Councils? And if we get regional councils will not somebody be asking: whatever happened to *local* government? He might even quote Kipling:

"Wider still and wider
Shall thy bounds be set . . ."

All this will require legislation. Accordingly, it is not going to happen tomorrow. The Queen's Speech on the opening of the new Parliamentary Session, November 12, 1986, made no mention of it. But the reader may care to bear these things in mind when he reads Chapters 4, 5 and 6 of this book. A consultation paper, "The Future of Development Plans," was issued by the Department of the Environment in September 1986.

11. Suggestions for the shape of planning things to come are given in three recent publications—the Fifth Report of the House of Commons Environment Committee, Session 1985–1986; the Government's response thereto entitled, "Planning: Appeals, Call-In and major Public Inquiries," and the Report (October 1986) of the Nuffield Foundation on "Town and Country Planning." These publications provide relevant additional reading for anyone interested in the contents of this ninth Edition but considered comment upon them in this "Outline" must await some further edition. Time alone will show whether they are to be acted upon or whether they are to be carefully, but irrevocably, filed.

* * * * * *

12. Finally, may I emphasise that the planning Circulars, issued from time to time by the Department of the Environment, are of the utmost importance to anyone owning, or thinking of owning, land. This is so, in my opinion, whether or not he is thinking of developing his land. These Circulars disclose, better than anything else I know, what, in any given case, is relevant government policy. Never forget, planning control of the land and its development *is rooted in government policy*. That is why these Circulars are so important. A full list of them is set out in the List of Circulars and Information appearing at page lxiii *et seq*.

13. I have made frequent reference to these Circulars in this Edition and I have quoted extensively from several of them. The Crown copyright material in this publication is reproduced with the kind permission of the Controller of Her Majesty's Stationery Office, for which permission I am grateful.

At the Sign of the Barbican,
In the City of London,
February 1987

CONTENTS

TABLE OF CASES

TABLE OF STATUTES

TABLE OF STATUTORY INSTRUMENTS

TOWN AND COUNTRY PLANNING
LIST OF MINISTERIAL CIRCULARS AND INFORMATION

from the Department of the Environment or its Predecessors

Ministry of Housing and Local Government Circulars

CIRCULAR NUMBER	
94/52	Town and Country Planning (Housing Accommodation) Direction 1952
42/55	Green Belts
46/55	The Recoveries from Acquiring Authorities Regulations, 1955
50/57	Green Belts
9/58	Report of the Committee on Administrative Tribunals and Enquiries
25/58	1. Planning Application for Petrol Stations 2. Control of Development Alongside Special Roads to be Provided by the Minister of Transport and Civil Aviation under the Special Roads Act, 1949
48/59	Town and Country Planning Act, 1959, with Explanatory Memorandum
44/61	Surface Development in Coal Mining Areas
49/62	Town and Country Planning Appeals (Inquiries Procedure) Rules, 1962
22/63	Design Bulletin: Landscaping for Flats with particular reference to High Density Schemes
33/63	Development near Railways; Risk of Fire Spread from Storage Areas; Notification to the Ministry of Aviation of Buildings, Works, etc. of 300 feet or Over
58/63	Recovery of Planning Compensation
58/65	Development Plans
73/65	Award of Costs at Statutory Inquiries
39/67	Town and Country Planning General Development Order 1963
12/68	Grants to local authorities: Comprehensive redevelopment and public open space
29/68	Planning control of radio masts
67/68	Planning Inquiry Commissions
15/69	Act of 1968—Part IV: Acquisition and disposal of land
33/70	Sports Facilities and the Planning Acts

Ministry Directions

Notification of applications for listed building consent, and decisions thereon (Circular 23/77, para. 54)

Town and Country Planning (Development Plans) (England) Direction 1981

Town and Country Planning (Control of Advertisements) Direction 1984

Town and Country Planning (Development Plans) (Greater London) Direction 1986

Welsh Office Circulars

30/80	Land for Private Housebuilding

WELSH OFFICE CIRCULARS—*cont.*

CIRCULAR NUMBER	
61/81	Historic Buildings and Conservation Areas—Policy and Procedure
47/84	Land for Housing in Wales
30/86	Housing for Senior Management

MINISTRY CIRCULAR LETTERS

3.6.1970	MHLG Directions under Article 4 of the General Development Order
30.1.1974	DOE Article 4 Directions

DEVELOPMENT CONTROL POLICY NOTES

1969/1	General principles
1969/2	Development in residential areas
1969/3	Industrial and commercial development
1969/4	Development in rural areas
1969/5	Development in town centres
1969/6	Road Safety and traffic requirements
1969/7	Preservation of historic buildings and areas
1969/8	Caravan sites
1969/9	Petrol filling stations and motels
1969/10	Design
1970/11	[Service Uses in Shopping Areas]
1972/12	Hotels and Motels
1972/13	Large New Stores
1974/14	Warehouses—wholesale, cash and carry, etc.
1975/15	Hostels and Homes
1985/16	Access for the Disabled

DEPARTMENT OF THE ENVIRONMENT CIRCULARS

82/70	Structure and Local Plans: a manual on form and content
56/71	Historic Towns and Roads
60/71	Town and Country Planning (Minerals) Regulations 1971
69/71	The Award of Costs at Statutory Inquiries—Determination of Amount in Case of Dispute
72/71	Disused railway lines in the Countryside
12/72	The Planning of the Undeveloped Coast
13/72	Development Control Policy Notes: Hotels and Motels
23/72	Planning Appeals and Applications—Forms
132/72	Planning Applications for Residential Development affecting the proposed line of a Trunk Road
10/73	Planning and Noise
12/73	Town and Country Planning General Development Order 1973
19/73	Building Regulations 1972; Town Centres and Shopping Precincts
24/73	Agricultural Dwellings (Annex only)
57/73	Lorries and the Environment
63/73	Local Government Act 1972: Administration of National Parks
71/73	Publicity for planning applications, appeals and other proposals for development
115/73	Long-distance lorries—National network of secure parks
38/74	Town and Country Planning (Inquiries Procedure) Rules 1974; Town and Country Planning Appeals (Determination by Appointed Persons) (Inquiries Procedure) Rules 1974

DEPARTMENT OF THE ENVIRONMENT CIRCULARS—*cont.*

CIRCULAR NUMBER	
62/74	Industrial and Commercial Developments
65/74	Local Government Act 1972: National Parks
79/74	New Streets
24/75	Housing—Needs and Action
4/76	Report of the National Parks Policies Review Committee
16/76	National Land Use Classification
20/76	The Petroleum and Submarine Pipe-Lines Act 1976
34/76	Consultation and consents for new electricity generating stations and overhead lines
71/76	Large New Stores
75/76	Development involving agricultural land
89/76	Town and Country Planning General Regulations
4/77	Town and Country Planning General Regulations 1976: Notification under reg. 11
17/77	Derelict Land
23/77	Listed Buildings and Conservation Areas
28/77	Gypsy Caravan Sites
43/77	New Towns Special Development Order 1976
49/77	Redevelopment of Contaminated Land
73/77	Guidelines for Regional Recreational Strategies
82/77	Town and Country Planning (Amendment) Act 1977
94/77	New Streets
96/77	Large New Stores
108/77	Nature Conservation and Planning
109/77	Enforcement of Planning Control—Established Use Certificates
125/77	Roads and Traffic: National Parks
1/78	Report of the Committee on Planning Control over Mineral Working
12/78	Report of the Mobile Homes Review
29/78	Control of Pollution Act 1974: Waste on Land
36/78	Trees and Forestry
37/78	Planning Permission—A Guide for Industry
57/78	Accommodation for Gypsies: Report by Sir John Cripps
58/78	Report of the Committee on Planning Control over Mineral Working
13/79	Local Government and the Development of Tourism
14/79	Town and Country Planning (Minerals) Regulations 1971: Time-limited planning permissions
26/79	Index to Circulars and Publications
22/80	Development Control—Policy and Practice
2/81	Development Control Functions: Act of 1980
8/81	Local Government, Planning and Land Act 1980—Various Provisions
9/81	Town and Country Planning General Development (Amendment) Order 1981; Town and Country Planning (National Parks, Areas of Outstanding Natural Beauty and Conservation Areas) Special Development Order 1981; Town and Country Planning (Fees for Applications and Deemed Applications) Regulations
12/81	Historic Buildings and Conservation Areas
26/81	Local Government and Planning (Amendment) Act 1981
32/81	Wildlife and Countryside Act 1981
38/81	Planning and Enforcement Appeals
39/81	Safeguarding of Aerodromes, Technical Sites and Explosives Storage Areas: Town and Country Planning (Aerodromes) Direction 1981

DEPARTMENT OF THE ENVIRONMENT CIRCULARS—*cont.*

CIRCULAR NUMBER	
1/82	Town and Country Planning (Minerals) Act 1981
10/82	Disabled Persons Act 1981
17/82	Development in Flood Risk Areas—Liaison Between Planning Authorities and Water Authorities
21/82	Guidelines for Aggregates Provision in England and Wales
1/83	Public Rights of Way
4/83	Wildlife and Countryside Act: Financial Guidelines for Management Agreements
13/83	Purchase Notices
22/83	Town and Country Planning Act 1971. Planning Gain. Obligations and Benefits which Extend Beyond the Development for which Planning Permission has been sought
23/83	Caravan Sites and Control of Development Act 1960
25/83	The Town and Country Planning (Fees for Applications and Deemed Applications) 1983
28/83	Publication by Local Authorities of Information about the Handling of Planning Applications
1/84	Crime Prevention
3/84	Opencast Coal Mining
8/84	Establishment of the Historic Buildings and Monuments Commission for England
9/84	Planning Controls over Hazardous Development
11/84	Town and Country Planning (Control of Advertisements) Regulations 1984
14/84	Green Belts
15/84	Land for Housing
16/84	Industrial Development
18/84	Crown Land and Crown Development
22/84	Memorandum on Structure and Local Plans: The Town and Country Planning Act 1971: Part II (as amended by the Town and Country Planning (Amendment) Act 1972, The Local Government Act 1972, and the Local Government, Planning and Land Act 1980)
23/84	Procedure for informing the Historic Buildings and Monuments Commission for England of Applications for Planning Permission and for Listed Building Consent
1/85	The use of conditions in planning permissions
2/85	Planning Control over Oil and Gas Operations
6/85	Compulsory Purchase Orders: Procedures
14/85	Development and Employment
15/85	Town and Country Planning (Compensation) Act 1985
16/85	Telecommunication Development
19/85	Town and Country Planning (Fees for Applications and Deemed Applications) (Amendment) Regulations 1985
20/85	Town and Country Planning Act 1971: Enforcement Appeals and Advertisement Appeals
24/85	Guidelines for the Provision of Silica Sand in England and Wales
25/85	Mineral Workings—Legal Aspects Relating to Restoration of Sites with a High Water Table
27/85	Review of the Economic Efficiency of National Park Authorities
28/85	Reclamation and Re-use of Derelict Land
29/85	Planning Development Grant

DEPARTMENT OF THE ENVIRONMENT CIRCULARS—*cont.*

CIRCULAR NUMBER	
30/85	Local Government Act 1985: Sections 3, 4 and 5: Schedule 1 Town and Country Planning: Transitional Matters
31/85	Aesthetic Control
2/86	Development by Small Businesses
3/86	Changes to the General Development Order
6/86	Local Government (Access to Information) Act 1985
8/86	Local Government Act 1985
11/86	Town and Country Planning (Minerals) Act 1981
17/86	Town and Country Planning (Agricultural and Forestry Development in National Parks etc.) Special Development Order 1986
18/86	Planning Appeals decided by Written Representations
19/86	Housing and Planning Act 1986: Planning Permissions
21/86	Town and Country Planning (Shopping Development) (England and Wales) Direction 1986
1/87	Town and Country Planning (Fees for Applications and Deemed Applications) (Amendment) Regulations 1987
2/87	Awards of Costs Incurred in Planning and Compulsory Purchase Order Proceedings

COMMAND PAPERS

NUMBER	
Cmnd. 9571	Lifting the Burden — (July 1985)
Cmnd. 9794	Building Businesses Not Barriers — (May 1986)
Cm. 43	Planning: Appeals, Call-in and Major Public Inquiries. The Government's Response to the Fifth Report from the Environmental Committee, Session 1985–86 — (December 1986)

TABLE OF ABBREVIATIONS AND INTERPRETATIONS

A.C.	Appeal Cases
All E.R.	All England Reports
C.A.	Court of Appeal
D.C.	Divisional Court
E.G.	Estates Gazette
H.L.	House of Lords
J.P.L.	Journal of Planning and Environmental Law
L.G.R.	Local Government Reports
L.T.	Lands Tribunal
P. and C.R.	Planning and Compensation Reports
Q.B.	Queen's Bench
R.V.R.	Rating and Valuation Reports
S.C.	Scottish Court
W.L.R.	Weekly Law Reports
D.O.E.	Department of the Environment at 2 Marsham Street, London SW1P 3EB. Telephone 01-212-3434.
Metropolitan County	One of the six Metropolitan Counties, *viz*., Greater Manchester, Merseyside, South Yorkshire, Tyne and Wear, West Midlands, West Yorkshire, established by the Local Government Act 1972, section 1, Schedule 1
Metropolitan District	A District within a Metropolitan County
Shire County	A County (there are 47 of them) which is *not* one of the six Metropolitan Counties established by the Local Government Act 1972, section 1, Schedule 1.
Shire District	A District within a Shire County
1947 Act	Town and Country Planning Act 1947
1949 Act	National Parks and Access to the Countryside Act 1949
1959 Act	Town and Country Planning Act 1959
1968 Act	Town and Country Planning Act 1968
1971 Act	Town and Country Planning Act 1971
1972 Act	Local Government Act 1972
1973 Act	Land Compensation Act 1973
1974 Act	Town and Country Amenities Act 1974
1977 Act	Town and Country Planning (Amendment) Act 1977
1980 Act	Local Government, Planning and Land Act 1980
1981 Act	Local Government and Planning (Amendment) Act 1981
1983 Act	National Heritage Act 1983
1984 Act	Town and Country Planning Act 1984
1985 Act	Local Government Act 1985
1986 Act	Housing and Planning Act 1986

TABLE OF DIAGRAMS

CHAPTER 1

HISTORICAL OUTLINE

1. The Public Health Code—1848 to 1987

THERE are three clear-cut yet interrelated codes of legislation on the Statute Book and these are (to quote them in chronological order of enactment) the public health code, the housing code and the town planning code. It is impossible to consider in detail any one of these codes without having at least a passing knowledge of the other two and, accordingly, in the historical outline given in this chapter reference is made to all of them. Each in its particular sphere is important, but there can be no doubt that the most important, the most comprehensive and the most far-reaching of all three is, since the passing of the Town and Country Planning Act 1947, the planning code. Indeed, public health and housing, though they still retain their separate legislative codes, are but two of the many facets of town planning, and the town planning code is, theoretically, large enough to embrace the other two.

The Industrial Revolution in England, the invention of machinery and the introduction of the factory system into methods of manufacture brought about a general exodus from the country into the town. The rural areas became more and more sparsely populated as the towns, or urban areas, filled to overflowing with the great influx of people seeking work in the new manufacturing centres. Congestion and overcrowding in the towns were rampant and cheap, insanitary dwellings were hurriedly erected, sometimes in the shadow of the factories themselves, in an effort to provide shelter for all. The erection of the new buildings was not subjected to supervision or control by local authorities, for such things as building by-laws did not exist, and the new dwellings in consequence were built in close and unregulated proximity with little or no regard to the requirements of proper ventilation and sanitation.

This form of development with all its natural and deplorable consequences to the health of the public was allowed to continue for the most part unchecked until Parliament intervened with its first general enactment dealing with the subject of public health, the Public Health Act 1848. Such Acts as the Towns Improvement Clauses Act, the Town Police Clauses Act, and the Waterworks, Gasworks, Cemeteries and Markets and Fairs Clauses Acts had been passed by Parliament in the previous year, 1847, with the object of bringing about developments and improvements in connection with the particular matters to which each of the Acts referred. But these Acts were not of general application. They formed ready-made codes of legislation lying dormant until incorporated, by reference, into local Acts of Parliament obtained as a result of local initiative, after which they came into operation within the particular area covered by the local Act.

The Public Health Act 1848, however, was the first of a series of general Acts dealing with the public health which culminated in that monumental enactment, the Public Health Act 1875, which repealed and consolidated former enactments on the subject and embodied further legislation for the protection and improvement of the public health. By-laws with respect to new streets and buildings could be made by local authorities and control could thereby be obtained over the erection of *future* buildings and the laying out of *future* streets. The powers conferred on local authorities with reference to sanitary matters, the making up of private streets, the construction of new buildings, infectious diseases, nuisances and other matters directly connected with the public health by the 1875 Act have since been augmented by the provisions of further Public Health Acts (largely adoptive) passed in 1890, 1907 and 1925. The Public Health Act 1936 is largely a consolidating enactment repealing and re-enacting most (but not all) of the earlier statutes dealing with the subject and is now the principal Act on this subject.

The Public Health Act 1936 is amplified or amended or affected by the Public Health Act 1961, the Health Services and Public Health Act 1968, the Public Health (Recurring Nuisances) Act 1969, the Health and Safety at Work, Etc., Act 1974, the Control of Pollution Act 1974, the Local Government (Miscellaneous Provisions) Act 1976, the Refuse Disposal (Amenity) Act 1978, the Vaccine Damage Payments Act 1979, the Residential Homes Act 1980, the Water Act 1981, the Disabled Persons Act 1981, the Health And Social Services And Social Security Adjudications Act 1983, the Public Health (Control of Disease) Act 1984, the Registered Homes Act 1984 and the Building Act 1984.

The Public Health Acts could prevent a repetition of the building horrors which followed the rush to the towns during the Industrial Revolution, but they did not even pretend to deal with the problem of removing the slums which developed in the wake of that upheaval. Moreover, it was characteristic of public health law to cater for the particular and not the general; that is to say, each man's plot of land was regarded as an isolated entity entirely shut off from its neighbours and having no connection with them whatsoever. A man could develop his own plot in accordance, of course, with the requirements of local building by-laws, but otherwise in a fashion which paid not the slightest regard to the sort of development which was taking place, or which was likely to take place, on adjoining or neighbouring land. One could not be prevented from erecting dwelling-houses in unhealthy industrial districts and it was possible for industrial buildings to intrude upon the quietude of residential areas. This sort of thing was beyond the scope of the Public Health Acts and was left, as were the slums of the post-Industrial Revolution period, to be dealt with by a different type of legislation.

2. The Housing Code—1890 to 1987

There had been earlier statutes such as the Artisans' and Labourers' Dwellings Act 1868 and the Artisans' and Labourers' Dwellings Improvements Acts 1875 and 1879, dealing with housing accommodation, but the first real assault on the slums was made by the Housing of the Working Classes Act 1890, an Act which marks the first important stage in the new type of legislation known as housing law, and passed with a view to remedying the deficiencies of public health law regarding the housing of the working classes.

The Act of 1890 made provision for the removal of insanitary dwellings and for the supply of new houses for the working classes and began a series of enactments on the subject of housing which culminated in the Housing Act 1925, which repealed and replaced the 1890 Act as the principal Act dealing with the law of housing.

The Housing Act 1925 was amended several times before yielding place, in 1936, to a further consolidating measure, the Housing Act 1936, which thereupon became the principal Act on the subject. This Act was, in its turn and after much amendment between 1936 and 1956, during which all references to "the working classes" were eliminated from the legislation, repealed (with the exception of certain financial and ancillary provisions) and replaced by a new consolidating measure, namely, the Housing Act 1957.

Financial matters relating to housing were themselves consolidated and dealt with in the Housing (Financial Provisions) Act 1958, the House Purchase and Housing Act 1959, the Housing Act 1980 and the Housing Act 1985.

The Housing Act 1957 and the Housing (Financial Provisions) Act 1958 were amended by the Housing (Underground Rooms) Act 1959, the Housing Act 1961, the Housing Act 1964, the Housing (Slum Clearance Compensation) Act 1965, the Housing Subsidies Act 1967, the Housing Act 1969, the Housing Act 1971, the Housing Finance Act 1972, the Housing (Amendment) Act 1973, the Furnished Lettings (Rent Allowances) Act 1973 the Housing Act 1974, the Housing Rents and Subsidies Act 1975 and the Housing (Homeless Persons) Act 1977, all of which could be cited together as the Housing Acts 1957 to 1977 (1977 Act, s.21(2)).

Notwithstanding all the foregoing statutory additions and amendments, the Housing Act 1957 remained the principal Act on housing until the enactment of the Housing Act 1985 on October 30, 1985.

The Housing Act 1985 came into operation on April 1, 1986 and is now the definitive legislative statement on housing matters. It is a monumental piece of work comprising 625 sections and 24 Schedules occupying some 353 pages of a Queen's Printer's copy of the Act. Its long title declares it to be,

> "An Act to consolidate the Housing Acts (except those provisions consolidated in the Housing Associations Act 1985 and the Landlord and Tenant Act 1985), and certain related provisions, with amendments to give effect to recommendations of the Law Commission."

It is not limited in its scope to any particular class of persons or income groups but is of general application to all sorts of persons.

Briefly the main purposes of the Housing Act 1985 may be said to be three in number, that is to say:

1. to make statutory arrangements for the *Provision of Housing* by legislating as to:
   (1) the provision of housing accommodation (Part II of the Act);
   (2) housing for the homeless (Part III) of the Act);
   (3) making tenancies secure and giving rights to secure tenants (Part IV of the Act); and
   (4) the provision of a right to buy (Part V of the Act);
2. to make statutory arrangements relating to *Housing Conditions* by legislating as to:
   (1) repair notices (Part VI of the Act);
   (2) improvement notices (Part VII of the Act);
   (3) area improvement (Part VIII of the Act);
   (4) slum clearance (Part IX of the Act);
   (5) overcrowding (Part X of the Act);
   (6) houses in multiple occupation (Part XI of the Act);
   (7) common lodging houses (Part XII of the Act); and
3. to make statutory arrangements concerning *Financial Provisions* relating to housing by legislating as to:
   (1) general financial provisions (Part XIII of the Act);
   (2) loans for the acquisition or improvement of housing (Part XIV of the Act);
   (3) grants for works of improvement, repair and conversion of houses (Part XV of the Act);

(4) assistance for owners of defective housing (Part XVI of the Act).

There are also two shorter consolidating Acts relating to housing. One is the Housing Associations Act 1985 (dealing with housing associations) and the other is the Landlord and Tenant Act 1985 (containing miscellaneous provisions affecting landlords and tenants which provisions were, in the main, formerly found in housing legislation).

Lastly, there is the Housing (Consequential Provisions) Act 1985 which deals with a number of technical matters—repeals, consequential amendments, transitional provisions and savings—all of which arise from the three housing consolidation Acts of 1985 above mentioned.

D.O.E. Circular 10/86, dated March 21, 1986 deals with the consolidation of housing law in these three Acts.

3. The Town Planning Code—1909 to 1987

If public health law and also, to a more limited extent, housing law were the product of the nineteenth century, town planning law is the creature of the twentieth. The Housing Acts, remedying one defect of the Public Health Acts, might deal with the slums and with the provision of new dwellings, but there was still (to put the matter quite shortly) the problem of the dwelling-house built in the shadow of the factory and of the factory erected in the midst of the garden suburb. Housing law did not cater for them any more than did public health law, but it was felt that the matter was associated more with the subject of housing than with that of public health and, accordingly, in 1909 it was housing law which introduced town planning law into the parliamentary arena in the Housing, Town Planning, etc., Act of that year, Part I of which dealt with the "Housing of the Working Classes" and Part II with "Town Planning."

The Housing, Town Planning, etc., Act 1909

The Act of 1909 is, in fact, the first enactment in Great Britain to deal with the subject of town planning. By section 54 of the Act local authorities were empowered to make a

> "town planning scheme . . . as respects any land which is in course of development or appears likely to be used for building purposes, with the general object of securing proper sanitary conditions, amenity and convenience in connection with the laying out and use of the land and of any neighbouring lands."

Here at last was an opportunity of controlling not merely the construction of individual buildings (that was possible under the Public Health Acts) but of building development *as a whole*, regarding the land of individual owners not as so many isolated plots but as parts of a greater whole and providing for the development of each plot not only in accordance with the requirements of local building by-laws but, in the words of section 54, with due regard to "amenity and convenience in connection with the laying out and use of the land and of any neighbouring lands." Thus residential districts could be safeguarded against the undesirable intrusion of industrial buildings (even though they *did* comply in all respects with the local building by-laws), and industrial areas could be set apart for the purpose of industrial development only.

These are some of the things which could be achieved by a local authority through the medium of a town planning scheme made under the 1909 Act. It was necessary for a local authoriy desirous of making a scheme first to obtain the approval of the Local Government Board to such course (1909 Act, s.54(2)), and the scheme itself, when made by the local authority, could not take effect until approved by the Board, which approval could not be given in certain circumstances until the scheme had been laid before Parliament (1909 Act, s.54(4)).

The Housing, Town Planning, etc., Act 1919

The planning machinery created by the Act of 1909 proved to be cumbersome and difficult of operation and improvements, which it was hoped would facilitate the making of schemes, were sought to be provided 10 years later by the Housing, Town Planning, etc., Act 1919, whereby the necessity of first obtaining the consent of the Local Government Board to the making of a scheme was in most cases removed (1919 Act, s.42), as was also removed the necessity of laying schemes before Parliament (1919 Act, s.44). Henceforth schemes were to come into force immediately upon being approved by the Board under section 54(4) of the 1909 Act.

Section 45 of the 1919 Act first introduced the subject of interim development whereby, during the preparation of a scheme, development of land might continue and the developer yet remain certain (assuming he followed the instructions of section 45) of obtaining compensation in respect of his development if it was later injuriously affected by the making of the scheme.

Section 46 of the 1919 Act attempted to stimulate the making of schemes by rendering it *obligatory* for certain local authorities with a population of 20,000 to prepare and submit planning schemes for approval within a specified period, and by section 47 it was open to the Local Government Board to *require* a local authority to prepare a scheme if satisfied that, in the circumstances, a scheme ought to be made. Voluntary planning was thus replaced in certain instances by compulsory planning and the first hint of regional planning appeared in a provision in section 42 to the effect that two or more authorities might agree to act together in the making of a town planning scheme and appoint a joint committee for that purpose.

The Ministry of Health Act 1919

In 1919 the Local Government Board was succeeded by the Ministry of Health established under the provisions of the Ministry of Health Act 1919 and all town planning matters which previously were referred by local authorities to the Local Government Board came under the control of the Ministry of Health, which remained the central authority for all matters appertaining to town planning until the establishment in 1943 of the Ministry of Town and Country Planning.

The Housing, etc., Act 1923

By the Housing, etc., Act 1923, Part II of which dealt with town planning, further slight amendments were made in planning law, the most important of which was the power given (1923 Act, s.20) to an authority responsible for the administration of a town planning scheme to withdraw or modify any provisions in the scheme which had given rise to an award of compensation in respect of injurious affection being made against the authority.

Until 1925 housing and town planning had gone hand in hand onto the Statute Book, but each of the subjects had assumed such large proportions and importance in 1925 that, when the law on the two matters was consolidated, a divorce was effected, housing being diverted into the Housing Act 1925 and town planning into the Town Planning Act 1925.

The Town Planning Act 1925

The 1925 Act consolidated the former planning enactments without introducing any remarkable new features, but further provisions of importance were enacted in the Local Government Act 1929.

The Local Government Act 1929

County councils had not so far been able to take any active part in the preparation of schemes except in a case where, under section

47(3) of the 1919 Act, the Local Government Board empowered a county council to act in place of a county district council which had failed to prepare a town planning scheme on being ordered so to do by the Local Government Board. But by the Local Government Act 1929, power was first given to county councils (1929 Act, s.40) to act jointly with other local authorities in the preparation of planning schemes and (1929 Act, s.42) to play the part of an authority responsible for enforcing and carrying into effect the provisions of a scheme. Moreover county district councils were entitled to relinquish to a county council their planning powers and functions under the 1925 Act (1929 Act, s.43).

Town and Country Planning Act 1932

Such was the state of affairs when the Town and Country Planning Act 1932 was passed. This Act repealed the whole of the former enactments dealing with town planning (including those sections of the Local Government Act 1929 previously mentioned) and re-enacted the law in consolidated form and with many important changes. It came into force on April 1, 1933.

The most remarkable feature of the 1932 Act was that it permitted the town planning of built-up areas and also of land not likely to be developed at all, whereas only unbuilt land actually being, or likely to be, developed was formerly within the scope of the Town Planning Acts. This was a sweeping extension of the town planning powers of local authorities. The 1932 Act reintroduced the necessity, abolished in 1919, of obtaining the consent of the Minister of Health (formerly the Local Government Board) to the making of a planning scheme and, once more, schemes had to be laid before Parliament before they could come into operation. The statutory obligation imposed on certain local authorities by the 1919 Act of preparing planning schemes within a limited period was repealed.

The 1932 Act secured control of development through the medium of town planning schemes (or planning schemes as they came to be called after 1932) made by local authorities and confirmed by the Minister of Health. When in operation the letter of a planning scheme was binding equally upon the authority who made it and upon those who sought to undertake development within the area to which it related. A planning scheme was by nature rigid and if, by effluxion of time, it became out of touch with what were for the time being the best ideas in planning, it could only be amended by some further planning scheme made in accordance with the involved machinery established by the 1932 Act for that purpose.

Prior to the coming into operation of a planning scheme

developers could develop under the protection of Interim Development Orders made under the 1932 Act. Interim development control was not, however, enforceable until the Town and Country Planning (Interim Development) Act 1943 came into force but if a developer developed in accordance with interim development control he could claim compensation when the relevant planning scheme ultimately came into operation if it was *then* found that his development contravened any provisions of the scheme and accordingly had to be removed or stopped.

Any person who sustained injurious affection by reason of the coming into operation of a planning scheme could claim compensation therefor from the local authority responsible for carrying out the scheme and, conversely, such authority could claim 75 per cent. of the increase in value (or betterment, as it was popularly called) of property resulting from the provisions of the scheme. In fact few planning schemes ever came into operation at all with the result that, on the one hand, little compensation ever came to be paid by responsible authorities (though the potential liability for it often led them to give decisions based not so much on the dictates of good planning as upon those associated with financial considerations) and, on the other hand, little betterment was ever recovered by them.

The extended scope of the 1932 Act, especially the application of its provisions to built-up areas, was responsible for the increased complexity of many of its sections. It was symbolic of the change which had taken place that the 1932 Act contained 58 sections and 6 Schedules as compared with the 22 sections and 4 Schedules of the Town Planning Act 1925. The 1932 Act remained the principal Act relating to planning until the coming into force on July 1, 1948, of the Town and Country Planning Act 1947, which, with its 120 sections and 11 Schedules, made the 1932 Act a small thing indeed.

The Minister of Town and Country Planning Act 1943

Under the Town and Country Planning Act 1932 the central authority for all planning matters remained the Minister of Health and throughout the Act of 1932 references to "the Minister" meant the Minister of Health. This continued to be the position until, by virtue of the Minister of Works and Planning Act 1942, the powers and duties of the Minister of Health in connection with planning assigned to him by the Town and Country Planning Act 1932 were, with slight exceptions, transferred to the newly appointed Minister of Works and Planning. This state of affairs was, however, altered by the Minister of Town and Country Planning Act 1943, whereby provision was made for the transfer of the powers and duties exercisable under the Town and Country Planning Act 1932 by the Minister of Works and Planning to the newly established Minister of Town and Country Planning, the Minister of Works and Planning being renamed "the Minister of Works" and the Minister of Works and Planning Act 1942 being retitled "the Minister of Works Act 1942." The central authority for planning matters became the Ministry of Town and Country Planning and references throughout the Town and Country Planning Act 1932 to "the Minister" had to be construed as references to the Minister of Town and Country Planning, except in the amended sections 32 and 51(3) of the 1932 Act, in each of which "the Minister" remained the Minister of Health.

Thus did planning, after 34 years as the slightly irregular offspring of the Ministry of Health, ultimately achieve legitimacy by being graced with a Minister whose interests were not divided but were concerned entirely with matters of town and country planning. This arrangement was, however, short-lived, for in 1951 the style and title of the Minister of Town and Country Planning were changed to the "Minister of Local Government and Planning" by the Transfer of Functions (Minister of Health and Minister of Local Government and Planning) (No. 1) Order 1951,[1] and were later, in the same year, further changed to the "Minister of Housing and Local Government" by the Minister of Local Government and Planning (Change of Style and Title) Order 1951.[2]

The general function of the Minister of Housing and Local Government was set out in section 1 of the Act of 1943 whereby he was charged with the duty of "securing consistency and continuity in the framing and execution of a national policy with respect to the use and development of land throughout England and Wales."[3] In pursuance of this policy the Minister had conferred upon himself, by subsequent planning legislation, an increasing number of powers until his control over the use of land in town and country is now very strong indeed.

The Town and Country Planning (Interim Development) Act 1943

The first enactment to be steered to the Statute Book by the new Minister was the Town and Country Planning (Interim Development

[1] S.I. 1951 No. 142.

[2] S.I. 1951 No. 1900. But see now, at pp. 35, 36, the Secretary of State for the Environment Order 1970 (S.I. 1970 No. 1681) and a short dissertation on the constitutional effect of this important Order.

[3] These words were of importance while they lasted. On them, see further the dissertation at p. 36.

Act 1943. This Act brought all land in England and Wales not already subject to an operative planning scheme under interim development control and gave, for the first time, power to all interim development authorities to enforce such control.

The Town and Country Planning Act 1944

Notwithstanding its title, the major portion of this Act dealt not so much with planning but with land acquisition and new powers of acquiring land compulsorily (and, in exceptional cases, very speedily) for a variety of purposes in areas of extensive war damage (blitzed areas) and their associated overspill areas and also in areas of bad layout and obsolete development (blighted areas) and their associated overspill areas.

This Act introduced the important new concept of *positive* town planning (as it has been called) by empowering local planning authorities to undertake themselves (subject to certain restrictions) the actual development of their own areas. It also introduced the "1939 standard" for compensation payable on the compulsory purchase of land, a standard later abolished by the Town and Country Planning Act 1947 and replaced by the principle of compensation based on the value of land for its existing use only. This latter principle, after modification under the Town and Country Planning Act 1954, was itself abolished under the Town and Country Planning Act 1959 and replaced (by provisions now to be found in the Land Compensation Act 1961) by the market value principle of compensation payable on the compulsory purchase of land.[4]

The Town and Country Planning Act 1947

The 1947 Act made an entirely new beginning by repealing all previous town planning legislation (re-enacting, however, in its own Eleventh Schedule some important provisions of the 1944 Act) and enacting principles entirely new to planning law. It was, on enactment, the principal Act relating to the control of land use in England and Wales.

It came into force on "the appointed day" which was July 1, 1948 (Town and Country Planning Act 1947 (Appointed Day) Order 1948).[5] It was amended by four subsequent Acts relating to town planning passed, respectively, in 1951, 1953, 1954 and 1959, and also by the Land Compensation Act 1961 on the particular matter of compensation payable on the compulsory purchase of land.

On the repeal, by the 1947 Act, of all previous town planning

[4] See Chap. 20.
[5] S.I. 1948 No. 213.

legislation, any town planning scheme operating under the Town and Country Planning Act 1932 or any of its predecessors—there were only a few of them covering a mere 4 per cent. of the land in England and Wales—ceased to function on July 1, 1948, the day when the 1947 Act began to operate.

The 1947 Act and its four town planning amending enactments were repealed and such of their provisions as had not become spent by lapse of time were consolidated in the Town and Country Planning Act 1962 which came into operation on "the commencement date," April 1, 1963 (1962 Act, s.225(1)). The 1962 Act thus became the principal Act relating to town and country planning in England and Wales until the further consolidating Act of 1971 (as to which more is said later in this chapter). It is the object of this historical review of town planning legislation, before reaching the 1962 Act, to trace, briefly, through the town planning Acts of 1951, 1953, 1954 and 1959, the development of town planning law from the principal Act of 1947 to its replacement by the principal Act of 1962.

It is impossible to exaggerate the importance of July 1, 1948, from the point of view of the local planning authority, the landowner or the building developer, for the 1947 Act (which, as stated, came into effect on that date) contained some of the most drastic and far-reaching provisions ever enacted affecting the ownership of land (which for this purpose includes buildings) and the liberty of an owner to develop and use his land as he thinks fit. Indeed, after July 1, 1948, ownership of land, generally speaking, carries with it nothing more than the bare right to go on using it for its existing purposes. The owner has no *right* to develop it, that is to say, he has no *right* to build upon it and no *right* even to change its use. Until the 1947 Act was amended by the Town and Country Planning Act 1954 a landowner selling his land could expect to obtain (in theory, at least) only its existing use value, because whatever development value the land had was expropriated by the State under the 1947 Act. The 1947 Act did not nationalise the land; what it did do was to nationalise the development value in land—a state of affairs which was reversed by the 1954 Act under which development value in land was returned to the landowner though, as will be seen later,[6] it is only development value which had accrued to land before January 7, 1947, which is compensated under the 1954 Act on the imposition of planning restrictions or on the compulsory purchase of land under a notice to treat served *before* October 30, 1958.

The objects of the 1947 Act may be grouped under seven headings and summarised as follows:

[6] See Chaps. 17 and 20.

(1) to replace the former system of planning control through the medium of rigid planning schemes by a new system of control through the medium of flexible development plans prepared by a greatly reduced number of planning authorities and subjected to constant review (Part II of the Act)[7];
(2) to prohibit (with exceptions) the carrying out of any kind of development whatsoever, and whether before or after the coming into operation of a development plan, without the consent of a local planning authority (Part III of the Act)[8];
(3) to provide for the levying by a new body, the Central Land Board, of development charges payable (with exceptions) on the carrying out of any kind of development (Part VII of the Act);
(4) to expropriate for the State the development value in all land and, in consequence, to enable landowners to make claims on a £300 million fund for loss of the development value of their land (Part VI of the Act);
(5) to confer upon local authorities wider powers for undertaking development themselves than they had ever previously held and, as a corollary to this, to confer upon such authorities wider powers for the compulsory acquisition of land (Part IV of the Act)[9];
(6) to provide increased financial assistance to local authorities to enable them to discharge their functions under the Act, including especially the acquisition of land and its development or redevelopment by the local authorities themselves (Part IX of the Act); and
(7) to amend the law relating to compensation for compulsory acquisition of land by abolishing the 1939 standard and substituting compensation based on existing use value only (Part V of the Act).

Objects numbered (3), (4) and (7) above have been substantially amended (as is shown below) by later legislation relating to town and country planning.

The Town and Country Planning (Amendment) Act 1951

This Act corrected certain drafting errors in the 1947 Act (particularly in relation to section 23 thereof) but did not disturb the main principles of the 1947 Act.

[7] See Chaps. 3, 4, 5, 6 and 7.
[8] See Chaps. 10 and 11.
[9] See Chaps. 19, 20 and 21.

The Town and Country Planning Act 1953

The financial portions of the 1947 Act relating respectively to the making of claims on the £300 million fund for loss of development value (Part VI of the 1947 Act) and to the payment of development charge before undertaking development (Part VII of the 1947 Act) were the subject of criticism between 1948 and 1952 with the result that the Government of the day produced the White Paper of November 1952 entitled, "Proposals for amending the Financial Provisions of the 1947 Act."[10]

The new financial structure for town planning, as outlined in the White Paper was brought into being first by the Town and Country Planning Act 1953, under which development charges were abolished for all development commenced on or after November 18, 1952 (the date of the introduction into Parliament of the Bill for the 1953 Act), and the distribution of the £300 million fund to successful claimants (a distribution due, under the 1947 Act, to take place in 1954) was suspended. The making of payments to those who suffered as a result of planning restrictions or requirements imposed in the public interest was left by the 1953 Act to be dealt with by subsequent legislation which followed in 1954.

The Town and Country Planning Act 1954

This Act, which came into force on January 1, 1955, completed the implementation, begun under the 1953 Act, of the provisions of the White Paper of 1952 by replacing the financial provisions of the 1947 Act with a new code of compensation payments. These payments were limited to the amount of the claims made under the 1947 Act on the £300 million fund but were to be paid not all at one given time (as was the arrangement under the 1947 Act) but only if and when a landowner was prevented from reaping the development value in his land by either:

(a) suffering the imposition of planning restrictions (subject to exceptions) which prevented or limited the development of his land; or

(b) having his land compulsorily acquired at its existing use value under a notice to treat served before October 30, 1958. (If the notice to treat is served on or after October 29, 1958, then the market value provisions of Part I of the Town and Country Planning Act 1959 will apply.)

The objects of the 1954 Act may be grouped under five headings and summarised as follows:

[10] Cmnd. 8699.

(1) to provide for the making of payments by the Central Land Board in respect of *past* matters and events (other than planning decisions occurring *before* the commencement of the Act (Part I of the Act);

(2) to provide for the payment of compensation by the Minister of Housing and Local Government in respect of *past* planning decisions occurring *before* the commencement of the Act (Part V of the Act);

(3) to provide for the payment of compensation by the Minister in respect of planning decisions occurring *after* the commencement of the Act (Part II of the Act)[11];

(4) to provide for the payment of compensation by public and local authorities in respect of *any* compulsory purchase of land under a notice to treat served *after* the commencement of the Act but *before* October 30, 1958 (Part III of the Act); and

(5) to provide for the payment of compensation by local planning authorities in respect of revocations or modifications of planning decisions occurring *after* the commencement of the Act (Part IV of the Act).

The Town and Country Planning Act 1959

After the coming into operation of the 1954 Act on January 1, 1955, there were two codes of compensation payable in respect of the acquisition of land. Development value in land having been, in effect, returned to the landowner by the operation of the 1953 Act in abolishing development charges, it followed that on a sale of his land a landowner had, after the commencement of the 1953 Act, clearly the right to sell not only the existing use rights in his land but also the development rights. Thus on a sale of land by private treaty the vendor could demand the current market value of the land. But on a sale of land to a public body purchasing under compulsory purchase powers the acquiring authority were precluded by the joint effect of the 1947 Act and the 1954 Act from paying more than the existing use value plus the 1947 development value of the land—in short, nothing was paid for post-1947 development values.

As time went on the discrepancy between the price payable under these two codes of compensation—the code applicable on a sale by private treaty and the code applicable on a sale under compulsory purchase powers—tended to get greater. This caused dissatisfaction which was commented upon in the Report of the Committee on

[11] See Chap. 17.

Administrative Tribunals and Inquiries 1957 (the Franks Report),[12] which declared (in para. 278):

> "One final point of great importance needs to be made. The evidence which we have received shows that much of the dissatisfaction with the procedures relating to land arises from the basis of compensation. It is clear that objections to compulsory purchase would be far fewer if compensation were always assessed at not less than market value. It is not part of our terms of reference to consider and make recommendations upon the basis of compensation. But we cannot emphasise too strongly the extent to which these financial considerations affect the matters with which we have to deal. Whatever changes in procedure are made dissatisfaction is, because of this, bound to remain."

Accordingly, the Government of the day decided in 1958 to bring to an end the double code of compensation payable on the acquisition of land and the result was the enactment of the Town and Country Planning Act 1959.

This Act came into force on August 16, 1959. Its objects may be grouped under six heads and summarised as follows:

(1) to provide for market value compensation (in lieu of compensation at the rate, under the 1954 Act, of existing use value plus 1947 development value) in the case of any compulsory purchase of land under a notice to treat served after October 29, 1958 (Part I of the Act)[13];

(2) to give local authorities and other public bodies greater freedom from Ministerial control in the acquisition, appropriation and disposal of land (Part II of the Act);

(3) to provide further opportunity for challenging in the courts certain orders made under the 1947 Act and certain decisions and directions of the Minister of Housing and Local Government under the Town Planning Acts 1947 to 1959 (Part III of the Act);

(4) to secure greater publicity for planning applications and to ensure that owners and agricultural tenants are informed of any planning applications affecting land owned or occupied by them (Part III of the Act)[14];

(5) to provide for the obligatory purchase by a local authority of an owner-occupier's interest in land detrimentally affected by

[12] Cmnd. 218.
[13] See Chap. 20.
[14] See Chap. 10.

town planning proposals—planning blight (Part IV of the Act)[15]; and

(6) to give local authorities additional powers to buy land in advance of their requirements (Part V of the Act).[16]

The Town and Country Planning Act 1962

As already mentioned the town planning Acts of 1947, 1951, 1953, 1954 and 1959 were repealed (except as to one or two details of minor importance) and the whole of their provisions (except those already spent) collected into one enactment as the Town and Country Planning Act 1962. The repeal of former legislation was, of course, without prejudice to anything done under it including the making of many orders, rules and regulations.

The Town and Country Planning Act 1962 came into operation on April 1, 1963 (1962 Act, s.225(1)), and thereupon became the principal Act relating to town and country planning in England and Wales. It continued so to be (although amended in 1963, 1965, 1966 and, quite substantially, in 1968) until the coming into operation of the further consolidating Act, namely, the Town and Country Planning Act 1971, on April 1, 1972. In the meantime, this historical review continues by making reference to the four amending Acts of 1963, 1965, 1966 and 1968 respectively.

The Town and Country Planning Act 1963

This Act modified the effect of Schedule 3 to the Town and Country Planning Act 1962. That Schedule specified eight classes of development which were regarded as falling within the notion of the "existing use" of land.

If planning permission for development falling within Part II of the aforesaid Schedule 3 was refused (or granted subject to conditions) then compensation might have to be paid, under section 123 of the 1962 Act, by the local planning authority.

Schedule 3 to the 1962 Act made reference (in paragraphs 3 and 7 respectively) to the enlargement of buildings by not more than one-tenth of their cubic content. It was this matter of enlargement up to one-tenth of cubic content which was modified by the 1963 Act.

The reason for this modification of Schedule 3 to the 1962 Act lay in the acceptance by the Government of the possibility that local

[15] See Chaps. 18 and 19.
[16] See Chap. 19.

planning authorities might be inclined to grant planning permission for office development (in cases where it ought, on planning grounds, to have been refused) owing to their fear of the burden of compensation to which refusal would render them liable. Such fear had been much increased in recent years since "Modern building methods . . . have made it possible for developers to get more floor space within a given building cube. With a 10 per cent. addition to the cube, the increase in floor space may well be of 40 per cent. in some cases."[17] This had produced a corresponding increase in the value of an existing office building where there was the right to rebuild or alter it with a 10 per cent. addition to the cubic content—and that was the measure of compensation for which the local authority might be liable if they refused planning permission for such development.

Accordingly, the Act of 1963 limited the increase by reference to *floor space* as well as *cubic content* and, in the case of buildings erected or rebuilt since July 1, 1948, removed altogether, from development which was to be taken into account, the right to enlarge the building.

The Control of Office and Industrial Development Act 1965

Part I of this Act imposed further restrictions on office development, whereby an office development permit (O.D.P.) from the Board of Trade needed to be obtained (in addition to the customary grant of planning permission from the local planning authority) before development involving the provision of office space of 3,000 square feet or more was commenced. Part I of this Act was to cease to function on August 4, 1972, unless Parliament otherwise determined.

The provisions of Part I of this Act were repealed by the Town and Country Planning Act 1971, s.292(2) and Schedule 25 but re-enacted as sections 73–86 and Schedules 12 and 13 of the 1971 Act. These provisions were extended until August 5, 1977, by section 5 of the Town and Country Planning (Amendment) Act 1972 and further extended to August 5, 1982 by the Control of Office Development Act 1977. This latter extension, however, did not live out its time because all this *ad hoc* control of offices was brought to an abrupt conclusion on August 6, 1979 by the Control of Office Development (Cessation) Order 1979.[18]

Part II of the 1965 Act enabled the exemption limit for industrial

[17] See Government White Paper "London-Employment: Housing: Land," App. 2, para. 4 (Cmnd. 1952, February 1963).

[18] S.I. 1979 No. 908.

development *not* requiring an industrial development certificate (I.D.C.) under the Town and Country Planning Act 1962 to be varied.

The Industrial Development Act 1966 (Part III)

This Part of this Act enacted further provisions relating to industrial development certificates granted under the Town and Country Planning Act 1962 and extended the meaning of "industrial building" (as used in the 1962 Act) by providing that an industrial development certificate should be required for a building used, or designed for use, for scientific research in the course of trade or business.

The Town and Country Planning Act 1968

The administrative process associated with town planning control over the development of land originally laid down in the 1947 Act came of age on July 1, 1969. The 1947 Act itself may be said to have been forced upon the country by the imperative need to do something about post-war redevelopment, for the aftermath of the Second World War, 1939 to 1945, had rendered it inescapable that something of this nature *should* be done. The 1947 Act was the answer.

But planning control of land development is a constantly evolving process. No sooner was the consolidating Act of 1962 on the Statute Book than recurrent voices prophesying (or demanding) change became increasingly noisy and the wind of change in the town planning world began to blow with increasing force. In 1965 a group, specially appointed by the Minister of Housing and Local Government and known as "The Minister's Planning and Advisory Group" (PAG), published their Report on a new styling for Town and Country Planning Control. Thereafter came the White Paper entitled, "Town and Country Planning," published in June 1967,[19] in which the case for change was advocated in the following terms:

> "Britain is fortunate in having had, for many years, the planning system established by the Town and Country Planning Act of 1947 (now consolidated in the Town and Country Planning Act 1962) and the Town and Country Planning (Scotland) Act of the same year. It was then, thanks to the care and foresight of Lord Silkin, the most advanced and complete system of land use planning in the world. It did much to help in the reconstruction of our war-damaged cities and it protected the countryside from a resumption of the uncontrolled urban

[19] Cmnd. 3333.

sprawl of the thirties. But the time has now come to profit from twenty years' experience and to make the changes required by new circumstances, new policies and new advances in planning techniques.

"Three major defects have now appeared in the present system. *First*, it has become overloaded and subject to delays and cumbersome procedures. *Second*, there has been inadequate participation by the individual citizen in the planning process, and insufficient regard to his interests. *Third*, the system has been better as a negative control on undesirable development than as a positive stimulus to the creation of a good environment.

"These are the main defects which the revision of the system must tackle and the Government propose to remedy them. To combine the safeguarding of individual interests with quicker decisions means streamlining; to emphasise the positive environmental approach requires a concentration of effort on what is vital, and less central control over detail; and in considering the changes necessary, we must recognise that planning now is operating in a very different context from that immediately after the war.

"When the Acts were being prepared, planning was based on the belief that our population was likely to remain stable and there was little appreciation at that time of the likely growth in the volume of motor traffic—and still less of the impact that this would have on the structure of our towns and on the countryside. Now, the best working assumption on population is that we may have to provide homes for perhaps 17½ million extra people in Great Britain by the end of the century—an increase of nearly a third. As well as building homes for a growing population, we must replace those houses which have come to the end of their useful life. While this is a continuing process, there already exists a need for about three million houses to replace slums and other old houses which are not worth rehabilitating. Not only must the occupiers be given new homes, but the cleared sites should be put to good use.

"Meanwhile, traffic problems will be mounting. The number of motor-cars on the road (already 9½ million in 1966) is expected to exceed 18 million in 1975, with even bigger increases to follow. The revised planning system must be able to cope justly, flexibly and swiftly with all this.

"A new factor has been introduced into planning by the Government's regional policies and by the setting up of the Economic Planning Councils in the regions and in Scotland and Wales. Some of these Councils have been publishing regional studies which should help to shape physical and economic development in the regions. The new planning process must take account of these evolving regional policies.

"The plans drawn up must also be realistic in financial terms and the demands they make on the main capital expenditure programmes must be reasonable in amount and in timing. However admirable they may be, plans which cannot be realised are positively harmful. They stand in the way of more realistic plans, and cause needless worries to people who fear that their interests may be affected.

"People must be able to participate fully in the planning process, and their rights must be safeguarded. Many changes have already been made in planning procedures following the Report (Cmnd. 218) of the Committee on Administrative Tribunals in 1957 (the Franks Committee) and the subsequent setting up of the Council on Tribunals. One of the Government's main aims in the present review of planning legislation is to ensure that there are greater opportunities for the discussion of important changes while they are still at the formative stage and can be influenced by the people whose lives they will affect. They intend also to maintain the rights of objectors—whether they are individuals or organisations—to argue their case at the formal stages.

"The problem is that safeguards built into the planning procedure automatically slow it up. Procedural safeguards, vital though they are, slow the progress towards decision, and there is growing impatience at present delays. These delays may hold up development that matters greatly to the people concerned and may be of economic importance for the country as a whole. While the preservation of proper rights of representation is of overriding importance, some streamlining of the system is essential if unfairness to those who wish to develop is to be avoided.

"There are therefore conflicting but basic requirements to be reconciled. On the one hand there is the desire for more consultation and wider association of the public with planning; on the other, there is the need for quicker decisions. The Government believe that the way to satisfy these requirements lies in devolution of responsibility for some planning decisions, and in simplification of procedures. With these aims in mind, the Government have decided to introduce legislation to improve and modernise the town and country planning system. . . ."

The promise of the White Paper was fulfilled in the Town and

Country Planning Act 1968. Its objects may be grouped under seven heads and summarised as follows:

(1) to provide for the making, for any area, of an overriding structure plan and consequential local plan (or plans) which, under the 1968 Act, were to constitute together the development plan (to use the old expression) for the area (Part I of the Act). Accordingly, Part II of the Town and Country Planning Act 1962 (relating to the making, approval and coming into operation of development plans) was totally repealed and replaced by Part I of the 1968 Act;

(2) to make alterations in the method of enforcement of planning control (Part II of the Act);

(3) to provide for certain planning appeals to the Minister to be determined, not by the Minister as before, but by an Inspector appointed by the Minister to hear the appeal and this was to be the position whether the appeal was by way of a private hearing or by way of a public local inquiry (Part III of the Act);

(4) to adapt the powers of compulsory acquisition, as contained in the Town and Country Planning Act 1962, to the new development plan provisions (which no longer provided for the designation of land in development plans as being subject to compulsory acquisition) and to enact new provisions relating to planning blight (Part IV of the Act);

(5) to make more effective provision for the preservation of buildings of special architectural or historic interest (Part V of the Act);

(6) to enact a variety of changes in planning law, some of them being quite novel and of great importance (Part VI of the Act); and

(7) to enact matters supplemental to the foregoing six Parts (Part VII of the Act).

The Town and Country Planning Act 1971

As to England and Wales all the provisions of the Town and Country Planning Acts 1962 to 1968 are now repealed (with a few exceptions) and re-enacted in consolidated form in the Town and Country Planning Act 1971 which received the Royal Assent on October 28, 1971. Its provisions came into operation, in general, on April 1, 1972—"the commencement date" (s.294(1)) except as to Part II of the Act (relating to the "new-style" development plans comprising structure plans and local plans) and this Part has come into operation from time to time and from place to place as has been appointed by order made by the Secretary of State under section 21 of the 1971 Act (*ibid.*). The legislative provisions as to "old-style" development plans, which continue to apply in any area until such time as Part II of the 1971 Act is applied thereto, are relegated to Schedule 5 to the Act. Certain provisions of the 1971 Act are modified by Schedule 6 pending the repeal of Schedule 5 in any area. Schedule 7 to the 1971 Act provides for the transition from Schedule 5 to Part II of the Act.

The Town and Country Planning Act 1971 is now the principal Act relating to town and country planning in England and Wales.

The Town and Country Planning (Amendment) Act 1972

Town planning law never stops! Within days of the consolidating Act of 1971 receiving the Royal Assent on October 28, 1971, a short amending Bill was introduced into Parliament on November 3, 1971. This Bill later became the Town and Country Planning (Amendment) Act 1972. This Act inserts certain new provisions into the Act of 1971 and also makes certain amendments to that Act, the purpose of the 1972 Act being:

(1) to provide for *joint* structure plans;
(2) to amend the procedure relating to structure plan inquiries by introducing a new concept of the "examination in public" in place of the conventional "public inquiry";
(3) to dispense with structure plans in London boroughs;
(4) to control demolition in conservation areas; and
(5) to extend for a further five years, that is to say, until August 5, 1977, the special control of office development first established under the Control of Office and Industrial Development Act 1965. (This special control was further extended to August 5, 1982 by the Control of Office Development Act 1977 but later brought to an end on August 6, 1979 by the Control of Office Development (Cessation) Order 1979.[20])

The Local Government Act 1972

Throughout England and Wales a reorganised system of local government, created by the Local Government Act 1972, came into operation on April 1, 1974. It was the biggest upheaval in local government administration since the invention of county councils

[20] See p. 26.

under the Local Government Act 1888. The long tussle for power between the county councils and the county borough councils—the latter being all-purpose authorities *solely* responsible, within their respective areas, for everything concerned with local government—ended in a win for the counties. County boroughs were abolished and a split-level form of local government (after the style of that which had previously existed since 1888 in the county areas of the country) was established everywhere throughout the land.

The new system in England and Wales (apart from Greater London to which the 1972 Act does not in general apply) consisted of the following authorities:

(1) 53 county councils, comprising six for the "metropolitan counties" (namely, Greater Manchester, Merseyside, South Yorkshire, Tyne and Wear, West Midlands, West Yorkshire) and 47 for the non-metropolitan counties (sometimes called—colloquially but not formally or officially—the "shire" counties);

(2) 369 district councils (those in the metropolitan counties being known as "metropolitan district councils"); and

(3) parish councils.

Diagrams 1 and 2 showing, respectively, the layout of local government before and after the April 1, 1974 reorganisation appear at pages 50 and 51.

The outcome of local government reorganisation in 1974 is mentioned deliberately in this historical outline of planning legislation because the responsibilities of a local planning authority, functioning under the Town and Country Planning Act 1971, were affected in several important particulars by the reorganisation. For instance, every county council and every district council was made a local planning authority in its own right. Thus, there were two local planning authorities, each wielding land planning powers, throughout every square inch of land in England and Wales. The division of duties and responsibilities between a county planning authority and a district planning authority is more fully commented upon in Chapter 2.[21] Suffice it to say here that (apart from Greater London) there were 141 local planning authorities before April 1, 1974, whilst on and after that date there were 422 such authorities.

In the sphere of land planning the reorganisation created by the Local Government Act 1972 achieved neither simplification of detail nor streamlining of administration. The arrangements for town and country planning and development control in England and Wales (outside Greater London), as established by the Local Government

[21] See pp. 41, 42, 43 and 44.

Act 1972, are set out in diagrammatic form in Diagram 4 at page 53.

The position of local government, as discussed in the preceding paragraph, in relation to planning control of land development, is now further amended by the Local Government Act 1985 (see later in this Chapter and see also Diagram 3 and Diagram 4 at pages 52 and 53 respectively) which, as from April 1, 1986 (the "abolition date"), abolished the Greater London Council and each of the six metropolitan county councils.

The Town and Country Amenities Act 1974

Notwithstanding its slightly different title, this Act, which came into operation on August 31, 1974 (s.13(3) of the Act) forms an integral part of the land planning legislation discussed in this historical outline as is evidenced by the fact that the Act may be cited, together with the Town and Country Planning Act 1971 and the Town and Country Planning (Amendment) Act 1972, as the Town and Country Planning Acts 1971 to 1974.

The Act re-wrote several sections of the Town and Country Planning Act 1971 (the principal Act) so as to make better provision for the preservation and enhancement of conservation areas, and of buildings of architectural or historical interest together with their surroundings and landscapes.

The Community Land Act 1975

A further Act which calls for brief mention in this historical outline (and which, in a preceding edition—the seventh edition—of this book, called for treatment in detail) was the Community Land Act 1975, now repealed (Local Government, Planning and Land Act 1980, s.101 and Schedule 17) but immediately largely resuscitated, for Wales only (*ibid.* and ss.102–111 and Scheds. 18–22). It is true that the Act stood outside the mainstream of planning legislation and was not to be cited as part and parcel of that legislation but, even so, the provisions of the Act did affect to a great extent the control of land development by making novel provision for the suspension of planning permissions in certain circumstances, conferring new and exceedingly wide *powers* (and, later on, *duties*) as to the compulsory acquisition of "development land" upon local authorities and enabling a local authority, when exercising such powers (or duties), to circumvent some of the safeguards for the landowner written into the Acquisition of Land (Authorisation Procedure) Act 1946.

Briefly, the avowed aims of the Community Land Act 1975 were two in number, that is to say:

(1) to enable the community to control the development of land in accordance with its needs and priorities; and

(2) to restore to the community the increase in value of land arising from its efforts.[22]

The Act had a short and highly controversial life and ceased to have effect as from November 13, 1980 by virtue of the Local Government, Planning and Land Act 1980 referred to above and also later in this chapter.

The Town and Country Planning (Amendment) Act 1977

This Act (which came into operation on August 22, 1977) extends the powers of local planning authorities to serve stop notices under section 90 of the Town and Country Planning Act 1971 to activities *other than* the carrying out of building, mining, engineering or other operations.

It also makes consequential amendments to the provisions of the 1971 Act concerning liability to compensation for loss due to the prohibition contained in a stop notice and gives local authorities and the Secretary of State power to require information concerning uses of land.

The Control of Office Development Act 1977

This Act (which came into operation on July 29, 1977) continued the special control over office development until August 5, 1982 and amended the Town and Country Planning Act 1971 accordingly.

Control of Office Development (Cessation) Order 1979[23]

The Control of Office Development Act 1977 was short-lived because the *ad hoc* control of office development introduced by the Control of Office and Industrial Development Act 1965 was terminated as from August 6, 1979, by the Control of Office Development (Cessation) Order 1979 made by the Privy Council under section 86(1) of the Town and Country Planning Act 1971. Since that date office development will run the same planning gauntlet, no more and no less, as does any other kind of development for which planning permission is needed and is sought.

[22] See Government White Paper (Cmnd. 5730) entitled, "Land," dated September 12, 1974, at para. 16.

[23] S.I. 1979 No. 908.

The Inner Urban Areas Act 1978

This Act calls for brief mention in this historical outline because it enacts provisions (in section 12) for the expedited making and adoption of local plans (under the Town and Country Planning Act 1971) which relate to any area which has become a designated district under the 1978 Act. In such a case the local plan may be brought into operation, if the Secretary of State so directs, even though he has not as yet given his approval to the structure plan for the designated district.

The Secretary of State, under section 1 of the 1978 Act, may designate any "inner urban area" to be a designated district if he is satisfied that:

(a) special social need exists in the area; and
(b) the conditions giving rise to that need could be alleviated by the exercise of powers created by the 1978 Act.

The Local Government, Planning and Land Act 1980

This Act received the Royal Assent on November 13, 1980. It makes important alterations and amendments to the law of planning control and land development as that law was enacted in the Town and Country Planning Act 1971 which is still the principal Act on the subject.

The 1980 Act is a weighty affair of 197 sections together with no less than 34 schedules. But, fortunately, not all this quantum of statutory enactment relates to matters of town planning. The latter are to be found in the 1980 Act principally in Part IX (Town & Country Planning); Part XVI (Urban Development) and Part XVIII (Enterprise, Zones); all as read along with Schedule 14 (Amendments Relating to Surveys and Plans), Schedule 15 (Further Planning Amendments), Schedule 23, Part IV (Amendments of Town & Country Planning Act 1971), Part V (Amendments of Local Government Act 1972) and Schedules 26, 27, 28, 29 and 31 (each relating to matters touching Urban Development Areas) and Schedule 32 relating to Enterprise Zones.

The Local Government and Planning (Amendment) Act 1981

This Act, passed on July 27, 1981, came into operation (s.2(3)) on August 27, 1981 except as to paragraph 6 of the Schedule (relating to the keeping of a register of enforcement notices and stop notices) which came into operation on November 27, 1981 (s.2(2)).

The Act amends sections 87 and 88 of the Town and Country Planning Act 1971 (relating to enforcement notices and appeals against them) by replacing them in the 1971 Act with four new sections (sections 87, 88, 88A and 88B). It also amends sections 96 and 97 of the 1971 Act (relating to listed building enforcement notices and appeals against them) by replacing them in the 1971 Act with three new sections (sections 96, 97 and 97A). It carries further amendments to the 1971 Act relating to the protection of trees, the tidying of waste land and it increases, in several cases, maximum penalties for breaches of planning control.

The Town and Country Planning (Minerals) Act 1981

This Act, passed on July 27, 1981, will come into operation (s.35 of the Act) on such dates as the Secretary of State appoints. It amends the Town and Country Planning Act 1971 with respect to the mining and working of minerals and the reinstatement of land after mineral working has ceased. This *Outline* does not purport to deal with planning control relating to minerals which is now (under the Town and Country Planning (Minerals) Act 1981) a highly specialised form of control outside the general mainstream of planning control over land development.

The Local Government and Planning (Amendment) Act 1981

This Act, passed on July 27, 1981 and operative as from November 27, 1981, provides amendments to the Town and Country Planning Act 1971 and to Schedule 16 to the Local Government Act 1972. Where these amendments are relevant to the contents of this book they have been "picked up" and "worked into" the pages which follow.

The Planning Inquiries (Attendance of Public) Act 1982

This Act requires that evidence at planning inquiries held under the Town and Country Planning Act 1971 shall be given in public subject to certain exceptions where the Secretary of State gives a direction to the contrary so as to secure better protection for the national interest, for national security or for preventing the disclosure of information relating to the security of premises or property.

The Local Government (Miscellaneous Provisions) Act 1982

This Act, as its title suggests, is a hotch potch of amendments to earlier legislation but four sections affect planning law. They are section 33 (relating to the enforceability by a local authority of positive covenants relating to land and replacing section 126 of the Housing

Act 1974), section 34 (relating to local land charges registers and computerisation, etc.), section 35 (relating to the acquisition of land, etc., by planning boards) and section 36 (relating to advertisements and the control of fly-posting).

The Town and Country Planning Act 1984

The general rule is that the 1971 Act does not bind the Crown (s.266). Thus the Crown does not require planning permission for its own development.[24] In these days when a grant of planning permission can add so much additional value to land which is being offered for sale this privilege of the Crown was an embarrassment as well. This 1984 Act remedies this difficulty. It allows the Crown to obtain planning permission for development other than its own development and thereby be able to sell Crown land with a formal grant of planning permission attached thereto. The Act also allows enforcement action to be taken in respect of Crown land where the development complained of was not carried out by, or on behalf of, the Crown or by right of a private interest in the land. D.O.E. Circular 18/84 and the memorandum accompanying the Circular which is dated August 3, 1984 and entitled, "Crown Land and Crown Development" give a descriptive account of the effect of the 1984 Act. Under the Act the Secretary of State for the Environment has made the Town and Country Planning (Crown Land Applications) Regulations 1984[25] and the Town and Country Planning (Special Enforcement Notice) Regulations 1984.[26]

The Local Government (Access to Information) Act 1985

This Act (which came into operation on April 1, 1986) is not specifically about planning and development but is mentioned in this historical outline of planning law because its provisions could be helpful to an applicant for planning permission, or an appellant against planning conditions or a refusal of planning permission, who needs, for the furtherance of his case, information from the local planning authority or a sight of local authority documents. The Act writes into the Local Government Act 1972 eleven new sections to be known respectively as sections 100A, 100B, 100C, 100D, 100E, 100F, 100G, 100H, 100I, 100J and 100K together with a new Schedule to be known as Schedule 12A. The long title to the Act shows its scope when it refers to the Act as, "An Act to provide for greater public access to local authority meetings, reports and documents

[24] *Ministry of Agriculture, Fisheries and Foods* v. *Jenkins* (1963) 2 Q.B. 317.
[25] S.I. 1984 No. 1015.
[26] S.I. 1984 No. 1016.

subject to specified confidentiality provisions, to give local authorities duties to publish certain information; and for related purposes."

The Town and Country Planning (Compensation) Act 1985

This Act amends sections 165 and 169 of the Town and Country Planning Act 1971 so as to restrict a local planning authority's liability to pay compensation first, where planning permission, automatically granted by a development order, is withdrawn by the revocation or amendment of that order and, secondly, in relation to the refusal of planning permission, or the conditional grant of such permission, for the enlargement (under the authority of Schedule 8, Part II, of the 1971 Act) of blocks of flats erected before July 1, 1948—the date when the Town and Country Planning Act 1947 came into operation.

The Local Government Act 1985

This Act abolished, as from April 1, 1986 (the "abolition date"), the Greater London Council and the six metropolitan county councils (Greater Manchester, Merseyside, South Yorkshire, Tyne and Wear, West Midlands and West Yorkshire) transferring, in the main, their planning powers and duties to the London boroughs (in Greater London) and to the metropolitan districts (in the metropolitan counties) but in some instances transferring such powers and duties to other bodies as, for example, in Greater London, to the Historic Buildings and Monuments Commission for England. In the London boroughs and in the metropolitan districts current structure and local plans will be replaced progressively by a new kind of development plan to be known as a unitary development plan.

The arrangements for local government in England and Wales (outside Greater London) after the abolition of the Greater London Council and the six metropolitan county councils is set out, in diagrammatic form, in Diagram 3 at page 52. The arrangements for the discharge of planning and development control in England and Wales (outside Greater London) after the aforesaid abolitions are set out diagrammatically (a) in Diagram 4 at page 53, and (b) in Diagram 5 following page 53.

The Town and Country Planning (Amendment) Act 1985

This Act amends section 62 of the 1971 Act relating to the replanting of protected trees in an area of woodland where the trees have been removed or destroyed or have died.

The Housing and Planning Act 1986

This Act is a mixture. It relates to housing (Part I of the Act); simplified planning zones (Part II of the Act); financial assistance for urban regeneration (Part III of the Act); hazardous substances (Part IV of the Act); opencast coal (Part V of the Act); and Miscellaneous Provisions (Part VI of the Act).

Parts II, IV, and VI carry important enactments relating to control of land development by making additions to, and amendments of, several of the provisions of the Town and Country Planning Act 1971.

Briefly, the changes in the 1971 Act made by the 1986 Act are as follows:

(1) section 25 (in Part II) of the 1986 Act inserts into the 1971 Act, five new sections, (namely, sections 24A, 24B, 24C, 24D and 24E) relating to simplified planning zones[27];

(2) sections 30, 31 and 32 (in Part IV) of the 1986 Act, relates to the control of hazardous substances[28] by a "hazardous substances authority" (*i.e.* generally speaking, the council of the district or London borough in which the hazardous substance is situtated) whose duty it is to grant or refuse "hazardous substances consent" to the presence of a hazardous substance on, under or over land. These sections, 30, 31 and 32 of the 1986 Act, insert 15 new sections into the Town and Country Planning Act 1971, all dealing with the subject of hazardous substances and their control. These 15 new sections of the 1971 Act are numbered, respectively, sections 1A, 1B, 58B, 58C, 58D, 58E, 58F, 58G, 58H, 58J (there is no 58I), 58K, 58L, 58M, 58N and 101B;

(3) section 40 (in Part VI) of the 1986 Act and Part I of Schedule 9 to that Act together amend the provisions of the 1971 Act, concerning listed buildings[29] and conservation areas[30] in respect of the following matters:

  (a) the treatment of free-standing objects and structures within the curtilage of a listed building;

  (b) the grant of listed building consent subject to the subsequent approval of detail;

  (c) applications for the variation or discharge of conditions attached to listed building consent;

[27] See Chap. 25.
[28] See Chap. 10 at pp. 245–248.
[29] See Chap. 14.
[30] See Chap. 9.

(d) the power of a local authority, the Secretary of State or the Historic Building Monuments Commission for England to carry out urgent works for the preservation of a building;
(e) the control of demolition in a conservation area;
(f) the form of an application for listed building consent; and
(g) the powers of the Secretary of State with respect to applications for listed building consent.

(4) section 41 (in Part VI) of the 1986 Act and Schedule 10, Part I, of that Act amend the provisions of Part II of the 1971 Act relating to local plans[31] by substituting, for the eight existing sections, sections 10C to 15B inclusive of the 1971 Act, 13 new sections numbered, respectively, sections 11, 11A, 11B, 12, 12A, 12B, 13, 14, 14A, 14B, 15, 15A and 15B of the 1971 Act.
(5) section 45 (in Part VI) of the 1986 Act provides for the definition of "experimental areas" in which to assess the effect on amenity or public safety of certain advertisements.
(6) section 46 (in Part VI) of the 1986 Act substitutes, for the existing section 65 of the 1971 Act, a new section 65 relating to waste land or land adversely affecting the amenity of a neighbourhood; and
(7) section 49, (in Part VI) of the 1986 Act makes miscellaneous amendments (to the 1971 Act) set out in Part I of Schedule 11 to the 1986 Act which amendments relate to:
(a) the operation of the Town & Country Planning (Use Class) Order 1972 on the subdivision of the planning unit;
(b) the provison which may be made by development orders[32];
(c) the construction of references to certain documents relating to access for the disabled[33];
(d) applications to vary or revoke conditions attached to planning permission[34];
(e) the procedure on appeals[35] and applications disposed of without a local inquiry or hearing;
(f) purchase notices[36];
(g) local inquiries[37];
(h) the determination of appeals by inspectors[38]; and

[31] See Chap. 5.
[32] See Chap. 10 at pp. 160–177 inclusive.
[33] See Chap. 10 at p. 202.
[34] See, as to planning conditions, Chap. 10 at p. 218 and Chap. 11.
[35] See Chap. 10 at p. 219.
[36] See Chap. 18.
[37] See Chap. 10 at p. 220.
[38] See Chap. 10 at p. 230.

(i) daily penalties for offences.

The Housing and Planning Act 1986 was enacted on November 7, 1986. All the foregoing provisions of the Act will, however, come into force only on "an appointed day" (1986 Act, s.40(3)) which means such day as may be appointed by the Secretary of State (*ibid.* s.40(4)) who may appoint different days for different provisons (*ibid.*).

At the date of this writing the Secretary of State has made the Housing & Planning Act (Commencement No. 1) Order 1986—S.I. 1986 No. 2262(C.92)—as a result of which the following *planning* provisions of the 1986 Act came into operation on January 7, 1987:

Section 44: overhead electricity lines

Section 45: control of advertisements: experimental areas

Section 46: land adversely affecting amenity of neighbourhood

Section 48: repeal of unnecessary enactments:

(a) grants for the removal of temporary defence works

(b) industrial development certificates

(c) planning redevelopment grants

Section 49 and Schedule 11: minor and consequential amendments: repeals:

paragraph 1:	subdivision of the planning unit
paragraph 2:	development orders
paragraph 3:	disabled persons: construction of references to certain documents
paragraph 4:	application to vary or revoke conditions attached to planning permission
paragraphs 5–7:	purchase notices
paragraph 10:	procedure on applications and appeals disposed of without inquiry or hearing
paragraph 11:	power to return appeal for determination by Inspector
paragraph 12:	appointment of assessors
paragraph 13:	increase of daily penalties for offences
paragraph 14:	clarification of section 1(2A) of the Town and Country Planning Act 1971

Section 54: effect of modification or termination of enterprise zone scheme

Section 55: discrimination in exercise of planning functions.

D.O.E. Circular 19/86, dated December 17, 1986 describes the foregoing provisions in detail.

It is intended that paragraph 8 of Schedule 11 to the Act will be brought into effect on March 1, 1987. The paragraph provides for decisions on applications for costs in respect of "transferred" planning appeals to be taken by the Inspector who decides the appeal. A separate circular on costs policy and procedure, is to be issued shortly.

Other planning provisions of the 1986 Act will be brought into effect during 1987. These are Part II (Simplified Planning Zones), Part IV (Hazardous Substances), Part V (Opencast Coal), and in Part VI (Miscellaneous Provisions) those sections dealing with Listed Buildings and Conservation Areas, Local Plans and Unitary Development Plans, and other miscellaneous provisions not commenced on January 7, 1987.

* * * * * *

The Town and Country Planning Act 1971 (amended, as above mentioned, in 1972, 1974, 1977, 1979, 1980, 1981, 1982, 1984 above, 1985 and 1986) when conjoined with the host of Orders, Rules and Regulations made under it, and under earlier legislation now replaced by the 1971 Act, together comprise the Town and Country Planning Code under which the development and use of all land in England and Wales is now controlled. It is that Code which is dealt with in the following chapters of this book.

It may be added that a comparable control is available in Scotland under the Town and Country Planning (Scotland) Act 1972 as amended.

* * * * * *

Before concluding this historical outline I cannot forbear the following comment.

The time, surely, has now come for the statutory enactments relating to planning and development control (as outlined in the following pages of this book and as currently set out in the 1971 Act and its 10 successive (and substantial) statutory amendments) to be consolidated in a new principal Act where the sections can be numbered *numerically only* and without the need to add almost half the alphabet as adjuncts to the numbering of new sections inserted into the 1971 Act by subsequent Acts.

"'Tis a consummation devoutly to be wished."

Chapter 2

CENTRAL GOVERNMENT AND LOCAL GOVERNMENT ADMINISTRATION OF PLANNING CONTROL

1. The Secretary of State for the Environment

The Minister of Town and Country Planning was, under the Town and Country Planning Act 1947, the central authority for the administration of land planning throughout England and Wales. The Minister's style and title has had the habit, over the years, of changing[1] but, by whatever name he was called, he remained charged (at least until November 12, 1970), by virtue of section 1 of the Act which created his office, namely, the Minister of Town and Country Planning Act 1943, "with the duty of securing consistency and continuity in the framing and execution of a national policy with respect to the use and development of land throughout England and Wales." These words were of great importance because, while they gave the Minister the last word (subject only to Parliament itself) in all matters of policy relating to the control of land use in England and Wales, they also imposed constraint on what was allowed, by law, to constitute that last word, that is to say, on what could be, under the law, the policy of the Government of the day relating to the use and development of land in England and Wales.

Under the Secretary of State for the Environment Order 1970[2] all the functions and property of the Minister of Housing and Local Government (as successor in title to the Minister of Town and Country Planning) were (*inter alia*) transferred to the Secretary of State (art. 2) and the Ministry of Housing and Local Government was dissolved (*ibid.*). Thus, central control over all matters relating to town and country planning in England and Wales is now handled by the Secretary of State who heads the Department of the Environment, that is to say, by the Secretary of State for the Environment.

The question is: whatever happened to the important words (quoted above) of section 1 of the Minister of Town and Country Planning Act 1943 after the Secretary of State for the Environment Order 1970 came into operation on November 12, 1970 (art. 1(5))?

[1] See pp. 9 and 10.
[2] S.I. 1970 No. 1681. The Order came into operation on November 12, 1970 (art. 1(5)).

On this I quote an extract from a commentary of mine which appeared in the "Journal of Planning and Environment Law" (1984) at pp. 76 *et seq*.

> "6. The Secretary of State for the Environment Order 1970 (S.I. 1970 No. 1681) provides categorically in article 5(3) of, and Schedule 4 to, the Order that the Minister of Town and Country Planning Act 1943, s.1 is (*inter alia*) repealed. (Incidentally, I did wonder at one time how a mere Statutory Instrument could repeal the very words of the Sovereign Parliament as set out in a Statute, *i.e.* in an Act of Parliament itself. The answer is simple—wonders never cease. The Ministers of the Crown (Transfer of Functions) Act 1946, s.1(3) provides power, by means of an Order in Council, to make "such incidental, consequential and supplemental provisions as may be necessary or expedient" for the purposes of the transfer of functions from one Minister to another. This authority has, it would seem, been regarded as sufficient to bring about the entire *repeal*, by Order in Council, of section 1 of the Minister of Town and Country Planning Act 1943. To complete this particular part of a confused picture it may be added that the Ministers of the Crown (Transfer of Functions) Act 1946 was itself repealed by the Ministers of the Crown Act 1975 which latter Act provided no saving for Orders made under the repealed Act of 1946.)
>
> "7. But if section 1 of the 1943 Act has gone by virtue of the 1970 Order, that Order further provides (or *did* provide in its day) (art. 2(1)) that "all *functions* [my italics] of the Minister of Housing and Local Government . . . are hereby transferred to the Secretary of State." Leaving aside the nice question of whether there is a distinction between *functions* and *duties*, I would say that, if the *functions* transferred to the Secretary of State for the Environment by the 1970 Order included the former undoubted *duty* of the Minister of Housing and Local Government under section 1 of the 1943 Act, then all is well. But did they? If it is the case (and I think it is) that the 1943 Act, s.1, was indeed repealed by the 1970 Order, is it not fair comment to say that, the 1943 Act section 1 having gone with the wind, the question then is: What function (or duty) under that section 1 of the 1943 Act remained for, and was capable of, transfer from the Minister of Housing and Local Government to the new Secretary of State?
>
> "8. To put the whole matter another way and to seek to discover where on earth, in the whole of this planning brouhaha,

the Secretary of State stands today, it could be argued as follows.

"9. Under the 1943 Act there is no doubt that the Minister for Planning Control (by whatever title known) was under the *duty* of "securing consistency and continuity in the framing and execution of a national policy with respect to the use and development of land throughout England and Wales." This was his statutory *duty*. It meant that, in the manner in which he discharged his statutory planning *functions* (functions specifically saddled upon him by one Act of Parliament after another), he had a *duty* to discharge those functions in such a way as would ensure "consistency and continuity in the framing and execution of a national policy, etc., etc." If this duty has now gone then the question is: What today *is* the basic, fundamental, last-analysis end-product, which it is *now* the Secretary of State's *duty* to secure when he is discharging his *functions*—his statutory functions—as to planning control?

"10. In short, what is it, in the last analysis, that the Secretary of State is adoing of as he goes about, up and down the country, discharging his planning functions? Today local authorities, as of old, are constrained (and to a substantial extent) by things called structure plans and local plans, that is to say, by development plans. But what is the Secretary of State constrained by? The answer, surely, must be: He is constrained by government policy and government policy may not *necessarily* be directed to 'securing consistency and continuity in the framing and execution of a national policy with respect to the use and development of land throughout England and Wales.' It may well be that government policy *is*, in fact, so directed (and I do not say at all that today it is *not* so directed) but the point—the *vital* point—is that government policy, since the repeal of section 1 of the 1943 Act, *need not necessarily be so directed*. Thus, constitutionally the situation is vapid, at large, unclear. It was never thus while we still had the 1943 Act with us to make clear beyond all doubt what exactly was the *duty* of the Minister (or the Secretary of State) as, day by day, he went around dutifully discharging his planning *functions*."

In this matter, generally, of government policy being paramount in the making of planning decisions relating to the control of land development, reference should be made to *Greater London Council* v. *Secretary of State for the Environment and Grey Coat Commercial Estates Ltd.* (the "*Coin Street Case*") (1983) J.P.L. 793 where it was held that, in coming to a planning decision, the Secretary of State had followed his own policy which he was entitled to do, had acted within his powers and had given sufficient reasons for his decision. In this case Stephen Brown J. said (at (1983) J.P.L. 798):

> "It had been made clear on many occasions that the role of the court in proceedings of this nature was a limited one: it was to examine whether the Minister had acted within his powers. It had no jurisdiction to pronounce upon or, indeed, to comment upon the merits of the Minister's decision in the general sense. It could not assume the role of the Minister or act as a Court of Appeal from him on the merits of the proposals approved by him. It had been generally acknowledged in the course of this hearing that the Minister was entitled to have a policy, even though it may be a policy which was objectionable to various parties. He was satisfied that the Minister did have a policy and that he stated it quite clearly in 1980, after it had been evolved through a lengthy inquiry which related substantially to the same sites now under consideration. He did not consider that he had been shown to have exceeded his powers or to have failed to give sufficient reasons for his decision."

This case was approved on appeal to the Court of Appeal ((1984) J.P.L. 263).

It will be noted that if the Secretary of State, in pursuance of government policy, does find it necessary to give a decision which conflicts with the policies set out in the relevant development plan, he must give reasons for his action (*Ynystaw, Ynyforgan and Glais Gypsy Site Action Group* v. *Secretary of State for Wales and West Glamorgan County Council* (1981) J.P.L. 874.

The Town and Country Planning Act 1971 confers upon the Secretary of State discretionary powers of a wide nature. The earlier exercise of such powers under the Town and Country Planning Act 1944 and the New Towns Act 1946 has been under judicial review in a number of cases to which reference may usefully be made when the exercise of similar powers under the Town and Country Planning Act 1971 is under consideration. The cases are as follows:

1. Decisions under the Town and Country Planning Act 1944:
   (1) *Phoenix Assurance Company* v. *Minister of Town and Country Planning*[3];
   (2) *Robinson* v. *Minister of Town and Country Planning*[4]; (overruling the *Phoenix* decision, *supra*).

[3] [1947] 1 All E.R. 454.
[4] [1947] 1 All E.R. 851; Lord Greene, M.R. at p. 857.

2. Decisions under the New Towns Act 1946:
   (1) *Fletcher* v. *Minister of Town and Country Planning*[5];
   (2) *Rollo* v. *Minister of Town and Country Planning*[6];
   (3) *Franklin* v. *Minister of Town and Country Planning*[7]—a decision of the House of Lords.

The foregoing cases show that, in the discharge of his town planning functions and duties, it is now well established law that the Secretary of State is acting in a purely administrative capacity. The town planning process is an administrative process—it is *not* a justiciable process. As Lord Thankerton said in 1947 in *Franklin's* case ((1948) A.C. at page 102):

> "In my opinion, no judicial or quasi-judicial, duty was imposed on the respondent, and any reference to judicial duty, or bias, is irrelevant in the present case. The respondent's duties under . . . [the New Towns Act 1946] . . . are, in my opinion, purely administrative, but the Act prescribes certain methods of, or steps in, discharge of that duty. . . . I am of opinion that no judicial duty is laid on the respondent in discharge of these statutory duties, and that the only question is whether he has complied with the statutory directions to appoint a person to hold the public inquiry, and to consider that person's report."

Further authority on the attitude of the courts in a case where a Minister of the Crown has power to act (as the Secretary of State frequently has under various sections of the 1971 Act) if he "is satisfied" as to something or other, may be found in *Thorneloe & Clarkson Ltd. and Others* v. *Board of Trade*.[8]

2. Local Government—New Format from April 1, 1986

The changing format of local government in England and Wales since before April 1, 1974 up to the present day (1987) is shown in diagramatic form in diagrams 1, 2 and 3 on pages 50, 51 and 52 respectively. The arrangements for planning and development control throughout the same period are shown in diagrams 4 and 5 on

[5] [1947] 2 All E.R. 496.
[6] [1948] 1 All E.R. 13.
[7] [1948] A.C. 87.
[8] [1950] 2 All E.R. 245; Sellers J. at p. 248 quoting Lord Greene, M.R. See also *Liversidge* v. *Anderson* [1942] A.C. 206; *Point of Ayr Collieries Ltd.* v. *Lloyd-George* [1943] 2 All E.R. 546; Lord Greene, M.R. at p. 547; his dictum applied in *Commissioners of Customs and Excise* v. *Cure and Deeley* [1962] 1 Q.B. 340; [1961] 3 W.L.R. 798.

pages 53 and following respectively. These diagrams may usefully be consulted when the remaining paragraphs of this chapter are being read.

For the 12 years prior to April 1, 1986, the local government arrangements for (a) the making of development plans (*i.e.* structure plans and local plans) and (b) the conduct of control over land development (*i.e.* the day-to-day grant or refusal of planning permission for development) was as set out in Diagram 4 on page 53. On April 1, 1986, by virtue of the Local Government Act 1985, there came a dramatic change in the local government format for England and Wales. On that date—April 1, 1986, the "abolition date" (Local Government Act 1985, s.1)—the Greater London *Council* (but not Greater London itself) and each of the six Metropolitan County *Councils* (but not the metropolitan counties themselves) were abolished, section 1 of the 1985 Act providing, it its terse fashion, that they "shall cease to exist."

Thus today, whenever planning matters are being considered, a distinction has now to be drawn between Greater London plus the six metropolitan counties (none of which has a county council at all) and the remaining 47 non-metropolitan counties in England and Wales in each of which the county council continues to exist.

The six metropolitan counties are (Local Government Act 1972, s.1 and Sched. 1):

1. Greater Manchester;
2. Merseyside;
3. South Yorkshire;
4. Tyne and Wear;
5. West Midlands; and
6. West Yorkshire.

The remaining 47 non-metropolitan counties in England and Wales are, in common parlance (and much more picturesquely), described as "shire counties." They are so referred to in this book.

It will be noted that in Greater London and in the metropolitan counties there is now only one level of local government (one tier) and that is in the hands (in Greater London) of the 32 London boroughs plus the Corporation of the City of London, and (in the metropolitan counties) in the hands of the metropolitan district councils, such boroughs and councils each becoming an all-purpose planning authority—see Diagrams 3 and 5 on pages 52 and following 53 respectively.

On the other hand, in the shire counties local government continues to function in split-level (or two-tiered) fashion, the upper level being in the hands of the shire county council and the lower level in the hands of the shire district councils.

The difference in the local government format in metropolitan counties and in shire counties is illustrated in Diagram 3 on page 52.

3. Local Planning Authorities and Allocation of Planning Functions

The Town and Country Planning Act 1971 (as amended from April 1, 1974, by the Local Government Act 1972, from January 13, 1981 by the Local Government, Planning and Land Act 1980 and from April 1, 1986, by sections 2 and 3 of the Local Government Act 1985) now provides (s.1(1)) that:

(1) *in a shire county* the county council shall be the county planning authority for the whole county and the shire district councils shall each be the district planning authority for their own district (s.1(1)(*a*));

(2) *in a metropolitan county* (which, after April 1, 1986, it will be remembered, has no county council at all) each of the metropolitan district councils shall be the (one and only) planning authority for their own district (s.1(1)(*b*)); and

(3) *in Greater London* (for which, after April 1, 1986, there is no longer the Greater London Council) each of the 32 London boroughs shall be the (one and only) planning authority for their own borough (s.1(1)(*c*)). The expression "London borough" includes the City of London (s.290(1)) where the Common Council of the City is the (one and only) planning authority.

Thus it is only in a shire county that there are now two local planning authorities (the county planning authority and the district planning authorities) for every piece of land (s.1(2A)).

Diagram 5 showing the current arrangements for town and country planning control in England and Wales outside Greater London appears on page following 53.

Parish councils are *not* local planning authorities but they are *entitled* to be consulted about certain applications for planning permission to carry out development of land in their areas (Local Government Act 1972, Sched. 16, para. 20 and Town and Country Planning General Development Order 1977, art. 17).[9]

The division of planning labours in a shire county, as between the county planning authority and each of the district planning authorities, is dealt with in the Local Government, Planning and Land Act 1980 which, as from January 13, 1981, made radical changes in

[9] S.I. 1977 No. 289.

the allocation of planning and development control functions outside National Parks (Local Government Act 1972, Sched. 16, para. 15(4)) and outside Greater London (*ibid.* para. 52). The law on this is found in:

(a) Schedule 16 to the Local Government Act 1972 (as amended by section 86 of the Local Government, Planning and Land Act 1980), particularly paragraphs 15, 16 and 32;

(b) articles 15, 15A and 16 of the Town and Country Planning General Development Order 1977 (article 15A being inserted by the Town and Country Planning General Development (Amendment) Order 1980)[10]; and

(c) the Town and Country Planning (Prescription of County Matters) Regulations 1980.[11]

D.O.E. Circular 2/81, dated January 9, 1981, entitled, "Town and Country Planning: Development Control Functions," (now applicable only in shire counties) deals with the allocation of development control functions as between county planning authorities and district planning authorities.

As from January 13, 1981 *all* applications for planning permission for development in a shire county will be made to the district council (Local Government Act 1972, s. 182, Sched. 16, para. 15(3)) and the responsibility of determining all those applications rests also with the district council *except* in the case of a "county matter," (*ibid.* para. 15(2)).

If the application appears to the district council to relate to a "county matter" they must send a copy of the application, within seven days, to the county planning authority (*ibid.* para. 15(3A)). If the application does *not* appear to the district council to relate to a "county matter," they must send a copy of the application as soon as may be, to the local highway authority (*ibid.* para. 15(3B)) unless the local highway authority do not wish to have it (*ibid.* para. 15(3C)).

In all of this the vital question is: What constitutes a "county matter?" The answer to this is found in paragraph 32 of Schedule 16 to the Local Government Act 1972 which provides (in great detail) that a "county matter" includes any application:

(a) for mineral working and related development (including cement works);

(b) for any development which straddles a National Park, *i.e.* development partly in and partly outside a National Park; and

[10] S.I. 1980 No. 1946.
[11] S.I. 1980 No. 2010.

(c) for any development prescribed in regulations made under the 1971 Act and under this head the Town and Country Planning (Prescription of County Matters) Regulations 1980[12] make applications for waste disposal in England a "county matter."

In more detail "county matters" are any application for planning permission which relates to:

(1) Minerals including
   (a) mineral workings;
   (b) the erection of buildings, plant or machinery to be used for mineral working, or for the treatment or disposal of minerals on land adjoining mineral workings;
   (c) the erection of buildings, plant or machinery (or the use of land) for any process of preparing or adapting a mineral for sale or manufacturing a product from it where—
      (i) the development is on or adjoining the mineral workings, or
      (ii) the mineral is to be brought from the mineral workings by pipeline, conveyor belt, aerial ropeway or similar plant or machinery, or by private road, private waterway or private railway;
   (d) the erection of buildings, plant or machinery which a mineral operator proposes to use for the grading, washing, grinding or crushing of minerals (no matter where they are sited);
   (e) the use of land for any purpose required in connection with rail or water transport for aggregates (including artificial aggregates) and the erection of associated buildings, plant and machinery;
   (f) the erection of buildings, plant or machinery for use for coating roadstone, producing concrete or concrete products or artificial aggregates where—
      (i) the development is on land forming part of or adjoining mineral workings, or
      (ii) the development is on land forming part of or adjoining land used in connection with rail or water transport of aggregates;
   (g) searches and tests for mineral deposits (and the erection of associated buildings, plant and machinery);
   (h) disposal of mineral waste;
   (i) cement works;
   (j) any development, on a current or disused mineral

[12] S.I. 1980 No. 2010.

working site, which would conflict with or prejudice compliance with a restoration condition imposed in respect of the mineral working;

(2) Development straddling the boundaries of a National Park; and

(3) Waste disposal sites (in England only) including waste transfer stations and similar facilities for treating, storing, processing or disposing of refuse or waste materials.

The shire county council will be responsible for determining any application for planning permission which relates to a "county matter" (Local Government Act 1972, Sched. 16, para. 15(2)). Since the operation (as from January 13, 1981) of the Local Government, Planning and Land Act 1980, county planning authorities no longer have the power to *direct* planning authorities to refuse a planning application for development on the grounds (as formerly) that it would substantially and adversely affect their interests as a local planning authority (Local Government Act 1972, s.86(2)). Instead, provision is now made whereby the district planning authority must *consult* with the county planning authority for their area on any application for planning permission which raises matters of concern to the county authority (Local Government Act 1972 s.182, Sched. 16, para. 19).

4. Consultation between Shire County Planning Authorities and Shire District Planning Authorities

What are the matters which may be said to be of concern to the shire county planning authority, ever watchful that the shire district planning authority, in the exercise of their powers of development control, do not drive a "coach and pair" through the intricately worked structure plan made (or being made) by the county planning authority? Very detailed enactment is made to ensure that the district planning authority behave themselves in this particular sphere and provision is made (*ibid.* para. 19) for the district council to consult with the county council in the case of any application for planning permission for the carrying out:

(a) of any development of land which would materially conflict with or prejudice the implementation—
   (i) of any policy or general proposal contained in a structure plan which has been approved by the Secretary of State;
   (ii) of any policy or general proposal contained in a structure plan which has been submitted to the Secretary of State for approval;

(iii) of any proposal to include in a structure plan any matter to which the county planning authority have given publicity under section 8 of the 1971 Act (publicity in connection with preparation of structure plans) or under that section as applied by section 10 of the 1971 Act (alteration of structure plans);

(iv) of a fundamental provision of a development plan which has been approved by the Secretary of State (whether under Part I of Schedule 5 of the 1971 Act or under any enactment replaced by that Part of that Schedule) so far as the development plan is in force in the district planning authority's area;

(v) of any proposal contained in a local plan which has been prepared by the county planning authority (whether or not the plan has been adopted by the authority or approved by the Secretary of State);

(vi) of any proposal to include, in a local plan which the county planning authority are preparing, any matter to which they have given publicity under section 12 of the 1971 Act (publicity in connection with preparation of local plans);

(vii) of any proposal to include, in alterations which the county planning authority are proposing for a local plan, any matter to which they have given publicity under that section 12 as applied by section 15 of the 1971 Act (publicity in connection with alteration of local plans);

(b) of any development of land which would, by reason of its scale or nature or the location of the land, be of major importance for the implementation of a structure plan which has been approved by the Secretary of State;

(c) of any development of land in an area which the county planning authority have notified to the district planning authority, in writing, as an area in which development is likely to affect, or be affected by, the winning and working of minerals, other than coal;

(d) of any development of land which the county planning authority have notified the district planning authority, in writing, that they themselves propose to develop;

(e) of any development of land which would prejudice the carrying out of development proposed by the county planning authority and notified to the district planning authority under paragraph (d) above;

(f) of any development of land in England in respect of which the county planning authority have notified the district planning authority, in writing, that it is proposed that it shall be used for waste disposal;

(g) of any development of land which would prejudice a proposed use of land for waste disposal notified to the district planning authority under paragraph (f) above.

Having received the representations of the county planning authority, the district planning authority must take them into account before determining the planning application (*ibid.* para. 19(7)).

Consultation can be avoided in any case where the county planning authority direct that it need not take place (*ibid.* para. 19(3)(4)).

Moreover, consultation need not go on for ever! It does *not* mean arriving at agreement—as is sometimes thought. In any case where it is required that consultation shall take place, the district council are precluded from determining a planning application before the expiration of 28 days after the county planning authority have been given notice by the district planning authority that the latter propose to consider the application and a copy of the application has been sent to the county planning authority (*ibid.* para. 19(5)(6) and the Town and Country Planning General Development Order 1977, art. 15A).[13] The period of 28 days can be extended only by written agreement by the district council (*ibid.*).

It is the duty of any local planning authority, when considering any application for planning permission for development to seek the achievement of the general objectives of the structure plan for the time being in force for their area (Local Government, Planning and Land Act 1980, s.86(3)). This provision, one would think, again discloses fear on the part of the county planning authority that the district planning authority, in the exercise of their powers of development control, may not "do the right thing" by the county planning authority's own structure plan.

A Code of Practice for consultation between district and county planning authorities under paragraph 19 of the Local Government Act 1972 in connection with development control has been worked out in some detail between the Department of the Environment and the local authority associations and is now set out in full in Appendix B of D.O.E. Circular 2/81 dated January 9, 1981.

5. Joint Planning Boards

The Secretary of State may constitute, as the county planning authority for the areas (or parts of the areas) of any two or more *shire*

[13] S.I. 1977 No. 289.

county councils (there are no longer any *metropolitan* county councils), a joint planning board (s.1(2) and Sched. 1). He may likewise constitute a joint board as the district planning authority for the areas (or parts of the areas) of any two or more district councils, whether metropolitan or shire district councils (*ibid.*). He may not, however, make the order constituting such a joint planning board *except* after holding a public local inquiry *unless* all the local government councils concerned consent to the making of the order (*ibid.*).

A joint planning board was constituted for the Lake District by the Lake District Planning Board Order 1951[14] and for the Peak District by the Peak Park Planning Board Order 1951.[15] Both boards were subsequently reconstituted in 1973 by the Lake District Special Planning Board Order[16] and the Peak Park Joint Planning Board Order.[17] This latter Order was revoked and replaced by the Peak Park Joint Planning Board Order 1986[18] as from April 1, 1986.

The Peak Park has its own structure plan prepared by its own Joint Planning Board. The plan is wholly separate from those made by metropolitan and non-metropolitan (or shire) county councils for those parts of their respective areas which lie outside the Peak Park boundary. The Peak Park is retained as a separate and single entity for planning and development control purposes and the new powers to make unitary development plans (explained in Chapter 6) will not extend to any part of a metropolitan district which lies within the boundary of the Peak Park.

6. Local Planning Authorities in Greater London

Within Greater London (defined in section 2(1) of the London Government Act 1963) each of the 32 London boroughs is the local planning authority for all purposes within its own area (section 1(1)(*c*) of the 1971 Act as substituted by section 3(1) of the Local Government Act 1985). The City of London is, for these purposes, included in the expression "London borough" (s.290(1)).

Planning and development control in Greater London is further dealt with in Chapter 7.

7. Planning Committees and Delegation of Powers to Officers

A local planning authority may arrange for the discharge of their planning functions under the 1971 Act by a Committee (Local

[14] S.I. 1951 No. 1491.
[15] S.I. 1951 No. 1533.
[16] S.I. 1973 No. 2001; amended by S.I. 1982 No. 991.
[17] S.I. 1973 No. 2061; amended by S.I. 1982 No. 992.
[18] S.I. 1986 No. 561.

Government Act 1972, ss.101 and 102) whilst a joint advisory committee may be established by two or more local planning authorities for the purpose of advising such authorities on the discharge of their functions under the 1971 Act (Local Government Act 1972, s.102(4)).

A local planning authority may appoint such sub-committees as they may determine for the discharge of any of their functions (Local Government Act 1972, ss.101 and 102).

A local planning authority may, if they so wish, delegate planning functions to an *officer* of the authority (Local Government Act 1972, s.101) in which event the decision of the officer becomes automatically the decision of the authority. (This matter is more fully discussed in Chapter 8 to which reference should be made). The local planning authority may not, however, delegate planning functions to a single *member* (as distinct from a single *officer*) of the authority even though that member happens to be the chairman of the planning committee of the authority.[19]

8. The Lands Tribunal

The Lands Tribunal is an authority which figures so much in connection with the settlement of disputes about compensation for planning restrictions and for the compulsory purchase of land, that brief mention of the Tribunal may usefully be made here although the Tribunal is not, strictly speaking, part or parcel of either the central or local administration of matters relating to town and country planning.

The Lands Tribunal is the creation of the Lands Tribunal Act 1949 and was established on January 1, 1950, as a piece of machinery for settling disputes involving the valuation of interests in land. Prior to 1950 such disputes had been settled by Official Arbitrators appointed under the Acquisition of Land (Assessment of Compensation) Act 1919.

The jurisdiction of the Tribunal is specified in section 1 of the 1949 Act. The Tribunal consists of a President (who must be a person who has held judicial office under the Crown—whether in the United Kingdom or not—or a barrister-at-law of at least seven years standing) and such number of other members (being barristers-at-law or solicitors of the like standing or surveyors appointed after consultation with the president of the Royal Institution of Chartered

[19] *R.* v. *Secretary of State for the Environment, ex p. London Borough of Hillingdon* (1986) 1 W.L.R. 192.

Surveyors) as the Lord Chancellor may determine and appoint (1949 Act, s.2).

The procedure of the Tribunal and the matter of appeals, costs and fees associated with it are governed by section 3 of the 1949 Act and the Lands Tribunal Rules 1975.[20] The jurisdiction of the Tribunal may be exercised by any one or more of its members (1949 Act, s.3). The decision of the Tribunal is final, but there is an appeal by way of case stated on a point of law direct to the Court of Appeal (1949 Act, s.3(4)(11)(*a*)).

[20] S.I. 1975 No. 299. See also The Lands Tribunal (Amendment) Rules 1977 (S.I. 1977 No. 1820), the Lands Tribunal (Amendment) Rules 1981 (S.I. 1981 No. 105), the Lands Tribunal (Amendment No. 2) Rules 1981 (S.I. 1981 No. 600) and the Lands Tribunal (Amendment) Rules 1984 (S.I. 1984 No. 793).

DIAGRAM OF LOCAL GOVERNMENT BEFORE REORGANISATION ON APRIL 1, 1974

Diagram 1

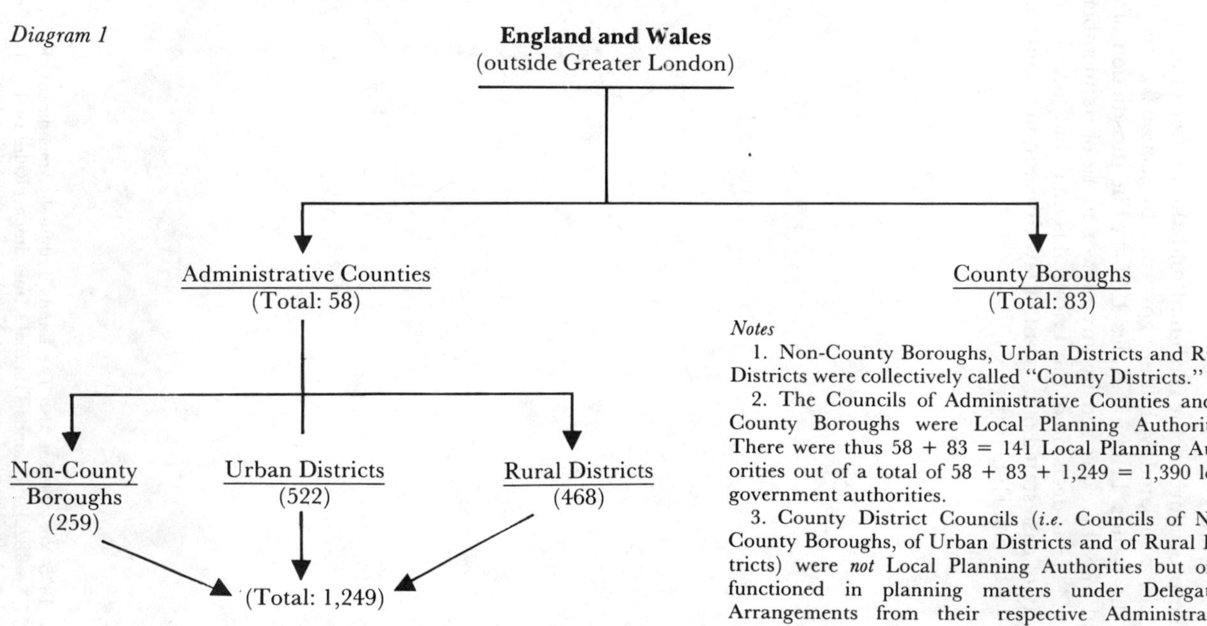

Notes

1. Non-County Boroughs, Urban Districts and Rural Districts were collectively called "County Districts."

2. The Councils of Administrative Counties and of County Boroughs were Local Planning Authorities. There were thus 58 + 83 = 141 Local Planning Authorities out of a total of 58 + 83 + 1,249 = 1,390 local government authorities.

3. County District Councils (*i.e.* Councils of Non-County Boroughs, of Urban Districts and of Rural Districts) were *not* Local Planning Authorities but often functioned in planning matters under Delegation Arrangements from their respective Administrative County Councils.

DIAGRAM OF LOCAL GOVERNMENT ON AND AFTER REORGANISATION ON APRIL 1, 1974

Diagram 2

England and Wales
(outside Greater London)

↓

New Counties
Total: 53—that is to say, 6 Metropolitan Counties *plus* 47 "Shire" or Non-Metropolitan Counties.

↓

New Districts
Total: 369—that is to say, 36 Metropolitan Districts (*i.e.* those Districts within a Metropolitan County) *plus* 333 "Shire" Districts (*i.e.* those Districts within a "Shire" County).

Split-level local government—County Level and District Level—throughout England and Wales.

Notes

1. The councils of the New Counties (whether Metropolitan or "Shire") and the councils of the New Districts (whether Metropolitan or "Shire") were all Local Planning Authorities.

2. There were thus 53 + 369 = 422 Local Planning Authorities, *i.e.* 53 County Planning Authorities and 369 District Planning Authorities.

3. Parish Councils were not Local Planning Authorities but were entitled to be consulted about certain planning applications (Local Government Act 1972, Sched. 16, para. 20 and General Development Order 1977, art. 17).

DIAGRAM OF LOCAL GOVERNMENT
ON AND AFTER FURTHER REORGANISATION
(THAT IS, THE ABOLITION OF THE GREATER LONDON COUNCIL AND THE SIX METROPOLITAN COUNTY COUNCILS)
ON APRIL 1, 1986.

Diagram 3

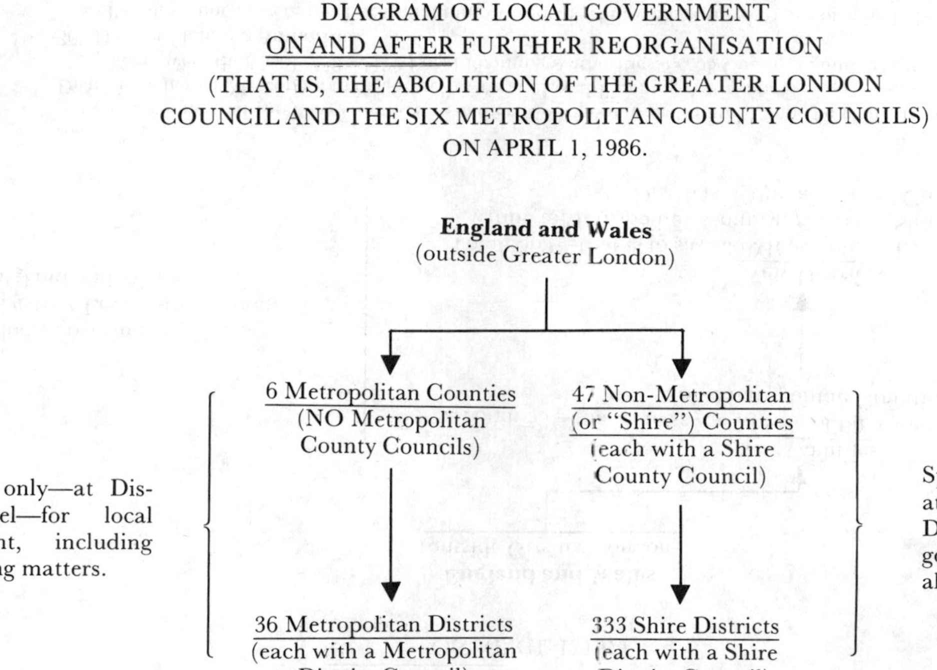

…ENTRY PLANNING AUTHORITIES …
… GREATER LONDON …
…FOLLOWING THE …
… GOVERNMENT …

…responsible … control.

Planning and …
Plan Making …
Metropolitan Districts
the Unitary
Development Plan is
made by the
the Metropolitan
District Council
grants or refuses
Planning Permission for
development
2. Unitary Development
Plan prepared by
Metropolitan District
Council
3. … Development
Plan submitted for
Public Participation
4. … Objections or
representations sent to
Metropolitan District
Council
5. Public Local Inquiry
held by Metropolitan
District Council …
objections
6. Formal Adoption of
Unitary Development
Plan by resolution of
Metropolitan District
Council with or without
modification

…there is no County Council on and after April 1, 1986 (Local Government Act …)
…Structure Plan and no Local Plan(s) but only one Unitary Development Plan.
…as set out in this Diagram 3 will apply as and when the new planning procedures under Part I …
…from time to time and place to place (Local Government Act 1985, s.4 …), brought
…by the Secretary of State.

Diagram 5

DIAGRAM SHOWING [illegible]

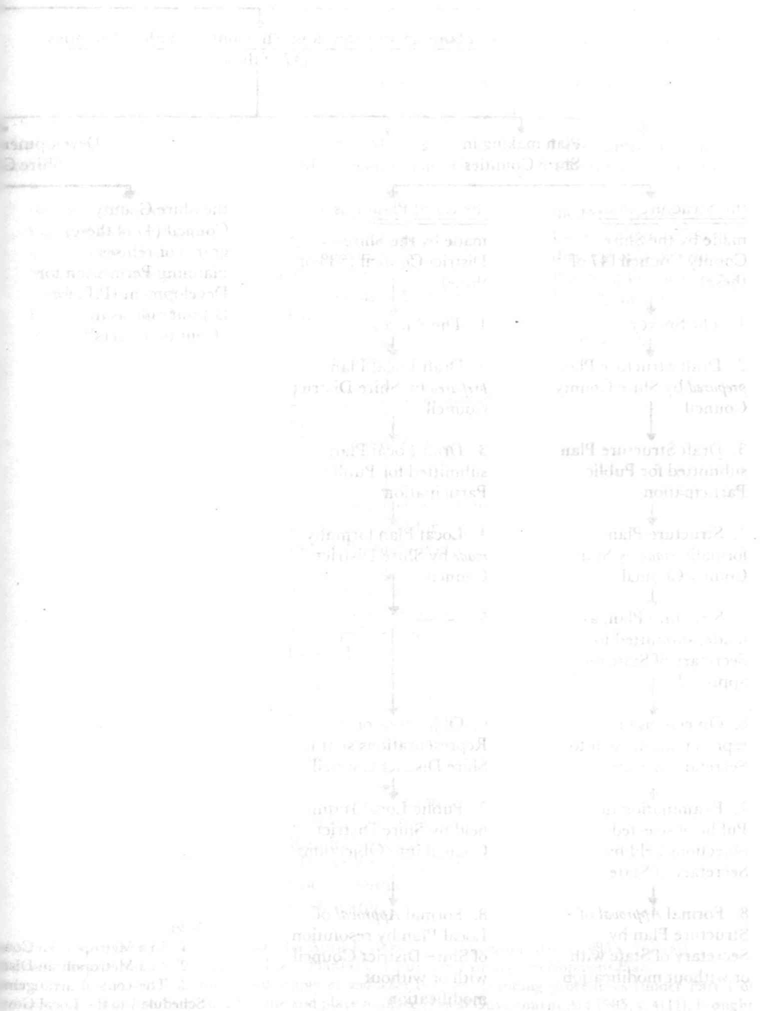

[illegible]

MAKING OF A COMPLETE [illegible]

PARTICULAR AREA) PART [illegible] SCHEDULE

The Secretary of State for the Environment [illegible]

relating to [illegible] of planning

[illegible]

[illegible] plan making in [illegible]

Shire Counties [illegible]

Structure Plans	Local Plans	[illegible]
made by the Shire County Council [illegible]	made by the Shire District Council [illegible]	the Shire County Council (and the [illegible]) [illegible] Planning Permission for Development [illegible]
1. [illegible]	1. [illegible]	
2. Draft Structure Plan prepared by Shire County Council	2. Draft Local Plan prepared by Shire District Council	
3. Draft Structure Plan submitted for Public Participation	3. Draft Local Plan submitted for Public Participation	
4. Structure Plan formally made by Shire County Council	4. Local Plan formally made by Shire District Council	
5. Structure Plan as made submitted to Secretary of State for approval	5. [illegible]	
6. Objections or representations sent to Secretary of State	6. Objections or Representations sent to Shire District Council	
7. Examination in Public of selected objections held by Secretary of State	7. Public Local Inquiry held by Shire District Council into Objections	
8. Formal Approval of Structure Plan by Secretary of State with or without modification	8. Formal Approval of Local Plan by resolution of Shire District Council with or without modification	

DIAGRAM SHOWING ARRANGEMENTS FOR TOWN AND COUNTY PLANNING AND DEVELOPMENT CONTROL IN ENGLAND AND WALES (OUTSIDE GREATER LONDON) ON AND AFTER APRIL 1, 1974 UNTIL THE MAKING, AFTER APRIL 1, 1986, OF A COMMENCEMENT ORDER BRINGING INTO FORCE (IN ANY PARTICULAR AREA) PART I OF SCHEDULE 1 TO THE LOCAL GOVERNMENT ACT 1985.

Diagram 4

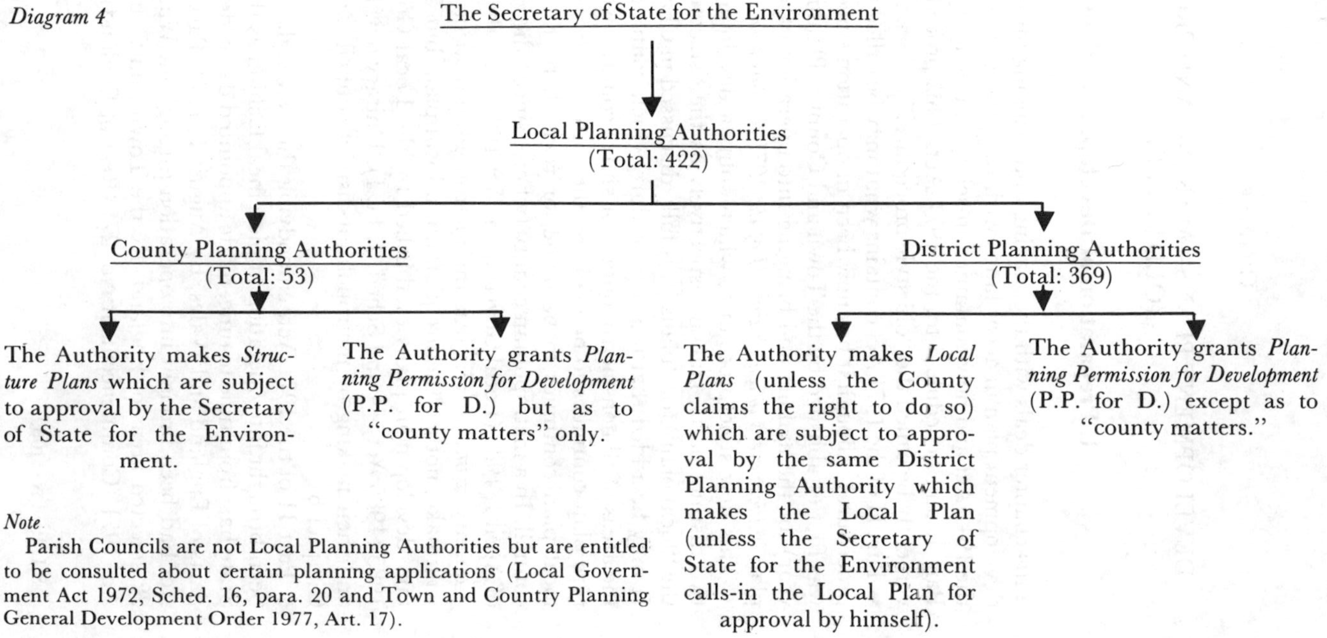

The Secretary of State for the Environment

↓

Local Planning Authorities
(Total: 422)

County Planning Authorities
(Total: 53)

- The Authority makes *Structure Plans* which are subject to approval by the Secretary of State for the Environment.
- The Authority grants *Planning Permission for Development* (P.P. for D.) but as to "county matters" only.

District Planning Authorities
(Total: 369)

- The Authority makes *Local Plans* (unless the County claims the right to do so) which are subject to approval by the same District Planning Authority which makes the Local Plan (unless the Secretary of State for the Environment calls-in the Local Plan for approval by himself).
- The Authority grants *Planning Permission for Development* (P.P. for D.) except as to "county matters."

Note

Parish Councils are not Local Planning Authorities but are entitled to be consulted about certain planning applications (Local Government Act 1972, Sched. 16, para. 20 and Town and Country Planning General Development Order 1977, Art. 17).

CHAPTER 3

DEVELOPMENT PLANS—MAKING AND PROCEDURE (OLD STYLE)

1. Preparation of Development Plans

THIS chapter deals with the making and bringing into operation of a development plan in accordance with the procedure first enacted in the 1947 Act and now contained in section 21 of, and in Schedule 5, Part I, and Schedule 6 to, the 1971 Act. This procedure may conveniently be called the "old style procedure."

Part II of the 1971 Act contains what may be called the "new style procedure" (though it has now been in operation since 1968 when it was first established by the Town and Country Planning Act of that year) for the making and bringing into operation of a development plan *in those areas to which Part II of the 1971 Act has been made applicable.*

This new style procedure, which splits a development plan into two distinct parts, known respectively as the "structure plan" and the "local plan" (or "plans"), is fully discussed in Chapters 4 and 5. It may be added that it is a procedure which continues to apply in the areas of all non-metropolitan (or shire) counties where the structure plan continues to be made by the shire county council and the local plan continues to be made, or revised, by the shire district council. In a metropolitan county (where, since "the abolition date" of April 1, 1986 (Local Government Act 1985, s.1), there is no longer a county *council* at all) it is the metropolitan district council which will make, not a structure plan nor a local plan, but one of the unitary development plans established by the Local Government Act 1985 (1985 Act, s.4 and Sched. 1, Pt. I). Unitary development plans and their making by metropolitan district councils are discussed in Chapter 6.

Part II of the 1971 Act, embodying the new style procedure, has been brought into operation in piecemeal fashion as the Secretary of State has, from time to time, made appointed day orders for different parts of England and Wales. By August 1, 1974, Part II of the 1971 Act had been brought into operation throughout Wales and also in 22 selected areas of England. By the Town and Country Planning Act 1971 (Commencement No. 27) (Rest of England) Order 1974,[1]

[1] S.I. 1974 No. 1069.

the remainder of England came under the provisions of Part II of the 1971 Act as from August 1, 1974.

In addition to the above, and as, since July 1, 1948, almost all local planning authorities have, by now, discharged their duties under the 1947 Act to carry out a survey of their area and submit to the Secretary of State a structive plan based on such survey, it is felt that in this, the 9th edition of this work, it will still be useful to include some explanation of the old style procedure for the making of development plans if only to get the historical record clear and thereby enable the reader to form his own judgment as to the comparative merits (or demerits) of the two procedures. But it must be remembered, when reading this chapter, that the old style procedure prescribed under the 1971 Act, Schedule 5, Part I, and any development plan made under that procedure, will cease to have effect (s.21(1)(*b*)) when a structure plan (for the area of the old style development plan) made under Part II of the 1971 Act becomes operative (*ibid.*).

It will be noted that the old style procedure and the new style procedure for the making and bringing into operation of a development plan are mutually exclusive procedures. Details as to the transition from the old style procedure (as now embodied in section 21 of, and in Schedule 5, Part I and Schedule 6 to, the 1971 Act) to the new style procedure (as embodied in Part II of the 1971 Act) are to be found in section 21(3) of, and Schedule 7 to, that Act.

The transition from the old style procedure to the new style procedure is complex and accordingly, it is good to discover that (by virtue of an amendment to the 1971 Act introduced by the Local Government, Planning and Land Act 1980) the Secretary of State is to keep an up-to-date register open to the public so that members of the public can readily discover for themselves the date when the provisions of Part II of the 1971 Act, relating to the making of development plans, came into effect in any particular area (s.21(7A)).

* * * * * *

The town planning schemes of former planning enactments determined and ceased to function on the coming into operation, on July 1, 1948, of the 1947 Act. Such schemes were progressively replaced by development plans made under the procedures (brand new in 1948) of the 1947 Act.

Under these procedures every local planning authority had to carry out, as soon as might be after July 1, 1948, a survey of their area and, thereafter had to prepare a development plan based on the survey.

Paragraph 1(1) of Schedule 5 to the 1971 Act (which Schedule is entitled, "Development Plans: Provisions in Force until Superseded by Part II of this Act"), requires any local planning authority (Local Government Act 1972, Sched. 16, para. 6) who have not already submitted to the Secretary of State a development plan for their area to do so within such period as the Secretary of State may allow.

Such a development plan is a plan indicating (Sched. 5, para. 1(2)):

(a) *the manner* in which the land covered by the plan is to be used (whether by the carrying out of development or not); and
(b) *the stages* by which the development is to be carried out.

A development plan may be prepared for part only of a local planning authority's area (Sched. 5, para. 1(5)) in anticipation of the making of a development plan for the whole of the area.

Details as to the form and content of these development plans are prescribed in the 1971 Act (s.21, Sched. 5, para. 6(2)) and in Part II of the Town and Country Planning (Development Plans) Regulations 1965.[2]

Generally speaking, a development plan will consist of a basic map and a written statement (both of which are obligatory in all cases) together with such other map or maps as may be appropriate to the proposals contained in the aforesaid maps and statement. Such other maps may, for example, include a town map, an inset map, a comprehensive development area map, a street authorisation map, and a programme map (showing the stages by which the proposals contained in the written statement should be carried out).

A development plan must include such maps and such descriptive matter as are necessary to illustrate, with such particularity as may be appropriate, whatever proposals it contains for the future development of the land to which it relates (Sched. 5, para. 1(3)). In particular a development plan may:

(1) *define the sites* of proposed roads, buildings, airfields, parks, pleasure grounds, nature reserves and other open spaces (*ibid.*);
(2) *allocate areas* for agricultural, residential, industrial or other purposes (*ibid.*); and
(3) *define as an area of comprehensive development* any area which should be developed or redeveloped as a whole (Sched. 5, para. 1(4)).

If a development plan covers land across which is to be constructed a trunk road by virtue of an order of the Secretary of State (under the Highways Act 1959 or the Highways Act 1980) or on

[2] S.I. 1965 No. 1453.

which a new town is to be developed by order of the Secretary of State (under the New Towns Act 1981 or its predecessors), the development plan is to have effect as if the provisions of the foregoing orders were included in the development plan itself (Sched. 5, para. 5).

2. Objections to, and Approval of, Development Plans

Before a development plan can come into operation it must be approved under the 1971 Act by the Secretary of State (Sched. 5, para. 2) and details as to the procedure for the submission to, and approval of plans by, the Secretary of State are contained (Sched. 5, para. 6(2)) in Part III of the Town and Country Planning (Development Plans) Regulations 1965.[3]

Under the foregoing Regulations it is provided, *inter alia,* that notice of the submission of a development plan to the Secretary of State must be given (reg. 17 and Sched. 2, Pt. I of the Regulations) in the *London Gazette* and in each of two successive weeks in at least one local newspaper circulating in the locality in which the land to which the development plan relates is situated (reg. 2(1)). Persons who object to the plan may send their objections in writing to the Secretary of State within whatever period is specified in the advertisement (reg. 18). This period may not be less than six weeks from the date of the first local advertisement (Sched. 2, Pt. I) and whilst the Secretary of State must consider all objections duly made he is not obliged to hold any public local inquiry (reg. 18). If he dispenses with such an inquiry he must afford a private hearing before one of his inspectors to any person who has made an objection and at any such private hearing the local planning authority is entitled to be heard (*ibid.*).

The Secretary of State may approve the development plan with or without modifications (Sched. 5, para. 2). In doing so he will be acting administratively and not judicially or quasi-judicially[4] and, accordingly, can permit himself, notwithstanding objections which have been duly made to him and duly considered by him, to be influenced by matters of policy. He is expressly authorised (Sched. 5, para. 6(3)) to hold discussions with the local planning authority or any other authority or person "behind the backs" (as it were) of objectors to the development plan. He may thus do under the 1971 Act what was held to be improper in *Errington* v. *Minister of Health.*[5]

[3] S.I. 1965 No. 1453.
[4] See *ante*, pp. 38 and 39.
[5] [1935] 1 K.B. 249.

Provision is made as to the date of operation (Sched. 5, para. 7) and the right of an aggrieved party to challenge the legal validity of a development plan in the High Court (s.244, as applied by Sched. 6, para. 3).

3. Review of Development Plans

A development plan *must* be reviewed by the carrying out of a new survey by the local planning authority at least once in every five years after the date of its approval by the Secretary of State (Sched. 5, para. 3(1)) though it *may* be reviewed at any time (Sched. 5, para. 3(2)). Thus a development plan never really achieves finality. The plan is under constant review and in this way is the better calculated to represent what, at any given moment, are the latest concepts relating to planning control over the development of land.

Whenever a review has taken place the local planning authority must submit to the Secretary of State a report of the new survey together with proposals for such alterations or additions to the development plan as the new survey calls for (Sched. 5, para. 3(1)).

The procedure which follows upon the review of a development plan is similar to that (described above) which applies on the first making, and submission to the Secretary of State for approval, of a development plan (Sched. 5, para. 6(2)). Thus the provisions of the Town and Country Planning (Development Plans) Regulations 1965[6] apply.

4. End of Designation of Land in Development Plans

It will be seen that many things may be provided for in a development plan. One of its most important features, formerly, was the designation of land as being liable to compulsory puchase by local authorities and other public bodies. By virtue, however, of the Town and Country Planning Act 1968 designation of land in a development plan as being subject to compulsory purchase ceased (1968 Act, s.27(*b*)). Any local authority needing land for town planning purposes or, to be more precise, needing land for:

(a) development, re-development and improvement;
(b) for a purpose which it is necessary to achieve in the interests of proper planning (s.112(1)(1A)(1B));

can now, without any prior designation of the land, resort to the

[6] S.I. 1965 No. 1453.

powers of section 112 of the 1971 Act to obtain the land. This is a matter more fully discussed in Chapter 19.

5. Default Powers of the Secretary of State with Respect to Development Plans

If a local planning authority fail in their duty under the 1971 Act to prepare and submit to the Secretary of State for approval a development plan, or an amendment to a development plan, the Secretary of State may himself take the requisite action to make the development plan (Sched. 5, para. 4(1)). Alternatively, the Secretary of State may authorise some neighbouring or other local planning authority to act in the place of the authority who are in default (Sched. 5, para. 4(2)). In either case the Secretary of State may recover any expenses incurred by him from the authority in default (Sched. 5, para. 4(5)). Similarly, a local planning authority acting in the place of an authority who are in default may recover *their* expenses from the latter authority (Sched. 5, para. 4(6)).

6. Modification of Provisions in their Application to Greater London

The foregoing provisions of this chapter relating to the preparation and bringing into operation of an "old style" development plan (or any amendment thereof) were made applicable (Sched. 5, para. 8(1)) to Greater London subject to modifications set out in Part II of Schedule 5 to the 1971 Act and in the Town and Country Planning (Development Plans for Greater London) Regulations 1966[7] as amended by the Town and Country Planning (Development Plans for Greater London) (Amendment) Regulations 1968[8] and the Town and Country Planning (Development Plans for Greater London) (Amendment) Regulations 1975.[9]

The result of the foregoing provisions was that any development plans relating to any part of Greater London and operative on March 31, 1965, became (together) "the initial development plan" for Greater London as from April 1, 1965 (Sched. 5 para. 8(2)). Thereafter the Greater London Council prepared the Greater London Development Plan approved (after a very lengthy public inquiry) by the Secretary of State on July 9, 1976 after which the

[7] S.I. 1966 No. 48.
[8] S.I. 1968 No. 815.
[9] S.I. 1975 No. 1680.

provisions of Part II (relating to Greater London) of Schedule 5 to the 1971 Act were revoked on October 8, 1976 by the Town and Country Planning (Repeal of Provisions No. 7) (Greater London) Order 1976.[10]

[10] S.I. 1976 No. 1162.

CHAPTER 4

DEVELOPMENT PLANS IN SHIRE COUNTIES—MAKING AND PROCEDURE—STRUCTURE PLANS

1. Introductory

THE old-style procedure for making a development plan is described in the previous chapter—a procedure first established on July 1, 1948 by the Town and Country Planning Act 1947. This continued until July 1, 1969, when the Town and Country Planning Act 1968, split the development plan into two parts—a structure plan made by a county council and a local plan (or plans) made by a district council under the aegis of the overriding county structure plan. (Until they were abolished on April 1, 1974, by the Local Government Act 1972 the 83 county boroughs in England and Wales, being *all-purpose* local government authorities, made both the structure and the local plan (or plans) for their own areas.)

The Local Government Act 1985, s.1, abolished on April 1, 1986, the six metropolitan county councils[1] (established by the 1972 Act) and also the Greater London Council (established by the London Government Act 1963). Thus no further structure plans will be made in the metropolitan counties nor in Greater London because there is no metropolitan county council to make them in any of the six metropolitan counties and no Greater London Council to make one for Greater London. Instead, in the metropolitan counties[1] and in Greater London[2] a new style of development plan to be known as a unitary development plan (Local Government Act 1985, s.4(1) and Sched. 1, Part I, para. 2(1)) will, in due course, when Schedule 1, Part I of the 1985 Act replaces Part II of the Town and Country Planning Act 1971 (Local Government Act 1985, s.4(1)) come to be made.

The non-metropolitan (or shire counties) are not touched by these new arrangements for unitary development plans. The shire county councils will continue to make studies, plans or, rather, alterations to existing structure plans (for England and Wales are now generally covered by structure plans) and the shire district councils will continue to make local plans for their own areas.[3] This chapter deals

[1] See Chap. 2 at p. 40; and see Chap. 6.
[2] See Chap. 6.
[3] See Chap. 5.

with the making (or alteration) of *structure plans* in *shire counties* while the next chapter (Chapter 5) deals with the making of *local plans* in *shire districts*. Chapter 6 deals with the making of *unitary development plans* in *metropolitan districts* while Chapter 7 deals with the making of *unitary development plans* in *the 32 London boroughs and the City of London* which together constitute Greater London.

Part II of the Town and Country Planning Act 1971 relates both to structure plans and local plans. Structure plans are dealt with under sections 6 to 10B of the 1971 Act and thereby become the responsibility of the shire county planning authority. This arrangement is provided for by section 183(1) of the Local Government Act 1972. Accordingly, in this chapter when the expression "local planning authority" or "county planning authority" is used in connection with instituting a survey or the making, alteration or withdrawal of a structure plan, it will be understood that the expressions refers to the council of a *shire* county and not a *metropolitan* county.

The Local Government, Planning and Land Act 1980 modified the statutory procedures for the preparation of structure plans by a county planning authority and for the consideration and approval of structure plans by the Secretary of State. The views and comments of the Secretary of State on all of this are contained in D.O.E. Circular 22/84 dated September 7, 1984 and in the Memorandum thereto.

2. Instituting the Survey

Under Part II of the 1971 Act every county planning authority *must institute* a survey of their area (s.6(1)) or, maybe, part of their area (s.6(5)), if they have not already done so. In so doing, their duty is to examine those matters which may be expected to affect the development of their area or the planning of its development (s.6(1)). Such matters must be kept under constant review (*ibid.*). The local planning authority *may*, if they wish, institute a fresh survey of their area at any time (s.6(2)).

It will be noted that the 1971 Act refers to the duty to *institute* a survey as distinct from to *carry out* a survey, the verb "to carry out" being the one used in the 1962 Act. This change is deliberate. The current idea is that it may be helpful for a local planning authority occasionally to employ the services of outside consultants to undertake surveys. Thus, while the local planning authority would be responsible for instituting a survey (*i.e.* for setting one in motion) they would not actually be carrying it out.

In making one of the foregoing surveys what are the particular points to which the county planning authority should give attention?

A good deal of instruction on this very important matter is given in the 1971 Act (s.6(3)) which provides that the matters to be examined and kept under review by the authority *must* include the following, namely:

(a) the principal physical and economic characteristics of the area of the authority (including the principal purposes for which land is used) and, so far as they may be expected to affect that area, of any neighbouring areas;
(b) the size, composition and distribution of the population of that area (whether resident or otherwise);
(c) without prejudice to paragraph (a) above, the communications, transport system and traffic of that area and, so far as they may be expected to affect that area, of any neighbouring areas;
(d) any consideration not mentioned in any of the foregoing paragraphs which may be expected to affect any matters so mentioned;
(e) such other matters as may be prescribed or as the Secretary of State may in a particular case direct;
(f) any changes already projected in any of the matters mentioned in any of the foregoing paragraphs and the effect which those changes are likely to have on the development of that area or the planning of such development.

If, in connection with a survey, a county planning authority needs to examine matters relating to the area of another such authority, the county planning authority must do such examination only in consultation with the other authority (s.6(4)).

3. Preparing a Structure Plan

Having made a survey of their area, the next duty of the county planning authority is to prepare and send to the Secretary of State for his approval a structure plan for their area, (s.7(1)). This submission of the structure plan must be done within such period as the Secretary of State may direct in any particular case (*ibid.*). A structure plan may be submitted for a part of the area of a county planning authority (s.7(7)).

The expression "structure plan" is not defined in the 1971 Act. The structure plan is, however, an important instrument because it is from the structure plan that the whole styling of future development control may stem.

A structure plan will (indeed it *must*) take the form of a written statement which (s.7(1A)):

(a) formulates the county planning authority's policy and

general proposals "in respect of the development and other use of land" in the area of the plan (including measures for the improvement of the physical environment and the management of traffic); and

(b) contains such other matters as may be prescribed or as the Secretary of State may in any particular case direct.

It will be noted that it is only those policies of the county planning authority which are associated with the development and other use of *land* which are to be included in the written statement of a structure plan. Today's planning and development control system, rooted in the Town and County Planning Act of 1947 (which first introduced the system) and now contained in the Town and County Planning Act 1971, is a system inseparably associated with the land, its development and its use.

In other words, town and country planning is about the land and is not to be treated as some sort of nostrum or *vade-mecum* for every sling and arrow of outrageous fortune.

In so far as a structure plan purports to set out the planning and development policies of the county planning authority, the decision of the House of Lords in the important case of *Great Portland Estates plc* v. *City of Westminster* (1985) J.P.L. 107 is relevant. It is true that this decision relates not to a structure plan but to a local plan (see later at page 80) but, even so, it is submitted that the principles enunciated in the case with respect to a local plan apply also, *mutatis mutandis*, to a structure plan.

In formulating their policy and general proposals as aforementioned, the county planning authority must secure (s.7(4)) that such policy and proposals are justified by the results of the survey earlier made under section 6 of the 1971 Act and by any other information which they may obtain and shall have regard:

(a) to current policies with respect to the economic planning and development of the region as a whole;
(b) to the resources likely to be available for the carrying out of the proposals of the structure plan; and
(c) to such other matters as the Secretary of State may direct them to take into account.

The written statement *must* be illustrated by any such diagrams as may be prescribed all of which will be treated as forming part of the plan (s.7(6)).

The structure plan *must*, in addition, be accompanied by an explanatory memorandum which *may* contain such illustrative material as the county planning authority may think to be appropriate (s.7(6A)).

The explanatory memorandum *must* (*ibid.*):

(a) summarise the reasons justifying each and every policy and general proposal formulated in the plan;
(b) state the relationship of any such policy or general proposal to expected development and other use of land in neighbouring areas (where relevant); and
(c) contain such other matters as may be prescribed.

An expression new to planning enactments since 1968 is the expression "the physical environment" (s.7(1A)(*a*)) which is not defined in the 1971 Act. A straightforward meaning of the expression is—the surroundings in which one lives, moves, works and generally has one's being. These surroundings are coming to be regarded as of increasing importance in the last decades of the twentieth century and their improvement is now declared by statute, for the first time, to be something to which planning control *must* give attention. It is perhaps significant that the 1971 Act speaks of "the improvement of the physical environment and the management of traffic" (s.7(1A)(*a*)) in, as it were, the same breath because the assault on the physical environment by traffic of all kinds is relentless and increasing. Accordingly, with Treasury consent, the Secretary of State may make grants to promote research and education about the planning and design of the physical environment (s.253).

A joint structure plan may be made by combination of two or more county planning authorities in respect of their combined area (Local Government Act 1972, s.101(5)).

Provision is made for the withdrawal of a structure plan by the county planning authority after it has been submitted to the Secretary of State for his approval and for the consequences of any such withdrawal (s.10B).

It will be seen that the structure plan is very much in the nature of a statement of general policy showing trends and tendencies and illustrating a broad basic pattern for future development. It will comprise (as already mentioned) two distinct elements, namely,

(1) a "written statement" illustrated by such diagrams as may be prescribed (s.7(1A) and (6)); and
(2) an "explanatory memorandum" (s.7(6A)).

In other words, there will be no *map* (ordnance survey or otherwise) associated with a structure plan.

> "A structure plan is almost a misnomer because it is not a plan in the way that people think of a plan, namely, a map. It is a written statement"—Mr. Niall MacDermot, Minister of State, Ministry of Housing and Local Government, *Hansard*, Standing Committee G, February 20, 1968, col. 86.

In preparing their structure plan a county planning authority may well be imbued with high ideals and grand concepts. Nevertheless, with their heads, maybe, well up in the air, the 1971 Act expressly requires them (s.7(4)) to keep their feet firmly on the ground. The Act requires that both *the policy* and the *general proposals* of the county planning authority must:

(a) *be justified* by the survey carried out under section 6 of the Act and by any other information which they may obtain; and

(b) *have regard* to current regional economic planning policies, to the resources likely to be available for the carrying out of the proposals of the structure plan and to such other matters as the Secretary of State may direct shall be taken into account (*ibid.*).

Thus, whatever may have been the situation in the past, local planning authorities now find themselves, under the procedures of the 1971 Act, injuncted by Act of Parliament *not* to provide for more town planning control than they can afford.

4. Approval or Rejection of Structure Plan by Secretary of State—Procedure

A structure plan having been prepared by a county planning authority requires submission to, and approval by, the Secretary of State before it can come into operation (s.9(1)). The plan may be approved in whole or in part and with or without modifications or reservations (*ibid.*) or the Secretary of State may reject it (*ibid.*). Before finally determining its content for submission to the Secretary of State, the county planning authority must take such steps as will in their opinion secure (s.8(1)):

(a) that adequate publicity is given in their area to the matters which they propose to include in the plan and to the proposed content of the explanatory memorandum relating to each such matter;

(b) that persons who may be expected to desire an opportunity of making representations to the authority with respect to those matters are made aware that they are entitled to an opportunity of doing so; and

(c) that such persons are given an adequate opportunity of making such representations;

and the authority must consider any representations made to them within the prescribed period.

What constitutes an "adequate opportunity" for the making of representation—"citizen (or public) participation" as this is popularly called—is not defined in the Act and when it comes to the matter of the county planning authority considering such representations the Act is again silent as to the *modus operandi*. Provision, however, is made (s.18(1)(*c*)) whereby the Secretary of State, by regulations, may do some filling-in of these important gaps by making provision with respect to the making of, and the consideration of, representations relating to any matter to be included in a structure plan. In this connection the Secretary of State has made the Town and Country Planning (Structure and Local Plans) Regulations 1982.[4]

Not later than the submission of the structure plan to the Secretary of State for approval, the local planning authority must make copies of the plan and of the explanatory memorandum available for public inspection and each copy must be accompanied by a statement of the time within which *objections to the plan may be made to the Secretary of State* (s.8(2)).

In connection with a structure plan the county planning authority and the Secretary of State are entitled to disregard (s.16) representations or objections with respect to development authorised by or under certain other enactments, namely, the Highways Act 1980 (replacing the Highways Act 1959), the Highways (Miscellaneous Provisions) Act 1961, or the Highways Act 1971 and the New Towns Act 1981. Duplication of procedures is thus avoided.

The county planning authority must by means of a statement accompanying the structure plan, inform the Secretary of State (s.8(3)):

(a) of the steps they have taken to give adequate publicity to their actions in preparing their structure plan and the accompanying explanatory memorandum;
(b) of the consultations which they have had with persons making representations about the plan; and
(c) of their consideration of any such representations.

If not satisfied with the local authority's information about these matters the Secretary of State may decline to consider the structure plan and return it to the local authority with suitable directions about further publicity and resubmission of the plan (s.8(4)(5)).

In considering whether to approve or reject a structure plan the Secretary of State has a fairly free hand. His function is an administrative function.[5] He may take into account any matters which he thinks relevant whether or not these were taken into account in the preparation of the plan as submitted to him (s.9(2)). He may also consult with, and consider the views of, *any* local planning authority

[4] S.I. 1982 No. 555.

[5] See pp. 38 and 39, *ante*. See also reference to Goverment policy in Chap. 2 at pp. 36 and 37, *ante*.

or other person but he is not obliged to do so (s.9(7)). Clearly, in all of this the Secretary of State will be guided by what is, for the time being, government policy as to planning control over land development.[5]

After consideration, the Secretary of State may reject a structure plan or he may approve it in whole or in part and with or without modifications or reservations (s.9(1)). The Secretary of State must give such statement as *he* considers appropriate of the reasons governing his decision (s.9(8)).

If the Secretary of State decides that he will reject a structure plan outright he may do so without further ado and without considering any objections which have been made to it. If, however, he does *not* decide to reject it outright then, before determining whether or not to approve it, he must (s.9(3)):

(a) consider any objections made in accordance with regulations[6] under Part II of the 1971 Act; and

(b) cause a person (or persons) appointed by him to hold an *examination in public* of such matters affecting his consideration of the plan as *he* considers ought to be so examined.

Thus not *all* objections will be the subject of an examination in public, but only those selected for such examination by the Secretary of State (s.9(5)). This is an important qualification.

The "examination in public," to be held as mentioned in the previous paragraph, is in substitution (as from July 27, 1972, the date of the passing of the Town and Country Planning (Amendment) Act 1972) for the "public inquiry" which formerly would generally have been held in connection with the consideration by the Secretary of State of objections to a structure plan. The nature of an "examination in public" is very much a matter for the discretion of the Secretary of State who has set forth his views and intentions in D.O.E. Circular 22/84 dated September 7, 1984, at paragraphs 2.36 and 2.37 of the Memorandum associated with the Circular in which he refers to D.O.E. booklet entitled "Structure Plans: The examination in public—a guide to procedure 1984." The most important part of the booklet is Section 2 which is a Code of Practice setting out the arrangements leading up to the examination in public and the way in which the examination will be conducted.

The Secretary of State, after consultation with the Lord Chancellor, may make regulations as to procedure at any "examination in public" (s.9(4)). His power to do this is dependent upon section 9(4)

[5] See pp. 38 and 39, *ante*. See also reference to Goverment policy in Chap. 2 at pp. 36 and 37, *ante*.

[6] See the Town and Country Planning (Structure and Local Plans) Regulations 1982 (S.I. 1982 No. 555).

of the 1971 Act being first brought into operation (s.9(4A)). In the meantime the Secretary of State has issued the non-statutory code of procedure (above mentioned) for examinations in public entitled "Structure Plans: The examination in public—A guide to procedure 1984."

An "examination in public" will constitute a statutory inquiry for the purposes of section 1(1)(*c*) of the Tribunals and Inquiries Act 1971 but not for any other purpose of that Act (s.9(6)).

It will be noted that no local planning authority nor anybody else can *demand a right* to appear at any "examination in public"; appearance is by invitation only of the Secretary of State (s.9(5)). But if such authority or person is *not* accorded, by the Secretary of State, an opportunity to appear, then in such a case the person (or persons) appointed by the Secretary of State to hold the examination may nevertheless allow any such authority or person the opportunity to be heard (*ibid.*). This discretion may be exercised at any time before or during the examination (*ibid.*).

The provisions of the 1971 Act as to "examinations in public" apply *only to structure plans*; they do *not* apply to the consideration of objections to local plans (s.13).[7]

D.O.E. Circular 22/84 dated September 7, 1984 (previously mentioned) is an important Circular relating to the whole development plan system of structure and local plans. It gives basic guidance to local planning authorities but is of equal importance to any one seeking to make representations or objections to a structure plan. It is a substantial document and carries a "Memorandum on Structure and Local Plans" followed by ten Annexes (Annexes A to J) of which Annexes A, C, D, E and I relate to structure plans. The Circular and the Memorandum (which together comprise some 88 pages) will repay close study. The memorandum should be treated as the principal document for reference (a) when preparing a structure plan or proposals for its alteration, repeal or replacement, or (b) when seeking to influence the contents of such a plan or to object to its being approved by the Secretary of State.

No landowner or land developer should fail to pay attention to the contents of a proposed structure plan nor to lodge an objection to those contents if he has reason to disagree with them. He must never forget that whenever he (or anyone else) comes to apply for planning permission for development (as dealt with later in Chapter 10) it may be that it is the contents of the structure plan which preclude him from getting the planning permission for development which he

[7] See p. 90.

so greatly desires. It is true that the contents of a structure plan do not *necessarily and in all circumstances* bind a planning authority when considering an application for planning permission but the authority are bound in law (s.29(1)) to "have regard to the provisions of the development plan" (which includes the structure plan) along with "any other material considerations" in coming to a conclusion on the planning application. Moreover, it is the statutory *duty* of any local planning authority, when considering a planning application, to seek the achievement of the general objectives of any relevant structure plan (Local Government, Planning and Land Act 1980, s.86(3)).

5. Regulations and Directions as to Details and Procedure

Further details

(a) as to the form and content of a structure plan and
(b) as to the procedure to be followed in connection with its preparation, submission, withdawal, approval, adoption, making, alteration, repeal and replacement

are found in regulations (the Town and Country Planning (Structure and Local Plans) Regulations 1982[8]) made by the Secretary of State under the provisions of the 1971 Act (s.18(1)).

Such regulations make provision as to:

(1) publicity in connection with the preparation of a structure plan, the sale of documents and the prescribed period for the making of representations ("public participation") about such a plan (Pt. II of the Regulations);
(2) consultation in connection with the making a structure plan (Pt. III of the Regulations);
(3) the form and content of a structure plan and prescribed matters to be set out in an explanatory memorandum (Pt. IV of the Regulations);
(4) action areas: prescribed period (usually 10 years) for purposes of section 11(4A) of the 1971 Act (Pt. VI of the Regulations);
(5) the procedure for the approval, withdrawal or rejection of a structure plan (Pt. VII of the Regulations);
(6) the availability and sale of documents, the register and the index map, associated with a structure plan (Pt. IX of the Regulations);
(7) the alteration, repeal and replacement of a structure plan (Pt. X of the Regulations);

[8] S.I. 1982 No. 555.

(8) the preparation and making of a structure plan by the Secretary of State (Pt. XI of the Regulations);
(9) the reconciliation of contradictions in a structure plan (Pt. XII of the Regulations);
(10) forms of notices (Sched. to the Regulations).

But if there are to be *regulations* (as there are)[9] there may also be *directions* because the 1971 Act provides that, subject to any regulations made as mentioned above, the Secretary of State may give directions (s.18(3)) either to local planning authorities in general, or to any one authority in particular,

(a) for formulating the procedure to be carried out by them in connection with the preparation and approval of a structure plan; and
(b) for requiring them to give him such information as he may need to help him to discharge his functions relating to structure plans.

6. Operation, Validity, Alteration, Repeal or Replacement of a Structure Plan

Subject to the provisions of section 242 of the 1971 Act (relating to the validity of development plans) a structure plan will become operative on a date appointed for the purpose in the relevant notice of approval by the Secretary of State (s.18(4)).

At any time after a structure plan has come into operation the county planning authority may submit to the Secretary of State proposals for alterations to the plan and they *must* submit such proposals if required to do so by the Secretary of State (s.10(1)).

Similarly, the county planning authority may submit proposals for the repeal and replacement of the structure plan (s.10(2)); but if this is done the proposals must be accompanied by the replacement structure plan (s.10(3)).

Any proposals for alteration or for repeal and replacement of a structure plan must be accompanied by an explanatory memorandum summarising the reasons of the county planning authority justifying the alteration or the replacement of the plan (s.10(4)) and giving other relevant information (s.10(5) and (6)).

The procedure for the submission and approval of structure plans as discussed above applies also to the alteration, or the repeal and replacement, of a structure plan (s.10(7) applying ss. 8 and 9 of the 1971 Act and para. 8 of Sched. 16 to the Local Government Act

[9] See the Town and Country Planning (Structure and Local Plans) Regulations 1982 (S.I. 1982 No. 555).

1972) except that there is no need for the holding of an examination in public where it appears to the Secretary of State that nothing in the proposals for alteration, or for repeal and replacement, of the structure plan calls for such an examination (s.10(8)).

Where proposals for the alteration or replacement of a *structure* plan have been submitted to the Secretary of State, he may, on the application of a local planning authority who are proposing to make, alter, repeal or replace any *local* plan, direct (after consultation (s.15A(3)) with the county planning authority or, as the case may be, the district planning authority) that it shall be assumed that the structure plan proposals have been approved by him subject to such modifications, if any, as may be proposed by him and notified to the county planning authority (s.15A(1)). Any such direction will cease to have effect if the Secretary of State rejects the proposals for the alteration or replacement of the structure plan (s.15A(2)).

7. Joint Structure Plans

A joint structure plan may be made by two (or more) county planning authorities under the provisions of section 101(5) of the Local Government Act 1972 which enables two or more local authorities to discharge *any* of their functions jointly. Details as to the form and content of a joint structure plan, and the procedure for the preparation, alteration, repeal or replacement of such a plan, are found in Schedule 16, paragraphs 8 to 14, of the Local Government Act 1972. All the matters contained in the aforesaid paragraphs 8 to 14 follow closely the corresponding provisions of sections 6 to 10B of the Town and Country Planning Act 1971 relating to the form and content and the procedure for preparing, altering, repealing or replacing, a structure plan prepared by a single county planning authority and described in the previous paragraphs of this chapter.

8. Withdrawal of Structure Plan

Section 10B of the 1971 Act allows a local planning authority to withdraw any structure plan they have submitted to the Secretary of State, *at any time before* it has been approved. Steps taken in connection with a plan which is withdrawn may be taken into account when a further plan is prepared (s.10B(3)).

9. Nature and Effect of a Structure Plan

Structure plans (as has already been mentioned) are by nature statements of broad policy illustrated by diagrams and descriptive matter.

The preparation and bringing into operation of a structure plan will bring a local planning authority face to face with the Secretary of State. Thus, central control over all structure plans is always on hand. To put the matter another way would be to say that in every instance (*i.e.* without exception) it is the Secretary of State who will have the last say in the form and content of a structure plan and he will be guided by what is, for the time being, government policy in the general field of planning and development control.[10]

The question for the man in the street, of course, is: *What will he be able to learn from a structure plan*? He will certainly not be able to learn as much as he has been able to learn from the "old style" development plan. Indeed, it is not the intention that he should do. Structure plans (which always need the Secretary of State's approval) are not to be cluttered with the detail to be found in old style development plans.

It may be repeated that the object of a structure plan will be to sketch out trends and tendencies, to lay down general lines and to show broadly and without detail how development could shape-up within the area of the structure plan.

Any person (landowner or developer) seeking further and better particulars about the shape of development yet to come in the future and on his own particular plot will need to move on from the structure plan to an investigation of what is known under the 1971 Act as a local plan.[11]

The broad nature of the structure plan system was highlighted by Mr. Niall MacDermot, Ministry of Housing and Local Government (*Hansard,* Standing Committee G, February 22, 1968, col. 107), when he said:

> "The broad picture of the new structure plan system, compared with present development plans, has now emerged fairly clearly. We envisage it as a system which will broaden the spectrum of the development plans; which will give first expression to the concept of two levels of responsibility for the approval of the development plan; and which will change the nature of the development plan—in that the structure plan will be a written statement supported by a diagram and not a map . . . .
>
> "What we have done is to spell out in much more detail than was done in the previous Act what shall be the matters to be covered by the Survey on which the structure plan is to be based. Clause 2(3) and clause 1(3) (now ss.7(3) and 6(3)

[10] See Chap. 2 at pp. 35–39 inclusive.
[11] See Chap. 5.

respectively of the 1971 Act) combined give an indication of the contents of the structure plan. Their effect is to indicate that, although a structure plan will be basically about land use, *it will deal with the subject in terms of the policies applicable to the major uses* . . . such as housing, education, recreation, industry and commerce and relating the broad intentions about the land use represented by those policies to the traffic policies, and to policies for the movement of people and of goods—the whole plan being framed with regard to its relationship to neighbouring areas."

10. Conformity (or Conflict) between Structure Plans and Local Plans

On the approval, by the Secretary of State, of proposals for the alteration or replacement of a structure plan, it straightway becomes the *duty* of the county planning authority to consider whether any local plan, adopted by a district planning authority *or* approved by the Secretary of State, conforms generally with the structure plan as altered or, as the case may be, with the new structure plan replacing the previous one (s.15A(4)).

Within one month from the date of the approval of proposals for altering or replacing a structure plan, the county planning authority must send to the Secretary of State and to any affected district planning authority lists showing all local plans which:

(a) conform to the structure plan; or
(b) do not so conform (s.15A(5)).

Where there is any conflict between a local plan and a structure plan both functioning in the same area, it is the contents of the local plan which are to prevail for all purposes (s.15B(1)). This statutory provision, however, will not apply in a case where a local plan is being altered, repealed or replaced in order to conform with an altered or replaced structure plan until the requisite alteration, repeal or replacement plan has come into force (s.15B(2)).

11. The Structure Plan becomes "the Development Plan"

Finally, the question may be asked: How does a structure plan (as discussed above) ever become "the development plan" (as the old expression goes) for any particular area? The answer is to be found in section 20 of the 1971 Act whereby "the development plan" for the purposes of the 1971 Act, or any other Act relating to town and country planning, the Land Compensation Act 1961 and the Highways Act 1980, is to be the structure plan (plus any alterations thereto) together with any local plan or plans (plus any alterations thereto) for the time being in force, together with the Secretary of State's notice of approval of the structure plan and the local planning authority's resolution adopting any local plan.

Thus "the development plan"—the outcome of the procedures under Part II of the 1971 Act—is a conglomeration of all the aforementioned documents.

12. The Secretary of State's Default Powers

The Secretary of State has certain default powers with respect to structure plans whereby he himself or, where he so appoints, some other local planning authority, may perform any of the duties and functions imposed on a county planning authority under Part II of the 1971 Act (s.17).

13. Modification of Provisions in their Application to London

All the provisions of Part II of the 1971 Act relating to structure plans are made applicable to Greater London subject to the provisions of Schedule 4 to the 1971 Act (s.19). This state will continue until Part I of Schedule 1 to the Local Government Act 1985 replaces in Greater London the provisions of Part II of the Town and Country Planning Act 1971 by the bringing into force of the aforesaid Part I of Schedule 1 to the 1985 Act by means of a commencement order made by the Secretary of State under the authority of section 4(1) of the 1985 Act.[12]

14. Regulations

The Secretary of State has made the Town and Country Planning (Structure and Local Plans) Regulations 1982.[13] These Regulations (repealing and re-enacting with amendments earlier Regulations of a like kind) were rendered necessary by the several amendments to the 1971 Act brought about by the Local Government Act 1972 and the Local Government, Planning and Land Act 1980.

These regulations (discussed earlier in this chapter) make provision with respect to the form and content of structure plans prepared under Part II of the 1971 Act, and with respect to the procedure to be followed in the preparation, submission, withdrawal,

[12] See Chap. 6.
[13] S.I. 1982 No. 555.

approval, adoption, making, alteration, repeal and replacement of such plans.

The 1982 Regulations apply to Greater London subject to certain exemptions and modifications (reg. 1(2) and (3)).

15. The Prospect Before Us

The Secretary of State, Mr. Nicholas Ridley, on September 15, 1986, (D.O.E. Press Notices Nos. 487 and 488 of that date) announced to the Royal Town Planning Institute Town and County Planning Summer School "major reforms to simplify and improve the development plan system:

They include:

(1) replacing the present two-tier system of structure and local plans in non-metropolitan (*i.e.* of shire) areas by a single-tier system of development plans drawn up by districts;

(2) the creation of a new statutory definition for environmentally important areas in the countryside, to be known as "rural conservation areas"; and

(3) the preparation by county councils of strategic policies on a range of planning issues which would provide part of the framework for the preparation of district development plans.

Mr. Ridley said:

> "The present two-tier system of structure and local plans is too cumbersome. Plans have become overburdened with unnecessary detail and they take far too long to prepare. We must make the system more responsive to present and future needs for economic growth and to protect and conserve sensitive environmental areas.
>
> "Cutting out structure plans and having a single-tier of development plans in all parts of England and Wales will mean that plan-making will be simpler and the plans more effective. It will bring planning closer to local people, where it belongs."

It will all require legislation *not* expected to be introduced during the current Parliament.

The proposals are set out in, "The Future of Development Plans," a consultation paper, published September 15, 1986, by the D.O.E. The consultation period lasts until March 14, 1987.

Chapter 5

DEVELOPMENT PLANS IN SHIRE COUNTIES—MAKING AND PROCEDURE—LOCAL PLANS

1. Introductory

Before embarking on any consideration of this chapter, the reader is referred to the three opening paragraphs of Chapter 4—particularly paragraph 3. In short, local plans will continue to be made under the provisions of sections 11 to 15B of the Town and Country Planning Act 1971 each of which sections has been substituted (by the Housing and Planning Act 1986, section 41 and Schedule 10, Part I) for earlier corresponding sections in the 1971 Act. As stated in paragraph 3 of Chapter 4, notwithstanding the new arrangements for unitary development plans to be made by the councils of metropolitan districts, the councils of shire districts will continue to have the duty of preparing local plans. Accordingly, in this chapter the expression "district planning authority" means the council of a shire district—not a metropolitan district.

2. Local Plan Schemes—Who Makes the Local Plan?

The making of local plans is dealt with in sections 11 to 15B of the Town and Country Planning Act 1971, 13 sections substituted (as mentioned) by the Housing and Planning Act 1986, section 41 and Schedule 10, Part I for the previous eight sections 10C to 15B of the 1971 Act.

If the responsibility for the making of a structure plan is exclusively that of the shire county planning authority (Local Government Act 1972, s.183(1)), the responsibility for the making of a local plan (or plans) is primarily and generally (but not necessarily exclusively) that of the shire district planning authority (Town and Country Planning Act 1971, ss.11(6) and 11A(2)(*c*)).

This statement as to the *general* position of a district planning authority in relation to the making of a local plan is qualified by the fact that the preparation of a local plan is subject to the provisions of a "local plan scheme" (s.11A). This scheme is to be prepared by the county planning authority in consultation with the district planning authorities (s.11A(4)) and its purpose is to set out a programme for the preparation of local plans (s.11A(1)) and to designate either the county planning authority or a district planning authority as the authority responsible for the preparation of each such plan (s.11A(2)(*c*)). The scheme must also specify the title and nature of each local plan and the area to which it applies and, where appropriate, its relationship with other local plans provided for by the scheme (s.11A(2)(*a*)(*b*)). The local plan scheme must be lodged by the county planning authority with the Secretary of State (s.11A(5))and may be amended from time to time (s.11A(3)(4)).

When a district planning authority is dissatisfied with a local plan scheme, they may complain about this to the Secretary of State who may himself amend the scheme (s.11A(6)).

From the foregoing statutory provisions relating to local plan schemes made pursuant to section 11A of the Town and Country Planning Act 1971, it will be understood that when, in connection with a local plan, reference is made in this chapter to the "local planning authority" the reference will relate to the particular planning authority (whether shire county or shire district) to whom, in the circumstances as set out in the local plan scheme, it falls to prepare, under Part II of the 1971 Act, a local plan or plans.

D.O.E. Circular 22/84, dated September 7, 1984, is an important Circular relating to the whole development plan system of structure plans and local plans. Primarily intended for the guidance of local planning authorities, (to whom alone it is addressed), it is of equal importance to anyone seeking to make representations or objections to a local plan.

The Local Government, Planning and Land Act 1980 modified the statutory procedures for the preparation of local plans by a local planning authority (the shire district planning authority). The views and comments of the Secretary of State on all of this are contained in the above mentioned D.O.E. Circular 22/84 and in the Memorandum and the ten Annexes thereto.

3. What is a Local Plan?—Preparation and Adoption—Procedure

A local plan is a plan prepared by a local planning authority under the aegis of an overriding structure plan. The prime distinguishing feature of a local plan is that at no time in its preparation and its being brought into operation does the local planning authority *necessarily* come face to face with the Secretary of State. Nevertheless it is from the local plan rather than from the structure plan that the private individual will really be able to learn what the local planning authority's planning proposals for the future mean to him and his property. If there is no local plan in operation (and not the whole of England and Wales is, as yet, covered by local plans) he will have to glean what he can from the structure plan which applies to his property and then proceed to ask questions of the district planning authority.

A local plan must consist of (s.11(1)):

(a) a *written statement* formulating, in such detail as the local planning authority think appropriate, their proposals for the development and other use of land in their area, or for any description of development or other use of such land including in either case such measures as the authority think fit for the improvement of the physical environment and the management of traffic;

(b) a *map* showing the foregoing proposals; and

(c) such *diagrams*, *illustrations* or other *descriptive matter* as the authority think appropriate to explain or illustrate the proposals in the plan, or as may be prescribed.

This specification for the content of a local plan set out in section 11(1)(*a*)(*b*) and (*c*) of the Town and Country Planning Act 1971 may be compared with the specification for the content of a structure plan as given in section 7(1A)(*a*) and (*b*) of the 1971 Act and referred to in the previous chapter.[1]

In formulating in a local plan their proposals about development, the district planning authority must have regard to any information or considerations which appear to be relevant or which are prescribed by the Secretary of State (s.11(3)) who, in any particular case, may direct what matter shall be taken into account (*ibid.*). The proposals must, in any case, be in general conformity with the structure plan subject to which the local plan is made (s.11(4)).

For the purpose of discharging their functions relating to local plans, a district planning authority may examine all or any of the matters which it is the duty (under section 6(1) and (3) of the Town and Country Planning Act 1971) of the county planning authority to examine when the county authority are making a survey of their area (s.11(6)).[2]

In preparing a local plan the district planning authority must take into account the provisions of any scheme relating to land in their area which has been designated as an enterprise zone (s.11(7)).[3]

Different local plans may be prepared for different purposes for the same area (s.11(2)).

The Secretary of State is empowered to direct the making,

[1] See Chap. 4, p. 63.
[2] See Chap. 4, pp. 62 and 63.
[3] See Chap. 24.

alteration, repeal or replacement of a local plan after consultation with the district planning authority concerned (s.11B(1)). The direction must specify the nature of the plan which is to be made or the nature of the alteration which is required (s.11B(2)). The district planning authority must comply with the direction as soon as possible (s.11B(3)) and the county planning authority must make such amendments to the relevant local plan scheme as appear to them to be appropriate in consequence of the giving of the direction (s.11B(4)).

A local plan, of whatever kind, may be regarded as a statement of further and better particulars than are to be found in a structure plan demonstrating a more detailed working-out of some particular aspect of town planning which, in the structure plan, is merely sketched as a matter of policy and not worked out in any detail.

In setting out in a local plan their "proposals for the development and other use of land," a district planning authority will be wise to set out such proposals as fully as possible and not leave some of them unmentioned in the local plan and left to be later dealt with in non-statutory guidelines to be prepared after the adoption of the plan. This is the outcome of the House of Lords decision in *Great Portland Estates plc.* v. *City of Westminster* (1984) 3 All E.R. 744; (1985) J.P.L. 107. In this case the Westminster City Council, in their local plan, divided the City of Westminster into two zones—the central activities zone and the rest of the city—and provided that, as a matter of policy, in the "rest of the city" office development would be allowed only in "exceptional" and "special" circumstances which were not particularised in the local plan because they were "best dealt with through non-statutory guidelines for different locations in the city."

In doing this the House of Lords held that the omission from the statutory local plan of the council's policies as to what were exceptional or special circumstances for allowing offices in Westminster outside the central zone constituted a failure by the council to comply with Schedule 4, paragraph 11 of the Town and Country Planning Act 1971. The council were not to introduce land-use policies additional to those proposed in the local plan by means of supplementary planning guidance which should, by law, have been included in the local plan so that all interested parties could know what would be the policy of the council in granting (or refusing) planning permission for office development outside the centre zone of the city. As Lord Scarman said in his judgment (1985) J.P.L. 107 at 114), "By excluding from the plan its proposals in respect of office development outside the centre activities zone the council deprived persons such as the respondents (Great Portland Estates Plc.) from raising objections and securing an inquiry into such objections."

The use of the words "exceptional" and "special" in the statutory local plan acted as "cover for policies excluded from the plan."

For further reading on this important matter relating to plan making, reference may be made to D.O.E. Circular 22/84, dated September 7, 1984, paragraph 1.13, which declares that

> "Any plan containing proposals for the development and other use of land which is not included in the development plan scheme as a local plan, or as proposals for the alteration of a local plan, and which has not been subject to any of the stages in the statutory procedures . . . can have little weight for development control purposes. It cannot be treated as an emerging local plan. Where there is a need to devote resources to the preparation of proposals for the use of land, these should be settled in the statutory plan."

However, the Circular does concede (paras. 1.14 and 1.15) that there is:

> "a continuing role for planning guidance which supplements the policies and proposals contained in structure and local plans. This may include, for example, practice notes for development control requirements, development briefs and detailed or sketch lay-outs for such development as housing or open space. These documents should be published separately from the policies and proposals of the statutory development plan for the area and kept publicly available. They should be consistent with the structure plan and any local plan for the area."

4. Regulations as to Details and Procedure

Further details (a) as to the form and content of a local plan, and (b) as to the procedure to be followed in connection with its preparation, adoption, abandonment, approval or rejection, alteration or repeal, are found in the Town and Country Planning (Structure and Local Plans) Regulations 1982[4] made by the Secretary of State under the 1971 Act (s.18(1)). These Regulations make provision as to:

(1) publicity in connection with the preparation of a local plan, the sale of documents and the prescribed period for the making of representations ("public participation") about such a plan (Part II of the Regulations);

(2) the form and content of a local plan (Part V of the Regulations);

[4] S.I. 1982 No. 555.

(3) the procedure for the adoption, abandonment, approval or rejection of a local plan (Part VIII of the Regulations);
(4) the availability and sale of documents, the register and the index map, associated with a local plan (Part IX of the Regulations);
(5) the alteration, repeal or replacement of a local plan (Part X of the Regulations);
(6) the preparation and making of a local plan by the Secretary of State (Part XI of the Regulations);
(7) the reconciliation of contradictions in a local plan (Part XII of the Regulations);
(8) forms of notices (Schedule to the Regulations).

5. Action Area Plans

Several types of local plan can be made (s.11(2)). One type of local plan which is given particular mention in the 1971 Act is the "action area plan." This is a type of local plan which *may* be prepared by the local planning authority (they are not bound to prepare one) relating to any part of their area which they *have selected for comprehensive treatment* by development, redevelopment or improvement within a *prescribed period* (s.11(5)).

If the local planning authority are going to have an action area plan, then the plan *must* set out the nature of the treatment which has been selected by the authority to secure the comprehensive treatment of the area (*ibid.*).

The comprehensive treatment to be visited upon an action area will need to be commenced within the period of time (10 years) prescribed (s.290(1)) in the 1982 Regulations (reg. 14). The object of the Act is clearly to provide that action areas shall be those areas where action in the planning field is required *not only on a comprehensive basis but also at an early date.*

As to the period of time to which action areas could relate the Minister of State, Ministry of Housing and Local Government, said on February 20, 1968, during the Committee stage of the Bill for the 1968 Act (*Hansard,* Standing Committee G, cols. 80 *et seq.*):

> "With regard to the span of time to which action areas could relate, to be prescribed by the Minister, we have in mind, as a sort of outside limit, a ten-year period. The period relates to the period from the time when the structure plan is approved, but I think that that would be the outside limit. As I have said, these are meant to be the areas which are envisaged for early treatment, early development, redevelopment and improvement. Nevertheless, there will be different types of action area plans

and they will themselves have to be phased if there are several action areas indicated in one plan. As we have had occasion to make clear earlier, some action area plans will themselves be very detailed. Other action area plans will give general indications of the kind of development that is to take place. That will be so particularly where it is envisaged that the development will be by a private developer and one wants to leave scope for him to put forward his own detailed plans.

"Even when one gets to the stage of publication of the action area plan itself, its precise effect and the degree to which it would indicate to property owners how their property would be affected will vary according to the nature of the action area plan."

6. Structure Plans and Local Plans—Relationship and Interplay

The relationship of a structure plan to a local plan and the interplay between these two kinds of differing plans was discussed at length in the Committee stage of the Bill for the Town and Country Planning Act 1968. Some very informative statements about all this were made on behalf of the Government by the Minister of State, Ministry of Housing and Local Government, who put the matter in the following terms on February 29, 1968 (*Hansard,* Standing Committee G, cols. 186 *et seq.*):

"These amendments raise an important question, involving, as they do, the nature of local plans and the amount of detail which should appear in them. It is, of course, one of the main purposes of separating structure plans from local plans to rid the central Government of the responsibility for a mass of detail which is better dealt with and decided at local level. Of necessity, therefore, one expects local plans to be more detailed in their nature. That, indeed, follows from a number of provisions in the Bill, including the fact that the local plan, unlike the structure plan, will be primarily a map. There will be written explanatory material but it will primarily be a map or series of maps—maps drawn on ordnance survey maps.

"We then come to the question which the amendments raise, which is whether we should try to write into the Bill a requirement or definition of the amount of detail that should appear in the maps. Here again I wish to make a plea to the Committee for flexibility, and for very good reasons, I think. Local plans, as we envisage them, will vary considerably in their type and scope, and we should be losing some of the benefits of the change that we are making if we tried to prescribe too rigidly the requirements that would apply to all local plans, particularly in this matter of detail.

"Some local plans—in particular, for example, a local plan setting out a development which it is proposed should be carried out by a local authority—should set out and specify in considerable detail what it is in mind to do. That might be so whether the plan was for a comprehensive redevelopment of an area or perhaps for an improvement for an old area. People should know precisely what it is that the authority intends to be done.

"Another class of local plan, and a very important one in my view, would be of a much more general nature, and in these the planning authority would indicate the kind of development or redevelopment which it had in mind but where the intention was that it should be done by private developers. The authority would want to leave some scope and freedom to the private developer and his architects to make proposals about the detail of the plan.

"I think we are agreed that one of the defects of the present system is its negative nature and that planning authorities are not able to play the useful and constructive role in positive planning which we would like to see them play. We believe that some of the local plans of the kind that I have been indicating—that would give general broad indications for the developer—would take the form, as it were, of a brief for the developer and his architect. It might, for example, state the general objectives of the plan and the broad outlines of the way in which the planning authority envisaged that they would be achieved. The proper grouping of usages within the area, the density and height of buildings on the site, provision for proper circulation of vehicles and foot passengers—matters of this kind will be indicated in the plan. It does not follow by any means that in such a case the planning authority would need to, or would want to, lay down at the plan-making stage the details of the buildings that it wants to see on the site to achieve the objectives of good design and satisfactory treatment of the environment. I think it will generally be considered advantageous to leave scope within the main framework for the imagination and initiative of private developers.

"If we were to insist on full detail in every case we should be forfeiting one of the main improvements which the Bill seeks to introduce. Also, there would be a certain inconsistency if the local planning authority were to be charged with the responsibility, in the general run of cases, of considering objections to a plan and deciding whether to adopt it formally or not, and we then denied the planning authority the right to judge what is appropriate as to its content and form. The authority will, of course, exercise its judgment in this matter in the light of the regulations made by the Minister and any directions or guidance given by him.

"But there is a remedy if the position were reached where a planning authority put forward a plan which was really wholly inadequate as to its detail and attracted objections on that ground—the remedy is the power of the Minister to intervene, either by requiring that an inquiry be held by a person of his choice or by calling in the plan for his own decision.

"All these plans will be sent to the Minister and, naturally, we shall want to examine them, not in all their detail but generally, to be satisfied that, first, they conform with the structure plan, and, secondly, that they contain sufficient detail to be meaningful, having regard to the nature of the local plan."

7. How Many Local Plans will there Be?

Under current procedures one structure plan (stating broad planning policy in outline) could be the progenitor of a litter of local plans each dealing in greater detail with its own pet aspect of planning control (s.11(2)). Here again it is wise to pay attention to the Government's own view of the matter as explained by the Minister of State on February 29, 1968 (*Hansard*, Standing Committee G, cols. 190 *et seq.*), in the following way:

"I had expected that this was in the nature of a probing amendment. It gives me an opportunity to explain a little further the variety and flexibility of local plans which we envisage. Local plans will be either plans with a varying degree of detail about a particular part of the area of the planning authority or plans which have a particular function or cover a particular aspect of planning for a rather wider area. It is because of this that one may get more than one local plan relating to and bearing upon the same piece of land.

"First of all, area plans; there will be action area plans designated in the structure plan. These will be the plans of areas for early and intensive development or redevelopment. . . .

"Then we envisage that there may be district plans covering a larger part of the area of the planning authority. The basic purposes of these will be to state more fully the working features of the locality within the structure plan area and to show the principal land uses as a guide for development control. But, having made the district plans for a district, there is no reason why at a later stage one should not have a much smaller local plan dealing with a particular problem of some area within the district. I have mentioned before the possibility of a local plan for a village, dealing with, say, a scheme for the expansion of a village. There would be no need to repeal or amend the original district plan because one proceeded to elaborate in more detail plans for a village falling within that district.

"Again, one might have a different kind of local plan which would be in the nature of a special policy or project plan. It might be a plan to deal with opportunities for access to the countryside or facilities for recreation. This plan also could overlap areas covered by other local plans. One might have a plan for the progressive and phased working of minerals within an area. This, again, could go on in more detail than was done in the district plans or other local plans.

"It will, of course, be important and necessary to ensure that these different types of local plan are mutually compatible and do not conflict with each other. This is another argument for retaining for the planning authority the power to make and approve local plans and not to delegate its powers. One local planning authority will be responsible for all the local plans within its area. It will be primarily its responsibility, subject to supervision by the Ministry, to ensure that the local plans are mutually compatible. It would be a ground for rejection of any local plan if it appeared to be inconsistent with and to conflict with another plan. I think that if we were not to have the power which the subsection points to and if we were to compel local authorities to combine all possible different matters in a single local plan, it would lead to a considerable loss of simplicity, clarity and flexibility.

"Again, on the point of clarity, I think that an advantage of separating local plans in this way is that they will be much clearer to people than the present plans. We know the confusion that arises from trying to overload a plan with too much detail on different matters. For these reasons we think that the system will work and not cause confusion. On the contrary, it will facilitate planning."

8. Making Representations about a Local Plan—Publicity

A local planning authority who propose to make, alter, repeal or replace a local plan must take such steps as will ensure "adequate publicity" of the matters which it is proposed to include in the plan and that persons who may be expected to have an interest in such matters are made aware that they are entitled to make *representations* within a prescribed period of six weeks (Town and Country Planning (Structure and Local Plan) Regulations 1982[5] reg. 5) about such matters and are afforded an "adequate opportunity" of making such representations to the local planning authority in respect of them (ss.12(1) and (2)).

The local planning authority making a local plan must also consult the county planning authority or, as the case may be, the district planning authority and afford them a reasonable opportunity to express their views (s.12(3)). Any such views must be taken into consideration by the authority making the local plan (*ibid.*).

The authority making the local plan, having prepared all the relevant documents, that is, the proposed plan, alterations, instrument of repeal or replacement plan (as the case may be), and having got any certificate required by section 15 of the 1971 Act (certificate of conformity with structure plan), must then make copies of the documents available for public inspection at their offices, send copies to the Secretary of State and send copies to the district or county planning authority as the case may require (s.12(4)). Each copy of the documents made available for inspection must be accompanied by a statement of the time within which objections can be made (s.12(5)).

If the Secretary of State is not satisfied about the adequacy of the the publicity and consultation associated with the making of the local plan, he may direct that no further steps are taken with the plan until he is himself satisfied that such further steps about publicity and consultation as he may specify have all been taken (s.12B).

A shortened procedure relating to publicity and consultation is available (s.12A) where a local planning authority propose, not to make, but to alter, repeal or replace a local plan and it appears to the Secretary of State that the issues involved are not of sufficient importance to warrant the full procedure of section 12 outlined above.

This right to make representations *before* the ideas of the local planning authority have fully crystallised is an instance of that citizen participation of which so much has been heard in connection with the 1971 Act. By making representations the local citizen is enabled to "put in his oar" at a time when the local plan is at a formative stage and before the local planning authority have completely made up their mind about the plan.

[5] S.I. 1982 No. 555.

The putting in of *representations* about a local plan to the district planning authority must not be confused with the right (which comes later) to put in *objections* to a local plan when the plan has been *prepared* by the planning authority but not yet *adopted* by them. Representations must be made *before* the local plan is prepared by the authority. Objections are made *after* the plan has been *prepared* by the authority but *before* the plan has been *adopted* by the authority. (It is helpful to note the distinctive use of the two different verbs: *to prepare* and *to adopt*.)

If representations about a local plan are in fact duly made to the district planning authority, then the authority must consider them (s.12(2)). The question is: What will be the manner of such consideration? As the 1971 Act itself stands, such consideration may be carried out in private by a committee of the local planning authority, the person making the representation having no right of audience either for himself or his representative before the committee.

A county or a district planning authority to whom it falls to prepare a local plan must (s.12(3)):

(a) consult the district planning authority or the county planning authority, as the case may be, with respect to the contents of the plan;
(b) afford that authority a reasonable opportunity to express their views; and
(c) take those views into consideration.

9. Making Objections to a Local Plan

Once a local plan has been *prepared* by the local planning authority (and before it is *adopted* by the authority) the authority must have copies of the local plan made available for public inspection at their office (s.12(4)) and each copy must be accompanied by a statement of the time namely, six weeks (1982 Regulations, reg. 5) within which *objections* to the plan may be made to the local planning authority (s.12(5)). *Objections, it will be noted, to a local plan must be sent to the local planning authority who prepared it and not to the Secretary of State as is the case with a structure plan.*

As with a structure plan, no landowner or land developer should fail to pay attention to the contents of a proposed local plan nor to lodge an objection to such contents if he has reason to disagree with them. He must never forget that whenever he (or anyone else) comes to apply for planning permission for development (see later in chapter 10) it may be that it is the contents of the local plan (or plans) which preclude him from getting that planning permission. It is true that the contents of a local plan do not *necessarily and in all circumstances* bind a planning authority when considering an application for planning permission but the authority are bound in law (s.29(1)) to "have regard to the provisions of the development plan" (which includes any local plan or plans) along with "any other material considerations" in coming to a determination of the planning application.

The local planning authority is entitled to disregard (s.16) representations or objections to a local plan if they relate to certain development authorised under the Highways Act 1959, the Highways (Miscellaneous Provisions) Act 1961, the Highways Act 1971 and the Highways Act 1980 or the New Towns Act 1981.

The local planning authority must send a copy of the local plan as prepared by them to the Secretary of State (s.12(4)) and to the district or county planning authority, as the case may require (*ibid.*).

A copy of a local plan sent to the Secretary of State under the foregoing provisions (namely, section 12(4) of the 1971 Act) must be accompanied by a statement (s.12B(1)):

(a) of the steps which the authority have taken to comply with the provisions of section 12(2) of the 1971 Act relating to the giving of publicity to any matters proposed to be included in the local plan; and

(b) of the authority's consultations with, and their consideration of the views of, other persons.

If the Secretary of State is *not* satisfied with the statement as sent to him by the authority he may, within 21 days of the receipt of the statement, intervene and direct the authority *not* to take any further steps for the adoption of the plan without first taking such action as he may specify in the direction (s.12B(3)). Any local planning authority who receive such a direction from the Secretary of State must forthwith withdraw all copies of the local plan which have been made available for inspection and notify any person who has made objections to the plan that the Secretary of State has given a direction as already mentioned (s.12B(4)).

The sending to the Secretary of State of a copy of the local plan and its accompanying statement is primarily for information because a local plan *prepared* by a local planning authority and later formally *adopted* by them does not normally need any approval from the Secretary of State. Objections to the local plan, it will be remembered, are to be sent to the local planning authority themselves and not to the Secretary of State (s.12(5)).

Accordingly, the next question is: How does the local planning authority handle the objections to their local plan when they have received them?

10. How Does the Local Planning Authority Deal with Objections?

This is a very important matter and the 1971 Act goes on to provide (s.13) that in such a case a local planning authority *may*, if they wish (s.13(1)), and *shall* (s.13(2)) in the case of objections made in accordance with regulations under Part II of the 1971 Act, cause a public local inquiry (Town and Country Planning (Structure and Local Plans) Regulations 1982,[6] reg. 27) or a private hearing to be held into any objection (s.13(1) and (2)) except when *all* the objections indicate in writing that they do not wish to appear (s.13(2)).

The public local inquiry or the private hearing will be held by a person (an Inspector) appointed either by the Secretary of State or (in prescribed cases only) by the local planning authority. (s.13(3)). The Secretary of State has decided that, for the time being, he himself should appoint the Inspector in all cases and, accordingly, the 1982 Regulations make no provision for the local planning authority to appoint a person of their own choice. Section 250(2) and (3) of the Local Government Act 1972 (relating to the power to summon and examine witnesses) will apply to any such public local inquiry (s.13(5)) as also will (s.13(6)) the provisions of the Tribunals and Inquiries Act 1971.

The procedure to be followed at any such public local inquiry is set out in the Code of Practice to be found in Section 2 of the booklet "Local plans: Public local inquiries—A guide to procedure 1984." The booklet is issued by the Department of the Environment and is referred to in D.O.E. Circular No. 22/84 dated September 7, 1984 at paragraph 3/68 of the Memorandum associated with the Circular.

The Code deals with such matters as making objections to a local plan, consideration of objections by the local planning authority by means of written representations or by a public local inquiry, evidence, site visits, the public local inquiry and the inspector's report, adoption of the local plan and challenge of the plan in the High Court. As with the structure plan, all objections to local plans lodged within the objection period are to be placed on deposit with copies of the local plan both before and during the inquiry, the object being to encourage objectors with common interests to group together and make a joint representation. Unlike a structure plan *examination in public*, however, appearance at a local plan *public local inquiry* is to be as of right and not to depend upon invitation.

As mentioned earlier, D.O.E. Circular No. 22/84 dated

[6] S.I. 1982 No. 555.

September 7 1984, with its "Memorandum on Structure and Local Plans" is an important Circular relating to the whole development plan system of structure plans and local plans. It gives basic guidance to local planning authorities *but is of equal importance to any one seeking to make representations or objections to a local plan.* Its "Memorandum on Structure and Local Plans" is followed by ten Annexes (Annexes A to J) of which Annexes B, C, F, G and J relate to local plans. The whole Circular, Memorandum and Annexes will repay close attention.

11. Adoption of a Local Plan by the Local Planning Authority

If no objections to an advertised local plan are received within the appropriate time the local planning authority may then proceed to the next step which is formally to adopt the plan by resolution of the authority (s.14(1)).

If objections to a local plan are made in due time, then "after considering the objections"—(*i.e.* after considering them with, or without, the holding of a public local inquiry or a private hearing as discussed above)—the local planning authority may proceed formally, by resolution, to adopt the plan either as originally prepared or as modified in the light of any objections that have been made and considered by the authority (s.14(1) and (2)). The authority cannot however, adopt any proposals which do not conform generally with the structure plan subject to which the local plan is made (s.14(3)).

If, after copies of the proposed local plan have been sent to him (s.12(4)(*b*) and before the plan is adopted, the Secretary of State concludes that the proposals are unsatisfactory he may direct the authority who are making the plan to consider modifying it as directed by him (s.14(4)) in which event the authority must not adopt the plan until they satisfy him that they have made the requisite modifications or his direction is withdrawn (s.14(5)).

Subject to the foregoing it is to be noted that the local planning authority are completely at liberty to adopt their own local plan in the form in which they prepared it notwithstanding that objections have been duly made to the plan, that a public local inquiry has been held and that the Inspector holding that enquiry has, in his report on the inquiry to the local planning authority, recommended modification of the plan, as prepared by the authority.[7]

If an objection to the local plan has been made by the Minister of

[7] *R.* v. *Hammersmith and Fulham Borough Council, ex p. People Before Profit Ltd.* [1981] J.P.L. 869; also noted at [1981] J.P.L. 778.

Agriculture, Fisheries and Food, and if the local planning authority making the plan do *not* propose to modify the plan so as to meet the objection (s.14(6)), then the local planning authority must send particulars of the objection to the Secretary of State along with a statement of their reasons for not meeting the objection and must not adopt the plan unless the Secretary of State authorises them to do so (*ibid.*). Where the Minister of Agriculture, Fisheries and Food has objected to the plan it is the duty of the Secretary of State to direct the local planning authority (under section 14A(3)) not to make the plan unless the Minister no longer objects to it (*ibid*).

If the local planning authority making, altering, repealing or replacing the local plan is a *district* planning authority, the local plan cannot be adopted by the district planning authority unless the county planning authority issues a certificate that the local plan *does* conform with the approved structure plan (s.15(1)(2)).

Again, in the case of a local plan made by a *district* planning authority, if the county planning authority will not, on the request of the district planning authority, issue a certificate as to the conformity of the local plan with the approved structure plan, then the matter will go for determination to the Secretary of State (s.15(3)(5)).

Irrespective of any argument (as to conformity) breaking out between the district planning authority (who made the local plan) and the county planning authority, the Secretary of State can always reserve to himself the determination of whether or not the local plan does generally conform to the structure plan (s.15(4)(5)).

12. Call In and Approval of Local Plan by Secretary of State

If the Secretary of State so desires he can always take out of the hands of the local planning authority responsibility for approving a local plan which they have prepared (ss.14(4), (5), (6) and 14A). As previously mentioned, the Secretary of State must always receive from the local planning authority a copy of any local plan which they have prepared (s.12(4)(*b*)). Thus advised about the contents of the local planning authority's local plan, the Secretary of State may, at any time before the plan has been formally adopted by the local planning authority, direct the authority to consider modifying the plan in such respects as are indicated in the direction (s.14(4)) in which event the authority must not adopt the plan until they have modified it accordingly or the Secretary of State has withdrawn his direction (s.14(5)).

In addition to the foregoing the Secretary of State may call in the plan by directing that it shall not have effect unless it is approved by him (s.14A(1)). If the Secretary of State does give such a direction (under section 14A(1)) the authority must not take any further steps for the adoption of the plan and in particular must not hold or proceed with a public local inquiry in respect of the plan (s.14A(2)(*a*)). In such a case the plan will not have effect unless it is *approved* by the Secretary of State (s.14A(2)(*b*)) in which case it will not require any *adoption* by the authority (*ibid.*).

Where the Secretary of State has given a direction under section 14A(1) of the 1971 Act calling in a local plan for his consideration, he may approve the plan in whole or in part and with or without modifications or he may reject it (s.14B(1)). The Secretary of State has rejected a local plan only once. In 1986 he rejected the North Southwark Local Plan prepared by the London Borough of Southwark on the ground (*inter alia*) that it conflicted with national policy as set out in Circular 22/84 on industrial development (see (1986) J.P.L. 399).

If the Secretary of State gives any direction (under section 14(4) or section 14A(1)) that the local planning authority shall not adopt the plan, then the Secretary of State must himself, before determining whether or not to approve the local plan (with or without modifications), consider all objections to the plan made in accordance with regulations under Part II of the 1971 Act and offer any person so objecting either a public local inquiry or a private hearing (s.14B(1)(2) and (3)) but he is not obliged to do any of these things if the local planning authority have already considered the objections and offered the objector either a public local inquiry or a private hearing (s.14B(3)).

When a local plan comes before the Secretary of State pursuant to a direction given by him to the local planning authority he may, in considering the plan, take account of any matters he thinks are relevant whether or not they were earlier considered by the local planning authority (s.14B(2)).

He may also (but is not obliged to) consult with, or consider the views of, any local planning authority or other persons (s.14B(4)). In the course of any such consultation or consideration of views he is not obliged (except as provided in section 14B(3) mentioned above) to afford any further opportunity for the making of representations or objections or for the holding of any public local inquiry or hearing (s.14B(4))).

This matter of the Secretary of State's power to "call in" a local plan for final approval (or rejection) by him is bound up with the right of a local planning authority to reject a recommendation made to them in his report by the Inspector appointed to hold a public local inquiry or a private hearing into objections made to a local plan. A local planning authority are no more bound to accept such a recommendation than is the Secretary of State in the case of a recommendation made to *him* by an Inspector. Accordingly, there could conceivably be a disagreement between what the Inspector recommends and what the local planning authority thinks is right. What is the position then?

This was the subject of debate on March 7, 1968, during the Committee stage of the Bill for the Town and Country Planning Act 1968, when the Minister of State said (*Hansard*, Standing Committee G, cols. 299 *et seq.*):

> "A difficult position could arise if, even after an inquiry, even after a recommendation by the inspector, the local authority still says, that the matter raises what is, for them, and [*sic*] that they, the locally elected planning authority, are the people to decide policy for this area, within the overall policy of the approved structure plan, and that their decision is so-and-so.
>
> "The Ministry could not consider the issue in isolation. It would have to consider it in relation to the whole of that local plan, considering all the policy underlying it in relation to the rest of the detail of that local plan; that would require very detailed consideration by the Ministry. We shall have our power of 'call in' and there will be cases where we think it right to use it. An issue of this kind might be a case in which the power would be used. And we still have the power of 'call in' even after the provisional resolution by the local authority rejecting a recommendation of the inspector has been made. But the discretion whether the issue should be decided at Ministry level ought to rest with the Minister, not with the objector. To give the objector the right to impose upon the Ministry the duty of going into all that detail is too heavy. The Minister should be left to decide. There will be time, even after a local authority has rejected the inspector's recommendation and given its reasons for doing so, for the Minister to decide whether to call it in if he is asked to do so at that stage.
>
> "It has been suggested that I might argue that there is always the remedy of the courts. I have never suggested that remedy. I do not recall using that argument on this kind of issue. It was certainly a slip if I did, because this kind of issue could not go to the courts. The appeal to the courts is on whether the proper procedure has been followed.[8] But on the matter of substance, which would be an issue of policy, there would be no appeal to the courts.[8]

[8] See p. 38 and Town and Country Planning Act 1971, s.242(1)(*a*).

"It is easy to say with horror in one's voice that a local authority is not bound to accept and can even reject the recommendation of the inspector. We all have the greatest respect for inspectors, but they are not democratically elected planning authorities. They are a very good vehicle for ensuring that objections are properly heard, that an independent, qualified and expert mind is brought to bear and to express an opinion, but when that has been done the decision should rest with the democratically elected authority which may be either the Minister or the local authority.

"Essentially, what we are considering here are local issues and local policies. If a matter raises more than local policy, it is an issue which will come up in the structure plans and will, therefore, be decided by the Minister, but what we are dealing with here is, *ex hypothesi,* a local matter raising a local question of policy. It is said—and again I quote one of my hon. Friend's phrases—that the local authority may be hell-bent to get its plans through. It may be hell-bent, but it will be subjected to some rigorous procedures as the Bill stands. I do not want to go over them again—hon. Members will remember the provisions for publicity and consultation in the formative stages and so on. What a local authority does and its reasons for doing so at every stage will be exposed to publicity—and local publicity—and it will have to answer for its actions at the end of the day.

"The amendment raises the basic issue of whether we want to delegate to local planning authorities the power to determine local plans, subject to the supervision and the power of 'call in' of the Minister. If the attitude of mind about which hon. Members are worried really exists, that fact will become patent if, unreasonably and through sheer obstinacy and with no valid policy, a local authority rejects substantial objections and recommendations of the inspector, without giving convincing reasons for doing so. That is the kind of case in which the Minister would exercise his power of 'call in.' But the decision on that must rest with the Minister and not with the objector, and it would not be right, therefore, to give the objector the right of appeal which the Amendment suggests."

13. Conformity (or Conflict) between Structure Plans and Local Plans

Where there is any conflict between a local plan and a structure plan both functioning in the same area, it is the contents of the local plan which are to prevail for all purposes (s.15B(1)). This statutory provision, however, will not apply, in a case where a local plan is being altered, repealed or replaced in order to conform with an altered or replaced structure plan, until the requisite alteration, repeal or replacement plan has come into force (s.15B(2)).

14. Operation and Validity of a Local Plan

Subject to the provisions of section 242 of the 1971 Act (relating to the validity of development plans) a local plan will become operative on a date appointed for the purpose in the relevant resolution of the local planning authority adopting the plan (s.18(4)).

15. The Local Plan becomes "the Development Plan"

The manner in which an operative local plan becomes "the development plan" for any particular area is dealt with in section 20 of the 1971 Act about which reference may be made to Chapter 4.[9]

16. The Secretary of State's Default Powers

In connection with local plans the Secretary of State has certain default powers enabling the Secretary of State himself or, where he so appoints, some other local planning authority to perform any of the duties or functions imposed upon a local planning authority with respect to local plans (s.17).

17. Modification of Provisions in their Application to Greater London

All the provisions of Part II of the 1971 Act relating to local plans are made applicable to Greater London subject to the provisions of Schedule 4 to the 1971 Act (s.19).[10] This state will continue until Part I of Schedule 1 to the Local Government Act 1985 replaces in Greater London the provision of Part II of the Town and Country Planning Act 1971 by the bringing into force of the aforesaid Part I of Schedule 1 to the 1985 Act by the making of a commencement order by the Secretary of State under the authority of section 4(1) of the 1985 Act.[11]

[9] See p. 74.
[10] See Chap. 7.
[11] See Chap. 7.

18. Regulations

Under the 1971 Act the Secretary of State has made the Town and Country Planning (Structure and Local Plans) Regulations 1982[12] repealing and re-enacting with amendments earlier Regulations of a like kind. The amendments are rendered necessary by the several amendments to the 1971 Act brought about by the Local Government Act 1972 and the Local Government, Planning and Land Act 1980.

These regulations (discussed earlier in this chapter) make provision as to the form and content of local plans prepared under Part II of the 1971 Act and with respect to the procedure to be followed in the preparation, withdrawal, approval, adoption, making, alteration, repeal and replacement of such plans.

The 1982 Regulations do not apply to Greater London. (reg. 1).

19. The Prospect Before Us

Reference should be made to the comment hereon appearing in Chapter 4 at page 76, *ante*.

[12] S.I. 1982 No. 555.

CHAPTER 6

DEVELOPMENT PLANS IN METROPOLITAN DISTRICTS—MAKING AND PROCEDURES—UNITARY DEVELOPMENT PLANS

NOTE. In this chapter "L.G. Act 1985" means the Local Government Act 1985 and "H. and P. Act 1986" means the Housing and Planning Act 1986. All other section references are to the principal Act, the Town and Country Planning Act 1971, unless otherwise stated.

1. Introductory—Transitional Arrangements

With the six metropolitan county councils abolished on April 1, 1986—the abolition date (L.G. Act 1985, s.1)[1] —a new style of development plan is introduced for the areas of those metropolitan counties (L.G. Act 1985, s.4 and Sched. 1, Pt. I). It is enacted (*ibid.*) that the 36 metropolitan district councils (the single tier, all-purpose planning authorities in the six metropolitan counties on and as from April 1, 1986) shall each make for their own area a new-style development plan to be known as a "unitary development plan" (*ibid.* para. 2).

These new arrangements for development plans in the metropolitan districts which will replace the structure and local plan provisions of Part II of the Town and County Planning Act 1971 (L.G. Act 1985, s.4(1)), do *not* come into force straightway on the abolition of the metropolitan county councils on April 1, 1986, but will be brought into operation, from time to time and from area to area, on such successive dates as may be appointed by commencement orders made by the Secretary of State for the Environment (*ibid.*). In the meantime any structure plan or local plan or old development plan in force in a metropolitan district on the abolition date will continue in force until a unitary development plan for the district comes into operation under Part I of Schedule 1 to the Local Government Act 1985 (L.G. Act 1985, Sched. 1, Part II, Transitional Provisions, para. 18). In this context "old development plan" means any pre-1968 development plan which is still in force on April 1, 1986 by

[1] See p. 30.

virtue of Schedule 7 to the Town and Country Planning Act 1971 (L.G. Act 1985, Sched. 1, Part II, para. 18(3)).

It is further provided that, in the interim period between the abolition date and the coming into force of a unitary development plan, any existing *structure* plan[2] may be revoked in whole or in part by the Secretary of State after consultation with the district planning authority (*ibid.* para. 19) while any existing *local* plan[3] will automatically be incorporated (without further discussion) in the unitary development plan (*ibid.* para. 21) subject to such alterations as may be specified in Part II of the plan (*ibid.* para. 21(1)).

D.O.E. Circular 30/85 entitled, "Local Government Act 1985: Section 3, 4 and 5: Schedule 1 Town and Country Planning: Transitional Matters," dated December 20, 1985, gives, in detail, the transitional arrangements for the making of development plans and the execution of development control by metropolitan district councils after the abolition of the metropolitan county councils on April 1, 1986. The Annex to the Circular sets out:

(a) the arrangements for development control in the period immediately proceeding the abolition of the metropolitan county councils; and
(b) the arrangements for development plans prior to the making of commencement orders (by the Secretary of State) for the preparation of unitary development plans.

2. Unitary Development Plans—Their Features in Outline

The new unitary development plan will contain the elements of the structure and the local plan all rolled into one. The plan will, in general, not only be prepared but also *adopted* by the district planning authority which has prepared it (L.G. Act 1985, Sched. I, paras. 2 and 5) although the Secretary of State has power to call in all or any part of a unitary development plan (*ibid.* para. 7) for consideration by himself after which the plan (if not rejected by him) will be *approved* by him (*ibid.* para. 8).

The unitary development plan will be in two parts (*ibid.* para. 2(2)). Part I will reflect the ideas and style of a structure plan while Part II will get down to the details customarily found in a local plan. Any proposals in Part II of a unitary development plan *must* be in general conformity with the contents of Part I of the plan (*ibid.* para. 2(5)).

[2] See Chap. 4.
[3] See Chap. 5.

3. Procedure for Making and Bringing into Operation a Unitary Development Plan by a Metropolitan District Council

The procedure for the making and bringing into operation of a unitary development plan is set out in detail in Schedule 1, Part I to the Local Government Act 1985 which Part I is shortly amended by the four paragraphs of the Housing and Planning Act 1986, Schedule 10, Part II.

(1) *The survey*

The making of a unitary development plan *must* start with a review by the district planning authority of the matters which can be expected to affect the development of their area and *may* include the institution of a survey for the examination of those matters (L.G. Act 1985, Sched. 1, Part I, para. 1). It will be noted that the institution of a survey is optional whereas in the case of a structure plan a survey is obligatory (s.6(1)).[4]

In reviewing the matters which can be expected to affect the development in their area, the district planning authority are required specifically (and without prejudice to the review of other matters) to review the following matters which are identical with those for a structure plan survey[5] (L.G. Act 1985, Sched. 1, Part I, para. 1(2)), namely:

(a) the principal physical and economic characteristics of the area of the authority (including the principal purposes for which land is used) and, so far as they may be expected to affect that area, of any neighbouring areas;

(b) the size, composition and distribution of the population of that area (whether resident or otherwise);

(c) without prejudice to paragraph (a) above, the communications, transport system and traffic of that area and, so far as they may be expected to affect that area, of any neighbouring areas;

(d) any considerations not mentioned in any of the foregoing paragraphs which may be expected to affect any matters mentioned in them;

(e) such other matters as may be prescribed or as the Secretary of State may in a particular case direct;

(f) any changes already projected in any of the matters mentioned in any of the foregoing paragraphs and the effect

[4] See pp. 62, 63 and 77.

[5] See p. 63.

which those changes are likely to have on the development of that area or the planning of such development.

(2) *Preparation of unitary development plan by metropolitan district council*

The district planning authority *must*, (they have no option), after the coming into force in their area of Part I of Schedule 1 to the Local Government Act 1985 by the making of a commencement order by the Secretary of State (L.G. Act 1985, s.4(1)), set about preparing a unitary development plan (L.G. Act 1985, Sched. 1, Pt. I, para. 2(1)). The plan *must* comprise two parts (*ibid.* para. 2(2)), namely:

(a) *Part I* which shall consist of—
    a written statement formulating the authority's general policies in respect of the development and other use of land in their area (including measures for the improvement of the physical environment and the management of traffic); and

(b) *Part II* which shall consist of—
    (i) a written statement formulating in such detail as the authority think appropriate (and so as to be readily distinguishable from the other contents of the plan) their proposals for the development or other use of land in their area or for any description of development or other use of such land;
    (ii) a map showing those proposals on a geographical basis;
    (iii) a reasoned justification of the general policies in Part I and of the proposals in Part II; and
    (iv) such diagrams, illustrations or other descriptive or explanatory matter in respect of the general policies in Part I or the proposals in Part II as the authority think appropriate or as may be prescribed.

A unitary development plan must also contain such other matters as may be prescribed by regulations or as the Secretary of State may, in any particular case, direct (*ibid.* para. 2(3)); and Part II of the plan *must* at all times conform generally with Part I of the plan (*ibid.* para. 2(5)).

In their formulation of the general policies set out in Part I of the plan, the district planning authority *must* have regard to any strategic guidance which is given to them by the Secretary of State, to current national and regional policies, to the resources likely to be available and to any other matters which the Secretary of State may direct them to take into account (*ibid.* para 2(4)). Today a metropolitan district council may well be rid of interference and "busy-bodying" from a county council (because they don't any longer have any county council to contend with) in the preparation of their development plan for their area (their very own unitary development plan), but they are certainly not entirely a free agent in such preparation; the Secretary of State is always going to be on the horizon (if not nearer) with good advice, "wise saws and modern instances," given through the medium of statutory directions which brook no gainsaying!

Part II of a unitary development plan may designate land as an action area (*i.e.* an area to be comprehensively developed, redeveloped or improved during a prescribed time limit) (*ibid.* para. 2(6)) and in preparing their plan the district planning authority must take into account the contents of any scheme for an enterprise zone[6] prepared under Schedule 32 of the Local Government, Planning and Land Act 1980 (*ibid.* para. 2(7)).

(3) *Publicity in connection with preparation of unitary development plan by metropolitan district council*

Before finally determining the contents of their unitary development plan the district planning authority must give (*ibid.* para. 3(1)):

(a) adequate publicity to the matters to be included in the plan;
(b) to persons expected to wish to make representations about the plan, notice that they are *entitled* to an opportunity of doing so, and
(c) an adequate opportunity to such persons of making such representations within a period to be presented by regulations made by the Secretary of State.

The district planning authority must send a copy of their plan to the Secretary of State before they themselves adopt it and put copies of it on deposit at their offices for public inspection (*ibid.* para. 3(2)). Each copy deposited for public inspection must disclose the time within which objections to the plan may be made (*ibid.*).

The copy of the plan sent to the Secretary of State must describe what steps have been taken to comply with the requirements of subparagraphs (*a*), (*b*) and (*c*) above and the consultations which have taken place with objectors and the consideration which has been given by the district planning authority to any objections made to the plan (*ibid.* para. 3(3)). If the Secretary of State is not satisfied with the publicity given to the plan he may direct the district planning authority *not* to take any further steps for adoption of the plan

[6] See Chap. 24.

until they have taken such further steps as he may specify in order better to achieve the purposes set out in the aforementioned subparagraphs (*a*), (*b*) and (*c*) (*ibid.* para. 3(4)). If the Secretary of State directs the taking of further steps to achieve the purposes of the aforementioned subparagraphs (*a*), (*b*) and (*c*), the district planning authority must withdraw the copies of their unitary development plan made available for public inspection and notify any person who has objected to the plan that the Secretary of State has given directions as above mentioned (*ibid.* para. 3(5)).

The Secretary of State, having received a copy of a unitary development plan as above mentioned, may, if he regards the plan as in any way unsatisfactory, direct the district planning authority, before adopting the plan, to consider modification of the plan on the lines stated in the direction (*ibid.*, para. 6A, added by H. and P. Act 1986, Sched. 10, Part II). If the Secretary of State does so direct, then the district planning authority may not adopt the plan unless they first satisfy the Secretary of State that they have modified their plan so as to conform with his direction or he himself withdraws the direction (*ibid.*)

(4) *Public local inquiry, or hearing, prior to adoption of unitary development plan by metropolitan district council*

If there are objections to a unitary development plan the district planning authority *may*, and *shall* in the case of objections made in accordance with regulations, arrange for a public local inquiry or other hearing to be held by an Inspector appointed by the Secretary of State to consider the objections unless all objectors indicate in writing that they do not wish to attend such an inquiry (*ibid.* para. 6). Any such public local inquiry will be conducted on the same lines as a public local inquiry into a local plan[7] with the Secretary of State's Inspector reporting to the district planning authority who prepared the plan.

(5) *Adoption of unitary development plan by metropolitan district council*

The district planning authority who prepared the unitary development plan may, by resolution of the authority, formally *adopt* their plan after the period for making objections to the plan has expired or, in a case where objections to the plan have been duly made, after considering such objections and the report of the Inspector holding the public inquiry (if any) into the objections (*ibid.* para. 5(1)). The plan can be adopted as originally prepared or as modified to take

[7] See Chap. 5.

into account objections made to the plan and any other material considerations (*ibid.*) but the plan cannot be adopted if Part II of the plan is *not* in general conformity with Part I of the plan (*ibid.* para. 5(2)).

The unitary development plan will become operative on the date it is adopted subject to challenge as to its validity as provided for in section 242 of the Town and Country Planning Act 1971 (*ibid.* para. 5(4)).

(6) *Withdrawal of unitary development plan by metropolitan district council*

A unitary development plan *may* be withdrawn by the district planning authority which prepared it at any time before it is adopted by the authority[8] (or approved by the Secretary of State[8]) and it *must* be withdrawn if the Secretary of State so directs (*ibid.* para. 4(1)). All copies of the plan made available for public inspection must be withdrawn (*ibid.* para. 4(2) and will be treated as never having been made available to the public at all (*ibid.* para. 4(4)) but any steps which have been taken to publicise the withdrawn plan may be taken into account with respect to some other (and, presumedly, later) unitary development plan (*ibid.* para. 4(3)).

(7) *Calling in of unitary development plan by Secretary of State*

At any time between deposit and adoption of a unitary development plan by the district planning authority, the plan, or any part of the plan, may be called in by the Secretary of State for his own consideration and approval or rejection (*ibid.* paras. 7(1) and 8(1)). Where this is done the district planning authority must forthwith stop all further work on the plan (*ibid.* paras. 7(1) and (3)).

(8) *Public local inquiry, or examination-in-public, prior to approval of unitary development plan by Secretary of State*

Before approving any unitary development plan called in by him, the Secretary of State must consider any objection to the plan duly made in accordance with regulations made under Part I of Schedule 1 to the Local Government Act 1985 (*ibid.* para. 9(1)).

Where the Secretary of State calls in:

(a) the whole of a unitary development plan; or
(b) the whole or part of Part II of the plan; or
(c) the whole or part of Part I along with any part of Part II, or the whole of Part II along with any part of Part I of the plan,

[8] See *ante*, p. 103 and this page at heading (7), *supra*.

he *must* hold a public local inquiry or other hearing for the purpose of considering objections made to the plan (*ibid.* para. 9(2)) unless the objections have already been considered at an earlier inquiry held by the district planning authority (*ibid.* para. 9(3)) or he decides to reject the plan (*ibid.*). But where it is the whole or part of Part I only of the plan (*i.e.* not the whole or any part of Part II of the plan) which is called in by the Secretary of State, he *may* hold an examination in public[9] of such matters as *he* considers should be so examined (*ibid.* para. 9(4), (5)). The difference, shortly, between the public local inquiry and the examination in public is that in the case of the former any objector will be heard but with the latter it is (in the main) only those objectors who are *invited* to appear by the Secretary of State who will be heard (*ibid.* para. 9(6)). The Inspector holding the examination in public has, however, a discretion to invite other persons to take part in it (*ibid.*).

(9) *Approval or rejection of unitary development plan by Secretary of State*

The Secretary of State, after considering a unitary development plan (or any part of such a plan) called in by him and after holding, as required, such a public local enquiry or examination in public as is mentioned above, may either approve the plan, in whole or in part and with or without modification, or he may reject it. (*ibid.* para. 8(1)(2) and (3)).

Where the Secretary of State approves the whole or part of Part I of a unitary development plan with modifications, the district planning authority, before adopting the remainder of the plan, must make all such modifications to Part II of the plan as may be necessary to bring Part II into general conformity with Part I of the plan (*ibid.* para. 8(4)).

A unitary development plan, or any part of such a plan, called in for consideration and approval by the Secretary of State, will become operative on such date as he may appoint, subject to challenge as to its validity as provided for in section 242 of the Town and Country Planning Act 1971 (*ibid.* para. 8(5)).

4. Procedure for Alteration or Replacement of Unitary Development Plan

A district planning authority *may* at any time, and *must* if so directed by the Secretary of State, make proposals for the alteration or replacement of any unitary development plan adopted by them or

[9] See p. 68.

approved by the Secretary of State (*ibid.* para. 10(1)). The authority may not, however, make any alteration or replacement of any plan, or part of a plan, which has been approved, as above described, by the Secretary of State himself without first getting his consent (*ibid.*). No provision is made for the repeal of any operative unitary development plan without replacement. Thus, once a district planning authority have proceeded to make and bring into operation, as they are obliged to do (*ibid.* para. 2(1)), a statutory unitary development plan for their area, they are not, thereafter, ever to be left without such a plan.

A district planning authority are obliged to make, as soon as practicable, all such consequential alterations to their unitary development plan, as they consider to be necessary following the coming into operation of an enterprise zone[10] (in whole or in part) in their area (*ibid.* para. 10(3)).

The procedure for altering or replacing a unitary development plan follows the procedure (above described) set out in paragraphs 2 to 9 of Schedule 1 to the Local Government Act 1985 for the preparation and adoption of such a plan (*ibid.* para. 10(2)). But if it appears to the district planning authority that the issues involved in any such alteration or replacement are not of sufficient importance to warrant the full procedure, as given in the aforesaid paragraphs 2 to 9, for the alteration or replacement of a unitary development plan, a short, expedited procedure is available (*ibid.* para. 10A added by H. and P. Act 1986, Sched. 10, Part II).

5. Joint Unitary Development Plans

A joint unitary development plan may be prepared by two or more district planning authorities in a metropolitan county and the provisions of Part I of Schedule 1 to the Local Government Act 1985 (as described in previous paragraphs of this chapter) will apply subject to slight amendment (*ibid.* para. 12). The joint plan will come into operation on a date jointly agreed between all the authorities preparing the plan (*ibid.* para. 12(8)).

6. Meaning of "Development Plan" in Metropolitan Counties

For the purposes of the Town and Country Planning Act 1971, the development plan for any district in a metropolitan county is to be (*ibid.* para. 15):

(a) the unitary development plan for the time being in force

[10] See Chap. 24.

together with the district planning authority's resolution of adoption or (as the case may be) the Secretary of State's notice of approval, or, where part of the plan has been adopted and part approved, the resolution of adoption and the notice of approval; and

(b) any alteration to the plan together with the district planning authority's resolution of adoption of the alteration or (as the case may be) the Secretary of State's notice of approval of the alteration, or, where part of the alteration has been adopted and part approved, the resolution of adoption and the notice of approval.

7. Secretary of State's Default Powers

If the Secretary of State is satisfied, after holding a public local inquiry or other hearing, that a metropolitan district planning authority are not taking the requisite steps to discharge their statutory duty to prepare a unitary development plan (as described in the previous paragraphs of this chapter), he may himself prepare and make the plan and the expenses of so doing will be payable on demand to the Secretary of State (*ibid.* para. 13).

Chapter 7

DEVELOPMENT PLANS FOR GREATER LONDON—MAKING AND PROCEDURE—UNITARY DEVELOPMENT PLANS

1. London—Historical Dissertation

NOTE. In this chapter "L.G. Act 1985" means the Local Government Act 1985 and "H. and P. Act 1986" means the Housing and Planning Act 1986. All other section references are to the principal Act, the Town and Country Planning Act 1971, unless otherwise stated.

Local Government in London has always been the exception to the rule. In 1888 a Liberal Government reformed (or reorganised) local government in the geographical counties of England and Wales by establishing for the first time—

(a) *county* local government through the medium of elected councils for each of the administrative counties (there were 58 of them) and

(b) *county borough* local government through the medium of elected county borough councils for each of the county boroughs (there were 83 of them)

—all done under the statutory authority of the Local Government Act 1888 (see Diagram 1 on page 50).

There were more administrative counties than geographical counties because some of the latter were over-large for administrative purposes—or, at least, were thought to be. Thus, Yorkshire was divided into three thirdings (or thriddings or riddings or ridings) namely, North Riding, East Riding and West Riding—but never a South Riding. Lincolnshire, again, was divided into three portions each one of which was called a "Parts"—the Parts of Holland, the Parts of Lindsay and the Parts of Kesteven. And there were other divisions of the ancient, geographical counties.

London was made, by the 1888 Act, exceptional to all this. Pieces of Kent, Surrey and Middlesex, all clustering around the capital town, were carved off from their respective geographical counties to make the artificial County of London (artificial because it never fielded a cricket team—no one ever played cricket "for London"!) presided over by the London County Council. Incidentally, there might never have been a London County Council at all if the Corporation of the City of London—a corporation by prescription, of immemorial foundation for no one knows when it began—had taken the opportunity (readily available at the time) to become the local government authority for the new County of London. But the City Corporation, rightly or wrongly—the debate continues to this day under the Doctrine of the Lost Opportunity—would not extend the boundaries of their *modern* local government powers beyond the Square Mile of the City of London even though (being an unreformed local government authority untouched by the Municipal Corporations Act 1835) it had peculiar and exceptional powers the exercise of which could function in areas far removed from the City—it bought (out of its private monies (not the rates)) and today still governs and controls, for example, the nine square miles of Epping Forest in Essex and the unique Burnham Beeches in Berkshire and it contributed (again out of its private monies) to the building of the first Underground Railway, opened by the Lord Mayor in 1863, from Paddington to Farringdon—the first bit of today's Circle Line.

Thus London got its own Council, the London County Council, in 1888. In 1899 a Conservative Administration sub-divided the County of London into 28 Metropolitan Boroughs (London Government Act 1899) each with their Metropolitan Borough Council. This had an emasculating effect on the London County Council (as it was intended to have) by introducing split-level local government—the county level and the metropolitan borough level—throughout the County of London.

In 1965, under the London Government Act 1963, London was subjected to further reorganisation. The area of the County of London was enormously expanded (into some 620 square miles with a population at that time of around eight million) at the expense of Kent, Essex, Surrey, Hertfordshire and Middlesex and the county boroughs of Croydon, East Ham and West Ham. The Royal Commission, which advised on all of this, carefully avoided referring to the new, expanded area as a county. It was called "Greater London" *simpliciter* and given a "Council for Greater London" which speedily established themselves under the style and title of "the Greater London Council." The 28 Metropolitan Boroughs were abolished and the new area of Greater London subdivided into 32 London boroughs plus the Corporation of the City of London for the square mile of the City. All this began on April 1, 1965.

This split level arrangement for local government in Greater London was copied for the whole of England and Wales when local government was re-organised by the Local Government Act 1972 (operating from April 1, 1974) by a Conservative Administration. It was the 1972 Act which established the six metropolitan counties[1]

[1] See pp. 23 and 24.

with their 36 metropolitan districts. Within 10 years another Conservative Administration went to work to unpick a lot of what had been done under the 1972 Act. The Local Government Act 1985 abolished, as from April 1, 1986, not only the six metropolitan county councils but also the Greater London Council. For the first time in 98 years London ceased to have one overall comprehensive local government authority.

Thus, in the metropolitan counties local government control came to function at a single level (the metropolitan district council level) while, on the disappearance of the Greater London Council, local government in Greater London came to function, similarly, at a single level (the London borough council level).

2. Planning and Development Control in Greater London

And where, in all of the foregoing "strange eventful history," did (and does) planning and development control stand in Greater London? From July 1, 1948, when the foundations of today's planning and development control of land development began under the Town and Country Planning Act 1947, there has always been split level control in London (or Greater London since 1965) divided, first, between the London County Council and the 29 metropolitan borough councils and then (as from April 1, 1965) between the Greater London Council and the 32 London borough councils plus the Corporation of the City of London.

3. Transitional Arrangements

With the Greater London Council abolished from April 1, 1986 (L.G. Act 1985, s.1) a new style of development plan is to be prepared by each of the 32 London boroughs plus the Corporation of the City of London (L.G. Act 1985 s.4(1) and Sched. 1, Part I). It will be called a unitary development plan (*ibid.* para. 2(1)). But these new arrangements for 33 unitary development plans will not come into force on the abolition date, April 1, 1986, because the enabling statutory provisions (namely, the Local Government Act 1985, s.4 and Schedule 1, Part I) will not come into force until some later date (or dates) when the Secretary of State feels the time has come to make a commencement order (*ibid.* s.4(1)) bringing the aforesaid statutory provisions into operation in Greater London.

In the meantime, until the new unitary development plans for Greater London come into force, all existing development plans for Greater London will continue to function (L.G. Act 1985 s.4(2) and Sched. 1, Part II paras. 18 and 20). In this context "structure plan" in relation to Greater London means the Greater London Development Plan (*ibid.* para. 18(3) and see 1971 Act, s.290(1)).

D.O.E. Circular 30/85 entitled, "Local Government Act 1985: Sections 3, 4 and 5: Schedule 1 Town and Country Planning: Transitional Matters" gives in detail an explanation of the transitional arrangements for unitary development plans and development control in Greater London.

4. Unitary Development Plans for Greater London

When the time comes for the provisions of the Local Government Act 1985 section 4 and Schedule 1 Part I to be brought into operation in Greater London by means of a commencement order made by the Secretary of State (L.G. Act 1985 s.4(1)), the then existing arrangements for development plans in Greater London (all done under the authority of the Town and Country Planning Act 1971, Part II) will cease to have effect because Part II of the 1971 Act will be replaced by Part I of Schedule 1 of the Local Government Act 1985 (L.G. Act 1985 s.4(1)). As is the case with unitary development plans for metropolitan districts,[2] the unitary development plans for Greater London will be a kind of amalgam between the structure plans and the local plans which will continue to be made in the shire counties.[3]

5. Procedure for Making and Bringing into Operation Unitary Development Plans for Greater London

The procedure for making and bringing into operation of unitary development plans for Greater London follows the lines of such procedure when used for a unitary development plan in a metropolitan district. No useful purpose would be served by repeating here (for Greater London) what has already been dealt with in connection with unitary development plans in metropolitan counties. Accordingly the reader is referred, at this stage, to Chapter 6, pages 100 to 105 where details are given as to:

(1) the general features of a unitary development plan;
(2) the survey for such a plan;
(3) the preparation of the plan;
(4) publicity for the plan;

[2] See Chap. 6.
[3] See Chaps. 4 and 5.

(5) the public local inquiry or hearing prior to the adoption of the plan;
(6) the adoption of the plan by a metropolitan district council;
(7) the withdrawal of the plan by a metropolitan district council;
(8) the calling in of the plan for consideration by the Secretary of State;
(9) the public local inquiry or the examination in public prior to the approval of the plan by the Secretary of State; and
(10) the approval or rejection of the plan by the Secretary of State.

6. Alteration or Replacement of Unitary Development Plans for Greater London; Joint Unitary Development Plans for Greater London; Secretary of States Default Powers

Again, these matters follow the lines of the comparable procedures for similar matters in connection with unitary development plans in metropolitan districts and the reader is, accordingly, referred to Chapter 6, pages 105 to 107 inclusive.

7. Meaning of "Development Plan" in Greater London

For the purposes of the Town and Country Planning Act 1971, the development plan for any London borough is to be:

(a) the unitary development plan for the time being in force together with the London borough's resolution of adoption or (as the case may be) the Secretary of State's notice of approval, or, where part of the plan has been adopted and part approved, the resolution of adoption and the notice of approval; and
(b) any alteration to the plan together with the London borough's resolution of adoption of the alteration or (as the case may be) the Secretary of State's notice of approval of the alteration or, where part of the alteration has been adopted and part approved, the resolution of adoption and the notice of approval.

8. Regulations

The Secretary of State for the Environment, on August 2, 1983, made the Town and Country Planning (Local Plans for Greater London) Regulations 1983[4] relating to the form and content, the procedures for adoption, abandonment, approval or rejection,

[4] S.I. 1983 No. 1190.

alteration, repeal or replacement of local plans in Greater London. These regulations (amended by the Town and Country Planning (Local Government Reorganisation) (Miscellaneous Amendments) Regulations 1986[5] consequential on the enactment of the Local Government Act 1985) remain currently in force until, presumably, the coming into operation of section 4 and Schedule 17 Part I to the 1985 Act when the duty to prepare unitary development plans for Greater London will become operative.

9. Joint Planning Committee for Greater London

As was earlier mentioned[6] the Local Government Act 1985, on April 1, 1986, brought to an end an unbroken period of 98 years during which there was an overall, comprehensive local government authority (first the London County Council and then, since 1965, the Greater London Council) for London as a whole. Local government (including planning and development control) in London is now in the hands of the 32 London boroughs plus the Corporation of the City of London. Thus 33 new unitary development plans covering the whole of Greater London are due for making in the fullness of time.

The architects of the 1985 Act are clearly alive to the need to inject into the planning system for Greater London some element of comprehensiveness, of looking at London *as a whole*. Accordingly, the 1985 Act provides that there shall be a joint planning committee for Greater London (L.G. Act 1985, s.5).

All the local planning authorities for Greater London, that is to say all the councils of the 32 London boroughs plus the Common Council of the City of London, are obligated to establish a joint planning committee (*ibid.*, s.5(1)) whose responsibility (*ibid.* s.5(2)) is to:

(a) consider and advise those authorities on matters of common interest relating to the planning and development of Greater London;

(b) inform the Secretary of State of the views of those authorities concerning such matters including any such matters as to which he has requested their advice; and

(c) inform the local planning authorities for areas in the vicinity of Greater London, or any body on which those authorities and the local planning authorities in Greater London are represented, of the views of the local planning authorities in

[5] S.I. 1986 No. 443.

[6] See pp. 30, 108–109 inclusive.

> Greater London are represented, of the views of the local planning authorities in Greater London concerning any matters of common interest relating to the planning and development of Greater London and those areas.

This joint planning committee for Greater London was due for appointment "not later than the abolition date" (*ibid.* s.5(1)), that is to say, April 1, 1986. In fact it held its first meeting on November 20, 1985.

Chapter 8

THE MEANING OF "DEVELOPMENT"

1. Meaning of "Development" Summarised

NOTE. In this Chapter a good deal of attention is given, at pages 129 to 133 inclusive, to the Town and Country Planning (Use Classes) Order 1972. This Order is currently (February 1987) under review with the object of its being re-enacted with considerable amendment. The review has been going on for two years. A new Order is expected around Eastertide 1987.

It may be said that *development* (*i.e.* the development of land which here includes buildings, structures and erections) is the very essence of the Town and Country Planning Act 1971—the pivot on which the whole of the Act turns and depends. Accordingly, an understanding of the meaning of "development," as that expression is used in the 1971 Act, is of prime importance for a full appreciation of the comprehensive and extensive scope of the law relating to town and country planning.

It is from section 22 of the 1971 Act (as read in the light of the definitions contained in section 290(1)) that a knowledge of "development" and all that it means for the purposes of the Act is to be gleaned. Indeed, with this Act it is especially advisable to consider at length the interpretation section (s.290) before turning to the rest of the Act, because this section provides special, and sometimes remarkably extended, meaning for no less than 88 expressions used throughout the Act.

The far-reaching effect of the interpretation section on the scope and extent of the 1971 Act will be realised when it is mentioned that each of the expressions set in bold type in the following paragraphs dealing with the meaning of "development" is given specialised definition (to which reference should be made) in, *inter alia*, section 290(1) of the Act.

"Development" is defined (ss.22(1) and 290(1)) as:

(1) the carrying out of **building operations, engineering operations, mining operations** or other operations[1] in, on, over or under **land,** or

[1] In *Chesire C.C.* v. *Woodward* [1962] 2 Q.B. 126, it was held that there is no one test to find out what physical characteristics constitute development of land—it depends on all the circumstances and on the degree of permanency of the "building, engineering, mining or other operations." See also Lord Denning's comments on the difference between (a) the carrying out of "operations" on land, and (b) the

(2) the making of any material change in the **use**[2] of any **buildings** or other **land.**

As to "mining operations" it is enacted (s.22(3A) added by the Town and Country Planning (Minerals) Act 1981 s.1(1) as from May 19, 1986 by S.I. 1986 No. 760) that such operations shall include—

(a) the removal of material of any description—
  (i) from a mineral working deposit;
  (ii) from a deposit of pulverised fuel ash or other furnace ash or clinker; or
  (iii) from a deposit of iron, steel or other metallic slags; and
(b) the extraction of minerals from a disused railway embankment.

It is enacted specifically by the 1971 Act that the following three matters *shall constitute development*:

(1) the **use** of a single dwelling-house for the purpose of two or more separate dwellings (s.22(3)(*a*));
(2) the deposit of refuse or waste materials on an existing dump if *either* (a) the superficial area of the dump is extended or (b) the height of the dump is extended and exceeds the level of the **land** adjoining the dump (s.22(3)(*b*));
(3) the display of **advertisements** on the external part of a **building** not normally used for such display (ss.22(4) and 64).

It is enacted specifically by the 1971 Act that the following six matters *shall not constitute development*:

(1) internal or external improvements, alterations, or maintenance works (not constituting the making good of **war-damage**) none of which materially affects the external appearance of the **building** so treated, provided that any works, begun[3] after December 5, 1968, for the alteration of a building by providing additional space in the building below ground level *will* constitute development (s.22(2)(*a*)); and

making of a "material change of use" of land in *Parkes* v. *Secretary of State for the Environment* [1978] 1 W.L.R. 1308. Are the two prongs of the definition mutually exclusive? Refuse dumping for land improvement may cause problems—see *Northavon D.C.* v. *Secretary of State for the Environment and D.R. Osborne* [1981] J.P.L. 114.

[2] As to whether activities on land constitute operations or uses, see *Parkes* v. *Secretary of State for the Environment and the Peak Park Planning Board* [1979] 1 All E.R. 211, C.A. and the comment thereon in *Journal of Planning and Environment Law* [1978] at p. 319.

[3] As to when works are begun, see s.43 of the 1971 Act and p.215 *post*. See also *United Refineries Ltd.* v. *Essex C.C.* [1976] J.P.L. 110.

provided further that, in the case of a *listed building*,[4] internal improvements, alterations or maintenance works will require "listed building consent"[4] even though they do not materially affect the external appearance of the building;

(2) maintenance or **improvement** works carried out by a **local highway authority** to, and within the boundaries of, a road (s.22(2)(*b*));

(3) the breaking open of streets, etc., for the inspection, repair or renewal of sewers, mains, pipes, cables, etc., by a **local authority** or by **statutory undertakers** (s.22(2)(*c*));

(4) the **use** of any **buildings** or other **land** within the curtilage of a dwelling-house for any purpose incidental to the enjoyment of the dwelling-house as a dwelling-house (s.22(2)(*d*));

(5) the **use** of **land** for **agriculture** or forestry (including afforestation) and the **use** for such purposes of any **building** occupied with land so used (s.22(2)(*e*));

(6) in the case of **buildings** or other **land** used for a purpose of any class specified in an Order made by the Secretary of State, the use thereof for any purpose in the same class (s.22(2)(*f*) (as amended by the Housing and Planning Act 1986 s.49(1)(*a*) and Sched. 11, Pt. I, para. 1.) and the Town and Country Planning (Use Classes) Order 1972.)[5]

Thus, as any building operation or change of use which falls under one or other of the items numbered (1) to (6) respectively in the previous paragraph is declared by the Act *not* to constitute development, it follows that the need to obtain planning permission in respect of it cannot arise. It is also to be noted that, in the case of items (4) and (5) of the previous paragraph, by virtue of the definition of "use" in section 290(1) of the Act, the *erection* of new buildings for any of the purposes mentioned in those two items *will* constitute development.

It is further enacted, by the 1971 Act that the following six matters, though they may constitute development, *shall not require planning permission*:

(1) the resumption—provided the resumption was *before* December 6, 1968—of the normal **use** of **land** which, on July 1, 1948 (the date when the Town and Country Planning Act 1947 came into operation), was being used temporarily for some different **use** (s.23(2));

[4] See Chap. 14.

[5] S.I. 1972 No. 1385. This order is currently (January 1987) under review with a view to a new Order being made around Eastertide 1987.

(2) the **use,** *before* December 6, 1968, for an occasional purpose of **land** which, on July 1, 1948, was normally used for one purpose but which was also used (whether at regular intervals or not) for the said occasional purpose, provided (in the case of any resumption of the occasional use taking place on or after December 6, 1968) that there has been at least one such resumption *since* July 1, 1948, and *before* January 1, 1968 (s.23(3));

(3) the **use** of **land** unoccupied on July 1, 1948 (provided it had been occupied at some time on or after January 7, 1937), for the purpose for which it was last used before July 1, 1948 (s.23(4))[6];

(4) the resumption, on the expiration of a **planning permission** to develop **land** granted for a limited period, of the **use** of the **land** for the purpose for which it was normally used before the limited planning permission was granted, provided that such normal use does not contravene Part III of the 1971 Act or previous planning control (s.23(5)(6)(10));

(5) the resumption, where **planning permission** to develop **land** subject to limitations has been granted by a **development order,** of the normal **use** of the **land,** provided that such normal **use** does not contravene Part III of the 1971 Act or previous planning control (s.23(8)(10));

(6) the resumption, after the issue of an enforcement notice in respect of any unauthorised **development** of **land,** of the **use** of the **land** for the purpose for which, under Part III of the 1971 Act, it could lawfully be used if the unauthorised development had not been carried out (s.23(9)).[7]

However, as to the **use** of **land** for a caravan site, it is to be noted that the freedom conferred under items (1), (2) and (3) in the previous paragraph from the need to obtain planning permission for such **use** does not apply unless the **land** has been used as a caravan site on at least one occasion during the period of two years ending on March 9, 1960 (s.23(7)).

It is further enacted specifically by the 1971 Act that, whilst the following two matters *do* constitute development, planning permission in respect of them *shall be deemed to be granted*:

(1) the display of **advertisements** in accordance with regulations made under section 63 of the 1971 Act (s.64 and the

[6] See *Cubitt Estates* v. *Westminster Corporation* (1952) 2 P. & C.R. 316 (L.T.)

[7] As to reversion to an earlier use *not* authorised by planning permission but immune from enforcement action by lapse of time, see *LTSS Print & Supply Services Ltd.* v. *London Borough of Hackney and Another* [1976] 1 All E.R. 311. See also *Bulco Transport Services Ltd.* v. *Secretary of State for the Environment* [1982] J.P.L. 177.

Town and Country Planning (Control of Advertisements) Regulations 1984.[8]

(2) certain development by a local authority or by a statutory undertaker which has been authorised by a government department (s.40).

An effort will now be made to break down the definition of "development" into its various components and to examine each of these in turn to see what it amounts to having regard to provisions of the interpretation section (section 290) of the 1971 Act.

2. Building Operations

The expression "building operations" includes (s.290(1)):

(1) rebuilding operations;
(2) structural alterations of buildings;
(3) structural additions to buildings; and
(4) other operations normally undertaken by a person carrying on business as a builder.

The special definition of "building operations" leads in turn to the special definition of "building" which includes (s.290(1)) any structure or erection, and any part of a building, structure or erection, but does not include plant or machinery comprised in a building, structure or erection. A model village (Bekenscot) is a "structure or erection"[9] but swingboats are not a "building."[10]

Apart from the building and the rebuilding of buildings, structures or erections and the making of structural alterations or additions to buildings, structures or erections, other operations normally undertaken by a builder would include *ancillary* demolitions in connection with rebuilding and in connection with alterations. This and similar operations will be caught by the expression "building operations" and will accordingly constitute development under the Act.[11]

The erection of a crane, 89 feet in height, which ran on wheels has been held to be development.[12]

3. Engineering Operations

"Engineering operations" includes (s.290(1)) the formation or laying out of means of access to highways and "means of access"

[8] S.I. 1984 No. 421; see Chap. 12.
[9] *Bucks C.C.* v. *Callingham* [1952] 2 Q.B. 515, C.A.
[10] *James* v. *Brecon C.C.* (1963) 15 P. & C.R. 20.
[11] *L.C.C.* v. *Marks and Spencer* [1953] A.C. 535, H.L.
[12] *Barvis Ltd.* v. *Secretary of State for the Environment* (1971) 22 P. & C.R. 710, D.C.

includes (again s.290(1)) any means of access, whether private or public, for vehicles or for foot passengers, and includes a street. Thus it follows that engineering operations could include such a modest matter as the making of a gateway in the rear wall of a factory giving egress for pedestrians only from the factory yard into the back street.

4. Mining or Other Operations—Demolition

This *Outline* does not purport to deal with mining operations or mineral working all of which are very specialised matters.

As to "other operations," it may be mentioned that nowhere does the 1971 Act declare that demolition works (as distinct from building works) constitute development. Under the Act (except in instances of *special* control such as the demolition of a listed building[13] or the demolition of any building in a conservation area[14]) demolition work is not prohibited.

Even so, a demolition may be so large as to constitute an "engineering operation" or it may, in a particular case involving the removal of embankments surrounding ammunition magazines, amount to a "building operation."[15]

On the other hand, demolition of nissen huts and a lean-to hut has been held *not* to be development.[16]

Irrespective of the law of planning control however, demolition work of the whole or part of a building must be first notified to the local authority (there are exceptions to this rule) under the provisions of public health law (Public Health Act 1936, s.29 and Local Government (Miscellaneous Provisions) Act 1982, s.28).

5. Land

"Land" means (s.290(1)) any corporeal hereditament including a building, a structure or an erection.

If land, occupied with a building, is used for the same purpose as the building, it can be regarded, in a planning sense, as one unit with the building; but if it is not so used, it cannot be.[17]

[13] See Chap. 14.
[14] See Chap. 9.
[15] *Coleshill and District Investment Co. Ltd.* v. *Minister of Housing and Local Government* [1969] 1 W.L.R. 746; 20 P. & C.R. 679, H.L.
[16] *Iddenden* v. *Secretary of State for the Environment* [1972] 1 W.L.R. 1433, C.A.
[17] *Brooks and Burton Ltd.* v. *Secretary of State for the Environment* [1977] 1 W.L.R. 1294, C.A.

6. Material Change of Use

All the foregoing matters relate to development as dealt with in sub-paragraph (1) of the definition of "development" as given on page 115, which sub-paragraph envisages the carrying out of some positive operation in, on, over or under any land, building, structure or erection.

But it is not essential that land, buildings, structures or erections should themselves be subjected to any such positive operation at all before their development may be said to have occurred for the purposes of the 1971 Act, for, under sub-paragraph (2) of the definition as given on page 116, development may take place when any material change occurs, not in the land or the building, structure or erection itself but in *the use* to which the land, building, structure or erection is for the time being put. The 1971 Act contains no definition of the expression "material change" as here used, although for the avoidance of doubt two examples of what may be said to constitute a material change are quoted in section 22(3) and will be referred to later.

The Town and Country Planning Act 1932 employed the expression "change in the use." The 1971 Act (following the precedent of the 1947 Act) employs the same expression but qualifies it with the word "material." It is clear from this that no slight or trivial change of use will amount to development but it is difficult to draw any hard and fast line. It may well be that whilst material change of use is difficult to define theoretically it will be readily recognisable when in practice it occurs. If there is doubt in any particular case provision is made in section 53 of the 1971 Act for resolving this (see page 133).

Although the expression "material change" is not defined in the 1971 Act, two examples of what may be regarded as a material change are given in section 22(3) of the Act "for the avoidance of doubt." It seems that the question of what amounts to a material change is a question of fact and degree to be determined in the light of given circumstances.[18]

The Secretary of State takes the view that for a change of use to be a *material* change of use the new use must be *substantially* different from the old use. In *Palser* v. *Grinling*,[19] "substantial" was accepted

[18] *Howell* v. *Sunbury-on-Thames U.D.C.* (1964) 62 L.G.R. 119, C.A; *Barling (David W.) Ltd.* v. *Secretary of State for the Environment* [1980] J.P.L. 594.
[19] [1948] A.C. 291, H.L.

as meaning "considerable, solid or big," the other meaning of the word (which is "not unsubstantial," *i.e.* just enough to avoid the *de minimis* principle) not being accepted in that case.

If a house, formerly occupied by a *single* family, is let out in flats to a *number* of families, there may be a material change, as a matter of degree and fact, notwithstanding that the use of the house remains residential throughout.[20]

Difficulties arise when there has been an interruption in the use of land. It is a question of fact whether a particular use has been continuous or whether there has been a discontinuance of the use followed by a resumption or repetition of the use for the same purpose. Factors to be taken into consideration are the length of the interruption, and whether the land was put to any other use during the interruption.

Thus in *Postill* v. *East Riding County Council*,[21] land used as a riding school and for grazing was used, under a planning permission, for a circus, subject to a condition that the circus user should cease in September. The circus user ceased in accordance with the condition. It was held (a) that the resumption *10 months later* of the circus user was not a continuance of the same user and did not amount to a breach of the condition; and (b) that discontinuance did not necessarily mean permanent discontinuance.

On the other hand in *Fyson* v. *Bucks County Council*,[22] resumption in 1956 of a use for storage to which premises had last been put prior to 1949 was held not to be a material change of use. *Postill* v. *East Riding County Council, supra,* was distinguished on the ground that in the *Fyson* case the plaintiff had owned the land since 1951 and there had never been any use of the land since 1943 except for the storage of materials.

In *Klein* v. *Whitstable Urban District Council*,[23] there was held to be no discontinuance where caravans which had been removed from agricultural land in compliance with an enforcement notice were brought back onto the land six weeks later.

Difficulties also arise where there has been an intensification of a use. In *Guildford Rural District Council* v. *Fortescue, Same* v. *Penny*,[24] the

[20] *Birmingham Corporation* v. *Minister of Housing and Local Government and Habib Ullah* [1964] 1 Q.B. 178; 15 P. & C.R. 404, D.C. See also *Borg* v. *Khan* (1965) 63 L.G.R. 309, D.C.; *Clarke* v. *Caterham and Warlingham U.D.C.* (1966) 18 P. & C.R. 82, D.C.

[21] [1956] 2 Q.B. 386, D.C. And see *Cynon Valley Borough Council* v. *Secretary of State for Wales and Aï Mee Lam* (1986) J.P.L. 283; reversed on appeal (1986) J.P.L. 760.

[22] [1958] 1 W.L.R. 634, D.C.

[23] [1958] 10 P. & C.R. 6, D.C.

[24] [1959] 2 Q.B. 112, C.A.

court declined to accept as a general proposition that mere intensity of user or occupation could never be relevant. Without deciding the point, the court indicated that whether an intensification of user amounted to a material change of use would depend on the particular circumstances of the particular case. The justices having found that the increase in the number of caravans using a one-and-a-half-acre site from eight to 27 did *not* amount to a material change of use, the Court of Appeal refused to disturb their finding.[25]

On intensification of user it has been held by the Court of Appeal—reversing the decision of the Divisional Court—that intensification will not of itself amount to such a material change of use as will take a use out of the ambit (and protection) of a use class specified in the Town and Country Planning (Use Classes) Order 1972.[26]

Where a group of buildings is used together for a single purpose, it may be that the use of any particular building should be disregarded, the use being that of the group as a whole.[27] So also where a building on a nursery garden hitherto used for sales of produce grown on the nursery becomes used also for sales of produce *not grown thereon,* this may amount to development since the former use was ancillary to the agricultural use of the land and the building which were one unit.[28]

The question whether there is a material change of the use to which part of a house has been put when that use is extended to another part of the house, is a question of fact and degree. The proper unit for consideration may be the house as a whole.[29]

There is clearly a material change in the use when the *nature* of the use is changed, as when a residential user is converted to a business user by turning a private dwelling-house into a shop. The position is

[25] See also *Brookes* v. *Flintshire C.C.* (1956) 6 P. & C.R. 140; *Washington U.D.C.* v. *Gray* (1958) 10 P. & C.R. 264, D.C.; *Marshall* v. *Nottingham Corporation* [1960] 1 W.L.R. 707; *Finch* v. *Leatherhead U.D.C.* (1961) 13 P. & C.R. 97: *Horwitz* v. *Rowson* [1960] 1 W.L.R. 803; *George Cohen 600 Group* v. *Minister of Housing and Local Government* [1961] 1 W.L.R. 944; D.C.; *Devon C.C.* v. *Allen's Caravans (Estates) Ltd.* (1962) 14 P. & C.R. 440; *Brooks and Burton Ltd.* v. *Secretary of State for the Environment* [1977] 1 W.L.R. 1294; *Emma Hotels Ltd.* v. *Secretary of State for the Environment* [1979] J.P.L. 390, D.C. and (1980) 41 P. & C.R. 255, D.C.

[26] S.I. 1972 No. 1385; and see *Brooks and Burton Ltd.* v. *Secretary of State for the Environment* [1977] 1 W.L.R. 1294, C.A.; *Bromsgrove District Council* v. *Secretary of State for the Environment and Edward Attwood* [1977] J.P.L. 797.

[27] *Vickers-Armstrong* v. *Central Land Board* (1957) 9 P. & C.R. 33, C.A.; *Trentham (G. Percy) Ltd.* v. *Gloucester C.C.* [1966] 1 W.L.R. 506; *Brazil (Concrete) Ltd.* v. *Amersham R.D.C.* (1967) 18 P. & C.R. 396, C.A.

[28] *Williams* v. *Minister of Housing and Local Government* (1967) 18 P. & C.R. 514, D.C.

[29] *Brooks* v. *Gloucestershire C.C.* (1967) 19 P. & C.R. 90.

not so clear when the nature of the use remains constant but its type is changed, *e.g.* when the type of business user is changed and the change does not fall squarely within one of the classes in the Schedule to the Town and Country Planning (Use Classes) Order 1972[30] (referred to later in this chapter). The fact that it does not fall within the Order does not preclude consideration of the question whether or not there is a material change of use. The important matter is the character of the use, rather than the purpose of the particular occupier.[31]

If the activity carried out on land remains the same, a mere change in the identity of the person carrying on the activity, or a mere change in the ownership or source of supply of the articles treated on the land, will not amount to a material change of use.[32]

Nice questions can arise when there is a material change of use in a case where the original use was of a mixed kind involving a dominant use and an ancillary use, the one, say, residential and the other, say, industrial. On this, useful judicial comment is given in *Frank Vyner and Son Ltd.* v. *Secretary of State for the Environment and London Borough of Hammersmith.*[33]

Many changes of use are excepted from the definition of development by the Town and Country Planning (Use Classes) Order 1972.[34] Thus the changing of a butcher's shop into a baker's shop, a greengrocer's shop or a hairdresser's shop (but not, be it noted, into a shop for the sale of hot food, a tripe shop or a cats' meat shop) does *not* constitute development; nor does the changing of a solicitor's office into an accountant's office or into a bank.

It is to be noted, however, that even though such changes do not in themselves constitute development it is clear (since the decision in *Corporation of City of London* v. *Secretary of State for the Environment and Another*[35] that, on granting planning permission, the local planning authority can, at that time, impose conditions which preclude the use of the land for which planning permission is granted being changed (except of course, with further planning permission) from the use stated in the planning permission to any other use even though such other use is within the same use class as is the use

30 S.I. 1972 No. 1385.

31 *East Barnet Urban District Council* v. *British Transport Commission* [1962] 2 Q.B. 484, D.C.

32 *Lewis* v. *Secretary of State for the Environment* (1971) 23 P. & C.R. 125, D.C. See also *Snook* v. *Secretary of State for the Environment* (1975) 237 E.G. 723.

33 (1977) 243 E.G. 597; [1977] J.P.L. 795.

34 S.I. 1972 No. 1385.

35 (1971) 23 P. & C.R. 169.

covered by the planning permission and, accordingly, is not, technically, development at all!

7. Section 22, subsections (3) and (4)

After the definition of development has been dealt with generally in subsection (1) of section 22, of the 1971 Act, subsections (3) and (4) of section 22 proceed to give examples of three uses of land which are declared specifically to involve a material change of use and which accordingly constitute development under the Act. These three uses are summarised as follows.

(1) The subdivision of *domestic* premises, *ie* the use as two or more separate dwelling-houses of any building previously used as a single dwelling-house (s.22(3)(*a*)).

As to what constitutes "two or more separate dwelling-houses" reference may usefully be made to cases decided under the "Rent Acts,"[36] in which it was held that the letting of two rooms with the use jointly of other rooms and amenities was, in effect, a sharing of the house and not a letting of a "separate dwelling."[37]

The rooms shared must be essential living rooms such as a kitchen,[38] or even a "kitchenette."[39] A sharing of accommodation other than living accommodation, such as a bathroom and water-closet, which are essential by modern standards, does not involve a sharing of the house.[40] But the rule applies whether the sharing is between tenant and landlord or between tenant and tenant.[41] Two self-contained flats, capable of being let as separate flats, were held to be capable of being let as a single "dwelling-house" within the meaning of the Rent and Mortgage Interest (Restrictions) Act 1933, s.16(1).[42] Many of these cases were reviewed in *Baker* v. *Turner*.[43]

Incidentally, it should be mentioned at this point that the Housing and Planning Act 1986 makes it clear (s.49(1)(*a*) and Sched. 11, Pt. I, para. 1) that the subdivision of *non-domestic* premises does *not* constitute a change of use and accordingly, does *not* constitute

36 *Neale* v. *Del Soto* [1945] K.B. 144, C.A.

37 See also *Sharpe* v. *Nicholls* [1945] K.B. 382, C.A.; *Krauss* v. *Boyne* [1946] 1 All E.R. 543; *Stevenson* v. *Kenyon* [1946] 2 All E.R. 595, C.A.

38 *Neale* v. *Del Soto, supra.*

39 *Winters* v. *Dance* [1949] L.J.R. 165, C.A.

40 *Cole* v. *Harris* [1945] K.B. 474, C.A.

41 *Banks* v. *Cope-Brown* [1948] 2 K.B. 287, D.C.; *Llewellyn* v. *Hinson* [1948] 2 K.B. 385, C.A.

42 *Langford Property Co.* v. *Goldrich* [1949] 1 K.B. 511, C.A.

43 [1950] A.C. 401.

development which requires planning permission. It is claimed by the Government that this arrangement will give greater freedom to industry to carry out development and create jobs without endangering the environment. "A Step by Step Guide to Planning Permission for Small Businesses" was published by the Department of the Environment in March 1985 and is available from the Department at 2 Marsham Street, London SW1P 3EB.

(2) The deposit of refuse or waste materials, even though they are deposited on a site which is already used for the purpose, provided that either, (a) the superficial area of the deposit is thereby extended, or (b) the height of the deposit is thereby extended so as to exceed the level of adjoining land (s.22(3)(*b*)). Thus one can apparently continue to dump waste materials into existing holes in the ground (caused, for example, by mining or quarrying) until the holes are filled to the surface of the surrounding land.

(3) Control over the display of advertisements is dealt with in detail in the Town and Country Planning (Control of Advertisements) Regulations 1984,[44] made under section 63 of the 1971 Act but, without prejudice to the provisions of those regulations, the display of advertisements on the external part of a building which is not normally used for such display is to be treated as a material change of use and therefore development of the building (s.22(4)) which provision will have the effect of preventing any recurrence of the decision in *Mills & Rockleys* v. *Leicester Corporation.*[45]

In connection with this provision "advertisement," it may be noted, is very widely defined (in section 290(1) of the 1971 Act) so as to mean any word, letter, model, sign, placard, board, notice, device or representation, whether illuminated or not, in the nature of, and employed wholly or in part for the purposes of, advertisement, announcement or direction and, without prejudice to the foregoing provision, the word includes any hoarding or similar structure used or adapted for use for the display of advertisements.

8. Section 23, subsections (2), (3), (4), (5), (6), (7), (8), (9) and (10)

Subsections (2) to (10) inclusive of section 23 of the 1971 Act deal with six types of case which, whilst strictly constituting development, can yet be undertaken without obtaining the planning permission which (were it not for the provisions of these nine

[44] S.I. 1984 No. 421; see Chap. 12.
[45] [1946] K.B. 315, D.C.

subsections) would otherwise be required under the provisions of subsection (1) of section 23.

These six types of case have already been referred to (see pages 117 and 118) and, in considering them further, comment under the following heads may be offered.

(1) In the first place it will be remembered that, whenever the use of land is mentioned in connection with these six cases, land includes buildings, structures or erections (s.290(1)).

(2) Secondly, when, in connection with the first of these six cases, reference is made to land being used "temporarily," it will be remembered that "temporarily" does not necessarily mean for a few years only; it means something that "may, within the reasonable contemplation of the parties, come to an end some day."[46]

(3) Thirdly, it is important to note that, so far as the use of land as a caravan site is concerned, this privilege of freedom from the need to apply for planning permission conferred, by subsections (2), (3) and (4) of section 23 of the 1971 Act, on the first three of these six types of case, does *not* apply to the use of land as a caravan site *unless* the land has been used as a caravan site on at least one occasion during the two-year period ending on March 9, 1960 (s.23(7)). What constitutes an "occasion" will be a question of fact; user for one day only would appear to be sufficient.

9. Section 22, subsection (2)

Turning now to subsection (2) of section 22, it is found that this subsection gives examples of *three operations* and *three uses* which are *not* to constitute development. These will now be examined in turn.

As to the *three operations*, the position is as follows.

(1) The carrying out of works of maintenance, improvement or other alteration to any building, structure or erection is not development, *provided* such works affect only the interior of the building or do not materially affect its external appearance, are not done by way of repairing war damage and do not constitute works begun after December 5, 1968, for the provision of additional space in the building but below ground level. (However, if the building is a *listed building*, "listed building consent" may be needed before any such works of maintenance, improvement, or alteration are carried out).[47]

Thus the carrying out of internal conversions will not constitute development provided it can be done without materially affecting the outside of the building concerned. In this connection it is

[46] *Burrows* v. *Lang* [1901] 2 Ch. 502.
[47] See Chap. 14.

necessary to bear in mind that the making of additional windows and doorways to a building in association with internal conversion may well be said to affect materially the external appearance of the building and thereby bring the internal conversions within the category of development for which consent will be required.

It will be noted that, whilst the carrying out of internal conversions (as mentioned in the previous paragraph) may not constitute development, nevertheless any material change in *the use* of the building, consequential upon such conversions, *will* of itself constitute development.

It is further to be noted that, since January 1, 1969, any expansion of a building below ground level (even if it does not materially affect the external appearance of the building) *will* constitute development (1971 Act, s.22(2)(*a*)).

(2) The carrying out of maintenance and improvement works to highways by a local highway authority is not development (s.22(2)(*b*)).

(3) The breaking open of streets, etc., for the inspection, repair or renewal of sewers, mains, pipes, cables, etc., by a local authority or by statutory undertakers is not development (s.22(2)(*c*)).

As to the *three uses*, the position is as follows.

(1) The use of any land or any buildings, structures or erections, within the curtilage of a dwelling-house for purposes incidental to the enjoyment of the dwelling-house as a dwelling-house is not development (s.22(2)(*d*)).

Here it is important to note that, by virtue of section 290(1), the word "use" in relation to land does not include the use of land by the carrying out of building operations or any other operations on the land. Thus, it follows that the *construction* of new buildings, structures or erections, even though they are within the curtilage of a dwelling-house, and even though they are to be used in connection with the enjoyment of the dwelling-house as a dwelling-house, does constitute development, although it must be added that much of this sort of "curtilage development" comes within the category of "permitted development" by reason of its being included in Class I of the First Schedule to the Town and Country Planning General Development Order 1977.[48]

As to the meaning of "curtilage," in *Sinclair-Lockhart's Trustees* v. *Central Land Board*[49] the Court of Session held that "the ground

[48] S.I. 1977 No. 289.

[49] (1950) 1 P. & C.R. 195; affirmed (1951) 1 P. & C.R. 320. See also *Stephens* v. *Cuckfield R.D.C.* [1960] 2 Q.B. 373, C.A.

which is used for the comfortable enjoyment of a house or other building may be regarded in law as being within the curtilage of that house or building, and thereby as an integral part of the same although it has not been marked off or enclosed in any way. It is enough that it serve the purpose of the house or building in some necessary or reasonably useful way."

(2) The use of land for agriculture or forestry, and the use for any of those purposes of any building, structure or erection occupied with the land so used is not development (s.22(2)(*e*)).

Again (and for reasons given above) this provision does not cover *new* agricultural or *new* forestry buildings, structures or erections the construction of which *does* constitute development. But the erection of many agricultural and forestry buildings is "permitted development" under Class VI and Class VII of the First Schedule to the Town and Country Planning General Development Order 1977[50] the scope of which two classes is now restricted, in certain aesthetically "sensitive areas," by the provisions of The Town and Country Planning (Agricultural and Forestry Development in National Parks etc.) Special Development Order 1986 (S.I. 1986 No. 1176).

It will be remembered that "agriculture," by section 290(1), includes horticulture, fruit growing, seed growing, dairy farming, the breeding and keeping of livestock (including any creature kept for the production of food, wool, skin or fur, or for the purpose of its use in the farming of land), the use of land as grazing land, meadow land, osier land, market gardens and nursery grounds, and the use of land for woodlands where that use is ancillary to the farming of land for other agricultural purposes.

(3) The Secretary of State is empowered under section 22(2)(*f*) to make an order specifying different classes of use. Under this authority he has made the Town and Country Planning (Use Classes) Order 1972[51] whereby, in the case of land or buildings used for a purpose of any class specified in the Order, a change of use to any other purpose of the same class will *not* constitute development. This Order is examined more fully in the following paragraphs.

10. The Town and Country Planning (Use Classes) Order 1972

In reading this section 10 of this chapter the reader is first referred to the italicised Note on page 115 *ante*.

[50] S.I. 1977 No. 289. But see, as to Class VI and Class VII of the General Development Order 1977, The Town and Country Planning (Agricultural and Forestry Development in National Parks etc.) Special Development Order 1986 (S.I. 1986 No. 1176).

[51] S.I. 1972 No. 1385. See also fn. 5, *supra*, at p. 117.

This Order which came into operation on October 23, 1972 (art. 1) has been amended by the Town and Country Planning (Use Classes) (Amendment) Order 1983 (S.I. 1983 No. 1614) which came into operation on May 1, 1984 (1983 Order, art. 1(2)). The two Orders may be cited together as the Town and Country Planning (Use Classes) Orders 1972 and 1983 (1983 Order, art.1(1)).

The 1972 Order specifies 18 different classes of use. Many of the expressions used in the Order, when dealing with the different Use Classes, are given extended meaning by the definitions in article 2(2) of the Order. Certain of these definitions merit special mention here.

(1) There is, for example, what may be termed a basic definition of the expression "industrial building" and this is followed by even more refined definitions of "light industrial building," "general industrial building" and "special industrial building."

(2) The word "office" is defined so as to include a bank but not a post office or a betting office.

(3) The word "shop" means a building used for the carrying on of any retail trade or retail business wherein the primary purpose is the selling of goods by retail.

(4) The following, *inter alia,* also constitute shops under the Order: a hairdresser's establishment, an undertaker's establishment, an agency supplying railway, theatre and other tickets, a place for receiving articles for washing, cleaning or repairing.

(5) The following do *not* constitute shops under the Order; a fun fair, a garage, a launderette, a petrol-filling station, an office, a betting office, an hotel, restaurant, snackbar, cafe or any other premises licensed for the sale of intoxicating liquors for consumption on the premises.

Under the Use Classes Order 1972, art. 2(3) a building may include land provided the land is occupied with the building *and* used for the same purposes.[52]

With the foregoing definitions in mind, attention may now be paid to article 3 and to the Schedule to the Order, the short effect of which is that (subject to any exceptions specified in the classes themselves and subject also to the decision in *Corporation of City of London* v. *Secretary of State for the Environment and Another*)[53] the use of a building for any purpose specified in one of the 18 classes may be changed to any other purpose falling *within the same class* without the need to

[52] *Brooks and Burton Ltd.* v. *Secretary of State for the Environment* [1977] 1 W.L.R. 1294, C.A.

[53] (1971) 23 P. & C.R. 169.

obtain planning permission because any change of use which still leaves the use within its original class does not constitute development under the 1971 Act (s.22(2)(*f*)).[53a]

The foregoing paragraph (and indeed the whole of the 1972 Order) must now be read in the light of the decision in the *Corporation of London* case just mentioned. This decision demonstrates that conditions attached to a grant of planning permission can validly restrict further changes in the use of land even though such changes would not constitute development by virtue of the provisions of the 1972 Use Classes Order.

An enforcement notice was served alleging a material change of use without planning permission. However, the original use and the new use both came within Class X of the Use Classes Order 1972. On appeal to the Secretary of State for the Environment against the enforcement notice the Inspector upheld the notice. This was challenged in the courts (as a matter of law) under section 245 of the 1971 Act. It was held there had been no development therefore no planning permission was required; that the Inspector had erred in presuming to consider whether the change of use which had, in fact, occurred was a material change of use; and that a planning authority could only exclude the operation of the Use Classes Order (as in the *Corporation of the City of London* case above) by some express condition contained in a grant of planning permission.[54]

Special reference is now made to certain (but not all) of the 18 Use Classes specified in the Schedule to the 1972 Order.

CLASS I

It follows from the provisions of Class I that, provided a building was used on July 1, 1948, as a shop, it may change its use to a totally different kind of shop without any need of planning permission, provided always that it does not transform itself into a shop for the sale of hot food, a tripe shop, a shop for the sale of pet animals or birds, a cats' meat shop, or a shop for the sale of motor vehicles.

Thus a grocer's shop can, without planning permission, become a butcher's shop, or a greengrocer's shop, or a hairdressing establishment, or a ticket agency, or a dry cleaner's receiving office. Whilst it is clear that a grocer's shop cannot, without permission, transform itself into a shop for the sale of hot food, it may be asked whether,

[53a] A change of use from one use class to another does not *necessarily* constitute development. It will not do so unless the change of use is a material change: *Rann* v. *Secretary of State for the Environment* (1980) 40 P. & C.R. 113.

[54] *Carpet Decor (Guildford) Ltd.* v. *Secretary of State for the Environment and Guildford Borough Council* [1981] J.P.L. 806.

conversely, a shop for the sale of hot food can transform itself into a grocer's shop without planning permission. Such a change would, it is submitted, constitute a material change of use but although it is not authorised by the Town and Country Planning (Use Classes) Order 1972,[55] it *is* authorised as "permitted development" under the Town and Country Planning General Development Order 1977,[56] article 3(1), and the First Schedule, Class III(*b*).

Class II

Class II of the Use Classes Order makes it clear than an auctioneer's office (for example) may transform itself into a solicitor's office or into a bank without the need for planning permission. If the predominant use of premises has been as offices, the use of the premises *as a whole* may be as an office and within this use class.[57]

Class III

Under Class III of the Order a light industrial building used for a particular purpose may transform itself into a light industrial building used for another type of purpose provided always that it remains throughout a light industrial building as defined in article 2(2) of the Order. The meaning of "light industrial building" is dealt with in *Crisp from the Fens Ltd.* v. *Rutland C.C.*[58]

Class IV

Under this class, a general industrial building may similarly transform itself provided that it remains throughout a general industrial building as defined in article 2(2) of the Order. As has already been mentioned, if a use leaps from one class into another class, it puts itself beyond the protection of the Order. Accordingly, a general industrial building may not, so far as this Order is concerned, so change the purposes for which it is used as to transform itself into a light industrial building, but it is to be noted that such a change *is* authorised, as "permitted development" by the Town and Country

[55] S.I. 1972 No. 1385
[56] S.I. 1977 No. 289.
[57] *Shephard* v. *Buckinghamshire C.C.* (1966) 18 P. & C.R. 419.
[58] (1949) 1 P. & C.R. 48, C.A.

Planning General Development Order 1977,[59] art. 3(1), and the First Schedule, Class III(*a*).

Other Use Classes

Referring briefly to some of the other 18 classes, it appears that under Class XIV a hospital can become an institution for old people and under Class XV a health centre can become a day nursery.

So far as this Order is concerned a health centre (being in Class XV) cannot transform itself into a nursing home (which is in Class XIV) for the Order does not authorise a use to leap from one class to another. But such a change *can* take place independently of the provisions of this Order and without planning permission if it can be proved that the change of use (from a health centre to a nursing home) does *not* constitute a material change of use.

Similarly, under Class XVI an exhibition hall can become a public library and under Class XVII a theatre can become a cinema. At least one local planning authority who, being wishful to maintain within their area the number of "live" theatres, gave planning permission for the demolition of a theatre and the erection on the site of an office block subject to the condition that the new block would contain within itself "a theatre," was dismayed to find the theatre, which had opened as a "live" theatre, shortly thereafter changed its use into that of a cinema. The question here is whether the local planning authority, in granting planning permission for a use which itself fell neatly within Use Class XVII (namely use as a theatre), ought to have added a condition which prevented any change of the live theatre into a cinema even though, by virtue of this Order, such a change does not of itself constitute development. (See *Corporation of City of London* v. *Secretary of State for the Environment and Another*.[60])

11. Determination of what Constitutes "Development"

From the foregoing paragraphs of this chapter it will be seen that the determination of whether a particular operation or change of use constitutes "development" within the meaning of the 1971 Act may be a nice point.[61] The Act recognises this and makes provision for the determination of doubtful cases by application to the local planning authority (s.53(1)), from whose decision there is an appeal to

[59] S.I. 1977 No. 289.

[60] (1971) 23 P & C.R. 169.

[61] *George Cohen 600 Group* v. *Minister of Housing and Local Government* [1961] 1 W.L.R. 944, D.C.; *Horwitz* v. *Rowson* [1960] 1 W.L.R. 803.

the Secretary of State (ss.53(2) and 36). The decision of the Secretary of State may be the subject of further appeal on a point of law to the High Court (s.247).

The procedure for obtaining a determination under section 53 is contained in article 6 of the Town and Country Planning General Development Order 1977.[62]

In addition to the foregoing manner of ascertaining under section 53 of the 1971 Act what constitutes "development," application may be made to the High Court for a declaration as to whether proposed operations or change of use constitutes development and the jurisdiction of the court to make such a declaration is not ousted by section 53 of the 1971 Act: *Pyx Granite Co.* v. *Ministry of Housing and Local Government.*[63]

12. The Meaning of "New Development"

Section 22 of the 1971 Act contains five subsections. The first four of these deal with the definition of "development" and have been dealt with in the foregoing paragraphs of this chapter.

It remains to add that subsection (5) of section 22 gives a specialised definition of "new development" which means any kind of development (as defined by subsections 22(1), (2), (3) and (4) of the 1971 Act and as discussed in this chapter) *other than* development specified in the Eighth Schedule to the Act. This latter kind of development (sometimes called "Eighth Schedule Development" or "Existing-Use Development"—it used, formerly, to be called "Third Schedule Development") is development falling within the ambit of the existing use of land. "New Development" is development which goes outside the bounds of existing use.

Whilst under the 1971 Act no development (whether new development or not) can be undertaken without planning permission, (s.23(1))[64] certain classes of existing-use development (namely, those six classes appearing in Part II of the Eighth Schedule to the Act) have always carried with them a right to compensation (under Part VIII of the 1971 Act)[65] in case of a refusal of planning permission (s.169). Compensation (under Part VII of the 1971 Act) on a refusal of planning permission for *new* development is a much more uncertain affair.[66]

[62] S.I. 1977 No. 289.
[63] [1958] 1 Q.B. 554; C.A.; [1960] A.C. 260, H.L.
[64] See Chap. 10.
[65] See Chap. 17, pp. 376–379.
[66] See Chap. 17 pp. 366–373.

It must be added that the obligation of a local planning authority to pay compensation, under section 169 of the 1971 Act, is now limited in favour of the local planning authority by the Town and Country Planning (Compensation) Act 1985 in respect of any enlargement (under the authority of Schedule 8, Part II, of the 1971 Act) of a block of flats erected before July 1, 1948—the date when the 1947 Act came into operation.[67]

[67] See Chap. 17, pp. 377–379. See also *Peaktop Properties (Hampstead) Ltd.* v. *London Borough of Camden* (1983) 45 P. and C.R. 177. The Town and Country Planning (Compensation) Act 1985 reverses the decision of the Court of Appeal in this case—that decision being "wholly unacceptable to the Government" (Mr. Neil Macfarlane M.P., *Hansard* 72 H.C. Debates 900; February 5, 1985).

Chapter 9

CONSERVATION AREAS: NATIONAL PARKS AND AREAS OF OUTSTANDING NATURAL BEAUTY

1. Introductory

In 1975 I was invited to deliver the Hamlyn Lectures. These are an annual series of four governed by the Hamlyn Trust set up in 1948. They were delivered at Law Society's Hall, London, in November 1975 and later published, under the Title "The Land and the Development; or, the Turmoil and the Torment," by Stevens & Sons, under the auspices of the Trust. The environment and its conservation figured prominently in the lectures and, accordingly, I would like to open this chapter with an extract from my concluding words in the first lecture—an extract which sets the background to the detailed legal particulars which follow in this chapter. May I repeat that the lectures were delivered in 1975. Today (1987) I find no cause to alter what I then said:

> "My second point, as I come to my conclusion tonight, is to refer to this matter of the environment.
>
> " 'Environment' is now the 'in' word and the Government were quick to cash in on this newly and popularly accepted epithet when, in 1971, they restyled the dear old Ministry the 'Department of the Environment.'
>
> "We now see an almost obsessive interest on the part of John Citizen in the environment and its preservation. Formerly, the environment did not mean a thing until Sir Colin Buchanan fired it into blazing life in his moving and thought-provoking *Traffic in Towns*. From the date of that book (1963) the environment has never looked back. This does not necessarily mean that it has always gone forward—not at all. But at least John Citizen, and one or two planning authorities, have now realised that the environment is not automatically here to stay. It is here only as long as valiant efforts are made to preserve it and, with it, that 'quality of life' (another 'in' phrase today) which becomes daily increasingly dear to some of us as some of us daily (and increasingly) realise that the thing is in danger of disappearing before our very eyes and being replaced by what I would call (and not for the first time) the milk-shake, tinned-peas way of life in which nothing tastes of anything at all and cellophane is paramount. If you do not

follow me in all this, take a trip abroad—particularly to the new world—and observe what is going on in one country after another.

"Let me say at once that planning control under the law is well able to take care of the environment. Please do not let me hear any more outcry for new laws to do this and that. The laws are here with us right now—all that is lacking is the political will to use them.

"The laws concerning the control of pollution do not run into hundreds; but they do run into scores. Look them up sometime; I have done so. Maybe new, dramatic efforts are going to be made to use them. The curse of the concrete jungle of the past 20 years is coming home to roost. That democratic process (to which I earlier referred) has a lot to answer for when we consider the concrete jungle, the unhuman scale of building and the barefaced vulgarity of a deal of development since the 1948 watershed made control of all this sort of thing entirely possible under the law.

"But notice how the bitter lesson is progressively being learnt. No wonder stronger measures were enacted in 1968, with respect to conservation areas and buildings of special significance. These measures were *enacted*—it remains to see how much the democratic process will use them—and use them intelligently. . . .

"[All land development is controllable under the law.] The question is: Do you want to control it? The question is: What sort of city do you want? The question is: Do you want a city at all? I rely on that democratic process (to which I earlier referred) to answer these questions for me. I hope the democratic process will come up with an answer before it is too late, that is, before the gracious city—the civilised city—has disappeared. I am now, thankfully, beginning to think that it will, so imbued, today, with the preservation of the environment has John Citizen become. The trouble with John is that he is at once a passionate and a fickle creature. Today I believe he is in danger of overdoing his understandable backlash against the concrete jungle which has emerged in the past 20 years and of leaping much too far out to the other extreme—namely preservation at all costs. (Oh yes, I shall be coming to Liverpool Street Station in a later lecture.) It is all a matter of being reasonable and steering a middle course; but steering a middle course must not be confused (as it so often is) with sitting on the fence with no aptitude for the taking of a decision."

* * * * * *

The control of the development of land by the grant or refusal, by a local planning authority, of planning permission for development is dealt with, generally and at length, in the next chapter. This chapter seeks, at the risk of possible repetition of matters dealt with in dispersed fashion elsewhere in these pages, to bring together all in one place (in one chapter) the three subjects, namely, conservation areas, National Parks and areas of outstanding natural beauty, which have been singled out by the law for sensitive attention and special protection when applications for planning permission for development, or the making of compulsory purchase orders for land, are under consideration.

2. Conservation Areas

(1) *Circulars and policy notes*

The Town and Country Planning Act 1971 deals with Conservation areas in three sections, namely, sections 277, 277A and 277B. These should be read along with the plethora of information, advice and policy statements contained in:

(a) the following five D.O.E. Circulars, namely, Circulars 12/73 (dated January 23, 1973) Appendix D, paragraphs 3 to 6 entitled "Conservation Areas"; Circular 23/77 (dated March 16, 1977) (as amended by Circulars 12/81 and 8/84), Part II entitled "Conservation Areas" and Appendix II; Circular 12/81 (dated March 24, 1981), entitled "Historic Buildings and Conservation Areas" paragraphs 28 and 45 to 47; Circular 8/84 (dated March 28, 84) entitled "Establishment of the Historic Buildings and Monuments Commission for England," paragraph 6; Circular 23/84 (dated September 14, 84) entitled "Procedure for Informing the Historic Buildings and Monuments Commission for England of Applications for Planning Permission and for Listed Buildings Consent," paragraph 3 and Appendix; and also in

(b) paragraphs 6 to 8, "Development in Conservation Areas," in Number 7, entitled "Preservation of Historic Buildings and Areas," of the Development Control Policy Notes issued by the Department of the Environment in 1969.

Anyone contemplating development in a conservation area would do well first to digest the relevant contents of the Circulars and the Number 7 Policy Note quoted above—all of which are obtainable from Her Majesty's Stationery Office or from the Department of the Environment, 2 Marsham Street, London, SW1P 3EB.

By way of setting the stage on which a developer in a conservation area will need to "play out" his application for planning permission, it will be in point at this juncture to quote an extract from the aforementioned Number 7 Policy Note. The extract comprises paragraphs 6 to 8 of the Policy Note. These three paragraphs set out what may be called the *mise-en-scène* against which the developer's planning application will be made; they are in the following terms.

"6. Conservation areas designated under section 1 of the Civic Amenities Act 1967 [now under section 277 of the Town and Country Planning Act 1971] are by definition "areas of special architectural or historic interest the character or appearance of which it is desirable to preserve or enhance." Further, the local planning authorities and the Minister are required to pay special attention to the character or appearance of the area when exercising their planning control functions in a conservation area. The first consideration on any proposal for development in a conservation area must therefore be its effect on the character of the area as a whole, and whether or not it would serve to "preserve or enhance" its character. This would normally preclude large scale or comprehensive development schemes and the emphasis will usually be on the selective renewal of individual buildings.

"7. There will be many different kinds of conservation area and they will vary greatly in size; so that development control policies will vary from one to another. In some, for example those comprising a Georgian square or Regency terrace, consistency of architectural style will be the dominant feature and there will be a presumption against any new development which would break the architectural unity. More often, the conservation area will contain less formal groupings of buildings of different ages and sizes, which will allow more scope for new building and greater freedom in design. Generally, the emphasis will be on control rather than prohibition, to allow the conservation area to remain alive and prosperous while ensuring that any new development accords with its special architectural and visual qualities. Every new building should be designed not as a separate entity, but as part of a larger scene with a well defined character of its own. The bulk and height of the building, its materials and colours, should all be considered with care.

"8. Proposals for new development that are likely to affect the character of a conservation area to any significant extent may be of general public concern. The Civic Amenities Act [now section 28 of the Town and Country Planning Act 1971] recognises this by requiring planning authorities to give public notice of such applications, indicating the nature of the development proposed, and to consider any representations they may receive when deciding whether or not to give permission. The Minister will also take account of such representations in the cases he has to decide."

(2) *Designation of conservation areas*

Section 277 of the 1971 Act deals with the designation of an area of land as a conservation area (s.277(1)). Every local planning authority must determine—after consultations (s.277(5)(c))—from time to time (the duty is on-going) which part of their local government area (if any) is "of special architectural or historic interest the character or appearance of which it is desirable to preserve or enhance" (*ibid.*). If such a part is found, then the local authority *must* (they have no option) designate that part as a conservation area (*ibid.*).

The local planning authorities carrying the foregoing responsibility are (s.277(10)):

(a) in Greater London, the council of a London borough and the Common Council of the City of London;
(b) in a National Park, the county planning authority; and
(c) elsewhere, the district planning authority.

Outside a National Park, a county planning authority may also exercise the function of designating a conservation area (*ibid.*).

It is the further duty of a local planning authority to review, from time to time, their past exercise of functions under section 277 and to determine whether any parts (or further parts) of their area should be designated a conservation area (s.277(2)).

The Secretary of State for the Environment may himself designate land as a conservation area but must first consult the local planning authority (s.277(4)).

A local planning authority must give notice to the Secretary of State of any designation by them of land as a conservation area and of any variation or cancellation of such designation (s.277(6)). Similarly, the Secretary of State must notify the relevant planning authority of any designation (or variation or cancellation of designation) by him of any land as a conservation area (*ibid.*).

Where designation of land as a conservation area affects land in England, notice of the designation must be given (s.277(6A)) to the Historic Buildings and Monuments Commission for England established under section 32 of the National Heritage Act 1983.

Notice of the designation of an area as a conservation area must be publicised in the *London Gazette* and in a local newspaper (s.277(7)) and the designation must be registered as a local land charge (s.277(9)).

(3) *Development in conservation areas*

When an application for planning permission for development within a conservation area is under consideration the local planning authority are in duty bound to pay special attention to the desirability of preserving or enhancing the character of the area (s.277(8)). This provision of the law is clearly calculated to render it harder to get planning permission for development in a conservation area than elsewhere. On this the commentary in paragraphs 6 and 7 (quoted, *ante*, at pages 138 and 139) of the Number 7 Development Control Policy Note issued by the Secretary of State may usefully be read. So can paragraphs 38 to 41 entitled, "Control of development in conservation areas," (set out in Part II—Conservation Areas) of D.O.E. Circular 23/77.

Publicity is to be given to any application for planning permission for development in a conservation area if the development will, in the opinion of the local planning authority, "affect the character or appearance of a conservation area" (s.28(1) and Policy Note No. 7, para. 8). (It is difficult to see how *any* development can be carried out without it affecting at least the *appearance* of the area.) The local planning authority must publish a notice indicating the nature of the proposed development and naming a place (within the locality) where the application and all plans and documents submitted with it may be inspected by the public (s.28(2)). It is the responsibility of the planning authority (not the developer) to publish the notice which must appear in a local newspaper and must also appear as a site notice (for not less than seven days) on or near the site of the proposed development (*ibid.*). All this is to enable the public to make representations about the proposed development and its effect on the conservation area—which representations can be made at any time within 21 days of the publication of the aforesaid notice in a local newspaper (*ibid.*). The local planning authority must take into account any representations made by the public before the application for planning permission is determined by the authority (s.29(4)).

If the conservation area is in England notice of the proposed development must also be given by the local planning authority to the Historic Buildings and Monument Commission for England (s.28(2A)). This latter requirement, however, does not apply in all cases. The Secretary of State (acting under section 28(2B)) has absolved the local planning authority from notifying the Commission as mentioned above except in those cases notified in D.O.E. Circular 23/84 paragraph 3 and the Appendix.

The Town and Country Planning General Development Order 1977[1] was amended (as from April 1, 1981) by the Town and Country Planning General Development (Amendment) Order 1981[2] which extended the scope of "permitted development" (*i.e.* development for which planning permission is automatically

[1] S.I. 1977 No. 289.
[2] S.I. 1981 No. 245.

granted by the 1977 Order itself).[3] But it is to be remembered that this liberalising of the scope of "permitted development" does *not* apply to development in a conservation area *if* the conservation area was designated *before April 1, 1981* the date on which the Town and Country Planning (National Parks, Areas of Outstanding Natural Beauty and Conservation Areas) Special Development Order 1981[4] came into operation.[5]

The Special Development Order of 1981 was revoked and re-enacted with additions by the Town & Country Planning (National Parks, Areas of Outstanding Natural Beauty and Conservation Areas, etc.) Special Development Order 1985[6] which came into operation on November 1, 1985[7] (see this Order, arts. 1, 2 and 3). This 1985 Order prevents the aforementioned liberalising of the scope of "permitted development" from applying to development in a conservation area if the area was designated a conservation area *before November 1, 1985*. November 1, 1985 is undoubtedly a most important date for anyone seeking to carry out development in a conservation area.

(4) *Buildings in conservation areas*

Buildings in conservation areas receive special protection whether they are listed buildings or not. Listed buildings have their own code of protection[8] but an unlisted building, provided it is in a conservation area, is specially protected by section 277A (particularly subsection (8) as substituted by section 40 of, and Schedule 9, Part I, paragraph 8 to, the Housing and Planning Act 1986) of the Town and Country Planning Act 1971 (relating to control of demolition in conservation areas), by the Town and Country Planning (Listed Buildings and Buildings in Conservation Areas) Regulations 1977[9] (article 10 relating to the demolition of unlisted buildings in conservation areas) and by the Housing and Planning Act 1986, section 40 and Schedule 9, Part I, paragraph 8.

Putting the matter shortly, the protection given by the 1971 Act to a listed building is projected generally to cover any sort of building (unless it is an excepted building) if it is in a conservation area. Circular 23/77 dated March 16, 1977, referred to previously in this

[3] See Chap. 10 "Control of Development" at pp. 160 to 177 inclusive.
[4] S.I. 1981 No. 246.
[5] See further, Chap. 10 at p. 166.
[6] S.I. 1985 No. 1012.
[7] See further, Chap. 10 at p. 166.
[8] See Chap. 14, pp. 302–318.
[9] S.I. 1977 No. 228.

Chapter,[10] deals (in paragraphs 68, 70, 71, 72 and 73) with the position. "Listed building consent" will be required before any such building can be demolished even though it is not a listed building. However, this constraint does *not* apply to any building which the Secretary of State, acting under section 277A(4) of the 1971 Act, has directed shall not be given the protection otherwise accorded to it by section 277A of the 1971 Act. Under this authority the Secretary of State has directed (Circular 23/77 paragraphs 71, 72) as follows:

"71. Consent is not needed under section 277A [of the 1971 Act] for the demolition of listed buildings, a building protected under the ancient monuments legislation, or for the partial demolition of an ecclesiastical building . . . and the Secretary of State may direct that the section shall not apply to certain buildings or descriptions of buildings. In pursuance of his powers under section 277A(4) of the 1971 Act the Secretary of State hereby directs as follows.

(1) Section 277A shall not apply to the following descriptions of buildings:

(a) any building with a total cubic content not exceeding 115 cubic metres or any part of such building;

(b) any building if development consisting of the erection of that building would be development permitted by classes I, II, IV, VI or VIII of Schedule 1 to the Town and Country Planning General Development Order 1977 and article 3 of that order or would be so permitted but for a direction given under that Order;

(c) any building required to be demolished by virtue of a discontinuance order made under section 51 of the Act;

(d) any building required to be demolished by virtue of any provision of an agreement made under section 52 of the Act;

(e) any building in respect of which the provisions of an enforcement notice served under section 87 or section 96 of the Act require its demolition, in whole or in part, however expressed;

(f) any building required to be demolished by virtue of a condition of planning permission granted under section 29 of the Act;

[10] See p. 138, *ante*.

(g) any building included in an operative clearance order or compulsory purchase order made under Part III of the Housing Act 1957 or to which a demolition order made under Part II of that Act applies [see now the Housing Act 1985 Part IX];

(h) any building purchased by a local authority by agreement where Part III of the Housing Act 1957 applies to that building [see now the Housing Act 1985;]

(i) a redundant building (within the meaning of the Pastoral Measure 1968) or part of such a building where the demolition is in pursuance of a pastoral or redundancy scheme (within the meaning of that Measure).

(2) In these directions "the Act" means the Town and Country Planning Act 1971 and except in paragraph (1)(a) above "building" has the meaning assigned to it by section 290 of the Act.

"72. Note: Paragraph (1)(b) of the direction means that consent is not required for the demolition of buildings of the type described whenever erected, if the re-erection of what has been demolished would be permitted development under the specified classes of the General Development Order, *e.g.* any wall less than 1 metre high abutting a highway or 2 metres elsewhere."

A local planning authority are not required to notify the Secretary of State before granting consent to an application for the demolition of an unlisted building in a conservation area. However, any application of their own for such consent must be made to the Secretary of State (D.O.E. Circular 23/77, para. 73).

(5) *Urgent works for preservation of unoccupied buildings in conservation areas*

If the Secretary of State takes the view an unoccupied building which is not a listed building but which stands in a conservation area (s.101(3)) needs to be preserved in order to maintain the character or appearance of the conservation area, he may (after consultation with the Historic Buildings and Monuments Commission for England in the case of a building situated in England) direct (s.101(2)(*b*)) that section 101 of the 1971 Act shall apply to it (*ibid.*). If he does so the unoccupied building gets the protection of subsections (4)(5)(5A) and (5B) of section 101 of the 1971 Act whereby, after giving seven days notice to the owner of the building, the local authority or the Secretary of State or the Commission (for a building in England), as the case may be, can carry out urgent works for the preservation of the building (*ibid.*) and may require the owner to pay the expenses of so doing (s.101(6)) subject to the owner's right to make representations to the Secretary of State against any such requirement (s.101(7)(8) and (9)).

The seven day notice to the owner should specify in detail the works believed to be urgently necessary.[11] The object of the notice is to allow the matter to be discussed with, as the case may be, the local authority or the Secretary of State or the Commission and to give this owner a chance to do the works himself if he so wishes.

(6) *Trees in conservations areas*

Section 61A(2) of the Town and Country Planning Act 1971 applies to *any* tree in a conservation area not already protected by a tree preservation order[12] the protection which would have been afforded to it had it been the subject of a tree preservation order (s.61A(1)).

Section 61A(3) of the 1971 Act, in effect, requires any one proposing to do work on a tree which is in a conservation area but which is not the subject of a preservation order, to give the local planning authority six weeks notice of his intentions. A register, open to free public inspection, of notices has to be kept by the relevant district council or London borough council (s.61A(7); D.O.E. Circular 23/77 para. 42 and D.O.E. Circular 36/78, Memorandum, Section VIII entitled "Trees in Conservation Areas," para. 64). The foregoing is the general position but the Secretary of State may exempt from protection such trees in a conservation area as are specified in regulations made by him (s.61A(4)). The Secretary of State has made the Town and Country Planning (Tree Preservation Order) (Amendment) and (Trees in Conservation Areas) (Excepted Cases) Regulations 1975[13] regulation 3 of which provides that section 61A of the 1971 Act shall not apply to:

(i) the cutting down, uprooting, topping or lopping of a tree in the circumstances mentioned in subs. (6) of s.60 of the 1971 Act;

(ii) the cutting down of a tree in the circumstances mentioned in

[11] *R.* v. *Secretary of State for the Environment, ex parte Hampshire County Council* (1981) J.P.L. 47; *R.* v. *London Borough of Camden, ex parte Comyn Ching and Co. (London) Ltd.* (1983) 47 P. & C.R. 417.

[12] See Chap. 14 at p. 299.

[13] S.I. 1975 No. 148.

para. (1) or (2), or the cutting down, uprooting, topping or lopping of a tree in the circumstances mentioned in para. (3), of the Second Schedule to the Form of Tree Preservation Order contained in the Schedule to the Town and Country Planning (Tree Preservation Order) Regulations 1969 (as amended by these regulations);

(iii) the cutting down of a tree in accordance with a felling licence granted by the Forestry Commissioners;

(iv) the cutting down, uprooting, topping or lopping of a tree on land in the occupation of a local planning authority and the act is done by or with the consent of that authority;

(v) the cutting down, uprooting, topping or lopping of a tree having a diameter not exceeding 75 millimetres, or the cutting down or uprooting of a tree having a diameter not exceeding 100 millimetres where the act is carried out to improve the growth of other trees, the reference to "diameter" herein being construed as a reference to the diameter, measured over the bark, at a point 1·5 metres above the ground level.

(7) *Advertisements in conservation areas*

The powers of a local planning authority with respect to outdoor advertising are dealt with in detail in chapter 12. So far as advertising in conservation areas is concerned all that needs to be mentioned here is that the Department of the Environment seems, or, in 1977 (to be more accurate) *seemed*, to be in some fear that the controlling powers of local planning authorities may be exercised too zealously because paragraph 43 of D.O.E. Circular 23/77 declares:

> "43. It is important that, in conservation areas, local planning authorities use their powers under the Control of Advertisement Regulations flexibly, taking account of the fact that many conservation areas include thriving commercial centres and at the same time the particular need to ensure that advertising displays do not detract from the appearance of areas of architectural and historic interest. [See also paras. 45 and 46 of Circular 12/81]."

The reference in the above quotation to paragraphs 45 and 46 of D.O.E. Circular 12/81 is important. When the Bill for the Local Government, Planning and Land Act 1980 was going through the House of Lords, the Government gave an undertaking to urge local planning authorities to make the fullest use of their powers in the Town and Country (Control of Advertisements) Regulations 1969 (now the Town and Country Planning (Control of Advertisements)

Regulations 1984[14]) to improve the quality of outdoor advertising in conservation areas (D.O.E. Circular 12.81 para. 45).

(8) *Schemes of enhancement for conservation areas and grants-in-aid*

It is the duty of a local planning authority to formulate and publish, from time to time, proposals for the preservation and enhancement of any part of their area which has been designated a conservation area (s.277B(1)). Any such proposals must be submitted for consideration to a public meeting in the area to which they relate (s.277B(2)) and the planning authority are obliged to have regard to any views of the public expressed at the meeting about the proposals of the authority (*ibid*).

The Department of the Environment is clearly wishful that there shall be the fullest public participation in connection with preservation and enhancement schemes for conservation areas. All this is made clear in paragraphs 46 and 47 of D.O.E. Circular 23/77 where it is roundly stated that, "Public interest and participation is . . . essential for success in conservation." Accordingly, local planning authorities are invited to seek advice specifically from local residents and amenity groups, residents' associations and Chambers of Trade or Commerce. Attention is drawn to the Civic Trust's publication entitled, "Pride of Place" obtainable from the Civic Trust at 17 Carlton House Terrace, London, SW1Y 5AW.

Grants (or loans) may be payable, since April 1, 1984, by the Historic Buildings and Monuments Commission for England, acting under the provisions of section 3A the Historic Buildings and Ancient Monuments Act 1953 for the upkeep of land *in* England which is regarded as land of outstanding historic interest (as land in a conservation area might be) whether or not the land is attached to a building of outstanding architectural or historic interest.

The Secretary of State may make similar grants (or loans) in respect of historic land *not* situated in England *i.e.* in Scotland or in Wales (1953 Act s.4 as extended to loans by the Civic Amenities Act 1967 s.4(10)).

Grants (or loans) may also be made by the Secretary of State (in respect of conservation areas *outside* England) and by the Historic Buildings and Monuments Commission for England (in respect of conservations areas *in* England) for the defraying of expenses incurred in the preservation or enhancement of the character or appearance of any conservation area provided the Secretary of State or (as the case may be) the Commission are of the opinion that such

[14] S.I. 1984 No. 421. See Chap. 12.

expenses will make a significant contribution towards preserving or enhancing the character of the conservation area (Town and Country Planning (Amendment) Act 1972 s.10 as amended by the Local Government, Planning and Land Act 1980, Sched. 15, para. 27).

3. National Parks

(1) *The Countryside Commission and the designation of National Parks*

National Parks are established under the authority of Part II of the National Parks and Access to the Countryside Act 1949 as amended by the Countryside Act 1968, the Wildlife and Countryside Act 1981 and the Wildlife and Countryside (Amendment) Act 1985. Part II of the 1949 Act does not apply to Scotland nor to Northern Ireland (1949 Act s.115(2)).

The 1949 Act section 1 established the National Parks Commission, renamed the Countryside Commission by the Countryside Act 1968 section 1(1)(5). The Countryside Commission is charged (1949 Act s.1) with the duty of exercising their several functions under the 1949 Act with a view to "the preservation and enhancement of natural beauty in England and Wales," and particularly in National Parks or areas of outstanding natural beauty (*ibid.*). In the discharge of this duty the Commission have identified "extensive tracts of country in England and Wales" which it is felt, by reason of their natural beauty and the opportunities they afford for open-air recreation (1949 Act s.5), ought to be designated (in Orders made by the Commission and approved by the Secretary of State for the Environment) as National Parks (1949 Act ss.5 and 7 and the National Parks and Access to the Countryside Regulations 1950, Part IV—S.I. 1950 No. 1066).

Before submitting a designation order for confirmation by the Secretary of State, the Commission must follow the procedure for so doing set out in Part I of the First Schedule to the 1949 Act which requires the giving of publicity in the London Gazette, in the national press and the local press about the making of the order so that public representations or objections about it can be made to the Commission. If any such representations or objections are duly made the Secretary of State must hold a public inquiry or a private hearing before he confirms the designation order (1949 Act, Sched. I, Part I). The Secretary of State may, if he thinks fit, confirm a designation order with or without modifications (*ibid.*).

The following 10 areas have, at the date of this writing (February 1987), been designated as National Parks:

Name of National Park	*Date of designation order*	*Date of confirmation of order*	*Area in sq km*
Peak Districk	28 December 1950	17 April 1951	1,404
Lake District	30 January 1951	9 May 1951	2,243
Snowdonia	6 February 1951	18 October 1951	2,171
Dartmoor	15 August 1951	30 October 1951	945
Pembrokeshire Coast	20 December 1951	29 February 1952	583
North York Moors	12 February 1952	28 November 1952	1,432
Yorkshire Dales	7 December 1953	12 October 1954	1,761
Exmoor	27 January 1954	19 October 1954	686
Northumberland	20 September 1955	6 April 1956	1,031
Brecon Beacons	20 September 1955	17 April 1957	1,344
		Total	13,600

The Peak District National Park and the Lake District National Park each have a planning board—known respectively as the Peak Park Joint Planning Board (S.I. 1973 No. 2061) and the Lake District Special Planning Board (S.I. 1973 No. 2001)—to supervise their day-to-day operations, established under section 1 of the Town and Country Planning Act 1971 by the Secretary of State. In the other National Parks, administration is in the hands of a national park committee established in each case by the relevant county council (Local Government Act 1972, s.184 and Sched. 17, para. 5; Wildlife and Countryside Act 1981 s.72(10)).

(2) *Development in a National Park*

The general duties of the Countryside Commission in relation to National Parks include not only the designation from time to time of areas of land in England and Wales as National Parks (1949 Act s.6(1)(2) and (3)) but also (*inter alia*) the giving of advice to the Secretary of State as to proposals for development of land in a National Park (1949 Act s.6(4)(e)) and to the appropriate planning authority as to the preparation or amendment of a development plan or in connection with any application for planning permission for the development of land in a National Park (*ibid.*; see also, Local Government Act 1972 s.182(4)(5) and (6)).

Thus, whenever it is sought to carry out development of land which is in a National Park, amenity and environmental considerations are going to loom large upon the development control scene and a developer will need to bear all this in mind when preparing his development proposals. Nor are the local planning authority to be allowed to forget these matters of amenity and conservation when they come to consider an application for planning permission for development of land in a National Park because section 11 of the Countryside Act 1968 declares (with admonitory, if pious, overtones) that:

> "In the exercise of their functions relating to land under any enactment every minister, government department and public body" (a local planning authority is clearly one) "shall have regard to the desirability of conserving the natural beauty and amenity of the countryside."

This exhortation, it is true, is in the widest possible terms—so wide in fact that it possibly has no specific legal effect—but that does not necessarily render its enactment a vain thing. It is in the nature of a cautionary tale for planning authorities seeking to do the right thing when faced with an application for planning permission for development in "the countryside," an expression not defined in the Act but to be read, it would appear, in contra-distinction to such expressions as "the townscape" or "the urban scene." Incidentally, it will be noted that the exhortation contained in section 11 of the Countryside Act 1968 is not limited in its effect to land in a National Park but applies "to land under any enactment."

The powers of a local planning authority in relation to a National Park are to be exercised so as to secure the accomplishment of any of the purposes set out in section 5(1) of the 1949 Act, that is to say, "the purpose of preserving and enhancing the natural beauty of the areas" designated as National Parks and for "the purpose of promoting their enjoyment by the public" (1949 Act s.11(1)). All this is, again, something which a developer, seeking planning permission for development of land in a National Park, must bear in mind when making his planning application. In this connection paragraph 5 of Development Control Policy Note No. 4 entitled "Development in Rural Areas," issued by the Department of the Environment, should be noted. It is in the following terms:

> "5. *In National Parks and Areas of Outstanding Natural Beauty.* The design and appearance, as well as the location, of any new development will be subject to special scrutiny, to ensure that it fits properly into its surroundings. Attention should be paid not only to the natural scenery, but also to the traditional character of buildings in the area and the use of local materials."

The Town and Country Planning General Development Order 1977[15] was amended (as from April 1, 1981) by the Town and Country Planning General Development (Amendment) Order

[15] S.I. 1977 No. 289.

1981[16] which extended the scope of "permitted development" (i.e. development for which planning permission is automatically granted by the Order itself[17]). But this extension does *not* apply to development in a National Park *if* the Park was designated before April 1, 1981 the date on which the Town and Country Planning (National Parks, Areas of Outstanding Natural Beauty and Conservation Areas) Special Development Order 1981[18] came into operation. This Order was revoked and re-enacted with additions by the Town and Country Planning (National Parks, Areas of Outstanding Natural Beauty and Conservation Areas, etc.) Special Development Order 1985[19] which came into operation on November 1, 1985 (see this Order, arts. 1, 2 and 3).

Finally, as to the carrying out of development in a National Park, attention may be drawn to D.O.E. Circular 4/76, dated January 12, 1976, giving, in the Annex to the Circular, the conclusions of the Secretary of State for the Environment and the Secretaty of State for Wales on the Report of the National Park Policies Review Committee set up in July 1971 under the chairmanship of Lord Sandforth. Paragraph 47 of the Annex is in the following terms:

> "47 The Secretaries of State endorse the Committee's view (5.11) that in the face of growing pressures stricter development control policies need to be applied in the national parks. Such policies are already more stringent in the parks than in the countryside generally but a further opportunity for strengthening them, where this is thought necessary, will be provided in structure plans,[20] which require the Secretary of States approval, and in local plans."[21]

Clearly, the getting of planning permission for development in a National Park is not going to be a walkover![21a]

4. Areas of Outstanding Natural Beauty (A.O.N.B's)

(1) *Designation of areas of outstanding natural beauty*

Any area of land in England or Wales, not already designated as a National Park, may be designated by order made by the Country-

[16] S.I. 1981 No. 245.

[17] See Chap. 10, "Control of Development" at pp. 160–177.

[18] S.I. 1981 No. 246. See also pp. 178 and 179, *ante*, as to National Parks designated before November 1, 1985.

[19] S.I. 1985 No. 1012. See also pp. 178 and 179, *ante*, as to National Parks designated before November 1, 1985.

[20] See Chap. 4. [21] See Chap. 5.

[21a] The Government are considering whether National Park Authorities should be given power to make *Landscape* Conservation Orders (analogous to *Nature* Conservation Orders) under the Wildlife and Countryside Act 1981, s. 29. A Consultation Paper dated December 1986 has been issued by the D.O.E. for comment by anyone interested.

side Commission as an area of outstanding natural beauty (1949 Act s.87(1)). Before making any such designation order the Commission must consult with every local authority (*i.e.* joint planning board, county council or county district council (1949 Act s.87(6)), functioning in the area to be designated and must advertise their proposals in the London Gazette and in one or more local newspapers mentioning, in the advertisements, that representations (from the public) about the proposals may be made to the Commission who must consider any representations duly made (1949 Act s.87(2)). The designation order cannot come into operation until it is confirmed by the Secretary of State (1949 Act s.87(3)) who may confirm it with such modifications as he thinks expedient (1949 Act s.87(4)). If he proposes to refuse to confirm the designation order, or to confirm it with modifications, he must first consult with the Commission and with every local authority affected by the order (1949 Act s.87(5)). The Commission (and also the Secretary of State) may from time to time vary the designation order but if they do so they must first carry out the statutory routine (above described) relating to the original making of the order (1949 Act s.87(7)).

It is the duty of the Countryside Commission to have available copies of any designation order made by them so that the public may inspect the order (1949 Act s.87(8)). These copies of the order must be available at the offices of the Commission (which are at John Dower House, Crescent Place, Cheltenham GL50 3RA), and also at the offices of each local authority affected by the order (*ibid.*).

At the time of this writing (February 1987) the following areas have been designated areas of outstanding natural beauty:

Area of Outstanding Natural Beauty	*Date of designation order*	*Date of confirmation of order*	*Area in sq km*
Gower	9 May 1956	10 December 1956	189
Quantock Hills	9 May 1956	1 January 1957	99
Lleyn	13 September 1956	28 May 1957	155
Northumberland Coast	22 January 1958	21 March 1958	129
Surrey Hills	13 September 1956	8 May 1958	414
Cannock Chase	4 June 1958	16 September 1958	68
Shropshire Hills	29 July 1958	11 March 1959	777
Dorset	31 December 1957	29 July 1959	1,036
Malvern Hills	25 March 1959	22 October 1959	104
Cornwall	22 April 1959	25 November 1959	932
North Devon	10 September 1959	25 May 1960	171
South Devon	10 September 1959	2 August 1960	332
East Hampshire	13 June 1961	26 September 1962	391
East Devon	30 January 1963	20 September 1963	267
Isle of Wight	27 March 1963	20 September 1963	189

Area of Outstanding Natural Beauty—cont.	*Date of designation order—cont.*	*Date of confirmation of order—cont.*	*Area in sq km—cont.*
Chichester Harbour	7 July 1963	4 February 1964	75
Forest of Bowland	27 February 1963	10 February 1964	803
Solway Coast	10 September 1964	12 December 1964	107
Chilterns	26 May 1964	16 December 1965	800
Sussex Downs	22 June 1965	7 April 1966	981
Cotswolds	22 February 1966	19 August 1966	1,507
Anglesey	20 December 1966	13 November 1967	215
South Hampshire Coast	30 May 1967	18 December 1967	78
Norfolk Coast	28 November 1967	8 April 1968	450
Kent Downs	19 December 1967	23 July 1968	845
Suffolk Coast and Heaths	23 October 1969	4 March 1970	391
Dedham Vale	26 February 1970	20 May 1970	57
Extension	20 February 1978	21 August 1978	15
Wye Valley	24 February 1971	13 December 1971	325
North Wessex Downs	6 December 1971	1 December 1972	1,738
Mendip Hills	14 February 1972	1 December 1972	202
Arnside and Silverdale	4 July 1972	15 December 1972	75
Lincolnshire Wolds	6 February 1973	17 April 1973	560
Scilly Isles	16 October 1975	18 February 1976	16
		Total	14,493

On September 12, 1986 (D.O.E. Press Notice 486 of that date) the Environment Minister, Mr. William Waldegrave, announced that "a large part" (some 900 square miles) of the North Pennines is to be designated an Area of Outstanding Natural Beauty by the Countryside Commission.

(2) *Development in areas of outstanding natural beauty*

Several of the provisions of the National Parks and Access to the Countryside Act 1949 are applied to areas of outstanding natural beauty (1949 Act, s.88). Thus section 6(4)(*e*) of the Act relating to applications for planning permission for development in an area of outstanding natural beauty is applied (1949 Act, s.88(1)). So also are the provisions of section 11 of the 1949 Act—"General powers of local planning authorities in relation to National Parks"—in so far as they confer powers for preserving and enhancing natural beauty (1949 Act, s.88(2)). In addition the pious words of section 11 of the Countryside Act 1968[22] must not be forgotten by those seeking planning permission for development in an area of outstanding natural beauty.

The extended scope of "permitted development" under the Town and Country Planning General Development Order 1977[23] (as with

[22] See p. 150, *ante*.
[23] S.I. 1977 No. 289.

development in a National Park)[24] does *not* apply to areas of outstanding natural beauty designated before April 1, 1981, the date on which the Town and Country Planning (National Parks, Areas of Outstanding Natural Beauty and Conservation Areas) Special Development Order 1981[25] came into operation. This Order was revoked and re-enacted with additions by the Town and Country Planning (National Parks, Areas of Outstanding Natural Beauty and Conservation Areas, etc.) Special Development Order 1985[26] which came into operation on November 1, 1985 (see this Order, arts. 1, 2 and 3).

When development in an area of outstanding natural beauty is being considered the provisions of paragraph 5 of Policy Note "No. 4—Development in Rural Areas" should be borne in mind.[27]

The Countryside Commission have reviewed the policy which, in their opinion, ought to be applied to the question of development proposed to be carried out in an area of outstanding natural beauty. This review led to a Parliamentary Statement of Government policy by the Secretary of State for the Environment on July 29, 1982 (Hansard, H.C. Deb., Vol. 28, Cols. 707–710) in which he declared (*inter alia*):

"*Planning, management, development control*

'Confirmation of an A.O.N.B. designation order confers formal recognition by the Government that the natural beauty of the landscape in the area identified is of national importance; and that we expect this to be reflected by local authorities in their preparation of structure and local plans and exercise of development control. Though development plans must remain the definitive means of setting out local policies for the development and other use of land, the Government believe that the 'statements of intent' for A.O.N.B.s which the Countryside Commission have encouraged authorities with such responsibilities to prepare, can, taking account of their special needs, be a worth while, informal aid to the planning and management of these areas. We have noted the commission's advocacy of the preparation of management plans for some areas. The Government accept that it may sometimes be useful for local authorities to play an active role in seeking to resolve conflicts of

[24] See p. 149, *ante*.
[25] S.I. 1981 No. 246. See also p. 151, *ante*.
[26] S.I. 1985 No. 1012. See also p. 151 *ante*, as to areas of outstanding natural beauty designated before November 1, 1985.
[27] See these provisions as quoted on p. 150, *ante*.

interest against the background of statements of intent, and consider that their existing powers are adequate for this purpose.

"Major development

'The Government agree with the commission's view that, in general, it would be inconsistent with the aims of designation to permit the siting of major industrial and commercial development in A.O.N.B.s. Only proven national interest and lack of alternative sites can justify any exception. But each individual case must be determined on its merits—that is a fundamental rule of our planning system. We believe the environmental effects of new proposals should be a major consideration in all such circumstances . . . .

"Minor industrial development

'In the A.O.N.B. context the commission draws a distinction between the scope for large and small scale industrial development, and the Government endorse this approach. Modern agriculture is capital intensive and can no longer be looked to as a major source of employment in rural areas. Small industries have a vital role to play here, and the Government's wish to encourage such activities was stressed in a recent circular issued jointly by my Department and the Welsh Office. There may be opportunities for small businesses to take over existing premises—redundant farm buildings, for example—and we believe that, subject to certain safeguards, such opportunities should be seized. Where new building is required in a A.O.N.B. the Government expect such development to be in sympathy with the architecture and landscape of the area."

5. Town and Country Planning (Agricultural and Forestry Development in National Parks etc.) Special Development Order 1986

There is one further order which needs to be referred to here. The order is the Town and Country Planning (Agricultural and Forestry Development in National Parks etc.) Special Development Order 1986.[28] It revokes the Town and Country Planning (Landscape Areas Special Development) Order 1950[29] which came into operation on May 22, 1950 (art. 1(3)).

[28] S.I. 1986 No. 1176.
[29] S.I. 1950 No. 729.

The new Order of 1986 (which came into operation on November 1, 1986) gives a local planning authority (art. 3) power to control the design and external appearance of certain kinds of "permitted development" in England or Wales automatically granted planning permission under article 3 of, and Class VI (Agricultural buildings, works and uses) or Class VII (Forestry buildings and works) of Schedule 1 to, the Town and Country Planning General Development Order 1977[30] provided (art. 1(1)) that these buildings, works or uses are in one or other of the areas of land specified in the Schedule to the 1986 Order.

The areas specified in the Schedule to the 1986 Order are the following, namely:

1. land which is on November 1, 1986, within the boundary of any of the following National Parks:

Brecon Beacons,
Dartmoor,
Exmoor,
Lake District,
Northumberland,
North York Moors,
Peak District,
Pembrokeshire Coast,
Snowdonia, or
Yorkshire Dales;

2. in England, land outside the boundaries of a National Park listed above which is, on November 1, 1986, within the parishes listed below:–

in the district of Allerdale:

Blindcrake, Bothel and Threapland, Bridekirk, Brigham, Broughton, Broughton Moor, Camerton, Crosscanonby, Dean, Dearham, Gilcrux, Great Clifton, Greysouthen, Little Clifton, Loweswater, Oughterside and Allerby, Papcastle, Plumbland, Seaton, Winscales;

in the borough of Copeland:

Arlecdon and Frizington, Cleator Moor, Distington, Drigg and Carleton, Egremont, Gosforth, Haile, Irton with Santon, Lamplugh, Lowca, Lowside Quarter, Millom, Millom Without,

[30] S.I. 1977 No. 289.

Moresby, Parton, Ponsonby, St Bees, St Bridget's Beckermet, St John's Beckermet, Seascale, Weddicar;

in the district of Eden:

Ainstable, Asby, Bandleyside, Bolton, Brough, Brough Sowerby, Brougham, Castle Sowerby, Catterlen, Clifton, Cliburn, Crackenthorpe, Crosby Garrett, Crosby Ravensworth, Culgaith, Dacre, Dufton, Glasonby, Great Salkeld, Great Strickland, Greystoke, Hartley, Hesket, Hillbeck, Hunsonby, Hutton, Kaber, Kings Meaburn, Kirkby Stephen, Kirkby Thore, Kirkoswald, Lanwathby, Lazonby, Little Strickland, Long Marton, Lowther, Mallerstang, Milburn, Morland, Mungrisdale, Murton, Musgrave, Nateby, Newbiggin, Newby, Orton, Ousby, Ravenstonedale, Shap, Skelton, Sleagill, Sockbridge and Tirril, Soulby, Stainmore, Tebay, Temple Sowerby, Thrimby, Waitby, Warcop, Wharton, Winton, Yanwath and Eamont Bridge;

in the borough of High Peak:

Chapel-en-le-Frith, Charlesworth, Chinley Buxworth and Brownside, Chisworth, Green Fairfield, Hartington Upper Quarter, Hayfield, King Sterndale, Tintwistle, Wormhill;

in the district of South Lakeland:

Aldingham, Angerton, Arnside, Barbon, Beetham, Blawith and Subberthwaite, Broughton West, Burton, Casterton, Docker, Egton-with-Newland, Fawcett Forest, Firbank, Grayrigg, Helsington, Heversham, Hincaster, Holme, Hutton Roof, Killington, Kirkby, Ireleth, Kirkby Lonsdale, Lambrigg, Levens, Lower Allithwaite, Lower Holker, Lowick Lupton, Mansergh, Mansriggs, Middleton, Milnthorpe, Natland, New Hutton, Old Hutton and Holmescales, Osmotherley, Pennington, Preston Patrick, Preston Richard, Scalthwaiterigg, Sedgwick, Skelsmergh, Stainton, Strickland Ketel, Strickland Roger, Urswick, Whinfell, Whitwell and Selside;

in the district of West Derbyshire:

Aldwark, Birchover, Stanton; and

3. in Wales land outside the boundaries of a National Park listed above which is on November 1, 1986

(a) within the communities listed below:–

in the borough of Aberconwy:

Caerhun, Dolgarrog;

in the borough of Arfon:

Betws Garmon, Bontnewydd, Llanberis, Llanddeiniolen, Llandwrog, Llanllyfni, Llandwnda, Waunfawr;

in the district of Meirionnydd:

Arthog, Corris, Llanfrothen, Penrhyndeudraeth; and

(b) within the specified parts of the communities listed below:–

in the borough of Aberconwy, those parts of the following communities which were on March 31, 1974 within the former rural district of Nant Conway:

Conwy, Henryd, Llanddoged and Maenan, Llanrwst, Llansanffraid Glan Conwy;

in the borough of Arfon, those parts of the following communities which were on March 31, 1974 within the former rural district of Gwyrfai:

Caernarfon, Llandygai, Llanrug, Pentir, Y Felinheli;

in the district of Dwyfor, that part of the community of Porthmadog which was on March 31, 1974 within the former rural district of Deudraeth and those parts of the following communities which were on that date within the former rural district of Gwyrfai:

Clynnog, Dolbenmaen, Llanaelhaearn;

in the district of Glyndwr, those parts of the following communities which were on March 31, 1974 within the former rural district of Penllyn:

Llandrillo, Llangwm;

in the district of Meirionnydd, those parts of the following communities which were on March 31, 1974 within the former rural district of Deudraeth:

Ffestiniog, Talsarnau;

and those parts of the following communities which were on that date within the former rural district of Dolgellau:

Barmouth, Mawddwy;

and that part of the community of Llandderfel which was on that date within the former rural district of Penllyn.

The 1986 Order, modifying the automatic planning permission granted under article 3 of, and Classes VI or VII of Schedule 1 to, the Town and Country Planning General Development Order 1977,[31] imposes conditions (art. 3) on the carrying out of development covered by those Classes. The conditions require the developer, before starting the development, to give the local planning authority (defined in article 2(3) of the order) specified information (art. 3(2)(a)(b)(c)) about the proposed development. If that authority, within 28 days of receipt of that information, give the developer notice in writing to that effect, development is not to be carried out without the authority's prior approval as to specified details of the development (*ibid*). One condition also imposes a time limit of five years (art. 3(2)(d)) on the carrying out of the development.

This new control over development comprising farm or forestry buildings in areas set out in the aforesaid Special Development Order 1986 is dealt with in D.O.E. Circular 17/86.

[31] S.I. 1977 No. 289.

CHAPTER 10

CONTROL OF DEVELOPMENT OF LAND BY GRANT OR REFUSAL OF PLANNING PERMISSION

1. The Need for Planning Permission—Town and Country Planning General Development Order 1977

ONCE a developer has satisfied himself that what he proposes to do constitutes development under the Town and Country Planning Act 1971 (a matter discussed in the preceding chapter), he will bear in mind that, if his land is *not* in a simplified planning zone (as to which, see Chapter 25 *post*), he should not undertake such development except with planning permission granted under Part III of the 1971 Act (s.23(1)). However, if he does carry out such development without the appropriate grant of planning permission (and thereby commits a breach of planning control) he does not, *ipso facto*, commit a criminal offence. Only if he fails to comply with an enforcement notice served upon him under Part V of the 1971 Act will he find himself liable to prosecution.

In this context it may be remembered that a local planning authority is never *obliged* to serve an enforcement notice in connection with a breach of planning control—the authority always have a discretion in this matter. The authority *may* serve an enforcement notice "if they consider it expedient to do so" (s.87(1)).

The system of development control by the grant or refusal of planning permission for development was established on July 1, 1948, the "appointed day" under the Town and Country Planning Act 1947 (now the 1971 Act—see s.290(1)).

Any permission relating to the development of land in force on July 1, 1948 lapsed with the repeal (by the 1947 Act) of the Town and Country Planning Act 1932 except interim development permissions granted on or after July 21, 1943 (under the Town and Country Planning (Interim Development) Act 1943) which were saved by section 77 of the 1947 Act—now section 292 and Schedule 24, paragraph 90 of the 1971 Act.

Under section 24 of the Town and Country Planning Act 1971 (which section is amended by the Housing and Planning Act 1986 section 49(1)(b), Schedule 11, Part I, paragraph 2) the Secretary of State for the Environment has made the Town and Country Planning General Development Order 1977.[1] This Order, which came

[1] S.I. 1977 No. 289.

into operation on March 29, 1977, is the general order, applicable to all land in England and Wales, providing, pursuant to the provisions of section 24 of the 1971 Act, for the grant of planning permission for the development of land under Part III of the Act. The Order has been amended seven times, first by the Town and Country Planning General Development (Amendment) Order 1980[2]; secondly, by the Town and Country Planning General Development (Amendment) Order 1981[3]; thirdly, by the Town and Country Planning General Development (Amendment)(No. 2) Order 1981[4]; fourthly, by the Town and Country Planning General Development (Amendment) Order 1983[5]; fifthly, by the Town and Country Planning General Development (Amendment) Order 1985,[6] sixthly by the Town and Country Planning General Development (Amendment) (No. 2) Order 1985[7] and seventhly, by the Town and Country Planning (Local Government Reorganisation) (Miscellaneous Amendments) Order 1986[7a] Schedule 1. The Orders (with the exception of the Miscellaneous Amendments Order 1986) may be cited together as the Town and Country Planning General Development Orders 1977 to 1985 (1985 (Amendment) (No. 2) Order, art. 1(1)).

Accordingly, all references in this chapter to the 1977 General Development Order are to the provisions of that Order as amended (from January 13, 1981) by the 1980 Amendment Order, (from April 1, 1981) by the 1981 Amendment Order (from November 27, 1981) by the 1981 (No. 2) Amendment Order, (from May 1, 1984) by the 1983 Amendment Order, (from November 1, 1985) by the 1985 Amendment Order, (from March 1, 1986) by the 1985 (Amendment) (No. 2) Order and (from April 1986) by the Miscellaneous Amendments Order 1986. D.O.E. Circular 3/86, dated February 24, 1986, deals with recent changes in the General Development Order 1977.

It is to be mentioned that the provisions of the General Development Order 1977 have been under review since 1983—a review which is still (February 1987) continuing. It would seem that the Order and its many amendments are now ripe for re-enactment in consolidated form.

Schedule 1 to the General Development Order 1977 sets out in

[2] S.I. 1980 No. 1946.
[3] S.I. 1981 No. 245.
[4] S.I. 1981 No. 1569.
[5] S.I. 1983 No. 1615.
[6] S.I. 1985 No. 1011.
[7] S.I. 1985 No. 1981.
[7a] S.I. 1986 No. 435.

detail the 30 classes of development for which planning permission is granted *by the order itself* under the provisions of article 3 (subject to the restrictive provisions of article 4).

Provision is made by articles 5 to 9 for the manner in which application for planning permission (and certain other applications under Part III of the Act of 1971) are made and dealt with, and for the procedure in relation to the making of appeals to the Secretary of State in respect of such applications (art. 20).

Articles 10 to 18 provide for consultation and directions affecting the grant of planning permission; article 19 requires notice to be given to the applicant where an application has been referred to the Secretary of State for him to determine; and article 21 deals with planning registers.

Article 22 makes provision for the manner in which applications for established use certificates are made and dealt with and for the procedure in relation to the making of appeals to the Secretary of State in respect of such applications.

Schedules 2 to 6 set out the prescribed forms which *must* be used for the purposes of the provisions of the 1971 Act.

Attention is directed to the use in the General Development Order 1977 of expressions which are given special and extended meaning by the interpretation provisions of article 2 of the Order.

An informal booklet (*i.e.* it is neither a Statutory Instrument and, accordingly, does not rank as subordinate legislation, nor is it an Official Circular of the Department of the Environment) is published by the Department and is entitled, "Planning Permission—A Guide for Householders." It was last reprinted September 1983 and is intended (as it declares on page 1) "to help you if you want to carry out some development on your house or the land around it."

A similar informal booklet is published by the Department of the Environment and is entitled, "Planning Permission—A Guide for Industry." It is dated 1984.

Both the foregoing informal booklets are obtainable free of charge from the Department of the Environment, 2 Marsham Street, London SW1P 3EB, or from the Central Office of Information, London or H.M. Stationery Office, London.

2. The Thirty Classes of "Permitted Development"

The General Development Order of 1977 itself automatically authorises the carrying out of thirty classes of development (s.24(2)(*a*)). Permission for any such development derives directly from the General Development Order itself and there is no need for a developer undertaking this kind of development to make any application for planning permission in respect of it.

But it is to be remembered that today (February 1987) the effect, scope and general impact of the 1977 Order are materially and importantly restricted in the case of development in a National Park, in an area of outstanding natural beauty, in a conservation area—see, generally chapter 9, and see also pages 166 and 167 of this chapter—and in any area of land set out in the Schedule to the Town and Country Planning (Agricultural and Forestry Development in National Parks etc.) Special Development Order 1986 (S.I. 1986 No. 1176) if the development happens to fall within Class VI or Class VII (farm and forestry buildings) of the General Development Order 1977—as to which, see chapter 9 at page 155 *ante*, and pages 171 and 172, *post*, of this chapter.

Moreover the automatic grant of planning permission by the 1977 Order has been limited, as from May 1, 1984, by amendments made (by S.I. 1983 No. 1615) to the 1977 Order relating to the manufacture, processing, keeping or use of a "notifiable quantity" of a "hazardous substance" (1977 Order, art. 3(1) proviso) or the construction of a "notifiable pipeline" (art. 3(2A)). The words within inverted commas in the preceeding sentence are specially defined in article 2 of the 1977 Order as that article is now to be read since its amendment, as from May 1, 1984, by S.I. 1983 No. 1615. As to hazardous substances reference should be made to page 245, *post*.

Subject to the foregoing *caveats*, by virtue of article 3(1) of the 1977 Order, planning permission is automatically given for all the 30 classes of development set out in Schedule 1 to the Order, which classes are, accordingly, referred to in the Order under the general heading of "permitted development." If development can be brought within the confines of any one or other of these 30 different classes, then no application for planning permission in respect of it need be made to any local planning authority, the General Development Order itself constituting sufficient planning authorisation therefor.

If, however, express planning permission has been granted by a local planning authority for the erection of a building, on an application therefor made under Part III of the 1971 Act, the provisions of article 3 of the General Development Order 1977 and of Schedule 1 to the Order do *not* permit the developer to depart from the details of the building as shown on the plans submitted to the local planning authority (art. 3(2)).

The automatic planning permission granted for permitted development under the General Development Order is granted subject to any limitation and to any condition imposed by Schedule 1 in relation to any specified class of permitted development (art. 3(1)). Moreover, any such planning permission for permitted development shall not (except with respect to Classes IX, XII and XIV of permitted development) authorise any development which involves the formation, laying out or material widening of a means of access to a trunk or classified road or which creates an obstruction to the view of persons using any highway used by vehicular traffic at or near any bend, corner, junction or intersection so as to be likely to cause danger to such persons (art. 3(3)).

No useful purpose would be served in setting out here details of all the 30 classes of permitted development. Certain comments, however, may usefully be offered upon a number of these classes.

Class I

Development within the curtilage of a dwelling-house. Paragraph 1 of this class relates to development occurring within the curtilage of a dwelling-house, including the enlargement, improvement or other alteration of the dwelling-house provided that:

(a) the external cubic content of the original house (as ascertained by external measurement) is not exceeded by more than—
   (i) in the case of a "terrace house" (as defined in article 2), 50 cubic metres or 10 per cent., whichever is the greater; or
   (ii) in any other case, 70 cubic metres or 15 per cent., whichever is the greater

   subject (in either case) to a maximum of 115 cubic metres;

(b) the height of the building as so enlarged, improved or altered shall not exceed the height of the highest part of the roof of the original dwelling-house;

(c) no part of the building as so enlarged, improved or altered shall project beyond the forwardmost part[8] of any wall of the original dwelling-house which fronts on a highway;

(d) no part of the building as so enlarged, improved or altered which lies within a distance of two metres from any boundary

[8] *Bradford Metropolitan District Council* v. *Secretary of State for the Environment and Others* (1977) 76 L.G.R. 454; (1977) 35 P. & C.R. 387; in the case of an L-shaped building two walls (one further back than the other) may front the highway—*North West Leicestershire District Council* v. *Secretary of State for the Environment* (1982) J.P.L. 777.

of the curtilage of the dwelling-house shall have, as a result of the development, a height exceeding four metres;

(e) the area of ground covered by buildings within the curtilage (other than the original dwelling-house) shall not thereby exceed 50 per cent. of the total area of the curtilage excluding the ground area of the original dwelling-house.

It is to be noted that a garage or coachhouse, a stable or loosebox erected within the curtilage of a dwelling-house is to count as an enlargement of the dwelling-house itself if any part of it is within a distance of five metres from the dwelling-house.

"Terrace house" is defined (in article 2 of the Order) as a dwelling-house:

(i) situated in a row of three or more buildings used, or designed for use, as single dwelling-houses; and

(ii) sharing a party wall with, or having a main wall adjoining the main wall of, the dwelling-house (or building designed for use as a dwelling-house) on either side of it,

but including the dwelling-houses at each end of such a row of buildings as is mentioned.

Under Class I are authorised (Class I paragraph 3) a number of other outbuildings (other than a dwelling, a stable or a loose-box), incidental to the *the enjoyment of a dwelling-house as such,* and frequently found within the curtilage of a house, *e.g.* summer-houses, green-houses, tool sheds, beehives, dog kennels, dovecotes, poultry houses, provided that

(a) no part of such outbuilding projects beyond the forwardmost part of any wall of the original dwelling-house which fronts on a highway;

(b) in the case of a garage or coachhouse, no part of the outbuilding is within a distance of five metres from any part of the dwelling-house;

(c) the height does not exceed, in the case of a building with a ridged roof, four metres or, in any other case, three metres;

(d) the area of ground covered by buildings within the curtilage (other than the original dwelling-house) does not thereby exceed 50 per cent. of the total area of the curtilage excluding the ground area of the original dwelling-house.

Enlargement, improvement or other alteration can only be to a dwelling-house *already in existence* when the operations were carried out; Class I does not cover the rebuilding of a house.[9]

As to the meaning of "curtilage," reference may be made to page 128.

[9] *Sainty* v. *Minister of Housing and Local Government* (1964) 15 P. & C.R. 432, D.C.

"Dwelling-house" has been held *not* to cover a Georgian house most of which was used as a residence but two ground-floor rooms of which were used for the business of an estate agent.[10]

It is further to be noted that the provisions as to permitted development set out (as above) in paragraphs 1 and 3 of Class I of the Schedule to the General Development Order 1977 apply to certain areas of land *with the restricted modifications* originally set out in the Town and Country Planning (National Parks, Areas of Outstanding Natural Beauty and Conservation Areas) Special Development Order 1981.[11] This Order, which operated as from April 1, 1981, applied (art. 1(1)) to development of land which, *on April 1, 1981,* was within:

(a) the area of a National Park;
(b) an area of outstanding natural beauty; or
(c) a conservation area.

If any of these three types of area were in existence on April 1, 1981, then the full scope of permitted development, under paragraphs 1 and 3 of Class I the General Development Order 1977, within them is *not* available.

The Special Development Order of 1981 was revoked and re-enacted with additions by the Town and Country Planning (National Parks, Areas of Outstanding Natural Beauty and Conservation Areas, etc.) Special Development Order 1985—S.I. 1985 No. 1012—which operates as from November 1, 1985 and which was itself slightly amended as from March 1, 1986, by the Town and Country Planning (National Parks, Areas of Outstanding Natural Beauty and Conservation Areas, etc.) Special Development (Amendment) Order 1986 (S.I. 1986 No. 8).

The provisions of the 1981 Order which are re-enacted in the 1985 Order without amendment (article 3(a), (b) and (c)) modify Schedule 1 to the General Development Order 1977 in its application to any land in any of the aforementioned areas by providing that:

(a) in Class I.1 (the enlargement, improvement or other alteration of a dwelling-house) the permitted increase in the size of a dwelling-house is 50 cubic metres or ten per cent. of the content of the original dwelling-house, whichever is the greater (instead of 70 cubic metres or 15 per cent.); and the erection of a garage or coachhouse *anywhere* within the curtilage

[10] *Scurlock* v. *Secretary of State for Wales* (1976) 238 E.G. 47, D.C.

[11] S.I. 1981 No. 246; revoked and re-enacted with additions by the Town and Country Planning (National Parks, Areas of Outstanding Natural Beauty and Conservation Areas, etc.) Special Development Order 1985—S.I. 1985 No. 1012—which operates as from November 1, 1985.

is to be treated as the enlargement of the dwelling-house (under the provisions of the General Development Order, only a garage or coachhouse which is erected within 5 metres of the dwelling-house is so treated);

(b) the erection, construction or placing and the maintenance, improvement or alteration of garages and coachhouses are excluded from Class I.3 (the erection and alteration of buildings and enclosures in the curtilage of a dwelling-house); and

(c) in Class VIII.1 (the carrying out of certain operations by industrial undertakers) the permitted increases in the size of a building are reduced from 20 per cent of the cubic content to 10 per cent and from 750 square metres of floorspace to 500 square metres.

The environmentally sensitive areas to which the Special Development Order of 1981 denied the extended scope of "permitted development"—that is to say, "permitted development" as extended in scope by the Town and Country Planning General Development (Amendment) Order 1981 (S.I. 1981 No. 245)—were those areas namely, those National Parks, those areas of outstanding natural beauty and those conservation areas, which were in existence on April 1, 1981. The Town and Country Planning (National Parks, Areas of Outstanding Natural Beauty and Conservation Areas, etc.) Special Development Order 1985 (S.I. 1985 No. 1012) as amended by the Town and Country Planning (National Parks, Areas of Outstanding Natural Beauty and Conservation Areas, etc.) Special Development (Amendment) Order 1986 (S.I. 1986 No. 8), now denies the aforesaid extended scope of "permitted development" to any National Park, any area of outstanding natural beauty or any conservation area (and, it may be added, any area specified for the purposes of the Wildlife and Countryside Act 1981 section 41) which was in existence on November 1, 1985 (1985 Order, arts. 1(1) and (2)).

Hardstanding for vehicles (provided it is used for a purpose incidental to *the enjoyment of the dwelling-house as such*) and oil storage tanks (not exceeding 3,500 litres in capacity) are also authorised (subject to conditions) under Class I, paragraphs 4 and 5 respectively of the 1977 Order.

Help in the interpretation of Class I will be found (as has already been mentioned) in the booklet of 20 pages, designed on the question and answer principle of disseminating information, entitled, "Planning Permission—A Guide for Householders." It is prepared by the Department of the Environment, 2 Marsham Street, London, SW1P 3EB, from where it is obtainable free. It was last reprinted in September 1983.

Class II

Sundry minor operations. Gates, fences, walls and other means of enclosure are authorised by this class provided they do not exceed one metre in height when abutting on a highway used by vehicles or two metres in height in any other case.[12]

External painting of a building is also authorised provided it is not in the nature of an advertisement.

Class III

Changes of use. Under this Class many changes of use (mentioned in the Town and Country Planning (Use Classes) Order 1972)[13] become permitted development. Such changes of use are any change of use,

(a) *to* use as a light industrial building as defined by the Use Classes Order *from* use as a general industrial building as so defined;

(b) *to* use as a light industrial building as defined by the Use Classes Order *from* use for any purpose included in Class X in the Schedule to the Use Classes Order;

(c) *to* use for any purpose included in Class X in the Schedule to the Use Classes Order *from* use as a light industrial building or *from* use as a general industrial building (as defined respectively by the Use Classes Order);

(d) *to* use as a shop for any purpose included in Class I in the Schedule to the Use Classes Order *from* use as:

  (i) a shop for the sale of hot food;
  (ii) a tripe shop;
  (iii) a shop for the sale of pet animals or birds;
  (iv) a cats' meat shop; or
  (v) a shop for the sale of motor vehicles

provided that paragraphs (b) and (c) above apply only where the total amount of floor space in the building used for the purposes of the undertaking does not exceed 235 square metres.

It will be noted that there is no authorisation here for a change of use *from* one of the five kinds of shops, etc., above specified *to* another one of those five kinds.

[12] As to when a fence may be said to abut on a highway, see *Simonds and Others* v. *Secretary of State for the Environment and Rochdale Metropolitan D.C.* [1981] J.P.L. 509.

[13] S.I. 1972 No. 1385.

Class IV

Temporary buildings and uses. Under this Class is authorised the erection of buildings, plant and machinery needed temporarily in connection with the carrying out of development (other than mining operations) for which planning permission has been granted, or deemed to have been granted, under the 1971 Act or for which planning permission is not required—as, for example, the carrying out of certain Government contracts.

This Class also authorises the use of land *not* within the curtilage of a building, for *any* purpose or purposes (except as a caravan site) on not more than 28 days in total in a calendar year and the erection or placing of movable structures on the land in connection with such use.[14] If, however, the temporary use is for motor car and motor-cycle racing or if it is for the holding of a market, then the 28 days in any year is reduced to 14 days.

The use of a field for an agricultural show and the erection of a marquee, etc., in association therewith, would be authorised as a temporary use under Class IV.

The effect upon planning permission and enforcement notices[15] of the provision as to 28 days in connection with this class of permitted development was raised in *Postill* v. *East Riding County Council*,[16] in *Francis* v. *Yiewsley and West Drayton Urban District Council*,[17] in *Miller-Mead* v. *Minister of Housing and Local Government*[18] and in *Cater* v. *Essex County Council*.[19] As a result of the decision in the latter case it appeared impossible to enforce the 28-day limitation imposed in connection with this class of permitted development, but section 38(2) of the Town and Country Planning Act 1959 (now s.24(6) of the 1971 Act) remedied this defect in the law.

Class V

Uses by members of recreational organisations. Under this Class land *not* within the curtilage of a dwelling-house may be used for recreation and instruction involving the use of tents (but not caravans) by members of a recreational organisation which holds a certificate of exemption under section 269 of the Public Health Act 1936.

[14] *Godstone R.D.C.* v. *Brazil* [1953] 1 W.L.R. 1102, D.C.
[15] See Chap. 15.
[16] [1956] 2 Q.B. 386, D.C.
[17] [1958] 1 Q.B. 478, C.A., affirming [1957] 2 Q.B. 136.
[18] [1963] 2 W.L.R. 225.
[19] [1960] 1 Q.B. 424, D.C.

Class VI

Agricultural buildings, works and uses. This Class is important from the farmer's point of view for it authorises the carrying out, on "agricultural land" of more than one acre *and* comprised in an "agricultural unit", of building or engineering operations requisite for the purposes of agriculture. "Agricultural land" and "agricultural unit" are defined in article 2(1) of the General Development Order 1977 and have the meanings respectively given to them in the Agriculture Act 1947.

Buildings covered by this class are limited in size (not exceeding 465 square metres) and height (not exceeding 12 metres—or 3 metres if within 3 kilometres of the perimeter of an aerodrome) by the conditions subject to which planning permission for their erection is permitted by the Order. A further condition requires that no part of any building may stand within 25 metres of the metalling of a trunk or classified road. Moreover, such buildings must be designed *for the purposes of agriculture.* Thus old bus bodies, tramcars, or railway carriages are not allowed under the permission.

Under this Class are also authorised roadside stands for milk churns (but not when they would abut on a trunk road or a classified road) and the winning and working upon land occupied with agricultural land of minerals reasonably required for the purposes of the agricultural land (*e.g.* for fertilisation and for the improvement of agricultural buildings) so long as no excavation is made within 25 metres of the metalling of a trunk or classified road.

The provision of, and the alteration of, dwellings are not covered by this Class. Nor is an aircraft hangar used in connection with the business of breeding and training horses for show-jumping—such business not being requisite for the use of land for agriculture.[20]

It was claimed that Class VI only applies if the building or engineering operations which are to take place are intended for an existing agricultural activity on the land. The Court of Appeal held this was not so and that there was no call for the building to be ancillary to some activity carried out on the remainder of the land.[21]

Class VI will not apply if *part* of the building or engineering operations (as, for example, a reservoir) lies within 25 metres of a trunk or classified road.[22]

[20] *Belmont Farm* v. *Minister of Housing and Local Government* (1962) 13 P. & C.R. 417, D.C. Tipping of waste materials on land to improve it for agricultural purposes *may* be permitted development under Class VI depending on the facts: see *Northavon District Council* v. *Secretary of State for the Environment* (1980) 40 P. & C.R. 332.

[21] *Jones* v. *Metropolitan Borough of Stockport* (1984) J.P.L. 274.

[22] *Faynewood Fish Farms* v. *Secretary of State for the Environment* (1984) J.P.L. 267.

It may be that while farmers, building a reservoir for irrigation purposes, can get the benefit of permitted development therefor under Class VI for their building or engineering operations, they may yet find themselves in need of a formal grant of planning permission by the local planning authority when they come to carry out the *mining operation* involved in the excavation of *large* quantities of gravel to make space for the reservoir. In *West Bowers Farm Products* v. *Essex County Council*,[23] Lord Justice Donaldson, Master of the Rolls, declared, " . . . some activities may constitute a change of use or an operation, according to what is the object of the activity. . . . The same activity may also constitute both an operation and a change of use . . . the digging of foundations for a building which, incidentally, involves the extraction of relatively small quantities of minerals, could not possibly be described as a mining operation. Nor could most 'cut and fill' operations involved in road building. It is a question of fact and degree in each case."

In those areas of natural beauty specified in the Town and Country Planning (Landscape Areas Special Development) Order 1950,[24] no agricultural development authorised under Class VI could be carried out without notification to the local planning authority, who had 14 days in which to intervene with requirements as to the design and external appearance of such development.

The 1950 Order was revoked by the Town and Country Planning (Agricultural and Forestry Development in National Parks etc.) Special Development Order 1986 (S.I. 1986 No. 1176) (art. 4) which came into operation on November 1, 1986 (art. 1(1)). The areas of land to which the 1986 Order applies are set out in the Schedule to the Order and are fully quoted, *ante*, in Chapter 9 at pages 156 to 158. The 1986 Order imposes conditions on the carrying out of development covered by Class VI as to which reference should be made to Chapter 9 at page 155.

Class VII

Forestry buildings and works. Under this Class are authorised the carrying out on land used for forestry purposes of building and other operations (but not the building or alteration of dwelling-houses) needed for those purposes and the making of private roads on such land.

The restrictive conditions of the Town and Country Planning

[23] *West Bowers Farm Products* v. *Essex County Council* (1985) J.P.L. 857.
[24] S.I. 1950 No. 729.

(Agriculture and Forestry Development in National Parks etc.) Special Development Order 1986 (as to which, see this Chapter at page 171 *ante*, and Chapter 9 at page 155, *ante*) apply (art. 3) to development authorised by this Class if the development is in one of the areas of land specified in that Order.[25]

Class VIII

Development for industrial purposes. This class applies to development of the following descriptions, carried out by an "industrial undertaker" (as defined in article 2(1)), on land used (otherwise than (i) in contravention of previous planning control or (ii) without planning permission granted, or deemed to be granted, under Part III of the 1971 Act) for the carrying out of any "industrial process," (as defined in article 2(1)), and for the purposes of such process, or on land used (otherwise than as aforesaid) as a dock, harbour or quay for the purposes of an industrial undertaking:

(i) the provision, rearrangement or replacement of private ways or private railways, sidings or conveyors;

(ii) the provision or rearrangement of sewers, mains, pipes, cables or other apparatus;

(iii) the installation or erection, by way of addition or replacement, of plant or machinery, or structures or erections of the nature of plant or machinery, not exceeding 15 metres in height or the height of the plant, machinery, structure or erection so replaced, whichever is the greater;

(iv) the extension or alteration of buildings (whether erected before or after July 1, 1948), so long as the height of the original building is not exceeded and the cubic content of the original building (as ascertained by external measurement) is not exceeded by more than 20 per cent. nor the aggregate floor space thereof by more than 750 square metres,

so long as:

(a) in the case of operations carried out under subparagraphs (iii) or (iv), the external appearance of the premises of the undertaking is not materially affected;

(b) in the case of operations carried out under subparagraph (iv), no part of the building is, as a result of the development, within a distance of 5 metres from any boundary of the curtilage of the premises; and

[25] See *ante* under Class VI at p. 170.

(c) in the case of operations carried out under subparagraph (iv), no certificate would be required under section 67 of the 1971 Act if an application for planning permission for the development in question were made:

Provided that the erection on land within the curtilage of any such building of an additional building to be used in connection with the original building shall be treated as an extension of the original building, and where any two or more original buildings comprised in the same curtilage are used as one unit for the purposes of the undertaking, the reference in the permission to the cubic content shall be construed as a reference to the aggregate cubic content of those buildings, and the reference to the aggregate floor space as a reference to the total floor space of those buildings.

As to the reference in paragraph (c) above to a certificate under section 67 of the 1971 Act, no industrial development certificates have been, or can be, issued after January 9, 1982 by virtue of the Town and Country Planning (Industrial Development Certificates) (Prescribed Classes of Building) Regulations 1981 (S.I. 1981 No. 1826). No building is now prescribed under section 67 of the 1971 Act and thus no industrial development certificate is, since January 9, 1982, required for any building.

The "permitted development" otherwise authorised by Class VIII (under item (iv) above) became limited in the case of land which, on November 1, 1985 was situated in a National Park, in an area of outstanding natural beauty, or in a conservation area, by the provisions of the Town and Country Planning (National Parks, Areas of Outstanding Natural Beauty and Conservation Areas) Special Development Order 1981 (S.I. 1981 No. 246) now revoked and re-enacted, with additions, by the Town and Country Planning (National Parks, Areas of Outstanding Natural Beauty and Conservation Areas, etc.) Special Development Order 1985 (S.I. 1985 No. 1012) which operates from November 1, 1985, with the result that the permitted increases in the size of buildings allowed under item (iv) above are reduced from 20 per cent. of the cubic content to 10 per cent. and from 750 square metres of floor space to 500 square metres.

This position is continued as from March 1, 1986 subject to the amendments to the 1985 Special Development Order provided by the Town and Country Planning (National Parks, Areas of Outstanding Natural Beauty and Conservation Areas, etc.) Special Development (Amendment) Order 1986 (S.I. 1986 No. 8) which came into operation on March 1, 1986.

Class VIII also applies to the deposit by an "industrial undertaker" of refuse resulting from an "industrial process" on any land comprised in a site which was used for such deposit on July 1, 1948, whether or not the superficial area or the height of the deposit is thereby extended.

Class IX

Repairs to unadopted streets and private ways. Under this Class abutting owners (*inter alia*) are authorised to repair the highway (as yet unadopted by the local authority) on which their own premises abut.

Class X

Repairs to service. This Class authorises the repair of sewers, underground telephone wires and similar services, by the appropriate authorities.

Class XI

War-damaged buildings, works and plant. Under this Class is authorised the replacement of war-damaged buildings, works or plant, provided the cubic content thereof is not increased beyond the limits authorised under Class I or Class VIII, and provided further that the replacement does not, except with the permission of the local planning authority, involve any material alteration of the previously existing external appearance.

In connection with development falling within this class, reference should be made to the observations later in this chapter relating to the making of a Direction (under article 4 of the General Development Order 1977) by the Secretary of State *excluding* certain kinds of development from this particular class of permitted development.

Class XII

Development under local or private Acts, or Orders. This Class authorises the carrying out (subject to important reservations), as development permitted under the 1971 Act, of any development of land which is authorised by a local or private Act, or an Order approved by both Houses of Parliament, provided that the Act or Order designates specifically both the nature of the development and the land upon which it may be carried out.

In *Pyx Granite Co.* v. *Ministry of Housing and Local Government,*[26] it was held that a company which was authorised by a special Act of Parliament to quarry over a specified area of land did not, as a result of the provisions of Class XII, require express planning permission to carry out further quarrying in the specified area.

Classes XIII to XXV

These classes of permitted development relate to development by local authorities, local highway authorities, drainage authorities, water authorities, sewerage and sewage disposal authorities, statutory undertakers, mineral undertakers and the National Coal Board (Classes XIII to XX), to the use of aerodrome buildings (Class XXI), to the use of land as a caravan site (Class XXII)[27] to development required by the conditions of a site licence in force under Part I of the Caravan Sites and Control of Development Act 1960 (Class XXIII)[27] to development by Telecommunications Code System Operators (Class XXIV) and to other telecommunications development (Class XXV).

Classes XXIV and XXV were added to Schedule 1 of the General Development Order 1977 by the Town and Country Planning General Development (Amendment) Order 1985 (S.I. 1985 No. 1011) which operates as from November 1, 1985. Limitations on the amount of development permitted by these two new use Classes are made by the Town and Country Planning (National Parks, Areas of Outstanding Natural Beauty and Conservation Areas, etc.) Special Development Order 1985 which also came into force on November 1, 1985. These limitations are as follows:

(a) an additional condition and an additional limitation are imposed on Class XXIV (development by telecommunications code system operators) which (i) require the operator (except in an emergency) to give 8 weeks' notice to the local planning authority before installing any apparatus on his own land, and (ii) exclude from the class (except in a case of emergency) the installation or alteration of microwave antennas and the replacement of an existing antenna by an antenna which is different from the original one; and

(b) Class XXV (other telecommunications development) does not apply in the areas covered by the aforesaid Special

[26] [1960] A.C. 260, H.L.
[27] See Chap. 13.

Development Order 1985 relating to National Parks, Areas of Outstanding Natural Beauty and Conservation Areas, etc.

Classes XXVI to XXX

These remaining five classes of permitted development are added to the quantum of permitted development under the 1977 Order by the Town and Country Planning General Development (Amendment) (No. 2) Order 1985 (S.I. 1985 No. 1981) which came into operation on March 1, 1986 and may be cited with the earlier orders as the Town and Country Planning General Development Orders 1977 to 1985.

The five new classes of permitted development added to Schedule 1 of the General Development Order of 1977 by the Town & Country Planning General Development (Amendment) (No. 2) Order 1985 (S.I. 1985 No. 1981) are as follows:

(1) a new Class XXVI which grants permission for small-scale temporary exploration for the purposes of exploiting minerals;

(2) a new Class XXVII which grants permission for the removal of material from stockpiles and from small or temporary mineral-working deposits;

(3) a new Class XXVIII which permits the extension of existing warehouses similar to the permission available in relation to industrial buildings—see class VIII;

(4) a new Class XXIX which permits the provision and rearranging of small buildings and equipment within existing amusement parks; and

(5) a new Class XXX which permits the Historic Buildings and Monuments Commission for England to carry out minor development in connection with the preservation of buildings or monuments for which they have responsibility.

3. Exclusion from "Permitted Development"

The Secretary of State or a local planning authority may make a Direction which will have the effect of removing from the category of permitted development any development specified in the Direction (art. 4(1)). Any such Direction made by a local planning authority will generally (but not always) require the Secretary of State's approval (art. 4(2) and (3)). Any such Direction made under an earlier Development Order in force on the commencement of the

General Development Order 1977 (on March 29, 1977) is further continued in force under article 4(8) of the 1977 Order.

This is important in connection with development falling within Class XI (see page 174, *ante*) relating to the replacement of war-damaged buildings, works or plant because some local planning authorities have had this particular class of development *excluded* from the category of permitted development (and thereby made subject to control by the local planning authority) by means of a Direction made and approved under the Town and Country Planning (General Interim Development) Order 1946 (now repealed). In those areas where this has been done, the local planning authority will continue to have control over the replacement of war-damaged buildings, works and plants, notwithstanding that these matters are included in Class XI of the General Development Order 1977.

Action by a local planning authority, under the provisions of article 4 of the General Development Order of 1977, to remove specified development from the category of permitted development could lead to the liability of the local planning authority to pay compensation under section 165 of the 1971 Act (see Chapter 17 at page 374) to an aggrieved applicant for planning permission. This liability is now materially restricted by the Town & Country Planning (Compensation) Act 1985, section 1(1) which adds a new subsection (6A) to section 165 of the 1971 Act—again, see Chapter 17 at page 374.

4. Buying Land for Development—Checklist of Things to Question

Assuming that development which it is sought to undertake is development within the meaning of the 1971 Act for which planning permission is *not* automatically granted (s.24(2)(*a*)) by the General Development Order 1977, it will be necessary for a formal grant of planning permission to be obtained for the development from the local planning authority (s.24(2)(*b*)).

Before, however, going into details of the procedures which will need to be followed in the course of getting a formal grant of planning permission for development, it may be useful to ponder the checklist of things which, today, will *call for careful consideration by any person thinking of buying land for development*. The various matters which will find a place in any such checklist are briefly itemised below. In each case reference is made to other pages in this book where further and fuller particulars about each item may be found.

The onset of planning and development control (as we have it today, February 1987) from "the appointed day" (July 1, 1948) under the Town and Country Planning Act 1947, has made it necessary for the person who contemplates buying land for development to ask a lot of questions *before* he commits himself to any contract for sale and purchase of the land. Among the many questions he must ask are, at least, the following 16 questions all relating to matters of *planning control* and all in addition to the usual questions asked, and searches made, in accordance with the normal rules and practices of good *conveyancing*.

(1) If and when he has purchased the land, is that which he seeks to do in, on, over or under it, "development" as defined in the 1947 Act, now the 1971 Act, s.22? (see Chapter 8).

(2) If it is development, is it "permitted development," under the Town and Country Planning General Development Order 1977? (see page 162, *ante*).

(3) Is the site in a *Shire County*? If it is he will need to consider not only the Structure Plan for the County but also the Local Plan (or Plans), if any, for the County District where the land is (see Chapters 4 and 5).

(4) Is the site in a *Metropolitan County*? If it is he will need to consider the Unitary Development Plan for the Metropolitan County District where the land is (see Chapter 6).

(5) Is the site a cleared site?

(6) If not, does the site contain:

(a) a tree and, if so, is the tree a protected tree under sections 59 to 62 of the 1971 Act? (see Chapter 14);

(b) a building and, if so, is the building protected as a listed building under sections 54 to 58A of the 1971 Act? (see Chapter 14).

(7) Is the site in a Conservation Area and, if so, was the Area designated under section 277 of the 1971 Act by a local planning authority, before, *or* on or after November 1, 1985? (see Chapter 8).

(8) Is the site in an Area of Outstanding Natural Beauty (A.O.N.B.) and, if so, was the Area designated, under section 87 of the National Parks and Access to the Countryside Act 1949, by the Countryside Commission before, *or* on or after, November 1, 1985? (see Chapter 8).

(9) Is the site in a National Park and, if so, was the National Park designated, under sections 5(3), 6, and 7 of the National Parks and Access to the Countryside Act 1949, by the Countryside Commission before, *or* on or after, November 1, 1985? (see Chapter 8).

(10) Is the site in an area of land specified in the Schedule to the Town and Country Planning (Agricultural and Forestry

Development in National Parks etc.) Special Development Order 1986 (S.I. 1986 No. 1176) which came into operation on November 1, 1986? (see Chapter 9 at page 155; see also pages 171 and 172 of this Chapter, *ante*).

(11) Is the site in an Urban Development Area designated, under section 134 of the Local Government, Land and Planning Act 1980, by the Secretary of State for the Environment? (see Chapter 23).

(12) Is the site in an Enterprise Zone designated, under section 179 of, and Schedule 32 to, the Local Government, Land and Planning Act 1980, by the Secretary of State for the Environment? (see Chapter 24).

(13) Is the site in an area demarcated as a Simplified Planning Zone under the Housing and Planning Act 1986? (see Chapter 25).

(14) Is the site the subject of a still-operative grant of planning permission for development and, if so, what kind of development? (see page 211—Duration of Planning Permission).

(15) Is the site the subject of an outstanding enforcement notice or a stop notice? (see Chapter 15).

(16) Have the local planning authority delegated, under section 101 of the Local Government Act 1972, to their officer the right to determine an application for planning permission? (If so the decision of the officer becomes automatically that of the local planning authority—see Chapter 2.)

The significance of the date November 1, 1985 in questions (7) (8) and (9) above, derives from the provisions of the Town and Country Planning (National Parks, Areas of Outstanding Natural Beauty and Conservation Areas) Special Development Order 1981 (S.I. 1981 No. 246) revoked and re-enacted with additions by the Town and Country Planning (National Parks, Areas of Outstanding Natural Beauty and Conservation Areas, etc.) Special Development Order 1985 (S.I. 1985 No. 1012). The effect of these orders is to put restrictions, in the respective areas to which they apply, on the amount of development falling within the scope of permitted development under Class I (development within the curtilage of a dwelling-house) and Class VIII (development for industrial purposes) of the Town and Country Planning General Development Order 1977 (S.I. 1977 No. 289 as amended).

Finally, *before* buying land for development the purchaser will be wise to discover whether, if and when he has purchased the land, he will then be able, notwithstanding the long arm of planning control, to carry out the development he has in mind. There is only one sure way to discover this most important information and that is to make formal application to the local planning authority for a grant of planning permission in outline (see *infra*, this page). Of course, if the proposed development is clearly permitted development under the General Development Order of 1977 (see pages 162 *et seq.*) the need to apply for outline planning consent will not arise.

5. Method of Applying for Planning Permission—Full Planning Permission—Outline Planning Permission

Returning now to the business of getting planning permission for development, it may be repeated that if the development which it is sought to undertake is development within the meaning of the 1971 Act for which planning permission is *not* automatically granted (s.24(2)(*a*)) by the General Development Order 1977 (*i.e.* assuming it is *not* "permitted development" under the 1977 Order and as earlier described in this chapter), then, in such case, it will be necessary for a formal grant of planning permission to be obtained for the development from the local planning authority (s.24(2)(*b*)).

Any applicant for planning permission, seeking guidance as to planning policy, may advisedly consider the various "Development Control Policy Notes" which have been published from time to time by the Department of the Environment or its predecessors in title. The publication of these Notes was first announced in Ministry Circular 23/69, dated March 18, 1969. This Circular has since been rescinded by D.O.E. Circular 26/1979, dated October 25, 1979 but without prejudice to the Notes themselves.

Each of these Policy Notes is prefaced by the observation that:

> "These notes set out current Ministerial policy and their purpose is to give general guidance to intending developers. Policies are not rigid and from time to time new Notes will be issued in this series taking account of changes in emphasis in policy or new policy decisions.
>
> "Each application or appeal is treated on its merits and the application of a general policy to the particular case must always be a matter calling for judgement.
>
> "Any legal views stated in these Notes have no statutory force and should not be relied upon as authoritative interpretations of the law.
>
> "A list of other current Notes in this series can be obtained free from the Ministry of Housing and Local Government or the Welsh Office."

A list of the Policy Notes issued to date (February 1987) appears in the Table of Ministerial Circulars and Information, *ante*.

Any application to a local planning authority for planning permission must be made in such manner as is prescribed by regulations (s.25).

Details as to the method of applying for planning permission are dealt with in articles 5, 6 and 7 of the General Development Order 1977. The application is to be made on a form issued by the local planning authority and obtainable from that authority or from the council with whom the application is to be lodged (art. 5(1)).

In the case of land in the City of London the application is to be lodged with the Common Council of the City, and in the case of other land in Greater London, with the council of the London borough in which the land is situated (art. 7(1)).

Where the land is not in Greater London the application is to be lodged with the district planning authority (art. 7(1)).

The application is to include such particulars as the application form requires to be supplied. It is also to be accompanied by a plan sufficient to identify the land together with such other plans and drawings as are necessary to describe the development (art. 5(1)). There must also be lodged such additional copies (not exceeding three) of the application, plans and drawings, as may be required by the directions printed on the application form. The local planning authority may require such further information as is requisite to enable them to determine the application (*ibid.*).

Either before he buys his land or before he incurs the cost of preparing detailed plans, a developer may wish to know whether his proposed development will be likely to get planning permission if he applies for it. A developer may make an application (art. 5(2)) for "outline planning permission" which can be granted subject to a condition that there shall be subsequent approval by the local planning authority of any "reserved matters" (art. 2(1)) relating to siting, design and external appearance of buildings. The developer thus gets to know, before he incurs undue expense, whether *in principle* his proposed development is acceptable to the local planning authority. If, however, the local planning authority feel that the application for planning permission ought not to be considered separately from the reserved matters above mentioned, then the authority can call for further particulars and, in the meantime, can decline to entertain the application (art. 5(2) proviso). There is a right of appeal within six months to the Secretary of State against such action by a local planning authority (*ibid.*).

Once an outline application is granted, the local planning authority are committed to allowing the proposed development in some form or other, the only matters requiring subsequent approval by the authority being such as are specifically reserved in the permission granted on the outline application.

The Secretary of State formerly took the view[28] that once matters, reserved by a grant of outline planning permission for subsequent approval, have in due course been approved by the local planning authority, they cannot then be revised or varied by a further submission for approval of reserved matters under the same grant of outline planning permission. This view was overruled by the Court of Appeal in *Heron Corporation Ltd.* v. *Manchester City Corporation*[29] where it was held that when planning permission has been granted in outline and subject to the subsequent approval of reserved matters, it is open to the applicant to make, in succession, more than one application to the planning authority for the approval of matters reserved for subsequent approval in the original grant of planning permission in outline. Lord Denning M.R. said:

> "Though the planning authority might at an early stage have given its approval in respect of reserved matters, there was no reason why the applicant should not make another and different application for approval in respect of that selfsame matter. A second application could be granted, leaving the first approval still standing. In that case the applicant could use whichever approval he liked; or the planning authority could grant the new application, subject to the first not being proceeded with."

Outline planning permission was granted for a major scheme of redevelopment which included a bus garage and a library. Later there was an application for the approval of details (*i.e.* of reserved matters) but this application made no reference to the bus garage and the library both of which the developer sought to abandon. Was an application for the approval of detail which omitted a use of land earlier approved in outline in order? It was held by the Court of Appeal that it *was* in order. In the circumstances of the case the omission of the bus garage and the library did not put the application for approval of details beyond the ambit of the original outline planning permission (*R.* v. *London Borough of Hammersmith and Fulham and Bredero Consulting Ltd., ex parte Greater London Council* (1986) J.P.L. 528). Reference may also be made to *Sunland Development Company Ltd* v. *Secretary of State for the Environment and Lewes*

[28] See [1975] J.P.L. at pp. 555 and 556.
[29] [1978] J.P.L. at p. 471.

District Council (1986) J.P.L. 759 where 44 houses were granted outline planning permission but only 35 came to be granted full planning permission.

It would appear that if a local planning authority wishes to insure that, when they grant outline planning permission for development set out in the outline application, *all* of that development (and not merely some part of it chosen at the discretion of the developer) is, in fact, ultimately carried out when planning permission for the approval of reserved matters comes to be granted,—the planning authority, in granting the outline permission, must grant it subject to some condition that, later on, the application for approval of reserved matters will embrace *all* of the development covered by the outline permission.

Paragraphs 42–51 inclusive of the Memorandum to Ministry Circular No. 48/59, dated August 11, 1959, together with the Appendix entitled "Notes for Applicants," to that Memorandum, provided guidance not only to local authorities but also to developers seeking to obtain a grant of planning permission for development. The notices and certificates formerly included in the "Notes for Applicants" have been superseded by the provisions of the Town and Country Planning General Development Order 1977, No. 289, Schedule 3.

6. Notification of Planning Application to Owners and Agricultural Tenants

An applicant for planning permission does not need to have a legal interest in the land to which the application relates; the application may be made (and frequently is—especially in the case of an application for "outline planning permission" as referred to earlier) by a prospective purchaser or lessee. Formerly the application could be made without the knowledge of the owner of the land,[30] but this is no longer the case.

It was the subject of adverse comment that an application for planning permission could be made behind the back, as it were, of the owner of the land concerned, who thus might never hear anything about the matter at all until there was, for example, an appeal to the Secretary of State against a refusal of planning permission. This state of affairs is now, to some limited extent, remedied by section 27 of the 1971 Act.

Any application for planning permission *must* be accompanied by

[30] *Hanily* v. *Minister of Local Government and Planning* [1952] 2 Q.B. 444.

a certificate in one or other of four different forms, and if it is not so accompanied, then the local authority receiving it "shall not entertain" it (s.27(1)). The choice of which of the four forms of certificate is used depends on the circumstances of the case but section 27(1)(*a*)(*b*)(*c*) and (*d*) of the 1971 Act indicate which form is to be used while article 9(1) of, and Part I of Schedule 4 to, the Town and Country Planning General Development Order 1977[31] set out each of the four forms of certificate from which the selection of one is to be made. These four forms of certificate are referred to in Part I of Schedule 4 to the General Development Order 1977 as (respectively) Certificate A, Certificate B, Certificate C and Certificate D.

If the circumstances of the case require that the certificate shall be in the form of Certificate C or Certificate D, then the certificate *must* contain a statement that a notice (as set out in the certificate itself) has been published on a specified date in a local newspaper circulating in the locality in which the land in question is situated (s.27(2)), the form of this notice being set out in Part II of Schedule 4 to the General Development Order 1977.

Whatever form of certificate is used the certificate *must* contain one or other of the alternative statements relating to agricultural holdings set out in section 27(3) of the 1971 Act.

In any case where the applicant for planning permission is himself the "owner" (as defined in section 27(7) of the 1971 Act) in fee simple of *all* the land comprised in the planning application (s.27(1)(*a*)), then a certificate in the form of Certificate A will be the appropriate one to use, with the result that the applicant for planning permission will not be under any obligation to give notification of his application to any third party, unless the land comprised in the application constitutes or forms part of an "agricultural holding" (as defined in s.27(7) of the 1971 Act), in which case any person who, at the beginning of the period of 21 days ending with the date of the planning application, was a tenant of the agricultural holding must be notified of the application (s.27(3)(*b*)).

If, however, the applicant is unable, on the facts, to accompany his planning application with a certificate in the form of Certificate A, then he must accompany it with a certificate in the form of Certificate B, or Certificate C, or Certificate D, as the case may require.

If any one of these three kinds of certificate is used, (*i.e.* Certificate B or Certificate C or Certificate D), or if the certificate discloses (pursuant to s.27(3)(*b*)) that notification of the application has been given to the tenant of an agricultural holding any part of which is

[31] S.I. 1977 No. 289.

comprised in land to which the application relates, then the local planning authority must not determine the application until the end of a period of 21 days from the date (as disclosed in the certificate accompanying the application) of the service of the notice of the making of the application or, as the case may be, of the publication of the notice of the making of the application, whichever date is the later (s.27(4)). If, during this period of 21 days, the authority receive any representation about the application, the authority must take such representation into account before determining the application (s.29(3)(*a*)), provided that the authority are satisfied that the representation is made by a person who is either an "owner" (as defined in s.27(7)) of any of the land to which the application relates or is the tenant of an "agricultural holding" (as defined in s.27(7)) any part of which is comprised in that land.

Having determined the application the local planning authority must give notice of their decision not only to the applicant but to any person who made representations which the authority was obliged to take into account (s.29(3)(*b*)).

Any person who issues a certificate which contains a statement which he knows to be false or misleading in a material particular, or who recklessly issues a certificate which is false or misleading in a material particular, is liable on summary conviction to a fine not exceeding level 3 on the standard scale *i.e.* £400 (s.27(5), Criminal Justice Act 1982, s.37 and the Criminal Penalties etc. (Increase) Order 1984 (S.I. 1984 No. 447).

7. Newspaper Advertisement and Site Notices for Certain Planning Applications—"Bad Neighbour" Development

It is provided in section 26 of the 1971 Act that a planning application in respect of any of those nine classes of development prescribed in article 8 of the General Development Order 1977,[32] must be advertised in the local press, and be the subject of a site notice displayed on the land affected by the development, so that representations concerning the development can be sent to the local planning authority within 21 days (s.26 and art. 8 and Sched. 3, Pts. I, II and III of the General Development Order 1977).[32] If any representations are so made they must be taken into account by the local planning authority (s.29(2)).

The Secretary of State has stated that this procedure for giving publicity to planning applications will be used only in the case of

[32] S.I. 1977 No. 289.

"very limited types of development which might be considered bad neighbours" and the nine classes of development so far prescribed in the General Development Order 1977, are as follows:

(a) construction of buildings for use as a public convenience;
(b) construction of buildings or other operations, or use of land, for the disposal of refuse or waste materials or as a scrap yard or coal yard or for the winning or working of minerals;
(c) construction of buildings or other operations (other than the laying of sewers, the construction of pumphouses in a line of sewers, the construction of septic tanks and cesspools serving single dwelling-houses or single buildings in which not more than 10 people will normally reside, work or congregate, and works ancillary thereto) or use of land for the purpose of the retention, treatment of disposal of sewage, trade waste or sludge;
(d) construction of buildings to a height exceeding 20 metres;
(e) construction of buildings or use of land for the purposes of a slaughter-house or knacker's yard; or for killing or plucking poultry;
(f) construction of buildings and use of buildings for any of the following purposes, namely, as a casino, a funfair or a bingo hall, a theatre, a cinema, a music hall, a dance hall, a skating rink, a swimming bath or gymnasium (not forming part of a school, college or university), or a Turkish or other vapour or foam bath;
(g) construction of buildings and use of buildings or land as a zoo or for the business of boarding or breeding cats or dogs;
(h) construction of buildings and use of land for motor car or motor cycle racing;
(i) use of land as a cemetery.

If any person makes a representation concerning any of the foregoing classes of development and the representation is received by the local planning authority before the end of 21 days from the date of the application, then the authority is bound to consider the representation before deciding the application (s.29(2)). A person making such a representation is, however, not entitled to appear before the local planning authority but must content himself with expressing his views in writing.

8. Site Notices

If, under the foregoing provisions of the 1971 Act a site notice needs to be displayed, it is the duty of the applicant for planning permission to post the notice on the site (s.26(2), (3)) unless he is prevented (and certifies accordingly—s.26(2)(*b*)(ii)) from doing so by lack of rights of access to the site or of other rights.

The notice must be posted for not less than seven days during the month immediately preceding the application for planning permission (s.26(3)(*b*)), and must be in the form prescribed (s.26(3)(*a*) and art. 8 and Sched. 3, Pt. III of the General Development Order 1977).[33] The notice must be firmly fixed and displayed so as to be easily visible by the public without going on the site (s.26(4)) and it must state that application for planning permission is to be made (s.26(3)(*a*)) and name a place *within the locality* where a copy of the application and of all plans and other documents will be open to public inspection at reasonable hours during a period of not less than 21 days after the posting of the notice (s.26(6)). It will be noted that it is the applicant's responsibility (and not that of the local planning authority) to make the plans and other documents open for inspection by the public at some place in the locality of the site.

Having done all the foregoing the applicant must sign a certificate (in the prescribed form—s.26(9)) to that effect and send it, with his application for planning permission, to the local planning authority who cannot entertain the application in the absence of the certificate (s.26(2)(*b*)). If an applicant is unable to carry out all the foregoing requirements he must certify accordingly (*ibid.*).

An applicant issuing a false certificate is liable on summary conviction to a fine not exceeding level 3 on the standard scale *i.e.* £400 (s.26(8), Criminal Justice Act 1982 s.37 and the Criminal Penalties (Increase) Order 1984 (S.I. 1984 No. 447)).

An applicant is excused if, without fault or intention of his, a site notice, duly posted, is removed, obscured, or defaced before the requisite seven days have elapsed, *provided* that the applicant has taken reasonable steps for its protection and, if need be, its replacement (s.26(5)).

9. Information about Planning Applications—Access to Information by General Public

Since April 1, 1986 when the Local Government (Access to Information) Act 1985 came into operation (1985 Act s.5) the right of the general public to know what is going on in the world of development and planning control is substantially increased.

The 1985 Act amends the Local Government Act 1972 by writing into that Act (1985 Act s.1) no less than 11 new sections now numbered

[33] S.I. 1977 No. 289.

in the 1972 Act, respectively as sections 100A, 100B, 100C, 100D, 100E, 100F, 100G, 100H, 100I, 100J and 100K together with a new Schedule now numbered, in the 1972 Act, Schedule 12A relating to "exempt information", *i.e.* information *not* to be made public.

These new enactments greatly strengthen the hands of any seeker after planning and development information when he approaches the appropriate local planning authority in his search for knowledge.

He now has access to meetings of the planning authority and to committees and sub-committees of the authority (1972 Act, ss. 100A and 100E); to agendas and connected reports (*ibid.* 100B); to minutes and other documents prepared after the conclusion of meetings (*ibid.* s.100C); to inspection of background papers (*ibid.* s.100D) and the register of additional information to be prepared and maintained by the authority (*ibid.* s.100G).

All the aforementioned documents must be open to inspection at all reasonable hours at the offices of the authority (*ibid.* ss. 100C and 100D usually without payment (*ibid.* s.100H). A member of the public may make copies or extracts from the documents without payment (*ibid.* s.100H(2)) or can require to be supplied with a photographic copy or extract on payment of a reasonable fee (*ibid.* s.100H). No information, however can be demanded in the case of "exempt information" (*ibid.* s.100I and Schedule 12A).

D.O.E. Circular 6/86 gives a detailed explanation of all the forgoing new provisions.

10. Fees for Planning Applications

A fee will be payable (under section 87 of the Local Government, Planning and Land Act 1980 and the Town and Country Planning (Fees for Applications and Deemed Applications) Regulations 1983)[34] to the local planning authority on submitting an application for planning permission for development or for approval of matters reserved in an outline planning permission or for consent to display an advertisement (reg. 3). D.O.E. Circular 25/83 dated November 22, 1983 should be read in association with the Fees Regulations of 1983.

Fees payable for planning applications were first introduced in 1981 by S.I. 1981 No. 369 and were amended in 1982 by S.I. 1982 No. 716. Both these Statutory Instruments are now revoked and replaced by the Fees Regulations of 1983 which came into operation

[34] S.I. 1983 No. 1674.

on December 1, 1983 (reg. 1) and which apply to planning applications made on or after that date (reg. 2).

The object of having fees payable in connection with applications for planning permission was to inhibit frivolous applications and also to recover the costs of the administration needed for operating the development control system.

The Fees Regulations of 1983 remain in force today (February 1987) but the fees as set out in these Regulations have been increased, as from August 26, 1985, by the Town and Country Planning (Fees for Applications and Deemed Applications) (Amendment) Regulations 1985 (S.I. 1985 No. 1182). In this connection the Department of the Environment have issued D.O.E. Circular 19/85 dated August 12, 1985. The Fees Regulations 1983 are now further amended by the Town and Country Planning (Fees for Applications and Deemed Applications) (Amendment) Regulations 1987 (S.I. 1987 No. 101) which came into force on February 25, 1987—see hereon D.O.E. Circular 1/87 dated February 5, 1987.

The 1987 Fee Regulations increase still further the fees payable on making planning applications. They also provide for refund of fee in certain cases; for exemption from fee in respect of certain mineral working permissions and consents to display of advertisements; for multiple applications for approval or reserved matters; for a fee of £30 (£33 if it is due on or after July 1, 1987) on application, under section 31A of the 1971 Act for permission to develop without complying with conditions earlier attached; for land in the area of two or more authorities; and for development in connection with oil or gas exploration.

The fees payable under the 1983 Fees Regulations as amended by the 1985 Fees Amendment Regulations and the 1987 Fees Amendment Regulations 1987 are as set out below.

New Part II of Schedule 1 to the Fees Regulations 1983 Showing Scale of Fees on or after July 1, 1987.

Category of development	Fee payable
1. Operations	
1. The erection of dwelling houses (other than development within category 6 below).	(*a*) Where the application is for outline planning permission, £66 for each 0.1 hectare of the site area, subject to a maximum of £1,650; (*b*) in other cases, £66 for each dwellinghouse to be created by the

1. Operations—continued

Category of development	Fee payable
	development, subject to a maximum of £3,300.
2. The erection of buildings (other than dwellinghouses, buildings coming within category 3, category 4 or category 7 or buildings in the nature of plant or machinery).	(*a*) Where the application is for outline planning permission, £66 for each 0.1 hectare of the site area, subject to a maximum of £1,650; (*b*) in other cases:— (i) Where no floor space is to be created by the development, £33; (ii) where the area of gross floor space to be created by the development does not exceed 40 sq metres, £33; (iii) where the area of gross floor space to be created by the development exceeds 40 sq metres but does not exceed 75 sq metres, £66; and (iv) where the area of gross floor space to be created by the development exceeds 75 sq metres, £66 for each 75 sq metres, subject to a maximum of £3,300.
3. The erection, on land used for the purposes of agriculture, of buildings (other than glasshouses) to be used for agricultural purposes.	(*a*) Where the application is for outline planning permission £66 for each 0.1 hectare of the site area, subject to a maximum of £1,650; (*b*) in other cases:— (i) where the area of gross floor space to be created by the development does not exceed 465 sq metres, nil; (ii) where the area of gross floor space to be created by the development exceeds 465 sq metres but does not exceed 540 sq metres, £66; (iii) where the area of gross floor space to be created by the devel-

1. Operations—continued

Category of development	Fee payable
	opment exceeds 540 sq metres, £66 for the first 540 sq metres and £66 for each 75 sq metres in excess of that figure, subject to a maximum of £3,300.
4. The erection of glasshouses on land used for the purposes of agriculture.	(*a*) Where the area of gross floor space to be created by the development does not exceed 465 sq metres, nil; (*b*) where the area of gross floor space to be created by the development exceeds 465 sq metres, £390.
5. The erection, alteration or replacement of plant or machinery.	£66 for each 0.1 hectrare of the site area, subject to a maximum of £3,300.
6. The enlargement, improvement or other alteration of existing dwellinghouses.	(*a*) Where the application relates to one dwellinghouse, £33; (*b*) where the application relates to 2 or more dwellinghouses, £66.
7. (*a*) The carrying out of operations (including the erection of a building) within the curtilage of an existing dwellinghouse, for purposes ancillary to the enjoyment of the dwellinghouse as such, or the erection or construction of gates, fences, walls or other means of enclosure along a boundary of the curtilage of an existing dwellinghouse; or (*b*) the construction of car parks, service roads and other means of access on land used for the purposes of a single undertaking, where the development is required for a purpose incidental to the existing use of the land.	£33.
8. The carrying out of any operations connected with exploratory drilling for oil or natural gas.	£66 for each 0.1 hectare of site area, subject to a maximum of £4,950.

I. Operations—continued

Category of development	Fee payable
9. The carrying out of any operations not coming within any of the above categories.	£33 for each 0.1 hectare of the site area, subject to a maximum of:— (*a*) in the case of operations for the winning and working of minerals, £4,950; (*b*) in other cases, £330.

II. Uses of Land

Category of development	Fee payable
10. The change of use of a building to use as one or more separated dwellinghouses	(*a*) Where the change is from a previous use as a single dwellinghouse to use as two or more single dwellinghouses, £66 for each additional dwellinghouse to be created by the development, subject to a maximum of £3,300; (*b*) in other cases, £66 for each dwellinghouse to be created by the development, subject to a maximum of £3,300.
11. (*a*) The use of land for the disposal of refuse or waste materials or for the deposit of material remaining after minerals have been extracted from land; or (*b*) the use of land for the storage of minerals in the open.	£33 for each 0.1 hectare of the site area, subject to a maximum of £4,950.
12. The making of a material change in the use of a building or land (other than a material change of use coming within any of the above categories).	£66.
13. The continuance of a use of land, or the retention of buildings or works on land, without compliance with a condition subject to which a previous planning permission has been granted (including a condition requiring the discontinuance of the use or the removal of the building or works at the end of a specified period).	£33.

SCHEDULE 2

SCALE OF FEES IN RESPECT OF APPLICATION FOR CONSENT TO DISPLAY ADVERTISEMENTS

Category of advertisement	*Fee payable*
1. Advertisements displayed on business premises, on the forecourt of business premises or on other land within the curtilage of business premises, wholly with reference to all or any of the following matters:— (*a*) the nature of the business or other activity carried on on the premises; (*b*) the goods sold or the services provided on the premises; or (*c*) the name and qualifications of the person carrying on such business or activity or supplying such goods or services.	£14
2. Advertisements for the purpose of directing members of the public to, or otherwise drawing attention to the existence of, business premises which are in the same locality as the site on which the advertisement is to be displayed but which are not visible from that site.	£14
3. All other advertisements.	£53

Fees in respect of applications are payable to the authority with whom the application is lodged (*i.e.* the district planning authority or, in Greater London, the London borough council or the Common Council of the City of London). Where, however, an application for planning permission or for approval of reserved matters, falls to be dealt with by a different local planning authority, the fee must be remitted to that authority (reg. 3(4)). The fee in respect of an application for consent for the display of an advertisement within a National Park must be remitted (reg. 9) to the county planning authority (who will be the local planning authority determining the application).

No fees are payable in respect of planning appeals unless an appeal against an enforcement notice is treated as an application for planning permission for development (reg. 8(1), (3)).

In all of this matter of fees in connection with planning applications the contents of D.O.E. Circular 25/83 are worthy of close study, particularly paragraphs 2 and 3 (which deal with the scope of the fee system) and paragraphs 4 to 17 (which deal with exemptions—of which there are several—from the need to pay fees at all and with concessions which reduce the full impact of the fee system).

11. Planning Permission in Conservation Areas

Sections 277, 277A and 277B of the 1971 Act are designed to secure the preservation of *areas* (as distinct from *buildings*) of special architectural or historic interest the character or appearance of which it is desirable to preserve. Such areas are called "conservation areas" (s.277(1)).

D.O.E. Circulars 23/77 dated March 16, 1977 and 12/81 dated March 24, 1981 deal, *inter alia*, with government policy and advice on conservation areas and greatly fill out the bare bones of sections 277, 277A and 277B of the 1971 Act.

The functions of a local planning authority in relation to conservation areas acting under section 277 of the 1971 Act, are exercisable since April 1, 1986 (s.277(10)) as amended by the Local Government Act 1985 s.6 and Sched. 2, para. 1(14)):

- (a) in Greater London, by the Historic Buildings and Monuments Commission for England and by the council of a London borough (which includes the Common Council of the City London);
- (b) in a metropolitan county, by the local planning authority;
- (c) in any part of a National Park outside a metropolitan county, by the county planning authority; and
- (d) elsewhere by the district planning authority.

But outside a National Park a county planning authority can also exercise these functions (*ibid.*).

Every local planning authority (s.277(10)) must determine from time to time whether any part of their area is to be designated a conservation area (s.277(1), (2)). Once a conservation area is designated the planning authority must formulate and publish proposals for the preservation and enhancement of the conservation area (s.277B(1)) which proposals must be submitted to a public meeting and the views on the proposals of any person at the meeting must be considered by the authority (s.277B(2)).

The Secretary of State may himself, after consultation with the local planning authority, designate an area of land as a conservation area (s.277(4)).

The local planning authority must notify the Secretary of State of the designation by them of any conservation area and of any variation or cancellation of such designation (s.277(6)). Similarly, the Secretary of State must give notification to the local planning authority of any designation by him (or variation or cancellation of designation) of any area as a conservation area (*ibid.*). If the designated area is in England, the Historic Buildings and Monuments Commission for England must also be notified (s.277(6A)).

Notice of the designation of any area as a conservation area must be publicised in the *London Gazette* and in a local newspaper (s. 277(7)).

The designation of any area as a conservation area is to be a local land charge (s.277(9)).

The Annual Report of the Historic Buildings Council for England for the year 1983/84 discloses that at December 12, 1984 there were "well over 5000" such areas in England. The year 1983–84 marked the final year of the Historic Buildings Council which ceased to exist on April 1, 1984. Its responsibilities were transferred to the new Historic Buildings and Monuments Commission for England (popularly known as "English Heritage") created by the National Heritage Act 1983 whose address is Fortress House, 23 Saville Row, London W1X 2HE.

Grants and loans for the preservation or enhancement of the character or appearance of conservation areas may be made by the Secretary of State or, in the case of a conservation area in England, by the Historic Buildings and Monuments Commission for England, in any case where, in his or the Commission's opinion, expenditure spent on the area has made, or will make, a significant contribution towards preserving or enhancing the character of the area (Town and Country Planning (Amendment) Act 1972, s.10(1), (1A) and (1AA) and D.O.E. Circular 12/81, dated March 24, 1981, paras. 31–39 which are now substituted for paras. 112 to 120 of D.O.E. Circular No. 23/77).

If any area is designated a conservation area the later grant of planning permission for development in the area could be a somewhat delicate matter. Accordingly, when any application for planning permission for development in a conservation area is made, special attention is to be paid by the planning authority to the desirability of preserving or enhancing the character of the conservation area (s.277(8)).

Again, where an application for planning permission relates to development, which would, in the opinion of the local planning authority, affect the character or appearance of a conservation area, or where the development would, in the opinion of the local planning authority, affect the setting of a listed building,[35] the application must be advertised by the planning authority (not by the applicant—contrast s.26) in the local press and additional publicity must be given to any such application through the medium of "site notices" posted on or near the land to which the application relates (s.28(1) and (2)). This will give a further opportunity for representations about the application for planning permission to be made to the local planning authority who must allow time for this to be done (s.28(3)). If any representations are made the local planning authority must take them into account when determining the application (s.29(4)).

[35] See Chap. 14.

A local planning authority, having reached an agreement under section 52 of the 1971 Act—see Chapter 11—involving demolition of existing buildings and development of their site, could not, when they later extended a conservation area so as to include the site, seek to prevent, under section 277A(2) of the 1971 Act, demolition of the buildings without the consent of the authority. "There was nothing in principle to prevent the exercise of a statutory power being limited by a previous exercise of another statutory power"—Fox J.[36] But this decision was reversed on appeal in *Royal Borough of Windsor and Maidenhead* v. *Brandrose Investments Ltd.* (1983) 1 All E.R. 818 in which it was held that, on the true construction of section 52(3) of the 1971 Act, a local planning authority was *not* empowered by that section to bind themselves by an agreement under that section *not* to exercise the powers conferred on them by section 277 of the 1971 Act to designate areas as conservation areas which powers they had a public duty to exercise. Lawton L.J. (at page 823) observed: "Whatever section 52(3) means, and we share the bemusement of counsel for the plaintiffs, it cannot in our judgment be construed as empowering a local planning authority to bind themselves not to exercise the powers given to them by section 277 of the Act."

Further consideration of Conservation Areas appears in Chapter 9.

12. Caravan Site Development

Where development involves the use of land as a caravan site the law has made special provision relating to the obtaining of planning permission for development. These special provisions are dealt with later.[37]

13. By-law Approval for Development

In connection with the need to obtain planning permission under the 1971 Act for all development, a developer must not lose sight of the fact that the code of planning law and the code of public health law still run their separate courses side by side and, accordingly, in addition to whatever planning permission it is necessary to obtain *under planning law* before development is undertaken, it still remains necessary for a developer to obtain, *under public health law* and its

[36] *Royal Borough of Windsor and Maidenhead* v. *Brandrose Investments Ltd.* [1981] J.P.L. 669; reversed, Court of Appeal, (1983) 1 All E.R. 818.

[37] See Chap. 13.

associated building by-laws, the approval of the appropriate by-law authority to the plans of any buildings involved in his proposed development.

14. Method of Handling Applications for Planning Permission

The method of handling applications for planning permission for development is dealt with in the Town and Country Planning General Development Order 1977[38] and in section 29 of the 1971 Act.

Upon receipt of an application for planning permission, (along with all attendant documents including the fee (if any) payable (art. 7(6B) and (6C)) under the Town and Country Planning (Fees for Applications and Deemed Applications) Regulations 1983), the receiving authority must, as soon as may be, send to the applicant an acknowledgment of his application (art. 7(3)) in the terms (or substantially in the terms) set out in Part I of Schedule 2 to the General Development Order 1977.

If the application for planning permission falls to be dealt with by the county planning authority, the district planning authority must send it on to the county planning authority and notify the applicant accordingly (art. 7(4)).

If the application for planning permission is regarded as invalid the applicant must be notified accordingly as soon as may be (art. 7(5)).

Where an application for planning permission consists of a number of separate and divisible elements, it is lawful for the planning authority to deal with them separately, granting planning permission for so much of the development as they think should be permitted.[39]

The period during which a local planning authority must give notice of its decision on a valid application for planning permission will be *eight weeks* from the receipt in due form of the application (art. 7(6) and (6A)) but this period may be extended by agreement in writing between the parties (*ibid.*). The requirement as to this period is directory and not mandatory and a notice of decision given after the expiration of the statutory period is not ineffective if accepted and acted upon by the applicant.[40]

Where application is made to a local planning authority for any consent, agreement or approval required by a condition in a planning

[38] S.I. 1977 No. 289.

[39] *Kent C.C.* v. *Secretary of State for the Environment* (1976) 241 E.G. 83; [1976] J.P.L. 755.

[40] *James* v. *Secretary of State for Wales* [1968] A.C. 409, H.L.

permission (*other* than an application for approval of reserved matters) the authority must give notice of their decision within *eight weeks* from the date of the receipt of the application by the authority (art. 7A).

If the applicant does not hear from the local planning authority within the appropriate period, then he has a right to appeal to the Secretary of State "as if" his application had in fact been refused (s.37).

In dealing with an application for planning permission for development a local planning authority *must* have regard to the provisions of the relevant development plan (so far as material to the application s.29(1)) but are not confined solely to the plan because it is further provided that the authority *must* also have regard to "any other material considerations" (*ibid.*).

In *South Oxfordshire D.C.* v. *Secretary of State for the Environment* (1981) 1 W.L.R. 1092 it was held that a previous grant of planning permission is capable of being a material consideration even if it has expired. But a local planning authority can undergo a change of heart and if they do, they may change their mind (*R.* v. *Yeovil Borough Council, ex parte Trustees of Elim Pentecostal Church* 23 P. & C.R. 39; *R.* v. *West Oxfordshire D.C., ex parte Pearce Homes Ltd.* (1986) J.P.L. 523).

The statutory requirement to "have regard to" the provisions of the development plan does not mean that the local planning authority must slavishly adhere to the plan. It requires the authority to consider the development plan but it does not oblige them necessarily to follow it.[41]

A local planning authority are authorised by the General Development Order 1977 (art. 14), and subject to the directions of the Secretary of State, to ignore, in such cases and subject to such conditions as may be prescribed by the directions aforesaid, the provisions of their development plan and grant permission for development which is contrary thereto (s.31(1)(*b*)); General Development Order 1977, art. 14).

If, however, the local planning authority *are* minded to grant planning permission which is a departure from the development plan, the authority must give attention to the procedures given in the

[41] See comment by Lord Guest in *Simpson* v. *Edinburgh Corporation* [1960] S.C. 313; *Enfield London Borough Council* v. *Secretary of State for the Environment* (1974) 233 E.G. 53; *Niarchos (London) Limited* v. *Secretary of State for the Environment and Westminister (City) London Borough Council* (1977) 76 L.G.R. 480; *Ynystaw Ynyforgan and Glais Gypsy Site Action Group* v. *Secretary of State for Wales and West Glamorgan County Council* (1981) J.P.L. 874 and (1984) J.P.L. 265. See also *Ynys Mon Isle of Anglesey Borough Council* v. *Secretary of State for Wales and Parry Bros. (Builders) Co. Ltd.* (1984) J.P.L. 646. See also page 199, *post*.

Town and Country Planning (Development Plans) (England) Direction 1981 referred to in paragraphs 9 to 19 inclusive of, and set out in Appendix D to, D.O.E. Circular 2/81, dated January 9, 1981, and made by the Secretary of State under articles 7, 10 and 14 of the Town and Country Planning General Development Order 1977. There is a separate Direction for Wales. The 1981 (England) Direction does not apply to Greater London (para. 1) which is dealt with in the Town and Country Planning (Development Plans) (Greater London) Direction 1986.

In *R.* v. *St Edmundsbury Borough Council, ex parte Investors in Industry Commercial Properties Ltd.* (1985) 3 All E.R. 234; (1985) J.P.L. 595 and (1986) J.P.L. 38, it was held that failure to comply with the (England) Direction 1981 was not fatal to the grant of planning permission for development which departed from the terms of the development plan because the Direction was to be regarded as directory and procedural but not mandatory. A similar decision was given in *R.* v. *Carlisle City Council and the Secretary of State for the Environment, ex parte Cumbrian Co-operative Society Ltd.* (1986) J.P.L. 206.

Under the head of "other material considerations" it has been held that it is lawful for the planning authority to take into consideration the desirability of whether an existing authorised use should continue (though there can be no certainty that it will) rather than that a new use for which planning permission is sought should be instituted.[42]

This matter of a local planning authority being required (s.29(1)), when deciding how to deal with an application for planning permission for development, to have regard (a) to the provisions of the development plan and (b) to any other material considerations, is the subject of incisive comment by the Secretary of State in paragraph 5 of D.O.E. Circular 14/85 dated July 16, 1985 which is set out in Annex 2 to the White Paper of July 1985 (Cmnd. 9571) entitled, "Lifting the Burden." The provisions of paragraph 5, which disclose current Government thinking in this important sphere of planning control of land development, are in the following terms.

> "5. In dealing with applications for planning permission, Section 29(1) of the Town and Country Planning Act 1971 requires that the authority *shall have regard to the provisions of the development plan, so far as material to the application, and to any other material considerations*. Development plans are therefore one, but only one, of the material considerations that must be taken into account

[42] *Clyde and Co.* v. *Secretary of State for the Environment* [1977] 1 W.L.R. 926.

in dealing with planning applications. Many development plans were approved or adopted several years ago, often several years after they had been prepared and based on even earlier information. The policies which they contain, and the assumptions on which they were based, may therefore be out of date and not well related to today's conditions. They cannot be adapted rapidly to changing conditions, and they cannot be expected to anticipate every need or opportunity for economic development that may arise. They should not be regarded as overriding other material considerations, especially where the plan does not deal adequately with new types of development or is no longer relevant to today's needs and conditions—particularly the need to encourage employment and to provide the right conditions for economic growth."[42a]

D.O.E. Circular 14/85 is more fully quoted at page 208, *post*.

Whatever it is that a local planning authority allow to influence their decision when considering a planning application, they are "not to discriminate" against any person. This is a new statutory injunction to be found in the Race Relations Act 1976, section 19A—inserted into the 1976 Act by the Housing and Planning Act 1986, section 55. D.O.E. Circular 19/86 dated December 17, 1986, Annex paragraph 22, refers to this matter.

The General Development Order 1977 contains further provisions relating to:

(1) the giving of directions by the Secretary of State restricting the right of a local planning authority to grant planning permission (art. 10);
(2) planning permission for development affecting certain highways (existing or proposed) (art. 11);
(3) directions which may be issued by a local highway authority restricting the grant of planning permission (art. 12);
(4) the application of by-laws in relation to the construction of new streets (art. 13);
(5) development *not* in accordance with the development plan (art. 14);
(6) the holding of consultations with specified bodies before planning permission is granted (art. 15 and art. 15A);
(7) planning applications in respect of "county matters" (art. 16);
(8) notice to parish and community councils (art. 17);
(9) notice about applications referred to the Secretary of State (art. 19);

[42a] See now *Surrey Health Borough Council* v. *Secretary of State for the Environment* (*The Times*, November 3, 1986).

(10) appeals to the Secretary of State in respect of planning decisions by a local planning authority (art. 20);
(11) the register of applications (art. 21); and
(12) established use certificates (art. 22).

How does a local planning authority "consult" other bodies? It is provided that where a local planning authority is required to consult with a specified body under the foregoing provisions, the body to be consulted must be given 14 days' notice that the planning application is to be considered (art. 15(5)). During that time the body consulted can make representations and these must be taken into account when the local planning authority is determining the application (*ibid.*). Thus consultation is not something which needs to go on for ever.

When a district planning authority are prohibited (Local Government Act 1972, Sched. 16, para. 19(5)(*b*)) from determining, for a prescribed period, any planning application on which they are required (*ibid.* para. 19(1)(2)) to consult the county planning authority, the prescribed period has been fixed at 28 days from the date of the notice of the application given to the county planning authority, or such longer period as may be agreed in writing by the district planning authority (General Development Order 1977, art. 15A).

Notice must be given by the district planning authority of the receipt of any application for planning permission of which a parish council or a community council are entitled to be informed (Local Government Act 1972, s.182 and Sched. 16) and there is then a period of 14 days during which the parish or community council can make representations about the application (art. 17). Any representations so made must be taken into account by the local planning authority which is responsible for determining the application (*ibid.*).

A parish or community council are *entitled* to be informed about any application for planning permission which relates to land in the parish or community, and of every application for the approval of "reserved matters" associated with an outline planning permission earlier granted in respect of land in the parish or community, *provided that* the parish or community council have notified the district planning authority accordingly and in writing (Local Government Act 1972, Sched. 16, para. 20 and G.D.O. 1977, art. 17).

The manner in which local planning authorities handle applications for planning permission has been made the subject of a formal Code of Practice which came into operation on April 1, 1984 and which appears as Annex A to D.O.E. Circular 28/83 dated December 29, 1983. The Code deals with the publication of information by local planning authorities about their handling of planning applications and has been prepared and issued by the Secretary of State for the Environment under powers conferred on him by the Local Government Planning and Land Act 1980 section 2.

The object of publishing information under the Code is:

(1) to give wider publicity to the time taken by local planning authorities in handling planning applications; and

(2) to help elected members, especially the chairman of committees and sub-committees which deal with planning applications, to ensure that there are effective management arrangements within their authorities for avoiding unnecessary delay.

The Code has been agreed by the Secretary of State with the local authority associations.

15. Decision of the Local Planning Authority

The planning decision of the local planning authority may be one of three kinds. The authority may:

(a) grant permission unconditionally; or

(b) grant permission subject to such conditions "as they think fit"; or

(c) refuse permission (s.29(1)).

In giving a decision granting planning permission, the local planning authority must, in the case of certain types of development, draw the attention of the applicant to his duties, under legislation relating to disabled persons, to cater for the needs of such persons (1971 Act, ss.29A and 29B—as slightly amended by the Housing and Planning Act 1986, section 49(1)(*c*) and Schedule 11, Part I, paragragh 3—inserted by the Disabled Persons Act 1981, s.3).

The decision of the local planning authority must be in "writing" (G.D.O. 1977, art. 7(7)), which expression, by virtue of section 5 of, and Schedule 1 to, the Interpretation Act 1978, includes printing, lithography, photography, and other modes of representing words in visible form.

It has been held that this written notice to an applicant of the grant of planning permission (and not the resolution of the planning committee) is the planning permission.[43] D.O.E. Circular 28/83

[43] *Cooperative Retail Services Ltd.* v. *Taff-Ely Borough Council* (1978) 38 P. & C.R. 156; (1979) 39 P. & C.R. 223, C.A. On appeal the Court of Appeal held that the notice purporting to grant planning permission had, in this case, been issued by the clerk of the council without authority and was, on that account, a nullity (1979) 39 P. & C.R. 223, C.A. The House of Lords confirmed the decision of the Court of Appeal—*The Times,* February 7, 1981. See also *R.* v. *West Oxfordshire D.C., ex parte Pearce Homes Ltd.* (1986) J.P.L. 523. See further, article at [1975] J.P.L. 184 by Desmond Heap and Rodney Davis.

dated December 29, 1983 has a comment on what constitutes the date of a grant of planning permission. Paragraph 15 of the Circular declares:

> "15. A number of authorities take the determination date as that when the committee decides an application rather than when a decision is issue. To ensure consistency in the preparation of statistics on the time taken to determine planning applications, local planning authorities seemed to be the date of determination as the date when notice of the decision is issued to the applicant."

The date of a planning decision is important because (to mention one reason only) the period of six months during which an appeal against the decision can be made to the Secretary of State for the Environment (see *post* at pages 219 *et seq.*) begins to run from that date.

There is no call for a local planning authority to hold up a planning decision merely because the relevant local plan is not, as yet, in operation although the holding of the public inquiry into the plan is imminent.[44]

If conditions are attached to the grant of permission, or if there is a refusal of permission, the reasons therefore must be given in writing, together with a notification set out in the terms of Part II of Schedule 2 to the General Development Order 1977 (art. 7(7)).

A permission for the erection of a building may specify the purposes for which the building shall be used and, if it does not, the building may be used for the purposes for which it was designed (s.33(2)).

A grant of planning permission for development may also cover permission for the *retention* of buildings or works already constructed before the application for permission is made and for the *continuance* of any use of land instituted before that day (s.32).

If an application is made for planning permission for one kind of development, as specified (as it must be) in the application, the question arises as to whether planning permission can rightly be granted for some other kind of development or must the grant be, at all times, for development the same as, or substantially the same as, that for which planning permission is applied? In *Bernard Wheatcroft Ltd.* v. *Secretary of State for the Environment* (1980) 257 E.G. 934, the application was for permission to develop 35 acres of land with 420 houses. In the event planning permission was granted, on appeal to the Queen's Bench Division (and after the Secretary of State had

[44] *Allen* v. *Corporation of London and Another* [1981] J.P.L. 685.

declared himself powerless to agree), to develop 25 acres with 250 houses, the court holding that it was permissible to grant planning permission subject to a condition which merely reduced the development to be carried out *provided* such reduced development did not differ substantially from the development proposed in the original application to the local planning authority.

Is it in order for a local planning authority (or, indeed, the Secretary of State on an appeal to him) to consider the possibility of a recognised and accepted need for development as proposed in the planning application (*e.g.* hotel development) to be met *not* on the site proposed in the application but elsewhere on some alternative site? It was held, in *Trusthouse Forte Hotels Ltd.* v. *The Secretary of State for the Environment and Northavon District Council* (1986) J.P.L. 834 that it *was* in order for this to be done and to be done even though the alternative site was unspecified. On this particular point—the matter of the alternative site—reference may further be made to the decision of the Court of Appeal in *Greater London Council* v. *Secretary of State for the Environment and London Docklands Development Corporation and Cablecross Projects Ltd.* (1986) J.P.L. 193.

A register of all applications for planning permission and of the local planning authority's decisions is to be kept and to be open for public inspection (s.34 and G.D.O. 1977, art. 21). The register of planning applications must contain copies of the application and any plans or drawings submitted with them (s.34(2)).

Any person interested in buying land may ascertain what planning permission or permissions (if any) have been granted in respect of the land by searching the planning register. Any such search will be additional to the usual conveyancing searches made in registers of local land charges kept under the Land Charges Act 1925.

16. Development Control—Policy and Practice—the Political Stance

For the general guidance of local planning authorities dealing with applications for planning permission D.O.E. Circular 22/80 dated November 28, 1980, entitled "Development Control—Policy and Practice," contains some "straight talking." The Circular contains much that any applicant for planning permission should undoubtedly know about. It includes the following important comments:

> "1. The planning system balances the protection of the natural and the built environment with the pressures of economic and social change. The need for the planning system is unquestioned and its workings have brought great and lasting benefits.

In each of the countless decisions many compromises are struck.

"2. But the system has a price, and when it works slowly or badly, the price can be very high and out of all proportion to the benefits. Many cases could be dealt with more quickly than they are at present. The evidence from the statistical monitoring of the development control system and from case histories suggests that there is room for substantial improvements in efficiency in handling cases in both central and local government. . . . This circular is concerned with planning applications. It has two aims—the first is to secure a general speeding up of the system. The second is to ensure that development is only prevented or restricted when this serves a clear planning purpose and the economic effects have been taken into account. This does not mean a lowering of the quality of decision but it does mean a greater awareness of the economic costs of planning control.

"Efficiency and Speed in Decisions

'3. The planning system should play a helpful part in rebuilding the economy. Development control must avoid placing unjustified obstacles in the way of any development especially if it is for industry, commerce, housing or any other purpose relevant to the economic regeneration of the country. It is, and should be seen to be, part of the process of making things happen in the right place at the right time. Local planning authorities are asked therefore to pay greater regard to time and efficiency; to adopt a more positive attitude to planning applications; to facilitate development; and always to grant planning permission, having regard to all material considerations, unless there are sound and clear-cut reasons for refusal.[44a] . . .

"4. The Government's concern for positive attitudes and efficiency in development control does not mean that their commitment to conservation is in any way weakened: in particular, they remain committed to the need to conserve and improve the countryside, natural habitats and areas of architectural, natural, historical or scientific interest and listed buildings. There is no change in the policies on national parks, areas of outstanding natural beauty or conservation areas. The Government continue to attach great importance to the use of green belts to

[44a] *E.C. Gransden and Co. Ltd. and Falkbridge Ltd.* v. *Secretary of State for the Environment and Gillingham B.C.* (1986) J.P.L. 519. See *ante*, p. 200, n. 42[a].

contain the sprawl of built-up areas and to safeguard the neighbouring countryside from encroachment and there must continue to be a general presumption against any inappropriate development within them. Nor will the Government allow more than the essential minimum of agricultural land to be diverted to development, nor land of a higher agricultural quality to be taken where land of a lower quality could reasonably be used instead.

"5. Promptness, relevance and efficiency are characteristics of good planning. The benefits to the economy and to the individual from the businesslike handling of planning applications are very substantial. The vitality of the economy depends on new development. The magnitude of the investment at risk from delay is very large: the annual value of development passing through the planning system is of the order of £8 billion in England and Wales. Unnecessary delays in the development control system can result in wasted capital, delayed production, postponed employment, income, rates and taxes, and lower profitability. They can create a poor climate for future investment. Local planning authorities have a clear responsibility to minimise delay in determining planning applications. The elected members, especially the chairman of the planning committee, have a vital role to play in the system. It is their responsibility to see that the management arrangements within their authority for minimising delay are effective. The chairman of the planning committee should be satisfied that the reporting system brings cases of delay regularly and promptly to his attention. All cases where a decision is not taken within 8 weeks should be brought to the attention of elected members.

* * * * * *

"Aesthetic Control

18. The Secretary of State for the Environment's view on control of design was set out in his speech at York on 13 September 1979 to the Town and Country Planning Summer School of the Royal Town Planning Institute. He said:

> 'Far too many of those involved in the system—whether the planning officer or the amateur on the planning committee—have tried to impose their standards quite unnecessarily on what individuals want to do . . . Democracy as a system of government I will defend against all comers but as an arbiter of taste or as a judge of aesthetic or artistic

standards it falls far short of a far less controlled system of individual, corporate or institutional patronage and initiative . . . '

This view is endorsed by the Secretary of State for Wales.

"19. Planning authorities should recognise that aesthetics is an extremely subjective matter. They should not therefore impose their tastes on developers simply because they believe them to be superior. Developers should not be compelled to conform to the fashion of the moment at the expense of individuality, originality or traditional styles. Nor should they be asked to adopt designs which are unpopular with their customers or clients.

"20. Nevertheless control of external appearance can be important especially for instance in environmentally sensitive areas such as national parks, areas of outstanding natural beauty, conservation areas and areas where the quality of environment is of a particularly high standard. Local planning authorities should reject obviously poor designs which are out of scale or character with their surroundings. They should confine concern to those aspects of design which are significant for the aesthetic quality of the area. Only exceptionally should they control design details if the sensitive character of the area or the particular building justifies it. Even where such detailed control is exercised it should not be over-fastidious in such matters as, for example, the precise shade of colour of bricks. They should be closely guided in such matters by their professionally qualified advisers. This is especially important where a building has been designed by an architect for a particular site. Design guides may have a useful role to play provided they are used as guidance and not as detailed rules.

"21. Control of external appearance should only be exercised where there is a fully justified reason for doing so. If local planning authorities take proper account of this policy there should be fewer instances of protracted negotiations over the design of projects and a reduction in the number of appeals to the Secretaries of State on matters of design. When such appeals are made the Secretaries of State will be very much guided by the policy advice set out in this circular in determining them."

So much, then, for the "straight talking" of the Secretary of State in D.O.E. Circular 22/80 of November 28, 1980. It will be noted that in paragraph 2 and also in paragraph 3 of the Circular, Government Policy takes the stance that, when an application for planning permission for development is made to a local planning authority, *prima facie* it should be granted "unless there are sound and clear-cut reasons for refusal" (para. 3)

The Secretary of State takes up this theme once again (and five years later on) with, if anything, increasing force in D.O.E. Circular 14/85 dated July 16, 1985 in which the following comments appear.

"*Development and Employment*

1. The White Paper on *Lifting the Burden* (Cmnd. 9571) sets out the Government's overall approach to reducing controls and regulations in the interest of promoting enterprise. Chapter 3 explains the action that the Government is taking to simplify the planning system and improve it efficiency, and relates this to the broader context. This circular (which is reproduced as an annex to the White Paper) deals with policy on development control under the Town and Country Planning Acts.

"2. New development contributes to economic activity and to the provision of jobs. It is in the national interest to promote and encourage it. The planning system must respond positively and promptly to proposals for development. Delay adds to the costs of development.

"3. Development proposals are not always acceptable. There are other important objectives to which the Government is firmly committed: the need to preserve our heritage, to improve the quality of the environment, to protect the green belts and conserve good agricultural land. The planning system, however, fails in its function whenever it prevents, inhibits or delays development which could reasonably have been permitted. *There is therefore always a presumption in favour of allowing applications for development, having regard to all material considerations, unless that development would cause demonstrable harm to interests of acknowledged importance.*[44b]

"4. Authorities are obliged, under Article 7 of the Town and Country Planning General Development Order 1977, to give reasons whenever they refuse planning permission. Those reasons must be precise, specific and relevant to the application: they must demonstrate clearly why, in the local planning authority's view, the proposed development cannot be permitted. Without such a clear demonstration the developer will not know whether or not his proposal can be made acceptable, or the grounds on which he can base an appeal against refusal. As a result, valuable investment and new jobs, in construction, in commerce and in industry, may be delayed or lost.

[44b] See hereon *ante*, n. 42a at p. 200 and n. 44a at p. 205.

"5. In dealing with applications for planning permission, section 29(1) of the Town and Country Planning Act 1971 requires that the authority *shall have regard to the provisions of the development plan, so far as material to the application, and to any other material considerations*. Development plans are therefore one, but only one, of the material considerations that must be taken into account in dealing with planning applications. Many development plans were approved or adopted several years ago, often several years after they had been prepared and based on even earlier information. The policies which they contain, and the assumptions on which they were based, may therefore be out of date and not well related to today's conditions. They cannot be adapted rapidly to changing conditions, and they cannot be expected to anticipate every need or opportunity for economic development that may arise. They should not be regarded as overriding other material considerations, especially where the plan does not deal adequately with new types of development or is no longer relevant to today's needs and conditions—particularly the need to encourage employment and to provide the right conditions for economic growth.

"6. It is important that local planning authorities should have regard to the special needs of small firms and the self-employed. The planning system can present serious difficulties for those seeking to set up or expand their business, even on a very modest scale. Local authorities can do much to help both in assisting small firms to cope with the planning process and by avoiding unnecessarily onerous and complex controls. The Department of the Environment and the Welsh Office in consultation with the Local Authority Associations, will be issuing a further circular on this subject, together with an explanatory booklet for small firms.

"7. The Secretaries of State and their Inspectors will have regard to the terms of this circular in dealing with planning appeals and with any application that may be made to them for the award of costs."

The Secretary of State takes up again the specific matter of "aesthetic control" in D.O.E. Circular 31/85 dated December 10, 1985 in which he reminds local authorities of the advice given in D.O.E. Circular 22/80 (quoted *ante*, at page 206) and goes on to say:

"A large proportion of planning appeals involve detailed design matters, either as the principal grounds in which planning permission has been refused or as a subsidiary reason. Likewise far too many planning applications are delayed because the planning authority seek to impose detailed design alterations."

He then reiterates the advice he gave in paragraphs 19, 20 and 21 of Circular 22/80 to which reference may be made at page 207; *ante*.

Attention is also drawn to the White Paper, "Lifting the Burden" (Cmnd. 9571) dated July 1985 Chapter 3 of which, entitled "Planning and Enterprise," contains some pointed observations about Government policy relating to planning control and land development. Paragraphs 3.4 and 3.5 may be quoted. They read as follows.

> "3.4 It is an established principle of planning law that the developer is entitled to his permission unless there are sound relevant and clear-cut reasons for refusal: that is to say, permission is not to be refused for arbitrary or irrelevant reasons. Nor is the developer required to prove the case for the development he proposes to carry out; if the planning authority consider it necessary to refuse permission, the onus is on them to demonstrate clearly why the development cannot be permitted and the reasons must be precise, specific and relevant to the application.
>
> "3.5 There is therefore always a presumption in favour of development, unless that development would cause demonstrable harm to interests of acknowledged importance. These principles were clearly stated in a circular issued by the then Ministry of Town and Country Planning in 1949 and restated in a further circular in 1953 and amplified in Department of the Environment Circular 22/80 (Welsh Office Circular 40/80) "Development Control: Policy and Practice." The Secretaries of State for Environment and Wales are issuing a new circular reaffirming these principles. It is reproduced in Annex 2 to this White Paper."

The foregoing extensive quotations from D.O.E. Circulars 22/80, 14/85 and 31/85 respectively and from the White Paper "Lifting the Burden," have been deliberately included in these pages because of their crucial importance to (a) an applicant for planning permission, and (b) an appellant to the Secretary of State against the planning decision which he receives in response to his application. The "sting" in paragraph 7 of the Circular 14/85 is specially to be noted. Clearly the Government means business!

17. Planning Decisions by Officers of Local Authorities Acting Under Delegation

Section 101 of the Local Government Act 1972 enables a local planning authority to delegate planning functions to *an officer* of the authority if they wish to do so. The authority have a discretion whether to delegate or not. If they do delegate planning functions to an officer this will not prevent the authority from exercising such functions themselves (Local Government Act 1972), s.101(4)) provided, of course, the officer has not already formally acted on their behalf under his delegated powers

It is important to note that delegation to one of their officers by a local planning authority acting under section 101 of the Local Government Act 1972, is quite a different thing from a local planning authority (acting under their own standing orders) delegating to the Chairman of their planning committee the right to issue enforcement notices—see Chapter 15. Where this was done it was held that the enforcement notice was void. Delegation to a single individual, *other than an officer*, was not a delegation in accordance with section 101(1) of the Local Government Act 1972 to a committee or a sub-committee. There is no concept in law supporting the idea that there can be a committee of one. Thus the action of the Chairman was *ultra vires* and the council's standing orders, in so far as they authorised the Chairman to act, were also *ultra vires* (*R.* v. *Secretary of State for the Environment, ex parte Hillingdon London Borough Council* (1985) (1986) 1 W.L.R. 192); (1986) J.P.L. 363.

18. Duration of Planning Permissions

The Town and Country Planning Act 1971 provides that, without prejudice to any revocation or modification, a planning permission to develop land, once granted, will enure for the benefit of the land and of any person for the time being having an interest in the land unless the permission itself otherwise provides (s.33(1)). There may thus be more than one permission in existence in respect of the same piece of land.

But a planning permission, the implementation of which is not begun, whilst it may enure for the benefit of a series of different people in succession, will not itself enure for ever. It can be revoked or modified in certain circumstances by the local planning authority (see page 240) but whether it is or not, its duration is limited by the 1971 Act. The duration of a planning permission is controlled by sections 41 to 44 inclusive of the 1971 Act together with paragraphs 18 to 22 inclusive of Schedule 24 to the Act.

In considering time limits for planning permission a distinction has to be made between those permissions granted before April 1, 1969, and those granted on or after that date. April 1, 1969, is the date when the provisions of the Town and Country Planning Act 1968 (which first introduced statutory time limits for planning permissions) came into operation.

(1) *Time limits for planning permissions granted before April 1, 1969*

Any planning permission granted *before* April 1, 1969, is deemed to have been granted (if the development to which it relates had not been begun *before* the beginning of 1968) subject to a condition that the development must be begun within five years, that is to say, before April 1, 1974 (Sched. 24, para. 19). This condition will not, however, apply to any planning permission which was granted, or was deemed to be granted, before April 1, 1969, subject to an express condition that the development to which it relates should be begun, or be completed, not later than a specified date or within a specified period (Sched. 24, para. 19(2)(*a*)).

In calculating the period of five years referred to in the abovementioned condition, no account is to be taken of any period, after April 1, 1969, during which any planning permission to which the condition relates is deemed to be of no effect by reason of paragraph 1(4)(*a*) of Schedule 12 to the 1971 Act relating to office development in the metropolitan region (Sched. 24, para. 20A).

Thus if a planning permission is a permission granted *before* April 1, 1969, then, if development pursuant to that planning permission was begun *before* January 1, 1968, the planning permission does *not* come within the ambit of the 1971 Act at all. If this is the case, then the planning permission does not come within the ambit of section 44 of the Act either and it follows, therefore, that the development to which the permission relates can *never* be made the subject of a "completion notice" (as to which, see page 215 *post*) under section 44 of the Act.

(2) *Time limits for planning permissions granted on or after April 1, 1969*

For any planning permission granted *on or after* April 1, 1969, the limitation was formerly dealt with in section 65 of the Town and Country Planning Act 1968, now re-enacted in section 41 of the 1971 Act, under which the limitation is again five years from the grant, or the deemed grant, of planning permission (s.41(1)(*a*)). The development must be begun within this period of five years (s.41(2)). But the five-year period may be varied up or down if circumstances so warrant (s.41(1)(*b*)) and it will be for "the authority concerned with the terms of the planning permission" to bring about any variation in the basic five-year period (*ibid.*), this authority being specifically defined in section 43(4) of the 1971 Act.

It is to be noted that the foregoing provisions relating to the limited duration of planning permissions (whether granted before, on or after, April 1, 1969) do *not* apply (s.41(3)) in the following six cases:

(1) to any planning permission granted by a development order;
(2) to any planning permission granted by an enterprise zone scheme (as to which see page 454);
(3) to any planning permission granted for a limited period (within the meaning of section 30(2) of the 1971 Act);
(4) to certain planning permissions relating to minerals;
(5) to any planning permission granted under section 32 of the 1971 Act on an application relating to buildings or works completed, or a use of land instituted, before the date of the application; and
(6) to any outline planning permission (as to which, see s.42 of the 1971 Act).

Any conditions relating to time limits imposed on a grant of planning permission may be the subject of an appeal to the Secretary of State under section 36 of the 1971 Act against the decision of the local planning authority (s.43(6)).

If a time limit runs out before that which was required to be done within the limit has actually been carried out, then anything done thereafter is declared to be unauthorised or otherwise out of order (s.43(7)).

(3) *Time limits for outline planning permissions granted* *__before__* *April 1, 1969*

Time limits applicable to outline planning permissions (as defined in s.42(1) of the 1971 Act) are dealt with separately from those refered to above.

If an outline planning permission for building or other operations has been granted *before* April 1, 1969, but the development to which it refers has not been begun *before* the beginning of 1968, then:

(a) application for approval of any matter reserved by the permission for later approval must be made within three years of April 1, 1969, and
(b) the development itself must be begun within five years of April 1, 1969, or within two years of "the final approval" of any reserved matter, whichever of these two periods is the longer (Sched. 24, para. 20(1)).

Such a matter may be said to have been fully approved when either the application for approval is granted by the local planning authority or, in the case of an appeal, when it is granted by the Secretary of State (s.43(5) and Sched. 24, para. 21).

It is to be noted that none of the foregoing provisions applying time limits to an outline planning permission granted *before* April 1, 1969, is to apply if the planning permission is granted subject to an express condition that the development to which it relates is to be begun or completed by a specified date, or that application for approval of any reserved matter is to be made by a specified date (Sched. 24, para. 20(2)).

In calculating the periods (referred to above) of three years, five years or two years respectively, no account is to be taken of any period, after April 1, 1969, during which any planning permission to which any one of the said periods relates is deemed to be of no effect by reason of paragraph 1(4)(*a*) of Schedule 12 to the 1971 Act relating to office development in the metropolitan region (Sched. 24, para. 20A).

(4) *Time limits for outline planning permissions granted on or after April 1, 1969*

As to an outline planning permission granted *on or after* April 1, 1969, the permission is to be granted (and will be deemed to be granted in a case where the planning authority fails to carry out this requirement (s.42(3)) subject to conditions which apply time limits of three years, five years and two years respectively (as mentioned above) (s.42(2)) so, however, that "the authority concerned with the terms of the planning permission" (as to which, see s.43(4)) may vary these time limits (making them shorter or longer) as they consider appropriate (s.42(4)). Before varying these time limits the authority must have regard to the provisions of the development plan and to any other material considerations (s.42(6)).

Any conditions relating to time limits required by section 42 of the 1971 Act to be imposed in connection with a grant of outline planning permission, or the later approval thereunder of any reserved matter, may be the subject of an appeal to the Secretary of State under section 36 of the 1971 Act against the decision of the local planning authority (s.43(6)).

Again, if a time limit included in a grant of outline planning permission runs out before that which was required to be done within the limit has actually been carried out, then anything done thereafter is declared to be unauthorised or otherwise out of order (s.43(7)).

(5) *No compensation for time limits*

Compensation is not claimable in respect of a time-limiting condition (s.147(3)) and any such condition may also be ignored for certain other purposes relating to compensation and the right to serve a purchase notice (ss.169(7), 180(4) and 237(5)).

(6) *When is development said to be begun?*

In connection with the foregoing time limits reference is frequently made to the beginning of development. When is a project of development to be regarded as having been begun? This is an important question and the answer is that a project of development must be regarded as having been begun on the earliest date on which a "specified operation" is begun to be carried out (s.43(1)).[45]

A specified operation means (s.43(2)):

(a) any work of construction in the course of the erection of a building;
(b) the digging of a trench which is to contain the foundations, or part of the foundations, of a building[46];
(c) the laying of any underground main or pipe to the foundations, or part of the foundations, of a building or to any such trench as is mentioned in the last preceding paragraph;
(d) any operation in the course of laying out or constructing a road or part of a road as, for example, marking out the line and width of a proposed estate road with pegs (*Malvern Hills District Council* v. *Secretary of State and Robert Barnes & Co. Ltd.* (1982) J.P.L. 439);
(e) any change in the use of any land, where that change constitutes "material development" (as defined in s.43(3) of the 1971 Act).

(7) *Termination of planning permissions—completion notices*

If there are time limits for the *beginning* of development, there are also to be time limits for its *completion.*

The 1971 Act provides for the termination of planning permission by reference to a time limit (s.44). Local planning authorities are empowered to serve a "completion notice" terminating a planning permission if the development has been begun, but has not been completed, before the expiration of the time limit contained in the permission and it appears unlikely to the local planning authority that it will be completed within a reasonable period thereafter (s.44(2)).

The completion notice must be served on the owner and occupier

[45] *United Refineries Ltd.* v. *Essex C.C.* (1976) 241 E.G. 389; [1978] J.P.L. 110.

[46] The digging of a trench must be related to the development covered by the planning permission which it is sought to implement—see *South Oxfordshire D.C.* v. *Secretary of State for the Environment and Faherty Bros. Ltd.* [1981] J.P.L. 359. As to whether digging a trench, later back-filled with the excavated soil, is a "specified operation", see *High Peak Borough Council* v. *Secretary of State for the Environment and Courtdale Developments Ltd.* [1981] J.P.L. 366.

of the land affected and also upon any other person likely, in the opinion of the local planning authority, to be affected by the notice (s.44(3)(*a*)).

The completion notice will state that the planning permission will cease to have effect on such date as may be specified in the notice and this date must not be earlier than 12 months from the date of the notice (s.44(2)). If and when the notice ultimately takes effect the planning permission referred to in it will cease to have effect except so far as it authorises development carried out up to and including any such date (s.44(5)).

The completion notice will not take effect until confirmed by the Secretary of State who may substitute a longer period for completion than the period stated in the notice (s.44(3)(*b*)).

Any person served with a completion notice may require to be heard by an Inspector (appointed by the Secretary of State) before the Secretary of State confirms the notice (s.44(4)). This requirement may be made within 28 days of receiving the notice or within such longer period as the notice may state (*ibid.*).

Having served a completion notice a local planning authority may change their mind, in which case they are entitled to withdraw the completion notice. This can be done at any time before the date on which the notice declares that the planning permission to which it refers is to cease to have effect (s.44(6)).

(8) *Renewal of time-limited planning permissions*

In connection with all these time limits it may be remembered that, if any particular limit is running out, it is always open to a person to apply for a renewal of the planning permission which contains the time limit. Whether it *will* be renewed is, of course, a matter for the local planning authority and, on appeal, the Secretary of State. On this matter of renewals the Government position was given by the Minister of State during the Committee Stage of the Bill for the Town and Country Planning Act 1968 (*Hansard,* Standing Committee G, April 4, 1968, col. 956) when he said:

> " . . . there is no bar to renewal of the [planning] permission. I accept that cases will arise when, for perfectly good reasons outside his control, the owner will not have been able to start his development within the expected time. It may be due to a falling off of demand in the area and because the builder has stocks of land on his hands. It may be due to difficulties over capital, although if that is so, it does not necessarily follow that he should get an extension, for it may be that he ought to convey

the land to somebody who is able to develop it—if it is land which ought, according to proper planning needs, to be brought forward earlier for development. All these are matters which can be considered and adjudicated upon fairly."

19. Abandonment of Planning Permission

Apart from the limitations on the life of a planning permission discussed in the previous paragraphs, the question has been raised as to whether a planning permission, once embarked upon (*i.e.* the development authorised by the permission has been begun), can thereafter, by non-user of the permission, be regarded as having been abandoned by the holder for the time being of the permission so that the permission can no further enure for the benefit of the land and of any successor in title to the land (s.33(1)). After much discussion of this point over the years the matter is now made clear in law by the decision in *Pioneer Aggregates (U.K.) Ltd.* v. *The Secreatry of State for the Environment* [1985] A.C. 132 in which the House of Lords held, unanimously, that there is no principle in planning law that a valid planning permission capable of being implemented according to its terms can be abandoned. Lord Scarman's comments (in his judgment) are comprehensive. He declared (*inter alia*):

"On the question of abandonment he (Lord Scarman) agreed with both courts below that there was no such general rule in the planning law. In certain exceptional situations not covered by legislation, the courts have held that a landowner by developing his land can play an important part in bringing to an end or making incapable of implementation a valid planning permission. But he was satisfied that the Court of Appeal in *Slough Estates Ltd.* v. *Slough Borough Council (No. 2)* (1969) 2 Ch. 305; in House of Lords at (1971) A.C. 1958, erred in law in holding that the doctrine of election between inconsistent rights was to be incorporated into planning law either as the basis of a general rule of abandonment or (which the courts below were constrained to accept) as an exception to the general rule that the duration of a valid planning permission was governed by the provisions of the planning legislation.

"Planning control was a creature of statute. It was an imposition in the public interest of restrictions upon private rights of ownership of land. The public character of the law relating to planning control had been recognised by the House in *Newbury District Council* v. *Secretary of State for the Environment* [1981] A.C. 578. It was a field of law in which the courts should not introduce principles or rules derived from private law unless it be expressly authorised by Parliament or necessary in order to give effect to the purpose of the legislation. Planning law, though a comprehensive code imposed in the public interest, was of course, based on land law. Where the code was silent or ambiguous, resort to the principles of the private law (especially property and contract law) might be necessary so that the courts might resolve difficulties by application of common law or equitable principles. But such cases would be exceptional. And, if the statute law covered the situation, it would be an impermissible exercise of the judicial functon to go beyond the statutory provision by applying such principles merely because they might appear to achieve a fairer solution to the problem being considered. As ever in the field of statute law it was the duty of the courts to give effect to the intention of Parliament as evinced by the statute, or statutory code, considered as a whole.

"Parliament had provided a comprehensive code of planning control. It was currently to be found in the Town and Country Planning Act 1971, as subsequently amended. Section 33(1) was of crucial importance.

> 'Without prejudice to the provisions of this Part of this Act as to the duration, revocation or modification of planning permission, any grant of planning permission to develop land shall (except in so far as the permission otherwise provides) enure for the benefit of the land and of all persons for the time being interested therein.'

"The clear implication was that only the statute or the terms of the planning permission itself could stop the permission enuring for the benefit of the land and of all persons for the time being interested therein."

20. Conditions Attached to Planning Permissions

Statistics show that the majority of applications for planning permission are granted. It is, naturally, the "big" applications which catch the headlines and, when any of these is refused, the consequent appeal to the Secretary of State (with its elaborate public inquiry) can take upon itself all the attributes of the *cause célèbre*. But, as stated, the facts show that the majority—the run of the mill stuff—of applications is granted. They are, however, rarely granted without some kind of condition or conditions against which there is an appeal to the Secretary of State (see page 219). Thus, over the years, the matter of conditions—their type, their relevance, their fairness—has become, increasingly a bone of contention between the applicant for planning permission and the local planning authority.

In short, planning conditions and the related matters of planning bargaining and planning gain have, in recent years, taken on an importance which merits their being dealt with in a separate chapter. Accordingly, discussion of these matters will be found in Chapter 11 of this book.

21. Planning Appeal to the Secretary of State—Decision by the Secretary of State

(1) *Decision by the Secretary of State*

Where an application is made to a local planning authority

(a) for planning permission for development;

(b) for any consent, agreement or approval of the authority required by a condition imposed on a grant of planning permission (as, for example, a condition that reserved matters—set out in a grant of outline planning permission—shall be subject to the approval of the authority *before* any development is commenced); or

(c) for any approval of the authority required under a development order,

and that permission, consent, agreement or approval is refused by the local planning authority or is granted subject to conditions unacceptable to the applicant, then, in any such case, the aggrieved applicant has a right of appeal within *six months* (General Development Order 1977,[47] Art. 20), to the Secretary of State (s.36(1)). There is a similar right of appeal in respect of the failure of the local planning authority to give a decision at all within the requisite period of *eight weeks* (s.37 and art. 7(6) of the General Development Order 1977.

Guidance as to the attitude which the Secretary of State might be expected to adopt on appeal being made to him is obtainable from the Bulletins of Selected Appeal Decisions issued from time to time by the Department of the Environment and also from "Ministerial Planning Decisions" published monthly in the *Journal of Planning and Environment Law* (Sweet and Maxwell Ltd., London).

On the subject generally of planning appeals reference may usefully be made to the booklet, "Planning Appeals—A Guide," published free and reprinted May 1 1984, by the Department of the Environment, 2 Marsham Street, London, SW1P 3EB.

[47] S.I. 1977 No. 289.

Attention must be drawn at this point to the Government's Response to the Fifth Report from the House of Commons Environment Committee, Session 1985–1986. The Response is entitled, "Planning: Appeals, Call-In and Major Public Inquiries" (Cm 43, dated December 1986). It was issued by the Department of the Environment and presented to Parliament by the Secretary of State for the Environment.

The Response shows the new measures which the Government have in mind to improve the efficiency of planning appeal procedures. These measures include the setting of strict timetables for the various stages of an appeal and for a revision of the Town and Country Planning (Inquiries Procedure) Rules 1974 (as to which, see Chapter 16).

A Consultation Paper about the proposed revision of the 1974 Rules and about a new Code of Practice for major planning inquiries was announced in the Commons, by the Secretary of State for the Environment, on December 17, 1986. The texts of these proposals are appended to the Command Paper (Cm 43) above mentioned. It is emphasized that all of the foregoing is, at the time of this writing (February 1987), in the realm of discussion and consultation.

The notice of a planning appeal must be given to the Secretary of State within *six months* of the receipt of the local planning authority's decision or of the expiry of the appropriate period of time within which such decision ought to be given (s.36(2) and art. 20 of the General Development Order 1977).[47a] "Month" is not defined in the General Development Order 1977 but, by virtue of article 2(2) of the Order, applying section 5 of, and Schedule 1 to, the Interpretation Act 1978, the expression "month" means a calendar month.

On an appeal to him against the decision of a local planning authority the Secretary of State may allow or dismiss the appeal or may reverse or vary *any* part of the local planning authority's decision and may deal with the application as if it had been made to him in the first instance (s.36(3)).

Thus appellants will bear in mind that, by appealing to the Secretary of State, they put before him *the whole* of their application for planning permission and not merely that part of the local planning authority's decision in respect of which they feel aggrieved.

In exercising his right to reverse or vary the local planning authority's decision the Secretary of State may himself add more onerous conditions than were imposed by the local planning authority in the first place. Indeed, he may go to the extent of refusing planning permission altogether in a case where, in his view, the local planning authority were wrong in granting the permission.

[47a] S.I. 1977 No. 289.

Before deciding an appeal the Secretary of State must, if either the applicant or the local planning authority so request, afford each of them an opportunity of being heard by a person appointed by the Secretary of State for the purpose—the Secretary of State's Inspector (s.36(4)). If the Secretary of State grants such a request, the hearing will be private to the two parties. Neither party can demand a public local inquiry although the Secretary of State frequently decides to hold such an inquiry.[48]

The provisions of the 1971 Act relating to:

(1) the notices to be given to owners and to agricultural tenants (s.27);
(2) the grant of planning permission (s.29(1) and (3)); and
(3) the imposition of conditions affecting other land or requiring the removal of buildings at the end of a specified period (s.30(1)),

are made applicable in the case of an appeal to the Secretary of State (s.36(5)).

The Secretary of State may decline (s.36(7)) to determine an appeal if satisfied that planning permission for the proposed development:

(a) could not have been granted at all; or
(b) could have been granted subject only to the conditions of which complaint is made,

in view of the provisions:

(1) of sections 29 and 30 of the 1971 Act (relating to the determination of planning applications and the conditional grant of planning permission); and
(2) of the Town and Country Planning General Development Order 1977 and any directions given under that order.

(2) *Finality of decision of Secretary of State—"persons aggrieved"—judicial review of Secretary's decision in High Court—rules of natural justice*

The decision of the Secretary of State on an appeal "shall be final" (s.36(6)) but, notwithstanding this, a "person aggrieved"[49] may within *six weeks* challenge the decision on *a point of law* in the

[48] Further discussion on planning inquiries and private hearings held by the Secretary of State in connection with appeals follows in Chap. 16.

[49] As to "persons aggrieved," see *Ealing B.C.* v. *Jones* [1959] 1 Q.B. 384, D.C.; *R.* v. *Dorset Quarter Sessions Appeals Committee, ex parte Weymouth Corporation* [1960] 2 Q.B. 230, D.C.; *Buxton* v. *Minister of Housing and Local Government* [1961] 1 Q.B. 278; *Turner* v. *Secretary of State for the Environment* (1973) 28 P. & C.R. 123; *Bizony* v. *Secretary of State for the Environment* (1975) 239 E.G. 281; *Coop Retoné* v. *Secretary of State for the Environment* (1980) 39 P. & C.R. 223; *Greater London Council* v. *Secretary of State for the Environment and Harrow London Borough Council* (1985) J.P.L. 868. See also [1960] J.P.L. 702; [1978] J.P.L. 739.

High Court (ss.242(1)(*e*), (3)(*b*) and 245(1)(*b*), (3)(4)(7)). A local authority may not necessarily be, in this context, a person aggrieved but they may nevertheless be able to challenge the decision on the ground that they are an "authority directly concerned with . . . action on the part of the Secretary of State" (s.245(2)).

The period of six weeks is absolute and begins to run on the date the decision letter of the Secretary of State is signed by him (or on his behalf) and not on the date it is received by the person aggrieved (*Griffiths* v. *Secretary of State for the Environment* (1983) J.P.L. 237 (H.L.)).

The challenge on a point of law will be that the decision of the Secretary of State is not within the powers of the 1971 Act—i.e. the decision is *ultra vires*—or that "relevant requirements"—i.e. procedural requirements—have not been complied with and the applicant's interests have thereby been "substantially prejudiced" (s. 245(4)(7)).

As to the decision of the Secretary of State on an appeal being final (s.36(6)), cases like *J. Sainsbury Ltd.* v. *Secretary of State for the Environment and Colchester Borough Council*[50] show that the present tendency of the courts is to scrutinise the decisions of Ministers in greater detail than formerly and with increasing reference to the rules of natural justice.[51] Even so, the underlying principle remains intact, namely, that the controlling process of town and country planning over the development of land is an *administrative* (and not a *justiciable*) process[52] and that the Secretary of State is to have the last

[50] [1978] J.P.L. 379.

[51] See *J.J. Steeples* v. *Derbyshire County Council* [1981] J.P.L. 582; *Covent Garden Community Association Ltd.* v. *Greater London Council* [1981] J.P.L. 183; *I.R.C.* v. *National Federation of Self-Employed and Small Businesses Ltd.* [1981] 2 All E.R. 65; *R.* v. *North Hertfordshire D.C., ex parte Sullivan* [1981] J.P.L. 625 and 752; *Furmston* v. *Secretary of State for the Environment and Kent County Council* (1983) J.P.L. 49; *R.* v. *St. Edmundsbury Borough Council, ex parte Investors in Industry Commercial Properties Ltd.* (1986) J.P.L. 38; *R.* v. *Lambeth London Borough Council, ex parte Sharp* (1986) J.P.L. 207; *Ainley* v. *S. of S. for E. and Fylde B. C.* (1987) J.P.L. 33; *London Borough of Southwark* v. *S. of S. for E. and Waterhouse* (1987) J.P.L. 36; *Vikoma International Ltd.* v. *S. of S. for E. and Woking B. C.* (1987) J.P.L. 38.

[52] *Dimsdale Developments (South East) Ltd.* v. *Secretary of State for the Environment and Hounslow L.B.C.* (1986) J.P.L. 276 including "Comment" at p. 279; and see comments of Stephen Brown J. in Chap. 2, *ante*, p. 38. See also cases quoted in Chap. 2 *ante* at pp. 38 and 39, and cases quoted in n. 8 at p. 39, *ante*, particularly the comments of Lord Greene, M.R., and Lord Thankerton. In *R.* v. *Sevenoaks District Council, ex parte Terry* (1984) J.P.L. 420 the court declined to follow the decision in *J.J. Steeples* (above note 51) ruling that, where a local planning authority had granted planning permission for development of land in which they themselves held an interest, the correct test was whether the planning committee were still in a position to exercise their planning discretion in a proper fashion. The whole matter was one of administrative discretion not justiciable precision. The *Sevenoaks* decision was followed in *R.* v. *St. Edmundsbury Borough Council, ex parte Investors in Industry Commercial Properties Ltd.* (1986) J.P.L. 38.

word because, *in the ultimate analysis, it is government policy*[52] *which is being placed in issue when an appeal to the Secretary of State is lodged*—a matter more fully discussed in Chapter 2 at page 36 where there is quoted some paragraphs from a commentary of mine in the "Journal of Planning and Environment Law" (1984) pages 74 *et seq.* to which reference may be made—particularly to paragraph 10 of that commentary.

It is to be emphasized that challenge in the High Court of a local planning authority's planning decision must be on a point of law. The *planning merits* of the decision are not for the courts.

On this, reference may be made to the comments of Stephen Brown J. in *Greater London Council and Others* v. *Secretary of State for the Environment and Greycoat Commercial Estates Ltd.* (the "*Coin Street* case") (1983) J.P.L. 793 at 798 as quoted *ante*, at page 38, *ante*.

Again, the words of Glidewell J. in the case (unreported) of *Pickvance* v. *Secretary of State for the Environment* may be quoted. The learned Judge said:

> "This is not a Court of Appeal from the Inspector. My only task is to decide under section 245 whether the Inspector, on behalf of the Secretary of State, has failed to comply with the provisions of the Town and Country Planning Act 1971: in other words, whether he has gone wrong in law in some material respect . . ."

The judgment of O'Connor L.J. in the Court of Appeal may also be quoted. In *R.* v. *London Borough of Harringay, ex parte Barrs and Faherty* (1983) the learned Lord Justice said:

> "Architectural standards of the development cannot be dealt with on judicial review unless there is so striking a difference that no one could accept it. We are not a Court of Appeal from the Planning Committee. We cannot substitute our views for that of the Planning Committee."

The foregoing quotation from this appeal case (which reverses the decision in *R.* v. *London Borough of Harringay, ex parte Norman Clifford Barrs and Another* (1983) J.P.L. 54 and which has likewise gone unreported) is taken from a transcript of Lord Justice O'Connor's judgment a copy of which, having been personally involved in the case, I have.

As to the rules of natural justice (whatever these are) reference may be made to *Fairmount Investments Ltd.* v. *The Secretary of State for the Environment* [1976] 1 W.L.R. 1255 (a case relating to a compulsory purchase order made under the Housing Act 1957 in respect of housing unfit for human habitation) in which case Lord Russell of Killowen said in the House of Lords:

> "I am satisfied that if the true conclusion is that the course which events followed resulted in that degree of unfairness to Fairmount [who owned the houses] that is commonly referred to as a departure from the principles of natural justice, it may equally be said that the order is not within the powers of the Act [the Housing Act of 1957] and that a requirement of the Act has not been complied with. For it is to be implied, unless the contrary appears, that Parliament does not authorise by the Act the exercise of powers in breach of the principles of natural justice and that Parliament does by the Act require, in the particular procedures, compliance with those principles."

His Lordship went on to say:

> " . . . in this case I am unable, consonant with the essential principles of fairness in a dispute, to uphold this compulsory purchase order. All cases in which principles of natural justice are invoked must depend on the particular circumstances of the case. I am unable, my Lords, in the instant case, to generalise. I can only say that in my opinion, in the circumstances I have outlined, Fairmount has not had—in a phrase whose derivation neither I nor your Lordships could trace—a fair crack of the whip. A passage at page 682 of *Rex* v. *Paddington and St. Marylebone Rent Tribunal, Ex parte Bell, London & Provincial Properties Ltd.* [1949] 1 K.B. 666 on being taken by surprise is of relevance here . . .
>
> "I do not wish to be thought to impute any moral blame to the inspector [who held the local inquiry into the compulsory puchase order] by my conclusion that the procedure in this case involved unfairness: no one can be expected to be perfect in all circumstances and he may take comfort from the fact that one judicial mind thought that he was in no way at fault."

Judicial challenge on matters of law and the rules of natural justice and the interplay of these two important matters on planning control and appeals to the Secretary of State by disappointed applicants for planning permission, came up for considerable contention and review in *Reading Borough Council* v. *The Secretary of State for the Environment and Commercial Union Properites (Investments) Ltd.* (1986) J.P.L. 115. Any one thinking of raising the rules-of-natural-justice routine in a planning appeal would do well to consider this case closely. Extracts from the case appear below.

Planning permission having been refused and an appeal lodged, the Inspector recommended the Secretary of State to allow the appeal. Before any decision on this recommendation was made there was correspondence between the applicant for planning permission and the Secretary of State who then allowed the appeal. The local council (who had refused planning permission in the first place) alleged breach of natural justice and defective reasoning in the Secretary of State's decision letter. They took the matter to law and succeeded. The High Court (Mr. David Widdicombe Q.C., sitting as a deputy Judge) quashed the decision of the Secretary of State and gave a lengthy review of the case law on natural justice and its interplay with the inquiry-procedure routines of planning appeals.

The judgment of the learned deputy judge falls neatly into two separate parts. It is the second part of the judgment at (1986) J.P.L. 117 which deals so comprehensively with the matter of natural justice and it is that second part of the judgment which now follows in full.

> "*Natural Justice*
>
> As this was a separate ground of the application, and in case he (the deputy Judge) was wrong in his judgement on the first point, he would deal with the natural justice issue.
>
> "Mr. Lowe's complaint (Mr. Lowe appeared for the Borough Council) was that the two letters from the company to the Secretary of State, both dated September 20, 1984, were not disclosed by the Secretary of State to the Borough Council, who therefore had no chance to answer the points made in them. He accepted that in matters dealt with by written representations (see, *post*, at page 234) there had to be finality at some point, but said there were matters of substance in the company's letters to which the Borough Council would have wanted to reply. He relied on the affidavit of Mr. M. A. Thackeray, Planning Officer, in paragraph 10 of which Mr. Thackeray spelt out in detail what the Borough Council would have wished to say in reply to the company's letter if they had had the chance to do so. Mr. Lowe referred to Wade on Administrative Law, 5th Edition, pp. 479–480 and p. 483, *Fairmount Investments Ltd.* v. *Secretary of State for the Environment* (1976) 1 W.L.R. 1255; *Performance Cars Limited* v. *Secretary of State for the Environment* (1977) 34 P. & C.R. 92; *Peak Park Joint Planning Board* v. *Secretary of State for the Environment* (1980) 39 P. & C.R. 361; *Simmons* v. *Secretary of State for the Environment* (1985) J.P.L. 253, and *Errington* v. *Minister of Health* (1935) 1 K.B. 249. He claimed that the Borough Council had been substantially prejudiced by the breach of natural justice.
>
> "Mr. Laws for the Secretary of State said that the Borough Council had made representations to the Secretary of State after the close of the inquiry and that the company had replied

to them. The principle of fairness did not compel the Secretary of State to disclose the company's letters unless they contained new factual assertions or possibly new arguments. Here there were no new facts or arguments. With written representations, there had to be an end at some point; the 'roundabout' did not have to be kept wound up for ever. There was no such thing as a technical breach of natural justice. Proof of substantial prejudice was required whether the breach arose under the Inquiry Procedure Rules (see Chapter 16) or under the general principle of natural justice. In addition to the cases cited by Mr. Lowe, Mr. Laws had referred to *Binney* v. *Secretary of State for the Environment* (1984) J.P.L. 871.

"Mr. Milner for the company adopted Mr. Laws' argument. He referred in addition to *Lake District Special Planning Board* v. *Secretary of State for the Environment* (1975) 236 E.G. 417; *Hambledon and Chiddingfold Parish Councils* v. *Secretary of State for the Environment* (1976) J.P.L. 502; *David Rea* v. *Minister of Transport* (1982) J.P.L. 108; and *George* v. *Secretary of State for the Environment* (1979) 38 P.C.R. 609.

"He drew attention particularly to what Kerr, J. (as he then was) said in *Lake District Planning Board* v. *Secretary of State for the Environment* at page 419 of the Estates Gazette report: 'The alternative submission was that the failure to send a copy of the letter of April 1 to the applicants constituted a denial of natural justice. A complainant inevitably faces a heavy burden in seeking to establish a breach of the rules of natural justice when the allegation related to something comprised within the scope of a statutory procedure which was in itself designed to lay down the requirements which must be complied with to ensure that justice was done. He (Kerr J.) accepted the submission to Mr. Woolf that a breach of natural justice was not made out *ipso facto* by the mere receipt by the Minister of some further representations after the close of an inquiry and the failure to circulate to everybody concerned. Cases which bore out these views were *Local Government Board* v. *Arlidge* (1915) A.C. 120; *Ridge* v. *Baldwin* (1964) A.C. 40; and *Maxwell* v. *Department of Trade and Industry* (1974) 2 W.L.R. 338. In the circumstances of the present case, and in the light of the authorities, he (his Lordship) was unable to find that any breach of the rules of natural justice had been established.

"Ackner J. (as he then was) had agreed with the sentence about burden of proof in *Hambledon & Chiddingfold Parish Councils* v. *Secretary of State for the Environment, supra.*

"It appeared to him [David Widdicombe, Q.C.] that the

cases established three propositions which had to form the starting point for determination of this issue in this case.

"(1) The Inquiry Procedure Rules did not exhaust the requirements of natural justice. In *Fairmount Investments Ltd.* v. *Secretary of State for the Environment* (1976) 1 W.L.R. 1255, Lord Russell with whom Lords Diplock, Simon of Glaisdale and Edmund-Davies agreed, said at page 1263: 'There was a certain amount of discussion before your Lordships on the significance and applicability of the phrase 'may quash' and on the difference between the phrase 'not within the powers of this Act' and 'the interests of the applicant have been substantially prejudiced by any requirement of this Act not having been complied with'. In my view the instant appeal does not require discussion of these points: for I am satisfied that if the true conclusion is that the course which events followed resulted in that degree of unfairness to Fairmount that is commonly referred to as a departure from the principles of natural justice it may equally be said that the order is not within the powers of the Act and that a requirement of the Act has not been complied with. For it is to be implied, unless the contrary appears, that Parliament does not authorise by the Act the exercise of powers in breach of the principles of natural justice, and that Parliament does by the Act require, in the particular procedures, compliance with those principles.'

"This was cited by Lord Denning in *George* v. *Secretary of State for the Environment* (1979) 38 P.C.R. 609, at p. 617 and applied by the Court of Appeal in that case. It was common ground that the present case was not covered by the Rules and the application was therefore made on the grounds that the Secretary of State's decision was not within the powers of the Act.

"(2) There was no such thing as a technical breach of natural justice—Kerr J. in *Lake District Special Planning Board* v. *Secretary of State for the Environment, supra* and *George* v. *Secretary of State for the Environment* (1979) 38 P. & C.R. 609 per Lord Denning, M.R. at page 617.

"(3) Whether the breach alleged was a breach of the rules or a breach of natural justice on general principles, the complainant had to show 'substantial prejudice.' In *George* v. *Secretary of State for the Environment, supra*, Lord Denning said at page 617: 'One should not find a breach of natural justice unless there has been substantial prejudice to the applicant as a result of the mistake or error that has been made.'

"He did not, however, accept Mr. Milner's further proposition that where a breach of natural justice was alleged outside the scope of the Inquiry Procedure Rules, there was a heavy burden of proof on the complainant. He differed from the views of Kerr J. and Ackner J. (as they then were) on this point naturally with great diffidence, but he felt free to do so because when Lord Denning, M.R. in *George* v. *Secretary of State* cited from the judgment of Kerr J. in *Lake District Special Planning Board* v. *Secretary of State for the Environment*, he, in his view significantly, did not cite the sentence about burden of proof, although it could have been relevant to the circumstances of the *George* case. Nor of course was there any suggestion of a different standard of proof in *Fairmount Investments Ltd.* v. *Secretary of State for the Environment*. His own view was that the Inquiry Procedure Rules were not intended to cover all possible natural justice situations. The cases demonstrated a number of situations not covered by the Rules and no doubt in the course of time more would emerge. In his view natural justice cases outside the scope of the Rules fell to be dealt with by reference to the normal standard of proof.

"Was there a breach of natural justice in this case? The Borough Council had written to the Secretary of State, and the company had responded. In his judgment it was not automatic that the Secretary of State had then to give the Borough Council the right to reply to the company. As Mr. Laws said, there had to be finality at some time. The Secretary of State was entitled to draw the line at that point if it could be done without unfairness to the Borough Council.

"So he asked himself whether in all the circumstances of this case it was unfair to the Borough Council for the Secretary of State to have proceeded to a decision without disclosing to the Borough Council the two letters from the company.

"Having carefully considered the contents of the company's two letters and an affidavit submitted by the Senior Planning Officer, in the context of the whole appeal, in his judgment the two letters did raise matters which in fairness called for a right of reply by the Borough Council. The Borough Council was entitled to be heard in reply, and on matters which they had something of substance to say. In his judgment therefore the Borough Council had been substantially prejudiced by a breach of natural justice in this case. For that reason he was satisfied that the Secretary of State's decision was not within the powers of the Act.

"Pursuant to section 245(4) of the Act the court had a discretion whether to quash the decision. Whether if the Borough

Council had been allowed to reply to the company's letters the decision would have been any different, he found it impossible to say. it might well be that the Secretary of State would have rejected the further arguments of the Borough Council and reached the same conclusion anyway. But he could not be sure of that and he therefore, on that ground also, quashed the decision of the Secretary of State."

Where any action on the part of the Secretary of State is, on appeal, quashed by the court under section 245(4)(*b*) of the 1971 Act, it is not open to the court to substitute any other order and the appeal to the Secretary of State revives and is pending.[53]

Notwithstanding the foregoing *statutory* provisions of ss.242 and 245 the 1971 Act as to challenge in the High Court, the Secretary of State's decision *may* be quashed on *certiorari*.[54] Where a local authority by resolution granted to themselves (under regulation 4(5) of the Town and Country Planning General Regulations 1976)[55] a deemed planning permission for development which departed from the provisions of the local plan, an incorporated body, representative of local residents' interests, was held to have a sufficient interest to give it *locus standi* to apply to the courts for *certiorari* to quash the local authority's resolution.[56]

For a summary of the principles of judicial review (on challenge in the Courts) of administrative decisions taken by the Secretary of State for the Environment, reference may be made to the observations of Forbes J. in *Seddon Properties Ltd. and James Crosbie and Sons Ltd.* v. *Secretary of State for the Environment and Another* (1978) 248 E.G. 950; (1978) J.P.L. 835 in which his Lordship concluded with the words:

"Therefore, although he had had to reject a number of counsel's grounds of challenge, he did consider that there had been both a failure to give adequate reasons as required by rule 13 of

[53] *Hartnell* v. *Minister of Housing and Local Government* [1964] 2 Q.B. 510, C.A.; affirmed [1965] A.C. 1134, H.L.; *Price Bros. (Rose Heath) Ltd.* v. *Secretary of State for the Environment* [1979] J.P.L. 387; see also comment of O'Connor, L.J., in *R.* v. *London Borough of Harringay, ex parte Barrs and Faherty* (1983) unreported but quoted at p. 223, *ante*.

[54] See comment on *certiorari* appearing, at p. 238.

[55] S.I. 1976 No. 1419.

[56] *Covent Garden Community Association Ltd.* v. *Greater London Council* [1981] J.P.L. 183. See, for unsuccessful challenges to grant of planning permission, *R.* v. *Hammersmith and Fulham Borough Council, ex p. People Before Profit Limited* [1981] J.P.L. 778 and 869 and *R.* v. *St. Edmundsbury Borough Council ex parte Investors in Industry Commercial Properties Ltd.* (1986) J.P.L. 38.

the Inquiries Procedure Rules and that the Secretary of State had taken into account irrelevant considerations or failed to take into account relevant considerations, *i.e.* his action was unreasonable and not within the powers of the Act. The distinction might be of some importance because under section 245(4) of the Act of 1971 where the failure complained of was a failure to comply with the relevant requirements the Court must be satisfied that the interests of the applicant had been substantially prejudiced thereby. Mr. Sullivan argued that there was no substantial prejudice to the applicants arising out of the failure of the Secretary of State to give adequate reasons in this case. In this connection it was worth quoting a passage from the judgment of Lord Denning M.R. in *Earl of Iveagh* v. *Minister of Housing and Local Government* [1964] 1 Q.B. 393: 'The whole purpose of the enactment is to enable the parties and the courts to see what matters he (the Minister) has taken into consideration and what view he has reached on the points of fact and law which arise.' The value to a developer of knowing the reasons for a decision by the Secretary of State was well demonstrated in this case by the importance attached by all parties (and the Secretary of State himself) to his previous decision in 1973. If a land-owner did not know precisely why his appeal had been turned down he cannot plan the future of his land with any precision and this must be, and he considered was, on the facts of this case, a substantial prejudice to the land-owner. Even if this were not so there was no statutory necessity to show substantial prejudice in the case of an order which was not within the powers of thc Act and that had been proved.

"In the circumstances Counsel's application succeeded and the decision must be quashed."

22. Planning Appeal to the Secretary of State—Decision by an Inspector

(1) *Decision by an Inspector*

In order to relieve pressure at the Department of the Environment, section 36(8) of, and Schedule 9 to, the 1971 Act provide for certain appeals to be heard and *determined* by an Inspector appointed by the Secretary of State. Where an Inspector is thus empowered the Secretary of State may appoint one or more assessors to sit with him at any hearing or public local inquiry which the Inspector may hold in connection with any appeal which he is to determine, in order to advise him on technical or scientific aspects of the matters to which the appeal relates (1971 Act, Sched. 9, para. 5(1A) added by the Housing and Planning Act 1986 s.49(1)(*h*), Sched. 11, Pt. I, para. 12).

Schedule 9 to the 1971 Act applies (Sched. 9, para. 2(1)) to the following appeals:

(1) an appeal relating to a planning decision (s.36(8));
(2) an appeal against an enforcement notice (s.88(9));
(3) an appeal relating to the certification of an established use (s.95(7));
(4) an appeal against a listed building enforcement notice (s.97(7));
(5) an appeal against an enforcement notice relating to duties as to replacement of trees (s.103(4)); and
(6) an appeal against the refusal of listed building consent, or the grant thereof subject to conditions (Sched. 11, para. 8(6)).

Out of the whole sum total of all the foregoing types of appeal the Secretary of State may prescribe by regulation certain classes of appeal (Sched. 9, para. 1) and, if he does so prescribe, then any appeal falling within a prescribed class may be determined by an Inspector appointed for the purpose by the Secretary of State instead of being determined, as hitherto, by the Secretary of State (*ibid.*).

The Secretary of State has made the Town and Country Planning (Determination of Appeals by Appointment Persons) (Prescribed Classes) Regulations 1981[57] whereby, as from July 1, 1981, *all* appeals under sections 36 and 37 of the 1971 Act (appeals in respect of applications for planning permission) and *all* appeals under section 88 of the Act (appeals against inforcement notices) are transferred for determination by an Inspector instead of by the Secretary of State (1981 Regulations, reg. 3). The foregoing does not however, apply to appeals by statutory undertakers which fall to be dealt with jointly by the Secretary of State and "the appropriate Minister" because they relate to the development of land to which section 225(1) of the 1971 Act applies (reg. 4).

In addition to the appeals to the Secretary of State referred to in the previous paragraph, the Town and Country Planning (Determination of Appeals by Appointed Persons) Regulations 1986 (S.I. 1986 No. 623) prescribe further classes of appeal which, from May 1, 1986, can not only be heard, but also determined, by an Inspector.

These further appeals are those (reg. 2(2)) concerned with listed building consent (see chapter 14, *post*), consent to demolish buildings

[57] S.I. 1981 No. 804.

in conservation areas (see chapter 9, *ante*) and enforcement notices related to cases where such consent is required (see chapter 15, *post*). Exceptions are made by regulation 2(3).

These 1986 Regulations do not apply to appeals relating to buildings in Wales.

The Lord Chancellor has made the Town and Country Planning Appeals (Determination by Appointed Persons) (Inquiries Procedure) Rules 1974[58] dealing with all procedural matters in a case where an Inspector is both hearing *and* determining a planning appeal.

Any Inspector who, under the foregoing arrangements, becomes empowered to determine an appeal is accorded the same powers and duties as the Secretary of State in relation to appeals (1971 Act, Sched. 9, para. 2(1)). Moreover, the parties to such an appeal have similar rights as to being heard by the Inspector as they have by the Secretary of State (*ibid.* para. 2(2)).

Where a local planning authority refused planning permission for housing development the applicant appealed to the Secretary of State. The appeal was heard *and determined* by an Inspector appointed by the Secretary of State. The Inspector allowed the appeal. The local planning authority then applied, under section 245 of the 1971 Act, to the Courts to quash the Inspector's decision. It was held that the Inspector had not made it clear whether or not he had taken account of a certain important matter, namely, the protection of Metropolitan Open Land and, further, that the Inspector's decision letter was not wholly clear and intelligible. In the circumstances and because the interests of the local planning authority had not been substantially prejudiced the court declined to quash the Inspector's decision.[59] Even so, this is a chastening decision for all Inspectors involved in the business of determining planning appeals, under the 1981 Regulations, in the name of the Secretary of State for the Environment. The need for adequate and intelligible reasoning in an Inspector's decision letter is the same as it is in the case of a decision by the Secretary of State.

In *Arlington Securities Ltd.* v. *Secretary of State for the Environment and Bromley London Borough Council* [1985] J.P.L. 550, outline planning permission for office development having been refused and, on appeal, the Inspector having upheld the refusal, the Divisional Court, in allowing the further appeal to the court, held that the Inspector's report was materially inadequate in its reasoning in that

[58] S.I. 1974 No. 420. See also Chap. 16.

[59] *London Borough of Greenwich* v. *Secretary of State for the Environment and Spar Environments Ltd.* [1981] J.P.L. 809.

it failed to spell out with sufficient clarity the sound and clearcut objection necessary to justify a refusal of planning permission.

Where the Secretary of State has appointed an Inspector to determine an appeal the Secretary of State has power, at any time before the appeal is determined, to substitute one Inspector for another if he so wishes (*ibid.* para. 4).

If, however, one Inspector is substituted for another, then the consideration of the appeal, or any inquiry or hearing in connection with the appeal if already begun, must be begun afresh (*ibid.* para. 4(2)) although, in such circumstances, it will not be necessary to give any person the opportunity either of making fresh representations or of modifying or withdrawing representations already made (*ibid.*).

The Secretary of State has power to direct that an appeal which would otherwise be given over for determination by an Inspector shall be withdrawn from such treatment and shall, instead, be referred to the Secretary of State for determination by him (*ibid.* para. 3). In any case, where the Secretary of State does this he has power to return, if he so desires, and by means of a further direction, the appeal for determination by an Inspector (*ibid.* para. 3A, added by the Housing and Planning Act 1986, s.49(1)(*h*), Sched. 11, Pt. I, para. 11).

Any direction by the Secretary of State restoring to himself the responsibility of determining any particular appeal (*ibid.* para. 3) must state the Secretary of State's reason for doing so and must be served on the Inspector appointed to hear the appeal (if one has actually been appointed), upon the appellant, upon the local planning authority and upon any person, being an owner or an agricultural tenant, who has made representations relating to the appeal which the local planning authority are required to take into account (*ibid.* para 3(2)).

If the Secretary of State's reasons for taking the determination of an appeal out of the hands of an Inspector raise matters on which representations have not so far been made, then all parties to the appeal have the right to make further representations and appear and be heard by an Inspector appointed by the Secretary of State for the purpose (*ibid.* para. 3(4)).

Similarly, if any party to the appeal had earlier expressed a wish, under paragraph 2(2) of Schedule 9 to the 1971 Act, to appear and be heard by the Inspector appointed to determine the appeal, then the Secretary of State, before himself determining the appeal, must afford any such person the right to appear before, and be heard by, an Inspector appointed by the Secretary of State for the purpose (*ibid.* para. 3(4) and (5)).

When an Inspector has been appointed by the Secretary of State to determine an appeal, the Inspector himself has a discretion (whether or not the parties have asked to be heard) to hold a public local inquiry before he determines the appeal (*ibid.* para 5). Such an Inspector is bound to hold such an inquiry if directed to do so by the Secretary of State in any particular case (*ibid.*).

When an appeal has been decided by an Inspector, his decision becomes that of the Secretary of State (*ibid.* para. 2(3)).

(2) *Finality of decision of Secretary of State given by an Inspector—"persons aggrieved"—judicial review of decision in High Court—rules of natural justice*

On this reference may be made to the commentary appearing, *ante.*, at pages 221 to 230 inclusive.

23. Planning Appeal to the Secretary of State—The Written Representations Process

In addition to planning appeals to the Secretary of State for the Environment where the decision is made by the Secretary of State (see page 219, *ante.*) and planning appeals to the Secretary of State where the decision is made on his behalf by an Inspector from the Inspectorate of the Department of the Environment (see page 230, *ante.*) it is becoming increasingly popular for a planning appeal to be made in neither of these ways.

This third method of dealing with a planning appeal is known as the "Written Representations Process". D.O.E. Circular 18/86 dated December 10, 1986 deals with the "Written Representations Process."

In a letter from the Department of the Environment dated May 14, 1985 to the Secretary of the Law Society it is stated that, out of all the planning appeals that are made (see page 242 for statistics), 85 per cent. of the appeals are now decided by the "written representations process" in which Inspectors from the Planning Inspectorate of the Department of the Environment issue decision letters having dealt with the case on the basis of written representations and a site visit but without holding an inquiry.

It has, however, to be remembered that in this simple, comparatively cheap and speedy method of appeal to the Secretary of State there is no confrontation with "the other side" and, accordingly, there is no means of testing, by the tempering fire of cross-examination, what the "other side" is saying. An appellant must ponder all this before he decides to accept the "written representations process".

In a planning appeal to him where the appeal is to be disposed of without a public local inquiry or a hearing (as, e.g., in the case of an appeal by the "written representations process"), the Secretary of State may, by regulations, provide for the procedure which is to be followed—including timetabling and cut-off for the receipt of evidence and supporting documents (s.282B added by the Housing and Planning Act 1986, s.49(1)(*h*), Sched. 11 Part I, para. 10). The Secretary of State on December 15, 1986 issued a consultation paper outlining proposed regulations for governing the procedure to be followed in planning appeals decided by way of written representations. Comments on them were to be sent to the Department of the Environment, 2, Marsham Street, London SW1P 3EB, not later than February 17, 1987.

24. Award of Costs in Planning Appeals[59a]

After a public local inquiry held in connection with a planning appeal, the Secretary of State is empowered to award costs (if he can be so persuaded) to the appellant (s.282(2), incorporating the Local Government Act 1972, s.250(5)). This discretionary power is now extended to an Inspector holding such an inquiry on behalf of the Secretary of State (Housing and Planning Act 1986, s.49(1)(*h*), Sched. 11, Pt. I, para. 9(2)).

Similarly, costs may be awarded to an appellant in a planning appeal to the Secretary of State which does not give rise to a public local inquiry (s. 282A—inserted by the Housing and Planning Act 1986 s.49(1)(*g*), Sched. 11, Pt. I, para. 9(1)). Thus, an appellant *may* be able to recover his costs in a case where his appeal leads to a private hearing (as distinct from a public local inquiry) or where it is dealt with through written representations (as to which, see page 334, *post*).

Where the Secretary of State holds a public local inquiry he may recover his own costs from such local authority or other party to the inquiry as he may direct (s.282(2)—incorporating the Local Government Act 1972, s.250(4)—and the Housing and Planning Act 1986, s.42). This provision applies also where an inquiry is cancelled (1986 Act, s.42(3)).

The House of Commons Environment Committee (appointed to examine the expenditure, administration and policy of (*inter alia*) the Department of the Environment) had some interesting *recommendations* to make about costs in their Fifth Report, Volume 1, for Session 1985–86, ordered, by the House of Commons, to be printed July 16, 1986. The Committee, in their Summary of Conclusions and Recommendations, at page lxxxi, *recommended* (and it is emphasized

[59a] See D.O.E. Circular 2/87 dated February 17, 1987.

that, at this stage, these are recommendations only and have no binding effect) as follows:

"2. We recommend that there should be a presumption that costs will be awarded against an unsuccessful appellant on a second or subsequent appeal for similar development on broadly the same site except where the Secretary of State is satisfied that, due to changes in policy or in the character of the development proposed, the behaviour of other parties to the appeal, or other relevant circumstances, an award should not be made.

"3. We recommend that costs be awarded against local planning authorities where an appeal is upheld against a refusal and the Secretary of State is satisfied that such refusal was made for reasons other than sustainable planning grounds.

* * * * * *

"5. We recommend that the Secretary of State should be prepared to award costs where at an inquiry no substantial evidence is brought by one of the parties to counter any material factual statement contained in the statement by the other party which has not been previously agreed.

"6. We also recommend that clear power should be taken for the Secretary of State to make a partial award of costs to introduce an element of flexibility in cases where there has been default on both sides and where the default of one party was not the sole cause of delay or of inconvenience to the other.

* * * * * *

"8. Third parties should neither receive costs, nor be liable to pay the costs of other parties.

"9. We recommend that the Secretary of State should undertake a thorough revision of his criteria and procedures on the award of costs, and should publish a new comprehensive circular giving detailed guidance as to the types of case where he would anticipate that costs would be awarded.

"*Compensation*

10. We recommend that a successful appellant should have the right to apply to the Lands Tribunal for an assessment of the compensation payable by the local planning authority in respect of all losses flowing directly from the action of the local planning authority in, without any planning justification, refusing a grant of planning permission, imposing a planning condition or failing to determine an application within the

prescribed time. In any such proceedings, the decision letter of the Secretary of State or his Inspector should be conclusive as to the facts found therein, but either side should be permitted at the discretion of the Tribunal to adduce further facts which were not before the Inspector or the Secretary of State."

25. Service of a Purchase Notice

On a refusal, either by a local planning authority or by the Secretary of State, of planning permission, or on the grant thereof subject to conditions, an aggrieved applicant, if an "owner" as defined in section 290(1) of the 1971 Act (and a freeholder who has let his land for less than a rack-rent is excluded by the definition[60]), may *in certain cases* require his interest in the land to be purchased by the council of the district where the land is situated (s.180). The requirement must be by a notice in writing called a "purchase notice."[61]

26. Planning Application Decided by the Secretary of State in the First Instance—the "Called-in Application"

Though applications for permission for development will normally be dealt with by local planning authorities, the Secretary of State may require any application to be referred to him for decision by himself (s.35 and General Development Order 1977, art. 19).[62] Such applications are sometimes referred to as "called-in applications." This power of determining an application in the first instance is quite distinct from the Secretary of State's power, under section 36 of the 1971 Act, to determine an appeal against the decision of a local planning authority.

The power of the Secretary of State to call in, under section 35 of the 1971 Act, an application for planning permission covers also an application for approval by a local planning authority of matters reserved in an outline planning permission earlier granted by the authority (s.35(1)).

Before deciding an application for planning permission the Secretary of State must, if either the applicant or the local planning authority so request (General Development Order 1977, art. 19), afford each of them an opportunity of a private hearing before a person appointed by the Secretary of State for the purpose—the Secretary of State's Inspector (s.35(5)).

[60] *London Corporation* v. *Cusack-Smith* [1955] A.C. 337, H.L.
[61] As to purchase notices, see Chap. 18.
[62] S.I. 1977 No. 289.

Where an application for planning permission is called in by the Secretary of State, certain sections of the 1971 Act relating to:

(1) the publication generally of notices of the planning application (s.26(2) and (7));
(2) the notices to be given to owners and to agricultural tenants (s.27);
(3) the grant of planning permission (s.29(1)(2) and (3)); and
(4) the imposition of conditions affecting other land or requiring the removal of buildings at the end of a specified period (s.30(1));

are made applicable to the matter (s.35(4)).

It is provided that the decision of the Secretary of State in a called-in application "shall be final" (s.35(6)) but, as in the case of an appeal to the Secretary of State from the decision of a local planning authority, a "person aggrieved" and a local "authority directly concerned with [the] action on the part of the Secretary of State" may, within six weeks, challenge the Secretary of State's decision in the High Court on a point of law (ss.242(1)(*e*), (3)(*a*) and 245(1)(*b*), (3)(4)(7)).[63]

Notwithstanding the foregoing *statutory* provisions of the 1971 Act as to challenge in the High Court, the Secretary of State's decision may be quashed on *certiorari* on the ground that in making it the Secretary of State has exercised his discretion so unreasonably as not to amount to an exercise of discretion at all. On this, reference may be made to the judgment of Lord Greene M.R. in *Associated Provincial Picture Houses* v. *Wednesbury Corporation.*[64] A court will not, however, go into the propriety of the policy considerations applied in any particular case.[65]

The inference drawn from *R.* v. *Northumberland Compensation Appeal Tribunal, ex parte Shaw,*[66] that a decision of the Secretary of State could be quashed by *certiorari* if there is an error of law on the face thereof has been established as law in *R.* v. *Medical Appeal Tribunal, ex parte Gilmore.*[67] It was said that the remedy of *certiorari* is not to be taken away by any statute except by the most clear and explicit words. "Final" means only without appeal, and not without recourse to *certiorari*.

[63] See cases quoted at p. 222.
[64] [1948] 1 K.B. 223, C.A.
[65] *R.* v. *East Kesteven R.D.C.* [1947] 1 All E.R. 310, D.C.; *R.* v. *London Borough of Harringay, ex parte Barrs and Faherty* (1983) unreported but mentioned, *ante*, at p. 223. See also *Pickvance* v. *Secretary of State for the Environment*, also unreported but quoted, *ante*, at p. 223.
[66] [1952] 1 K.B. 338, C.A. See also cases quoted in notes 51, 56 of this Chapter, *ante*.
[67] [1957] 1 Q.B. 574, C.A.

27. Planning Permission for Development by Local Authorities and Statutory Undertakers, and on Crown Land

The 1971 Act contains special provisions relating to planning permission for development by local authorities and by statutory undertakers (ss.40, 222–241, 270, 271 and 272).

Much of the development carried out by a local authority or a statutory undertaker in the normal course of their duties as public bodies is covered by Classes XIII to XXI, referred to in the Schedule to the Town and Country Planning General Development Order 1977,[68] and is accordingly "permitted development" under article 3 of that Order.

Under section 270 of the 1971 Act the Secretary of State has made the Town and Country Planning General Regulations 1976,[69] Part II of which relates to planning permission for development by local planning authorities.

As to planning control over development of Crown land, this is dealt with in section 266 of the 1971 Act and in the Town and Country Planning Act 1984 the latter Act being passed specially to remedy certain planning anomalies relating to Crown land. The traditional constitutional position that the planning Acts do not bind the Crown is maintained (and, accordingly, planning permission is not required by the Crown for its own development[70]) but the 1984 Act now allows the Crown to apply for planning permission for development (other than its own development) so that it can thereby sell land with the benefit of a planning permission which will have the effect of increasing the value of the land and, in consequence, the amount of the purchase money to be paid for the land. The 1984 Act also allows enforcement action (notwithstanding s.266(3) of the 1971 Act) to be taken in respect of the development of Crown land where the development is not by, or on behalf of the Crown, nor by right of a private interest in the land.

The Secretary of State has made, in respect of Crown land, the Town and Country Planning (Crown Land Applications) Regulations 1984[71] and the Town and Country Planning (Special Enforcement Notice) Regulations 1984.[72] He has also issued D.O.E. Circular 18/84 dated August 3, 1984 giving advice on, and a descriptive account of the provisions of, the 1984 Act.

[68] S.I. 1977 No. 289.

[69] S.I. 1976 No. 1419.

[70] *Ministry of Agriculture, Fisheries and Food* v. *Jenkins* (1963) 2 Q.B. 317; *R.* v. *Worthing Borough Council, ex parte Burch* (1984) J.P.L. 261.

[71] S.I. 1984 No. 1015.

[72] S.I. 1984 No. 1016; and see p. 345.

28. Revocation or Modification of Planning Permission

It has already been stated that planning permission once given enures (subject to limitations of time contained in the grant of permission itself or imported into the matter by sections 41 to 44 inclusive of the 1971 Act discussed earlier in this chapter) for the benefit of all persons for the time being interested in the land affected (s.33(1)) but this is subject to the right of a local planning authority to revoke or modify a planning permission by means of an order made by the authority and confirmed by the Secretary of State (s.45). Before confirming the order the Secretary of State must afford the owner and the occupier of land affected by the order an opportunity of being heard by the Secretary of State's Inspector (s.45(3)).

Under section 46 of the 1971 Act certain orders (but not all orders—s.46(6)) revoking or modifying planning permissions, which orders are unopposed, will continue to be made by the local planning authority but will not require confirmation by the Secretary of State (s.46 and Town and Country Planning General Regulations 1976,[73] reg. 19).

A local planning authority desirous of revoking or modifying a planning permission previously granted by them must do so either:

(a) before building operations authorised by the permission have been completed, in which case the revocation or modification is not to affect so much of the building operations as have been carried out; or

(b) before any change in use of land authorised by the planning permission has taken place (s.45(4)).

The validity of an order revoking or modifying a grant of planning permission may, within six weeks, be challenged on a point of law in the High Court by a "person aggrieved"[74] or by an "authority directly concerned"[74] (ss.242(1)(*d*), (2)(*a*) and 245(1)(*a*), (2), (3), (4), (7)).

Compensation may become payable on revocation or modification of a previous planning permission and this is considered in Chapter 17.

On the revocation or modification of a grant of planning permission a purchase notice may, in appropriate circumstances, be served, by the owner, upon the council of the London borough or county district where the land is situated requiring the purchase of land (s.188).[75]

[73] S.I. 1976 No. 1419.

[74] See pp. 221 to 230 inclusive.

[75] As to purchase notices generally, see Chap. 18.

29. Review of Planning Decisions Where Compensation Claimed

Under the provisions of Part VII of the 1971 Act (relating to compensation for planning decisions restricting new development) compensation *may* in limited circumstances[76] become payable. When this is the case it is open to the Secretary of State to review the planning decision which gives rise to the claim for compensation and to direct that a different decision be made so as thereby to remove (or to minimise) the claim for compensation (ss.38 and 39). Such a direction may require that the application be granted in terms "more favourable to the applicant" (s.38(2), (4)) or that planning permission be granted for some form of substituted development (s.38(3)).

30. Eighth Report of House of Commons Expenditure Committee 1977—Planning Procedures

On May 19, 1977 the Report of the Environment Sub-Committee of the House of Commons Expenditure Committee for Session 1976–1977 was ordered to be printed and published.[77]

It emerges from the Report that the "total cost to local authorities of administering the planning system was approximately £104 million in 1975–76, of which about £38 million was attributable to development control and £66 million to other planning work. On April 1, 1976 the local planning authorities employed nearly 17,500 staff, 38 per cent. in development control and 62 per cent. in other planning work. (The apportionment of staff and expenditure between development control and other planning work is a rough estimate, as many district authorities make no distinction between local plans and development control in their working arrangements.) In addition the Department of the Environment employed 656 staff on planning work (including appeals) at a total cost of just over £9.5 million. Thus the total public sector cost of development control and planning was approximately £113.5 million in 1975–76."

It will be noted that all the figures quoted in the previous paragraph relate to the year 1975–76. They are the latest available and are quoted here as a matter of interest.

[76] See Chap. 17.
[77] It was published by HMSO at 85p net, but is now out of print. The Government's Response to the Report is given in the White Paper, "Planning Procedures", dated January 1978, Cmnd. 7056.

31. Planning Appeals Statistics

Figures for planning appeals for England for the quarter ended June 30, 1986, have now (November 1986) been published. They show that the overall success rate for planning appeals in the quarter to be 40 per cent., 1 per cent. lower than in the previous three quarters.[78]

The most important statistics are as follows:

1. Appeals in hand at start of quarter	9615	(9099)
2. Appeals received during quarter	4538	(4652)
3. Appeals withdrawn during quarter	567	(610)
4. Appeals decided during quarter	3222	(3526)
5. Appeals in hand at end of quarter	10364	(9615)
6. Analysis of appeals decided:		
Secretary of State inquiry cases	87	(73)
Secretary of State written representation cases	163	(125)
Transferred inquiry cases	415	(318)
Transferred written representation cases	2455	(2902)
Transferred informal hearing cases	102	(108)
7. Appeals allowed (as a percentage of total decisions)	40%	(41%)

Figures for the previous March 1986 quarter are shown in brackets.

The median times for decisions given during the June 1986 quarter was as follows:

Secretary of State inquiry cases	60 weeks
Secretary of State written representation cases	35 ,,
Transferred inquiry cases	36 ,,
Transferred written representation cases	19 ,,
Transferred informal hearing cases	27 ,,

The success rates of each type of appeal proceedings were as follows:

Secretary of State inquiry cases	40%
Secretary of State written representation cases	41%
Transferred inquiry cases	52%
Transferred written representation cases	37%
Transferred informal hearing cases	49%

32. Section 52 Agreements Restricting or Regulating the Development of Land

Irrespective of the powers whereby a local planning authority may control development by the granting or withholding of planning permission, a local planning authority may enter into agreements with landowners restricting or regulating the development of land either permanently or for temporary periods (s.52(1)). Any such agreement may contain such incidental and consequential provisions (including provisions of a financial character) as appear to the local

[78] D.O.E. Press Notice 493 dated September 19, 1986.

planning authority to be necessary or expedient for the purposes of the agreement (*ibid*).

Any section 52 agreement is enforceable against persons deriving title under the person with whom the agreement was originally made (s.52(2)) thus avoiding the difficulty which arose in *London County Council* v. *Allen.*[79]

Further discussion on the scope and effect of a section 52 agreement will be found in Chapter 11 at pp. 258 to 263 inclusive to which reference should be made.

33. Stopping Up and Diversion of Highways

So that development may proceed in accordance with planning permission granted under Part III of the 1971 Act, Part X of the Act—sections 209 to 221 inclusive—makes provision for the stopping up or diversion of highways.[80]

What is popularly known as the "planning" method of closing or diverting public streets and roads has been increasingly resorted to in place of the more cumbersome procedure under sections 84 to 91 of the Highways Act 1835. These sections are repealed by the Highways Act 1959, Schedule XXVI, and the stopping up and diversion of highways is now dealt with in Part VI of the Highways Act 1959. It is, however, provided by section 115 of the latter Act that these provisions shall not prejudice a power to stop up or divert a highway contained in any other enactment as, for example, Part X of the Town and Country Planning Act 1971.

When the carrying out of development under a planning permission already granted requires that a public highway (whether a carriageway, bridleway or footway) shall be closed up or diverted, an order for such treatment can be made by the Secretary of State (ss.209 and 215). If the highway in question is a footpath or bridleway, the order may also be made (subject—unless the order is unopposed—to confirmation by the Secretary of State (s.217 and Sched. 20)), by a competent authority (s.210) which means a local planning authority (s.210(4)).

The making of a stopping-up or a diversion order for a highway takes time. Accordingly, the Secretary of State can, in certain circumstances, make a *draft* order stopping up or diverting a highway

[79] [1914] 3 K.B. 642, C.A. The Local Government (Miscellaneous Provisions) Act 1982, s.33, superseding s.126 of the Housing Act 1974, enables a local authority to enter into a "section 52 agreement", enforceable against successors, even though it contains *positive* (as distinct from negative) obligations.

[80] *Harlow* v. *Minister of Transport and Others* (1951) 2 K.B. 98, C.A.; *Lewis Thirkwell Ltd.* v. *Secretary of State for the Environment* [1978] J.P.L. 844.

notwithstanding that planning permission for the related development has not yet been actually granted (s.216). In short, the proceedings for the highway order and for the planning permission can go forward concurrently and this will lead to a saving of time. The highway order cannot, however, be *finally* made unless and until the related planning permission has been granted (s.216(5)). The circumstances when this concurrent procedure is available are set out in section 216(2), (3) and (4).

Another ground for closing or diverting a highway by the Secretary of State is where planning permission is granted for constructing or improving a highway (or the Secretary of State proposes to do this sort of thing) and some *other* highway crosses or enters the route of such highway. In these circumstances an order may be made stopping up or diverting such *other* intruding highway if it appears to the Secretary of State that it is expedient to do so in the interests of safety or in order to facilitate traffic movements (s.211).

Provision is made whereby, for the purpose of improving amenity, an order can be made by the Secretary of State changing a highway which carries vehicles as well as pedestrians into a highway restricted solely for use by pedestrians with or without horses (s.212). This could be useful in connection with the provision of what are sometimes called "shopping malls." Action rests in the first place with the local planning authority who must first consult the highway authority (if a different authority) and any other authority who are a local planning authority for the area in question (s.212(2)). The order, having been made, may be revoked or varied by a subsequent order (s.212(8)).

If any such restrictive change in the use of a highway is ordered, compensation for consequential injurious affection may be claimed from the local planning authority (s.212(5) and (6)) by any person who has "lawful access" (*i.e.* access authorised by a planning permission or access which needs no such permission (s.212(5)) to the highway. The claim for compensation must be made in the manner and within the time (six months) prescribed by regulations (s.212(6) and Town and Country Planning Regulations 1976,[81] reg. 14).

Where a local authority have acquired or appropriated land (ss.214(2) and 133(1)) and are holding it for planning purposes (s.214(1)) the Secretary of State may by order extinguish rights of way over that land, provided alternative rights are given or he is satisfied none is required (s.214(1)(*a*)). Similarly, if the right of way is a footpath or a bridleway (but not a carriageway) and provided an alternative right of way is given or the local authority are satisfied no

[81] S.I. 1976 No. 1419.

such alternative is needed, the local authority may by order extinguish the right of way (s.214(1)(*b*)). The order of the local authority requires confirmation (unless it is unopposed) by the Secretary of State (s.217 and Sched. 20).

34. Control of Hazardous Substances—Hazardous Substances Consent

Part IV of the Housing and Planning Act 1986, entitled "Hazardous Substances", contains only five sections which relate to England and Wales but they make masterful changes in the Town and Country Planning Act 1971 by inserting into that Act no less than 15 new sections, all dealing with hazardous substances about which the Secretary of State had earlier issued D.O.E. Circular 9/84, dated March 30, 1984, entitled "Planning Controls over Hazardous Development".

It is strange that the 1986 Act should seek to complicate the 1971 Act in this fashion. It is true that control of hazardous substances becomes increasingly important nowadays—what on earth *are* we going to do about nuclear waste?—but that does not seem a good reason for attaching a brand new system of control over an exclusive, not to say esoteric, matter, namely, hazardous substances, to the current, and now well-established, system of planning control over land development. Indeed, Part IV of the 1986 Act does not appear to deal with development at all; it deals *not* with the development of a hazardous substance but with the mere *having of it* "on, over or under land" (1971 Act, s.58A). The pitching into the 1971 Act of this new system of control our hazardous substances appears to fly in the face of ministerial comment in at least two D.O.E. Circulars. D.O.E. Circular 55/76, relating to the Control of Pollution Act 1974, declares:

> "2. . . . In the absence of specific control, conditions attached to a planning permission have, in the past, been used for the purpose of water protection and public health which are now met by the licensing system. *It has long been accepted that planning control should not be used to secure objectives for which provision is made in other legislation* (my italics) and conditions attached to new planning permissions should not therefore extend to matters which are more appropriate to the disposal licensing system."

Again, D.O.E. Circular 9/84 (mentioned above) declares:

> "5. *The planning system should not, however, be used to pursue objectives more appropriate to health and safety legislation* (my italics). The local planning authority's responsibility is to decide whether

development involving a hazardous installation is an appropriate use for the land, taking into account existing and prospective development in the vicinity, and to consider what planning conditions should properly be imposed restricting that use. The Health and Safety Executive are responsible for ensuring that the hazardous installation is operated, so far as is reasonably practicable, safely and without risk to health, in accordance with the requirements of the Health and Safety at Work etc. Act, 1974. The Executive will advise the local planning authority on the potential hazards of the proposed installations so that the authority can make a properly informed decision on its planning merits. Local planning authorities will wish to protect the communities they represent by imposing any conditions which may be appropriate, but in doing so they should endeavour to avoid duplicating the controls for which the Health and Safety Executive are responsible and in particular should not impose conditions which are at variance with them."

Notwithstanding all the foregoing, the Housing and Planning Act 1986 (as already stated) makes great changes (1986 Act, ss.30, 31 and 32) in the Town and Country Planning Act 1971 by inserting into that Act:

(1) two new sections, enumerated sections 1A and 1B respectively dealing with those authorities each of which are to be a "hazardous substances authority"—usually this will be the council of the district or London borough in which the substance is situated but in a shire county it will be the county council for land in a National Park or land used for mineral working or used (in England) for refuse and waste disposal, while
   (i) in an urban development area[82] it will be the urban development corporation[82] (if they have been made the local planning authority for all kinds of development),[82] and
   (ii) in the case of operational land of a statutory undertaker, it will be the appropiate Minister for the purposes of the undertaking;

(2) 12 new sections enumerated, respectively, sections 58B, 58C 58D, 58E, 58F, 58G, 58H, 58J, (there is no 58I) 58K, 58L, 58M and 58N, the gist of all of which is dealt with below; and

(3) one new section, enumerated section 101B, which relates to the power of a hazardous substances authority to issue a hazardous substances contravention notice if they think it

[82] See Chap. 23.

expedient so to do having regard to *any* material consideration.

What is a "hazardous substance?" This remains to be dealt with in regulations to be made by the Secretary of State for the Environment (1971 Act, s.58A) as also is the quantity which is to be the controllable quantity under the 1971 Act (*ibid.*).

Sections 58B to 58N inclusive of the 1971 Act (all inserted, it will be remembered by the Housing and Planning Act 1986, s.31) contain enactments which will ensure that certain provisions of the 1971 Act relating to administration and enforcement of development control are applied, *mutatis mutandis*, to the new form of "Additional Control in Special Cases" (Pt. IV of the 1971 Act), namely, hazardous substances control. Briefly, the 12 new sections of the 1971 Act 58B to 58N inclusive function as follows.

Sections 58B, 58C, 58D and 58E adapt for the purposes of applications for "hazardous substances consent" the provisions of the 1971 Act relating to the making and determination of planning applications, consultation, "call-in" of applications and appeals.

Section 58F provides for hazardous substances consent to be deemed to be given in cases where a government department authorises a development by a local authority or statutory undertaker.

Section 58G provides for applications to vary or revoke conditions attached to hazardous substances consents.

Section 58H enables a hazardous substance consent to be revoked or modified in certain circumstances.

Section 58J provides for the benefit of a hazardous substances consent to run with the land to which it relates, subject to special provisions which apply when control of that land is divided.

Section 58K provides that contraventions of hazardous substances control shall be offences.

Section 58L enables the Secretary of State to make a temporary direction in an emergency overriding hazardous substances control.

Section 58M provides for registers to be kept containing information concerning hazardous substances applications and consents.

Section 58N provides that where there is a conflict between a requirement imposed under the provisions of the 1971 Act relating to hazardous substances and a requirement under health and safety legislation, the latter shall prevail.

New section 101B of the 1971 Act (added by the Housing and Planning Act 1986 section 32) empowers a hazardous substances authority to issue a "hazardous substances contravention notice" requiring steps to be taken to remedy the contravention. The section also enables regulations to be made providing for an appeal to the Secretary of State against a hazardous substances contravention notice and to enable a stop notice to be issued.

The Housing Planning Act 1986 was passed on November 7, 1986 but Part IV of the Act (Hazardous Substances) will not come into operation until an appointed day (1986 Act, s.57(2)) which means such day (or days) as may be appointed by the Secretary of State for the Environment (*ibid.*).

Finally, it must be mentioned that, during a transitional period (*i.e.* the period of six months beginning with the date when Part IV of the Housing and Planning Act 1986 comes into operation—(1986 Act, s.34(10)) an existing keeper or user of hazardous substances may claim a hazardous substances consent. Where a valid claim is submitted, a consent is deemed to be granted for the same activities involving the presence of hazardous substances at the same level as before the commencement of the provisions (1986 Act, s.34).

35. Council of the European Communities—Environmental Assessment

This Chapter may conclude with a warning that the Council of the European Communities has adopted their first Directive relating (Article 1) to "the assessment of the environmental effects of those public and private projects which are likely to have significant effects on the environment." The Directive (85/337/EEC) is dated June 27, 1985. It emanates from Luxembourg and is addressed (Article 14) to the Member States. These include England and Wales. It was notified to the Member States on July 3, 1985 and the Member States have now (Article 12) three years from that date (*i.e.* until July 3, 1988) in which to take the necessary measures to comply with the Directive, that is to say, to adapt their planning legislation and procedures in order to obtain what the Directive sets out to achieve. This appears to be the first instance of the European Economic Community (the so-called "common market") seeking to influence the English system of planning control over land development. The Directive is set out in full at pages 10 *et seq.* of the *Journal of Planning and Environment Law* for January 1987.

CHAPTER 11

PLANNING CONDITIONS; PLANNING BARGAINING—SECTION 52 AGREEMENTS; PLANNING GAIN—THE USE AND MISUSE OF AUTHORITY

1. Planning Conditions

(1) *What are, and are not, lawful planning conditions*

WITHOUT prejudice to the general right under section 29(1) of the 1971 Act to grant planning permission subject to such conditions "as they think fit," a local planning authority may specifically grant planning permission subject to conditions:

(a) for regulating the development of *any* land under the control of the applicant, or requiring the carrying out of works on such land if these matters appear to the authority to be expedient in relation to the development for which planning permission is given (s.30(1)(*a*));

(b) for requiring the removal of buildings or works, or the discontinuance of any use of land, authorised by the planning permission at the end of a specified period (s.30(1)(*b*)) in which case the permission is known as a "planning permission granted for a limited period" (s.30(2));

(c) for requiring that the building or other operations permitted by the planning permission shall be *commenced* (not, it will be noted, *finished*) not later than a specified date (s.30(3)(*a*)) in which case any operations commenced after that date will be operations commenced and carried out without planning permission (s.30(3)(*b*)).

As to the general right under section 29(1) of the 1971 Act, of a local planning authority, when granting planning permission for development, to grant it "either unconditionally or subject to such conditions as they think fit," it is to be noted that in *Mixnam's Properties* v. *Chertsey Urban District Council* [1964] 1 Q.B.D. 214, (affirmed in the House of Lords, *sub nom., Chertsey Urban District Council* v. *Mixnam's Properties* [1965] A.C. 735), Willmer L.J. in the Court of Appeal stated four general limitations to which he said a statutory permission to impose conditions is subject. These limitations (he said) are:

(1) conditions must not be such as to effect a fundamental alteration in the general law;

(2) conditions must be limited by reference to the subject-matter of the Statute;

(3) conditions must not be unreasonable;
(4) conditions must be sufficiently certain and unambiguous.

A condition stipulating for the payment of an annual sum of money to a local planning authority as security for the final fulfilment of a number of conditions subject to which planning permission was granted has been held by the Secretary of State on appeal to be improper, the Secretary of State being advised that the general rule of law in such matters is that no money can be demanded from any person except on distinct authority laid down by statute.[1]

In exercising their discretion to add conditions to a grant of planning permission, a local planning authority cannot do *just as they please* and section 29(1) of the 1971 Act does not mean this when it says that a planning authority may add to a planning permission such conditions "as they think fit." This means that the conditions must be thought to be "fit" (*i.e.* meet, fit, proper, appropriate, apt, requisite, etc.) *from a planning point of view*. Statutory support for this assertion is to be found in subsection (1) itself of section 29 when it enacts that the "authority, in dealing with the application [for planning permission], shall have regard to the provisions of the development plan, so far as material to the application, and to any other material considerations."

It is well settled that a public body holding the privileged position of being able to exercise their discretion when coming to a decision must exercise that discretion reasonably and in good faith.[2] The exercise of an executive discretion in relation to the attaching of conditions to a grant of planning permission was scrutinised when *Pyx Granite Co. Ltd.* v. *Ministry of Housing and Local Government* was before the Court of Appeal.[3] In his judgment in the Court of Appeal Lord Denning said[4]:

> "The principles to be applied are not, I think, in doubt. Although the planning authorities are given very wide powers to impose 'such conditions as they think fit,' nevertheless the law says that those conditions, to be valid, must fairly and reasonably relate to the permitted development. The planning

[1] Case III/16, at p. 12 of the Ministry of Town and Country Planning Bulletin of Selected Appeal Decisions No. III, dated April 1948. See also D.O.E. Circular 1/85, dated January 7, 1985, entitled "The Use of Conditions in Planning Permissions," Annex, para. 63, "Planning Gain".

[2] See Lord Greene M.R. in *Associated Provincial Picture Houses Ltd.* v. *Wednesbury Corporation* [1948] 1 K.B. 223 at pp. 228, 233.

[3] [1958] 1 Q.B. 554, C.A.; reversed on other grounds [1960] A.C. 260, H.L.

[4] *Ibid.* at p. 572.

authority are not at liberty to use their powers for an ulterior object, however desirable that object may seem to them to be in the public interest. If they mistake or misuse their powers, however *bona fide*, the court can interfere by declaration and injunction: see *Sydney Municipal Council* v. *Campbell*[5]; *Roberts* v. *Hopwood*[6]; and *Smith* v. *East Elloe Rural District Council*."[7]

These words of Lord Denning were later approved in the House of Lords in *Fawcett Properties* v. *Buckingham County Council* [1961] A.C. 636 at page 674 by Lord Keith of Avonholm and at page 685 by Lord Jenkins; in *Mixnam's Properties* v. *Chertsey U.D.C.* [1965] A.C. 735 at page 751 by Lord Reid and at page 761 by Lord Guest; and also in *Newbury District Counil* v. *Secretary of State for the Environment* [1981] A.C. 578.

In *Fawcett Properties Ltd.* v. *Buckingham County Council*[8] the county council, in granting planning permission to erect a pair of semi-detached cottages, added a condition that: "The occupation of the houses shall be limited to persons whose employment or latest employment is or was employment in agriculture as defined by section 119(1) of the Town and Country Planning Act 1947, or in forestry, or in an industry mainly dependent upon agriculture and including also the dependents of such persons aforesaid." The local planning authority stated in writing (as required by the Town and Country Planning General Development Order 1950, art. 5(9)(*a*)) their reasons for imposing this condition. When this case was before the Court of Appeal, Pearce L.J. (as he then was) said[9]:

"The council are, by the terms of section 14 of the Town and Country Planning Act 1947 [now section 29(1)(*a*) of the 1971 Act] entitled to grant permission 'subject to such conditions as they think fit.' The *Wednesbury* case (*i.e. Associated Provincial Picture Houses Ltd.* v. *Wednesbury Corporation* [1948] 1 K.B. 223) makes it clear that the court will not interfere with that discretion unless it is shown that the authority did not take into account the right considerations, that is, that they disregarded something which they should have taken into account or regarded something which they should not have taken into account. The onus of showing this is on the person seeking to upset the condition imposed by the authority. That onus may

[5] [1925] A.C. 338 at p. 343.
[6] [1925] A.C. 578 at p. 613.
[7] [1956] A.C. 736 at pp. 762, 763.
[8] [1959] Ch. 543, C.A.; affirmed [1961] A.C. 636, H.L.
[9] [1959] Ch. 575 at p. 576.

> be discharged either by showing from the terms of the condition itself that the authority cannot have taken into account the right considerations or by extrinsic evidence to that effect . . .
>
> "When no reasons are given and decisions of the authority present what Lord Sumner called in another context 'the inscrutable face of a sphinx,' it is hard to discharge such an onus. However, in the case of conditions imposed under section 14 it has been provided (by a statutory instrument[10]) that reasons must be given. No doubt the purpose of that is to help and inform the persons on whom conditions are imposed. Moreover, by the last four lines of section 14(1) [now section 29(1) of the 1971 Act, reminding the local planning authority to pay attention to "the provisions of the development plan . . . and to any other material considerations"] indication has been given of the matters which the authority must take into account. But the general principle remains that the condition cannot be upset by this court unless it be shown that the authority have not taken into account the right matters . . .
>
> "The court will, of course, hold a condition *ultra vires* if it does not 'fairly and reasonably relate to the permitted development,'[11] but in this case it does so relate. Here there is no extrinsic evidence that the authority did not take the right matters into account."

This instructive dissertation by Pearce L.J. may be used as an authoritative yardstick by which to measure the validity of any condition attached to a grant of planning permission for development.

In *Hall & Co. Ltd.* v. *Shoreham-by-Sea Urban District Council,*[12] a condition which not only required landowners to build a road on their own land but also, in effect, to grant a public right of way over it without compensation was held by the Court of Appeal to be so unreasonable as to be *ultra vires*.

Similarly, conditions attached to an outline planning permission for residential development that the houses should be occupied by persons on the local authority's waiting list, with security of tenure

[10] Town and Country Planning General Development Order 1950 (S.I. 1950 No. 728), art. 5(9)—see now Town and Country Planning General Development Order 1977 (S.I. 1977 No. 289), art. 7(7).

[11] See Lord Denning's judgment in *Pyx Granite Co. Ltd.* v. *Ministry of Housing and Local Government* [1958] 1 Q.B. 554 at p. 572.

[12] [1964] 1 W.L.R. 240, C.A.; (1964) 1 All E.R. 1; See also *Britannia (Cheltenham) Ltd.* v. *Secretary of State for the Environment and Tewkesbury Council* [1978] J.P.L. 554; and *City of Bradford Metropolitan Council* v. *Secretary of State for the Environment and McClean Homes Northern Ltd.* (1986) J.P.L. 292 and 598.

for 10 years, were held to be unreasonable and *ultra vires* because they had the effect of relieving the local authority (in its capacity as a housing authority under the legislation relating to housing) from their *statutory* duty to provide houses and, as such, the conditions were not directed to the furtherance of any true planning purpose.[13]

Thus, it can be said that, whilst there are many yardsticks by which the lawfulness of a planning condition can be measured (including the four limitations cited above by Wilmer L.J. in *Mixnam's* case) it seems, from a general appreciation of all the cases quoted so far in this chapter, that a planning condition to be valid must (at least):

(1) fulfil a planning purpose (the *Royco Homes* case);
(2) be fairly and reasonably related to the development for which planning permission is granted (*Pyx Granite* case; but see *Grampian Regional Council* v. *City of Aberdeen* (1984) J.P.L. 590, where the planning condition (granted in *negative* form) was upheld by the House of Lords even though it related to danger at a road junction 1½ kilometres distant from the development site); and
(3) be clearly reasonable, that is to say, it must not be "so unreasonable that no reasonable planning authority could have imposed it" (see *Mixnam's* case, per Diplock L.J. at page 237; and *Kingston upon Thames Royal London Borough Council* v. *Secretary of State for the Environment* (1974) 1 All E.R. 193, per Lord Widgery C.J. at page 196).

(2) *Planning conditions—the views of the Secretary of State*

The views of the Secretary of State on the attaching of conditions to a grant of planning permission are now set out at length in D.O.E. Circular 1/85 dated January 7, 1985, entitled, "The Use of Conditions in Planning Permissions". This is a lengthy document of 31 pages but it is, undoubtedly, essential reading for any developer proposing to apply for planning permission or, more particularly, make an appeal to the Secretary of State against a planning decision by the local planning authority which either refuses him planning permission *in toto*, or grants it subject to conditions which the developer finds unacceptable.

In the body of the Circular the Secretary of State (para. 1) reminds the reader (in effect) that the wide power to impose conditions on a grant of planning permission may well be the enabling

[13] *R.* v. *London Borough of Hillingdon, ex p. Royco Homes Ltd.* [1974] 2 W.L.R. 805; 28 P. and C.R. 251.

key which opens the way ahead for many a scheme of development which otherwise might have had to be stopped. But the objectives of planning, the Circular adds (*ibid.*), are best served when the power to add conditions is exercised in such a way that "the conditions are seen to be fair, reasonable and practicable."

The Annex to the Circular (paras. 11–15) particularly stress the tests to be applied to planning conditions and itemises six tests each of which in turn is analysed in detail. The six tests are:

(1) necessity for the condition;
(2) relevance of the condition to planning;
(3) relevance of the condition to the development to be permitted;
(4) enforceability of the condition;
(5) precision of the condition; and
(6) reasonableness of the condition in all other respects.

The Annex (as stated) puts each of these six tests to close scrutiny, an analysis which need not be repeated here but which should certainly be read in full in the Circular itself. To take but one example (relating to test (1) about the necessity for a planning condition being imposed at all), the Annex, para. 12, declares:

> "*Test of need.*
>
> '12. In considering whether a particular condition is necessary, authorities should ask themselves whether planning permission would have to be refused if that condition were not to be imposed. If it would not, then the condition needs special and precise justification. The argument that a condition will do no harm is no justification for its imposition: as a matter of policy, a condition ought not to be imposed unless there is a definite need for it."

After the Annex, Circular 1/85 carries two Appendices. Appendix A carries a list of no less than 38 suggested models of planning conditions which, in appropriate circumstances, could be regarded as acceptable conditions. Appendix B, on the contrary, carries a list of 14 conditions which are unacceptable, the Appendix usefully going on to explain, in each case, the grounds of their unacceptability.

Paragraph 4 of the Circular makes an interesting suggestion in the following terms:

> "4. When applications come to appeal, the Secretaries of State or Planning Inspectors welcome reasoned suggestions from either of the parties as to conditions which they would find acceptable if permission were granted. Such suggestions will be fully examined and may or may not be adopted, but conditions

> will not be imposed if they are considered to be invalid or if they are unacceptable on policy grounds."

Extended reference in these pages has been made to Circular 1/85 because it would be hard to exaggerate its impact in the increasingly important field of planning conditions—are they, or are they not, legal?—should they, or should they not, be challenged? The field is increasingly important because statistics show that an enlarging number of planning applications is granted subject to conditions and that the conditions themselves are tending to proliferate.

It is not possible to conclude these references to Circular 1/85 (which gave a Grand, Advisory-Planning Opening of the New Year to all Chief Executive Officers—wherever they might be—embroiled in the day-to-day handling of planning applications) without quoting the rhetorical flourish of paragraph 3 of the Circular which speaks out in the following terms:

> "3. It is essential that the operation of the planning system should command public confidence. The sensitive use of conditions can improve development control and enhance that confidence. The use of conditions in an unreasonable way, however, so that it proves impracticable or inexpedient to enforce them, will damage such confidence and should be avoided."

(3) *Severability of planning conditions*

Assuming a planning condition is invalid the question arises: can the condition, subject to which planning permission has been granted, be severed from the permission itself, leaving the latter to stand on its own, free of the inhibiting restrictions caused by the invalid condition? Lord Justice Hodson (speaking *obiter*) in the *Pyx Granite* case said[14]:

> "The only remaining question is as to the conditions imposed by the Minister. I have nothing to add on this subject to the views expressed by my Lord as to the validity of the conditions generally. In any event it would, I think, be impossible to mutilate the Minister's decision by removing one or more of the conditions. The permission given has been given subject to those conditions, and *non constat* but that no permission would have been given at all if the conditions had not been attached. The

[14] [1958] 1 Q.B. 554 at pp. 578, 579.

consequence would be that if any of the conditions imposed were held to be bad as imposed without jurisdiction, the whole planning permission would fall with it, and the respondents would be left without any planning permission at all, for it would not be open to the court to leave the planning permission standing shorn of its conditions, or any of them."

It is worthwhile emphasising that in making the foregoing comment on the inseverability of a planning permission and its attendant conditions and on the wholly annihilating effect of one invalid condition upon an otherwise stainless planning permission, the learned judge was speaking *obiter*.

On this the comment may be quoted of Roxburgh J. in the Chancery Division in *Fawcett Properties Ltd.* v. *Buckingham County Council*[15] when, after quoting the observations (above) of Hodson L.J., he went on to say:

> "So that if there were twenty varied conditions attached to the permission to erect the house, and the house had been erected and yet one of them, however trivial, was *ultra vires*, there would be no planning permission for the erection of that house. Well, that is a very far-reaching *obiter dictum* and I am glad that I have been absolved from the duty of considering whether it is well-founded."

This particular matter came before the courts in *Hall & Co. Ltd.* v. *Shoreham-by-Sea Urban District Council.*[16] In this case the Court of Appeal, having held that a certain condition was invalid (as being *ultra vires*), the next question was: could the invalid condition be severed from the planning permission so as to leave the latter otherwise intact? Lord Justice Willmer referred to the remark (quoted above) of Roxburgh J. in the *Fawcett* case about "trivial" conditions but then added, "I do not think that any such problem arises in the present case, for here the conditions . . . are fundamental to the whole of the planning permission." Accordingly, it was held that the planning permission itself fell, dragged down by an invalid condition which was, however, *fundamental* to the permission and not a trivial attachment.

This important matter of the severability of conditions from planning permissions to which they are attached came before the Court of Appeal and thereafter the House of Lords in *Kingsway Investments (Kent) Ltd.* v. *Kent County Council.*[17]

15 [1958] 1 W.L.R. 1161, at p. 1167.

16 [1964] 1 W.L.R. 240; (1964) 1 All E.R. 1; and see also *Allnatt London Properties* v. *Middlesex C.C.* (1964) 15 P. & C.R. 288 and cases quoted in fn.12, *supra*.

17 [1971] A.C. 72; reversing [1969] 2 Q.B. 332.

In this case a condition (of a kind which had been attached to almost all outline planning permissions granted by the Kent County Council and other planning authorities since about 1950) providing that the permission "shall cease to have effect" after three years unless the planning authority, having received detailed plans from the developers, *had approved them and had notified their approval* to the developers within the three years, was held, by a majority of the Court of Appeal, to be unreasonable and invalid because the approval and the notification would be outside the control of the developer. The court also held (Davies and Winn L.JJ., with Lord Denning M.R. dissenting) that the invalid condition *could* be severed from the outline permission so that the permission remained in existence and could be acted on. The House of Lords, reversing the decision of the Court of Appeal by a three to two majority, held that the condition was valid, and that if the condition were void it could not have been deleted to leave the permission standing since it was of fundamental importance.[18]

It would appear from these decisions that, whether or not a planning permission is to be held wholly bad and of no effect by reason of the invalidity of some condition (or conditions) attached to it, is a matter to be decided on a basis of common sense and with particular inquiry as to whether the invalid condition is fundamental or trivial. There is some conflict (as the *Kingsway* case shows) of judicial opinion on the matter.

(4) *Development of land without compliance with earlier-attached planning conditions*

Section 31A of the Town & Country Planning Act 1971 was added to that Act by the Housing and Planning Act 1986, s.49(1)(*d*), Schedule 11, paragraph 4 which operates as from a day to be appointed by the Secretary of State for the Environment (1986 Act, s.57(2) and (3)). (Incidentally, subsection (3) of section 57 of the 1986 Act is misprinted as subsection "(5)" as the Queen's Printers' Copy of the Act.)

This new section 31A of the 1971 Act relates to planning applications for development of land without the need to comply with conditions subject to which a planning permission was earlier granted. Such an application for permission to carry out development freed from inhibiting acceptable or unacceptable conditions may now be made without fear (as was previously the case) of the

[18] [1971] A.C. 72. See also *R.* v. *London Borough of Hillingdon, ex p. Royco Homes Ltd.* [1974] 28 P. & C.R. 251.

developer losing the entire planning permission earlier granted to him. In other words, the local planning authority, when considering such an application to vary or revoke a planning condition, are now restricted to considering solely the condition in question. They cannot touch the planning permission as a whole—the general principle of the grant of permission is *not* to be re-opened.

2. Planning Bargaining—Section 52 Agreements

The lodging with the local planning authority of a formal application for planning permission for development is a first and most important step on the prickly road to the getting a grant of planning permission with or without conditions. It is much the practice, these days, for the applicant for planning permission to discuss with the planning officer or other authorised representative of the local planning authority a draft of the planning application *before* this important document is frozen into shape and formally lodged. These meetings with the planning officer can serve a useful purpose in that he may be able to make suggestions modifying the terms of the application which (in his view, at least) will give it a better chance of success when it ultimately comes before the local planning authority (or the authority's authorised committee) for formal determination. The applicant for permission may well be able to meet the modifications suggested by the planning officer without in any way prejudicing the integrity of the application.

All this sort of thing has come to be known (harshly) as "horse-trading" or (more elegantly) as "planning bargaining" and, within certain limits (relating, usually, to the attaching of conditions to the planning permission) there is nothing wrong with it. Indeed D.O.E. Circular 28/83 dated December 29, 1983, in paragraphs 8 and 9, positively recommends that this sort of thing should occur. It needs to be remembered, however, that, in the last analysis, it is *not* the word or opinion of the planning officer which carries the day—it is the view of the elected planning authority which is final and this need not necessarily coincide with the advice proferred to them by the planning officer.[19] Most planning committees of local authorities have now been thrown open to the public gaze so that an applicant for planning permission may attend (but not speak) and hear how his application is getting along.

[19] *Southend on Sea Corporation* v. *Hodgson (Wickford) Ltd.* (1962) 1 Q.B. 416. See also *Lever Finance Ltd.* v. *Westminster City Council* (1970) 21 P. & C.R. 1778; *Brooks & Burton Ltd.* v. *Secretary of State for the Environment* (1976) 75 L.G.R. 285, D.C.; *Western Fish Products Ltd.* v. *Penwith District Council and the Secretary of State for the Environment* (1978) J.P.L. 623.

If a planning officer finds himself in a position where his professional, technical advice on a planning application is rejected by the planning authority (and this is no new thing) this is no cause for discomfort on his part. He has discharged his professional duty to the best, no doubt, of his skill and ability but Parliament, under the 1947 Act (now the 1971 Act), made planning decisions the ultimate responsibility *not* of an appointed professional but of a committee of elected amateurs. The whole control is an administrative, democratic process. If the planning officer's advice is rejected then, clearly, the planning authority, if there is a planning appeal against their decision, must look elsewhere for a planning expert who will support their view. If they can't find one then the chairman (or some other elected member of the planning authority) will simply have to do his best.

It will be rare for the process of planning bargaining to go far before the question of a "section 52 agreement" rears its perplexing head.

Section 52 of the 1971 Act relates to "agreements regulating development or use of land." These are agreements *voluntarily* entered into between an applicant for planning permission and a local planning authority. Because they are agremeents between consenting parties many controls over the development of land can be achieved which the local planning authority could never have obtained by means of planning conditions attached to a grant of planning permission for the simple reason that the power to attach planning conditions is constrained and limited by law (as has already been explained and emphasised in earlier paragraphs of this chapter). Both the decision and the *obiter dicta* in the Court of Appeal in *City of Bradford Metropolitan Council* v. *Secretary of State for the Environment and McLean Homes Northern Ltd.* (1986) J.P.L. 598 make relevant and highly important reading on the question of whether that form of control over land development which *cannot* be achieved by a planning condition can *always and necessarily* be achieved by means of a section 52 agreement. In this case Lloyd L.J. declared:

> "If the proposed condition was manifestly unreasonable, then it was beyond the powers of the planning authority to impose it; and if it was beyond the powers of the planning authority to impose the condition, then it was beyond their power to agree [by a section 52 agreement] to impose it, *even if the developer consented.* As was stated in paragraph 35 of Circular 1/85: 'An unreasonable condition does not become reasonable because an applicant suggests it or consents to its terms.' If the condition was manifestly unreasonable, the willingness of

the developer was irrelevant. *Vires* could not be conferred by consent."

Under section 33 of the Local Government (Miscellaneous) Provisions Act 1982 (superseding section 126 of the Housing Act 1974) a section 52 agreement is enforceable against successors in title even though it contains *positive* (as distinct from negative) obligations.

Neither side (the local planning authority and the applicant for planning permission) can be *forced* into a section 52 agreement. It is the essence of the whole thing that it is voluntary. If the applicant can make no progress with a proposal for a section 52 agreement he can always fall back on his formally lodged application for planning permission (which must be dealt with within 8 weeks—or such extended period as may be agreed—from the receipt of the application by the local planning authority[20]) ever bearing in mind that it is not open to the authority to attach, to any grant of planning permission which they make, a condition that the applicant *shall* enter into a section 52 agreement. Such a condition is clearly unlawful because it breaches the test of reasonableness earlier mentioned in this chapter.[21]

Section 52 of the 1971 Act is not without its own problems. Subsection (1) of the section provides that a local planning authority may enter into an agreement (which, incidentally, requires no approval by the Secretary of State) between themselves and a person having an interest in land in their area, *restricting or regulating* the development or use of such land. Subsection (3)(*a*) of section 52 goes on to declare that:

> "Nothing in this section or in any agreement made thereunder shall be construed—
>
> (a) as restricting the exercise, in relation to land which is the subject of any such agreement, of any powers exercisable by any Minister or authority under this Act so long as those powers are exercised in accordance with the provisions of the development plan"—as to which see ss.290(1) and 20 of the 1971 Act—"or in accordance with any directions which may have been given by the Secretary of State as to the provisions to be included in such a plan."

The interpretation of this subsection is not easy. Can a local

[20] Town and Country Planning General Development Order 1977 (S.I. 1977 No. 289) art. 7(6).

[21] See D.O.E. Circular 22/83 dated August 25, 1983, entitled "Planning Gain." See also pp. 263 to 267 inclusive.

planning authority, by means of a section 52 agreement, fetter their powers under the 1971 Act?

A local authority made a section 52 agreement allowing the demolition of buildings. Later the authority under statutory powers conferred upon them by section 277 of the 1971 Act, designated the area where the buildings stood as a conservation area in which buildings could *not* be demolished *except* with the consent of the authority. Did this mean that the buildings referred to in the earlier-executed section 52 agreement could not be demolished without the consent of the authority who, having made the section 52 agreement, then went on to declare the area of the buildings a conservation area? It was held (but reversed on appeal) that it did not.[22] The learned judge (Fox J.) declared that in view of section 52(3) the planning authority could not use any of their statutory powers against the defendants to prevent the demolition of the buildings, unless what they were proposing was in accordance with the development plan. There had not been, and was not, any development plan. The result, in his view, was that the plaintiffs could not enforce their powers under section 277A in relation to the extension of the conservation area, so as to prevent the demolition of the buildings covered by the section 52 agreement.

This decision was reversed on appeal[23] when it was held that, on the true construction of section 52(3) of the 1971 Act, a local planning authority was not empowered by section 52(3) to bind themselves by an agreement not to exercise the powers conferred upon them by section 277 of the 1971 Act to designate areas as conservation areas which they had a public duty to exercise. Since neither section 52 itself nor the section 52 agreement could inhibit the local authority from including the defendant's land in the conservation area, the buildings on the defendants land were subject to the prohibition against demolition imposed by section 277A(2) of the 1971 Act.

As has been mentioned, a section 52 agreement may achieve for a local planning authority many matters (including what is popularly called "planning gain"—referred to later in this chapter) relating to, and arising out of, the control of land development which the authority could not achieve by a grant of planning permission for development loaded with conditions. It is emphasized once again that, in attaching conditions to a grant of planning permission, a local

[22] *Royal Borough of Windsor and Maidenhead* v. *Brandrose Investments Ltd.* (1981) J.P.L. 668; (1981) 3 All E.R. 38.

[23] *Windsor and Maidenhead Royal Borough Council* v. *Brandrose Investments Ltd.* (1983) 1 All E.R. 818.

planning authority, while they may attach such conditions "as they think fit," do not have a totally free hand.[24] Thus, there appears to be increasing resort to the use of a section 52 agreement to achieve what will satisfy the local planning authority when it comes to consider an application for planning permission for land development.

However, local planning authorities will need to remember that the completion of a section 52 agreement is not necessarily the end of their worries. What has been done freely by mutual agreement may, it appears, now be undone by unilateral action. In view of the decision of the Lands Tribunal in *Beecham Group Limited's Application* (LP/44/1979) it is to be remembered that the Tribunal is today prepared to assume jurisdiction (at least, in respect of negative covenants) to consider an application made by one of the parties to a section 52 agreement to have the constraints of the agreement set aside.

Application was made to the Lands Tribunal, under section 84(1) of the Law of Property Act 1925, to modify a restrictive covenant in a section 37 agreement (the predecessor of today's section 52 agreement) made in 1969 under the Town and Country Planning Act 1962 restricting the use of certain land to recreational use only. Application to the local planning authority had been made in 1979 for planning permission to develop the land by the erection of 45,000 square feet of building which permission had been granted by the Secretary of State on appeal to him and against the recommendation of his Inspector who had held a public local inquiry into the appeal. The Lands Tribunal demonstrated that it was not prepared to refuse the application to modify the restrictive covenant in the section 37 agreement either

(a) because the restrictive covenant was only 10 years old, or
(b) because the applicant for modification was one of the very parties who had entered into the section 37 agreement some 10 years earlier.

The restriction was modified accordingly.[25]

Where a third party (a neighbour) who was in no way associated with a duly negotiated and executed section 52 agreement, felt himself aggrieved by the grant of the planning permission on which the

[24] See "Planning Bargaining—the Pros and the Cons: or, How Much Can the System Stand?" by Desmond Heap and Antony J. Ward [1980] J.P.L. 631. For further discussion (judicial) on the interaction of planning permissions and section 52 agreements, see *McLaren* v. *Secretary of State for the Environment and Broxbourne Borough Council* [1981] J.P.L. 423.

[25] *Beecham Group Limited's Application, Estates Gazette,* November 22, 1980. See further, "Planning Agreements and the March of Time" by Antony J. Ward (1981) J.P.L. 557.

agreement was dependent, it was held that he had a sufficient interest to establish for him the requisite *locus standi* to enable him to challenge the legality of the planning permission—all which he did and the planning permission was declared null and void.[26]

3. Planning Gain—the Use and Misuse of Authority

Over the last 20 years or so the expression "planning gain" has increasingly come to be used in connection with conditions attached by a local planning authority to a grant of planning permission for development and also in connection with the execution of a "section 52 agreement" (referred to in the preceeding paragraphs of this chapter) made between an applicant for planning permission and the local planning authority to whom the application is made.

In October 1981 the Secretary of State for the Environment published the report entitled, "Planning Gain," prepared for him and at his request by his Property Advisory Group. The Secretary of State invited comment on the report from interested bodies and also from the general public. The report generated much interest, debate and disputation for strong (though greatly varying) feelings were held on the subject by local planning authorities, by developers, by politicians (of both the central government and of local government) by planning officers of local authorities and by town planning consultants in general. The outcome of all this was the issue of D.O.E. Circular 22/83 dated August 25, 1983 entitled, "Planning Gain."

What, then, is "planning gain?" It is a term which has come to be applied whenever, in connection with a grant of planning permission for development, the local planning authority seek to impose on the developer an obligation to carry out works not included in the development for which planning permission has been sought or to make some payment or confer some extraneous right or benefit in return for permitting development to take place. The local planning authority will seek to obtain these benefits or gains by means of planning conditions attached to the grant of planning permission or by means of a section 52 agreement "voluntarily" entered into by the developer or by a mixture of both these methods.

The whole of this procedure obviously has its uses but, equally obviously, it also has its misuses as, for example, when a developer

[26] *J.J. Steeples* v. *Derbyshire County Council* (1981) J.P.L. 582. See also *Covent Garden Community Association Ltd.* v. *Greater London Council* (1981) J.P.L. 183; *R.* v. *North Hertfordshire D.C., Ex parte Sullivan* (1981) J.P.L. 625 and 752; and House of Lords decision in *I.R.C.* v. *National Federation of Self-Employed and Small Businesses Ltd.* (1981) 2 All E.R. 65.

was told he could have his planning permission provided he entered into a section 52 agreement to spend many thousands of pounds on refurbishing a fine old church within the area of the planning authority but some three miles from the development site and having no association, historical or otherwise, with the site or the developer.

It has been felt, over recent years, that misuse of planning procedures (in order to obtain planning gains) was coming into the ascendant. This was putting the good name of planning and development control in jeopardy, something which was regarded, rightly, as a matter of grave importance. The outcome was D.O.E. Circular 22/83.

There is clearly a temptation for a local planning authority to jettison sound planning principles for getting (to put it crudely but simply) a share in the commercial advantages arising from the grant of planning permission for development. But commercial advantage (or gain) deriving from development for which the planning authority have granted permission (in the discharge, be it remembered, of their *statutory duty* under s.29 of the 1971 Act) is not (or should not be) a matter of interest to the planning authority. After all, the development may turn out to be a commercial disaster for the developer (the applicant for planning permission) but that is *his* business, *his* risk, and has nothing whatever to do with the planning authority. In this context the words of Lord Denning in *Pyx Granite Co. Ltd.* v. *Ministry of Housing and Local Government*[27] come echoing across the years whenever a local planning authority seek to step out of their statutory planning line in an endeavour to obtain some advantage or gain in which, on a true reading of planning law, it has neither interest nor *locus standi*:

> "Although the planning authorities are given very wide powers to impose 'such conditions as they think fit,' nevertheless the law says that those conditions, to be valid, must fairly and reasonably relate to the permitted development. *The planning authority are not at liberty to use their powers for an ulterior object, however desirable that object may seem to them to be in the public interest. If they mistake or misuse their powers, however bona fide, the court can interfere by declaration and injunction.*"[28]

Re-reading Lord Denning's comments (later approved by the House of Lords[29]) one wonders how the brouhaha about planning gain ever arose—but it certainly did.

[27] (1958) 1 Q.B. 554 at p. 572. See p. 250, *ante*.
[28] Emphasis (in italics) added.
[29] See p. 251, *ante*.

Today the latest official statement on the matter is found in D.O.E. Circular 22/83 earlier mentioned. The Circular declares (para. 4) under the heading, "General Policy":

> "4. It is a matter of law as well as of good administration that planning applications should be considered on their merits having regard to the provisions of the development plan and any other material consideration and that they should be refused only when this serves a clear planning purpose and the economic effects have been taken into account. By the same token, the question of imposing a condition or obligation—whether negative or positive in character—should only arise where it is considered that it would not be reasonable to grant a permission in the terms sought which is not subject to such condition or obligation. A wholly unacceptable development should not of course be permitted just because of extraneous benefits offered by the developer."

The Circular admits (para. 5) that, depending on circumstances, it might be reasonable to impose conditions on a grant of planning permission, or (where the planning authority's purpose cannot be achieved by means of a condition) to seek a section 52 agreement with the developer which agreement would be associated with whatever planning permission was granted.

> "But this does not mean" says the Circular, "that an authority is entitled to treat an applicant's need for permission as an opportunity to obtain some extraneous benefit or advantage or as an opportunity to exact a payment for the benefit of ratepayers at large. Nor should the preparation of such an agreement be permitted to delay unduly the decision on the application" for planning permission.

Appendix A of the Circular goes into some of the "Legal Aspects" of planning gain and the use of a section 52 agreement to get that which could not be obtained by means of a planning condition. Paragraph 3 of Appendix A declares:

> "3. Local authorities are given express powers under section 52 of the Town and Country Planning Act 1971 to enter into Agreements with persons having an interest in land for the purpose of "restricting or regulating the development or use of the land". The advantage of using section 52 is that provisions in such agreements which are in the nature of negative covenants are, by virtue of sub-section (2) enforceable by the local planning authority against successors in title of the person or body

who entered into the agreement. Positive covenants[30] can be included in such agreements provided that they achieve the purpose of restricting or regulating the use or development of the land. Incidental and consequential provisions (including provisions of a financial character) which are considered necessary or expedient for the purposes of the agreement may also be included. It should be noted that a developer cannot be required to enter into such an agreement by means of a planning condition."

That last sentence in the foregoing quotation from paragraph 3 of Appendix A emphasis what should never be forgotten, namely, that a developer cannot be coerced by a planning authority into entering into a section 52 agreement against his will. If the authority seek to do this sort of thing by refusing, for example, to deal with the developer's duly lodged application for planning permission, then the developer can appeal to the Secretary of State *as if* his application had been refused (1971 Act, s.37).

The whole of Circular 22/83 (it is a short affair of but five pages) together with the important comment about planning gain in paragraph 63 of the Annex to the more recent Circular 1/85 (earlier referred to in this chapter), will be found of much help and importance to any developer who finds himself "up against it" in the course of his planning bargaining with the local planning authority to whom he has made (or is going to make) an application for planning permission for his development. On this, one last quotation from this important Circular on planning gain may be made as the conclusion to this chapter. Paragraph 13 of Circular 23/83 concludes the circular with the words:

"13. This Circular is particularly intended to provide guidance to local authorities about the proper limits of their statutory development control powers . . . Should authorities seek to impose unreasonable obligations in connection with a grant of planning permission, the applicant may refuse to accept them and appeal to the appropriate Secretary of State against a subsequent refusal of permission, or imposition of a condition, or the non-determination of the application. Such appeals will be considered in the light of the advice given in this circular. Where an appeal has arisen because of what seems to the Secretaries of State to be an unreasonable demand on the part of the local planning authority in such a case, and an inquiry has been

[30] Positive covenants can be enforced against successors in title by virtue of section 33 of the Local Government (Miscellaneous Provisions) Act 1982.

held, they will consider sympathetically any application which may be made to them for the award of costs."

In the forgoing quotation the sting in the tail about costs[31] will (or, should) be noted by local planning authorities otherwise law-abiding but tending "to go off at a tangent" in their efforts to obtain planning benefits or gain to which, in law, they are not entitled. If they think they are being denied that which is their due, then their clear course is to get the law altered. But they must not be surprised if they find opposition in their tracks—the planning gain syndrome has many facets.

[31] See D.O.E. Circular 2/87 dated February 17, 1987 on award of costs in planning appeals.

CHAPTER 12

AMENITIES AND CONSERVATION: CONTROL OF ADVERTISEMENTS

1. The Advertisements Regulations 1984

THE Town and Country Planning (Control of Advertisements) Regulations, 1984[1] (hereinafter in this chapter referred to as the "Advertisements Regulations") form a substantial document containing 33 regulations and six schedules. They provide a complete *ad hoc* code relating to the display and control of outdoor advertisements.

The Secretary of State for the Environment has issued a comprehensive Circular on the Advertisement Regulations of 1984. It is D.O.E. Circular 11/84, dated April 9, 1984.

The sections of the Town and Country Planning Act 1971 relating to the control of advertisements are sections 63, 64, 109 and 109A. Insofar as the display of advertisements constitutes development (as to which reference may be made to section 22(4) of the 1971 Act), no application for planning permission in respect of such development is required, provided the display of the advertisement is in accordance with the Advertisements Regulations (s.64) in which case section 64 of the 1971 Act itself, and without more, grants automatically the requisite planning permission.

Section 63 of the 1971 Act is given a new subsection (3) by the Housing and Planning Act 1986, section 45. Regulations made by the Secretary of State for the purposes of section 63 of the 1971 Act may now make special provision with respect to:

(a) conservation areas,
(b) areas defined by the regulations as "experimental areas," and
(c) areas defined by the regulations as "areas of special control."

2. Penalties for Breach of Advertisements Regulations

Any person guilty of an offence against the Advertisements Regulations by displaying an advertisement in contravention thereof is liable, on summary conviction, to a fine not exceeding £200

[1] S.I. 1984 No. 421; and see D.O.E. Circular 11/84 and the Town and Country Planning (Control of Advertisements) Direction 1984.

(s.109(2) and reg.8) and, in the case of a continuing offence, a fine not exceeding £40 per day (s.109(2) and reg.8 as amended by Housing and Planning Act 1986 s.49(1)(i) and Sched. 11, Pt.I, para. 13(1) and (2)). Where an unauthorised advertisement is taken down but replaced a week later, this is not a continuing offence attracting a daily penalty—it is a fresh offence.[2]

With respect to *onus probandi* it is to be noted that a person is deemed to display an advertisement:

(a) if the advertisement is displayed on land of which he is either the owner or the occupier; or
(b) if the advertisement publicises his goods, trade, business or other concern (s.109(3)).

But it is open to any such person to prove that the offending advertisement was displayed without his knowledge or consent in which case he will not be guilty of an offence (*ibid.*). In *Preston* v. *British Union for the Abolition of Vivisection* (*The Times*, July 24, 1985) it was held that, if an advertisement was displayed initially without the knowledge or consent of the person whose goods it publicised, as soon as that person became aware of the advertisement and failed to remove it he became guilty of an offence under the Advertisement Regulations.

Further control over, for example, flyposting[3] is contained in section 109A of the 1971 Act (inserted by section 36 of the Local Government (Miscellaneous Provisions) Act 1982) whereby a district council and a London borough council can remove or obliterate without notice any advertisement displayed in contravention of the Advertisements Regulations which does not identify the person who displays it and, otherwise, after giving two days notice to such person.

3. Definitions

Turning now to the Advertisements Regulations themselves, the word "advertisement" is widely defined by the Regulations and should be specially noted. It means "any word, letter, model, sign, placard, board, notice, device or representation, whether illuminated or not, in the nature of, and employed wholly or in part for the purposes of, advertisement, announcement or direction (excluding any such thing employed wholly as a memorial or as a railway signal), and (without prejudice to the preceding provisions) includes any hoarding or similar structure or any tethered balloon used, or

[2] *Kensington & Chelsea Royal Borough* v. *Elmton Ltd.* (1978) 246 E.G. 1011.
[3] See p. 278, *post*.

adapted for use, for the display of advertisements, and references to the display of advertisements shall be construed accordingly" (reg. 2(1)). References in the Advertisement Regulations to the land, the building, or the site or premises on which an advertisement is displayed mean, in the case of a tethered balloon, the land, building, site or premises (as the case may be) to which the balloon is tethered (reg. 2(4)).

The extent and application of the Regulations is dealt with in regulation 3 whereby they are to apply to the display on land (and "land" includes (reg. 2(1)) buildings and land covered with water whilst "building" includes (*ibid.*) any structure or erection or any part of a building, structure or erection) of *all* advertisements (reg. 3(1)) subject to six exceptions as follows:

(a) an advertisement on "enclosed land" (as defined in regulation 3(2)(*b*)) and not readily visible from outside the enclosure or from any part of a public right of way over the enclosure or from any land on such enclosure to which the public have access (reg. 3(1)(*a*));
(b) an advertisement within (reg. 3(2)(*d*)) a building (which means displayed inside a structure and not outside on a forecourt[4]), subject, however, to the special control provided by regulation 12 with respect to certain advertisements displayed within a building but visible from outside the building (reg. 3(1)(*b*));
(c) an advertisement displayed upon or inside a moving vehicle or a vessel moving on an inland waterway (regs. 3(1)(*c*) and 3(2)(*c*));
(d) an advertisement displayed on, or which consists of, a tethered balloon flown above ground at a height of more than 60 metres (regs. 3(1)(*d*) and 2(1));
(e) an advertisement incorporated in, and forming part of, the fabric of a building (regs. 3(1)(*e*) and 3(2)(*e*));
(f) an advertisement displayed on an article for sale or on the package or other container of the article, or displayed on the pump, dispenser or other container from which the article is sold, provided always that the advertisement relates wholly to the article and is not an illuminated advertisement and does not exceed 0.1 square metre in area (regs. 3(1)(*f*) and 3(2)(*a*)).

It is to be noted that, for the purpose of item (c) of the foregoing exceptions, "vehicle" means (reg. 3(2)(*c*)) a vehicle normally

[4] *Dominant Sites Ltd.* v. *Berkshire C.C.* (1955) 6 P. & C.R. 10.

employed as a moving vehicle on a roadway or a railway and also a vessel normally employed as a moving vessel on an inland waterway. Thus omnibuses (provided they keep moving) can carry advertisements both within and without if the managers of these vehicles think fit.

With reference to a tethered balloon carrying an advertisement (item (d) of the foregoing exceptions) *one* such balloon can be flown (except in an area of special control (see section 4 of this chapter, *post*) or in a conservation area (see page 138, *ante*) or in a National Park (see page 148, *ante*) or in an area of outstanding natural beauty (see page 151, *ante*)) at any height (*i.e.* at less than 60 metres above ground) provided it is displayed on a site (reg. 3(4)) for not more than ten days in any calendar year (reg. 3(3)). The definition of "site" in regulation 3(4) is specially to be noted because it prevents the advertiser from getting the benefit of the aforementioned ten day exemption by the expedient of moving the tethered balloon around from one position to another position on one large site.

Control under the Advertisements Regulations over the display of advertisements can be considered mainly under two heads, namely, control within areas of special control, and control outside such areas.

4. Areas of Special Control

The definition of an area of special control is dealt with in section 63(3)(3A) and (3B), (4), (5) of the 1971 Act and in regulations 26 and 27 of, and Schedule 4 to, the Advertisements Regulations. It is for a district planning authority (Local Government Act 1972, Sched. 16, para. 25) to take the initiative in defining such an area. All district planning authorities are under a duty to consider such definition (reg. 26(1)) and to reconsider the matter at least once in every five years (reg. 26(4)). For this purpose the local planning authority is (reg. 26(6)):

(a) in the City of London, the Common Council;
(b) in a London borough, the council of the borough;
(c) outside Greater London and not within a National Park, the district planning authority; and
(d) in a National Park, the county planning authority.

The definition of an area of special control is achieved by means of an Order made by the district planning authority and approved by the Secretary of State (s.63(4), (5) and reg. 26(2) and Sched. 4). Such an Order may be made by the Secretary of State himself (reg. 28).

Provision is made for advertising the proposal to make such an

Order and for consultations by the district planning authority before making the Order; for the lodging of objections thereto; for the considering of such objections, and for the holding of a public local inquiry or a hearing before the Order is approved (s.63(5) and reg. 26(7), Sched. 4, and Sched. 5, Forms 1 and 2).

The exercise of the power to define an area of special control is to be discharged only in the interests of amenity (reg. 26(8)) and attention is to be paid to the general characteristics of the area, including the presence of any feature of historic, architectural or cultural interest (*ibid.*).

Within an area of special control the general rule will be that no advertisements whatever may be displayed (reg. 27). Such advertisements as are displayed will form exceptions to this general rule (reg. 27(1)(*a*) and (*b*), (2), (3)).

The object of regulation 27(2) of the Advertisements Regulations is to give a wider discretion to local planning authorities in permitting the display of certain advertisements and directional signs within areas of special control in the hope that thereby such authorities might be encouraged to apply special control over most of the countryside and in other places worthy of this protection. According to D.O.E. Circular 11/84, para. 35—

> "At present rather more than 40 per cent. of the total land area of England and Wales has been defined by LPAs as being within an area of special control; but there are some areas of high landscape quality (for example, some designated areas of outstanding natural beauty) which the respective LPAs have not hitherto proposed for inclusion in an area of special control. The LPA's decision whether an area should be defined as an area of special control may be approached in two ways. First, if it is a largely or wholly rural area there need be little doubt that a special control order is appropriate, though LPAs should still be willing to consult informally any local interested organisations, e.g. Chambers of Trade, or tourist organisations, or local branches of the Civic Trust, before formally proposing an order. Secondly, where the proposed area is entirely or substantially urban in character, LPAs must be able to show *to the Secretary of State's satisfaction* that there are relevant planning considerations justifying their view that the proposed area requires 'special protection on grounds of amenity.' "

An Order defining an area of special control may be challenged, by a "person aggrieved" or by an "authority concerned,"[5] within six

[5] See pp. 221–230.

weeks on a point of law by application in the High Court (ss.242(1)(*d*), (2)(*d*) and 245(1)(*a*), (2), (3), (4), (5) and (7).)

The 1971 Act, s. 63(3), (3A) and (3B) (as amended by the Housing and Planning Act 1986, s. 45) enables regulations to be made with respect to "experimental" areas in order to assess, over a prescribed period, the effect on amenity or public safety of advertisements of a prescribed kind.

5. Other Areas

With respect to areas which are not areas of special control the general rule is that no advertisements may be displayed without consent, which may be either "express consent" granted by a local planning authority or by the Secretary of State (reg. 6(1)) or "deemed consent" (reg. 6(2)), that is to say, consent which is deemed to be granted by the Advertisements Regulations themselves. Deemed consent is applicable to all advertisements falling within Part III of the Regulations (regs. 9–16).

6. Deemed Consent for Display of Part III Advertisements

Advertisements falling within Part III of the Advertisements Regulations are, first, those coming within the seven specified classes given in regulation 14 which cover the following:

Class I—Functional advertisements of local authorities, statutory undertakers and public transport undertakers, *e.g.* bus stop signs, signs indicating the way to railway stations, museums, art galleries.

Class II—Miscellaneous advertisements relating to premises on which they are displayed, (*e.g.* professional, business or trade plates attached to premises where the profession, business or trade is carried on) limited to one advertisement, not exceeding 0.3 square metres in area, in respect of each person, partnership or company, or, if the premises have entrances on different roads, one such advertisement at each of *two* such entrances.

Class III—Certain advertisements of a temporary nature, *e.g.* "For Sale" or "To Let" boards.

Class IV—Advertisements (subject to reservations—reg. 14(1), set out in the proviso to Class IV) on business premises relating *wholly* to the business carried on or to the goods sold or the services provided, together with the name and qualifications of the person carrying on the business, or selling the goods or supplying the services.[6]

[6] *Cooper* v. *Bailey* (1956) 6 P. & C.R. 261, D.C.; *Solosigns Ltd.* v. *Essex C.C.* [1956] J.P.L. 904; *Dominant Sites Ltd.* v. *Berkshire C.C.* (1956) 6 P. & C.R. 10; *Arthur Maiden Ltd.* v. *Lanark C.C.* (*No.* 1) [1958] J.P.L. 417; *Jones* v. *Merioneth County Council* (1968) 20 P. & C.R. 106; D.C.; *Heron Service Stations* v. *Coupe* (1973) 25 P. & C.R. 349, H.L.

Class V—Advertisements on any forecourt of business premises, relating wholly to all or any of the matters specified in Class IV above, provided that the aggregate area of such advertisements is not more than 4.5 square metres.

Class VI—Flag advertisements, *e.g.* a flag bearing only the name or device of the person occupying the building over which it flies from a single flagstaff in an upright position on the roof of a building.

Class VII—Certain advertisements on hoardings round building sites on land allocated in a development plan primarily for commercial, industrial or business purposes (but *not* if the building site is in a conservation area, an area of special control, a National Park or an area of outstanding natural beauty) the display being limited to two years (reg. 14(1) and Sched. 2).

Any advertisement falling within one or more of the foregoing classes can be excluded from such class by a direction of the Secretary of State made under regulation 15(1) of the Advertisement Regulations. If an advertisement *is* so excluded it cannot be (or continue to be) exhibited unless it first gets express consent from the local planning authority (*ibid.*). Before making such a direction, the Secretary of State must afford an opportunity for objections to be made to the proposed direction (reg. 15(2)) which objections must be taken into account by the Secretary of State when considering whether or not to make the direction (reg. 15(3)). If the Secretary of State makes the direction he must state in writing his reasons for so doing (reg. 15(4)). Notice of the making of the direction must be published by the local planning authority (reg. 15(5), (6)).

The Secretary of State has made a direction under regulation 15 of the Advertisement Regulations which requires, as from June 1, 1986, express consent to be obtained to the display of estate agents' boards (Class III of regulation 14) in certain areas within the two London boroughs of (a) the City of Westminster, and (b) the Royal Borough of Kensington and Chelsea.

Advertisements falling within Part III of the Advertisements Regulations are, secondly, those coming within reg. 9 relating to:

(a) a pending parliamentary, European Assembly, or local government election;

(b) advertisements displayed under statutory obligation, *e.g.* advertisements relating to the making of compulsory purchase orders under the 1971 Act; and

(c) advertisements in the nature of traffic signs such as traffic lights and "Give Way" and "Turn Left" signs.

Thirdly, a local planning authority may display advertisements without express consent upon any land within their area except in an area of special control (reg. 10(1)). The Secretary of State can, however, require the discontinuance of display of any such local planning authority advertisement (reg. 10(2)).

Fourthly, any advertisement displayed on August 1, 1948, may continue, without express consent, to be displayed (reg. 11).

Fifthly, certain advertisements displayed within a building but so as to be visible from outside the building may be displayed without express consent (reg. 12(2)). The "certain advertisements" here mentioned comprise (reg.12(1)):

(a) an illuminated advertisement;
(b) an advertisement in a building which is used principally for displaying advertisements;
(c) an advertisement within one metre of any external door, window or other opening through which it can be seen from outside the building.

Sixthly, advertisements displayed in the first place with express consent granted for a limited period, may continue to be displayed, after the expiration of the limited period, without express consent (reg. 13) subject to the power of the local planning authority to require discontinuance of the display (*ibid.*).

A local planning authority can require (by serving a "discontinuance notice") the discontinuance of the display of any advertisement (other than an advertisement specified in regulation 9 relating to election notices, statutory advertisements and traffic signs) displayed with deemed consent if they consider it expedient to do so in the interests of amenity or public safety (reg. 16) provided, however, that, in relation to an advertisement in a specified Class set out in regulation 14 and displayed in accordance with that regulation, a discontinuance notice may *not* be served unless the authority are satisfied that such a notice is required in order to remedy "a substantial injury to the amenity of the locality or a danger to members of the public" (reg.16(1), proviso).

The four Standard Conditions given in Schedule 1, Parts I and II, to the Advertisements Regulations will apply, obligatorily, to all advertisements displayed with deemed consent (reg. 7) with the exception that Standard Condition No. 1 relating to cleanliness and tidiness will not apply (reg. 9(3)) to an advertisement relating to a pending parliamentary, European Assembly or local government election and displayed pursuant to regulation 9(1)(*a*).

7. Express Consent for Display of Advertisements

Where express consent to the display of an advertisement is required (reg. 6(1)) application therefor can be made to the local planning authority on a form to be supplied by the authority (reg. 17).

Applications for express consent to the display of an advertisement are made (reg. 17(1) and (2)) to the local planning authority which means (reg. 2(1)):

(a) where the land is in the City of London, the Common Council;
(b) where the land is in a London borough, the council of the London borough;
(c) where the land is outside Greater London and is not within a National Park, the district planning authority; and
(d) where the land is in a National Park, the district planning authority (reg. 17(2)) who must transmit it to the county planning authority (*ibid.*).

In considering an application for express consent a local planning authority are to consider only the interests of amenity and public safety (reg. 5), are under a duty, before granting express consent, to consult certain other authorities (reg. 18) and, subject to these requirements, may:

(a) grant consent subject to the three obligatory Standard Conditions set out in Part I of Schedule 1 to the Advertisements Regulations together with such additional and optional conditions (if any) as they think fit to impose; or
(b) refuse consent (reg. 19).

As to the meanings of "amenity" and "public safety," reference may be made to *Re Ellis and Ruislip-Northwood U.D.C.*[7] in which Scrutton L.J. said that, "It appears to mean pleasant circumstances, features, advantages."

As to the display of advertisements in conservation areas the Secretary of State sounded a warning note to local planning authorities (D.O.E. Circular 23/77 dated March 16, 1977, para. 43) in the following terms:

> "It is important that in conservation areas, local planning authorities use the powers under the Control of Advertisement Regulations flexibly, taking account of the fact that many conservation areas include thriving commercial centres and at the same time the particular need to ensure that advertising displays do not detract from the appearance of areas of architectural and historic interest."

Every grant of express consent must be for a fixed term, that is to say, for a period of five years unless the local planning authority makes a grant for such shorter or longer period as they specify (reg.

[7] [1920] 1 K.B. 343, C.A.

20(1)). If the authority grant consent for less than five years, they must state in writing their reasons for so doing unless the application itself required a consent for less than five years (reg. 20(3)).

The grant or refusal of express consent must be in writing together with (in the case of a refusal or a grant subject to conditions—other than the standard conditions of Schedule 1) the reasons for the decision (reg. 21).

A local planning authority must give their decision on an application for express consent within two months unless such period is extended by agreement in writing made between the authority and the applicant (reg. 21(2)). If the decision is not given in the beforementioned period the application is to be regarded as having been refused (reg. 22(1), (3) and (4) applying s.37 of the 1971 Act as modified by reg. 22 of the Advertisement Regulations and set out in its modified form in Sched. 3, Pt. II, to the Regulations).

Every local planning authority is to keep a register containing particulars of their decisions on applications for express consent (reg. 31).

Provision is made for the revocation or modification of any grant of express consent to the display of an advertisement (regs. 24 and 25).

8. Appeal to the Secretary of State

An applicant for express consent who is aggrieved by the decision of a local planning authority refusing consent or granting the same subject to conditions may appeal to the Secretary of State (reg. 22(1)) within two calendar months from the receipt of the notification of the local planning authority's decision (reg. 22(1), (2) and (4) applying ss.36 and 37 of the 1971 Act as modified by reg. 22 of the Advertisements Regulations and set out in their modified form in Sched. 3 to the Regulations).

The notice of appeal must be accompanied by the following documents (reg. 22(1), (2) and (4) applying s.36 of the 1971 Act as modified):

(1) the application for express consent;
(2) all relevant plans and particulars submitted to the local planning authority;
(3) the notice of decision;
(4) all other relevant correspondence with the authority.

Within one month (or such longer period as the Secretary of State may allow) of being notified by him of an advertisement appeal, the local planning authority must submit to the Secretary of State two identical sets of photographs of the appeal site and its surroundings together with two copies of a plan showing the location and boundary of the site and the position from which the photographs were taken.[8]

The decision of the Secretary of State on an appeal is final (reg. 22(1), (2) and (4) applying s.36(6) of the 1971 Act as modified) subject, however, to challenge by a "person aggrieved" or by an "authority directly concerned"[9] within six weeks in the High Court on a point of law (ss.242(1)(*e*), (3)(*e*) and 245(1)(*b*), (2), (3), (4) and (7)).

With the object of improving the efficiency and effectiveness of advertisement appeals made to the Secretary of State under regulation 22 of the Advertisement Regulations, the relevant administrative arrangements have been reviewed. The new and revised arrangements are set out in D.O.E. Circular 20/85 dated August 30, 1985.

9. Fly-Posting

It is to be a condition of every consent to the display of an advertisement under the Advertisements Regulations that such display shall take place only with the permission of the owner of the land or other person entitled to grant permission in relation thereto (reg. 6(4)). This condition will apply to all consents whether the condition itself is expressly imposed or not (*ibid.*) although it will not apply (*ibid.*) to statutory advertisements displayed pursuant to regulation 9(1)(*b*). Breach of this condition, being a contravention of the Advertisements Regulations, is an offence for which a penalty is imposed (reg. 8).

Thus fly-posting (which has always been a trespass) becomes an offence prosecutable before a court of summary jurisdiction. Further control over fly-postings is contained in section 109A of the 1971 Act (inserted by the Local Government, Planning and Land Act 1980).

10. "Existing Advertisements"

"Existing advertisements," that is to say, advertisements which were on display on August 1, 1948, may continue to be displayed without express consent (reg. 11) but subject:

[8] Town and Country Planning (Control of Advertisements) Direction 1984.
[9] See pp. 221–230 inclusive.

(a) to the four Standard Conditions set out in Part I and Part II of Schedule 1 to the Advertisements Regulations (reg. 7);
(b) to the condition that there shall be no substantial increase or alteration of the advertising site from the state in which it stood on August 1, 1948 (reg. 11(2)(*a*));
(c) to the condition that the deemed consent for the display of the existing advertisement does not enure for the benefit of any successor building replacing that which was standing on August 1, 1948 (reg. 11(2)(*b*)); and
(d) to the requirement as to discontinuance by notice served by a local planning authority (regs. 11 and 16).

11. Compensation

Where, in order to comply with the Advertisements Regulations, works are carried out by any person:
(a) for removing an advertisement which was on display on August 1, 1948; or
(b) for discontinuing the use for the display of advertisements of any site which was being used for that purpose on August 1, 1948,

such person may claim compensation with respect to any expenses reasonably incurred by him in carrying out such works (s.176 and reg. 30). The claim must be submitted in writing to the local planning authority within six months of the completion of any such works (*ibid.*).

12. Miscellaneous Provisions

The Advertisements Regulations contain further provisions dealing with the "special case" of advertisements relating to travelling circuses and fairs (reg. 23).

The Advertisements Regulations empower the Secretary of State to call up for decision by himself (instead of by a local planning authority) any matter requiring decision under the Regulations (reg. 28).

13. Saving for Other Statutory Obligations

Neither the Advertisements Regulations nor consents granted under them will have the effect of discharging any obligation or liability relating to the display of advertisements which is imposed or incurred under any other enactment (reg. 33).

14. Decisions of the Courts and D.O.E. Advice Relating to Advertisements

When considering the provisions of the 1971 Act relating to advertisements and the Advertisements Regulations, reference may usefully be made to cases decided under earlier legislation relating to the display of advertisements. Such cases are:

(1) *United Billposting Co.* v. *Somerset C.C.* (1926) 24 L.G.R. 383, D.C.;
(2) *Gloucester Billposting Co. Ltd.* v. *Hopkins* (1932) 30 L.G.R. 488;
(3) *Royle* v. *Orme* (1932) 30 L.G.R. 494;
(4) *Horlicks Ltd.* v. *Garvie* [1939] 1 All E.R. 335, D.C.;
(5) *Mills & Rockleys Ltd.* v. *Leicester Corporation* [1946] K.B. 315, D.C.;
(6) *More O'Ferrall Ltd.* v. *Harrow U.D.C.* [1947] K.B. 66, D.C.;
(7) *Borough Billposting Co.* v. *Manchester Corporation* [1948] 1 All E.R. 807, D.C.;
(8) *Dominant Sites Ltd.* v. *Hendon Borough Council* [1952] 2 All E.R. 899, D.C.

Useful advice as to control over the display of advertisements is found in D.O.E. Circular 11/84 dated April 9, 1984 (previously mentioned) which contains an elaborate Explanatory Memorandum on the Advertisement Regulations 1984 including a specimen form of "Application for Consent to Display an Advertisement" and a statement of the relevant considerations to be taken into account by a local planning authority when assessing "public safety" factors arising from an advertisement application.

The Department of the Environment has issued two short brochures which helpfully discuss the whole matter of outdoor advertising. The two brochures are entitled, respectively, "Outdoor Advertisements And Signs—A Guide For Advertisers" and "Outdoor Advertising For Small Firms."

15. Proposed Amendments to the Advertisement Regulations 1984

The White Paper "Lifting the Burden,"[10] dated July 1985, declared (in Chapter 3, paragraph 3.6(iv)) that the Advertisement Regulations 1984 are being reviewed and specifically mentioned one aspect that warranted early attention, namely, the signposting in rural

[10] Cmnd. 9571.

areas of tourist facilities, hotel accommodation, craft workshops and similar establishments.

Accordingly, on November 29, 1985 the Department of the Environment issued a consultation paper setting out proposals for a new "deemed consent" for the display, *off highway land*, of suitably designed and sited directional advertising signs. The consultation paper is currently "going the rounds" of local planning authorities, professional bodies and other interested parties seeking their views on the new proposals.

On July 30, 1986 the Department of the Environment announced publication of a further consultation paper making 21 proposals for change in the present system of control over outdoor advertisements including a proposed reduction in the size of estate agents' boards and a new form of "deemed consent" for any advertisement which has been continuously displayed since at least April 1, 1974. This consultation paper is likewise "going the rounds" as mentioned in the previous paragraph.

It is emphasised that the contents of these consultation papers are not *law*. They do, however, show the way the wind is currently blowing in the matter of control of outdoor advertising.

CHAPTER 13

AMENITIES AND CONSERVATION: CONTROL OF CARAVANS

Note: In this chapter all section references are references to the Caravan Sites and Control of Development Act 1960 unless otherwise stated.

1. Summary

ONE particular form of development, namely, the use of land as a site for caravans caused more litigation under the Town and Country Planning Act 1947 between the years 1948 and 1960 than any other kind of development and in 1960 Parliament decided that there should be a new *ad hoc* statutory form of control relating solely to caravans and the *licensing* of caravan sites.

The outcome of this was the enacting of Part I of the Caravan Sites and Control of Development Act 1960. Part I of the Act (relating to caravan sites) currently, in 1986, contains 27 sections (ss.1 to 20 and 23 to 30—less s.27 which is now spent) none of which is affected in any way by the Town and Country Planning Act 1971. On the other hand, Part II of the 1960 Act (relating to the enforcement of planning control over development generally) is repealed and superseded by Part V of the 1971 Act.

Thus the *ad hoc* statutory form of licensing control over caravans and caravan sites introduced in 1960 continues to be found in Part I of the Caravan Sites and Control of Development Act 1960 and not in the Town and Country Planning Act 1971. This *ad hoc* form of control over caravans—which comprises a system of licensing of caravan sites by the local authority (s.3(1)), *i.e.*, the council of a London borough or a district, the Common Council of the City of London and the Council of the Isles of Scilly (s.29(1))—is a form of control which functions over and above (*i.e.* in addition to) the general control of development through the medium of planning permission granted under Part III of the Town and Country Planning Act 1971 and the enforcement provisions of Part V of that Act.

In short, planning permission for caravan sites is just as essential as ever it was, but a caravan site must now satisfy not only the Town and Country Planning Act 1971 but also the licensing provisions of Part I of the Caravan Sites and Control of Development Act 1960.

Part I of the Caravan Sites and Control of Development Act 1960 did not originally apply to the County of London (s.31 now repealed) but it was extended to Greater London as from April 1, 1965, by the London Government Act 1963, Schedule 17, paragraph 21.

The control of local authorities over moveable dwellings by means of licences granted under section 269 of the Public Health Act 1936 is now abolished in so far as it relates to caravans (s.30). The Minister of Housing and Local Government could, by order made before August 29, 1962 (*i.e.* within two years from the commencement of the 1960 Act on August 29, 1960—s.50(4)), repeal or amend any local enactment which appeared to him either to be superseded by, or to be inconsistent with, the 1960 Act (s.27—now spent).

It should be mentioned that the Caravan Sites Act 1968 was enacted primarily to restrict the eviction of occupiers of caravans from caravan sites and to secure the establishment of such sites by local authorities "for the use of gypsies and other persons of nomadic habit." This Act, accordingly, does not fall within the general stream of town planning legislation and is not therefore referred to in this chapter except in so far as it enacts a slight variation in the definition of "caravan"—a matter referred to on page 284.

2. Site Licences for Caravans

Under the 1960 Act the general rule is that no land may be used as a caravan site unless and until a site licence has been issued by the local authority (*i.e.* the council of a London borough or a district, the Common Council of the City of London or the Council of the Isles of Scilly (s.29(1)) to the occupier of the land comprising the site (s.1(1)). If an occupier of land contravenes this requirement he is liable (s.1(2)), on a first offence, to a fine of £100 and on a second or subsequent offence to a fine not exceeding level 4 on the standard scale, *i.e.* in 1987, £1,000 (Criminal Justice Act 1982, s.37 and Criminal Penalties etc. (Increase) Order 1984,[1] art. 2(4) and Sched. 4). In this context an occupier of land is the person who, by virtue of an estate or interest held by him in the land, is entitled to possession of the land or would be so entitled but for the rights of any other person under any licence granted in respect of the land (s.1(3)); provided, however, that where land amounting to not more than 400 square yards in area is let under a tenancy entered into with a view to the use of the land as a caravan site, the expression "occupier" means, in relation to that land, the person who would be entitled to possession of the land but for the rights of any person under that tenancy (*ibid.*).

[1] S.I. 1984 No. 447.

A "caravan site" is any land in which a caravan is stationed *for human habitation,* together with land used in conjunction therewith (s.1(4)).

A single caravan was installed on agricultural land in 1983 for the purpose of storing and mixing cattle feed, the buildings already existing on the land being insufficient for this purpose. The local planning authority issued an enforcement notice requiring the cessation of the use of the land for stationing the caravan. On appeal to the Secretary of State the Inspector found that the caravan was used for a purpose ancillary to agriculture and that no material change of use of the land from an agricultural use to some other use had occurred. The local planning authority appealed (under section 246 of the 1971 Act) to the High Court which upheld the decision of the Inspector.[2]

"Caravan" means any structure (not being a tent or a railway carriage standing on a railway) designed or adapted for human habitation which is capable of being moved from one place to another (by being towed or transported) including a motor-vehicle so designed or adapted (s.29(1)). This definition is *not* to include any railway rolling-stock (so long as it is on rails) nor a tent (*ibid.*). Nor is it to include (Caravan Sites Act 1968, s.13) a "twin-unit caravan" if its dimensions exceed *any* of the following limits, namely:

(a) length: 60 feet (18·288 metres);
(b) width: 20 feet (6·096 metres);
(c) overall height of living accommodation: 10 feet (3·045 metres).

Motor vehicles (*e.g.* a motor van) used for human habitation *but not designed for that purpose nor physically altered to fit that purpose* do not appear to be caravans within the above definition.[3]

3. Application for, and Issue of, Site Licence

An application for a site licence must be made in writing by the occupier of the land to the local authority (s.29) in whose area the land is situated (s.3(1)). The application must specify the land in respect of which the application is made and give such other information as the local authority may reasonably require (s.3(2) and the Caravan Sites (Licence Applications) Order 1960).[4]

Faced with an application for a site licence the local authority,

[2] *Wealden District Council* v. *Secretary of State for the Environment and Colin Day* (1986) J.P.L. 753.

[3] *Backer* v. *Secretary of State for the Environment* (1983) J.P.L. 602.

[4] S.I. 1960 No. 1474.

provided there has been a grant of planning permission *otherwise* than under and by virtue of a development order (s.3(3)), *must* issue the same within two months of receiving the particulars referred to in the previous paragraph or within such extended period as may be agreed (s.3(4)) unless the applicant has had a site licence revoked (s.9) within the previous three years (s.3(6)).

It is to be emphasised that a site licence is to be issued if, and only if, the requisite planning permission for the use of land as a caravan site has already been formally granted by the local planning authority who, before doing so, must first consult with the site licensing authority (Town and Country Planning Act 1971, s.29(5), (6)). Thus the general rule under the 1960 Act is that if there is in being the requisite planning permission for use of land as a caravan site, then the issue of a site licence under the 1960 Act for such land *must* follow—the real sting of the 1960 Act lying not in the granting or the withholding of a site licence, but in the number and style of conditions which may be attached to a site licence. If there is no such requisite planning permission in being, then the application for a site licence *must* be refused (s.3(3)).

If a site licence is not issued within the appropriate two months period (s.3(4)) to an applicant who is entitled to receive one, no offence is committed by the applicant under section 1 of the 1960 Act pending the issue of the site licence (s.6).

A register of site licences is to be kept by every site licensing authority and is to be open to public inspection (s.25(1)).

4. Transfer of Site Licence

The holder of a site licence who ceases to occupy the caravan site may, with the consent of the local authority, transfer it to the new occupier of the site (s.10(1)). The transferee *must* be the occupier of the site (*ibid.*). The name of the transferee must be endorsed on the site licence (s.10(2)) and an appropriate entry made in the register of site licences (s.25(2)).

The object of the need to get the local authority's consent to any transfer of a site licence is simply to secure that the local authority get to know of any transfer which might take place. Usually there will be no question of the local authority refusing consent to a transfer because if they did the new occupier of the site could at once apply for a new site licence in his own name and, if planning permission to station caravans on the site was still in existence, the site licence to the new occupier could not be refused. If however, the local authority took the view that the arrival of a new occupier provided a convenient occasion for reviewing the conditions attached to the site licence, they could refuse the transfer and leave it to the new occupier to apply for a new site licence in his own name, and to this new site licence the local authority could attach new conditions.

5. Duration of Site Licence

In general a site licence cannot be issued for a limited period (s.4(1)). The governing factor is again the planning permission subject to which the site licence is issued. Only if the governing planning permission is for a limited period may the site licence be granted for a limited period only—a period which *must* expire when the planning permission itself expires (*ibid.*).

Any variation in the governing planning permission made by the Secretary of State on appeal to him under section 36 of the Town and Country Planning Act 1971 will require the making of appropriate alterations in the site licence to ensure that its terms comply with the period (if any) for which the planning permission (as varied on appeal) is to subsist (s.4(2)).

6. Conditions Attached to Site Licence

A local authority have a wide discretion as to the attaching of conditions to a site licence but conditions must be such as the authority think it (a) necessary or (b) desirable to impose on the occupier of the land in the interests of (s.5(1)):

(1) caravan dwellers on the site itself, or
(2) any other class of persons; or
(3) the public at large.

In deciding what conditions (if any) to attach to a site licence a local authority must have regard (s.5(6)) to the "Model Standards for Caravans Sites" (with respect to the layout of caravan sites and the provisions of facilities, services and equipment in connection therewith) which have been issued by the Secretary of State under powers contained in the 1960 Act (*ibid.*).

Without prejudice to a local authority's power to impose conditions generally, a local authority are specifically authorised (s.5(1)) to impose conditions;

(a) for restricting the occasions on which caravans are stationed on land for human habitation, or the total number of caravans which are so stationed at any one time;
(b) for controlling, whether by reference to size, to state of repair or to any other feature other than the materials of which the caravans are constructed (s.5(2)), the types of caravan which are stationed on land;

(c) for regulating the positions in which caravans are stationed on land for human habitation and for prohibiting, restricting, or otherwise regulating, the placing or erection on such land, at any time when caravans are so stationed, of structures and vehicles of any description whatsoever and of tents;
(d) for securing the taking of any steps for preserving or enhancing the amenity of land on which caravans are stationed for human habitation, including the planting and replanting of the land with trees and bushes;
(e) for securing that, at all times when caravans are stationed on land, proper measures are taken for preventing and detecting the outbreak of fire, and adequate means of fighting fire are provided and maintained;
(f) for securing that adequate sanitary facilities, and such other facilities, services or equipment as may be specified by the local authority, are provided for the use of persons dwelling in caravans and that, at all times when caravans are stationed on land for human habitation, any such facilities and equipment are properly maintained.

As to conditions under subparagraph (e) above, relating to fire risks, the local authority must consult with the local fire authority as to the extent which any model standards relating to fire precautions (specified by the Secretary of State under s.5(6) are appropriate to the land on which the caravans are stationed (s.5(3A)). If no such standards have been specified, or if, being specified, are thought by the fire authority to be inappropriate to the land, the local authority must nevertheless consult with the fire authority as to what conditions relating to fire risks ought to be attached to the site licence (s.5(3B)).

No condition may be imposed controlling the types of caravan to be stationed on a licensed site by reference to the materials of which the caravans are constructed (s.5(2)).

A condition which *must* be attached to a site licence is that requiring a copy of the site licence to be conspicuously displayed on the site unless the site is restricted to three caravans or less (s.5(3)). Against this particular condition there is no appeal (s.7(1)).

Any conditions imposed under the foregoing provisions must be related, generally, to the *physical use of the land* on which the caravan site stands. For example, conditions relating to the rent of a place on the caravan site, to security of tenure or to the social lives of the caravan dwellers are *ultra vires* and therefore void.[5]

[5] *Chertsey Urban District Council* v. *Mixnam's Properties Ltd.* (1965) A.C. 735.

A condition attached to a site licence may require the doing of works on the site by the occupier within a specified period and may prohibit the bringing of caravans on the site until such works are completed to the satisfaction of the local authority (s.5(4)). If the works are not so completed within the specified period, the local authority may do the works and recover the cost thereof from the occupier who is in default (s.9(3)).

A condition attached to a site licence is perfectly valid notwithstanding that it requires the carrying out of works which the holder of the site licence is not entitled to carry out as of right (s.5(5)). The holder must either acquire such a right or forego the use of the land as a caravan site.

If an occupier of land fails to comply with any condition attached to a site licence, he is liable on a first offence to a fine of £100 and on a second or subsequent offence to a fine not exceeding level 4 on the standard scale (*i.e.* in 1987, £1,000 (Criminal Justice Act 1982 s.37 and Criminal Penalties etc. (Increase) Order 1984, art. 2(4) and Sched. 4). On a third or subsequent conviction for breach of a condition the court (*i.e. not* the local authority) may make an order revoking the site licence (s.9(2)). If the site licence is so revoked the local authority may not issue a further licence to the offending occupier until a period of three years has elapsed (s.3(6)).

7. Appeal Against Conditions Attached to Site Licence

Within 28 days of the issue of a site licence, there is a right of appeal to a magistrates' court by a person aggrieved[6] by a condition attached to a site licence (s.7(1)) and the court, if satisfied that the condition is "unduly burdensome,"[7] may vary or cancel the condition (*ibid.*).

"Unduly burdensome" is an expression not defined in the 1960 Act. The question whether a condition is "unduly burdensome" is the only matter which the court is entitled to consider and in doing so the court must have regard to the Secretary of State's "Model Standards for Caravan Sites" (s.7(1)).

[6] As to "a person aggrieved," see *Ealing Corporation* v. *Jones* [1959] 1 Q.B. 384, 390, D.C.; *R.* v. *Dorset Q.S. Appeals Committee, ex p. Weymouth Corporation* [1960] 2 Q.B. 230, D.C. See also [1960] J.P.L. 702. See further *ante*, pp. 221–230.

[7] See *Owen Cooper Estates* v. *Lexden and Winstree R.D.C.* (1964) 16 P. & C.R. 233, D.C.; *Esdell Caravan Parks* v. *Hemel Hempstead R.D.C.* [1966] 1 Q.B. 895, C.A.; *Llanfyllin Rural District Council* v. *Holland* (1964) 62 L.G.R. 459, D.C.

The way of appealing to a magistrates' court is by way of complaint for an order (Magistrates' Court Rules 1968 (S.I. 1968 No. 1920), r. 30).

As already mentioned, there is no appeal against the obligatory condition requiring a copy of the relevant site licence to be conspicuously displayed on the site (s.7(1)).

8. Alteration of Conditions Attached to Site Licence

A local authority may at any time and of their own volition (but only after allowing the licence holder an opportunity of making representations) alter, by the variation or cancellation of existing conditions, or by the imposition of new conditions, the conditions attached to a site licence (s.8(1)). The licence holder may himself apply for an alteration of such conditions (s.8(2)). In either case the local authority must *not* alter the conditions without first having regard to the Secretary of State's "Model Standards for Caravans Sites" (s.8(4)). The local authority must consult with the fire authority if there is to be any alteration of a condition relating to fire precautions (s.8(5)).

The holder of a site licence who is aggrieved[8] by any alteration of site licence conditions or by the local authority's refusal to agree to his application for an alteration of conditions may appeal to a magistrates' court (s.8(2)) and the court in considering the matter must have regard to the Secretary of State's "Model Standards for Caravan Sites" (s.8(4)).

When site licence conditions are altered, the licence holder must, if required, deliver up his site licence to the local authority for amendment[9] (s.11(1)) and if he fails, without reasonable excuse, to do so, he is liable to a fine of £10 (s.11(2)).

9. Temporary Exemptions for Existing Caravan Sites

The 1960 Act contains special provision (ss.13 to 20) relating to caravan sites in existence when the 1960 Act came into operation on August 29, 1960 (s.50(4)). Such "existing sites" (as defined in section 13) were temporarily relieved of the need to obtain a site licence but application for such a licence had to be made not later than October 29, 1960 (s.14). Further exemption until November 29, 1960, was accorded (s.15) to certain sites which were in being on August 29, 1960, but which were nevertheless technically not "existing sites."

[8] As to persons aggrieved, see *ante*, pp. 221–230.
[9] *Turner* v. *Garstang R.D.C.* (1965) 17 P. & C.R. 218.

10. Permanent Exemptions from Requirements as to Site Licences

All the foregoing provisions of this chapter relating to the need of a caravan site to be granted a site licence under the 1960 Act have no application (s.2) to a number of caravan sites more particularly described in the First Schedule to the Act.

Briefly, the 1960 Act has no application to the following 12 uses of land, namely:

(1) the use of land within the curtilage of a dwelling-house as a caravan site, such use being incidental to the enjoyment of the house;

(2) the use of any land as a site for a caravan for a period including not more than two nights, by a person travelling with the caravan, provided:
  (a) that at the time there is no other caravan for human habitation on the land (including any adjoining land in the same occupation); and
  (b) that during the previous 12 months there has not been any such caravan on such land on more than 28 days;

(3) the use as a caravan site of land comprising at least five acres (including any adjoining unbuilt land in the same occupation), provided that during the previous 12 months:
  (a) there has not been any caravan for human habitation on any part of the land on more than 28 days; and
  (b) there have not been more than three such caravans on the land at any one time;

(4) the use as a caravan site of land occupied and supervised for the purposes of recreation by an "exempted organisation," *i.e.* an organisation for promoting recreational activities which has been granted a certificate of exemption by the Secretary of State under paragraph 12 of the First Schedule to the 1960 Act;

(5) the use by not more than five caravans at a time of land where a certificate has been issued by an exempted organisation declaring the land as being approved by the exempted organisation for use by its members;

(6) the use as a caravan site under the supervision of an exempted organisation in connection with a meeting of its members, lasting not more than five days;

(7) the use of agricultural land as a caravan site for seasonal accommodation of agricultural workers employed on land in the same occupation;

(8) the use of any land as a caravan site for seasonal accommodation of forestry workers employed on land in the same occupation;

(9) the use as a caravan site for the accommodation of persons employed in connection with building or engineering operations on the same or adjoining land;

(10) the use as a caravan site by a travelling showman (being a member of an organisation of travelling showmen recognised by a certificate of the Secretary of State) either travelling for the purposes of his business or in winter quarters (October—March);

(11) the use as a caravan site of land occupied by the local authority in whose area the land is situated.

(12) the use of land occupied by a county council as a caravan site for gipsies.

The Secretary of State may, by order, exclude particular land from any of the foregoing exemptions numbered (2) to (10) inclusive (Sched. 1, para. 13).

Planning permission is granted under Class XXII of Schedule 1 to the Town and Country Planning General Development Order 1977 for the use of land as a caravan site in the circumstances of items (2) to (9) inclusive above and also in the circumstances of item (10) above (other than the circumstances relating to winter quarters).

11. Provision of Caravan Sites by Local Authorities

A local authority (including in this context a county council and the council of a joint planning board for an area which includes a National Park (s.24(8)) have power to provide caravan *sites* within their area and to manage them (s.24(1)), to acquire land compulsorily for such purposes (s.24(5) and (6)), and to make reasonable charges (s.24(3)) for the services provided by them at any site (s.24(2)). They must not exercise the power to provide a caravan site before consulting the fire authority (if they are not themselves such authority) of the area where the site is to be provided (s.24(2A)).

The aforesaid powers of a local authority with respect to caravan sites may be exercised as freely for those who do *not* normally live in the area of the local authority as for those who do (s.24(4)).

Whilst they may provide caravan *sites,* a local authority have no power to provide caravans (s.24(7)).

The foregoing *powers* to provide caravan sites are converted into *duties* to provide such sites insofar as they are needed for gipsies residing in or resorting to their areas by the provisions of the Caravan Sites Act 1968, section 6.

12. Caravans on Commons

A district council may by order prohibit (s.23(1), (2) and (7) and Sched. 2), either absolutely or except in specified circumstances, the stationing of caravans on a common including a town or village green (s.23(8)). Any person stationing a caravan in contravention of such an Order is liable on summary conviction to a fine not exceeding (s.23(3)) level 1 on the standard scale (*i.e.*) in 1987, £50 (Criminal Justice Act 1982 s.37 and Criminal Penalties etc. (Increase) Order 1984 (art. 2(4) and Sched. 4).[10]

The need for the foregoing provision against stationing caravans on a common arises from the fact that in the case of commons there may be no occupier who could be said to "cause or permit . . . the use of land as a caravan site" as mentioned in section 1 of the 1960 Act and, accordingly, no offence under that section could be committed. The provisions of section 23 of the Act are thus complementary to the site licensing system set up by the rest of Part I of the Act—a system which presupposes the existence of an identifiable occupier.

These powers of a district council do not apply (s.23(1)(*a*)) to commons or waste land falling under section 193 of the Law of Property Act 1925. That section mainly applies to urban commons. Nor do such powers apply (s.23(1)(*b*)) to land subject to a scheme under Part I of the Commons Act 1899 nor to land (s.23(1)(*c*)) for which a site licence is for the time being in force.

13. Entry on Land and Protection for Occupiers

An authorised officer of a local authority may (on giving 24 hours' notice to the occupier) enter upon a caravan site, or upon land with regard to which an application for a site licence has been made, in connection with the discharge of the local authority's powers under the 1960 Act (s.26). Any person wilfully obstructing such an officer in the execution of his duty is liable to a fine (s.26(5)) not exceeding level 1 on the standard scale (*i.e.*) in 1987, £50 (Criminal Justice Act 1982, s.37 and Criminal Penalties etc. (Increase) Order 1984 (art. 2(4) and Sched. 4).[10]

[10] S.I. 1984 No. 447.

Where an occupier of land grants to another a licence (not to be confused with a "site licence" granted by a local authority) to use land as a caravan site, or where land of not more than 400 square yards is the subject of a tenancy for use as a caravan site (in which two cases the licensor or the lessor remains (s.1(3) the "occupier" of the land) then if, in either of these cases, the licensee or the tenant does anything which would amount to an offence under the 1960 Act if done by the occupier, the occupier may terminate the licence or the tenancy and retake possession of the land notwithstanding the terms of the licence or tenancy (s.12(1)). Such an occupier may enter on the land and do any works necessary in order to comply with a site licence granted in respect of such land by a local authority (s.12(2)).

Chapter 14

AMENITIES AND CONSERVATION: CONTROL OF TREES AND WOODLANDS, OF SPECIAL BUILDINGS AND OF WASTE LAND

A. TREES AND WOODLANDS

THE provisions of the Town and Country Planning Act 1971 relating to control over trees and woodlands, special buildings and waste land are amended in important respects by the Local Government, Planning and Land Act 1980, the Local Government and Planning (Amendment) Act 1981 as from August 27, 1981 (1981 Act, s.1 and Sched. and s.2(3)), the Town and Country Planning Act 1984 (in relation only to tree preservation orders) as from August 12, 1984 (1984 Act, s.7(2)); the Town and Country Planning (Amendment) Act 1985 (in relation only to replacement of trees) as from September 22, 1985 (1985 Act, s.3(3)) and the Housing and Planning Act 1986, ss.40, 46, 49(1)(i) and Schedule 9, Pt. I and Schedule 11, Part I, paragraph 13 as from a date to be appointed by the Secretary of State for the Environment (1986 Act, s.57(2)). Any reference in this chapter to the 1971 Act is a reference to that Act amended as above mentioned.

1. Tree Preservation Orders

The 1971 Act makes provision for the preservation of trees, groups of trees or woodlands by means of tree preservation orders. Such an order (which operates independently of any development plan whether in course of preparation or in operation) is *made* by a local planning authority (s.60), usually a district planning authority (s.60(1A)). The order needs *confirmation* by the same local planning authority which made the order (and not, as formerly, by the Secretary of State) before it can take effect (s.60(4)).

D.O.E. Circular 36/78 dated May 3, 1978 contains full information as to the policy of the Department of the Environment relating to Trees and Forestry. The Circular is most comprehensive and carries a Memorandum, Section VI and Section VII of which relate especially to tree preservation orders—their application and the procedure for making them.

Before making a tree preservation order a local planning authority must be satisfied that it is expedient so to do *in the interests of amenity* (s.60(1)). In other words, matters of amenity are the only relevant factors for consideration in connection with the making of a tree preservation order.[1]

It is the *duty* of a local planning authority, when granting planning permission for development, to ensure, by the imposition of conditions, that adequate provision is made for the preservation or planting of trees (s.59(*a*)). To this end the authority may make such tree preservation orders as appear necessary (ss.59(*b*) and 60(3)).

As already stated, it will usually be a district planning authority which will make a tree preservation order because a county planning authority can make such an order only in limited circumstances (s.60(1A)), namely,

(a) if they make it in pursuance of section 59(*b*) (mentioned above) of the 1971 Act;
(b) if it relates to land which does not lie wholly within the area of a single district planning authority;
(c) if it relates to land in which the county planning authority hold an interest; or
(d) if it relates to land in a National Park.

2. Effect of a Tree Preservation Order

When in force a tree preservation order, subject to any exemptions mentioned in the order, will prohibit the cutting down, topping, lopping, uprooting, wilful damaging or wilful destruction of trees except with the consent (which may be given subject to conditions) of the local planning authority (s.60(1)(*a*)).The prohibitions set out in the order will not apply to trees which are dying or dead or have become dangerous nor will they prevent action which is necessary to prevent or abate a nuisance or comply with an Act of Parliament (s.60(6)).

A tree preservation order may also provide for the replanting of any woodland area which is felled in the course of forestry operations permitted by, or under, the tree preservation order (s.60(1)(*b*)) and for the payment by a local planning authority of compensation in respect of loss or damage caused or incurred in consequence of any refusal of consent as aforesaid by the local planning authority or arising out of the grant of any such consent subject to

[1] As to the meaning of "amenity," see *Re Ellis and Ruislip-Northwood U.D.C.* [1920] 1 K.B. 343, C.A. where Scrutton L.J. declared, (at page 370) "The word 'amenity' is obviously used very loosely; it is, I think, novel in an Act of Parliament, and appears to mean pleasant circumstances or features, advantages"; as to the meaning of "tree" see *Bullock* v. *Secretary of State for the Environment* [1980] J.P.L. 416.

conditions (s.174)[2] or out of a requirement as to the replanting of trees (s.175).

As to applications for a local authority's consent under a tree preservation order, the order may apply (subject to adaption and modification) the provisions (except ss.25, 26, 27, 28, 29(2) to (6), 34(2), 38, 39, 41 to 44 and 47 to 49) of Part III of the 1971 Act relating to planning permissions and applications for such permission and appeals to the Secretary of State (s.60(1)(*c*), (2)(*a*)).

A purchase notice requiring the purchase of the applicant's land may, in appropriate circumstances, be served in the event of any consent under a tree preservation order being refused (ss.60(2)(*b*) and 191(1)).[3]

3. Procedure for a Tree Preservation Order

The procedure for the making of a tree preservation order is dealt with (s.60) in the Town and Country Planning (Tree Preservation Order) Regulations 1969[4] as amended by the Town and Country Planning (Tree Preservation Order) (Amendment) and (Trees in Conservation Areas) (Exempted Cases) Regulations 1975,[5] art. 2 and the Town and Country Planning (Tree Preservation Order) (Amendment) Regulations 1981[6] whereby the order must be made in the form (or substantially in the form) set out in the Schedule to the 1969 Regulations (reg. 4) and must define the trees, groups of trees or woodlands to which it relates and for that purpose must include a map (*ibid.*).

On making the order the local planning authority must deposit for inspection, in the locality of the trees, a certified copy of the order and the map (reg. 5(*a*)) and send copies of these to the Conservator of Forests and the District Valuer (reg. 2(1)) together with a list of persons affected (reg. 5(*b*)).

The local planning authority must serve a copy of the order upon owners and occupiers of land affected by the order, and on any other person known to them as being entitled to work by surface working any minerals in the land affected by the order, or to fell any trees or woodlands affected by the order (reg. 5(*c*)).

With the copy of the Order there must also be served a notice stating

[2] *Cardigan Timber Co.* v. *Cardiganshire County Council* [1957] 9 P. & C.R. 158, L.T.
[3] As to purchase notices generally, see Chap. 18.
[4] S.I. 1969 No. 17.
[5] S.I. 1975 No. 148.
[6] S.I. 1981 No. 14.

(reg. 5(*c*)(i), (ii), (iii) and (v)) the grounds for making the order, the place where it can be inspected by the public, and that objections and representations about the order may be made to the local planning authority within 28 days of the service of the notice.

Every objection or representation must be made in writing and must state both the particular trees, groups of trees or woodlands to which it refers and also the grounds of the objection and, unless it does these things and is received by the local planning authority within the 28 days mentioned above, it will not be "duly made" (reg. 7).

Before confirming a tree preservation order the local planning authority must take into consideration any objections or representations which have been "duly made," and, if a public local inquiry into the matter is held, they must also take into consideration the Inspector's report of the inquiry (reg. 8(2)).

In a case of urgency, (*e.g.* where there is danger of the imminent felling of trees) a tree preservation order, as made by the local planning authority, may contain a direction that section 61 of the 1971 Act shall apply to it in which event the order will forthwith operate provisionally for a period of six months or until the date when the order is confirmed whichever first occurs (s.61(2)).

Notice of the confirmation of a tree preservation order must be served by the local planning authority on all owners and occupiers of land affected by it, on the Conservator of Forests and the District Valuer (reg. 2(1)) and on any other person known to them to be entitled to work, by surface working, any minerals in the land affected by the order or to fell trees affected by the order (reg. 9).

Tree preservation orders are registrable as local land charges under rule 3 of the Local Land Charges (Amendment) Rules 1948.[7]

A "person aggrieved"[8] by, or an "authority directly concerned"[8] with the making of a tree preservation order may, within six weeks, challenge, on a point of law, the validity of the order by application to the High Court (ss.242(1)(*d*), (2)(*c*) and 245).

On such an application the High Court may quash the order if satisfied that the order is not within the powers of the 1971 Act or that the interests of the applicant have been substantially prejudiced by failure to comply with the requirements of the Act (s.245(4)(*b*)). In addition the court may quash or (where applicable) suspend the operation of the order in whole or in part (s.245(5)).

The powers to make tree preservation orders and the circumstances in which they may be used are further explained in Section

[7] S.I. 1948 No. 1283.

[8] As to the meaning of these expressions, see *ante*, pp. 221–230.

VI of the Memorandum on Trees and Forestry which accompanies D.O.E. Circular No. 36/78 dated May 3, 1978. Section VII of the same Memorandum deals with the procedures for making a tree preservation order and for dealing with applications for consent made under such an order.

4. Penalties for Contravention of a Tree Preservation Order

If any person, in contravention of the provisions of a tree preservation order, cuts down, uproots or wilfully destroys a tree, or wilfully damages, tops or lops a tree in a manner likely to destroy it, he is liable on summary conviction to a fine not exceeding £2,000 or twice the value of the tree (whichever is the greater) whilst on conviction on indictment he is liable to a fine of unlimited amount in the calculation of which regard is to be had to any financial benefit accruing to the defendant (s.102(1)), Criminal Justice Act 1982, s.37 and Criminal Penalties (Increase) Order 1984 (S.I. 1984 No. 447).

The offence under section 102(1) of the 1971 Act is an absolute offence; liabiliy may be incurred even if the person charged had no knowledge of the existence of the tree preservation order.[9]

If any person contravenes the provisions of a tree preservation order otherwise than in the above-mentioned manner, then he is liable on summary conviction to a fine not exceeding level 4 on the standard scale, *i.e.* £1,000 (s.102(2)), Criminal Justice Act 1982, s.37 and Criminal Penalties etc. (Increase) Order 1984, (S.I. 1984 No. 447).

In the case of any continuing offence after conviction the offender is liable to a daily penalty of £5 per day (s.102(3)).

In addition to the forgoing penalties by way of fine, a local authority is able to resort to the remedy of an injunction in order to prevent a possible contravention of a tree preservation order.[10] This is because: "It is not just a case of taking action to prevent a criminal offence. It is a case of preventing interference with the areas of natural beauty which they [the local authority] have sought by their tree preservation orders to preserve."[10]

In *Barnet London Borough Council* v. *Eastern Electricity Board and Others* (1973) 1 W.L.R. 430, the defendants excavated a trench and in so doing damaged and severed the roots of six trees which were subject to a tree preservation order. In consequence the trees had

[9] *Maidstone Borough Council* v. *Mortimer* (1980) 256 E.G. 1013; but see also *Vale of Glamorgan Borough Council* v. *Palmer* (1984) J.P.L. 334.

[10] *Kent County Council* v. *Batchelor* [1978] 3 All E.R. 980, at p. 986.

reduced stability and life expectancy but there was no evidence they would die within a certain period. They were close to a public highway. The local authority felled four trees and replaced them. The defendants were charged with wilful destruction of the six trees. The magistrates dismissed the information and the local authority appealed to the High Court which allowed the appeal. It was held that the purpose of the legislation was the protection of trees for the amenities of giving pleasure, protection and shade and that a tree, the subject of a preservation order, was destroyed when an injury inflicted was such that the tree was no longer worth preserving as an amenity.

5. Trees in Conservation Areas

Under sections 277, 277A and 277B of the 1971 Act special provision is made with respect to conservation areas (that is, areas of special architectural or historic interest the character or appearance of which it is desirable to preserve or enhance) and such an area can be designated by a local planning authority (s.277).

Designation of land as a conservation area brings limited protection to certain (but not all) trees in the conservation area even though such trees are not protected by a tree preservation order (s.61A). The instant protection afforded is not to apply (s.61A(4)) in the five exempted cases set out in regulation 3 of the Town and Country Planning (Tree Preservation Order) (Amendment) and (Trees in Conservation Areas) (Exempted Cases) Regulations 1975.[11]

The five exempted cases set out in the aforesaid regulation 3 are as follows:

(i) the cutting down, uprooting, topping or lopping of a tree in the circmstances mentioned in sub-section (6) of section 60 of the 1971 Act;

(ii) the cutting down of a tree in the circumstances mentioned in paragraph (1) or (2), or the cutting down, uprooting, topping or lopping of a tree in the circumstances mentioned in paragraph (3), of the Second Schedule to the Form of Tree Preservation Order contained in the Schedule to the Town and Country Planning (Tree Preservation Order) Regulations 1969 (as amended by these 1975 regulations);

(iii) the cutting down of a tree in accordance with a felling licence granted by the Forestry Commissioners;

[11] S.I. 1975 No. 148.

(iv) the cutting down, uprooting, topping or lopping of a tree on land in the occupation of a local planning authority and the act is done by or with the consent of that authority;

(v) the cutting down, uprooting topping or lopping of a tree having a diameter not exceeding 75 millimetres, or the cutting down or uprooting of a tree having a diameter not exceeding 100 millimetres where the act is carried out to improve the growth of other trees, the reference to "diameter" being construed as a reference to the diameter, measured over the bark, at a point 1.5 metres above ground level.

6. Duties as to Replacement of Trees

If a tree in respect of which a tree preservation order is in force is removed, uprooted or destroyed in contravention of the order, or, (except in the case of a tree to which the order applies as part of a woodland), is removed, uprooted or destroyed or dies at a time when its cutting down or uprooting is authorised only because it is dying or is dead or has become dangerous (s.60(6)), then in any such circumstances it is the automatic *duty* of the owner of the land to plant another tree of appropriate size and species at the same place as soon as he reasonably can (s.62(1) as amended by Town and Country Planning (Amendment) Act 1985). This duty applies to any person who is, for the time being, the owner of the land and may be enforced against any such person (s.62(3)).

In the case of trees which form part of a woodland and which are removed, uprooted or destroyed because they are dying or are dead or have become dangerous (the only instances in which the replacement of trees *in a woodland* is called for), it is a sufficient compliance with the duty referred to in the preceding paragraph for such trees to be replaced by a similar number of trees either on or near the land from which the earlier trees have gone or on such other land as may be agreed between the local planning authority and the owner of the land, and (in either case) in such places as may be designated by the local planning authority (s.62(1A)).

Any person under a duty to replace a tree by planting another tree may be relieved of the duty at the discretion of the local planning authority (s.62(1)).

A tree planted by way of replacement will straightaway come under the automatic protection given by the tree preservation order which formerly applied to the tree which has gone (s.62(2)).

The local planning authority (within a period of four years of the failure to discharge the automatic duty mentioned above), by notice served on the owner of the land, are empowered to enforce the forgoing provisions subject to appeal to the Secretary of State (s.103) and to a further appeal (on law only) to the High Court (s.246(1A)).

Details as to the grounds of appeal to the Secretary of State are given in section 103(3) and (4) of, and Schedule 9 to, the 1971 Act. The grounds of appeal are as follows (s.103(3)):

(a) that the provisions of section 62 of the 1971 Act, or that any conditions subject to which a consent under a tree preservation order has been given which conditions require the replacement of trees, are not applicable or have been complied with;
(b) that the requirments of the notice served, (as mentioned above) on the owner of the land, are unreasonable in respect of the period within which trees are to be replaced or in respect of the size or species of tress specified in the notice;
(c) that the planting of a tree or trees in accordance with the notice is not required in the interests of amenity or would be contrary to the practice of good forestry;
(d) that the place on which a tree is, or trees are, required to be planted by way of replacement is unsuitable for that purpose.

The proceedure for the appeal is set out in section 103(3A), (3B), (3C), (3D), and (3F) of the 1971 Act.

7. Tree Preservation Orders in Anticipation of Disposal of Crown Land

Until the Town and Country Planning Act 1984, section 2 came into operation on August 12, 1984 no tree preservation order could be made in respect of any tree or trees growing on Crown Land. This was because of the Crown's constitutional immunity from planning control under the 1971 Act.

Section 2 of the 1984 Act alters this position by allowing a local planning authority (with the consent of the "appropriate authority" (1984 Act s.6(1)), *i.e.* the appropriate Crown authority (1971 Act, s.266(7)) to make a tree preservation order which will take effect when the land to which it relates ceases to be Crown Land or becomes subject to a private interest whichever first occurs (1984 Act, s.2(3)). Once this occurs the order takes immediate (but provisional) effect (*ibid.*) until the expiration of a period of six months or until it is confirmed by the local planning authority (1984 Act, s.2(4)) whichever first occurs. The Crown must, as soon as practicable, give notice in writing to the local planning authority of the name and address of the person who has become entitled to the land in question or to a private interest in it (1984 Act, s.2(5)). Time for confirming the order runs from date of that notice (*ibid.*).

Section 2 of the memorandum to D.O.E. Circular 18/84 gives further explanation of the effect of the 1984 Act as it applies to tree preservation orders.

8. Compensation in Connection with Tree Preservation Orders

As to compensation which may become payable to an owner in respect of action taken in pursuance of the provisions of a Tree Preservation Order, reference may be made to Chapter 17.

B. BUILDINGS OF SPECIAL ARCHITECTURAL OR HISTORIC INTEREST

1. Listing of Buildings Replaces Building Preservation Orders

The listing of a building under the Town and Country Planning Act 1971 is the key to its further protection under the provisions of Part IV of the 1971 Act and the Town and Country Planning (Listed Buildings and Buildings in Conservation Areas) Regulations 1977.[12]

The enactments (may it be said again) relating to listed buildings have recently been amended by the Housing and Planning Act 1986, s.40 and Schedule 9, Part I and Schedule 11, Pt. I, paragraphs 7(2) and 13. These several amendments are incorporated into the following paragraphs of this chapter.

The policy of the Secretary of State and the procedures relating to "Historic Buildings," their listing and their protection and preservation, are dealt with comprehensively in D.O.E. Circular 23/77[12] dated March 16, 1977 and in D.O.E. Circular 12/81 dated March 24, 1981—both circulars as amended by Appendix B of D.O.E. Circular 8/84. Amongst many other things these Circulars set out the principles which are used in the selection of buildings for listing (Circular 23/77, Appendix 1 and Circular 12/81, Appendix A).

Under sections 30 and 31 of the Town and Country Planning Act 1962 a building of special architectural or historic interest could be given protection if it were made the subject of a building preservation order made by a local planning authority and approved by the Secretary of State. If it were merely included in a list of buildings of special architectural or historic interest under section 32 of the 1962 Act it did not receive the same amount of protection.

Under the 1971 Act there are no more building preservation

[12] S.I. 1977 No. 228. The 1977 Regulations are to be revoked and replaced by new regulations now (February 1987) published in draft form. A new D.O.E. Circular updating Circular 23/77 (and its amendments) will follow.

orders but every building which was subject to such an order on January 1, 1969, but was not listed under the 1962 Act, will be deemed (s.54(10)) to be a building listed under the 1971 Act. The Secretary of State may at any time direct that this arrangement shall cease to have effect (*ibid.*) but before he does so he must consult with the local planning authority and with the owner and with the occupier of the building (s.54(11)).

2. A Set of Special Expressions

Part IV of the 1971 Act creates a number of expressions peculiarly relating to special buildings. These expressions are seven in number as follows: "listed building" (s.54(9)); "listed building consent" (s.55(3A)); "listed building purchase notice" (s.190(5)); "listed building enforcement notice" (s.96(2)); "building preservation notice" (s.58(1)); "repairs notice" (s.115(1)); and "direction for minimum compensation" (s.117(4)).

3. Lists of Special Buildings

With a view to guiding local planning authorities in the preservation of buildings of special architectural or historic interest the Secretary of State is to compile lists of such buildings or approve, with or without modifications, such lists compiled by the Historic Buildings and Monuments Commission for England or by other persons or bodies (s.54(1),(2),(3)) and deposit copies of such lists with the proper officer of the council of any London borough or county district affected and also with the Chief Officer of the Commission, (s.54(4),(5)). Any copy so deposited is to be a local land charge (s.54(6)) for the purposes of the Local Land Charges Act 1975 and the Local Land Charges Rules 1977.[13]

The Historic Buildings and Monuments Commission for England is a statutory body established under section 32 of, and Schedule 3 to, the National Heritage Act 1983. It succeeds the Historic Buildings Council for England and the Ancient Monuments Board for England (1983 Act, s.39) and, for brevity's sake, is hereafter referred to in this chapter as "the Commission." The establishment of the Commission is dealt with in D.O.E. Circular 8/84 dated March 28, 1984. The Commission advises the Secretary of State on (a) the listing of buildings (D.O.E. Circular 8/84, para. 7) and (b) the granting

[13] S.I. 1977 No. 985.

of "listed building consent" (D.O.E. Circular 23/77, para. 55 and D.O.E. Circular 8/84, para. 8) for the demolition, alteration or extension of a listed building as to which see page 308 *post*.

When considering whether or not to list a building the Secretary of State may take into account not only the building itself but also its relationship to other buildings and the desirability of preserving any feature of the building consisting of a man-made object or structure fixed to the building or forming part of the land and comprised within the curtilage of the building (s.54(2)). Thus, it is not only the building which is to be considered but the entire *mise en scène*.

The erection of a building (which term includes a structure or erection (s.290(1)) within the curtilage of a listed building may well need planning permission for development (s.23(1)). It will certainly need listed building consent (see page 308) before it can be demolished—*Cotswold District Council* v. *Secretary of State for the Environment and Pearson* (1985) J.P.L. 407.

If a building becomes a listed building then (a) any object or structure fixed to the building, and (b) any object or structure within the curtilage of the building which, although not fixed to the building (*i.e.* is free-standing), forms part of the land and has done so since before July 1, 1948 (the date the 1947 Act came into operation), must be treated as part of the building (s.54(9) as amended by the Housing and Planning Act 1986, s.40(*a*) and Sched. 9, Pt. I, para.1). As to the meaning of curtilage in this context, it was held in *Attorney-General, ex rel. Sutcliffe* v. *Calderdale Borough Council* (1983) J.P.L. 310 that, where a mill had become a listed building, a terrace of cottage houses (originally constructed as dwellings for the mill-workers) which was adjacent to the mill and linked to the mill by a bridge, was itself within the curtilage of the mill and therefore was "caught" by the listing of the mill (s.54(9)).

The owner and occupier of a listed building must be informed that the building has been listed or has been removed from the list (s.54(7)) but the Secretary of State is not obliged to consult either the owner or the occupier before listing any building though he must consult with such other persons as appear to him appropriate as having special knowledge of, or interest in, such buildings (s.54(3)) and, if the building is in England, he must also consult with the Commission (*ibid.*).

Is there any appeal against the listing of a building? The answer, strictly, is "No". But in the House of Lords on July 30, 1986 (in a debate on the Housing and Planning Bill 1986 then under consideration by the House) an interesting comment was made by Lord Elton, for the Government, when replying to the question of appeals against listing raised by Viscount Ridley. Lord Elton said:

> "My noble friend also raised the question of appeals against listing. He rightly said that such an appeal exists. It is true that it is not generally known. I was advised that this was the case when I took office and I then arranged that everyone whose house was subsequently listed should be advised that if he felt it was wrongly listed he had but to send his reasons to my right honourable friend to have it reviewed and, if appropriate, struck off the list. I believe that is quicker and cheaper than anything which could be achieved by statute" (*Hansard*, Vol. 479, col. 909).

Thus anyone who feels aggrieved should write to the Department of the Environment, Lambeth Bridge House, London SE1 7SB.

The Secretary of State must keep open for free inspection copies of all lists, and amendments of lists, compiled or approved by him and a local authority must likewise keep open for such inspection any portion of a list relating to their area (s.54(8)). The Commission must similarly keep open for inspection any list relating to buildings in Greater London (*ibid.*).

As has been mentioned, the Secretary of State, in deciding to list a building, need have no consultation or contact of any kind with the owner or occupier of a building. If such a person is thinking of carrying out development involving the building it will clearly be helpful to him to know whether or not it is going to be listed. This can be ascertained on application to the Secretary of State for a certificate stating that he does not intend to list the building (s.54A(1)). If the Secretary of State issues such a certificate then he is precluded from listing the building for the next five years and the local planning authority (and the Commission, with respect to a building in Greater London) are likewise precluded for that same period of five years from taking action under section 58 of the 1971 Act relating to the service of a building preservation notice in respect of an unlisted building (s.54A(2)).

Notice of the application made to the Secretary of State must be given to the local planning authority (or to the Commission, with respect to a building in Greater London) (s.54A(3) and (4)) and it is important to note that the application to the Secretary of State can be made only when either (a) an application has already been made for planning permission for development involving the alteration, extension or demolition of the building or (b) such planning permission has already been granted (s.54A(1)(*a*) and (*b*)).

Any person thinking of buying a building which is unlisted will do well to protect himself, by appropriate provisions in the contract for sale, against the consequences of any listing which may take place before the completion of the sale and purchase. In *Amalgamated Investment and Property Co. Ltd.* v. *John Walker and Sons Ltd.* (1976) 3 All E.R. 509, C.A., the day after a contract was signed to purchase a warehouse, the vendors were informed the warehouse had been selected for listing as being of special historic or architectural interest. On the following day this listing was given legal affect when the list was signed on behalf of the Secretarty of State. The purchasers had contracted to buy the property for re-development. The Court of Appeal rejected an action claiming recession of the contract on the grounds of common mistake or, alternatively, frustration.

4. Causing Damage to a Listed Building

The doing of any act causing, or likely to result in, damage to a listed building not being an ecclesiastical building or an ancient monument (s.56(1)) is an offence punishable with a fine on summary conviction not exceeding level 3 on the standard scale (*i.e* £200) (s.57(1)), (2)); Criminal Justice Act 1982, s.37 and Criminal Penalties etc. (Increase) Order 1984 (S.I. 1984 No. 447)). If a person, convicted of this offence, fails to prevent further damage resulting from the offence he is liable to a daily penalty of £40 (s.57(3) as amended by Housing and Planning Act 1986, s.49(1)(i) and Sched. 11, para.13(1)).

5. Urgent Works to Preserve Listed Buildings

A local authority or the Secretary of State may carry out works urgently necessary for the preservation of a listed building after giving seven days' notice of intent in writing to the owner (s.101(1)(*a*), (4)) and may recover from the owner the cost of so doing (s.101A(1), (2), (3)) subject to the right of the owner to make representations to the Secretary of State within 28 days of the demand for payment (s.101A(4), (5)). In all of this the Secretary of State must authorise the Commission to act in his stead if the listed building is in England (s.101(5)(c)).

The foregoing provisions as to urgent preservation works may be extended to an *unlisted* building if it is in a conservation area (s.277), by direction of the Secretary of State (s.101(1)(*b*), (2), (5)(*b*)).

If the building on which it is proposed to carry out urgent preservation works is occupied, such works may be carried out only to those parts which are not in use (s.101(3)). No works may be carried out in respect of an "excepted building" specified in section 58(2) of the 1971 Act.

The notice of intent to carry out urgent works must specify *in detail* the works regarded by the local authority or the Secretary of State as urgently necessary, the object of the seven days' notice to the owner of the building being to allow time for discussions as a result of which the owner might agree to do the works himself.[14] The need to specify *in detail* the remedial works which are regarded as necessary to preserve the listed building is important. It is not enough to specify the taking of "all such steps as may be necessary to preserve the structure of the building"; the steps need to be spelt out.[15]

Local authorities have power to contribute by way of grant or loan to the cost of preserving buildings of special architectural or historic interest (whether listed or not) under the provisions of the Local Authorities (Historic Buildings) Act 1962 (s.1(1)(*b*)) and the London Government Act 1963, s.2(4). Action by a local authority by way of grant or loan no longer needs the approval of the Secretary of State (Town and Country Planning Act 1968, s.58 which is not repealed by the 1971 Act).

The Secretary of State may make loans (Civic Amenities Act 1967 (s.4(1)) as well as grants under section 4 of the Historic Buildings and Ancient Monuments Act 1953 for the preservation of historic buildings not situated in England. The Commission may do the like for such buildings in England (Historic Buildings and Ancient Monuments Act 1953, s.3A(1) and (2) as inserted by the National Heritage Act 1983, Sched. 4, para. 3).

Before making a dangerous structure order (under section 77 or 79 of the Building Act 1984 or sections 62, 65 or 69 of the London Building Acts (Amendment) Act 1939) in respect of a listed building, a local planning authority must first consider whether they should, instead, carry out urgent preservation works themselves (under section 101 of the 1971 Act) or acquire the building as being in need of repair (under sections 114 and 115 of the 1971 Act) (s.56C as added by the Housing and Planning Act 1986, s.40(*f*) and Sched. 9, Pt.I, para. 6.

6. Building Preservation Notices for Unlisted Buildings

Where a building is *not* listed under the 1971 Act but nevertheless appears to the local planning authority (other than a county planning authority) to be of special architectural or historic interest and is threatened with demolition or alteration, the local planning authority

[14] *R.* v. *Secretary of State for the Environment, ex p. Hampshire County Council* [1981] J.P.L. 47.

[15] *R.* v. *London Borough of Camden, ex p. Comyn Ching & Co (London) Ltd.* (1983) 47 P. & C.R. 417.

may serve on the owner and occupier of the building a "building preservation notice" which subjects the building, for a maximum of six months, to the same protection and provisions as if it were listed (s.58(1), (3), (4)). In a case of urgency the local planning authority may serve a building preservation notice by fixing it conspicuously to the building (s.58(6)). The need for this power became evident in *Maltglade Ltd.* v. *St. Albans Rural District Council.*[16]

During the aforesaid period of six months the local planning authority may request the Secretary of State to consider including the building in a list (s.58(1)) compiled or approved under the 1971 Act. If the Secretary of State does so include it, or if he notifies the local planning authority in writing that he does not intend so to include it, then the building preservation notice at once ceases to have effect (s.58(3)). If the Secretary of State does in fact decline to list the building, the local planning authority may not, within the next 12 months, serve any further building preservation notice in respect of the building (s.58(5)).

So far as building preservation notices for unlisted buildings relate to buildings in Greater London, the Commission have, concurrently with the London boroughs, the functions of a local planning authority (s.58(7)).

A building preservation notice may *not* be served in respect of an "excepted building" (s.58(2)), that is to say, an ecclesiastical building for the time being in use for ecclesiastical purposes or a building listed in the Schedule to the Ancient Monuments and Archeological Areas Act 1979 (*ibid.*).

In a case where a building preservation notice ceases to have effect but the building to which the notice relates does not become a listed building—in other words, where the efforts of the local planning authority have failed—provision is made for the payment of compensation for loss or damage caused by the service of the building preservation notice (s.173(1), (2), (3)) including loss or damage for breach of contract relating to proposed works to the building (s.173(4)).

7. Listed Building Consent for Demolition, Alteration or Extension of Listed Building

Under section 55 of the 1971 Act it is an offence (s.55(1)) to demolish, or to alter or to extend so as to affect *its character as a building of special architectural or historical interest,* any listed building without a written grant of consent— known as "listed building consent"

[16] [1972] 3 All E.R. 129.

(s.55(3A))—granted by the local planning authority (in this instance the district planning authority, by virtue of the Local Government Act 1972, Sched. 16, para. 25) or by the Secretary of State (s.55(2), (3)). The offence is one of absolute liability. Thus there is no need to proof intent (*R.* v. *Wells Street Metropolitan Stipendiary Magistrate, ex parte Westminster City Council* (1986) J.P.L. 903.

A demolition contractor who negligently and mistakenly demolished a listed building instead of the building he should have demolished was ordered by the High Court to pay the costs of rebuilding the listed building—*Solihull Borough Council* v. *D. Doyle Contractors (Birmingham) Ltd. and Another* (1985) *Chartered Surveyor Weekly*, Nov. 28, at p. 766.

The penalty, on summary conviction, for the offence of demolishing, altering or extending a listed building without a grant of listed building consent is imprisonment not exceeding three months or a fine of £1,000 or both (s.55(5)(*a*) and Criminal Law Act 1977, s.28(2)). On conviction on indictment the penalty is imprisonment not exceeding 12 months or a fine or both and in determining the amount of the fine the court is to have particular regard to any financial benefit which has accrued, or appears likely to accrue, to the defendant in consequence of the offence (s.55(5)(*b*)).

It is also an offence (punishable as above mentioned) to carry out works on a listed building in breach of any condition subject to which listed building consent for the works was granted (s.55(4)).

In any proceedings for an offence it is a defence to prove (s.55(6) as substituted by Housing and Planning Act 1986, s.40(*b*) and Sched. 9, Pt.I, para. 2(1)):

(a) that works to the listed building were urgently necessary in the interests of safety or of health or for the preservation of the building;

(b) that it was not practicable to secure safety or health or, as the case may be, the preservation of the building by works of repair or works for affording temporary support or shelter,

(c) that the works carried out were limited to the minimum measures immediately necessary, and

(d) that notice in writing, justifying in detail the carrying out of the works was given to the local planning authority as soon as reasonably practicable.

In the case of an extension to a listed building (for which planning permission and listed building consent have been duly granted) the work of keying the extension to the original listed building may *in itself* constitute demolition (in part) of the listed building so that, in the absence of listed building consent for such demolition, a neighbour can obtain from the courts a grant of *certiorari* to quash the listed building consent (and also the planning permission) already granted by the local planning authority.[17]

The painting of the stonework of a listed building without listed building consent has been the subject of a listed building enforcement notice requiring the removal of the paint which notice was upheld by the Secretary of State on appeal to him against the notice.[18]

Listed building consent may be granted either with or without conditions (s.56(4), (4A), (5)) and must be distinguished from any grant of planning permission which may, or may not, also be required in the circumstances of any particular case.

Listed building consent may be granted subject to conditions including a condition reserving specified details of the works for subsequent approval (s.56(4B) as added by Housing and Planning Act 1986, s.40(*c*) and Sched. 9, Pt.I, para.3(1)). This will produce a kind of "outline listed building consent."

Where listed building consent has been granted subject to conditions, any person interested in the listed building may apply to the local planning authority to have the conditions varied or discharged (s.56B as added by Housing and Planning Act 1986, s.40(*d*) and Sched. 9, Pt.I, para.4).

Listed building consent may be granted so as to cover the *retention* of works for the demolition, alteration or extension of a listed building irregularly carried out without the requisite authority (s.55(2A)). The grant of listed building consent for retention of such works does not, however, protect a person from prosecution (as described above) for the offence of carrying out works without due authorisation in advance!

In deciding whether or not to grant planning permission or listed building consent with respect to the building of special architectural or historic interest, special regard must be paid to the desirability of preserving the building *or its setting* or of preserving any features of special architectural or historic interest which the building possesses (s.56(3)).

If a local planning authority propose to grant listed building consent they must notify the Secretary of State accordingly (1971 Act, s.56(6) of, and Sched. 11, para. 5 to, the 1971 Act—as amended by the Housing and Planning Act 1986, section 40(*j*) and Schedule 9, Part I, paragraphs 10 and 11—and D.O.E. Circulars 23/77, para. 55 and 8/84, para. 8). This is to enable him to decide whether or not he should call-in the application for listed building consent for his own

[17] *R.* v. *North Hertfordshire District Council, ex p. Sullivan* [1981] J.P.L. 752.
[18] [1979] J.P.L. 782.

decision (D.O.E. Circular 23/77, para. 55). The Secretary of State will then seek the advice of the Commission on all such applications (D.O.E. Circular 8/84, para. 8).

The attitude of the Secretary of State to the matter of granting listed building consent is set out in paragraph 17 of D.O.E. Circular 22/80 dated November 28, 1980. That paragraph declares:

> "The Government are determined to implement current policies to preserve the best of our heritage. The Secretaries of State will not be prepared to grant listed building consent for the demolition of a listed building unless they are satisfied that every possible effort has been made to continue the present use or to find a suitable alternative use for the building. They would usually expect to see evidence that the freehold of the building had been offered for sale on the open market. There would need to be exceptional reasons to justify the offer of a lease, or the imposition of restrictive covenants, which would unreasonably limit the chances of finding a new use for the building. They are particularly concerned about the number of applications to demolish which are being submitted by local authorities in respect of their own buildings. Local authorities are reminded of the advice in paragraph 24 of D.O.E. Circular 23/77 which draws attention to the help available from the Department of the Environment's Historic Buildings Bureau when owners are having difficulty in disposing of historic buildings. To ensure an economic future for old buildings it will often be essential to find appropriate alternative uses for them. Local planning authorities should therefore be flexible in dealing with applications for changes of use of buildings of architectural or historic interest."

8. Special Provisions for Listed Buildings in Greater London

The Secretary of State may, by regulations, provide that, whenever an application is made for planning permission for development which would affect a listed building in Greater London, the application shall first be referred to the Commission (s.58A(1), (2)). The Commission may then give to the local planning authority directions as to how the application should be dealt with (s.58A(3)).

9. Buildings Exempt from Protection

The aforementioned protective provisions of section 55 of the 1971 Act do *not* apply (s.56) to works for the demolition, alteration or extension of:

(a) an "ecclesiastical building" which is for the time being used[19] for ecclesiastical purposes or would be so used but for the works; or

(b) a building for the time being included in the Schedule of monuments compiled and maintained under section 1 of the Ancient Monuments and Archeological Areas Act 1979.

The aforementioned exemption from protection, under section 55 of the 1971 Act, of ecclesiastical buildings may itself now be restricted or excluded in such cases as the Secretary of State may, by order, specify (s.58AA as added by Housing and Planning Act 1986, s.40(*e*) and Sched. 9, Pt.I, para.4).

The expression "ecclesiastical building" is not defined in the 1971 Act but a building used by a minister of religion wholly or mainly as his residence for the performance of his duties as such minister is *not* to be treated as an ecclesiastical building (s.56(1)) overruling *Philips* v. *Minister of Housing and Local Government* (1965) 1 Q.B 156.

Monuments scheduled under Part I of the Ancient Monuments and Archeological Areas Act 1979, (which came into operation on October 9, 1981[20]) have their own system of control and protection under the 1979 Act.

10. Limited Duration of Listed Building Consent

A grant of listed building consent will last for five years or such other period (whether longer or shorter) as may be considered appropriate and be stated in the grant (s.56A(1)). If no period is stated in the grant then the consent will expire automatically at the end of five years from the date of the grant (s.56A(2)).

Provision is made for dealing with listed buildings consents already running when section 56A of the 1971 Act came into operation on November 13, 1980, the date when the Local Government, Planning and Land Act 1980 was passed. Such existing consents will get a life of five years before they lapse (s.56A(3), (4)).

Nothing in the 1971 Act relating (as above described) to the limitation on the duration of a listed building consent applies to such a consent granted (under section 55(2A) of the 1971 Act) for the *retention* of works for the demolition, alteration or extension of a listed building which have been irregularly carried out without the requisite listed building consent being first obtained (s.56A(5)).

[19] See *Att.-Gen. ex rel. Bedfordshire County Council* v. *Howard United Reformed Church Trustees, Bedford* (1975) 30 P. & C.R. 47, H.L.

[20] Ancient Monuments and Archeological Areas Act 1979 (Commencement No. 2) Order 1981 (S.I. 1981 No. 1300).

11. Applications, Appeals and Revocations Relating to Listed Building Consents

An application for listed building consent will be made in the first place to the local planning authority although the Secretary of State may direct that the matter shall be dealt with by him instead of by the local planning authority (s.56(6)). The functions of the local planning authority for the purpose of such an application will be discharged (outside Greater London) by the *district* planning authority (Local Government Act 1972, Sched. 16, paras. 25 and 52).

The detailed procedure for the making of an application for listed building consent and the form in which such an application is to be made, is dealt with in section 56(6) of, and Schedule 11, Part I, paragraphs 1 and 2 to, the 1971 Act (as amended by the Housing and Planning Act 1986, s.40(*i*) and Sched. 9, Pt.I, para. 9) and in the Town and Country Planning (Listed Buildings and Buildings in Conservation Areas) Regulations 1971.[21]

There is a right of appeal to the Secretary of State for the Environment in a case where the applicant for listed building consent is aggrieved by the decision of the local planning authority in refusing such consent or in granting it subject to conditions (s.56(6) of, and Sched. 11, Pt.I, paras. 8 & 9 to, the 1971 Act and the Town & Country Planning (Listed Buildings and Buildings in Conservation Areas) Regulations 1977).[22]

A listed building consent may be revoked or modified by the local planning authority in so far as it has not been acted upon (s.56(6) and Sched. 11, paras. 10–12).

12. Purchase Notices for Listed Buildings

If, having made an application for listed building consent in respect of a building and having got a decision which either refuses consent or attaches conditions to the grant of consent, or where listed building consent is revoked or modified—if in any of these circumstances the owner of the building—and, indeed, of other contiguous or adjacent land owned with the building, the use of which land is "substantially inseparable" from the use of the building (s.190(3))— claims that, in its present state, the listed building has become incapable of reasonably beneficial use, then he may serve on

[21] S.I. 1977 No. 228.
[22] S.I. 1977 No. 228.

the council of the London borough or the district where the listed building is situated a purchase notice (s.190(1))—called in the 1971 Act a "listed building purchase notice" (s.190(5))—requiring the council to purchase the listed building.

Details as to proceedings following the service of a listed building purchase notice are contained in Schedule 19 (as amended, as to para.1, by the Housing and Planning Act 1986, s.49(1)(*f*) and Sched. 11, para.5(2) and, as to para.3, by the 1986 Act, s.49(1)(*f*) and Sched. 11, para.7(2)) to the 1971 Act (s.190(1)) and in the Town and Country Planning (Listed Buildings and Buildings in Conservation Areas) Regulations 1977.[22]

If the application for listed building consent is an application *not* to demolish a building but merely to carry out alterations or extensions, and the application is refused, then in certain instances compensation is to be paid to the owner by the local planning authority (s.171 and the Town and Country Planning (Listed Buildings and Buildings in Conservation Areas) Regulations 1977).[22]

13. Enforcement Notices for Listed Buildings—Issue, Service and Appeals

For the record it should be stated that the issue of listed building enforcement notices and appeals against them was originally dealt with in sections 96 and 97 of the 1971 Act. These *two* sections are repealed by the Local Government and Planning (Amendment) Act 1981 as from August 27, 1981 (1981 Act, s.2(3)) and are substituted by *three* new sections, namely, sections 96, 97 and 97A of the 1971 Act (1981 Act, s.1 and Sched., para. 9).

It has already been mentioned that it is an offence to demolish, or to alter or extend a listed building in any manner which would affect its character as a building of special architectural or historic interest without first obtaining listed building consent (s.55(1), (4)). If unauthorised works to a listed building are carried out, then the local planning authority, (under section 96 of the 1971 Act) or the Secretary of State (under section 276(5A) of the Act), in addition to taking proceedings for the offence, may, if they consider it expedient to do so, issue (and serve upon the owner and the occupier of the building a copy of) an enforcement notice (s.96(1), (3))—called in the 1971 Act a "listed building enforcement notice" (s.96(2)).

A listed building enforcement notice may require the building to be restored to its former state (s.96(1)(*b*)(i)), *or*, where it is considered that restoration would not be reasonably practicable or

[22] S.I. 1977 No. 228.

would be undesirable, the notice may require the execution of such further works as are necessary to alleviate the effect of the unauthorised works already carried out (s.96(1)(*b*)(ii)).[23]

Additionally a listed building enforcement notice may require the building to be brought to the state in which it would have been if the terms and conditions of any listed building consent relating to the building had been complied with. (s.96(1)(*b*)(iii)).

Details as to the contents, the method of service and the taking effect, of a listed building enforcement notice are given in section 96 of the 1971 Act (s.96(1), (3), (4) and (7)).

A listed building enforcement notice can be withdrawn (without prejudice to the service of another one) at any time *before* it takes effect (s.96(5), (6)).

If listed building consent is granted after the issue of a listed building enforcement notice, the notice ceases to have effect insofar as it relates to works authorised by the listed building consent (s.99A).

Against the service of a listed building enforcement notice there is a right of appeal to the Secretary of State (s.97). Details as to the grounds of appeal, the proceedure on appeal and the decision on the appeal by the Secretary of State are given in section 97 of, and Schedule 9 to, the 1971 Act, in section 97A of the Act and in the Town and Country Planning (Enforcement Notices and Appeals) Regulations 1981,[24] Part III and Part IV (operative from January 11, 1982).

If, in connection with an appeal to the Secretary of State against the service of a listed building enforcement notice, the Secretary of State decides to hold a public local inquiry, the provisions of the Town and Country Planning (Enforcement) (Inquiries Procedure) Rules 1981[25] (operating from January 11, 1982) will apply (r. 2(1)(*c*)). The Rules follow substantially the provisions of the Town and Country Planning (Inquiries Procedure) Rules 1974,[26] (dealt with in Chapter 16), which have hitherto been applied, by custom but not by law, to listed building enforcement notices.

In the event of non-compliance with the terms of a listed building enforcement notice, the local planning authority may recover penalties from the person in default (s.98) and this might include a subsequent owner (s.98(2), (3)). The penalty on summary conviction is a fine not exceeding £2,000 (s.98(1), Criminal Justice Act 1982, s.37 and Criminal Penalties etc. (Increase) Order 1984 (S.I. 1984 No.

[23] *Bath City Council* v. *Secretary of State for the Environment* (1983) J.P.L. 737.
[24] S.I. 1981 No. 1742.
[25] S.I. 1981 No. 1743.
[26] S.I. 1974 No. 419.

447)) or, on conviction on indictment, a fine of unlimited amount (s.98(1)). There is a daily penalty of £200 (s.98(4) and Housing and Planning Act 1986, s.49(1)(*i*) and Sched. 11, Pt.I, para. 13) on summary conviction or a fine of unlimited amount on conviction or indictment if, after first conviction, the defendant does not do all in his power to secure compliance with the listed building enforcement notice (s.98(4)).

In addition the local planning authority may themselves take steps to implement a listed building enforcement notice which has not been complied with (s.99) and recover the costs of so doing (*ibid.*).

Similarly, the Secretary of State may himself (after consultation with the local planning authority and, where the listed building is in England, with the Commission) issue and serve a listed building enforcement notice (s.100(1)). In relation to any such notice the Secretary of State has the same powers under section 99 of the 1971 Act (relating to the execution of works in default and the recovery of the costs thereof) as has a local planning authority (s.100(2)).

The Commission have, throughout Greater London, concurrent functions under sections 96 to 99A of the 1971 Act with each of the London Boroughs (s.99B).

14. Compulsory Acquisition of Listed Buildings

Provision is made in the 1971 Act whereby the council of the county or county district or, in the case of a listed building in Greater London, the Commission or the London borough where the building is situated where a listed building is situated (s.114(1)) or the Secretary of State himself (s.114(2)) may acquire compulsorily any listed building which is not being properly preserved (s.114). The acquisition is by compulsory purchase order made or confirmed by the Secretary of State who, if the building is in England, must first consult with the Commission (s.114(3A)).

The foregoing power of acquisition may not be exercised until at least two months after the service upon the owner of the building of a "repairs notice" specifying the work which is considered to be necessary for the proper preservation of the building (s.115).

Any person having an interest in a listed building which it is proposed to acquire compulsorily can within 28 days after the service upon him of notice of intention to acquire, apply to a magistrates' court for the area in which the building is situated to stay the proceedings under the compulsory purchase order (s.114(6)), and if the court is satisfied that reasonable steps have in fact been taken for properly preserving the building, the court may make an order accordingly (*ibid.*) Against any such order a person aggrieved has a right of further appeal to the Crown Court (s.114(7)). Thus the question of whether or not proper and reasonable steps have been taken for preserving the building is a matter which will be argued out before the magistrates in the first place and the Crown Court in the second.

15. Compensation on Acquisition of Listed Building

If a listed building is compulsorily acquired the compensation to be paid to the owner of the building will, in general, disregard the depressive effect of the fact that the building has been listed (s.116).

If, however, it is established that the listed building has been allowed *deliberately* to fall into disrepair for the purpose of justifying redevelopment of the site, then provision is made whereby the council proposing to acquire the building (s.117(1)) or the Secretary of State (s.117(2)), as the case may be, may include in the compulsory puchase order authorising the acquisition of the building a direction for what is referred to as "minimum compensation" (s.117(1), (2), (3)).

The effect of the inclusion in the compulsory purchase order of a direction for minimum compensation is that the local authority (or the Secretary of State) will be able to buy the listed building compulsorily but at a price which disregards any profit which might have accrued from the redevelopment of the site (s.117(4)). Thus the effect of a direction for minimum compensation is to put a ceiling on the amount which the owner can get. In short, in the circumstances here discussed, "minimum compensation" represents the maximum amount receivable.

Against a direction for minimum compensation there is a right of appeal to the magistrates' court acting for the area where the building is situated (s.117(5)) with a further appeal to the Crown Court (s.117(6)).

16. Application to Local Authority Buildings and to Crown Land and Government Interests in Land

The controls and procedures relating to the preservation of special buildings are applied (subject to modifications) to the buildings of local planning authorities (s.271) and also to Crown land (s.266) to the extent to which any interest in such land is *not* held by or for the Crown.

"Crown land" includes land in which there is a "Crown interest" (s.266(7)) and "Crown interest" includes an interest belonging to a government department (*ibid.*). While in accordance with the customary rule of law, the 1971 Act does not bind the Crown, it is the practice of government departments, notwithstanding the legal position, to consult local planning authorities before undertaking development needing planning permission if done by a private individual.

D.O.E. Circular 18/84 entitled "Crown Land and Crown Developments" (particularly para. 4 and Part IV of the Memorandum which accompanies the Circular) deals with all this.

Reference should also be made to the Town and Country Planning Act 1984 and its provision for special enforcement notices relating to the enforcement of planning control over Crown Land—all of which is discussed in chapter 15 at pages 345 *et seq*.

C. WASTE LAND

Section 65 (as substituted *in toto* by the Housing and Planning Act 1986, section 46) together with sections 104–107 of the 1971 Act empower a district planning authority or a London borough to take action with regard to land the condition of which is adversely affecting the amenity of the neighbourhood. The current version of section 104 of the 1971 Act was substituted for the earlier version of the section by the Local Government and Planning (Amendment) Act 1981 as from August 27, 1981 (1981 Act s.1 and Sched., and s.2(3)).

If it appears to the local planning authority that the amenity of a part of their area is adversely affected by the condition of *any* land in their area, they may serve on the owner and occupier of the land (s.65(1)) a notice requiring the remedying of the condition of the land (s.65(2)) by the taking of such steps, and within such period, as may be specified in the notice (*ibid.*). Such a notice does not require confirmation by the Secretary of State and will take effect at the end of such period (not less than 28 days after service of the notice) as is specified in the notice (s.65(3)) subject to the provisions of Part V of the 1971 Act relating to the enforcement of control (*ibid.*). The 28 day period may be extended by the planning authority who served the notice (s.104(8)).

If, after the notice has taken effect, any owner or occupier of the land fails to take the requisite steps to comply with it, he is liable on summary conviction to a fine not exceeding level 3 on the standard scale (*i.e.* £400) (s.104(2); Criminal Justice Act 1982, s.37 and Criminal Penalties etc. (Increase) Order 1984).[27]

If proceedings are brought against a person as owner of the land

[27] S.I. 1984 No. 447.

and he has ceased to be owner, he is entitled to have the new owner brought before the court (s.104(3)). Similarly, an occupier of the land who is prosecuted but who has ceased to be occupier can have any new occupier brought before the court (s.104(4)). If there is no new occupier (*i.e.* the land is unoccupied) the occupier who is being prosecuted is entitled to have the person who was the owner of the land at the date of the notice brought before the court (s.104(5)).

If, in proceedings for failure to comply with a notice served under section 65 of the 1971 Act, the original defendant proves that such failure was due, in whole or in part, to the default of another person whom he specifies, that person may be convicted in lieu of the original defendant (s.104(6)).

If any person who has been convicted for failure to comply with a notice served under section 65 does not, as soon as practicable, do all he can to comply with the notice he will be guilty of a further offence and liable on summary conviction to a fine not exceeding £40 per day (s.104(7) as amended by the Housing and Planning Act 1986, s.49(1)(*i*), Sched. 11, Pt.I, para. 13).

If, within the requisite period, a notice under section 65 has not been complied with, the planning authority who served the notice may themselves enter on the land and take the appropriate action to comply with the notice, the cost of so doing being recoverable by the authority from the person who is then the owner of the land (s.107(1)).

Regulation 16 of the Town and Country Planning General Regulations 1976[28] applies sections 276, 289 and 294 of the Public Health Act 1936 to the steps required to be taken to comply with a notice under section 65 (ss.107(3) and 91(3), (4)).

Expenses incurred by an owner or occupier of land in complying with a section 65 notice, and sums paid by an owner in reimbursement of the costs of a planning authority in securing compliance with the notice, are deemed to be incurred or paid for at the request of the person who caused or permitted the land to be in such a state that the section 65 notice came to be served (s.107(2)).

A notice under section 65 may be the subject of an appeal to a magistrates' court (s.105) with a further appeal to the Crown Court (s.106). The notice is of no effect pending the final determination or withdrawal of the appeal (s.105(3)). The magistrates' court may correct any informality, defect or error in the notice if satisfied that it is not a material matter (s.105(4)). In determining the appeal the magistrates' court must give directions for giving effect to the court's decision (s.105(5)).

[28] S.I. 1976 No. 1419.

The grounds of appeal to the magistrates' court may be any of the following (s.105(1) as amended by the Housing and Planning Act 1986, s.49(1), Sched. 11, Pt.I, para. 20), namely:

(1) that the condition of the land does not adversely affect the amenity of any part of the area of the local planning authority who served the notice, or of any adjoining area;
(2) that the condition of the land is the ordinary result of development which is not a contravention of Part III of the 1971 Act;
(3) that the requirements of the notice exceed what is necessary for preventing the condition of the land from adversely affecting the amenity; and
(4) that the period allowed for the taking of the steps required by the notice falls short of what should reasonably be allowed.

Chapter 15

ENFORCEMENT OF PLANNING CONTROL

1. Enforcement of Control where Planning Permission Required for Development

The enforcement of planning control over the development of land is dealt with in Part V of the Town and Country Planning Act 1971. Important amendments to the provisions of that Part of the 1971 Act are enacted in the Local Government, Planning and Land Act 1980 and in the Local Government and Planning (Amendment) Act 1981. For example, this latter Act substitutes, for sections 87 and 88 of the 1971 Act, *four* new sections for the 1971 Act, namely, sections 87, 88, 88A and 88B. The amendments function as from August 27, 1981 (1981 Act, s.1 and Sched. and s.2(3)). Any reference in this chapter to the 1971 Act is a reference to that Act as amended by the 1980 Act and the 1981 Act.

The D.O.E. Circular 109/77 entitled "Enforcement of Planning Control—Established Use Certificates," dated November 4, 1977, and the Memorandum accompanying it contain useful information and advice on the enforcement of planning control generally and the granting of established use certificates by a local planning authority or by the Secretary of State. This Circular must now be read along with later D.O.E. Circulars, namely, Circular 38/81, entitled "Planning and Enforcement Appeals," dated December 18, 1981, and Circular 20/85 entitled "Enforcement Appeals and Advertisement Appeals," dated August 30, 1985. A revised enforcement appeal form is now available together with an explanatory booklet on enforcement appeals. Both of these documents will be sent with the copy of any enforcement notice issued by a local planning authority.

(1) *Issue and service of enforcement notice*

Section 87 of the 1971 Act provides for the issue by a local planning authority of enforcement notices. Under the Local Government Act 1972, Schedule 16, paragraph 24(1) (which does not apply to Greater London—para. 52) the responsibility for the issuing of enforcement notices rests primarily with the district planning authority who must first consult (*ibid.* para. 24(2)) the county planning council if it appears to the district authority that the matter in hand constitutes a "county matter" as defined in the 1972 Act, Sched. 16, para. 32. The non-metropolitan county planning authority may also issue an enforcement notice if it appears to them that the matter in hand constitutes a county matter (*ibid.* para. 24(3)). The council of a metropolitan district is a local planning authority for the purpose of issuing an enforcement notice (s.1(1)(*b*)) as also is the council of a London borough (s.1(1)(*c*)).

An enforcement notice cannot be served on the sole authority of the chairman of a local government planning committee. Where this was done the action of the chairman was held *ultra vires*; section 101 of the Local Government Act 1972 does not allow delegation of authority to a committee of one—*R.* v. *Secretary of State for the Environment, ex parte Hillingdon London Borough Council* (1986) J.P.L. 363.

A local planning authority may issue an enforcement notice in any instance where it appears to the authority that there has been *a breach of planning control after the end of 1963* (s.87(1), (2)). The authority are not *obliged* to issue an enforcement notice whenever it appears that there has been a breach of planning control. The authority have a discretion and must consider, in each case, whether it is *expedient* to issue such a notice having rcgard to:

(a) the provisions of the development plan; and
(b) any other material considerations (s.87(1)).

"Breach of planning control" is specially defined (s.87(3)) and relates to any development carried out, whether before or after the 1971 Act without planning permission, or to development which fails to comply with conditions or limitations subject to which planning permission for the development was granted.

(2) *The four-year rule*

The reference to "after the end of 1963,"[1] is worthy of note. December 31, 1963, was just about four years prior to the publication of the Town and Country Planning Bill on December 19, 1967—the Bill which became the Town and Country Planning Act 1968.

Under the law as it formerly stood under the Town and Country Planning Act 1962, it was well known that if irregular development could continue in being for a period of four years without getting itself subjected to an enforcement notice, then such development became automatically legitimated from a town planning point of

[1] As to establishment of use before December 31, 1963 and as to subsequent intensification thereof, see *Bromsgrove District Council* v. *Secretary of State for the Environment and Edward Attwood* [1977] J.P.L. 797 at p. 797. See also *Whipperman and Anor.* v. *Barking London Borough Council* [1966] 64 L.G.R. 97, Widgery J. at p. 102.

view by the effluxion of time, namely, the period of four years. Thereafter, under the 1962 Act, no enforcement notice could be issued in respect of such development.

This is still the position under the 1971 Act (s.87(4)) *if* the development complained of consists of:

(a) the carrying out without planning permission of building, engineering, mining or other operations in, on, over or under land; *or*

(b) the failure to comply with any condition or limitation which relates to the carrying out of such operations and subject to which planning permission was granted for the development of that land; *or*

(c) the making, without planning permission, of a change of use of any building to use as a single dwelling-house; *or*

(d) the failure to comply with a condition which prohibits, or has the effect of preventing, a change of use of a building to use as a single dwelling-house.[2]

In other words, the effect of section 87(4) of the 1971 Act is that in the case of development which involves *not operations* but only *change of use,* there is no time limit on the service of an enforcement notice *except* in the two instances (s.87(4)(*c*) and (*d*)) where, in each instance, the change of use constitutes a change of use of a building into use as a single dwelling-house, in both of which instances the four-year rule continues to apply.

It follows from the foregoing that if *any* originally irregular development has contrived, not later than December 31, 1967, (as to which date, see above), to "make the grade" by persisting for four years and thereby getting itself in order in the eyes of town planning law then no enforcement notice can touch it.

However, after the commencement, on April 1, 1969, of Part II of the 1968 Act there came a change. After that date, if change-of-use development is irregular at its inception no passage of time will make it regular. At all times it will be open to the local planning authority to issue and serve an enforcement notice notwithstanding that four, six, ten or, indeed, any other number of years have passed since the change-of-use development was originally carried out. The two exceptions to this rule are both changes of use of a building into use as a single dwelling-house (s.87(4)(*c*) and (*d*)); this sort of development still "makes the grade" after four years' existence without challenge by enforcement notice.

[2] See *Backer* v. *Secretary of State for the Environment* (1981) J.P.L. 357 and (1982) J.P.L. 516.

Where development has comprised both change of use and also building (or other) operations, the change of use may be outside the protection of the four-year rule and may thereby be the subject of an enforcement notice notwithstanding that the building (or other) operations are protected by the rule.[3]

(3) *Service, contents and effect of enforcement notice*

Under the 1971 Act a copy of an enforcement notice *must* be served, not later than 28 days *after the date* of its issue and not later than 28 days *before the date* on which (as specified in the notice) it is to take effect, on the owner and on the occupier of the land to which it relates and also upon any other person who has an interest in the land which interest, in the opinion of the authority, is materially affected by the notice (s.87(5)). It will be noted that an enforcement notice must specify two calendar dates, namely, the date of its issue and the date on which it is to take effect (*ibid.*).

The enforcement notice must specify the matters alleged to constitute a breach of planning control (s.87(6)) and must also specify (s.87(7)):

(a) any steps which are required by the local planning authority to be taken in order to remedy the breach; and
(b) any such steps as are required by the authority for the purpose (s.87(10)):
    (i) of making the development comply with the terms of any planning permission granted in respect of the land; or
    (ii) of removing or alleviating any injury to amenity caused by the development.

The enforcement notice must specify the period within which any of the forgoing steps is to be taken (s.87(8)) and different periods may be specified for different steps (*ibid.*).

Any period of time which is allowed for compliance with an enforcement notice means the period specified in the notice itself or such extended period as the local planning authority may allow (s.89(6)).

In the context of an issued enforcement notice the expression "steps to be taken in order to remedy the breach" means (as circumstances require) steps for the purpose (s.87(9)):

(a) of restoring land to its condition before the development took place; or
(b) of securing compliance with the conditions or limitations subject to which planning permission was granted,

[3] *Burn* v. *Secretary of State for the Environment* (1971) 219 E.G. 586, D.C.; *Murfit* v. *Secretary of State for the Environment* (1981) J.P.L. 755.

including—
(i) the demolition or alteration of any building or works;
(ii) the discontinuance of any use of land; and
(iii) the carrying out on land of any building or other operations.

Where it is the depositing of refuse or waste materials which is alleged in an enforcement notice to be the breach of planning control which is complained of, the notice may require the contour of the deposit to be modified by altering the gradient of its sides in such manner as may be specified in the notice (s.87(11)).

The Secretary of State may, by regulations, direct enforcement notices to specify additional matters as mentioned in the regulations (s.87(12)(*a*)) and to be accompanied by an explanatory note drawing attention to the right of appeal to the Secretary of State against the notice (s.87(12)(*b*)). All this the Secretary of State has now done in the Town and Country Planning (Enforcement Notices and Appeals) Regulations 1981,[4] Part II (operative from January 11, 1982). Under these Regulations a local planning authority must specify, in the enforcement notice; their reasons for issuing it and the precise boundaries of the land concerned (reg. 3). They must supply to any person served with a copy of the notice an explanatory note about sections 87, 88, 88A and 88B of the 1971 Act and about the right and manner of appeal to the Secretary of State against an enforcement notice (reg. 4).

An enforcement notice will take effect (subject to appeal to the Secretary of State under ss.88, 88A and 88B of the 1971 Act) on the date specified in it (s.87(13)). Where such an appeal is brought (see p. 328) the enforcement notice immediately becomes of no effect pending the final determination or the withdrawal of the appeal (s.88(10), and see p. 328). In the meantime, the stop notice procedures (see p. 335) under s. 90 of the 1971 Act remain available.

There is no prescribed form of enforcement notice and there has been much litigation about the form and content of such a notice. D.O.E. Circular 38/81, referred to above, relating to "Planning and Enforcement Appeals," contains model enforcement notices which may be adapted to cater for a variety of situations while Part II of the Town and Country Planning (Enforcement Notices and Appeals) Regulations 1981[5] (which came into force on January 11, 1982) sets out the matters to be specified in an enforcement notice (reg. 3) and the details of the accompanying explanatory note to an enforcement notice served by a local planning authority (reg. 4).

[4] S.I. 1981 No. 1742.
[5] S.I. 1981 No. 1742.

An enforcement notice must specify clearly and accurately the development which it is alleged has been carried out without planning permission or, in the case of a breach of conditions or limitations, the matters on which it is alleged that conditions or limitations subject to which planning permission was originally granted have not been complied with.[6] A notice which ignored the fact that planning permission had been granted for a limited period (which had expired at the time of the service of the notice) was held to have proceeded on a false basis and, accordingly, to be invalid.[7] But the failure to state the reason why the acts complained of amounted to development was held not to invalidate the notice.

If an enforcement notice is defective on the face of it, it will be a nullity and will thereby have no effect in law. Accordingly, there can be no right of appeal under section 88 of the 1971 Act to the Secretary of State against the provisions of such notice. But this does not mean the notice cannot be challenged by judicial review: *Rhymny Valley District Council* v. *Secretary of State for Wales*.[6]

A local planning authority are not, *as a general rule* estopped from serving an enforcement notice in respect of development simply because one of their chief officers has stated that planning permission was not required for that development—*Southend-on-Sea Corporation* v. *Hodgson* (*Wickford*) *Ltd.* [1962] 1 Q.B. 416. This case illustrates the danger of relying on statements made (doubtlessly in good faith) by the planning officer of a local planning authority. It is the decision of *the authority* which counts and the authority are not bound to accept the advice of their planning officer.

In a later case, however, it was decided that where a variation of the work permitted by a planning permission is authorised by an officer of the local planning authority acting within his ostensible authority, the local planning authority will be bound by the authorisation: *Lever* (*Finance*) *Ltd.* v. *Westminster City Council* (1970) 3

[6] *Keats* v. *L.C.C.* [1954] 1 W.L.R. 1357 D.C.; *Lincolnshire* (*Parts of Lindsey*) *C.C.* v. *Wallace Holiday Camp* [1953] 2 Q.B. 178, D.C.; *East Riding C.C.* v. *Park Estate* (*Bridlington*) [1957] A.C. 223, H.L.; *Miller-Mead* v. *Minister of Housing and Local Government* [1963] 2 Q.B. 196, C.A. where Upjohn L.J. said that the test is "does the notice tell him (the person on whom it is served) fairly what he has done wrong and what he must do to remedy it." See also comment by Templeman J. in *Eldon Garages Ltd.* v. *Kingston-upon-Hull County Borough Council* [1974] 1 W.L.R. 276; see, further, *Rhymny Valley District Council* v. *Secretary of State for Wales* (1985) J.P.L. 27. For two cases where enforcement notice held *not* to be a nullity, see *Coventry Scaffolding Co. (London) Ltd.* v. *John Brian Parker* (1987) J.P.L. 127 and *Epping Forest District Council* v. *Matthews* (1987) J.P.L. 132.

[7] *Francis* v. *Yiewsley & West Drayton U.D.C.* [1958] 1 Q.B. 478, C.A.

W.L.R. 732; 21 P. & C.R. 1778. But in *Brooks and Burton Ltd.* v. *Secretary of State for the Environment* (1976) 75 L.G.R. 285, D.C., the court deprecated any attempt to expand the doctrine of estoppel as applied in *Lever's* case. Lord Widgery C.J. observing (at page 296):

> "... local government officers should feel free to help applicants who come and ask them questions without all the time having the shadow of estoppel hanging over them and without the possibility of their immobilising their authorities by reason of some careless remark which produces such an estoppel."

This deprecation was later endorsed by the Court of Appeal in *Western Fish Products Ltd.* v. *Penwith District Council and the Secretary of State for the Environment* [1978] J.P.L. 623.[8]

An enforcement notice is registrable as a local land charge.[9] There will not be any question of removing an enforcement notice from the register after there has been compliance with the notice, since the notice is not discharged by such compliance (s.93(1)).

A local planning authority may extend the time for compliance with an enforcement notice *before* the specified time has expired (s.89(6)), but an extension *after* that time is an act of grace without legal consequences.[10]

Where an enforcement notice, issued because of the erection of a building or the carrying out of works without planning permission, requires steps to be taken under section 87(10)(*b*) of the 1971 Act—steps for removing or alleviating injury to amenity caused by the development—once such steps have been taken, planning permission for the retention of the building or works as they then stand is deemed to have been granted by the local planning authority. (s.87(16)).

(4) *Withdrawal of enforcement notice*

A local planning authority may withdraw an enforcement notice at any time *before it takes effect* (s.87(14)) and, if they do, they must forthwith give notice of the withdrawal to every person on whom the notice was served (s.87(15)).

This is a useful provision. There had been doubt as to whether an enforcement notice once served could in law be withdrawn by the local planning authority even if the local planning authority wished to do so.

[8] See also *Bedfordia Plant Ltd.* v. *Secretary of State for the Environment* [1981] J.P.L. 122.
[9] Local Land Charges (Amendment) Rules 1966, No. 579, r. 8.
[10] *Joyner* v. *Guildford Corporation* (1954) 5 P. & C.R. 30 (county court decision).

The withdrawal of an enforcement notice does not in any way preclude the service of a second one in respect of the same matter (s.87(14)).

(5) *Appeal to Secretary of State against enforcement notice*

Appeals against enforcement notices are dealt with in sections 88, 88A and 88B of the 1971 Act and in Part III of the Town and Country Planning (Enforcement Notices and Appeals) Regulations 1981,[11] (operative from January 11, 1982), made by the Secretary of State under section 88(5) of the 1971 Act. Reference may also be made to D.O.E. Circular 20/85 entitled "Town and Country Planning Act 1971: Enforcement Appeals and Advertisement Appeals" and dated August 30, 1985. The object of the Circular is to improve the efficiency and effectiveness of the planning appeals system. New and revised arrangements are set out in the Circular.

An appeal against an enforcement notice is to the Secretary of State for the Environment. It can be made, by any person having an interest in the land, at any time *before* the notice comes into effect (s.88(1)).

Dates and periods of time associated with the enforcement procedures of the 1971 Act need to be carefully observed. They can be crucial. An enforcement notice, having been duly served, was due to come into effect on February 16, 1984 as the notice, on the face of it, declared. The disappointed developer sought to appeal to the Secretary of State. All requisite appeal documents were prepared, dated February 13, 1984 but not posted until February 15, 1984. The appeal was received by the Secretary of State on January 16, 1984 the very date on which the enforcement notice took effect. The Secretary of State declined to deal with it because it had not been received by him *before* the date on which the enforcement notice took effect. This decision was upheld by the courts.[12]

Once an appeal is brought the enforcement notice is of no effect pending the final determination or the withdrawal of the appeal (s.88(10)).[13]

The Secretary of State has no power to reinstate an appeal when it has been validly withdrawn and the enforcement notice has thereafter taken effect—*R.* v. *Secretary of State for the Environment ex parte Monica Theresa Crossley* (1985) J.P.L. 632.

[11] S.I. 1981 No. 1742.

[12] *Lenlyn Ltd.* v. *Secretary of State for the Environment* (1984) Q.B. Division, Hodgson J., November 28, 1984; (1985) J.P.L. 482.

[13] As to "final determination" of an enforcement notice appeal, see p. 333.

The grounds of appeal against an enforcement notice are any of the following (s.88(2)(*a*) to (*h*)):

(a) that planning permission ought to be granted for the development to which the notice relates or, as the case may be, that a condition or limitation alleged in the enforcement notice not to have been complied with ought to be discharged;

(b) that the matters alleged in the notice do not constitute a breach of planning control;

(c) that the breach of planning control alleged in the notice has not taken place;

(d) in the case of a notice which, by virtue of section 87(4) of the 1971 Act, may be issued only within the period of four years from the date of the breach of planning control to which the notice relates, that that period had elapsed at the date when the notice was issued;

(e) in the case of a notice not falling within paragraph (d) above, that the breach of planning control alleged by the notice occurred before the beginning of 1964;

(f) that copies of the enforcement notice were not served as required by section 87(5) of the 1971 Act[14];

(g) that the steps required by the notice to be taken exceed what is necessary to remedy any breach of planning control or to achieve a purpose specified in section 87(10) of the 1971 Act;

(h) that the period specified in the notice as the period within which any step is to be taken falls short of what should reasonably be allowed.

The appeal is made by notice in writing to the Secretary of State (s.88(3)). The appellant must furnish, either with the notice of appeal or later, a statement in writing (s.88(4)):

(a) specifying the grounds of appeal; and

(b) giving all such further information as may be prescribed.

If the appellant fails to provide the foregoing information within the prescribed period, the Secretary of State may dismiss the appeal (s.88(6)(*a*)). Similarly, if the local planning authority fail to comply, within the prescribed period, with any requirement of the Enforcement Notices and Appeals Regulations 1981, the Secretary of State may allow the appeal and quash the enforcement notice (s.88(6)(*b*)).

[14] But failure to serve a copy of an enforcement notice on the *owner* as well as the *occupier* of the relevant land need not necessarily be fatal to the validity of the notice as the Secretary of State has a discretion, under s.88A(3) of the 1971 Act, to overlook such failure where a person has not been substantially prejudiced by the failure to serve him: *R.* v. *Greenwich London Borough Council ex parte Patel* (1985) J.P.L. 594.

The Secretary of State must, if either the appellant or the local planning authority desire it, afford them an opportunity of being heard by an Inspector appointed by the Secretary of State (s.88(7)) but he need not do this if he proposes to dismiss an appeal under section 88(6)(*a*) of the 1971 Act or if he proposes to allow the appeal and quash the enforcement notice under section 88(6)(*b*)) of the Act (s.88(8)).

Schedule 9 of the 1971 Act applies to any appeal against an enforcement notice (s.88(11)).

Since the coming into operation July 1, 1981 of the Town and Country Planning (Determination of Appeals by Appointed Persons) (Prescribed Classes) Regulations 1981 (S.I. 1981 No. 804), the Inspector who hears an enforcement notice appeal will not only hear it but will also determine it except where the appeal is by a statutory undertaker (s.225(1)(*b*) and reg. 4(*b*)) or the Secretary of State recovers for himself jurisdiction to determine the appeal (s.88(11) and Sched. 9, para. 3).

If, in connection with any appeal to him against an enforcement notice, the Secretary of State decides to hold a public local inquiry, then the provisions of the Town and Country Planning (Enforcement) (Inquiries Procedure) Rules 1981[15] (operative from January 11, 1982) will apply (r. 2(1)(*a*) and (*b*)) in relation to:

(1) notification of the inquiry (r. 4) and notification of the identity of the Inspector who is to hold the inquiry (r. 5);
(2) service of statements and inspection of documents before the inquiry (r. 6);
(3) the Inspector acting in place of the Secretary of State (r. 7);
(4) appearances at the inquiry (r. 8);
(5) representatives of government departments at the inquiry (r. 9);
(6) representatives of local authorities at the inquiry (r. 10);
(7) procedure at the inquiry (r. 11);
(8) site inspections (r. 12);
(9) report of the inquiry (r. 13);
(10) procedure after the inquiry (r. 14);
(11) award of costs (r. 15);
(12) notification of the decision (r. 16);
(13) service of notices by post (r. 17); and
(14) application of the Rules (as modified) to Greater London (r. 18).

[15] S.I. 1981 No. 1743.

The foregoing Rules follow substantially the provisions of the Town and Country Planning (Inquiries Procedure) Rules 1974[16] (dealt with in Chapter 16) which have hitherto been applied, by custom but not by law, to enforcement notices. D.O.E. Circular 38/81, relating to "Planning and Enforcement Appeals," explains current procedures on appeal.

On the appeal the Secretary of State may correct any informality, defect or error[16a] in the enforcement notice or give directions for varying its terms if he is satisfied that this can be done without injustice to the appellant or to the local planning authority (s.88A(2)). If a person who should be served with a copy of the enforcement notice is not so served, the Secretary of State may disregard this fact if neither the appellant nor the person not served has been substantially prejudiced (s.88A(3)).[17]

On determining the appeal the Secretary of State must give all such directions as are requisite for giving effect to his decision, whatever the decision may be (s.88A(1)). Amongst other things the Secretary of State may give directions quashing an enforcement notice or varying its terms (*ibid.*).

On the determination of an appeal the Secretary of State may—

(a) grant planning permission himself for the development, or for *part* of the development, *to which the enforcement notice relates*,[18] or for the development of *part* of the land to which the enforcement notice relates[19] (ss.88B(1)(*a*) and 92[20]);

(b) discharge any condition or limitation subject to which planning permission was granted; (ss.88B(1)(*b*) and 92);

(c) determine any purpose for which the land may, in the circumstances obtaining at the time of the determination, be lawfully used having regard to any past use of it and to any planning permission relating to it (ss.88B(1)(*c*) and 92).

In considering whether to grant planning permission himself the Secretary of State *must* pay attention to the provisions of the development plan so far as they are material to the subject matter of the enforcement notice and also to any other material considerations (s.88B(2)).

[16] S.I. 1974 No. 419.

[16a] *Epping Forest District Council* v. *Matthews* (1987) J.P.L. 132.

[17] *Patel* v. *Betts* (1978) J.P.L. 109; *Skinner and King* v. *Secretary of State for the Environment and Eastleigh District Council* [1978] J.P.L. 842.

[18] *Richmond on Thames London Borough Council* v. *Secretary of State for the Environment* (1972) 224 E.G. 1555.

[19] *Finlay* v. *Secretary of State for the Environment* (1983) J.P.L. 802; *Jillings* v. *Secretary of State for the Environment* (1984) J.P.L. 32.

[20] *Dudley Borough Council* v. *Secretary of State for the Environment* (1981) J.P.L. 181.

Any planning permission granted by the Secretary of State, as a result of an appeal against an enforcement notice, may be granted by him subject to such conditions as he thinks fit (s.88B(2)(*b*)) and may include permission to retain or to complete any buildings or works with or without complying with a condition attached to a previous planning permission (s.88B(2)(*a*)).

If, on an appeal against an enforcement notice, the Secretary of State discharges a condition or limitation he may substitute another condition or limitation, whether more or less onerous (s.88B(2)).

Any planning permission granted by the Secretary of State on appeal against an enforcement notice will be final (s.88B(3)(*b*)) and, for the purposes of the local planning authority's register of planning permissions, the Secretary of State's decision is to be treated as the decision of the local planning authority (s.88B(3)(*c*)).

Where a notice purporting to be an enforcement notice is one relating to non-compliance with conditions or with limitations attached to a grant of planning permission, the validity of the notice is not to depend on whether the non-compliance to which the notice relates was in fact a non-compliance with conditions or with limitations or with both (s.243(5)). If the notice has referred to "conditions" or to "limitations" or even to both of these things, then the notice is to be construed as applying to conditions or to limitations (or to both) as the facts of the case require (*ibid.*).

Once a person has appealed to the Secretary of State against an enforcement notice, neither he nor anyone else will be entitled, in any other proceedings instituted after the appeal, to claim that a copy of the enforcement notice was not duly served on the person who appealed against it (s.110(2)). This is a matter which must be taken on the appeal to the Secretary of State or not at all.

If, after service of an enforcement notice, planning permission is granted for the retention of buildings or works, or for continuance of a use of land, to which the notice relates, the notice ceases to have effect (s.92(1), (2)) but this is without prejudice to the liability of any person for an offence in respect of a failure to comply with the enforcement notice before it ceased to have effect (s.92(3)).

On an appeal against an enforcement notice the Secretary of State has power to award costs to either of the parties to the appeal (s.110(1)).

When the Secretary of State has given his "decision" (s.246(5)) on the appeal made to him against the enforcement notice, then:

(1) the appellant himself; or
(2) the local planning authority; or
(3) any person on whom the enforcement notice has been served,
may either appeal against the decision on a point of law to

the High Court or require the Secretary of State to state and sign a case for the opinion of the High Court (s.246(1)).

At any stage of the proceedings on an appeal to the Secretary of State, the Secretary of State may himself take the initiative and state any question of law which arises during the proceedings in the form of a special case for the decision of the High Court (s.246(2)) from whose decision there will be a further appeal to the Court of Appeal (*ibid.*).

An appeal to the High Court from the decision of the Secretary of State can only be on a question of law. The Court will not interfere with a finding on a question of fact or degree unless it can be said that the decision made thereon could not properly have been reached.[21] The onus of proof is on the appellant,[22] but there is no call for the appellant to prove his claim beyond all reasonable doubt—the normal civil standard of proof is sufficient.[23] It is open to an appellant to raise in court a point of law which was not earlier raised when the appellant was appealing against an enforcement notice to the Secretary of State—*John Pearcy Transport Ltd.* v. *Secretary of State for the Environment and Hounslow London Borough Council* (1986) J.P.L. 680.

(6) *When does an enforcement notice take effect?*

When does an enforcement notice take effect and what exactly do the words "pending the final determination . . . of the appeal" in section 88(10) of the 1971 Act mean? These questions have caused confusion in the past.[24] They are important questions because, where the notice specifies the period of time within which things have to be done to satisfy the requirements of the notice, that period of time clearly cannot begin to run until the notice has taken effect.

Moreover, if there is an appeal to the Secretary of State against the enforcement notice and the Secretary of State dismisses the appeal, is his letter of decision the "final determination . . . of the appeal" or must allowance be made for further appeal to the courts on a point of law under section 246 of the 1971 Act? Such further appeal under section 246 must be made within 28 days after the

[21] *East Barnet U.D.C.* v. *British Transport Commission* [1962] 2 Q.B. 484, D.C.

[22] *Nelsovil* v. *Minister of Housing and Local Government* [1962] 1 W.L.R. 404, D.C.

[23] *Thrasyvoulou* v. *Secretary of State for the Environment and Hackney London Borough Council* (1984) J.P.L. 732.

[24] *Garland* v. *Westminster London Borough* (1970) 21 P. & C.R. 555; *Griffiths* v. *Secretary of State for the Environment* (1983) 1 All E.R. 439; (1983) J.P.L. 237, H.L.

decision of the Secretary of State.[25] (Incidentally, the decision of the Secretary of State is the date of his letter of decision and not the date the letter is received by the appellant).[26]

Clarification of the disputed point as to the date when an enforcement notice takes effect (in the event of an appeal against the notice to the Secretary of State under section 88 of the Act) has now been achieved by the Divisional Court decision in *Dover District Council* v. *McKeen* (1985) J.P.L. 627 where it was held that, where an appeal against an enforcement notice had been dismissed by the Secretary of State, the enforcement notice took effect from the date of dismissal and not from the date when the time for appealing on a point of law to the High Court under section 246 had expired.

This decision has important consequences. Proceedings for non-compliance with an enforcement notice would now appear to be capable of being instituted without the local planning authority having to hold their hand waiting to see if there is going to be a further appeal on a point of law to the High Court under section 246 of the Act. In short, the period (set out in the enforcement notice) for compliance with the terms of the notice begins to run from the date of the Secretary of State's decision letter dismissing the appeal to him under section 88 of the Act and not (as some had thought) from a date several weeks later, *i.e.* the date when the time for appealing to the High Court has run out.

Before leaving the complicated matter of enforcement notices to enforce planning control over land development under the Town and Country Planning Act 1971, it is worth drawing attention to the quite different powers available to a local planning authority under section 222 of the Local Government Act 1972. The case of *Westminster City Council* v. *Jones* [1981] J.P.L. 750 has drawn attention to these powers.

Section 222 of the Local Government Act 1972 provides that:

(1) Where a local authority consider it expedient for the promotion or protection of the interests of the inhabitants of their area—

[25] Rules of the Supreme Court (S.I. 1965 No. 1776) Ord. 94, r. 12 and Ord. 55, r. 4(4). The 28 days limitation may be extended by the court under Ord. 3, r. 5. And see *Gill* v. *Secretary of State for the Environment and North Warwickshire District Council* (1985) J.P.L. 710.

[26] *Ringroad Investments Ltd.* v. *Secretary of State for the Environment* (1979) 40 P. & C.R. 99; *Griffiths* v. *Secretary of State for the Environment* (1983) 1 All E.R. 439; (1983) J.P.L. 237 H.L.—a House of Lords majority (4 to 1) decision, Lord Scarman dissenting.

(a) they may prosecute or defend or appear in any legal proceedings and, in the case of civil proceedings, may institute them in their own name, and
(b) they may, in their own name, make representations in the interests of the inhabitants at any public inquiry held by or on behalf of any Minister or public body under any enactment.

This enables a local authority to prosecute without the intervention (as was formerly the case) of the Attorney-General in a relator action.

Acting under the powers of section 222 the local authority, in the *Westminster* case, acted to prevent the operation of an amusement arcade causing nuisance and disturbance to a residential area. The defendant knew when he took a lease of the arcade premises that he needed planning permission for a new use but he chose to proceed before he got the permission. The planning authority served an enforcement notice and a stop notice. A summons for failure to comply with the stop notice was shortly to be heard. In the meantime the authority sought an interlocutory injunction, under section 222 of the Local Government Act 1972, against the defendant. The question was whether, in the court's discretion, it was proper to grant the relief sought. Rather than wait for the proceedings on the summons, for failure to comply with the stop notice, to work their way to a conclusion, the court granted the injunction which the local planning authority sought.

The principle, established by the *Westminster* case, that the service of an enforcement notice and a stop notice does not preclude a local planning authority from resorting to the civil remedy of injunction under the powers of section 222 of the Local Government Act 1972, was further reinforced by the decision of the Court of Appeal in *Runnymead Borough Council* v. *Ball* (1985) [1986] J.P.L. 288. In this case the court again took the view that, in the circumstances of the case, the local planning authority were justified in resorting to the civil remedy of an injunction (breach of which would amount to contempt of court) without first exhausting the enforcement provisions (of prosecution to recover a fine or fines) of the 1971 Act.

(7) *Stop notices*

Once a copy of an enforcement notice is served, the local planning authority may, at any time thereafter but before the enforcement notice takes effect, serve a notice known as a "stop notice" (s.90(1)). The stop notice must refer to the enforcement notice to which it is dependent and must have a copy of such enforcement notice annexed to it (*ibid.*). This provision is aimed at those appellants who, in time past, have been prepared to adopt delaying tactics in order to drag out as long as possible the ultimate determination of an appeal against an enforcement notice.

The effect of a stop notice is to prohibit any person on whom it is served from *carrying out any activity* (specified in the stop notice) which is alleged (in the earlier-served enforcement notice) to constitute a breach of planning control (s.90(1)).

However, there are three things which a stop notice cannot do. It cannot prohibit (s.90(2)):

(1) the use of any buildings as a dwelling-house;
(2) the use of land as the site of a caravan occupied by any person as his only or main residence ("caravan" here having the meaning given to it for the purposes of Part I of the Caravan Sites and Control of Development Act 1960); or
(3) the taking of specific steps needed in order to remedy the breach of planning control which is alleged in the enforcement notice.

Moreover, it is to be noted that if an activity began to be carried out (continuously or not) more than 12 months before the stop notice, then such an activity is protected from interference by the stop notice[27] unless it is itself a building, engineering, mining or other kind of operation or is the deposit of refuse or waste materials or is incidental to any of the foregoing matters (s.90(2)).

A stop notice may be served on any person who appears to the local planning authority to have an interest in the land, or to be engaged in any activity prohibited by the notice (s.90(5)). A local planning authority can *require* the occupier of premises or the person who receives the rent of the premises to provide such information as they need in order to ascertain the identity of persons having an interest in the land (s.284).

In addition, when a stop notice has been served, the authority may display a "site notice" on the land giving particulars of the service of the stop notice, the date it becomes effective and the requirements called for by the notice (s.90(5)).

A stop notice cannot take effect (and so cannot be contravened) until the date specified in the notice. This may not be earlier than three, nor later than 28, days from the day on which it is first served on any person (s.90(3)).

Any person who fails to comply with the provisions of a stop notice is guilty of an offence and liable on summary conviction to a fine not exceeding £2,000 or, on conviction on indictment, to a fine of

[27] *Scott Markets Ltd.* v. *London Borough of Waltham Forest* [1979] J.P.L. 96; 392.

unlimited amount (s.90(7); Criminal Penalties etc. (Increases) Order 1984[28]). If the offence is continued after conviction, then for every day on which it is continued such a person is liable to a further fine of not more than £200 on summary conviction (s.90(7); Housing and Planning Act 1986, s.49(1)(*i*) and Sched. 11, Pt. I para. 13) and to a further fine of unlimited amount on conviction on indictment (s.90(7)). In any proceedings it is a defence to prove the stop notice was not served on the accused person *and* that he did not know, and could not reasonably be expected to know, of its existence (s.90(8)).

A stop notice is not invalidated by reason of the fact that a copy of the enforcement notice to which it relates was not served precisely as required by section 87(5) of the 1971 Act, if it is shown that the local planning authority took all reasonable steps to effect proper service of the enforcement notice (s.90(9)).

A local planning authority may at any time withdraw a stop notice by serving notice to that effect on persons served with the stop notice and, if a site notice has been displayed, by displaying on the site a notice of withdrawal (s.90(6)).

A stop notice will cease to have effect (s.90(4)) when

(a) the related enforcement notice is either withdrawn or is quashed; or

(b) the period for compliance with the enforcement notice expires; or

(c) the stop notice itself is withdrawn as mentioned above.

If the activities complained about in the stop notice cease, in whole or in part, then, again, the stop notice will cease to have effect in whole or in part as the case may be (*ibid.*).

(8) *Compensation for loss or damage due to stop notice*

Compensation for loss or damage *directly* due to a stop notice can be claimed from the local planning authority by any person who has an interest in, or occupies, the land to which the stop notice relates (s.177(1)).

Compensation will be payable (s.177(2)) when (and only when):

(a) the enforcement notice to which the stop notice is related is itself quashed on grounds other than those mentioned in paragraph (*a*) of section 88(2) of the 1971 Act[29]; or

(b) the enforcement notice is varied, otherwise than on the

[28] S.I. 1984 No. 447.

[29] See p. 329. See also *Malvern Hills District Council* v. *Secretary of State for the Environment and Robert Barnes and Company Ltd.* (1982) J.P.L. 439; 46 P. & C.R. 58.

grounds mentioned in that paragraph (*a*) of section 88(2), so that the matters alleged to constitute a breach of planning control cease to include one or more of those activities which are prohibited by the stop notice; or

(c) the enforcement notice is withdrawn by the local planning authority (but not if this is done because planning permission is granted for the development to which the enforcement notice relates or for the retention or continuance of such development freed of any condition or limitation subject to which a previous planning permission was granted); or

(d) the stop notice itself is withdrawn.

Claims for compensation for loss or damage due to a stop notice must be made (s.177(4)) to the local planning authority in the manner prescribed and within the time (six months from the decision which gives rise to the claim) prescribed by regulation 14 of the Town and Country Planning General Regulations 1976.[30] Any such loss or damage may include a sum payable for breach of contract caused by the taking of action necessary to comply with the stop notice (s.177(5)). In assessing compensation account is to be taken of the extent (if any) to which the claimant's entitlement to compensation is attributable to his own failure to comply with a notice under section 284 of the 1971 Act (power of a local authority to require information as to interests in land) or to any mis-statement made by him in response to such a notice (s.177(6)).

(9) *Certification of established use of land*

As already explained, the 1971 Act (re-enacting the Town and Country Planning Act 1968) provides for the abolition of the four-year time limit on the service of an enforcement notice in respect of any development which constitutes an unauthorised change of use unless such change of use is the change of use of a building to use as a single dwelling-house, in which case the four-year time limit continues to function (s.87(4)(*c*) and (*d*)).

It has been recognised that this abolition of the four-year rule in the case of any unauthorised change-of-use development could lead to difficulties in the future because it will be open to a local planning authority *at any time* in the future—that is to say, days, months or even years ahead—to challenge a use of land as being unauthorised. If such challenge does not take place until many years after the commencement of the use of which complaint is made, it may well be

[30] S.I. 1976 No. 1419.

that, at that time in the future, it will be difficult for the person enjoying the use complained of to prove that such use was earlier established at a time which renders it immune from challenge.

Accordingly, sections 94 and 95 of, and Schedule 14 to, the 1971 Act make provision whereby a use of land may, on application, be certified by a local planning authority as *an established use* (s.94(2)) in which event the applicant is entitled to receive from the local planning authority an "established use certificate" (s.94(4)).

A use of land is to be regarded as established (s.94(1)) if:

(a) it was begun before the beginning of 1964 without planning permission and has continued ever since the end of 1963; or

(b) it was begun before the beginning of 1964 under a planning permission granted subject to conditions or limitation which have either never been complied with at all or have not been complied with since the end of 1963; or

(c) it was begun after the end of 1963 as the result of a change of use which did not require planning permission and since the end of 1963 there has been no change of use which did require planning permission.[31]

The benefit of this procedure is that an established use, certified as aforesaid, is not liable to challenge under the enforcement procedure of section 87 of the 1971 Act because under that section an enforcement notice may be served only in respect of a breach of planning control occurring "after the end of 1963" (s.87(1)).

It should be emphasised that these provisions relating to the certification of established uses are relevant only in the case of change-of-use development in respect of which the four-year limitation rule has been abolished by the 1971 Act.

Where the four-year rule continues to apply, as it does (s.87(4)) in the case of development which involves either the carrying out of operations affecting land or a change of use of a building to use as a single dwelling-house, then the four-year rule may continue to be relied upon by a developer in the future just as it always has been relied on under the Town and Country Planning Act 1947 and all its successors. This position is not affected by the certification procedure here discussed.

Any person who claims that a particular use of land in which he has in interest has become established can apply to the local planning authority for an established use certificate (s.94(2)) provided, however, that no such application can be made in respect of the use

[31] See 1971 Act, s. 23(9). See also *LTSS Print & Supply Services Ltd.* v. *London Borough of Hackney and Another* [1976] 1 All E.R. 311.

of land as a single dwelling-house, or in respect of any use of land which is not actually subsisting at the time of the application (*ibid.*).

An established use certificate may be granted either by a local planning authority under section 94 of the 1971 Act or by the Secretary of State under section 95 of the Act. In either event the grant may relate to the whole or part only of the land specified in the application, or to one or more uses in a case where the applicant claims to have more than one established use for the same piece of land (s.94(3)).

If, on application for a certificate, the local planning authority are satisfied that the applicant's claim is made out, then they *must* grant him an established use certificate (s.94(4)). If they are not so satisfied, then they *must* refuse the application (*ibid.*).

The application for an established use certificate must be made to the district planning authority and will, in general, be determined by them unless it appears to the district authority that the development in question relates to a "county matter" (Local Government Act 1972, Sched. 16, paras. 15, 16, 32—not applicable to Greater London, para. 52). The application will be made in accordance with the Town and Country Planning General Development Order 1977, article 22.

The application must be dealt with by the local planning authority within the period prescribed by the development order (*i.e.* eight weeks) or within such extended period as may be agreed in writing between the applicant and the local planning authority, and if not granted within such period the application is deemed to be refused (s.94(5) and Town and Country General Development Order 1977,[32] art. 22(7)).

Detailed provisions as to:

(1) the method of applying for an established use certificate;

(2) the method of appealing under section 95 of the 1971 Act against a refusal of a certificate; and

(3) the form of such a certificate

are given in section 94(6) of, and Schedule 14 to, the 1971 Act.

If the local planning authority refuse a certificate the applicant may appeal to the Secretary of State (s.95(2) and (7)) who may grant or refuse the certificate (*ibid.*) and whose decision is final (s.95(5)). Before determining such an appeal the Secretary of State must give the applicant and the local planning authority (if either so desire) an opportunity of being heard by a person appointed by the Secretary of State (s.95(4)).

[32] S.I. 1977 No. 289.

If, in connection with any appeal to him against the refusal of a local planning authority to grant an established use certificate, the Secretary of State decides (as he may) to hold a public local inquiry, then the provisions of the Town and Country Planning (Enforcement) (Inquiries Procedure) Rules 1981[33] (operative from January 11, 1982) will apply (r. 2(1)(*d*)).[34] These Rules follow substantially the provisions of the Town and Country Planning (Inquiries Procedure) Rules 1974[35] (dealt with in Chapter 16, *post*) which have hitherto been applied, by custom but not by law, to establish use certificate appeals. D.O.E. Circular 38/81, relating to Planning Enforcement Appeals, explains the current procedures on appeal.

Once granted, an established use certificate is, as regards any matters stated within it, to be conclusive for the purposes of any appeal to the Secretary of State against any enforcement notice a copy of which has been served in respect of the land to which the established use certificate relates, provided that the copy of the enforcement notice was served after the date on which the established use certificate was granted (s.94(7)).

An established use certificate is an important document. Thus any person who, with a view to obtaining such a certificate, knowingly or recklessly makes a false statement or, with intent to deceive, produces a false document or withholds material information, is liable on summary conviction to a fine not exceeding £1,000 or, on conviction on indictment, to imprisonment not exceeding two years or to a fine of unlimited amount or to both (s.94(8)).

For the purposes of being recorded in the Register of Decisions on Planning Applications kept by a local planning authority under section 34 of the 1971 Act an application for an established use certificate is to be regarded as an application for planning permission (s.94(6) and Sched. 14, para. 6).

(10) *Established use certificates—grant by Secretary of State*

Any application for an established use certificate made, as it always will be in the first place, to a local planning authority, may be called-in by the Secretary of State in order that he may deal with it instead of the authority (s.95(1)). Any decision by the Secretary of State on a called-in application for an established use certificate is final (s.95(5)).

Where the Secretary of State declines to grant an established use

[33] S.I. 1981 No. 1743.
[34] See pp. 351, 353–356.
[35] S.I. 1974 No. 419.

certificate he may, instead, grant planning permission for the use in respect of which the application for an established use certificate was made (s.95(3), (6)).

If, in connection with a called-in application for an established use certificate, the Secretary of State decides (as he may) to hold a public local inquiry, then the provisions of the Town and Country Planning (Enforcement) (Inquiries Procedure) Rules 1981[36] (operative from January 11, 1982) will apply (r. 2(1)(*d*)).[37]

(11) *Enforcement notice ignored: action by local planning authority*

If an enforcement notice which has come into operation requires specified steps to be taken (other than the discontinuance of a use of land) and those steps are not taken within the period specified in the notice (or within such extended period as the local planning authority may allow), the authority may enter on the land affected by the notice and carry out, by means of the demolition or alteration of buildings or works, the requirements of the enforcement notice and, having done so, may recover as a simple contract debt their reasonable expenses of so doing (ss.91 and 111). Any such expenses may become a charge on the land (s.91(5)).

The action for recovery of expenses incurred by a local planning authority in carrying out the requirements of an enforcement notice is taken against the person who is the owner (as defined in s.290(1) of the 1971 Act) of the land at the date when it is sought to recover the expenses (s.91(1)).

It will be noticed that a person against whom an action for the recovery of expenses is taken may not necessarily be the person who improperly carried out, without planning permission, the development of which complaint is made or who broke the conditions or limitations subject to which planning permission was originally granted, because action for the recovery of expenses is to be taken against "the person who is then the owner of the land" (s.91(1)). Any expenses, however, which are incurred either by an owner or occupier of land in complying with an enforcement notice, or any sums paid by an owner of land under section 91 of the 1971 Act in respect of the expenses of a local planning authority in taking steps to enforce the provisions of an enforcement notice, are deemed to have been incurred by, or to have been paid for the use and at the request of, the person by whom the development was originally carried out (s.91(2)) to whom recourse for reimbursement must be

[36] S.I. 1981 No. 1743.
[37] See p. 330.

made by any subsequent owner or occupier of the land who incurs expenses as a result of the service upon him of an enforcement notice.

The provisions of sections 276, 289 and 294 of the Public Health Act 1936 apply, with the necessary modifications, in relation to steps required to be taken by an enforcement notice (s.91(3), (4) and the Town and Country Planning General Regulations 1976,[38] reg. 16).

(12) *Penalties for non-compliance with enforcement notice*

In addition to the powers of the local planning authority to "step in" and carry out the requirements of an enforcement notice (s.91), it is provided that where the notice requires specified steps (other than the discontinuance of a use of land) to be taken, the person who was the owner of the land at the time the notice was served shall, if the aforementioned steps are not duly taken, be liable to a fine not exceeding £2,000 on summary conviction or to a fine of unlimited amount on conviction on indictment (s.89(1) and Criminal Penalties etc. (Increase) Order 1984).[39]

Such a person, if he has ceased to be the owner of the land before the end of the time allowed for complying with the enforcement notice, may, on giving at least three *clear* days' notice to the prosecution, have the person who had then become the owner of the land brought before the court (s.89(2)). If the original defendant proves that the failure to comply with the enforcement notice was due, in whole or in part, to the default of the subsequent owner, then the latter may be convicted and the original owner, if he proves that he himself took all reasonable steps to secure compliance with the order, *must* be acquitted (s.89(3)).

If a person, having been convicted under any of the above provisions for non-compliance with an enforcement notice, then fails to do everything in his power to comply with the notice as soon as practicable, he is liable to a daily penalty not exceeding £200 on summary conviction or a fine of unlimited amount on conviction on indictment (s.89(4); Housing and Planning Act 1986, s.49(*i*) and Sched. 11, Pt. I, para. 13).

Where an enforcement notice requires the discontinuance of a use of land, or compliance with conditions or limitations attached to a grant of planning permission, then if any person uses the land, or carries out operations in contravention of the notice, he will be liable to a fine not exceeding £2,000 on summary conviction or to a fine of

[38] S.I. 1976 No. 1419.
[39] S.I. 1984 No. 447.

unlimited amount on conviction on indictment together with (if the prohibited use is continued) a daily penalty not exceeding £200 on summary conviction or a fine of unlimited amount on conviction on indictment (s.89(5); Housing and Planning Act 1986, s.49(*i*) and Sched. 11, Pt. I, para. 13).

A person who, without planning permission, reinstates or restores buildings or works which have already been demolished or altered in pursuance of an enforcement notice, is liable on summary conviction to a fine not exceeding level 5 on the standard scale, *i.e.* £2,000 (s.93(5), Criminal Justice Act 1982, s.37 and Criminal Penalties etc. (Increase) Order 1984.[40]

(13) *Continuing efficacy of enforcement notice against subsequent development*

Compliance with the terms of an enforcement notice does not discharge the notice (s.93(1)). Thus the resumption of a use of land, after that use has been discontinued in compliance with an enforcement notice, will constitute a further contravention of the notice (s.93(2) and see, *Proser* v. *Sharp* (1985) J.P.L. 717). Similarly, if development of land, by way of reinstating or restoring buildings or works which have been demolished or altered in compliance with an enforcement notice, is carried out, the enforcement notice is deemed to apply to such reinstated buildings or works "notwithstanding that its terms are not apt for the purpose" (s.93(3)).

Where the local planning authority propose to take enforcement action under section 91 of the 1971 Act in respect of such irregularly reinstated buildings or works, they must give not less than 28 days' notice of their intention to the owner and the occupier of the land affected (s.93(4)).

(14) *Register of enforcement and stop notices*

Section 92A of the 1971 Act—added by the Local Government and Planning (Amendment) Act 1981, section 1 and Schedule, paragraph 6, and operative as from November 27, 1981 (1981 Act, s.2(2))—requires that district planning authorities and London boroughs shall each keep a register containing prescribed information about enforcement and stop notices in their areas. The information which is to be kept in such a register is specified in article 21A of the General Development Order 1977.[41]

The register kept under section 92A of the 1971 Act is to be open for public inspection at all reasonable hours (s.92A(4)).

[40] S.I. 1984 No. 447.
[41] S.I. 1977 No. 289.

(15) *Crown land—special enforcement notices*

No enforcement notice can be issued under section 87 of the 1971 Act in respect of development carried out by, or on behalf of, the Crown (s.266(3)). This is because, consitutionally, the 1971 Act does not bind the Crown. Thus the Crown could not, for example, apply for planning permission for development as well it might have wished to do if it wanted to dispose of Crown Land with such permission attached and at the higher figure which such permission would give to the land.[42]

The Town and Country Planning Act 1984 has made important changes into the forgoing position. So far as the enforcement of planning control over Crown land is concerned, this is dealt with in section 3 of the 1984 Act and applies to any development carried out after April 12, 1984, the date of the *passing* of the Act (1984 Act, s.7(2)(*b*)). It applies to development of Crown land carried out otherwise than by, or on behalf of, the Crown at a time when no person is entitled to occupy the land by virtue of a private interest (1984 Act, s.3(1)). Thus, it will apply to unauthorised development by trespassers as, for example, the setting up of mobile snack bars and other trading "outlets," to encampments and the like on the verges and lay-bys of trunk roads.

Again, the local planning authority are not *obliged* to take enforcement action but can do so if they think it expedient (1984 Act, s.3(2)). Action, if taken, is commenced by the issue of a "special enforcement notice" (*ibid.*) which can only be issued with the consent of the appropriate Crown authority (1984 Act, s.3(4)). The procedure thereafter follows approximately the enforcement procedure of the 1971 Act earlier described in this chapter.

The special enforcement notice must specify:

(1) the *matters* alleged to be development;
(2) the *steps* required to remedy anything of which complaint is made (1984 Act, s.3(4));
(3) the *date* on which it will take effect and the *period* within which the steps (just mentioned) are to be taken (1984 Act, s.3(5)).

A copy of the special enforcement notice must be served (1984 Act, s.3(6)) not later than 28 days *after* the date of the notice and at least 28 days *before* the date it takes effect upon:

(1) the person who carried out the development (if he can be found);
(2) the person occupying the land at the date of the notice; and
(3) the appropriate Crown authority.

[42] See further hereon, at p. 29.

There is a right of appeal to the Secretary of State against the special enforcement notice but only on the grounds (and here the special enforcement notice differs from other enforcement notices) that the matters specified in the notice have not taken place at all or, if they have, that they do not constitute development to which section 3 of the 1984 Act applies (1984 Act, s.3(7)). The appeal *must* be made *before* the date specified in the notice as the date when the notice will take effect (*ibid*).

A person occupying Crown land, not as holder of a property interest in the land but merely by virtue of a licence in writing, has also a right of appeal against a special enforcement notice (1984 Act, s.4).

The Secretary of State has made the Town and Country Planning (Special Enforcement Notices) Regulations 1984[43] and has also issued a Circular and Memorandum entitled, "Crown Land and Crown Development" (D.O.E. Circular 18/84 dated August 3, 1984). As to special enforcement notices attention should be given to section 3 (paras. 13–18 inclusive) of the Memorandum accompanying the Circular.

2. Enforcement of Control over Authorised Development

The commentary in this chapter has, so far, dealt with the enforcement of planning control over *unauthorised* development, *i.e.* development which wholly lacks planning permission, or development which is in breach of conditions or limitations subject to which planning permission has been granted. In the case of such unauthorised development the remedy (as already discussed) is by way of an enforcement notice.

But the proper planning of land may, from time to time, require the removal or prohibition of development originally undertaken *with* planning permission and in entire compliance with planning control. Accordingly, a local planning authority may by order, confirmed by the Secretary of State, require the alteration or removal of any *authorised* building or the discontinuance of any *authorised* use of land (s.51) but if this is done compensation, assessed (s.178) in accordance with the Land Compensation Act 1961, will be payable (s.170) to any person in respect of damage caused by:

(a) the depreciation in the value of his interest in the land; or

(b) the disturbance of his enjoyment of the land (s.170(2), (4)).

Such a person may also claim compensation for expenses reasonably incurred by him in complying with the requirements of a local planning authority respecting authorised development (s.170(3)).

[43] S.I. 1984 No. 1016.

Claims for compensation must be made in writing within six months of the order of the local planning authority (Town and Country Planning General Regulations 1976,[44] reg. 14).

The validity of an order made under section 51 of the 1971 Act may be challenged on a point of law within six weeks by application in the High Court by any person aggrieved by the order or by any authority directly concerned[45] with the order (ss.242(1)(*d*), (2)(*b*) and 245(1), (2), (3), (4), (7)).

If any person, without planning permission, uses land in contravention of an Order made under section 51 of the 1971 Act he will be liable to a fine not exceeding £2,000 on summary conviction or to a fine of unlimited amount on conviction on indictment (s.108(3); Criminal Justice Act 1982, s.37 and Criminal Penalties etc. (Increase) Order 1984).

In addition the local planning authority may, in default, take any steps required to be taken under the order for the alteration or removal of buildings or works (s.108(4)) and may sell materials removed (accounting for the proceeds of sale) under the authority of section 276 of the Public Health Act 1936 as applied by section 108(4) of the 1971 Act.

3. Enforcement of Control over Listed Buildings

Under section 54 of the 1971 Act the Secretary of State may prepare lists of buildings of special architectural or historic interest with a view to guiding local planning authorities as to their functions under the 1971 Act in relation to such buildings.

The enforcement of control over a listed building is discussed in Chapter 14.[46]

4. Enforcement of Control over Waste Land

Under section 65 (as substituted by the Housing and Planning Act 1986, s.46) together with sections 104–107 of the 1971 Act, a district planning authority or a London borough council may serve on the owner and on the occupier of land a notice requiring the taking of specified steps to remedy the condition of *any* land in their area which is adversely affecting amenity.[47] Subject to appeal to a magistrates' court, a notice under section 65 will take effect at the end of

[44] S.I. 1976 No. 1419.

[45] As to a "person aggrieved" or an "authority directly concerned" see pp. 221–230.

[46] See p. 314.

[47] See p. 318.

such period (which may not be less than 28 days after the service of the notice) as may be stated in the notice (s.65(2)).

The enforcement of control following the service of a notice under section 65 is discussed in Chapter 14.[48]

5. Enforcement of Tree Preservation Orders

The making of a tree preservation order for the preservation of trees and woodlands is dealt with earlier in Chapter 14.[49] So far as enforcement is concerned it needs only to be stated here that if any person contravenes the provisions of a tree preservation order[49] by cutting down, uprooting or wilfully damaging a tree, or topping or lopping a tree in a manner likely to destroy it, he is liable, on summary conviction, to a fine not exceeding £2,000 or twice the value of the tree (whichever is the greater) or, on conviction on indictment, to a fine of unlimited amount (s.102(1); Criminal Justice Act 1982, s.37 and Criminal Penalties etc. (Increase) Order 1984 (S.I. 1984 No. 447)).

If the contravention of the tree preservation order is otherwise than in the fashion mentioned in the preceeding paragraph, then the offender is liable on summary conviction to a fine not exceeding level 4 on the standard scale, *i.e.* £1,000 (s.102(2); Criminal Justice Act 1982, s.37 and Criminal Penalties etc. (Increase) Order 1984).

For a continuing offence under section 102 of the 1971 Act there is a further fine, on summary conviction, of £5 per day (s.102(3)).

In determining the amount of the fine on conviction on indictment, the court is to have particular regard to any financial benefit which has accrued or appears likely to accrue, to the defendant in consequence of his offence (s.102(1)(*b*)).

Notwithstanding the foregoing provisions of the Town and Country Planning Act 1971, a local authority, in order to prevent a feared breach of a tree preservation order, may, in certain instances, resort to enforcement by means of injunction with the attendant possibility of a sentence of imprisonment for breach of the injunction.[50]

6. Enforcement of Control over Advertisements

Advertisement control has been discussed earlier in Chapter 12.[51]

Regulations made under section 63 of the 1971 Act may make

[48] See p. 294.
[49] See p. 298.
[50] *Kent County Council* v. *Batchelor* [1978] 3 All E.R. 980; and see p. 298.
[51] See p. 268.

provision for enabling a local planning authority to require the removal of any advertisement displayed in contravention of the Town and Country Planning (Control of Advertisements) Regulations 1984[52] or the discontinuance of the use of any advertising site used in contravention of those regulations and, for that purpose, for applying any of the provisions of Part V of the 1971 Act with respect to enforcement notices (s.109(1)). It needs to be stated that the Advertisement Regulations 1984 have not, in fact, made any provision for applying the provisions of Part V of the 1971 Act with respect to enforcement notices.

A local planning authority have power under the 1984 Regulations, to require the discontinuance of the display of advertisements displayed with deemed consent in order to remedy injury to amenity or danger to the public (reg. 16).

It is to be remembered that a person is deemed to display an advertisement if:

(a) the advertisement is displayed on land of which he is the owner or occupier, or

(b) the advertisement gives publicity to his goods, trade, business or other concerns

unless, in either case, such person proves that the advertisement was displayed without his consent or knowledge (s.109(3)).

A person who displays an advertisement in contravention of the 1984 Regulations is liable on summary conviction to a fine of such amount as the regulations may prescribe (they, in fact, prescribe (reg. 8) a fine of £200) not exceeding level 3 on the standard scale, *i.e.* £400 (s.109(2); Criminal Justice Act 1982, s.37 and Criminal Penalties etc. (Increase) Order 1984 (S.I. 1984 No. 447)). In the case of a continuing offence such person is liable to a daily penalty of £20 (s.109(2) and the 1984 Regulations, reg. 8).

The former power to serve an enforcement notice in respect of a contravening advertisement is not continued under the 1984 Regulations. In some cases, however, the display of an advertisement may amount to development under section 22(1) and (4) of the 1971 Act and, if not in accordance with the 1984 Regulations, planning permission will not be deemed granted under section 64 of the Act, in which case the normal enforcement procedure under Part V of the 1971 Act will apply.

[52] S.I. 1984 No. 421.

Chapter 16

PLANNING INQUIRIES—PROCEDURE RULES

1. Rules of Procedure—the Franks Report

The holding of public local inquiries is an accepted part of the administrative process relating to town planning control over the development of land. The Secretary of State may cause a local public inquiry to be held for the purposes of the exercise of any of his functions under the 1971 Act (s.282(1)) and, if a local inquiry is so held, the provisions of the Local Government Act 1972 sections 250(2) to (5)—relating to the giving of evidence at, and defraying the cost of, local inquiries—will apply (s.282(2)).

Such a local inquiry may be held, for example, in connection with an appeal to the Secretary of State (under s.36 of the 1971 Act) against a planning decision or (under s.37 of the 1971 Act) in default of the giving of a planning decision, or (under ss.63(2)(*c*) and 60(2)(*a*) of the Act) against a decision relating to the display of an advertisement.

Such an inquiry may also be held in connection with the approval by the Secretary of State of a local plan called in by him (under s.14(3), (4)(*c*) of the 1971 Act) for his approval or of a compulsory purchase order for land, made in accordance with the procedure set out in the Acquisition of Land Act 1981, or of a designation order for the site of a new town made under the New Towns Act 1981.

Confirmation by the Secretary of State of a structure plan is done after the holding by him, *not* of a public local inquiry, but of an examination in public (under s.9 of the 1971 Act (see p. 68)).

The Report[1] of the Committee on Administrative Tribunals and Enquiries (the Franks Committee)—see Ministry Circular 9/58, dated February 27, 1958—recommended in July 1957 that in connection with these inquiries a "code or codes of procedure for Inquiries should be formulated by the Council on Tribunals (later established under the Tribunals and Inquiries Act 1958, now repealed and replaced by the Tribunals and Inquiries Act 1971) and made statutory; the procedure should be simple and inexpensive but orderly."

The result of these recommendations was the enacting of a statutory provision (now contained in s.11 of the Tribunals and Inquiries

[1] Cmnd. 218 of 1957; and see Ministry Circular 9/58.

Act 1971) which enables the Lord Chancellor, after consultation with the Council on Tribunals, to make rules of procedure for "statutory inquiries," as defined in section 19(1) and (2) of the Tribunals and Inquiries Act 1971, held by or on behalf of the Secretary of State.

The Lord Chancellor has made the Town and Country Planning (Inquiries Procedure) Rules 1974,[2] the Town and Country Planning Appeals (Determination by Appointed Persons) (Inquiries Procedure) Rules 1974[3] and the Compulsory Purchase by Public Authorities (Inquiries Procedure) Rules 1976.[4]

Of these three sets of rules the first set relates to town planning *applications and appeals* (r. 2(1)). The second set relates only to town planning *appeals* (r. 2(1)). Both sets of Rules came into operation on April 1, 1974 (r. 1(2) of each set of Rules). (Each set is amended in minor and consequential fashion, upon the abolition on April 1, 1986 of the Greater London Council and the six Metropolitan County Councils, by the Town and Country Planning (Various Inquiries) (Procedure) (Amendment) Rules 1986: S.I. 1986 No. 420.) Each set of Rules will apply additionally to any application, or (as the case may be) appeal which had not been determined when the Rules (revoking earlier Rules of a like kind made in 1968 and 1969) came into operation (rr. 1(2) and 17 of S.I. 1974 No. 419 and rr. 1(2) and 20 of S.I. 1974 No. 420).

The Compulsory Purchase by Public Authorities (Inquiries Procedure) Rules 1976 came into operation on June 17, 1976 but do *not* apply to any compulsory purchase order made before that date (r. 1(2)). Thus any such order will continue to be dealt with under the Compulsory Purchase by Local Authorities (Inquiries Procedure) Rules 1962[5] which are otherwise revoked by the 1976 rules (r. 12).

2. Scope of the Rules

The scope of these three sets of Rules of 1974 and 1976 respectively needs to be noted.

The Town and Country Planning (Inquiries Procedure) Rules 1974 apply in those cases in which the determination of the *application to* the Secretary of State or the *appeal to* the Secretary of State will be made *by* the Secretary of State.

[2] S.I. 1974 No. 419.
[3] S.I. 1974 No. 420.
[4] S.I. 1976 No. 746.
[5] S.I. 1962 No. 1424.

The Town and Country Planning Appeals (Determination by Appointed Persons) (Inquiries Procedure) Rules 1974 apply where, in the case of *an appeal* (and only in the case of an *appeal*) to the Secretary of State, the Secretary of State has delegated the determination of *the appeal* to an Inspector who thus not only hears the appeal but determines it as well—and in the name of the Secretary of State.

Each of the two foregoing sets of Rules of 1974 applies (r. 2 of each set of Rules) not only to public local inquiries but also to private hearings (r. 15 of S.I. 1974 No. 419 and r. 18 of S.I. 1974 No. 420).

The Town and Country Planning (Inquiries Procedure) Rules 1974 apply (r. 2):

(1) in connection with *applications* for planning permission referred to the Secretary of State under section 35 of the 1971 Act *or appeals* to the Secretary of State under sections 36 and 37 of the 1971 Act against a planning decision relating to development;

(2) in connection with *applications* for consent *or appeals* under tree preservation orders;

(3) in connection with *applications* for consent *or appeals* relating to listed building consents under Part I of Schedule 11 to the 1971 Act (including consent for the demolition of a building in a conservation area);

(4) in connection with *applications* for consent under the Town and Country Planning (Control of Advertisements) Regulations 1969,[6–7] relating to the display of advertisements *or appeals* to the Secretary of State under those Regulations.

The Town and Country Planning Appeals (Determination by Appointed Persons) (Inquiries Procedure) Rules 1974 apply in each of the four instances mentioned in the previous paragraph *but only in the case of an appeal* (r. 2). This distinction is to be noted; an Inspector appointed by the Secretary of State to hear *and determine* a matter can deal only with an *appeal* to the Secretary of State and not with an *application* referred to the Secretary of State.

The Compulsory Purchase Inquiries Rules 1976 apply (r. 2) to public local inquiries and private hearings into compulsory purchase orders made under the Acquisition of Land Act 1981. Thus they do *not* apply to orders made under Part II or Part III of the Housing Act 1985, or under the New Towns Act 1981.

[6–7] S.I. 1969 No. 1532 now revoked and replaced by the Town and Country Planning (Control of Advertisement) Regulations, 1984 S.I. 1984 No. 421; see *ante*, p. 268.

3. The Town and Country Planning (Inquiries Procedure) Rules 1974

The Town and Country Planning (Inquiries Procedure) Rules 1974 are currently (February 1987) under review. They are referred to in the Government's Response (Cm 43 dated December 1986) to the Fifth Report of the House of Commons Environment Committee, Session 1985–86 mentioned *ante* at page 220 to which reference should be made.

The 1974 Rules exclude (r. 2(1)) from the operation of the Rules all *appeals* given over (under the 1971 Act) for determination by an Inspector instead of by the Secretary of State except that in a case where the Secretary of State recovers (under Sched. 9, para. 3, to the 1971 Act) the right to determine an appeal himself, then the Planning Inquiries Rules 1974 will again apply to the proceedings (r. 2(3)).

4. The Town and Country Planning Appeals (Determination by Appointed Persons) (Inquiries Procedure) Rules 1974

If an *appeal* is to be determined by an Inspector instead of by the Secretary of State, then the procedure will be regulated, as already mentioned, *not* by the Town and Country Planning (Inquiries Procedure) Rules 1974 but by the Town and Country Planning Appeals (Determination by Appointed Persons) (Inquiries Procedure) Rules 1974.[8] These Rules follow closely the provisions of the Town and Country Planning (Inquiries Procedure) Rules 1974 and make provision as to procedure for all those classes of planning appeals which can be transferred for *determination* by an Inspector under Schedule 9 to the 1971 Act.

The Secretary of State has made the Town and Country Planning (Determination of Appeals by Appointed Persons) (Prescribed Classes) Regulations 1981.[9] These Regulations:

(1) re-enact with amendments the provisions of the earlier Town and Country Planning (Determination of appeals by appointed persons) (Prescribed Classes) Regulations 1972 to 1977;

(2) prescribe the classes of appeal which are to be determined by persons appointed for the purpose by the Secretary of State

[8] S.I. 1974 No. 420.

[9] S.I. 1981 No. 804.

(in accordance with the provisions of Schedule 9 to the 1971 Act) instead of being determined by the Secretary of State;

(3) prescribe certain classes of case within those prescribed classes of appeal which are to continue to be determined by the Secretary of State; and

(4) provide for publication by local planning authorities of any direction made by the Secretary of State under paragraph 1 of Schedule 9 to the 1971 Act which relates to directions specifying classes of case within the prescribed classes of appeal which are to continue to be determined by the Secretary of State.

Under these 1981 Regulations it is now provided that:

(a) *all appeals* under sections 36 and 37 of the 1971 Act (appeals in respect of applications for planning permission) and *all appeals* under section 88 of that Act (appeals against enforcement notices) are prescribed, by Regulation 3, as appeals to be determined by a person (an Inspector) appointed by the Secretary of State, in place of the more restricted classes of such appeals set out in former regulations; and

(b) the classes of case which are excepted (reg. 4) from determination by an Inspector are reduced to cover only appeals made by statutory undertakers which fall to be dealt with jointly by the Secretary of State and "the appropriate Minister" because they relate to the development of land to which section 225(1) of the 1971 Act applies (operational land or land which would become operational land if, in the decision on the appeal, planning permission were granted for its development).

This wholesale transfer of appeals for determination by Departmental Inspectors (instead of by the Secretary of State) has lessened the importance of the Town and Country Planning (Inquiries Procedure) Rules 1974[10] and greatly enhanced that of the Town and Country Planning Appeals (Determination by Appointed Persons) (Inquiries Procedure) Rules 1974.[11] Accordingly, the rest of this chapter is devoted generally to a consideration of the *latter* Rules.

5. Importance of the 1974 Rules

The Franks Committee advocated the provision of a right of appeal to a court of law whenever certain irregularities occurred in connection with a town planning appeal. In consequence of this, section

[10] S.I. 1974 No. 419.
[11] S.I. 1974 No. 420.

245 of the 1971 Act provides for challenging the validity of the Secretary of State's decision in a planning appeal on the ground that his action is *ultra vires* or that any of "the relevant requirements" have not been complied with (ss.245(1)(*b*), (3) and 242(3)(*b*)). The expression "the relevant requirements" means (s.245(7)), *inter alia,* any requirements of the Tribunals and Inquiries Act 1971 *or of any rules made under that Act.* Thus *all* the requirements of the Town and Country Planning (Inquiries Procedure) Rules 1974 as also those of the Town and Country Planning Appeals (Determination by Appointed Persons) (Inquiries Procedure) Rules 1974 become "relevant requirements" and if any one of these is not properly observed, any determination of the Secretary of State (or of an Inspector) which derives from them may be challenged in a court of law under section 245 of the 1971 Act. Thus the need for a close observance of the requirements of the Town and Country Planning (Inquiries Procedure) Rules 1974, as also of the requirements of the Town and Country Planning (Determination by Appointed Persons) (Inquiries Procedure) Rules 1974, is a matter of the greatest importance.

6. Town Planning Appeals—Their Importance

Town planning appeals increase both in importance and in number. Today the value of land depends pre-eminently on the kind of planning permission for development which can be got for it. Planning permission for development, once granted, runs with the land (s.33(1)) and every owner of land (except the owner who neither wishes to sell nor to develop his land) has every incentive for seeking to obtain the most generous grant of planning permission which it is possible to obtain. This has led to an increasing number of appeals to the Secretary of State against refusals of planning permission or against the grant of planning permission subject to conditions.

Not every appeal which is made to the Secretary of State is sustained to the end. Often a compromise is reached between the aspirations of the developer and the requirements of the local planning authority. The national figures for the last few years show how appeals have grown in number; they also show that the odds against winning an appeal are hardening with the years.[12]

The rewards which attend success are often sufficiently attractive

[12] See "Development Control Statistics 1978/79" available in booklet from the Directorate of Statistics (SPR Division), Department of the Environment, 2 Marsham Street, London, SW1P 3EB, price £1.00 net. See also p. 242.

to make an appeal seem a worthwhile effort to an applicant seeking planning permission to develop his land. Rural land with the benefit of planning permission for development may be worth £1,000 per acre; without such permission it may fetch only £100 per acre. Any payment of compensation for a refusal of planning permission is a mere consolation prize compared with the rewards which follow (subject, of course, to market demand) in the wake of a grant of planning permission for development.

7. The Town and Country Planning Appeals (Determination by Appointed Persons) (Inquiries Procedure) Rules 1974—Details

In view of the fact (already mentioned at page 354) that the Secretary of State has, as from July 1, 1981, delegated all planning *appeals* (under ss.36 and 37 of the 1971 Act)—except from statutory undertakers—and all enforcement notice *appeals* (under s.88 of the 1971 Act) to be determined by Inspectors appointed by him, the rest of this chapter confines itself to the provisions of the Town and Country Planning Appeals (Determination by Appointed Persons) (Inquiries Procedure) Rules 1974. But the commentary which follows in this chapter is, in general, equally applicable to the other 1974 set of Rules—The Town and Country Planning (Inquiries Procedure) Rules 1974—which apply when the determination of an *application* or an *appeal* is made by the Secretary of State and not by an Inspector.

8. Procedure before Inquiry

(1) *Preliminary information*

The Town and Country Planning Appeals (Determination by Appointed Persons) (Inquiries Procedure) Rules 1974[13] (hereinafter in this chapter referred to as "the 1974 Rules") begin to function with a letter from the Secretary of State addressed to the "local planning authority" which expression means (r. 3(1)) the county planning authority or the district planning authority, as the case may be.

On being notified by the letter from the Secretary of State of the appeal to the Secretary of State, the local planning authority must forthwith inform the Secretary of State and the appellant (r. 4(1)) of the name and address of any "section 29 party" (r. 3(1)), that is to say, of any party who has made representations to the local planning authority under sections 26, 27 or 28 of the 1971 Act, these being the

[13] S.I. 1974 No. 420.

sections which require an applicant for planning permission to give notice of his application in the case of certain types of "bad neighbour" development (s.26) or, if the applicant is *not* the owner of the land affected by the application, require him to serve notice of his application upon the owner of the land and upon any agricultural tenant of the land (s.27) or which require the local planning authority to advertise in the local press and publish a site notice in the case of development in a conservation area (s.28). Such third parties are referred to in the 1974 Rules as "section 29 parties" (r. 3(1)) because their rights in this context arise generally from section 29 of the Town and Country Planning Act 1971.

Where there is in force a direction given by either the Secretary of State or a local authority to the local planning authority restricting the grant of planning permission for the development which it is sought to carry out, the Secretary of State must, on hearing from the local planning authority that the direction is a relevant matter in the appeal, send a statement in writing to the local planning authority giving the reasons for the giving of the direction (r. 4(2)).

(2) *Notification of inquiry*

If the Secretary of State decides to hold a public local inquiry in connection with the appeal he must fix a date, time and place all of which can be varied—but not to suit the religious beliefs of an applicant[14]—by him for the holding of the inquiry and he must give not less than 42 days' notice in writing of this to the appellant, to the local planning authority and to all section 29 parties (r. 5(1)).

With the written consent of the appellant and the local planning authority the Secretary of State may give such shorter notice for the holding of the inquiry as may be agreed and he may vary the time or place fixed for the inquiry where he thinks is necessary or advisable (*ibid.*).

The Secretary of State may require the local planning authority to publicise the holding of the inquiry (r. 5(2)), and where the land involved in the inquiry is under the control of the appellant the latter must, if requested by the Secretary of State, affix firmly on the land a public notice of the inquiry (r. 5(3)).

(3) *Notification of identity of Inspector*

The Secretary of State must give to the appellant, to the local planning authority and to all section 29 parties written notice of the

[14] *Ostreicher* v. *Secretary of State for the Environment* [1977] J.P.L. 716 and [1978] J.P.L. 539.

name of the person (the Inspector) appointed by him to conduct the inquiry and determine the matter which is before the inquiry (r. 6). But if the Secretary of State switches the Inspector (as he can do under the 1971 Act, Sched. 9, para. 4) and it is not practical to give written notice of this change before the inquiry opens, then the Inspector holding the inquiry must announce his own name and his appointment as Inspector at the commencement of the inquiry (r. 6).

(4) *Written statement of submissions and list of documents*

Next comes the written statement of submissions. This statement is most important.

In the case of an appeal to the Secretary of State, the local planning authority must, not later than 28 days before the inquiry (or such later date as the Secretary of State may specify), serve on the appellant and all section 29 parties a written statement of any submission the authority propose to put forward at the inquiry (r. 7(1)). A copy of the written statement must be sent to the Secretary of State for transmission to the Inspector who is to hold the inquiry (*ibid.*).

The written statement must mention any direction given by a local authority restricting the grant of planning permission for development or directing the manner in which the application for planning permission shall be determined and must include a copy of any such direction and the reasons for its making (r. 7(2)).

Where a government department or a local authority have expressed in writing to the local planning authority the view that the application for planning permission should not be granted, or should be granted only subject to conditions, then, if the local planning authority propose to rely at the inquiry on any such expression of view, they must include such view in their written statement and must supply a copy of the statement to the government department or local authority concerned (*ibid.*).

The written statement of the local planning authority must be accompanied by:

(i) a list of all the documents (including maps and plans) to which the authority intend to refer, or which they intend to put in evidence, at the inquiry; and

(ii) a notice stating the times and place at which such documents may be inspected (r. 7(3)).

A reasonable opportunity[15] for inspection must be afforded to the

[15] As to "reasonable opportunity" see *Performance Cars Ltd.* v. *Secretary of State for the Environment* [1977] J.P.L. 585.

appellant and all section 29 parties all of whom must be allowed, where practicable, to take copies of the documents (*ibid.*).

Any other *person interested* must also be given a reasonable opportunity to inspect the aforementioned documents and, where practicable, to take copies of such documents and of the local planning authority's written statement (r. 7(4)).

If the Secretary of State and the local planning authority have to give a written statement about their case *before* the inquiry opens (in other words, if they have to give away their case to "the other side" before the shouting starts!) so also will this have to be done by the appellant if, *but only if,* the Secretary of State so requires (r. 7(5)). It is a matter of government policy whether an appellant shall be called upon to do for "the other side" what the other side are bound in all cases themselves to do for the appellant.

(5) *Appointed person may act in place of Secretary of State*

The Inspector appointed by the Secretary of State to hold the public inquiry and determine the appeal is himself given the same powers (r. 8) as has the Secretary of State (and can use such powers in place of the Secretary of State) with respect to:

(1) notification of the inquiry under rule 5;
(2) service of written statement of submissions on, and list of documents to, "the other side" under rule 7(1) or (5);
(3) summoning of representatives of government departments before the inquiry under rule 10(1) or (2); and
(4) summoning likewise of representatives of local authorities under rule 11(1) or (2).

(6) *Representatives of government departments at inquiry*

Where a government department has expressed in writing the view that the application for planning permission should not be granted in whole or in part, or should be granted only subject to conditions and the local planning authority (as required by r. 7(2)) have set out such view in their written statement—then the appellant may, not later than 14 days before the opening of the inquiry, apply in writing to the Secretary of State for a representative of the government department concerned to be available at the inquiry (r. 10(1)) and appropriate arrangements must be made accordingly (r. 10(2)).

The representative of a government department attending the inquiry in the foregoing circumstances will be called as a witness by the local planning authority, must state the reasons for the view of his department earlier expressed and will be liable to cross-examination[16] like any other witness (r. 10(3)) provided, however, that the Inspector taking the inquiry must disallow any question which, in his opinion, is directed to the merits of government policy (r. 10(4)).

(7) *Representatives of local authorities at inquiry*

Where a local authority have given to the local planning authority a direction restricting a grant of planning permission or directing the manner in which it should be determined, or where a local authority have expressed in writing to the local planning authority the view that the application for planning permission should not be granted in whole or in part or should only be granted subject to conditions and this view has been included in the written statement of the local planning authority (as required by r. 7(2))—then the appellant may, not later than 14 days before the opening of the inquiry, apply in writing to the Secretary of State for a representative of the local authority concerned to be available at the inquiry (r. 11(1)) and appropriate arrangements must be made accordingly (r. 11(2)). Such a representative will be called as a witness by the local planning authority, must state the reasons for the direction or the view earlier expressed by the local authoritiy and will be liable to cross-examination[17] like any other witness (r. 11(3)).

(8) *Who may appear at inquiry*

The persons *entitled as of right* under the 1974 Rules to appear at the inquiry are (r. 9(1)):

(a) the appellant;
(b) the local planning authority (as defined in r. 3(1));
(c) where the land is *not* in Greater London, the council of the administrative county where the land is situated, if such council is not the local planning authority;
(d) where the land is *not* in Greater London, the council of the district where the land is situated (or the Council of the Isles of Scilly, as the case may be) if such council is not the local planning authority;
(e) where the land is in a National Park, the National Park committee (if any); if not, the local planning authority;
(f) any joint planning board constituted under section 1 of the 1971 Act (or reconstituted under Pt. I of Schedule 17 of the

[16] As to the circumstances in which an objector has a right to cross-examine, see *Nicholson* v. *Secretary of State for Energy* (1977) 76 L.G.R. 693; (1977) 245 E.G. 139; [1978] J.P.L. 39; *The Times*, August 6, 1977; *Bushell* v. *Secretary of State for the Environment* (1980) 40 P. & C.R. 51, H.L.

[17] See *Bushell* v. *Secretary of State for the Environment* (1980) 40 P. & C.R. 51, H.L.

Local Government Act 1972) if such board is not the local planning authority;

(g) where the land is in an area designated as the site of a new town, the development corporation of the new town;

(h) section 29 parties;

(i) the council of the parish or community where the land is situated, if that council has made representations to the local planning authority;

(j) any persons on whom the Secretary of State or the Inspector has required notice to be served under rule 5(2)(*b*) of the 1974 Rules.

It will be noted that rule 9(1)(*c*) and (*d*) does *not* cater for land within the area of Greater London. The reason for this is that the 1974 Rules are modified in their application to Greater London by rule 19.

In addition to the foregoing parties and persons who appear at the inquiry *as of right* the Inspector may, at his discretion, allow *any* other person to appear (r. 9(2)).

Where there are two or more persons having a similar interest in the matter under inquiry, the Inspector may allow one or more persons to appear for the benefit of some or all of the persons so interested (r. 9(4)).

9. Procedure at Inquiry

Except as otherwise provided in the 1974 Rules the Inspector taking the inquiry can, at his discretion, choose the procedure to be followed at the inquiry (r. 12(1)).

Unless the Inspector with the consent of the appellant otherwise determines, the appellant will have the responsibility of beginning, that is to say, speaking first at the inquiry, and he will also have the right of finally replying, whilst all other persons, whether *entitled or merely permitted* to appear at the inquiry, will be heard in such order as the Inspector may determine (r. 12(2)).

The appellant, the local planning authority and the section 29 parties are *entitled* freely to call evidence at the inquiry and to cross-examine any person giving evidence, but any other person appearing at the inquiry may call evidence and cross-examination only to such extent as the Inspector permits (r. 12(3)).[18] The distinction here made may well, in practice, turn out to be more apparent than real because it is inconceivable that an Inspector would in any way

[18] As to the refusal of a planning officer to answer questions to cross-examination, see *The Accountancy Tuition Centre* v. *Secretary of State for the Environment* [1977] J.P.L. 792.

obstruct any person who has anything to say or bring out that which is germane to the inquiry.

The Inspector may neither require nor permit the giving or production of evidence which is contrary to the public interest (r. 12(4)) but, subject to the protection accorded to a witness representing a government department—who may not be asked questions touching the merits of government policy (r. 10(4))—any evidence may, at the discretion of the Inspector, be admitted at the inquiry (r. 12(4)). The Inspector may also direct that documents put in evidence may be inspected by any person *entitled or permitted* to appear at the inquiry and that facilities may be afforded to such a person to take or obtain copies of such documents (*ibid.*).

An important provision in the 1974 Rules is that which empowers the Inspector to allow both the local planning authority and the appellant to add to the submissions set out in their written statement served (under r. 7) earlier in the appeal and also to alter, or to add to, any list of documents which accompanied the written statement, so far as any such alterations or additions may be said to be necessary to determine the issues between the parties (r. 12(5)). But if any such alteration or addition is made then the Inspector must give the local planning authority, the appellant and the section 29 parties an adequate opportunity of considering any fresh submission or document, and to enable this to be done he must, if need be, adjourn the inquiry, in which case he may make a recommendation in his report as to the payment of additional costs incurred by any such adjournment (*ibid.*). Thus, those who fail to put into their written statement matters which, later, they wish to raise at the inquiry, may find that, whilst they are able to do this, they can only do it on making themselves responsible for any additional costs thereby caused.

If a person who is *entitled* to appear at the inquiry fails to appear the Inspector may, at his discretion, proceed with the inquiry notwithstanding the absence of any such person (r. 12(6)).

The Inspector is entitled, subject to disclosure thereof at the inquiry, to take into account any written representation or statement received by him before the inquiry from *any* person (r. 12(7)).

The Inspector may, from time to time, adjourn the inquiry and if the date, time and place for the re-opening of the inquiry are announced before its adjournment, then no further notice about the reopening of the inquiry need be given (r. 12(8)).

10. Application for Costs

If at any inquiry *any* person applies for an award of costs, the Inspector *must* report in writing to the Secretary of State the proceedings on the application (r. 15). In his report the Inspector *may* draw attention to any relevant considerations which might affect the decision of the Secretary of State whether or not to allow costs (*ibid.*).

On this it will be remembered that the Inspector may, at the inquiry, allow both the local planning authority and the appellant to alter, or add to, the submissions in any written statement of theirs earlier served (under r. 7) before the opening of the inquiry (r. 12(5)). If this leads (as well it may) to an adjournment of the inquiry, the Inspector may make to the Secretary of State a recommendation as to the payment of any additional costs brought about by the adjournment (*ibid.*).

As to the award of costs, reference may be made to chapter 10 and the commentary appearing at page 235.

11. Site Inspection

The Inspector may, either *before* or *during* the inquiry, and without giving notice of his intention to anybody, make an unaccompanied inspection of the land which is to be the subject of the inquiry (r. 13(1)).

The Inspector *may*, and if so requested by the appellant or by the local planning authority *before* or *during* the inquiry, *must* inspect the land *after the inquiry has closed* and where he decides to do this he must, during the course of the inquiry, announce both the date and the time at which he proposes to inspect the site (r. 13(2)).

At any inspection made after the close of the inquiry the appellant, the local planning authority and the section 29 parties are all entitled to be present, but the Inspector is not bound to defer his inspection if any person entitled to be present does not attend at the time appointed (r. 13(3)).

12. Procedure after Inquiry

If, after the close of the inquiry, the Inspector proposes to take into consideration any new evidence (and this includes *expert opinion* on a matter of *fact*) or any new issue of *fact* (not being a matter of government policy) which was not raised at the inquiry[19] and which he considers material to his decision, then he must not come to a decision without first notifying:

(1) the appellant;

[19] *Lake District Special Planning Board* v. *Secretary of State for the Environment* (1975) 236 E.G. 417; *French Kier Developments Ltd.* v. *Secretary of State for the Environment* [1977] 1 All E.R. 296.

(2) the local planning authority; and
(3) any section 29 party *who appeared at the inquiry*, of the substance of the new evidence or of the new issue of fact and affording all the foregoing persons and parties an opportunity (r. 14(1)):
 (a) of making representations thereon to him in writing within 21 days; or
 (b) of asking within 21 days for the reopening of the inquiry (*ibid.*).

If a request, as aforesaid, is made for the re-opening of the inquiry, the Inspector *must* arrange for this to be done r. 14(2)). Irrespective of this *obligation* to re-open the inquiry, the Inspector *may*, of his own volition, have the inquiry re-opened if he thinks fit to do so (*ibid.*)[20]

If the inquiry *is* to be re-opened, the Inspector *must* give not less than 28 days notice in writing to the appellant, to the local planning authority and to all section 29 parties of the date, time and place of the re-opening (*ibid.*). The Inspector *may* also require the local planning authority to give publicity to the re-opening of the inquiry (rr. 14(2) and 5(2)).

13. Notification of Inspector's Decision

The last step in the appeal is the Inspector's decision. This must be given by him in writing, together with reasons[21] supporting it, to the appellant, to the local planning authority, to all section 29 parties, and also to any person who, *having appeared at the inquiry*, has asked to be notified of the Inspector's decision (r. 16(1)).

Any person who is *entitled* to be notified of the Inspector's decision may apply to the Secretary of State, within six weeks of the notification, for an opportunity to inspect any documents, photographs or plans which are listed in the notification (r. 16(2)). Any such

[20] For a case where the Secretary of State (acting under the comparable r. 12 of the Town & Country Planning (Inquiries Procedure) Rules 1974) unsuccessfully sought, of his own volition and without request from either of the main parties, to exercise his discretion to re-open an inquiry and found himself prevented by the courts from so doing on the ground that his decision to re-open the inquiry was perverse—see *Niarchos (London) Ltd.* v. *Secretary of State for the Environment and Westminster City Council (No.* 2) [1981] J.P.L. 44.

[21] Reasons must be stated reasonably precisely and clearly and must not leave substantial doubts in the mind of an informed reader: See *Givandon & Co. Ltd.* v. *Minister of Housing and Local Government* [1967] 1 W.L.R. 250. See also *Hope* v. *Secretary of State for the Environment* (1975) 31 P. & C.R. 120; *Ellis* v. *Secretary of State for the Environment* (1975) 31 P. & C.R. 130; *The Accountancy Tuition Centre* v. *Secretary of State for the Environment and London Borough of Hackney* [1977] J.P.L. 792.

application to inspect documents must be allowed by the Secretary of State (*ibid.*).

14. Private Hearings in Connection with Appeals

The foregoing commentary on the 1974 Rules is dealt with on the basis that the Secretary of State, having received notification of a planning appeal, has decided to hold a public local inquiry. But the Secretary of State is *not* obliged to hold such an inquiry and may content himself with offering to the appellant and to the local planning authority a private hearing (ss.35(5) and 36(4)). If this is done, then the 1974 Rules—except those portions relating to the giving of public notice of the holding of a public local inquiry (r. 5(2) and (3)) and to the giving of notice of an inquiry to any particular person whom the Secretary of State or the Inspector has required to be notified (r. 9(1)(*j*))—are to apply to the private hearing in the same way as they apply to a public local inquiry (r. 18).

15. Appeals Dealt With by Written Representations

None of the 1974 Rules applies to any appeal which the appellant and the local planning authority agree shall be decided by written representations made to the Secretary of State.[22]

16. Application of Rules to Greater London

The 1974 Rules as detailed above are applied to the area of Greater London subject to the modifications set out in rule 19.

[22] See *ante*, p. 234.

CHAPTER 17

COMPENSATION FOR PLANNING RESTRICTIONS

1. Summary

COMPENSATION *may* be payable under the Town and Country Planning Act 1971 in respect of planning restrictions which either:

(1) prevent or hamper the development of land; or

(2) cause loss or damage or depreciation in the value of land.

It is essential in connection with this matter of compensation for planning restrictions to draw a clear distinction, as does the 1971 Act, between:

(1) compensation for planning restrictions on *new* development (Pt. VII of the Act); and

(2) compensation for planning restrictions on *other* development (Pt. VIII of the Act).

In this chapter compensation for restrictions on each of these two kinds of development is examined in turn.

2. Compensation for Planning Restrictions on "New Development"—Part VII of the 1971 Act

(1) *What is "new development"?*

Section 22(1) to (4) of the 1971 Act gives a long definition of the meaning of "development" and this is discussed at length in Chapter 8. Having defined development as being (briefly) either:

(1) the carrying out of operations in, on, over or under land; or

(2) the making of a material change in the use of land,

section 22(5) goes on to provide that "new development" means any development which does *not* fall within Schedule 8[1] to the Act. Schedule 8 to the Act gives various examples of development falling within the existing use of land and in respect of which special compensation rights attach (as discussed later in this chapter[2]). Thus new development is any development (as defined in s.22(1)–(4) of the 1971 Act) which lies *outside* the bounds of Schedule 8 to the Act

[1] As to Sched. 8 see pp. 134, 135 and 376.

[2] See p. 376.

and thus may be said to go beyond the ambit of the existing use of land. When land is developed in the normal and ordinary way from one kind of state into another and different kind of state (either because, for example, it is subjected to building operations which go beyond the point of merely replacing what (if anything) was already there, or because the use of land is changed from one kind of use to a materially different kind of use)—then it will be found, generally, that "new development" of the land has taken place.

"New development" (like any other kind of development) should not take place without planning permission being first obtained (s.23(1)) and, if planning permission is refused or is granted subject to conditions, compensation *may* become payable, under Part VII of the Act, by the Secretary of State (ss.146, 157).

If a developer anticipates the imposition of a planning condition by voluntarily providing, in his application for planning permission, for the doing of whatever would be required under the condition, then compensation may become payable in the same way as if that which the developer had chosen to do voluntarily had been imposed upon him by means of a condition attached to the grant of planning permission (s.150).

(2) *Unexpended balance of established development value*

It is a condition precedent to the getting of any compensation under Part VII of the Act for planning restrictions that there shall be an unexpended balance of established development value (ss.134, 135, 136, 139, 140) for the time being attaching to the land in question (s.134(2)). Whether there is such a balance depends on whether a claim in respect of the land was duly made, under the Town and Country Planning Act 1947, on the £300 million Fund set up under the 1947 Act and was formally accepted and established by the Central Land Board (s.135). If no such claim was ever made, or if it was made and was accepted by the Central Land Board but was excluded from satisfaction by the *de minimis* provisions of section 63 of the 1947 Act, then no compensation for any planning restrictions on the land can ever be paid under Part VII of the 1971 Act.

Provision is made for the Secretary of State to issue to any person a certificate showing what is, for the time being, the unexpended balance (if any) of established development value attaching to any particular land (s.145).

(3) *The amount of compensation*

The amount of the compensation (if any) will depend on how far the affected land is depreciated by the planning restriction (ss.146,

152, 153, 156), but it will not exceed the amount of the unexpected balance of established development value for the time being attaching to the land (s.152). Any compensation paid will go in reduction or complete extinguishment, as the case may be, of the unexpended balance attaching to the land (ss.139, 140, 141, 143, 144).

It may be added that, as the object of the 1971 Act is to compensate only for development value which, owing to planning restrictions, becomes incapable of being realised, the value of any "new development" taking place on or after July 1, 1948 (the date when the 1947 Act came into operation), and not made the subject of a development charge under the 1947 Act, will also go in reduction or extinguishment of the unexpended balance (s.141), the value of any such "new development" being calculated in accordance with Schedule 16 to the 1971 Act (*ibid.*).

The calculation of value for the purposes of Part VII of the 1971 Act will be (s.163) in accordance with Rules (2) to (4) of section 5 of the Land Compensation Act 1961.

The right to compensation vests in any person having an interest in the affected land and it so vests whether or not he was the applicant for planning permission (ss.146, 157), subject to certain exceptions (s.149).

Where a planning restriction affects land only part of which has an unexpended balance attaching to it, or affects land in which there is an interest which comprises part only of the land, then the land is to be treated as divided into appropriate units for the purpose of assessing compensation (s.152).

(4) *Exclusion of compensation*

The foregoing paragraphs set out the *general* position with respect to the payment of compensation under Part VII of the 1971 Act for planning restrictions on "new development." But it is necessary to bear in mind the many limitations in the Act on the payment of compensation in such circumstances. These fall under three main categories and are examined in succeeding paragraphs.

(i) First category of exclusion—section 147. In the first category comes the effect of section 147 of the 1971 Act. Under this section compensation is excluded in a variety of cases.

First, there is no compensation payable on a refusal of planning permission for any development which *consists of or includes* the making of any material change in the use of land or buildings (s.147(1)(*a*)). As most applications for planning permission in built-up areas are for change of use it follows that compensation will not often be payable in connection with such applications.

Secondly, there is no compensation on refusal of planning permission for the display of advertisements or on the grant of such permission subject to conditions (s.147(1)(*b*)).

Thirdly, compensation is excluded where the reason (or one of the reasons) for the refusal of planning permission is because the application for permission is premature having regard to either one or both of the following matters, namely:

(a) the order of priority, if any, indicated in the development plan for the area in which the land is situated for development in that area;

(b) any existing deficiency in the provision of water supplies or sewerage services, and the period within which any such deficiency may reasonably be expected to be made good (s.147(4)).

These two grounds are the only two on which prematureness of application can be used as a basis of refusal and compensation, at the same time, be avoided. The first ground may not always be available because development is not always staged (or programmed) in all parts of a development plan. Moreover, a planning application cannot in any case be "stood down" on the ground of prematureness for more than seven years from the date when it was first refused on this ground (s.147(4)).

Fourthly, there is no compensation on a refusal of planning permission to develop land liable to flooding or subsidence (s.147(5)).

For the purposes of any of the four instances quoted above of *refusal* of planning permission, any grant of planning permission subject to a condition prohibiting development of a specified part of the land is to be regarded as a refusal of planning permission with respect to that part of the land (s.147(6)).

Fifthly, there is a wide exclusion under section 147(2) of the 1971 Act of compensation in respect of planning permissions which are granted but which have conditions (some of them severe) attaching to them. These conditions relate to:

(a) the number or disposition of the buildings on the plot of land affected by the planning application—(thus if application is made for houses at ten to the acre but only three to the acre are permitted, no compensation will be payable);

(b) the dimensions, design, structure or external appearance of a building or the materials of which it may be constructed—(this gives a very wide power of control; under it stone may be required in place of brick, the number of floors in a building may be limited, the ratio of the size of the floor area to the size of the building plot may be reduced as the planning authority require, all of which things may or may not make a building an economic proposition in the eyes of the developer);

(c) the lay-out of land including provision of facilities for the parking, loading, unloading or fuelling of vehicles—(under this, basement car parks can be required in buildings without liability for compensation);

(d) the use of buildings or of land without buildings;

(e) the location or the design of a means of access to a highway or the materials of which it may be constructed;

(f) the winning and working of minerals.

(ii) Second category of exclusion—section 148. Section 147 of the 1971 Act is not the only section the function of which is to limit the liability for compensation for planning restrictions; section 148 must also be considered.

Under section 148 compensation is not to be paid (s.148(1)) on a refusal of planning permission "if, notwithstanding that refusal, there is available . . . planning permission to which this section applies," and section 148 applies to (s.148(3)):

> "any development of a residential, commercial or industrial character, being development which consists wholly or mainly of the construction of houses, flats, shop or office premises, or industrial buildings (including warehouses), or any combination thereof."

This section is a re-enactment of section 20 of the Town and Country Planning Act 1954, the object of which (as explained in the House of Commons by the Minister of Housing and Local Government[3]) was to provide that: " . . . compensation is not to be payable for refusal to allow one kind of development, let us say industrial, if another kind, let us say commercial or residential, is allowed. The principle is that, provided some reasonably remunerative development is allowed, the owner is not entitled to compensation because he is prevented from exploiting his land to the most remunerative development position."

(iii) The third category of exclusion—sections 38 and 39. The third category of limitation on the ability of the Secretary of State to pay compensation for planning restrictions is found in sections 38 and 39 of the 1971 Act, under which it is provided that whenever the planning decision of a local planning authority gives rise to a claim for compensation the Secretary of State may review the planning decision and, if he so desires, may give a direction

[3] *Hansard*, Vol. 525, col. 56.

(s.38) varying it so as to avoid the payment, either in whole or in part (s.155), of the compensation claimed.

Before the Secretary of State interferes in this way with the decision of a local planning authority he must give notice in writing of his proposed action to the authority and to the person whose proposed development will be affected by this decision and, if so required by either of them, must afford each of them an opportunity of appearing before, and being heard by, an Inspector appointed by the Secretary of State for the purpose (s.39).

As to the use of his powers under section 38, the Minister of Housing and Local Government (Mr. Harold Macmillan, later Lord Stockton) said in the House of Commons[4] (in connection with section 23 of the Town and Country Planning Act 1954, now re-enacted in section 38 of the 1971 Act):

> "There is a fear that the principle of 'pay as you go' [*i.e.* the payment of compensation as and when and not before the right to claim it arises] may mean that short term finance or even economy will dominate the planning. If I thought that, I should not have introduced the scheme. However, I must frankly admit that that is theoretically possible. Since the money has to be found as we go we have to pay as we go, and a Government could, if it wanted to, bring the whole thing to ruin by refusing to propose the necessary money supplies, or a House of Commons could do so by refusing to vote the money. . . .
>
> "I admit that, theoretically, this is inherent in paying as we go. Nevertheless, I do not think that we need fear that any Government will fail to ask for it or that any House of Commons will refuse to vote the supplies needed to finance compensation, always provided that we stick to the principle of paying only on established claims and so maintain a strict hold over the money that will be needed. . . .
>
> "The Government certainly have no intention whatever of subordinating the proper use of land to the need for budgetary economies."

(5) *Procedure for claiming compensation*

Claims for compensation under Part VII of the 1971 Act must be "duly made" (s.154(1)), that is to say, within six months of the relevant decision (s.154(2)) but the Secretary of State may extend this period in a particular case (*ibid.*). A claim must be made (s.154(3)) in the form set out in Schedule 1 to the Town and Country Planning

[4] *Hansard*, Vol. 525, col. 47.

(Compensation and Certificates) Regulation 1974,[5] and must be sent to the local planning authority for transmission to the Secretary of State (s.154(4)).

If it appears to the Secretary of State that the claim is not in order he must notify the claimant accordingly and invite the withdrawal of the claim (s.154(5)(*a*)). If the claim is not withdrawn the Secretary of State must give notice of it to every other person (if any) who appears to the Secretary of State to have an interest in the land affected (s.154(5)(*b*)).

Details as to the action to be taken by a local authority on receiving a claim, the supporting material to be supplied by a claimant, the determination of the amount payable and the reference of a disputed amount for determination by the Lands Tribunal, are given in Part II of the aforementioned Regulations of 1974.

(6) *Apportionment, registration and repayment of compensation*

When an award of compensation exceeds £20 it will be apportioned among different parts of the relevant land in accordance with the manner in which such parts are affected by it (s.158). The amounts charged to each part of the land will be registered by means of a "compensation notice" (s.159(1)) in the register of local land charges (s.158) and will thereafter become a charge on the land to which they relate.[6]

It is important for any purchaser of land on which compensation exceeding £20 has been paid to note that if, later, he wishes to carry out "new development"[7] on that land by:

(a) the construction of residential, commercial or industrial buildings (s.159(2)(*a*); or
(b) the mining or working of minerals (s.159(2)(*b*)); or
(c) any other form of development which is, in the Secretary of State's opinion, of such value to warrant the requirement (s.159(2)(*c*)),

then he must first *pay back* the compensation or so much as is attributable to the area of land which he seeks to develop (ss.159(1), 160). Any sum so repaid will be restored to the unexpended balance of established development value for the time being attaching to the land (s.161).

The Secretary of State, however, has power to remit any such

[5] S.I. 1974 No. 1242.

[6] As to the effect of failure to register a notice in the register of local land charges, see *Stock* v. *Wanstead and Woodford Borough Council* (1962) 2 Q.B. 479; and *Ministry of Housing and Local Government* v. *Sharp and Another* (1970) 2 Q.B. 223.

[7] See pp. 134, 135, 366 and 376.

repayment in whole or in part in any case where proper development of the land is unlikely to be carried out if it is not remitted (s.160(2)).

(7) *Mortgages, rentcharges and trusts of a settlement*

The Town and Country Planning (Compensation and Certificates) Regulations 1974,[8] relating to the application of payments and compensation made under section 162 of the 1971 Act must be considered in order to ascertain:

(i) who shall exercise the right to apply for compensation under Part VII of the 1971 Act;
(ii) who shall receive such compensation; and
(iii) how such compensation shall be applied,

in any case in which the right to apply for compensation is exercisable by reference to an interest in land which is:

(i) subject to a mortgage; or
(ii) subject to a rentcharge; or
(iii) subject to the trusts of a settlement.

3. Compensation for Planning Restrictions on Other Development—Part VIII of the 1971 Act

Part VII of the 1971 Act having dealt with the matter of compensation (payable by the Secretary of State out of central funds) in respect of planning restrictions on "new development," Part VIII of the Act proceeds to deal with compensation (payable by local planning authorities out of their own funds) for *other* planning restrictions. These other restrictions fall into ten separate categories each of which is examined in turn in the following paragraphs of this chapter.[9]

It is to be noted that compensation payable under Part VIII of the 1971 Act in respect of *other* planning restrictions is not dependent upon the land in question having attached to it an unexpended balance of established development value as is the case with compensation payable under Part VII of the Act in respect of planning restrictions on *new* development.

Compensation under Part VIII of the 1971 Act for any depreciation in the value of land will be assessed (s.178) in accordance with the rules set out in section 5 of the Land Compensation Act 1961, except (s.178(2)) in the case of compensation:

[8] S.I. 1974 No. 1242.

[9] As to special provisions relating to compensation where a stop notice is served, see p. 337.

(1) in respect of a tree preservation order[10] in which case compensation will be payable in accordance with the provisions of the order itself in respect of damage or expenditure arising from the refusal of any consent required under the order or from the grant of any such consent subject to conditions (s.174);

(2) in respect of a direction as to the replanting of trees given by the Secretary of State or the local planning authority in pursuance of provision made in a tree preservation order (s.175); and

(3) in respect of loss due to a stop notice (s.177).[11]

Questions of disputed compensation under Part VIII of the 1971 Act will be determined by the Lands Tribunal (s.179) except in so far as a tree preservation order may otherwise provide (*ibid.*).

Category (1): *Compensation on revocation or modification of planning permission—sections 164 and 165.*

As has been shown,[12] a planning permission once granted can, in certain circumstances, be later revoked or modified under section 45 of the 1971 Act by an order made by the local planning authority and confirmed by the Secretary of State, in which case compensation may be payable by the local planning authority for abortive expenditure (s.164(1)(*a*))—including expenditure on plans[13] (s.164(2))—and for loss or damage directly attributable to the revocation or modification (s.164(1)(*b*)). Loss or damage is not restricted to loss in value of land but includes loss of future business profits.[14]

The above provision also applies (s.165) when the planning permission which is revoked or modified is a permission granted, in the first instance, not by a local planning authority acting under section 29 of the 1971 Act, but by a development order under section 24 of the Act.

Compensation may arise under section 165 of the 1971 Act when a development order authorising development is revoked or modified or the scope of the order is restricted by the issue of a direction under the order (s.24(5)(*b*)).

The payment of compensation under the authority of section 165 of the 1971 Act is now materially restricted by the Town and

[10] As to tree preservation orders, see Chap. 14.
[11] As to stop notices, see pp. 335–338.
[12] See p. 240.
[13] *Holmes* v. *Bradfield R.D.C.* [1949] 2 K.B. 1, D.C.
[14] *Hobbs (Quarries) Ltd.* v. *Somerset County Council* (1974) 234 E.G. 829, L.T.

Country Planning (Compensation) Act 1985, section 1(1) which adds a new subsection (1A) to section 165 of the 1971 Act whereby such compensation will be payable only where an application for planning permission is made after January 23, 1985 (1985 Act s.3(3)) and within 12 months of the revocation or modification of the development order (s.165(1A) of the 1971 Act) or, in a case where such revocation or modification of the order has already occurred, within 12 months of the 1985 Act being enacted (1985 Act, s.3(2)). The 1985 Act received the Royal Assent on May 9, 1985.

D.O.E. Circular 15/85, entitled Town and Country Planning (Compensation) Act 1985 and dated July 25, 1985 deals with the effect of the 1985 Act on the limitation of the right to compensation when a development order is revoked or modified.

Compensation on revocation or modification of planning permission must be claimed in writing from the local planning authority within six months of the revocation or modification (ss.164(1), 165 and the Town and Country Planning General Regulations 1976,[15] reg. 14).

The compensation on revocation or modification of a planning permission is payable by the local planning authority (s.164(1)). Nevertheless that authority may receive from the Secretary of State an Exchequer contribution equal to the amount which the Secretary of State would have had to pay (under Pt. VII of the 1971 Act) by way of compensation if the planning permission had been refused in the first place, or, as the case may be, had been granted in the form in which it was later modified (s.167 and Pt. VI of the Town and Country Planning (Compensation and Certificates) Regulations 1974[16]). As the Secretary of State is only liable to make this contribution if he would have been liable under Part VII of the 1971 Act to pay compensation, it follows that a contribution from the Secretary of State can be called for only if the land in question has attached to it an unexpended balance of development value.

Any compensation payable on the revocation or modification of a planning permission and exceeding £20 will, where it is practicable so to do, be apportioned among the various parts of the land affected (s.166), will be registrable as a local land charge (s.166(5) applying s.158(4) to (6)) and will be recoverable by the Secretary of State on the subsequent carrying out (s.168 applying ss.159 and 160) of "new development" of a kind to which section 159 of the 1971 Act applies, that is to say, the kind of "new development" specified in section

[15] S.I. 1976 No. 1419.
[16] S.I. 1974 No. 1242.

159(2) of the 1971 Act.[17] The Secretary of State may, however, remit the recovery of the compensation in whole or in part (s.168 applying s.160). Any compensation recovered by the Secretary of State is payable by him to the local planning authority by whom the compensation was paid in the first place (s.168(2), (3)).

Category (2): *Compensation on refusal of planning permission, or on grant thereof subject to conditions, for development within Part II of Schedule 8—section 169*

Part II of Schedule 8 to the 1971 Act gives six classes of development which fall within the ambit of the existing use of land. If the Secretary of State refuses planning permission for this "existing-use development," or if he grants it subject to conditions, then compensation may be payable by the local planning authority if the value of the land is lessened by the refusal or the conditional grant (s.169(1), (2)).

The six classes referred to in Part II of Schedule 8 to the 1971 Act which qualify for compensation under section 169 (subject, as to Class (i) below, to (a) the provisions of section 278 of, and the condition set out in Schedule 18 to, the 1971 Act, and (b) to the restrictions now contained in the Town and Country Planning (Compensation) Act 1985 referred to later in this chapter) may be summarised as follows:

(i) the enlargement (Sched. 8, para. 11(a)), improvement or other alteration as often as required of
  (a) any building in existence on the "appointed day" (s.290(1)), *i.e.* July 1, 1948, or
  (b) any building substituted for a building which was in existence before July 1, 1948, but which has been destroyed or demolished after January 7, 1937,

(i) provided the cubic content, as ascertained by external measurement (Sched. 8, paras. 9 and 11(*b*)), of the original building is not increased in the case of a dwelling-house by more than one-tenth or 1,750 cubic feet (whichever is the greater), and in any other case by more than one-tenth (Sched. 8, para. 3);

(ii) the carrying out of building or other operations (Sched. 8, para. 4) for agricultural or forestry purposes (but not dwelling-houses or market garden or nursery buildings or buildings used for timber yards or other purposes *not* connected

[17] See pp. 134, 135, and 366.

with general farming or with the cultivation or felling of trees) on land which was agricultural or forestry land "at a material date"[18] (Sched. 8, para. 12);

(iii) the winning and working of minerals on land occupied along with agricultural land, provided such minerals are reasonably required for use on the agricultural land, *e.g.* for fertilisation or the repair of agricultural buildings (Sched. 8, para. 5);

(iv) where a building or land was used "at a material date"[18] for a purpose falling within any of the 22 general classes specified in the Town and Country Planning (Use Classes for Third Schedule Purposes) Order 1948[19] or, if unoccupied at all times on and since July 1, 1948, was last used (otherwise than before January 7, 1937) for any such purpose, the use of that building or land for any other purpose falling within the same general class (Sched. 8, para. 6);

(v) where part only of a building or land was, "at a material date,"[20] used for a particular purpose, the use for the same purpose of an additional part of the building or land not exceeding one-tenth of the cubic content of the part of the building (as ascertained by external measurement (Sched. 8, para. 9)) or, as the case may be, not exceeding one-tenth of the land, so used on that day (Sched. 8, para. 7);

(vi) where any land was, "at a material date,"[21] comprised in a site being used for the deposit of waste materials or refuse in connection with the working of minerals, the use for the same purpose of any additional part of the site reasonably required in connection with the working of such minerals (Sched. 8, para. 8).

The first of the foregoing six classes (namely, class (i) in the preceding paragraph) is importantly affected not only by section 278 of, and Schedule 18 to, the 1971 Act but also by the restriction on

[18] The expression "at a material date" is defined (Sched. 8, para. 12) so as to mean at *either* of the following dates, that is to say:

(*a*) the appointed day, *i.e.* July 1, 1948 (s. 290(1)); *or*

(*b*) the date by reference to which Schedule 8 to the 1971 Act falls to be applied in the particular case in question:

Provided that sub-para. (*b*) is not to apply in relation to any buildings, works, or use of land in respect of which, whether before or after the date mentioned in sub-para. (*b*), an enforcement notice served before that date has become, or does become, effective.

[19] S.I. 1948 No. 955. The Sched. 3 therein referred to has been repealed and replaced by Sched. 8 to the 1971 Act.

[20] See n. 18, *supra*.

[21] See n. 18, *supra*.

compensation enacted in section 169(6A) of the 1971 Act, a new subsection inserted by the Town and Country Planning (Compensation) Act 1985, section 1(2). Section 169(6A) is in the following terms:

> "(6A) For the purposes of subsection (1) of this section [*i.e.* section 169] paragraph 3 of Schedule 8 to this Act shall be construed as not extending to the enlargement of a building which was in existence on the appointed day if—
>
> (*a*) the building contains two or more separate dwellings divided horizontally from each other or from some other part of the building; and
>
> (*b*) the enlargement would result in an increase in the number of such dwellings contained in the building or an increase of more than one tenth in the cubit content of any such dwelling contained in the building."

In effect this means that, by virtue of this amendment to section 169 of the 1971 Act, compensation will not be payable under section 169 in relation to development consisting of the enlargement of a building which was in existence on the appointed day (1st July 1948) if the building contains two or more flats and the development would result in an increase in the number of flats. (The enlargement of buildings erected on or after the appointed day is already excluded from section 169, by the provisions of section 169(6)(*a*)). It is to be noted that the restrictive effect of the new subsection (6A) applies only to the enlargement of a building containing flats by the making of more flats. A claim for compensation can still be made in respect of other buildings falling within the ambit of item (i) above.

The restriction on compensation brought about by section 169(6A) of the 1971 Act applies to any refusal or conditional grant of planning permission on any application for planning permission made after January 23, 1985 (1985 Act, s.3(3)).

Section 169(6A) reverses (as from January 24, 1985) the effect of the decision in *Peaktop Properties* (*Hampstead*) *Ltd.* v. *Camden London Borough Council* (1983) 45 P. and C.R. 177; [1982] J.P.L. 453.

D.O.E. Circular 15/85 entitled Town and Country Planning (Compensation) Act 1985 and dated July 25, 1985, deals with the restrictive effect of the 1985 Act on compensation payable on a refusal of planning permission, or a grant thereof subject to conditions, for development falling within Part II of Schedule 8 to the 1971 Act.

It is a condition precedent to the recovery of compensation in any of the six classes above mentioned and appearing in Part II of Schedule 8 to the 1971 Act, that the applicant for planning permission shall challenge the decision of the local planning authority in refusing planning permission or in granting the same subject to conditions, by appealing against such decision to the Secretary of State under section 36 of the 1971 Act (s.169(1)).

Claims for compensation must be in writing and must be made within six months (or such extended period as the Secretary of State for the Environment may allow) of the refusal of planning permission or, as the case may be, the grant thereof subject to conditions (s.169(2) and Town and Country Planning General Regulations 1976,[22] reg. 14).

It will be noted that no compensation is payable in respect of a refusal of planning permission or the grant thereof subject to conditions, in respect of the two classes of development falling within Part I of Schedule 8 to the 1971 Act, which part relates to (a) the replacement of war-damaged buildings, and (b) the use of a single dwelling-house for the purpose of two or more dwelling-houses, *e.g.* for the purpose of flats. The remedy of an aggrieved person in these cases is by way of a purchase notice[23] served by him under section 180 of the Act whereby (if the Secretary of State confirms the notice) the local authority will be obliged to buy the land affected by the planning decision complained of.

Category (3): *Compensation for interference with authorised buildings or discontinuance of authorised uses—section 170*

Development plans are liable to alteration and notions as to what constitutes the proper planning of an area change with the passing of the years. Accordingly, the proper planning of land may require from time to time the removal, or prohibition, of development originally undertaken with all due planning permission and a local planning authority may, by order made by the authority and confirmed by the Secretary of State, require the alteration or the removal of any authorised building or the discontinuance of any authorised use of land (s.51). If this is done, compensation will be payable by the local planning authority to any person in respect of the depreciation in the value of his interest in the land or in respect of the disturbance of his enjoyment of the land (s.170(1), (2), (4)). Such a person may also claim compensation for expenses reasonably incurred by him in complying with the requirements of a local planning authority respecting authorised development (s.170(3)).

Claims for compensation must be in writing and made within six months (or such extended period as the Secretary of State for the Environment may allow) of the taking effect of the order requiring

[22] S.I. 1976 No. 1419.

[23] As to purchase notices see Chap. 18.

the alteration or removal of any authorised building or, as the case may be, the discontinuance of any authorised use of land (s.170(2) and Town and Country Planning General Regulations 1976,[24] reg. 14).

Category (4): *Compensation for refusal of consent to alteration or extension of a listed building—section 171*

Where listed building consent[25] is refused by the Secretary of State for the *alteration* or *extension* of a listed building (refusal of consent for *demolition* of a listed building does not apply) and the works either do not constitute development (as defined in section 22 of the 1971 Act) or, if they do, the development is such that planning permission for it is granted by a development order, then compensation may be claimed from the local planning authority in respect of any depreciation in the value of the property (s.171).

Claims for compensation must be made in writing within six months of the refusal of listed building consent or such extended period as the Secretary of State may allow (s.171(2) and Town and Country Planning (Listed Buildings and Buildings in Conservation Areas) Regulations 1977 (S.I. 1977 No. 228), reg. 7).

Category (5): *Compensation where listed building consent revoked or modified—section 172*

Where, on the revocation or modification of listed building consent, a person can show that:

(a) he has incurred expenditure in carrying out works which are thereby rendered abortive; or

(b) he has otherwise sustained loss or damage directly attributable to such revocation or modification;

the local planning authority must pay him compensation in respect of that expenditure, loss or damage (s.172).

These provisions are extended to the revocation or modification of consent for the demolition of an unlisted building in a conservation area by the provisions of the Town and Country Planning (Listed Buildings and Buildings in Conservation Areas) Regulations 1977 (S.I. 1977 No. 228) regulation 10 and Schedule 3.

Claims for compensation must be made in writing within six months of the revocation or modification complained of or within

[24] S.I. 1976 No. 1419.

[25] See Chap. 14.

such extended period as the Secretary of State may allow (s.172(1) and Town and Country Planning (Listed Buildings and Buildings in Conservation Areas) Regulations 1977 (S.I. 1977 No. 228) reg.7).

Category (6): *Compensation for loss or damage caused by building preservation notice—section 173*

Under section 58 of the 1971 Act a building preservation notice[26] can be served by a local planning authority in respect of an unlisted building. This gives temporary protection to the building pending consideration of whether or not it should be listed by the Secretary of State. This protection lasts for six months (s.58(3)) from the service of the notice but will cease earlier if the Secretary of State lists the building under section 54 of the 1971 Act or notifies the planning authority that he does not intend to do so (*ibid.*) In the event of the Secretary of State *not* listing the building compensation may be claimed by the landowner in respect of loss or damage directly attributable to the building preservation notice (s.173(3) and (4)).

Claims for compensation must be made in writing within six months of the date or decision in respect of which the claim is made or such extended period as the Secretary of State may allow (s.173(3) and Town and Country Planning (Listed Buildings and Buildings in Conservation Areas) Regulations 1977 (S.I. 1977 No. 228) reg. 7).

Category (7): *Compensation in respect of tree preservation order—section 174*

By means of a tree preservation order,[27] a local planning authority may prevent the cutting down, topping, lopping or wilful destruction of trees and woodlands which, in the interests of amenity, the authority feels should be preserved (s.60).

Compensation may become payable by the local planning authority subject to such exceptions and conditions as may be specified in the order, to any person in respect of damage or expenditure caused or incurred by reason of the fact that any consent required by the order to be obtained from the local planning authority is either refused by the authority or is granted subject to conditions (s.174).

Category (8): *Compensation in respect of requirement as to planting of trees—section 175*

A tree preservation order must provide that, where consent is given under the order for the felling of all or any part of a woodland

[26] See Chap. 14.
[27] See Chap. 14.

area, the replanting of the felled area shall be undertaken (s.175(1)). Compensation may be claimed in respect of loss or damage sustained by the owner of a woodland arising out of a direction as to replanting given by the local planning authority or the Secretary of State (s.175(2)).

The claim for compensation must be served on the local planning authority within 12 months of the giving of the aforesaid directions or, where there is an appeal to the Secretary of State against the action of the authority in giving the direction, within 12 months of the decision of the Secretary of State on the appeal (s.175(4)). The period of 12 months may be extended by the local planning authority (*ibid.*).

Category (9): *Compensation for expenditure on removal of certain advertisements—section 176*

The control of advertisements is dealt with in sections 63 and 64 of the 1971 Act and the Town and Country Planning (Control of Advertisements) Regulations 1984.[28] The expression "advertisement" is given wide definition by section 290(1) of the 1971 Act and regulation 2 of the aforementioned Regulations.

Any person who is required to remove an advertisement which was being displayed when the first Advertisements Regulations came into force on August 1, 1948, or who is required to discontinue the use for the display of advertisements of any site which was being used for that purpose on August 1, 1948, may claim compensation from the local planning authority with respect to any expenses reasonably incurred by him in carrying out works necessary in order to comply with such requirements (s.176). The claim must be submitted in writing to the local planning authority within six months of the completion of any such works (Advertisements Regulations 1984,[29] reg. 30(1)).

Category (10): *Compensation for loss due to stop notice—section 177*

A stop notice[30] can prohibit (s.90) the carrying out of any activity which, by an enforcement notice[30] issued in respect of it (s.87), is alleged to be a breach of planning control. If the stop notice is withdrawn or if the enforcement notice in which it is dependent is quashed, varied or withdrawn (s.177(2)), compensation may be payable by the local planning authority in respect of loss or damage

[28] S.I. 1984 No. 421; see Chap. 12.
[29] S.I. 1984 No. 421.
[30] See Chap. 15.

directly attributable[31] to the prohibition contained in the stop notice (s.177(1)(4)(5) and (6)). The claim must be submitted in writing to the local planning authority within six months from the date of the decision in respect of which the claim is made (s.177(4) and Town and Country Planning General Regulations 1976[32] reg. 14) or such extended period as the Secretary of State for the Environment may allow (*ibid.*).

4. Contributions by Ministers towards Compensation paid by Local Authorities

It will be noted that, while compensation in respect of restrictions on "new development" is payable by the Secretary of State,[33] compensation in respect of restrictions on "other development" is payable by the local planning authority.[34] Provision is made (s.254) whereby a local authority may be repaid, in whole or in part by the Exchequer, any compensation which they have been called upon to pay following a decision or order made under Part III or Part IV of the 1971 Act when the decision or order was in respect of action taken, wholly or partly, in the interest of a service provided by a Government department.

5. Compensation for Planning Restrictions—The Future

A News Release from the Department of the Environment dated April 16, 1986 declares that

> "A Government review of planning compensation provisions in the Town and Country Planning Act 1971 says that there should be no change to the basic framework of the existing law of planning compensation.
>
> "This is the conclusion of a Department of Environment consultation paper published today and announced by Lord Elton in the House of Lords.
>
> "The consultation paper does, however, propose the repeal of some outdated provisions.
>
> "In answer to a written question from The Lord Campbell of Alloway who asked whether Her Majesty's Government are now in a position to publish the results of their review of planning compensation, Lord Elton said:

[31] *J. Sample (Warkworth) Ltd.* v. *Alnwick District Council* (1984) J.P.L. 670.
[32] S.I. 1976 No. 1419.
[33] See p. 373.
[34] *Ibid.*

> 'A consultation paper on the compensation provisions of the Town and Country Planning Act 1971 is being sent to interested bodies today and copies are being placed in the Library.
>
> 'During the passage of the Town and Country Planning (Compensation) Act 1985, the Government undertook to review these provisions. The consultation paper concludes that there should be no change to the basic framework of the existing law of planning compensation, but proposes amendment of a number of the provisions.' "

The Consultation Paper is still (February 1987) going the rounds of professional, local government and other interested bodies.

Chapter 18

PURCHASE NOTICES AND PLANNING BLIGHT

1. Purchase Notices for Interests Affected by Planning Decisions or Orders

(1) *Service of a purchase notice*

On a refusal, either by a local planning authority or by the Secretary of State, of planning permission for development of land, or on a grant of planning permission subject to conditions, an aggrieved applicant, provided he is an "owner" as defined in section 290(1) of the 1971 Act (and a freeholder who has let his land for less than a rack-rent is excluded by the definition[1]), may, *in certain cases,* require his interest in the land affected by the planning decision to be purchased by the council of the London borough or county district for the area where the land is situated (s.180(1)). The requirement must be by a notice in writing called a "purchase notice" (s.180(7)) given within 12 months of the planning decision on which the service of the notice is founded (s.180(1) and Town and Country Planning General Regulations 1976,[2] reg. 14).

A purchase notice cannot be founded on a "deemed" refusal of planning permission operating under section 37 of the 1971 Act. In such a case an owner (provided he was the applicant for planning permission) must first appeal to the Secretary of State under section 37 and get a confirmation by the Secretary of State of the "deemed" refusal of permission, after which he will be able to serve a purchase notice under section 180 of the Act.

The law relating to purchase notices and the service of such a notice on a local authority by an owner of land who has been refused planning permission or had it granted subject to conditions is complex indeed. Much useful information about this sphere of planning law is to be found in the Memorandum to D.O.E. Circular 13/83.

(2) *Action by the Secretary of State*

Except when the council on whom a purchase notice is served are, of their own accord, willing to comply with it or can get some other

[1] *London Corporation* v. *Cusack-Smith* [1955] A.C. 377, H.L.; see also *Smart and Courtney Dale Ltd.* v. *Dover R.D.C.* (1972) 23 P. & C.R. 408.

[2] S.I. 1976 No. 1419.

local authority or statutory undertaker to comply with it (s.181(1)(*a*), (*b*)) and buy the interest referred to in it (s.181(2)), a purchase notice needs confirmation by the Secretary of State before it can become effective (ss.181(1)(*c*),(3), 182).

Before confirming a purchase notice (ss.182(1) and 183(1)) or taking any other action open to him in lieu of confirming the notice—such as granting planning permission for development as sought by the applicant (s.183(2)), or directing a grant of planning permission for some other kind of development on an application therefor being made (s.183(3)), the Secretary of State must give notice of his proposed action to the person who served the notice, to the council on whom it was served, to the local planning authority and to any other local authority who might be substituted for the council on whom the notice was served (s.182(2)). The Secretary of State must afford any of these persons or authorities which require it an opportunity of being heard by his Inspector before he takes action in the matter[3] (s.182(3)). However, where the Secretary of State has given notice of his proposed action and his Inspector has heard interested parties, the Secretary of State is *not* precluded from taking a different line of action if it appears to him to be expedient so to do (s.182(4)).

(3) *Special provisions as to compensation*

Where the Secretary of State, in lieu of confirming a purchase notice, takes one of the alternative courses open to him under section 183 and directs (under s.183(3)) that there shall be granted planning permission, not for the development sought by the owner, but for some other kind of development, compensation will become payable by the local planning authority (s.187(2)) if the permitted development value of the owner's interest is thereby shown to be less than its existing use value (s.187(2), (5)). The "permitted development value" of the owners's interest is the value attaching to it having regard to the amount of development which would be permitted under the Secretary of State's direction (s.187(5)), whilst the "existing use value" of that interest means the value attaching to it for its existing use and as if all the development regarded as falling within the ambit of the existing use of land and referred to in Schedule 8 to the 1971 Act were permitted (*ibid.*).

The claim for compensation must be made to the local planning authority within six months of the decision on which the claim is

[3] *Ealing Corporation* v. *Minister of Housing and Local Government* [1952] Ch. 856.

based (Town and Country Planning General Regulations 1976,[4] reg. 14).

(4) *Challenging Secretary of State's decision*

The decision of the Secretary of State either to confirm or not to confirm a purchase notice, or to grant planning permission in lieu of confirming a purchase notice, may be challenged within six weeks on a point of law by application in the High Court (ss.242(1)(*e*), (3)(*i*), (*j*), and 245). Where, upon any such challenge, the Secretary of State's decision is quashed, the purchase notice is to be treated as cancelled, but this is without prejudice to the right of the owner to serve a further purchase notice (s.186(4), (5)).

(5) *Grounds for confirming a purchase notice*

Before confirming a purchase notice the Secretary of State must be satisfied (ss.183(1) and 180(1), (2) and (3)):

(a) that the land to which it relates has become incapable of reasonably beneficial use in its existing state; *and*

(b) in a case where permission to develop the land has been granted subject to conditions, that the land cannot be rendered capable of reasonably beneficial use if the development is undertaken in accordance with these conditions; *and*

(c) in any case, that the land cannot be rendered capable of reasonably beneficial use by the carrying out of any other development for which permission

   (i) has been granted, *or*

   (ii) has been undertaken to be granted by the local planning authority or by the Secretary of State.

In the forgoing conditions (a), (b) and (c), when reference is made to "the land," this means the whole of the land to which the purchase notice relates. In other words, a purchase notice will be invalid if the person (or persons) who serve it does, (or do) not own *the whole* of the land in respect of which it has been served.[5] Moreover, it must, again, be *the whole* of the land (and not merely a part of it) which has become incapable of reasonably beneficial use and the Secretary of State has refused to confirm a purchase notice on the ground that *part* of the land (for which planning permission has

[4] S.I. 1976 No. 1419.

[5] *Smart and Courtenay Dale Ltd.* v. *Dover R.D.C.* (1972) 23 P. & C.R. 408.

earlier been refused) is still capable of reasonably beneficial use in its existing state.[6]

The decision of the Secretary of State as to whether the foregoing conditions precedent to the confirmation of a purchase notice—conditions (a), (b) and (c) set out above—have been satisfied can be challenged by *certiorari* if there is an error on the face of the order made by him; that is to say, if he makes a speaking order which discloses an error in law.[7]

It will be noted that section 180 of the 1971 Act requires it to be shown that "the land has become incapable of reasonably beneficial use in its existing state." The words "in its existing state" are of crucial importance both to the landowner and to the local authority because they narrow down the cases in which the landowner can "unload" his land on to the local authority.

The prime need for section 19 of the Town and Country Planning Act 1947 (the predecessor of s.180 of the 1971 Act) was to meet the case of a war-damaged plot of land (often near a city or town centre) the redevelopment of which was prevented by planning restrictions imposed because the blitzed area which incorporated the particular plot of land was to be relaid out and redeveloped as a whole consequent upon general war damage in the district. In such a case the war-damaged plot *in its existing state* (it was probably a heap of rubble or a hole in the ground) was clearly incapable of any beneficial use and therefore, under section 19 of the 1947 Act, was liable to have to be purchased by the local authority.

The question is, and always has been, to what kind of development is it appropriate and lawful to pay regard when deciding whether land is incapable of reasonably beneficial use in its existing state. There was a tendency, particularly where planning permission was refused for the development of green belt land which, being situated on the fringe of a town, could be said to be ripe for development, to pay attention to the possibility of the land's potential development into, for example, a residential suburb. But the law, as now contained in section 180 of the 1971 Act, requires that the owner who serves a purchase notice must make his case on one ground only—the uselessness of his land in its existing state. He must be able to show that his land, *quite apart from any potential value for development which it may have,* has become incapable of reasonably beneficial use in its existing state (s.180(2)).

[6] *Wain* v. *Secretary of State for the Environment and Wigan Metropolitan Borough Council and Another* (1982) J.P.L. 244, C.A.

[7] *R.* v. *Minister of Housing and Local Government, ex p. Chichester R.D.C.* (1960) 2 All E.R. 407.

The Memorandum (previously mentioned) to D.O.E. Circular 13/83 has some informative and helpful observations (particularly in paras. 12 and 13) on the manner in which the Secretary of State interprets the meaning of the highly important words, "the land has become incapable of reasonably beneficial use[8] in its existing state," and used in section 180(1)(*a*) of the 1971 Act. Paragraphs 12 and 13 of the Memorandum are in the following terms:

> "12. The question to be considered in every case is whether the land in its existing state, taking into account operations and uses for which planning permission (or listed building consent) is not required, is "incapable of reasonably beneficial use." The onus is on the server of the notice to show that this is so. No account is taken of any prospective use of the land which would involve the carrying-out of new development (see section 22 of the 1971 Act) or (in the case of a notice served under section 180 of the 1971 Act) would contravene the condition, which is contained in Schedule 18 to the 1971 Act, regarding the creation of floor space in buildings. In the case of a listed building purchase notice, no account is taken of any prospective use of the land which would involve the carrying out of new development or of any works which require listed building consent, other than works for which the local planning authority or the Secretary of State have undertaken to grant such consent.
>
> "13. In considering what capacity for use the land has, relevant factors are the physical state of the land, its size, shape and surroundings, and the general pattern of land-uses in the area; a use of relatively low value may be regarded as reasonably beneficial if such a use is common for similar land in the vicinity. It may sometimes be possible for an area of land to be rendered capable of reasonably beneficial use by being used in conjunction with neighbouring or adjoining land, provided that a sufficient interest in that land is held by the server of the notice, or by a prospective owner of the purchase notice land.

[8] As to "reasonably beneficial use" see, further, decisions and comments in *R.* v. *Minister of Housing and Local Government, ex parte Chichester R.D.C.* (1960) 1 W.L.R. 587; *Adams and Wade Ltd.* v. *Minister of Housing and Local Government* (1965) 18 P. & C.R. 60; *General Estates Company Ltd.* v. *Minister of Housing and Local Government* (1965) E.G. April 17; *Leominster Borough Council* v. *Minister of Housing and Local Government* (1971) 218 E.G. 1419; *West Bromwich County Borough Council* v. *Minister of Housing and Local Government* (1968) 206 E.G. 1085; *Purbeck District Council* v. *Secretary of State for the Environment* (1982) J.P.L. 640. See also "Journal of Planning and Environment Law" at (1958) J.P.L. 897; (1967) J.P.L. 299; (1967) J.P.L. 491; (1973) J.P.L. 604; (1976) J.P.L. 189; and (1977) J.P.L. 256.

Use by a prospective owner cannot be taken into account unless there is a reasonably firm indication that there is in fact a prospective owner of the purchase notice site. In this paragraph the word "owner" is used to include a person who has a tenancy of the land or some other interest which is sufficient to enable him to use the land. Profit *may* be a useful comparison in certain circumstances, but the absence of profit (however calculated) is not necessarily material: the concept of reasonably beneficial use is not synonymous with profit."

The Secretary of State may refuse to confirm a purchase notice where the land, in whole or in part, has a restricted use by virtue of a previous planning permission (s.184). This would occur in the following circumstances.

If land in respect of which a purchase notice has been served has *a restricted use* by reason of the fact that some previous planning permission has required that the land shall be used only for a restricted purpose (the reason for this being that the land in question is part of a larger area for which planning permission for development was previously granted subject to the condition that the land in respect of which the purchase notice was later served should not be developed at all or should be developed only in some restricted fashion) then, if the land is restricted in this fashion, the Secretary of State can decline to confirm the purchase notice if it appears to him that the land in question ought, in accordance with the previous planning permission, to remain undeveloped or restricted as to the manner of its development. This is the position notwithstanding the fact that, by virtue of the previous planning decision, the land in question has become incapable of reasonably beneficial use in its existing state (s.184(3)). The effect of section 184 of the 1971 Act is to nullify the decision in *Adams and Wade Ltd.* v. *Ministry of Housing and Local Government and Wokingham R.D.C.* (1965) 18 P. & C.R. 60.[9]

Where development has been carried out without planning permission but the breach is not enforceable by the local planning authority against the landowner (because of, for example, the passage of time), the landowner can rely on his own unlawful activity to establish that his land has no reasonable beneficial use—*Balco Transport Services Ltd.* v. *Secretary of State for the Environment and Maidstone Borough Council* (1985) J.P.L. 722; (1986) J.P.L. 123. In the Court of Appeal Glidewell, L.J. declared that the maxim that a man cannot take advantage of his own wrong had no application to the question

[9] See further, *Plymouth Corporation* v. *Secretary of State for the Environment* (1972) 24 P. & C.R. 88; *Sheppard* v. *Secretary of State for the Environment* (1974) 233 E.G. 1167; (1974) J.P.L. 38 and (1983) J.P.L. 753.

where the land has become incapable of reasonably beneficial use in its existing state.

(6) *Effect of Secretary of State's action*

When the Secretary of State confirms a purchase notice the local authority affected by the notice are deemed to be authorised to acquire compulsorily the interest of the "owner" who served the notice and to have served a notice to treat to acquire that interest (s.186(1)). Such a constructive notice to treat may not be withdrawn (s.208).

If the Secretary of State, within the "relevant period", that is to say, within the period of nine months of the service of the purchase notice or within six months of the transmission of a copy of the notice to the Secretary of State (whichever is the shorter period—(s.186(3)), has, on the one hand, neither confirmed the notice (nor taken alternative action in lieu of confirmation) nor, on the other hand, notified the "owner" who served the notice that he, the Secretary of State, does not intend to confirm it, then in such case the notice is deemed to have been confirmed at the end of the period above mentioned and the local authority on whom the notice was served are deemed to be authorised to acquire compulsorily the interest of the "owner" and to have served a notice to treat (which, again is incapable of being withdrawn (s.208)) to acquire that interest (s.186(2)).

The aforesaid "relevant period" will not run if the Secretary of State has before him at the same time both a copy of the purchase notice transmitted to him under section 181(3) of the 1971 Act and an appeal notice, under any of the following provisions of the Act, relating to any of the land to which the purchase notice relates—

section 36 (appeal against refusal of planning permission, etc.);
section 88 (appeal against enforcement notice);
section 95 (appeal against refusal of established use certificate);
section 97 (appeal against listed building enforcement notice); or
paragraphs 8 or 9 of Schedule 11 (appeal against refusal of listed building consent, etc.) (s.186(3A) added by Housing and Planning Act 1986 s.49(1)(f) and Sched. 11, Pt.I, para.7(1)).

(7) *Purchase notices in other cases*

A purchase notice may be served not only when there is a planning decision refusing planning permission for development or granting permission subject to conditions but also when an order is made under section 45 of the 1971 Act revoking or modifying an existing grant of planning permission (s.188 and Town and Country Planning General Regulations 1976,[10] reg. 14).

Similarly, a purchase notice may follow the making of an order under section 51 of the 1971 Act requiring the discontinuance of an existing use of land or the alteration or removal of existing buildings or works on land (s.189 and Town and Country Planning General Regulations 1976,[11] reg. 14).

The provisions of sections 180 to 183, 186 and 187 of the 1971 Act relating to purchase notices, together with regulation 14 of the Town and Country Planning General Regulations 1976[11] are also applied in the case of a Tree Preservation Order[12] (s.60(1)(*c*) referring to ss.60(2)(*b*) and 191(1)), and to the control of advertisements[13] (s.63(2)(*c*) referring to ss.60(2)(*b*) and 191(1)).

2. Owner-Occupiers Adversely Affected by Planning Proposals—Planning Blight

(1) *When planning blight arises*

The making and coming into effect under the Town and Country Planning Act 1971 of a development plan can have dramatic effects on the value of land. Whilst the development plan does not itself grant any permission for development, it does show the kind of thing for which permission may well be granted if it is sought. Thus a development plan may, merely by coming into operation, drain away development value from land or, conversely, may attract development value, to land.

The draining away of development value has been referred to, somewhat inelegantly, as "planning blight" and so important has this matter come to be regarded that the 1971 Act makes special provision to deal with it. There is good reason for this for a small symbol on a development plan may mean a great deal to the owner of the land to which the symbol is attached. If, for example, the symbol shows a new highway is to be constructed across a man's land, then he may find it impossible either to sell his land or to get planning permission to develop it himself, assuming he wants to do so. But whilst the development plan may show a proposed road it will not necessarily show the particular year in which the road is to be

[10] S.I. 1976 No. 1419.
[11] S.I. 1976 No. 1419.
[12] See Chap. 14.
[13] See Chap. 12.

constructed and, even if it does, it may yet turn out to be the case that, for one reason or another, the authority who are responsible for constructing the road are not able to get on with the work at the date contemplated by the development plan. In the meantime, what is to happen to the landowner whose land is blighted in this fashion? Sections 192 to 208 of the 1971 Act make provision for this by means of a procedure which may be termed "compulsory purchase in reverse."

Sections 192 to 208 of the 1971 Act must now be read together with Part V—"Planning Blight; Extension of Classes of Blighted Land"—of the Land Compensation Act 1973, and with section 147 of the Local Government, Planning and Land Act 1980 relating to planning blight in an urban development area designated under section 134 of that Act.[14]

All these enactments taken together provide statutory relief for *resident owner-occupiers of houses* and for *owner-occupiers of farms and small businesses* whose property has become unsaleable by reason of the incidence of any one of the 10 sets of circumstances itemised in section 192(1) of the 1971 Act, as extended by the provisions of Part V of the Land Compensation Act 1973 and section 147 of the Local Government, Planning and Land Act 1980. While these enactments are wide enough to catch more than provisions in development plans which have the effect of depressing land values, their ambit is not as wide as some had hoped and their limited scope needs to be watched closely.

Accordingly it is proposed first to examine those cases where planning blight comes within the ambit of sections 192 to 208 of the 1971 Act, secondly, to examine the extensions to these provisions enacted by Part V of the Land Compensation Act 1973 and section 147 of the Local Government, Planning and Land Act 1980, and, thirdly, to examine what persons can, in those cases, make a claim for compensation arising from planning blight.

By way of warning it should be mentioned that sections 192 to 208 of the 1971 Act are intricate in the extreme, containing a good deal of legislation in one section by reference to the contents of another section. Many expressions used in these 17 sections are given specialised definition, for which reference should be made to sections 203, 205, 206 and 207 of the 1971 Act. Special provisions as to hereditaments or agricultural units occupied by a partnership firm are contained in section 204 of the Act.

[14] See Chap. 23.

Part IV of the Memorandum to M.H.L.G. Circular 48/59 gives general advice on the obligation of a local authority to purchase, in certain instances, the interests of owner-occupiers affected by planning blight.

Turning then to the cases which fall within the ambit of sections 192 to 208 of the 1971 Act, it may be stated that there are 10 classes of proposal (not all of them associated with development plans) in respect of which a claim arising from planning blight can be made. The 10 classes are, briefly, where land is:

(1) land indicated in a structure plan in force for the district in which the land is situated either as land which may be required for the purposes of any functions of a government department, local authority or statutory undertakers, or of the National Coal Board, or of a telecommunication system, or as land which may be included in an action area (s.192(1)(*a*));

(2) land allocated for the purposes of any such functions by a local plan in force for the district in which it is situated, or is land defined in such a plan as the site of proposed development for the purposes of any such functions (s.192(1)(*b*));

(3) land indicated in a development plan as land on which a highway is to be constructed, improved or altered (s.192(1)(*c*));

(4) land on or adjacent to the line of a highway indicated in an order or scheme operating under Part II of the Highways Act 1980 or under the corresponding provisions of Part II of the Highways Act 1959, or section 1 of the Highways Act 1971, being land in relation to which compulsory acquisition may be exercisable under Part XII of the Highways Act 1980, the land being required for purposes of the construction, improvement or alteration of a highway as indicated in the aforesaid order or scheme (s.192(1)(*d*));

(5) land shown on plans approved by a resolution of a local highway authority as land comprised in a highway proposed to be constructed, approved or altered (s.192(1)(*e*));

(6) land on which the Secretary of State proposes to provide a trunk road or a special road and has given to the local planning authority written notice of his intention together with maps and plans (s.192(1)(*f*));

(7) land in respect of which there is in force a compulsory purchase order providing for the acquisition of rights over the land where the appropriate authority have power to serve, but have not served, notice to treat in respect of such rights (s.192(1)(*g*));

(8) land indicated under section 257 of the Housing Act 1985 as land proposed to be acquired under Part VIII of that Act as a general improvement area (s.192(1)(*h*));

(9) land authorised by a special Act of Parliament to be compulsorily acquired (s.192(1)(*i*));

(10) land in respect of which a compulsory purchase order is in force but no notice to treat has been served (s.192(1)(*j*)).

On the point of land (item (5), above) shown on a plan approved by resolution of a local highway authority, it may be noted that the Secretary of State, in the Memorandum to Ministry Circular No. 48/59 dated August 11, 1959, declared (in para. 57) that

> "... the attention of local highway authorities is drawn to paragraph (*f*) of [section 39(1) of the 1959 Act—now section 192(1)(*e*) of the 1971 Act], which refers to 'land shown on plans approved by a resolution of a local highway authority.' The Minister understands that decisions to carry out road schemes are sometimes taken without the formal approval of plans by resolution. He suggests that, where necessary, local highway authorities should review their procedures so as to ensure that owner-occupiers whose property is blighted by road schemes will not be deprived of the remedy offered by the [1971] Act."

The list of 10 classes set out above shows those instances of planning blight in respect of which something may be done under the 1971 Act.

These 10 classes of blight are now extended by sections 68 to 76 of the Land Compensation Act 1973. These sections give, in general, statutory effect to the advice formerly given to local authorities in Ministry Circular 46/70 dated June 5, 1970 now cancelled.

The effect of the extensions (10 in number) enacted by sections 68 to 76 of the Land Compensation Act 1973 is to give relief from blight in the case of land affected by:

(1) proposals in structure plans and alterations thereto where the plan or alteration has been submitted to the Secretary of State but has not come into force (1973 Act, s.68(1)(*a*) and (*b*));

(2) modifications proposed to be made by the Secretary of State in a submitted structure plan (1973 Act, s.68(1)(*c*));

(3) proposals in a local plan or proposals for alterations to such a plan where the plan or proposed alterations have been made available for inspection under the publicity arrangements in the 1971 Act (1973 Act, s.68(2)(*a*) and (*b*));

(4) modifications proposed to be made by the Secretary of State

or the local planning authority in a local plan (1973 Act, s.68(2)(*c*));

(5) proposals submitted to the Secretary of State for alterations to an "old style" development plan, in force until superseded by the current style of development plan (involving a structure plan and, maybe, also a local plan or plans), and by modifications proposed to be made by the Secretary of State in such proposals (1973 Act, s.68(3));

(6) highway orders or schemes submitted for confirmation to, or prepared in draft by, the Secretary of State where notice of the order has been published (1973 Act, s.69);

(7) compulsory purchase orders submitted for confirmation to, or prepared in draft by, a Minister where notice of the order has been published, including orders providing for the acquisition of rights over land (1973 Act, ss.70 and 75);

(8) an indication in a plan (other than a development plan) approved by the local planning authority for development control purposes that the land may be required for the purposes of a government department, local authority or statutory undertakers (1973 Act, s.71(1)(*a*));

(9) action which the local planning authority have resolved to take to safeguard the land for the purposes of development by such bodies, or by directions of the Secretary of State restricting the grant of planning permission in order to safeguard the land for such development (1973 Act, s.71(1)(*b*));

(10) the proposed exercise of powers under section 22(1) of the Land Compensation Act 1973 to acquire land for the purpose of mitigating any adverse effect which the existence or use of a new or improved highway may have on the surroundings of the highway (1973 Act, s.74).

To the foregoing 20 classes of blight—10 arising under the 1971 Act and 10 under the Land Compensation Act 1973—there must now be added one further class of blight and that is blight arising from the designation of land as an urban development area under section 134 (see also s.147) of the Local Government, Planning and Land Act 1980.

(2) *Owner-occupiers who are entitled to claim*

Once the narrowly defined cases of blight which are capable of being dealt with under the 1971 Act, as extended by the Land Compensation Act 1973, and the Local Government, Planning and Local Act 1980, have been appreciated, the next question to determine is what sort of persons can take action. Such persons are, generally speaking, *owners* of one kind or another and they fall into three categories as follows:

(1) the "resident owner-occupier" (see s.203(3)) of a hereditament" (see s.207(1)) wholly or partly contained in the blighted land which includes a private dwelling-house occupied by him (s.192(3), (4)(*b*));

(2) the non-resident "owner-occupier" (see s.203(1)) of a hereditament (see s.207(1))—other than a private dwelling-house—as, for example, a hereditament used for business purposes not exceeding the prescribed limit of annual value, namely, £2,250, which hereditament is wholly or partly contained in the blighted land (s.192(3), (4)(*a*) and Town and Country Planning (Limit of Annual Value) Order 1973[15]);

(3) the "owner-occupier" (see s.203(2)) of an "agricultural unit" (see s.207(1))—as, for example, a farm, grazing land, market garden, etc. (see definition of "agriculture" in section 290(1))—wholly or partly contained in the blighted land (s.192(3), (5)).

For the foregoing purposes an owner-occupier includes not only a freeholder but also a tenant having a tenancy granted (or extended) for a term of years certain of which at least three years remain unexpired (s.203(4)).

Before qualifying to make a claim an owner-occupier of a hereditament must have occupied the hereditament either *in whole or in part* for a period of at least six months immediately prior to making his claim, *or* for a period of at least six months before leaving the premises unoccupied for a period of not longer than 12 months immediately prior to making his claim (s.203(1)). If the occupation is of *part only* of a hereditament it must, nevertheless, be occupation of a *substantial part* (*ibid.*).

An owner who stopped living in his house some 10 years previously but who continued to store goods in three sheds in the garden of the house and in the garage is not such an owner-occupier of the house as brings him within the ambit of the blight provisions of the 1971 Act.[16]

A Nonconformist chapel not being liable, as a place of worship, to be assessed for rates (Rating and Valuation (Miscellaneous Provisions) Act 1955, s.7), was entered, in accordance with Rule 22 of the Valuation Lists Rule 1955,[17] in the local valuation list as

[15] S.I. 1973 No. 425.
[16] *Ministry of Transport* v. *Holland* (1962) 14 P. & C.R. 259.
[17] S.I. 1955 No. 1680.

"exempt." In other words, the annual value of the chapel was not entered as "nil." It was given, as the opinion of the court, that since no value was shown in the valuation list and the premises were entered as "exempt," it could not be said that their value was either greater or less than a specified sum, and hereditaments of that kind did not qualify for protection from blight.[18]

In the case of a claim by the owner-occupier of an agricultural unit, the owner-occupier must show that he has occupied *the whole* of the agricultural unit either for a period of at least six months immediately prior to making his claim; *or* for a period of at least six months ending not more than six months before the making of the claim (s.203(2)).

Apart from "owner" it is to be noted that a mortgagee is also given specific power (s.201) to take advantage of sections 192 to 207 of the 1971 Act relating to the obligatory purchase of land by a local authority on the ground of planning blight.

(3) *Service of purchase notice relating to planning blight*

If qualified as above mentioned, the owner-occupier of hereditament can require the whole of the hereditament to be taken off his hands whilst the owner-occupier of an agricultural unit can require action to be taken in respect of that part of the agricultural unit which falls within the area of blight (s.196).

The power to serve a blight notice is dealt with in section 193 of the 1971 Act. Provided a person is the owner-occupier (as detailed above) of land blighted (as detailed above) by planning proposals, then the 1971 Act authorises him to serve a blight notice (in accordance with the Town and Country Planning General Regulations 1976[19] reg. 18 and Sched. 1) requiring the acquisition of his interest in the blighted land by the "appropriate authority" (s.205), *i.e.* the authority which would, at some later date in the future, have come to acquire that interest compulsorily in accordance with the planning proposals which have currently brought about the blight (s.193(1)). In serving such a notice the owner-occupier must show that:

(1) he has, at some time (*i.e.* at any time), made reasonable efforts to sell his interest in the blighted land (s.193(1)(*c*) as amended by the Land Compensation Act 1973, ss.77(1), 186, Sched. 3); and
(2) that he could not have sold it except at a price substantially

[18] *Essex C.C.* v. *Essex Incorporated Congregational Church Union* [1963] A.C. 808, H.L.
[19] S.I. 1976 No. 1419.

lower than that for which it might reasonably have been expected to sell if no part of the land had been affected by the blight (s.193(1)(*d*) as amended by the Land Compensation Act 1973, s.77(2)).

Whilst the service of a blight notice is dealt with in subsection (1) of section 193 of the 1971 Act, the restrictive provisions of subsection (2) of section 193 need to be carefully noted. Section 193(2) carries an important proviso which precludes a person from serving a blight notice in respect of his interest in *part* of a hereditament or unit affected by blight if, in fact, he is entitled to an interest in the *whole* of the hereditament or the unit (s.193(2) proviso (*a*) and (*b*)). This complex matter was the subject of discussion before the Lands Tribunal in *Binns* v. *Secretary of State for Transport*.[20]

A blight notice served by an owner-occupier may be withdrawn by him at any time before compensation for the acquisition of his land has been determined by the Lands Tribunal *or* within a period of six weeks after any such determination (s.198(1)), but there can be no such withdrawal if the acquiring authority have entered on the land in pursuance of the notice to treat which is deemed to have been served in consequence of the blight notice (s.198(2)). No compensation is payable in connection with the withdrawal of the notice to treat which is deemed to be withdrawn on the withdrawal by the owner-occupier of the blight notice (s.198(3)).

If an owner-occupier dies after serving a blight notice his personal representatives take over his powers and responsibilities in the matter (s.200).

Where at the date of his death an owner-occupier was in a position to serve a blight notice, his personal representatives may do so (Land Compensation Act 1973, s.78).

(4) *Service of counter-notice by appropriate authority*

The question of whether the price which the owner-occupier could have got for his land in the open market is a price "substantially lower" than its price in the open market if it had not been affected by blight is a matter of valuation and opinion. Accordingly, provision is made for any blight notice served by an owner-occupier calling for the purchase of his land to be challenged or objected to within two months by the appropriate authority on whom the notice was served (s.194). Both the service of a blight notice by an owner-occupier upon the appropriate authority and the service by the appropriate

[20] Lands Tribunal (V. G. Wellings Esquire Q.C.) (1985) June 17, Ref.158/1984—(1985) J.P.L. 647.

authority of a counter-notice upon the owner-occupier, are referred to in the Town and Country Planning General Regulations 1976,[21] regulation 18 and Schedule 1.

A counter-notice may be served by the appropriate authority on one or more of the following grounds (s.194(2)), namely:

(1) that no part of the hereditament or agricultural unit required to be purchased is comprised in land directly affected by blight as specified above (see s.192(1)(*a*)–(*j*), Land Compensation Act 1973, ss.68–76 and Local Government, Planning and Land Act 1980, s.134);

(2) that the appropriate authority do not propose to acquire compulsorily any part of the hereditament or, in the case of an agricultural unit, any part of the area of that unit which is directly affected by the blight;

(3) that the appropriate authority propose to acquire a part of the hereditament or (in the case of an agricultural unit) a part of the affected area specified in the counter-notice, but do not propose to acquire any other part of that hereditament or that area;

(4) that in the case of land falling within section 192(1)(*a*) or (*c*) but not (*d*), (*e*) or (*f*) of thc 1971 Act—in other words, items (1) or (3) but not items (4), (5) or (6) on page 394, the appropriate authority do *not* propose to acquire any part of the hereditament, or (in the case of an agricultural unit) any part of the affected area, during a period of 15 years from the date of the counter-notice, or during such longer period from that date as may be specified in the counter-notice;

(5) that, on the date of the service of the blight notice by the owner-occupier upon the appropriate authority, the owner-occupier had no interest in the hereditament or agricultural unit;

(6) that (for reasons specified in the counter-notice) the owner-occupier is not a freeholder or a tenant with a term of at least three years yet to run;

(7) that the owner-occupier, making reasonable endeavours, could have sold his interest in the blighted land at a price which was not substantially lower than it would have been if no part of the land had been comprised in land affected by the blight.

An objection may not be made (s.194(3)) under item (4) above if it can be made under item (2) above.

[21] S.I. 1976 No. 1419.

The matter of the 15 years referred to under item (4) above is an important one because it allows the appropriate authority to neutralise the effect of a blight notice by declaring their intention to postpone action on the planning proposals which have caused blight to occur.

A counter-notice served under any of the foregoing provisions must specify the grounds on which the appropriate authority object to the blight notice (s.194(5)).

Where a counter-notice has been served the owner-occupier may, within a period of two months from the date of the service of the counter-notice, require the matter to be referred for decision by the Lands Tribunal (s.195(1)).

Except in a case where the appropriate authority deny that they have any intention to acquire any part of the blighted land (s.195(3)), any ground of objection set out in the appropriate authority's counter-notice *must* be upheld on appeal to the Lands Tribunal *unless* it is shown, to the satisfaction of the Tribunal, that the objection is *not* "well-founded" (s.195(2)). In other words, the onus is on the owner-occupier to show that any ground of objection set out in the appropriate authority's counter-notice is not well founded *except* in a case where the authority denies any intention to acquire the blighted land compulsorily in which case the onus is on the authority to show that their objection *is* "well founded" (s.195(3)). Thus any argument about whether or not a blight notice can be countered on the 15-year principle above quoted is a matter which can be referred for arbitration to the Lands Tribunal and the 15-year basis of objection is not to be upheld unless the Tribunal is satisfied that it is "well founded" (*ibid.*).[22]

(5) *Effect of valid purchase notice relating to planning blight*

If the Lands Tribunal determine not to uphold the counter-notice they must declare that the notice served by the owner-occupier is valid (s.195(4)) and the appropriate authority are then deemed to be authorised to acquire compulsorily the interest of the owner-occupier and to have served a notice to treat so to do (s.196(1)), the notice to treat being dated as specified in directions to be given by the Tribunal (ss.195(6), 196(2)(*a*)).

Similarly, where no counter-notice is served by an appropriate

[22] As to the limited extent of the jurisdiction of the Lands Tribunal when a matter of planning blight is referred to it for decision under section 195(1) of the 1971 Act, see the arguments set out in *Binns* v. *Secretary of State for Transport*, Lands Tribunal, June 17, 1985, Ref.158/1984; (1985) J.P.L. 647.

authority, the authority will be deemed to have served a notice to treat (s.196(1)) on a date which will be two months after the date on which the blight notice was served by the owner-occupier (s.196(2)(*b*)).

A constructive notice to treat (*i.e.* one which, in the foregoing circumstances, is *deemed* to have been served) may not be withdrawn (s.208) though where the blight notice requiring purchase is itself withdrawn (s.198), any notice to treat deemed to have been served in consequence of that notice is also deemed to have been withdrawn (s.198(1)) and no compensation is payable in respect of any such withdrawing (s.198(3)). But a blight notice cannot be withdrawn if the appropriate authority have already entered and taken possesion of land in pursuance of a notice to treat deemed to have been served in consequence of the blight notice (s.198(2)).

(6) *Compensation*

The price to be paid for the blighted land on compulsory acquisition pursuant to a blight notice served by an owner-occupier will be the "unblighted" price of the land in the open market (Land Compensation Act 1961, s.9) that is to say, the value of the land *not* (as was previously the case) at the date of the deemed notice to treat but (since the House of Lords decision in *Birmingham Corporation* v. *West Midland Baptist* (*Trust*) *Association* (*Inc.*)[23] at the date when compensation is agreed or assessed, or the date (if earlier) when possession is taken.

Compensation for severance and disturbance in connection with planning blight was formerly excluded by section 143 of the Town and Country Planning Act 1962, which section was repealed by the Town and Country Planning Act 1968. Thus, compensation under these two heads may now be claimed.

[23] [1970] A.C. 874.

Chapter 19

TOWN PLANNING AND COMPULSORY PURCHASE OF LAND

1. Powers as to Compulsory Purchase of Land

The statutory grounds on which a local authority or the Secretary of State for the Environment can acquire land compulsorily for the purposes of town and country planning are set out in sections 112 and 113 of the 1971 Act.

Section 112 confers compulsory purchase powers on the councils of counties and county districts, and the councils of London boroughs (s.112(5)). The Secretary of State may, under the 1971 Act (s.112(1)), authorise any of the foregoing local authorities to acquire compulsorily any land in their area being:

(a) land which is *suitable* for and is *required* in order to secure the carrying out of one or more of the following activities, namely, development, re-development and improvement; or

(b) land which is *required* for a purpose which it is necessary to achieve in the interests of the proper planning of an area in which the land is situated.

In considering whether land is *suitable* for development, re-development or improvement (as mentioned in the previous paragraph) both the local authority concerned and the Secretary of State must (s.112(1A)) have regard:

(a) to the provisions of the development plan so far as material;

(b) to whether planning permission for any development on the land is in force; and

(c) to any other considerations which, on an application for planning permission for development of the land, would be material for the purpose of determining that application.

Where a local authority is authorised, as mentioned above, by the Secretary of State to acquire land compulsorily, they are also empowered (s.112(1B)) to acquire compulsorily:

(a) any land adjoining that land which is required for the purpose of executing works for facilitating its development or use; or

(b) where that land forms part of a common or open space or fuel or field garden allotment, any land which is required for the purpose of being given in exchange for the land which is being acquired.

If a local authority do acquire land under the foregoing provisions of the 1971 Act, the authority are not obliged, in order to achieve those purposes for which the land was acquired, to undertake any activity themselves (s.112(1C)). The question of who does the work necessary to achieve the purposes of the acquisition is immaterial (*ibid.*).

In connection with the foregoing provisions the Secretary of State may authorise a local authority to acquire land which is within the area of another local authority (s.112(2)), but before doing this he must consult with the local authority for the area where the land is situated (s.112(3)).

2. Acquisition of Land by Compulsory Purchase Order

The procedure for acquisition will be by means of a compulsory purchase order made (s.112(4)) in accordance with the procedure set out in (a) the Acquisition of Land Act 1981 (which came into operation on January 30, 1982) as modified in several respects by section 132 of the 1971 Act, and (b) the Compulsory Purchase of Land Regulations 1982 (S.I. 1982 No.6).

If the Secretary of State certifies that possession of a house on land which has been acquired or appropriated by a local authority for "planning purposes" and is still being held for such purposes is immediately required for those purposes, then nothing in the Rent Act 1977 is to prevent its being taken possession of by the local authority (s.130(3)).

Any public inquiry or private hearing in connection with the compulsory purchase of land by a local authority will be conducted in accordance with the Compulsory Purchase by Local Authorities (Inquiries Procedure) Rules 1976.[1] These Rules follow generally the lines of the Town and Country Planning Appeals (Determination by Appointed Persons) (Inquiry Procedure) Rules 1974[2] discussed in Chapter 16, to which reference may be made.

Section 113 of the 1971 Act confers power upon the Secretary of State to acquire compulsorily any land necessary for the public service (s.113(1)). The expression "the public service" is nowhere defined in the Act and it would appear to be a far-reaching expression. Compulsory acquisition under section 113 includes power to acquire an easement or other right over land (s.113(2)).

If the acquiring authority enters upon and takes possession of the land (as they can (Compulsory Purchase Act 1965, s.11)) before

[1] S.I. 1976 No. 746.
[2] S.I. 1974 No. 420.

completion of the purchase, the authority must pay the vendor interest on the purchase money at the rate, as from August 14, 1985, of $12\frac{1}{4}$ per cent. per annum (Acquisition of Land (Rate of Interest after Entry) (No. 3) Regulations 1985.[3]

3. Speedy Acquisition of Land by General Vesting Declaration

Under Part II and Part III of the Compulsory Purchase (Vesting Declarations) Act 1981 an "acquiring authority" (Compulsory Purchase (Vesting Declarations) Act 1981 s.2(1)), whether the Secretary of State or a local authority, having obtained a compulsory purchase order (but not before), will be able to obtain not only possession but actual *ownership* of the land covered by the compulsory purchase order by the method of making a general vesting declaration (Compulsory Purchase (Vesting Declarations) Act 1981 s.1).

Under this procedure for the speedy acquisition of land by a public authority, details as to:

(1) preliminary notices before executing a vesting declaration;
(2) the form and execution of a vesting declaration;
(3) the effect of such a declaration when it has been executed;
(4) the vesting and right to enter and take possession of land; and
(5) the recovery by the acquiring authority of compensation overpaid;

—all these matters are dealt with in Part II, Part III and Part IV of the Compulsory Purchase (Vesting Declarations) Act 1981 and in the Compulsory Purchase of Land Regulations 1982.[4]

The forms prescribed by these 1982 Regulations include—

(1) the compulsory purchase order itself;
(2) the preliminary notice, *i.e.* the newspaper notice and the personal notice to owners, lessees and occupiers, describing the effect of the order and specifying how objections can be made;
(3) the notice of confirmation of the order;
(4) the notice that a certificate has been given under Part III of, or Schedule 3 to, the Acquisition of Land Act 1981;
(5) the general vesting declaration itself;
(6) the statement of the effect of the statutory provisions relating to a general vesting declaration;
(7) the notice that such a declaration has been made; and
(8) the notice of a proposed inquiry for the purposes of section 125(2) of the Local Government Act 1972.

[3] S.I. 1985 No. 1131.
[4] S.I. 1982 No. 6.

4. Compulsory Acquisition of Land for Highways

The Secretary of State or a local highway authority may be authorised to acquire land compulsorily (s.218(1)) for providing or improving any highway which is to be provided or improved in pursuance of an order made under sections 209, 211 or 212 of the 1971 Act (relating to the stopping up and diversion of highways and the conversion of a highway into a footpath or bridleway), or for any other purpose for which land is required in connection with such an order or for the purpose of providing any public right of way in lieu of a right of way extinguished under section 214(1)(*a*) of the 1971 Act (s.218(1)). Compulsory acquisition is by means of a compulsory purchase order made (s.218(2)) in accordance with the procedure under the Acquisition of Land Act 1981.

Proceedings required in connection with the acquisition of land under section 218 of the 1971 Act may be taken concurrently with any stopping up or diversion proceedings required to be taken under a stopping up or a diversion order made under section 209 of the Act (s.219 and the Stopping Up of Highways (Concurrent Proceedings) Regulations 1948[5]).

5. Extinguishment of Rights over Land Compulsorily Acquired[6]

Upon the completion of any compulsory purchase of land under Part VI of the 1971 Act, all *private* rights of way and rights of laying down, erecting, continuing or maintaining any apparatus on, under or over the land will be extinguished and any such apparatus will vest in the acquiring authority (s.118(1)). This provision will not apply to rights and apparatus belonging to a statutory undertaker (s.118(2)) the extinguishment of which rights is dealt with in section 230 of the 1971 Act—nor to any right conferred by the "telecommunications code" (Telecommunications Act 1984, s.10 and Sched. 2) on the operator of a telecommunications code system nor to any telecommunications apparatus installed for the purposes of any such system (s.118(2)).

Nor will the provisions of section 118(1) of the 1971 Act apply to other rights or apparatus in respect of which other arrangements are made by the acquiring authority (s.118(3)).

Any person suffering loss by the extinguishment of a right or the

[5] S.I. 1948 No. 1348.

[6] As to other powers of a local authority over land acquired for planning purposes, see Chap. 21.

vesting of apparatus under the provisions of section 118 of the 1971 Act is entitled to compensation from the acquiring authority (s.118(4)), the compensation being determined (s.118(5)) in accordance with the Land Compensation Act 1961.

The extinguishment of *public* rights of way over land held for planning purposes is dealt with in section 214 of the 1971 Act.

6. Acquisition by Agreement of Land Required by Local Authorities for Planning Purposes

A local authority may acquire by agreement (s.119) any land which they require for any purpose for which a local authority may be authorised to acquire land compulsorily under section 112 of the 1971 Act, that is to say, land needed for development, re-development and improvement, or needed to achieve the proper planning of their area.

7. Acquisition of Land for Purposes of Exchange

It is provided (s.120) that the power of a local authority under the 1971 Act to acquire land, whether compulsorily or by agreement, shall include power to acquire land required for giving in exchange for: (1) land appropriated under section 121 of the 1971 Act for planning purposes[7]; or (2) for Green Belt land within the meaning of the Green Belt (London and Home Counties) Act 1938 appropriated for any purpose specified in a development plan.

8. Compulsory Purchase or Appropriation of Open Spaces

A change in the law relating to the compulsory acquisition or appropriation of open space land is contained in Part III "Orders subject to special parliamentary procedure," of the Acquisition of Land Act 1981. Formerly, when open space land has been acquired or appropriated for other purposes, the acquiring authority had to submit the appropriate order to Special Parliamentary Procedure *unless* the Minister gave a certificate certifying either that equally advantageous land would be provided in exchange or that the land was needed for road improvements and no alternative land was necessary. Under section 19 of the 1981 Act the Secretary of State can give his certificate without the need for "exchange land," provided the open space land which is being taken does not exceed 250 square yards in extent *or* is required for the widening or drainage of an existing

[7] See Chap. 21.

highway (or for both of these things) *and* that the provision of "exchange land" is unnecessary.

9. Joint Body to Hold Land Acquired for Planning Purposes

If the Secretary of State, after consultation with the local authorities concerned, thinks it expedient, he may by order constitute a joint body (s.131) to hold land which has already been acquired for planning purposes (s.133(1)) by those local authorities. The order will provide for the transfer of the land from the local authorities to the joint body (s.131(1)) and may confer upon the joint body all or any of the powers of a local authority under the 1971 Act with respect to land acquired by such an authority for planning purposes (s.131(2)).

10. Effect of Acquisition on Unexpended Balance of Established Development Value

Where land is purchased compulsorily, or by agreement under threat of compulsion, any unexpended balance of established development value[8] attaching to the land will be extinguished unless all the interests in the land are *not* acquired, in which event the balance must be apportioned and will be reduced in value by the amount which is attributable to those interests which are in fact acquired (s.142).

[8] See p. 367.

Chapter 20

COMPENSATION PAYABLE ON COMPULSORY PURCHASE OF LAND

1. Historical Summary

The Acquisition of Land (Assessment of Compensation) Act 1919 laid down the principle of market value compensation as that which should be payable on a compulsory purchase of land. This basic principle was subsequently subjected by statute to three artificial distortions.

Part II of the Town and Country Planning Act 1944 introduced "the 1939 ceiling" value on compulsory purchase. This was followed by Part V of the Town and Country Planning Act 1947 which repealed "the 1939 ceiling" and enacted the principle of existing use value compensation on a compulsory purchase under a notice to treat served after July 1, 1948. Part III of the Town and Country Planning Act 1954 supplemented Part V of the 1947 Act by enacting that, on a compulsory purchase under a notice to treat served on or after January 1, 1955, compensation should be the existing use value of the land (in accordance with Part V of the 1947 Act) *plus* the 1947 development value of the land (in accordance with Part III of the 1954 Act).

After some 15 years of these artificial arrangements, Part I of the Town and Country Planning Act 1959 brought them to an end by enacting that, on a compulsory purchase under a notice to treat served after October 29, 1958, compensation should once again be the market value of the land (in accordance with the Acquisition of Land (Assessment of Compensation) Act 1919) but subject to modifications contained in the 1959 Act.

Thus, as time passes and notices to treat served before October 30, 1958, fulfil their purpose and compulsory purchases based upon them are completed (as, surely, most of them—indeed, maybe all of them—now are), it becomes less and less necessary to consider the provisions of the 1947 and 1954 Acts relating to compensation on the compulsory purchase of land. When all compulsory purchases based on such notices to treat have been completed (or the notices themselves have, by agreement, been withdrawn), Part V of the 1947 Act and Part III of the 1954 Act will become spent. Accordingly, most of Part V of the 1947 Act and all of Part III of the 1954 Act were formally repealed by section 58(5) of, and Schedule VIII to, the Town and Country Planning Act 1959 in respect of notices to treat served after October 29, 1958.

2. Compensation at Market Value

The whole of the Acquisition of Land (Assessment of Compensation) Act 1919, together with Part I of the Town and Country Planning Act 1959 (in so far as it relates to compensation on compulsory purchase of land), were repealed by the Land Compensation Act 1961, but their joint effect is re-enacted in the 1961 Act which came into operation on August 1, 1961 (1961 Act s.42(2)). The 1961 Act (including the repeals made by it) does not affect any compulsory purchase of land under a notice to treat served before August 1, 1961 (1961 Act, s.41).

Thus the statutory foundation for the amount of compensation to be paid on a compulsory purchase of land is now to be found in the Land Compensation Act 1961 which, to put the matter briefly, provides that such compensation shall be the market value[1] of the land (1961 Act, s.5) subject to the modifications contained in the Act and to the intricate provisions of the Act relating to assumptions concerning planning permission (1961 Act, ss.14, 15 and 16) and to the certification of appropriate alternative development (Part III of the 1961 Act).

3. The Four Modifications of the Market Value Principle

To the general proposition that compensation shall be the market value of the land—"the amount which the land if sold in the open market by a willing seller might be expected to realise" (1961 Act, s.5, rule (2))—there are now four statutory modifications. Not all of these are new, some of them being based on what has hitherto been custom.

The first and most important modification of the market value principle is to the effect that an acquiring authority shall not pay any *increase* in the value of the acquired land if the increase may be said to have been brought about by the scheme of development which gives rise to the need for the compulsory purchase (1961 Act, s.6). Nor, it may be added, is any account to be taken of any *diminuation* in the value of

[1] Since the House of Lords decision in *Birmingham Corporation* v. *West Midland Baptist (Trust) Association (Inc.)* [1970] A.C. 874, the date by reference to which the land is to be valued is the date when compensation is agreed or assessed, or the date (if earlier) when possession of the land is taken. See also *Washington Development Corporation* v. *Bramlings (Washington) Ltd.* (1984) 273 E.G. 980.

the acquired land which is, likewise, attributable to the carrying out of the scheme of development which brought about the need for the compulsory purchase (*ibid.*).

The important point in all of this is to define what, in any particular case, may be said to be the *scheme of development* and the effect of the 1961 Act is to widen the customary concept of this in three important instances.

The scheme of development is now to be regarded (1961 Act, s.6(1) and Sched. 1, Pt. I) as covering, for example, any development carried out in any part of an area of comprehensive development (*i.e.* an action area) for which a local plan is in force (1961 Act as adapted by the Town and Country Planning Act 1971, s.291(1) and Sched. 23, Pt. I) *or* in any part of an area delineated as the site (or, in certain circumstances, the extension of the site) of a new town (under the New Towns Act 1981) *or* in any part of an area delineated in a development plan as an area of town development (under the Town Development Act 1952) *or* in any part of an urban development area designated under section 134 of the Local Government Planning and Land Act 1980.[2]

The second modification secures that if on a compulsory purchase of land the scheme of development causes an increase in value of other "contiguous or adjacent" land belonging to the same owner, such increase shall be set off against the price paid for the land compulsorily acquired (1961 Act, s.7).

The third modification operates in favour of the vendor whose land has been taken compulsorily and ensures that any diminution in the value of the land caused by the threat of compulsory purchase shall be ignored (1961 Act, s.9).[3] This provision is important in connection with the contents of Part IX of the Town and Country Planning Act 1971, under which certain property which has become unsaleable due to the provisions of a development plan (that is to say, property suffering from "planning blight"[4]) can be required by the owner to be purchased by a local authority but at an "unblighted price."

Finally the fourth modification makes general what is already lawful under certain Acts, namely, the payment on any compulsory purchase of land to which the 1961 Act applies of a disturbance payment to cover costs of removal and trade losses sustained, as a result of the compulsory puchase, by the "little man" whose interest in the

[2] See Chap. 23.

[3] See *London Borough of Hackney* v. *MacFarlane* (1970) 21 P. & C.R. 324, C.A.; *Trocette Property Co. Ltd.* v. *Greater London Council* (1974) 28 P. & C.R. 408, C.A.; and *J. Davy Ltd.* v. *London Borough of Hammersmith* (1975) 30 P. & C.R. 469.

[4] See Chap. 18.

land acquired is not such as to entitle him to receive notice to treat (Land Compensation Act 1973, ss.37 and 38).[5] But if a tenancy is *surrendered* there is no compulsory acquisition.[6]

4. Special Cases

The return to market value compensation on compulsory purchase has necessitated special provisions in the 1961 Act relating to the acquisition of slum property (1961 Act, s.10), to the acquisition of land of statutory undertakers (1961 Act, s.11), to the acquisition of land in relation to which there is already outstanding a right to compensation for refusal of planning permission (1961 Act, s.12) and to the acquisition of war-damaged land (1961 Act, s.13).

So far as the owner-occupier of a slum house is concerned, the 1961 Act secures (1961 Act, s.10 and Sched. 2) that, though the house may be acquired under the Housing Act 1985 at its site value, the minimum payment by way of compensation on compulsory purchase shall at least be equal to the gross value of the house for rating purposes. There is thus established a "compensation floor" (as distinct from a "compensation ceiling") for owner-occupiers of private dwellings found to be unfit for human habitation under the provisions of the Housing Act 1985.

5. How to Calculate Market Value in an Era of Town Planning Control

In the comparatively simple days of 1919 the assessment of market value was little affected by the incidence of town planning control, for the simple reason that there was hardly any such control at all. But after the dramatic strokes of the Town and Country Planning Act 1947 (now re-enacted in the 1971 Act), which require planning permission to be obtained before any development of land, including material change of use, can take place, town planning control plays an important, perhaps the most important, part in establishing what a particular piece of land will fetch in the open market when sold for development.

Nowadays, under the current system of regulatory planning control backed by legal sanctions, the whole question of the market value of land depends largely upon what sort of planning permission would be granted for the development of the land if an application for planning permission were to be made. It is because of a desire to

[5] See *Prasad* v. *Wolverhampton Borough Council* (1983) 47 P. & C.R. 252.
[6] *R.* v. *Islington Borough Council, ex p. Knight* (1984) 1 All E.R. 154; (1984) J.P.L. 592.

help in the solution of this question that many of the complexities of the Land Compensation Act 1961 have arisen.

The 1961 Act provides that in assessing compensation for the compulsory purchase of land certain assumptions as to planning permission *shall* be made (1961 Act, s.14). There are seven of these assumptions; three are general and four are special.

6. The Three General Planning Assumptions

Taking the three general planning assumptions first, these require that upon any compulsory purchase it will be assumed that:

(1) planning permission will be granted for the development which brings about the need for the compulsory purchase (1961 Act, s.15(1), (2));

(2) planning permission will be granted for all development falling within the ambit of the "existing use of land" (1961 Act, s.15(3))—as to which reference should be made to the provisions of Schedule 8 to the 1971 Act—but not, of course, if the existing use value of the land has already been realised by the payment to the landowner of compensation (1961 Act, s.15(4)); and

(3) planning permission will be granted for "certificated development" that is to say, development in respect of which a certificate is issued under Part III of the 1961 Act[7] (1961 Act, s.15(5)).

7. The Four Special Planning Assumptions

Turning now to the four special planning assumptions (1961 Act, s.16) these, it may be said, all arise from insufficiencies in the development plan for the area where the compulsorily acquired land is situated. Attention is to be paid to the state in which the development plan exists at the date of the notice to treat, any amendment to the plan subsequent to that date being irrelevant.

The four special planning assumptions require it to be assumed that:

(1) where the current development plan defines the land (not being "land subject to comprehensive development" (1961 Act, s.16(8)) as a site for specified development—that planning permission will be given for that development (1961 Act s.16(1) and (6));

[7] See p. 414.

(2) where the development plan allocates the land (not being "land subject to comprehensive development" (1961 Act, s.16(8)) for some "primary use"—that planning permission will be granted for any development falling within the scope of that "primary use," *provided* it is development for which planning permission might reasonably be expected to be granted (1961 Act, s.16(2), (6) and (7));

(3) where the development plan allocates the land (not being "land subject to comprehensive development" (1961) Act, s.16(8)) for a range of two or more "primary uses"—that planning permission will be granted for any development falling within the scope of that range of uses, *provided* it is development for which planning permission might reasonably be expected to be granted (1961 Act, s.16(3), (6) and (7)); and

(4) where the land is in an action area (that is to say, is land which *is* subject to comprehensive development (1961 Act, s.16(8)) for which a local plan is in force (1961 Act as adapted by the Town and Country Planning Act 1971, s.291(1) and Sched. 23, Pt. I)—that, irrespective of the proposed layout of the area, planning permission will be given for any development falling within the range of uses allowed in the action area, *provided* it is development for which planning permission might reasonably be expected to be granted (1961 Act, s.16(4), (5), (6) and (7)).

It is to be noted that the first three of these four special assumptions do *not* apply to land in an action area, such land being catered for under the fourth special assumption.

It is further to be noted that while the 1961 Act requires the making of the foregoing planning assumptions (or such of them as are relevant to the matter in hand) the Act does not exclude the taking into account of other types of development to which the market in land might conceivably have regard (1961 Act, s.14(3)).

8. Certification of Development

Notwithstanding the making of the foregoing assumptions, there may still remain, under the current system of planning control, some difficulty in computing what would be the market value of land which is being compulsorily acquired. The relevant development plan may be unhelpful on the point if, for example, the acquired land happens to be in an area in respect of which the development plan has refrained from committing itself, that is to say, in an area sometimes referred to as "white land." Again, a development plan may provide that an area shall be zoned as a green belt. Although this usually means that no development in that area will be allowed at all, it is well known that, on occasion, certain kinds of development *are* permitted even in a green belt.

To deal with cases of this kind the 1961 Act makes further (and elaborate) provision (1961 Act, Pt. III, and the Land Compensation Development Order 1974[8]) whereby either the landowner or the authority seeking the compulsory purchase may apply (1961 Act, s.17) to "the local planning authority" (sometimes the county planning authority and sometimes the district planning authority—Local Government Act 1972, Sched. 16, para. 55) to issue a certificate stating the answer to a hypothetical question, namely: What, in all the circumstances, would be the kind of development (if any) for which planning permission might reasonably be expected to be granted if the land were not being compulsorily acquired by the acquiring authority and an application for planning permission for development were lodged in respect of the land? It is appropriate that the local planning authority should have the responsibility of answering this hypothetical question because it is a question closely related to the grant or refusal of an actual planning permission—all of which is a prime function of the local planning authority and not a function of the Lands Tribunal.[9]

The applicant for a certificate of appropriate alternative development must himself specify one or more classes of development which appear to him appropriate for the land in question (1961 Act, s.17(3); Local Government, Planning and Land Act 1980, s.121 and Sched. 24).

The local planning authority must issue a certificate (1961 Act, s.17(4)) declaring either the nature of the development which might have been permitted had it been applied for, or declaring that no development (other than that—if any—proposed by the acquiring authority) would have been permitted.

Any person aggrieved by any such certificate has a right of appeal to the Secretary of State (1961 Act, s.18). The steps in the appeal are regulated by the Land Compensation Development Order 1974.[10] The Secretary of State, before determining the appeal, must afford the landowner and the acquiring authority and also the local planning authority whose certificate is being appealed against an

[8] S.I. 1974 No. 539.

[9] See further hereon the protest by the President of the Lands Tribunal, Sir Douglas Frank Q.C., in *Williams and Stephens* v. *Cambridgeshire County Council* [1977] Lands Tribunal Decision, Ref. 143/1976; and see [1977] J.P.L. 529, 617.

[10] S.I. 1974 No. 539.

opportunity of being heard by a person appointed by the Secretary of State.

In an appeal against a certificate, where the Secretary of State does not accept the reasons given by the local planning authority, he may nevertheless confirm the certificate and give his own reasons; the essential matter of such a certificate is its conclusion, and the Secretary of State may well agree with the conclusion (for reasons of his own) even though he does not accept the reasons of the local planning authority because, for example, he finds them to contain inaccuracies of fact.[11]

It is to be noted that the procedure with respect to the certification of development does *not* apply if the land which is being compulsorily acquired is land in an action area *or* is in an area allocated primarily for residential, commercial or industrial purposes (or for a range of two or more such purposes) (1961 Act, s.17(1) as adapted by the Town and Country Planning Act 1971, s.291(1) and Sched. 23, Pt. I).

9. Ministerial Comment on Certification

Interesting comment on the working of the certificate system is to be found in paragraphs 2 to 7 of the Memorandum to Ministry of Housing and Local Government Circular 48/59 dated August 11, 1959, now rescinded.

The Minister said that he "thinks it important that the certificate system should be worked on broad common sense lines" and drew attention to the fact that a certificate could be at variance with the use shown by a development plan for the particular land in question. The Minister remarked that "a certificate is not a planning permission but a statement to be used in ascertaining the fair market value of land," its purpose being to state what, if any, other forms of development would have been allowed under town planning control had the land not been compulsorily acquired. In this connection the Minister commented that he "would expect the local planning authority to determine this question in the light of the character of the development in the surrounding area and the general policy of the development plan" and he quoteed, by way of example, the case where the land being compulsorily acquired is surrounded almost entirely by residential development, and observed that in such an instance a certificate of residential use would normally be appropriate.

[11] *Parrish* v. *Minister of Housing and Local Government* (1961) 13 P. & C.R. 32.

There is no doubt that all sorts of difficult questions can be propounded in connection with the working of the certificate system but the clue to its successful working appears to be to let common sense have full play and to avoid nice, legalistic refinements.

Chapter 21

ACQUISITION, APPROPRIATION, DEVELOPMENT AND DISPOSAL OF LAND FOR PLANNING PURPOSES—LOCAL AUTHORITIES' POWERS

1. Acquisition of Land for Planning Purposes

The acquisition of land by a local authority for development, redevelopment or improvement or which is necessary in order to achieve the proper planning of the area where the land is situated, is dealt with in sections 112 (compulsory purchase) and 119 (acquisition of land by agreement) of the 1971 Act. Such acquisition is discussed fully in Chapter 19, *ante*, and is, accordingly, not further referred to in this Chapter.

2. Appropriation for Planning Purposes of Land forming part of a Common, etc.

A local authority may, by Order confirmed by the Secretary of State, appropriate (s.121) for any purpose for which they can be authorised to acquire land, any land already held by them for other purposes and forming part of a common or fuel or field garden allotment (s.290(1)), including any such land which is specially regulated by any public, local or private enactment, provided it is *not* Green Belt land under the Green Belt (London and Home Counties) Act 1938.

The order appropriating any such land will be subject, by virtue of the provisions of section 121(2) of the 1971 Act, applying section 19 of the Acquisition of Land Act 1981, to "special parliamentary procedure," as dealt with in the Statutory Orders (Special Procedure) Act 1945, before it can come into operation *unless* the Secretary of State certifies that such special procedure is not necessary (1981) Act, s.19(1)). The Secretary of State cannot give this certificate unless he is satisfied (and certifies accordingly) that for the land appropriated equivalent open space land will be given in exchange *or*, in the case of open space land taken for road widening, that no such exchange is necessary (*ibid.*). However, the Secretary of State, acting under section 19(1)(*b*) of the Acquisition of Land Act 1981, can now give his certificate without the need for "exchange land" if the open space land which is being appropriated does not exceed 250 square yards in extent *or* is required for the widening or drainage of an existing highway (or for both of these things) *and* that the provision of "exchange land" is unnecessary.

3. Appropriation for Other Purposes of Land Held for Planning Purposes

When a local authority have either acquired or appropriated land for planning purposes and are currently holding it for such purposes, they may appropriate it for *other* purposes for which they are entitled to acquire land by any enactment other than Part VI of the 1971 Act (s.122). The consent of the Secretary of State is required (s.122(2), (2A)) for any such appropriation if the land to be appropriated is, or formerly was, part of a common and is held or managed by the local authority under a local Act.

It follows from the foregoing that land which, either by acquisition or appropriation, has once been brought under the "control" of the 1971 Act, may be "appropriated out" of that control and used for purposes other than the planning purposes for which it was originally acquired or appropriated.

On appropriating planning land to other purposes a local authority must have regard (s.125) to the desirability of preserving features of special architectural or historic interest including in particular any "listed building" (s.54(9)).

4. Development of Land by Local Authorities

Prior to the Town and Country Planning Act 1944 a local authority, whilst they could make a planning scheme and so control the development of land by other parties, could not, generally speaking, undertake development themselves. In other words, planning control was negative and a local authority could not implement the provisions of their own planning scheme by carrying out positive development of land in accordance with their scheme. The 1944 Act, however, introduced an entirely new and important principle by conferring on local authorities power to carry out development of land themselves.

This power is now found in the 1971 Act which provides that a local authority shall, on any land which was acquired or appropriated and is for the time being held for planning purposes, have power to erect, construct or carry out any building or work not being a building or work in respect of which statutory authority exists otherwise (s.124).

Once a local authority have completed a building or work under the foregoing powers, they are authorised to repair, maintain and insure it and generally to deal with it in a proper course of management (s.124(5)).

Instead of carrying out positive development themselves the local authority may enter into arrangements with an authorised association for such development to be carried out by the association (s.124(6)). "Authorised association" means (s.124(8)) any society, company or body of persons whose objects include the promotion, formation or management of garden cities, garden suburbs or garden villages, the erection, improvement or management of buildings for the working classes and others, and which does not trade for profit or whose constitution forbids the issue of any share or loan capital with interest or dividend exceeding the rate for the time being fixed by the Treasury.[1]

When carrying out positive development a local authority must have special regard to the need to preserve features and buildings of special architectural or historic interest (s.125).

5. Miscellaneous Powers Relating to Land Acquired, Appropriated or Developed by Local Authorities

In connection with the acquisition, appropriation or development of land under the 1971 Act by a local authority, the Act makes provision with respect to a number of consequential matters so as to facilitate such acquisition, appropriation or development. These consequential provisions relate, briefly, to:

(a) power to override easements and other rights (s.127);
(b) extinction of public rights of way (s.214);
(c) extinction of private rights of way and rights as to apparatus (s.118);
(d) extinction of rights of way and rights as to apparatus vested in statutory undertakers (ss.230 and 231);
(e) extension or modification of functions of statutory undertakers (ss.233, 234 and 236);
(f) relief of statutory undertakers from obligations rendered impracticable (ss.235 and 236);
(g) use and development of consecrated land and burial grounds notwithstanding restrictions (s.128);
(h) use and development of commons, open spaces, etc., notwithstanding restrictions (s.129);
(i) displacement of persons from land and the obtaining of

[1] See p. 422 as to a local authority participating in "joint venture" development with the private sector.

possession of occupied dwelling-houses and other buildings (s.130);

(j) stopping up and diversion of highways[2]; conversion of highways into footpaths and bridleways; extinguishment of rights of way, etc. (ss.209–221);

(k) alteration of telegraphic lines (s.220).

6. Disposal of Land by Local Authorities

Where a local authority have acquired or appropriated land for planning purposes and are for the time being holding the land for these purposes—in other words, where a local authority are possessed of "planning land"—they may, instead of developing it themselves, dispose of it to such person, in such manner and subject to such conditions as may appear expedient in order that the land may be developed by that person (s.123(1)). The disposal may be by way of sale, exchange or lease (s.290(1)).

The consent of the Secretary of State to any disposal of planning land is now required only in the following instances (s.123(2)):

(a) where the land is land which, immediately before the disposal, is land which consists or forms part of a common (or formerly consisted or formed part of a common) and is held or managed by a local authority in accordance with a local Act; or

(b) where the disposal is to be for a consideration *less* than the best that can reasonably be obtained and is not—

  (i) the grant of a term of seven years or less; or

  (ii) the assignment of a term of years of which seven years or less are unexpired at the date of the assignment.

If the planning land which is being disposed of consists or forms part of an open space (s.290(1)), then the local authority who are disposing of the land:

(a) must first publish a notice of their intention to do so for at least two consecutive weeks in a newspaper circulating in their area; and

(b) must consider any objections to the proposed disposal which may be made to them (s.123(2A)).

Where the planning land which is being disposed of is land acquired or appropriated for planning purposes for a reason men-

[2] See *Harlow* v. *Ministry of Transport and Others* [1951] 2 K.B. 98, C.A.; reversing [1950] 2 K.B. 175. See further as to highways, p. 243.

tioned in section 112(1)(*a*) and (*b*) of the 1971 Act, the power of disposal of such land must be exercised so as to secure, so far as may be practicable, that persons formerly living or carrying on business on such land before the local authority acquired it may be able to get reaccommodation on the land suitable for their reasonable requirements and at a price settled with due regard to the price at which such land was acquired from them (s.123(7)).

In determining the manner and the conditions subject to which "planning land" is to be disposed of for development, the motivation of the local authority should be directed (a) to securing the best use of the land (or other land) and buildings erected (or to be erected) on it, whether by the local authority themselves or other persons, *or* (b) to securing the erection of buildings or works needed for the proper planning of their area (s.123(1)).

It will be seen that, under the foregoing provisions as to the disposal of "planning land," land may be made available by a local authority to a private individual lacking compulsory purchase powers but wishful to carry out the development of land. Moreover, the words of section 123(1) are wide enough to allow a local authority disposing of "planning land" for development by a third party, to share in (by the use of appropriate terms in the instrument of disposal) the development as a joint venture on a basis to be agreed, the local authority relying on section 124 of the 1971 Act as their authority to undertake development of land themselves.

7. Former Restrictions on Right of Disposal Removed

Formerly, under section 19(5) of the Town and Country Planning Act 1944, the Secretary of State was precluded from consenting to a disposal of planning land by a sale of the freehold or by a lease for more than 99 years unless he was satisfied that there were "exceptional circumstances which render the disposal of the land in that manner expedient . . . in order to secure the best use of that or other land and any building or works which have been, or are to be, erected . . . thereon . . . or to secure the erection . . . thereon of any buildings . . . needed for the proper planning of the area of the [local] authority."

Section 19(5) of the 1944 Act was repealed by section 18 of the Town Development Act 1952, with the result that, in those few cases (s.123(2)) in which the consent of the Secretary of State is still needed before planning land can be disposed of by a local authority, he is no longer under any obligation to find exceptional circumstnces before consenting to a sale of the freehold or a lease for more than 99 years.

8. The Uthwatt Report

The principle formerly embodied in section 19(5) of the 1944 Act whereby the freehold of land, once it had been acquired by a local authority, was not thereafter to be disposed of by way of sale, derived from a recommendation of the Expert Committee on Compensation and Betterment (the Uthwatt Committee), who, in paragraph 147 of their Final Report of September 1942,[3] stated:

> "It may be possible for much of the work of rebuilding in the replanned area to be carried out by private enterprise and land should be made available to developers for approved development in accordance with the plan. In our view it is essential to secure that the land should not again be divided up among owners of small freeholds. We recommend, therefore, that once any interest in land has passed into public ownership it should be disposed of by way of lease only and not by way of sale, and that the authority should have the power to impose such covenants in the lease as planning requirements make desirable, breach of such convenants to be enforceable by re-entry.
>
> "Although this recommendation is made primarily in connection with Reconstruction Areas, we intend it to be of general application to any interest in land disposed of by a public authority."

9. The New Towns Report

The foregoing recommendation of the Uthwatt Committee was repeated by the New Towns Committee in paragraph 15 of their Second Interim Report of April 1946,[4] with the result that a new town development corporation operating under the New Towns Act 1946 (now repealed and replaced by the New Towns Act 1981) was formerly subject to the same restrictions (s.5 of the New Towns Act 1946) on the disposal of the freehold in, or the grant of a lease for more than 99 years of, any land which it held, as was a local authority operating under the Town and Country Planning Act 1944.

[3] Cmnd. 6386.
[4] Cmnd. 6794.

This restriction was likewise removed by section 18 of the Town Development Act 1952.

10. The Central Advisory Committee Report

As to the length of leases to be granted by a local authority, it is stated in paragraph 71 of the Report of the Central Advisory Committee on Estate Development and Management in War Damaged Areas (a report made to the Secretary of State in 1947) that "the time when the general run of buildings in a central area will become obsolete will almost certainly be reached considerably before the end of ninety-nine years," and in paragraph 72 it is recommended "that in the interest of good estate management, the general practice in regard to commercial and industrial buildings in central areas should be to grant ground leases for an average term of seventy-five years."

Chapter 22

PLANNING INQUIRY COMMISSIONS—AN ALTERNATIVE KIND OF PROCEDURE

1. Why Have an Alternative Procedure?

THREE sections of the Town and Country Planning Act 1971, namely, sections 47, 48 and 49, derive from the Town and Country Planning Act 1968 in which their content was first enacted. They contain provisions whereby the Secretary of State is empowered to set up Planning Inquiry Commissions to inquire into any matters referred to them. The motivating factor behind the reference of anything to a Planning Inquiry Commission is that the development which is the subject of the inquiry is development which raises considerations of national or regional importance or presents unfamiliar, technical or scientific aspects which merit a special inquiry. In connection with Planning Inquiry Commissions the Minister of Housing and Local Government issued Circular 67/68 dated December 9, 1968. It is still operative.

A Planning Inquiry Commission will constitute a "planning inquiry" for the purposes of the Planning Inquiries (Attendance of Public) Act 1982 (s.1(5) of that Act) with the result that, except where the Secretary of State for the Environment directs otherwise (s.1(2), (3) and (4) of the 1982 Act), oral evidence before the Commission must be heard in public and documentary evidence must be open to public inspection (s.1(1) of the 1982 Act).

The responsibility of setting up any particular Planning Inquiry Commission rests with the Secretary of State (s.47(1)). The customary single Inspector, so well known at public inquiries held in connection with planning matters, will be replaced, where a Planning Inquiry Commission is set up, by a team of investigators consisting of a chairman and not less than two or more than four other members (s.47(2)), thus making a minimum of three members and a maximum of five.

Once set up, the Commission will not be confined simply to the hearing of objections or representations. It will have something more in the nature of a roving commission to undertake a full examination of all problems associated with the matter which is laid before it.

The need for something more than the normal type of Departmental inquiry in certain types of case became apparent in the period preceding the passing of the Act of 1968 in connection with proposals such as those for a plant for processing natural gas at Bacton, Norfolk, a new London airport at Stanstead, Essex, a hovercraft terminal at Pegwall Bay, Kent, and a gas-holder at Abingdon, Berkshire. However, the Secretary of State has not, at the time of this writing, February 1987, had recourse to this alternative procedure for inquiring into development which is potentially controversial on a large scale. For example, it was not used at the public inquiry held in 1978 into the need to establish a nuclear reactor at Windscale in Cumbria nor at the public inquiry in 1983–1985 into the need for a nuclear power station at Sizewell in Suffolk.

2. Matters Capable of Treatment by the New Procedure

The 1971 Act specifies those particular matters which "the responsible Minister or ministers" (s.48(2)–(8))—and this expression includes the Secretary of State for the Environment—may refer for investigation to a Planning Inquiry Commision. These matters are four in number as follows (s.48(1)), namely:

(a) any application for planning permission which has been called in for decision by the Secretary of State himself under section 35 of the 1971 Act;
(b) any planning appeal to the Secretary of State under section 36 of the 1971 Act against a planning decision;
(c) any proposal that a government department should direct, under section 40 of the 1971 Act, that planning permission should be deemed to be granted for development by a local authority or by a statutory undertaker; and
(d) any proposal that development should be carried out by a government department.

The foregoing are the four matters (and the only four matters) which can be referred for investigation by a Planning Inquiry Commission.

Any two or more of the foregoing four matters may be referred at the same time to a Planning Inquiry Commission if they appear to relate to proposals to carry out development for similar purposes on different sites (s.48(3)).

A Planning Inquiry Commission may, with the approval of the Secretary of State (s.48(7)) and at his expense, arrange for the carrying out of research of any kind which appears to them to be relevant to the matter referred to them for inquiry and report (*ibid.*).

3. When is the New Procedure Applicable and Who Decides?

The next question is: When should the Secretary of State decide that a Planning Inquiry Commission should investigate any of the foregoing matters rather than that they should be dealt with under the other procedures of the 1971 Act? Whether or not any one of the foregoing matters should be referred to a Planning Inquiry Commission is to be decided by either the "responsible Minister or Ministers" (s.48(2)). Schedule 10 to the 1971 Act gives details as to who in any particular circumstances will be "the responsible Minister" (s.48(8)).

What are to be the considerations to be borne in mind before it is decided to refer a matter to a Planning Inquiry Commission? The answer to this question is found in section 48(2) of the 1971 Act. Before a reference can be made the Minister concerned must come to the conclusion that it is expedient for the reference to be made so as to ensure that the matter in hand becomes the subject of a special inquiry on either one or both of the following two grounds, that is to say:

(1) that there are considerations of national or regional importance which require evaluating but that a proper evaluation cannot be made *unless there is a special inquiry for the purpose;* and
(2) that the technical or scientific aspects of the proposed development are of so unfamiliar a character—so new, so strange—as to prejudice a proper determination of the question of whether or not the development should be permitted *unless there is a special inquiry for the purpose* (s.48(2)).

The 1971 Act caters specifically for the question of whether an alternative site for any proposed development should be considered, by providing that whenever a proposal to carry out developent on a particular site is referred to a Planning Inquiry Commission, the Commission can also consider the question of whether such development should be carried out instead on some alternative site (s.48(4)).

The Minister referring a matter for inquiry to a Planning Inquiry Commission *must* state in the reference the reasons why he does so and *may* draw the attention of the Commission to any points which seem to him to be relevant to the inquiry (s.48(5)).

4. What a Planning Inquiry Commission Must Do

When a Planning Inquiry Commission have a matter before them, their duty appears to fall under three headings, as follows (s.48(6)).

Their first duty is to *identify* those considerations or those technical or scientific aspects of the matter which are relevant to the question of whether or not the proposed development should be permitted and then *assess* the importance to be attached to such considerations or aspects (s.48(6)(*a*)).

When the foregoing is done their next duty is to afford to the applicant for planning permission and to the local planning authority and to other interested parties an opportunity of appearing before or being heard by one or more members of the Commission if any of these persons or parties desire to be heard (s.48(6)(*b*)). If a desire to be heard is expressed by the applicant for planning permission or by the local planning authority or by any other interested party, then the Planning Inquiry Commission *must* hold a local inquiry (s.49(3)) but they *may*, in any case and at their own discretion, hold such an inquiry if they think it necessary for the proper discharge of their functions (*ibid.*). Any local inquiry held as aforesaid by a Planning Inquiry Commission will come (s.49(5)) within the ambit of the Tribunals and Inquiries Act 1971. The provisions of the Local Government Act 1972, section 250, relating to the summoning of witnesses, the giving of evidence on oath, the production of documents and the costs incurred by the Minister causing the inquiry to be held, will also apply (s.49(6)).

Thirdly and lastly, the Planning Inquiry Commission must make a report on the matter referred to them to the Minister who initiated the reference (s.48(6)(*c*)).

When a Planning Inquiry Commission holds a local inquiry (s.49(3)) they may do so concurrently with some other ministerial inquiry into any cognate matter (s.49(4)), or, alternatively, the two inquiries may be combined (*ibid.*).

5. Notices about, and Timing for, a Reference to a Planning Inquiry Commission

Whenever a reference to a Planning Inquiry Commission is made, notice of the making of the reference is to be published in the *London Gazette* and in at least one newspaper circulating in the locality of the proposed development (s.49(2) and the Town and Country Planning (Planning Inquiry Commissions) Regulations 1968).[1] A copy of the notice is to be served on the local planning authority for the area in which the proposed development is to be carried out (*ibid.*). Notice of the reference is also to be served on other interested parties as, for example, the applicant for planning permission or any person who has made representations relating to the matter (*ibid.*).

A reference relating to development by a government department can be made to a Planning Inquiry Commission at any time

[1] S.I. 1968 No. 1911.

(s.49(1)). References of any other matter can be made before *but not after,* the relevant application for planning permission or the relevant appeal or the relevant direction has been determined or given (*ibid.*). It is worthy of note that any such reference may be made notwithstanding that there has already been held one of the conventional local inquiries or private hearings provided for under the 1971 Act (*ibid.*).

The question of whether the conventional and familiar procedures of inquiry under the 1971 Act shall be followed, or whether the procedure by way of a Planning Inquiry Commission shall be brought into operation, is a matter *not* for the applicant for planning permission but for "the responsible Minister or Ministers."

Attention may again be drawn to the fact that a reference to a Planning Inquiry Commission, can still be made notwithstanding that the conventional private hearing or public inquiry into the matter has already been held under the 1971 Act (s.49(1)). No such reference can, however, take place *if a decision has been given* following the holding of the aforementioned conventional hearing or public inquiry under the 1971 Act (*ibid.*).

6. How Will it all Work Out in Practice?—What the Minister Said

Developers will be interested to learn just how the procedure by way of a Planning Inquiry Commission is going to be handled in practice. Accordingly, it will be useful to conclude this chapter by quoting a statement made by the Minister of State, Ministry of Housing and Local Government, when the Bill for the Town and Country Planning Act 1968 was in Committee (*Hansard,* Standing Committee G.—April 2, 1968, cols. 903 *et seq.*):

> "We definitely envisage the work of these Commissions falling into two distinct parts. The first part is modelled on the procedures of a Royal Commission or a Departmental committee that is set up to investigate some particular problem. The second part is modelled on the public inquiry procedure with which we are all familar through planning applications.
>
> "As I explained a few moments ago, one of the reasons for our putting forward this procedure is that we feel that the kind of problems that we want to refer are such that the existing procedure is inadequate because the inspector at the inquiry often is not qualified to probe and investigate some of the issues involved. And the procedure of a public inquiry, which is a public inquiry to receive, hear and inquire into objections to the

proposals, does not enable the kind of highly technically qualified investigation in depth of the issues to be made which is needed in this type of case.

"We have had very much in mind, of course, the point about how to keep down the time that is going to be spent on these investigations, so that they do not produce intolerable delays in the planning procedure. Therefore, we envisage the first stage as what I shall call the stage of investigation by the Commission. . . .

"The way in which we envisage the commissions will work is that at this stage they will begin by receiving written memoranda from the applicant, from Government Departments which are concerned and affected, from outside bodies which have an interest; they may have to commission some research to investigate some aspect on which they have not adequate information, and receive a report from a research body.

"Having studied those memoranda, the Commission may wish them to hear oral evidence from the persons who have submitted memoranda, as, for example, a Royal Commission does. We envisage that the Commission will itself conduct the investigation, and will be qualified to do it. It will do the questioning; there will not be examination and cross-examination by legal representatives at this stage. This is a commission set up by the Government to investigate a problem in depth for itself, and it will be qualified to do it.

"Evidence will be taken at both stages, but in a different way, with a different procedure. . . .

"May I add a word here about alternative sites? It is at this stage that we envisage the Commission really being able to introduce helpfully a new element in the procedure. Let us suppose that, at the end of this stage, it forms the view that the development could equally well—perhaps better—be done at some site other than the one the applicant has applied for. It might well say to the applicant, 'We shall be greatly assisted if you would make an application in respect of this alternative site. We know it is not your first choice, but we are impressed by the objections against your site, and this looks to us to be one we would like to be able to consider and report on. We could, perhaps, have a public inquiry into that site as well as the one for which you have already applied.' The applicant is then confronted with this situation: if he refuses to take the hint, or accept the invitation, and he says, 'No; it is all or nothing on the site I have asked for,' he is in serious danger of having a recommendation against him, and he will fail to get his permission. On the other hand, if he is prepared, as second best but perhaps under protest, to put in an alternative application, he has a chance of getting finality then, and, at the end of the day, getting a decision in his favour either for site A or for site B.

"So much for the moment for the first stage. Then comes the second stage of the public inquiries. In our anxiety to cut short time, we wondered whether the first stage would be enough and one could avoid, as it were, the second stage. But I think people have come so much to accept the public local inquiry as a necessary and proper part of the machinery for investigating these controversial cases that we thought we must retain it. But we want to avoid, if we can, too much duplication between the two stages and having to go over all the same evidence again. So what we propose . . . is that all the evidence which has been collected, both the written evidence and the oral evidence at the first stage, will be made available to the parties at the public inquiry at the second stage. Then it will be up to the inspector who is conducting the inquiry, and to legal representatives, counsel and others who are involved in the second stage, to avoid time-wasting repetition of evidence which is all there on the record. But, of course, there may be matters in that evidence which they want to investigate and probe further, cross-examine on at the second stage, and they will be free to do so. They will not be prevented from doing so. It is at this stage that people who wish to be legally represented and be able to cross-examine and probe the evidence in that way would be able to do so. That is, broadly speaking, how we envisage the two stages."

7. Possible Use of a Planning Inquiry Commission

The possibility that a Planning Inquiry Commission or similar form of inquiry might be held before planning permission is granted for any nuclear fast-breeder reactor on a commercial scale is indicated in the Government's response to the Sixth Report of the Royal Commission on Environmental Pollution.

In its Report the Commission recommended that a special procedure for public consultation should be established in respect of major questions of nuclear development to enable decisions to "take place by explicit political process." The Government say that in the case of "specific projects" there are provisions for public inquiries to be held. The Government fully accepts the need, however, for a proper framework for a wider public debate, and it is to consider the most suitable kind of special procedure to achieve this.[2] If the form of debate chosen were to be a Planning Inquiry Commission, the first stage would allow for debate on general policy issues, the second being the traditional planning inquiry to consider specific proposals for a particular site.

However (and as stated earlier in this Chapter), at the moment of writing (February 1987) no Government has yet seen fit to set up a Planning Inquiry Commission to inquire into anything at all.

[2] Nuclear Power and the Environment: Cmnd. 6820.

Chapter 23

URBAN DEVELOPMENT CORPORATIONS

Note: In this chapter all section and schedule references are to the Local Government, Planning and Land Act 1980 unless otherwise stated.

1. Introductory

The Local Government, Planning and Land Act 1980 Part XVI and Part XVIII break new ground in the sphere of land development and planning control over such development by providing, respectively, for the establishment of urban development corporations and enterprise zones. Urban development corporations are dealt with in this chapter and enterprise zones in the next chapter—Chapter 24.

The Secretary of State is empowered to designate an area of land as an "urban development area" and to establish an urban development corporation to regenerate the area. All this is done by means of an order made by the Secretary of State and approved by affirmative resolution of each House of Parliament. On November 14, 1980, the Minister for Local Government and Environmental Services, Mr. Tom King, M.P. declared:

> "We shall shortly be bringing forward Orders under powers in the Local Government, Planning and Land Act to set up Urban Development Corporations as single-minded agencies to spearhead the regeneration of the London and Merseyside docklands and to introduce the bold new experiment of Enterprise Zones, where business can be freed from such detailed planning control and from rates."

The requisite orders for the Merseyside and for the London docklands came into operation on March 25, 1981[1] and on July 2, 1981[2] respectively. The Merseyside Development Corporation and London Docklands Development Corporation are, at the time of this

[1] The Merseyside Development Corporation (Area and Constitution) Order 1980 (S.I. 1981 No. 481).

[2] The London Docklands Development Corporation (Area Constitution) Order 1980 (S.I. 1981 No. 936); and The London Docklands Development Corporation (Area and Constitution) (Amendment) Order 1981 (S.I. 1981 No. 937).

writing (January 1987), the only urban development corporations so far established under the provisions of the Local Government, Planning and Land Act 1980.

However, it was announced on October 8, 1986 by the Environment Secretary, Mr. Nicholas Ridley, that four new urban development corporations are to be set up during the next two years. They will function

(1) at Trafford Park in Greater Manchester;
(2) on Teeside;
(3) in the Black Country within the four boroughs of Dudley, Sandwell, Walsall and Wolverhampton; and
(4) in the metropolitan county of Tyne and Wear.

These are all places with major concentrations of derelict or disused land formerly used for industrial purposes.

2. Urban Development Areas

With a view to regenerating areas of derelict, run-down land (often the inner cores of old towns) by means of an urban development corporation, appointed *ad hoc* for that one single purpose, the Secretary of State *may* designate an area of land as an urban development area (s.134(1)). Under the Local Government, Planning and Land Act 1980 as originally enacted, if the area of land was in England (as distinct from Scotland or Wales) then the land had also to be either within a metropolitan district or within an inner London borough (including land partly in an outer London borough having a common boundary with an inner London borough (s.134(2)).

A "metropolitan district" is a district situated within a metropolitan county (Local Government Act 1972, s.1, Sched. 1). There are, in all, six metropolitan counties, as follows:

1. Greater Manchester;
2. Merseyside;
3. South Yorkshire;
4. Tyne & Wear;
5. West Midlands; and
6. West Yorkshire (*ibid.*).

An "inner London borough" is one of the 12 London boroughs (Interpretation Act, 1978, ss.5, 22(1) and Sched. 1) specified in the London Government Act 1963, Sched. 1. The 12 inner London boroughs are the London boroughs of:

1. City of Westminster;
2. Camden;
3. Islington;

4. Hackney;
5. Tower Hamlets;
6. Greenwich;
7. Lewisham;
8. Southwark;
9. Lambeth;
10. Wandsworth;
11. Hammersmith and Fulham; and
12. Kensington and Chelsea.

The foregoing restriction on the places in England which could be designated urban development areas under the Local Government, Planning and Land Act 1980 has now been removed by the Housing and Planning Act 1986, section 47 which enacts that section 134(2) of the 1980 Act shall be omitted. *Any* land *anywhere* in England can now be designated an urban development area.

An urban development area may comprise any number of separate parcels of land (s.134(3)) and the order of the Secretary of State designating the area must, before it can function, be approved positively by resolution of each House of Parliament (s.134(4)).

The motivating factor for the Secretary of State in designating an urban development area is "the national interest" (s.134(1)). The sole question for him is: Is it expedient in the national interest that an urban development area be designated (*ibid.*)? Thus, an area designated as an urban development area will be an area superimposed upon existing local government boundaries. It follows that the regeneration of the urban development area by one of the new urban development corporations, *appointed* by the Secretary of State and not *elected* by anybody, cannot do other than lead to a diminishment of local government authority and functioning within the area of the urban development corporation—as the following paragraphs of this chapter will disclose.

3. Urban Development Corporations

As mentioned, the Secretary of State *may* (he has a discretion) designate land as an urban development area. Having done so he *must* then proceed (at the same time or later (s.135(2)) to procure its regeneration by means of an *ad hoc* body called an "urban development corporation" (s.135(1))—a body corporate by such name as is prescribed in the order which establishes it (s.135(4)). Such an order is made by statutory instrument (s.135(1)) and requires positive approval by resolution of each House of Parliament (s.135(3)).

An urban development corporation will consist of a chairman, a deputy chairman and additional members (not less than five nor more than eleven) as the Secretary of State may prescribe (s.135(5) and Sched. 26, para. 1). The members of the urban development corporation are not elected in any way—they are all the appointees of the Secretary of State (Sched. 26, para. 2(1)). In appointing members of an urban development corporation the Secretary of State must have regard to the desirability of securing the services of people who have special knowledge of the locality (Sched. 26, para. 2(2)) and, before making any appointment, he must consult with such local authorities as appear to him to be concerned with the regeneration of the area (Sched. 26, para. 2(3)). The Secretary of State must appoint two members to be chairman and deputy chairman respectively (Sched. 26, para. 2(4)).

To a large extent the tenure of office of members of a development corporation will depend upon the particular terms of their appointment by the Secretary of State (Sched. 26, para. 3) but the Local Government, Planning and Land Act 1980 itself makes provision with respect to certain matters affecting tenure of office.

The chairman or deputy chairman of a corporation must cease to act as such if they cease to be members of the corporation (Sched. 26, para. 4) and any member of a corporation can resign by giving notice in writing to the Secretary of State (Sched. 26, para. 5), such member being eligible for reappointment (Sched. 26, para. 7).

In case of bankruptcy, illness, absence from meetings for more than three consecutive months without permission, or inability or unfitness for duty, the Secretary of State may remove a member of a development corporation from office (Sched. 26, para. 6).

Members of a development corporation are to be paid such remuneration as the Secretary of State, with the consent of the Minister for the Civil Service, may fix and there is provision for pensions and for compensation on expiration of office (Sched. 26, paras. 9 and 10).

A development corporation may, with the approval of the Secretary of State, appoint such officers and servants as it needs and may remunerate them, pay them pensions and compensate them for loss of office on such terms and conditions as the corporation may determine (Sched. 26, paras. 11 and 12).

The arrangements relating to the conduct of business at meetings of a development corporation and the quorum of the corporation are matters which the corporation may determine for themselves, subject to any directions given by the Secretary of State (Sched. 26, para. 13). Any vacancy among members or any defect in the appointment of members will not invalidate the proceedings of a corporation (Sched. 26, para. 14).

Special provision is made as to the sealing and execution of documents by, or on behalf of, a development corporation and as to the receiving of such documents in evidence (Sched. 26, paras. 15–17).

4. Object of an Urban Development Corporation

The object of a development corporation is to secure the regeneration of its area (s.136(1) and (7)) and it is to achieve this object (s.136(2)) by (in particular):

(1) bringing land and buildings into effective use;
(2) encouraging the development of new industry and commerce;
(3) creating an attractive environment; and
(4) ensuring that housing and social facilities are available to encourage people to live and work in the area.

5. General Powers of an Urban Development Corporation

In order that a development corporation may achieve its statutory object wide powers are conferred upon it (s.136(3), (6), (7)) to:

(1) acquire, hold, manage, reclaim and dispose of land and other property;
(2) carry out building and other operations;
(3) seek to ensure the provision of water; electricity, gas, sewerage and other services;
(4) carry on any business or undertaking for the purposes of the object; and
(5) generally do anything necessary or expedient for the purposes of the object or for purposes incidental to those purposes.

In addition to the foregoing an urban development corporation may, with the consent of the Secretary of State and the concurrence of the Treasury, make contributions towards:

(1) the costs of any local authority or statutory undertakers incurred in the discharge of their statutory functions (including costs in the acquisition of land); and
(2) the costs in the provision of amenities (s.136(5)).

Any of the functions exercisable by an urban development corporation may be excluded from its purview, either as to the whole or any part of its area, by appropriate provision made by the Secretary of State in the order (Local Government, Planning and Land Act, 1980, s.135) establishing the corporation (s.137).

Moreover, the exercise of any of its powers by an urban development corporation may be restricted by direction of the Secretary of State given after consultation with the corporation (s.138).

In exceptional circumstances the Secretary of State may, by

order, direct that the functions of an urban development corporation shall be performed by some other urban development corporation (s.139(1)). Again, the Secretary of State may, by order, transfer the functions of one urban development corporation to another corporation (whether already established or newly established to receive such functions) and dissolve the corporation from which the functions are transferred (s.139(2)). Any order re-allocating or transferring functions from or to a corporation must first be the subject of consultation between the Secretary of State and the corporation (s.139(4)). The order will require positive approval by resolution of each House of Parliament (s.139(7)).

The finances, accounts and reports of an urban development corporation are regulated by section 164 of, and Schedule 31 to, the Local Government, Planning and Land Act 1980.

It is to be noted that an urban development corporation is *not* a local authority within the meaning of section 270(1) of the Local Government Act 1972[3] and, accordingly, does not have the power (available to a local authority under section 222 of that Act) to take proceedings for the protection of local inhabitants without first seeking the intervention of the Attorney-General in a relator action.

6. Specific Powers of an Urban Development Corporation

Apart from the general powers of a development corporation referred to above, the Local Government, Planning and Land Act 1980 confers specific powers on such a corporation in order to facilitate the regeneration of the area for which it is established.

(1) *Acquisition of land*

To enable an urban development corporation to get on with its object of regenerating its area, the Secretary of State may shift land which is vested in a local authority, in a statutory undertaker or in any other public body and vest it in the urban development corporation (s.141). The vesting is done by means of an order[4] made by the Secretary of State in the form of a statutory instrument (s.141(1)) and the order has the same effect (s.141(4)) as a declaration under Part III of the Compulsory Purchase (Vesting Declarations) Act 1981. The vesting order requires positive approval by resolution of each House of Parliament (s.141(6)).

[3] See *London Docklands Development Corporation* v. *Rank Hovis McDougall Ltd.* (1985) J.P.L. 593; (1986) J.P.L. 826.

[4] See, *e.g.*, The London Docklands Development Corporation (Vesting of Land) (Port of London Authority) Order 1981 (S.I. 1981 No. 941); also The London Docklands Development Corporation (Vesting of Land) (Greater London Council) Order 1981 (S.I. 1981 No. 942).

Compensation for the land will be paid in accordance with the Land Compensation Act 1961 and will be assessed by reference to values current at the date of vesting (s.141(5) and Sched. 27).

In addition to obtaining land by vesting order, a development corporation may acquire land by agreement (ss.142(1), 144(1), (3) and Sched. 28, Pt. II) or, on being authorised by the Secretary of State, compulsorily (ss.142(1)(3)(4), 144(1)(2) and Sched. 28, Pt. I).

Land may be acquired (s.142(1)) if it is:

(a) land in the urban development area;
(b) land adjacent to the area which the corporation requires for purposes connected with the discharge of the corporation's functions in the area; or
(c) land, whether or not in or adjacent to the area, which the corporation requires for the provision of services in connection with the discharge of the corporation's functions in the area.

If the development corporation cannot acquire any necessary land by agreement it is authorised to acquire it compulsorily by means of a compulsory purchase order made by the corporation and confirmed by the Secretary of State (s.142(1) and (2A)) in accordance with the procedure of the Acquisition of Land Act 1981 as modified (s.144(2)) by Part I of Schedule 28 of the Local Government, Planning and Land Act 1980.

Provision is made (Sched. 28, Pt. III) in connection with the acquisition of land (whether by compulsory purchase or vesting as mentioned above) for the extinguishment of rights over the land, the overriding of easements, the treatment of consecrated land and burial grounds, open spaces, telegraph lines and the rights of statutory undertakers, the displacement of persons and the extinguishment of public rights of way.

A local highway authority can be authorised to acquire any land compulsorily *outside* an urban development area for the construction or improvement of a road if this will further the regeneration of the urban development area or provide proper means of access to it (s.143).

Compensation for land acquired by an urban development corporation in the discharge of its functions will be payable under the provisions of the Land Compensation Act 1961 as amended by section 145 of the Local Government, Planning and Land Act 1980 (ss.6 and 7, Sched. 1).

(2) *Disposal of land*

Subject to any directions which the Secretary of State may give, an urban development corporation may dispose of any land which has been vested in it or acquired by it, to such persons and in such manner and subject to such covenants and conditions as the corporation thinks expedient for securing the regeneration of its area (s.146(1)).

In disposing of land a development corporation is under a duty to provide, as far as is practicable, for the re-accomodation of persons who were living or carrying on business or other activities on the land and who wish to obtain accommodation on land belonging to the corporation (s.144(2)). The land offered by the corporation must be suitable to the reasonable requirements—provided these do not relate to the sale of intoxicating or alcoholic liquor (s.146(3))—of such persons and must be offered on terms which are settled with due regard to the price at which land has been purchased from such persons by the corporation (s.144(2)). Such persons must be ready to comply with any requirements of the development corporation as to the development and use of the land on which they are re-accommodated (*ibid.*).

A development corporation in disposing of land must have regard to the need for preserving features of special architectural or historic interest, and in particular any building listed under section 54 of the Town and Country Planning Act 1971, and the Secretary of State is under the duty of giving to a development corporation such directions as he thinks necessary or expedient for ensuring that the corporation discharges its obligations in these respects (s.148(3)).

(3) *Planning and development control*

An urban development corporation, when it has determined what is best in order to secure the realisation of its prime function, namely, the regeneration of its area, may submit to the Secretary of State proposals for the development of any land within its area (s.148(1)). After consultation with the local planning authority within whose area such land lies and with any other local authority who appear to be concerned, the Secretary of State may approve such development proposals with or without modification (*ibid.*). Thereafter the Secretary of State may make a special development order,[5] under section 24 of the Town and Country Planning Act

[5] See, *e.g.*, The Town and Country Planning (Merseyside Urban Development Area) Special Development Order 1981 (S.I. 1981 No. 560); The Town and Country Planning (London Docklands Urban Development Area) Special Development Order 1981 (S.I. 1981 No. 1082). Both these Orders are amended by the Town and Country Planning (Local Government Reorganisation)(Miscellaneous Amendments) Order 1986 (S.I. 1986 No. 435) to take account of the abolition of the Greater London Council and the six metropolitan county councils on April 1, 1986 by the Local Government Act 1985, s.1.

1971, granting automatic planning permission for any development of land which is in accordance with the proposals earlier approved by him (s.148(2)). Such automatic planning permission may be given by the special development order subject to conditions as set out in the order itself (*ibid.*). One of these conditions may require that details of the permitted development be submitted to the local planning authority (s.148(2) and (4)). Subject to this requirement (which will function only if the special development order so provides), it will be noted that the local planning authority are relieved of all responsibility for considering what shall, and what shall not, take place by way of development in order to secure the regeneration of the urban development area. That matter is the prime function of the urban development corporation; indeed, it is the very *raison d'être* of the corporation.

The Secretary of State may give an urban development corporation directions calculated to ensure that, in the carrying out of development by the corporation, features of special architectural or historic interest and, in particular, any building listed under section 54 of the Town and Country Planning Act 1971, will be preserved (s.148(3)).

The two preceding paragraphs relate to the carrying out of "permitted development" in an urban development area. But what is to happen in the case of a developer wishing to carry out development *not* permitted by any special development order relating to the urban development area (or, if it comes to that, not permitted by the Town and Country General Development Order 1977). Such development will need an *ad hoc* grant of planning permission. This will emanate from the local planning authority *unless* the Secretary of State has created the urban development corporation the local planning authority for the whole or any portion of their area so far as concerns those purposes of Part III of the Town and Country Planning Act 1971 as are prescribed by him (s.149(1)). This the Secretary of State can do by an order[6] which is subject to annulment by resolution of either House of Parliament (s.149(12)).

[6] See, *e.g.*, The Merseyside Development Corporation (Planning Functions) Order 1981 (S.I. 1981 No. 561); The London Docklands Development Corporation (Planning Functions) Order 1981 (S.I. 1981 No. 1081). These orders (both of which are amended by the Town and Country Planning (Local Government Reorganisation)(Miscellaneous Amendments) Order 1986 (S.I. 1986 No.435)) make the Merseyside Development Corporation and the London Docks Development Corporation, within their respective designated areas, the local planning authority in relation to *all* kinds of development for *all* the purposes of Part III of the Town and Country Planning Act 1971. Thus any application for planning permission for development within the designated areas will be made direct to the appropriate Urban Development Corporation. But the aforesaid development corporations are not local authorities for the purposes of section 270(1) of the Local Government Act 1972—see p. 438, and footnote 3, *ante*.

Any order by which the urban development corporation becomes (so far as is prescribed in the order) the development control authority for its own area (so ousting the powers of the local government planning authority for the area), may provide for the application (or non-application) to the urban development corporation of enactments relating to local planning authorities (s.149(2)).

It may also provide that the functions conferred by such of the following provisions of the Town and Country Planning Act, 1971 as are specified in the order shall be exercised by the corporation (s.149(3)(*a*),(4) and Sched. 29, Pt. I) in place of any other authority (except the Secretary of State)—the aforesaid "following provisions" being:

section 55 (control of works of demolition, alteration or extension of listed buildings);

section 58 (building preservation notice in respect of building not listed);

section 59 (planning permission to include appropriate provision for preservation and planting of trees);

section 60 (tree preservation orders);

section 61 (provisional tree preservation orders);

section 61A (trees in conservation areas);

section 62 (replacement of trees);

section 63 (control of advertisements);

section 65 (proper maintenance of waste land);

section 87 (power to serve enforcement notice);

section 90 (stop notices);

section 91 (execution and cost of works required by enforcement notice);

section 96 (power to serve listed building enforcement notice);

section 99 (execution and cost of works required by listed building enforcement notice);

section 101 (urgent works for preservation of certain unoccupied buildings);

section 103 (enforcement of duties as to replacement of trees);

section 107 (execution and cost of works required by notice as to waste land);

section 109 (enforcement of control as to advertisements);

section 114 (compulsory acquisition of listed building in need of repair);

section 115 (repairs notice as preliminary to compulsory acquisition under s.114);

section 117 (minimum compensation in case of listed building deliberately left derelict);

section 126 (management etc. of listed buildings acquired by local authority or Secretary of State);

section 271 (application to local planning authorities of provisions as to listed buildings);

section 277 (designation of conservation area);

section 277A (control of demolition in conservation area);

section 277B (formulation and publication of proposals for preservation and enhancement of conservation area); and

Schedule 11 (control of works for demolition, alteration or extension of listed buildings).

The order may also provide that the provisions of the Town and Country Planning Act 1971, set out in Part II of Schedule 29 to the 1980 Act (or such of them as are specified in the order) shall apply to the urban development corporation subject to such modifications as are specified in the order (s.149(3)(*b*), (4) and Sched. 29, Pt. II).

If, under the foregoing enactments, an urban development corporation becomes, in effect, the local planning authority for its own area, this does *not* require it to be treated as such for the purposes of paragraph 17 of Schedule 16 to the Local Government Act 1972, whereby a local highway authority can, in certain circumstances, impose restrictions on the grant, by the local planning authority, of planning permission for certain kinds of development (s.150(1)). The urban development corporation, acting as local planning authority, is thus freed from control by the local highway authority which control might otherwise affect its planning decisions. But the Secretary of State (if he so wishes) can restore this kind of control by the local highway authority by including appropriate provision in any development order which he may make relating to the urban development area (s.150(2)).

Planning blight in an urban development area is dealt with in section 147 of the Local Government, Planning and Land Act 1980, whereby all the provisions of sections 192 to 208 of the Town and Country Planning Act 1971 (relating to the interests of owner-occupiers blighted by planning proposals and the service of blight notices (see, *ante*, pp. 392–402)) are made to apply to land (s.147(1)(*a*) and (*b*)):

(1) which is land in an area *intended* to be designated as an urban development area by a designation order which has been made but which has not yet come into operation; *or*

(2) which is land in an area so designated by an order which has not only been made but which has come into operation.

The difference in the two foregoing alternatives is that if the land in respect of which it is sought to serve a blight notice is land in an urban development area designated as such by an order which has been made but which has not yet come into operation—in such a case the blight notice can *not* be served after the designation order has come into operation (s.147(2)).

Until such time as an urban development corporation is established for the urban development area in respect of which the blight notice is served, it will be the Secretary of State who will have to act upon (*i.e.* "pick-up") the blight notice (s.147(3)). Accordingly, he is authorised to acquire compulsorily any land which has been blighted (s.147(4)). Having acquired it he *may* dispose of the land as he thinks fit (s.147(4)(*b*)) unless (before he disposes of it) the land becomes land in an area designated as an urban development area by an order which has not only been made but which has come into operation in which case he *must* dispose of this land to the urban development corporation established for the urban development area (s.147(4)(*a*)).

(4) *Other controls*

To enable an urban development corporation the better to discharge its functions, the Local Government, Planning and Land Act 1980 makes provision for a variety of further powers and duties to be conferred (either directly by the Act itself or by orders made from time to time by the Secretary of State) upon an urban development corporation (ss.151–163 and 167, 168). These further powers and duties relate to the following matters, namely:

(1) building control (s.151);
(2) fire precautions and home insulation (s.152);
(3) housing authority functions (s.153);
(4) rent rebates (s.154);
(5) rents and removal of protection therefor afforded by section 14 of the Rent Act 1977 (s.155);
(6) the urban development corporation acting, under the Housing Act 1980, as a housing authority (s.156);
(7) declaration of a street as a highway maintainable at the public expense (s.157);
(8) sewerage functions (s.158);
(9) public health (s.159);
(10) loans for building by any person to whom an urban development corporation has sold or let land (s.160);
(11) loans made by an urban development corporation in pursuance of building agreements (s.161);
(12) powers relating to inner urban areas, that is to say, covering land which is at one and the same time in both a "designated district" under the Inner Urban Areas Act 1978, and an urban development area (s.162);

(13) supply of goods and services (under the Local Authorities (Goods and Services) Act 1970) by a local authority to a public body (s.163);
(14) surveying of land (s.167); and
(15) service of notices (s.168).

7. Transfer of Urban Development Corporation's Undertaking

It is not the idea that any urban development corporation should last forever. Such a corporation is a transient or temporary affair even though it may last for several years. Its object is to secure the regeneration of its area (s.136). When this is done its work is completed and it may depart the scene.

The Local Government, Planning and Land Act 1980 accordingly provides that an urban development corporation may "transfer" the whole or part of its undertaking (s.165). This is done by agreement, upon such terms as may be prescribed in the agreement, made by the development corporation with any local authority (s.165(1)(*a*), (9)) or with any statutory undertakers (s.165(1)(*b*))—the agreement being made with the approval of the Secretary of State and the concurrence of the Treasury (s.165(1)).

Where an agreement for a transfer is made, or is about to be made, with a local authority (s.165(1)(*a*)) and when, after the transfer, only liabilities will remain vested in the corporation, then in such case the Secretary of State may vest the liabilities in himself (s.165(3)).

Where an agreement for transfer is made, or is about to be made, and the Secretary of State is satisfied that it is expedient that the liability of the development corporation in respect of advances made to it by himself should be reduced, he may, by order made with the consent of the Treasury, reduce the liability as specified in the order (s.165(7)). Such an order needs positive approval by resolution of each House of Parliament (s.165(8)).

The right of a development corportion to *transfer* the whole or part of its undertaking to a local authority or to a statutory undertaker does not prejudice in any way its right to *dispose* of any of its property including any trade or business which it may be carrying on (s.165(2)).

As mentioned, any agreement by a development corporation to *transfer* the whole or part of its undertaking must carry the approval of the Secretary of State (s.165(1)) who, before giving approval, must consult each local authority in whose area all, or part, of the urban development area lies (s.165(4)) except when the local authority is the actual authority with whom the agreement for transfer is being made (*ibid.*).

Where any transfer is sought the Secretary of State must publish in the *London Gazette* (the *Edinburgh Gazette* in Scotland) and in one or more newspapers circulating in the urban development area, notice of the agreement for transfer and that it has been submitted to him for approval together with a description of its general effect (s.165(5)). If, within 28 days of publication of the notice in the *Gazette*, any statutory undertaker functioning within the urban development area (or in an area adjacent to it) and carrying on a statutory undertaking similar to that proposed to be transferred—if any such statutory undertaker lodges objection to the transfer, then the agreement for transfer must be approved *not* by the Secretary of State but by the "appropriate Minister" (s.165(6)), that is, the Minister of government having central responsibility for the statutory undertaking (s.170(3)).

8. Dissolution of Urban Development Corporation

When all the property and all the undertakings of an urban development corporation have been transferred either to one or more local authorities or to one or more statutory undertakers (or to a mix of all these) under the procedures described above—when all this has happened the work of the urban development corporation is done. It is then provided that it may be dissolved (s.166). This is done by order made by the Secretary of State (s.166(1)). Before making any such order he must consult each local authority in whose area all or part of the urban development area lies (s.166(2) and (5)).

When the dissolution order comes into force the development corporation must cease to act except only for the purpose of preparing its final accounts and report and winding up its affairs (s.166(3)). The actual dissolution of the corporation will take place, without more, either on a date specified in the order of dissolution or on a date ascertainable by reference to such order (s.166(4)).

9. Code of Practice for Development Corporations—Consultation with Local Authorities

It will be seen from the foregoing paragraphs of this chapter that an urban development corporation, *appointed* by the Secretary of State and not *elected* of the people, and all its functioning cannot be other than an encroachment upon the preserves of the local authority (or authorities) into whose area the development corporation steps. There is a precedent for this in the New Towns Act 1946, (now the

New Towns Act 1981), which established new town development corporations to carry out the development of new towns rather than leave this to the routines of established, elected local government authorities. Such authorities did not welcome this incursion into their areas of the single-purpose, ministerially appointed new town development corporations. There is no reason to believe that the new urban development corporations will be better welcomed. Indeed, the first two orders establishing urban development corporations for London's docklands and for Merseyside were vigorously opposed by local government authorities who felt prejudiced by these new "single-minded agencies to spearhead the regeneration" of their respective areas.

All this being so, it is not surprising that the Local Government, Planning and Land Act 1980 deliberately provides for consultation between urban development corporations and local government authorities.

Within 12 months of being established an urban development corporation *must* prepare (s.140(1), (5)) and complete (s.140(3)) a code of practice as to consultation with all "relevant local authorities" (that is, all local authorities the whole or any part of whose area is included (s.140(2)) in the urban development area) about the exercise of their powers by the development corporation (s.140(1)). This code of practice may from time to time be revised, in whole or in part, by the development corporation (s.140(4), (5)). No provision is made for the enforcement by law of any of the provisions of the code of practice.

It will be noted that both the preparation and any revision of their code by an urban development corporation is to be done in consultation with the relevant local government authorities (s.140(5)). However, consultation is one thing; getting agreement is another. Consultation can go on for some time. The Local Government, Planning and Land Act 1980 has not failed to notice this. Hence the provision (s.140(3)) that the preparation of a code of practice *must* be completed within 12 months from the date of the establishment of the corporation. In short, there may be *talk*—the on-going dialogue—but it is talk which is not allowed to go on for ever.

Chapter 24

ENTERPRISE ZONES

Note: In this chapter all section and schedule references are to the Local Government, Planning and Land Act 1980 unless otherwise stated.

1. Government Policy

Section 179 and Schedule 32 of the Local Government, Planning and Land Act 1980 make new and unprecedented provision about planning control and the levying of rates in certain areas of land which are designated under Schedule 32 of the Act as enterprise zones (EZs).

The Minister for Local Government and Environmental Services, Mr. Tom King M.P., speaking on November 14, 1980 about the 1980 Act referred to, "the bold new experiment of enterprise zones where business can be freed from much detailed planning control and from rates."

In a pamphlet issued by the Department of the Environment[1] and dated April 1981, it is stated at page 3 that:

> "The Government is setting up a number of Enterprise Zones. The idea is to see how far industrial and commercial activity can be encouraged by the removal of certain tax burdens, and by relaxing or speeding up the application of certain statutory or administrative controls. The Zones will last for 10 years and it is hoped that the first ones will come into effect this summer.
>
> "Eleven sites have been announced as prospective Enterprise Zones. They vary widely, but all contain land ripe for development. In size they range from about 50 to over 400 hectares (about 125 to over 1000 acres). Enterprise Zones are not part of regional policy, nor are they directly connected with other existing policies such as those for inner cities or derelict land. The sites chosen will continue to benefit from whatever aid is available under these policies.
>
> "The Enterprise Zone sites are in Corby, Dudley, Hartlepool

[1] "Enterprise Zones" unpriced, available from: Inner Cities Directorate, Room P2/108, Department of the Environment, 2 Marsham Street, London, SW1P 3BE.

the Isle of Dogs (in London's docklands), Newcastle/Gateshead, Salford/Trafford, Speke (Liverpool) and Wakefield in England; the lower Swansea Valley in Wales; Clydebank in Scotland; and Belfast, Northern Ireland." (A fuller list of Enterprise Zones designated up to October 10, 1986 appears at page 452, *post.*)

The pamphlet goes on to say that:

"The following benefits are available, for a 10-year period from the date each Zone comes into effect, to both new and existing industrial and commercial enterprises in the Zones:

i. Exemption from Development Land Tax; (this tax was, in any event, abolished in the Budget arrangements of April 1985);
ii. Exemption from rates on industrial and commercial property;
iii. 100% allowances for Corporation and Income Tax purposes for capital expenditure on industrial and commercial buildings;
iv. Applications from firms in Enterprise Zones for certain customs facilities will be processed as a matter of priority and certain criteria relaxed;
v. Industrial Development Certificates are not needed; (Industrial Development Certificates were, in any event, abolished as from January 9, 1982 by the Town and Country Planning (Industrial Development Certificates) (Prescribed Classes of Buildings) Regulations 1981)[2];
vi. Subject to the passage of the Employment and Training Bill, employers will be exempt from industrial training levies and from the requirement to supply information to Industrial Training Boards;
vii. A greatly simplified planning regime; developments that conform with the published scheme for each Zone will not require individual planning permission;
viii. Those controls remaining in force will be administered more speedily;
ix. Government requests for statistical information will be reduced."

Further information about enterprise zones is obtainable from the "Green Pamphlet" (undated) on "Enterprise Zones" and from the seven page note entitled, "Advice on the Enterprise Zone Planning System in England and Wales" dated November 1983, both

[2] S.I. 1981 No. 1826.

lished by ICD 3, Department of the Environment P2/102, 2 Marsham Street, London SW1P 3EB.

2. Invitation to Prepare Scheme for an Enterprise Zone

There are three steps to the creation of an enterprise zone. These are:

(1) invitation to prepare a scheme for an enterprise zone;
(2) preparation and adoption of the scheme;
(3) designation of the enterprise zone.

The invitation to prepare a scheme for an enterprise zone is given by the Secretary of State (Sched. 32, para. 1(3), (4), (5)). It *must* specify the area of the proposed zone (Sched. 32, para. 1(5)(*a*)) and it *may* contain directions about the drawing up of the scheme (Sched. 32, para. 1(5)(*b*)) and as to publicity for the scheme (Sched. 32, para. 1(6)).

Only certain specified bodies may be invited to draw up a scheme and these bodies, in England and Wales, are (Sched. 32, para. 1(1), (7)):

(1) a district council;
(2) a London borough;
(3) a new town corporation; and
(4) an urban development corporation.

(County councils, it will be noted, have no *locus standi* in this new matter of enterprise zones).

3. Preparation of Draft Enterprise Zone Scheme

A body which is invited by the Secretary of State to prepare an enterprise zone scheme is not obliged to do so; it *may* do so if it so wishes but if it does it *must* do so in accordance with the terms of the invitation (Sched. 32, para. 2(1)). If it does so prepare a scheme, then it must give adequate publicity about it so that representations about it may be made (Sched. 32, para. 2(2)). If any representation is made within the specified period for making representations it must be considered by the scheme-making body insofar as it is made on the ground that development within the area of the scheme should not be granted automatic planning permission in accordance with the terms of the scheme (Sched. 32, para. 2(3)).

4. Adoption of Enterprise Zone Scheme

After the time for making representations has run out and after representations (if any) have been considered, the draft enterprise zone scheme may be formally adopted (with or without modification) by resolution of the scheme-making body (Sched. 32, para. 3(1), (2), (3)). Notice of adoption must be advertised (Sched. 32, para. 3(4), (7), (8)) and a copy of the adopted scheme sent to the Secretary of State and also placed on deposit at the principal office of the scheme-making body (Sched. 32, para. 3(4)).

The public may inspect the enterprise zone scheme and have copies of it at a reasonable cost (Sched. 32, para. 3(5), (6)). This latter provision is important because the scheme itself is an "in house" document made by the scheme-making authority—it is not a document in the form of a statutory instrument (purchaseable from H.M. Stationery Office) as is the later-made order designating the area to which the scheme relates to be an enterprise zone. The scheme itself is crucial if only because it is from the scheme that the important details will be learned as to what forms of development are, and what are not, granted automatic planning permission by the later-made order designating the area of the scheme to be an enterprise zone.

The validity of a scheme may, within six weeks, be questioned in the High Court by any person aggrieved (Sched. 32, para. 4(1) and (4)) and the court may order either that the Secretary of State shall *not* designate the area of the scheme as an enterprise zone or shall not so designate it until specified steps have been taken to obviate substantial prejudice to the aggrieved person (Sched. 32, para. 4(2)).

5. Designation of Enterprise Zone

Once an enterprise zone scheme has been adopted by the scheme-making body the Secretary of State, if he thinks it expedient to do so—he has a discretion—may, by order in the form of a statutory instrument, made with Treasury consent and liable to annulment by resolution of either House of Parliament (Sched. 32, para. 5(3)), designate the area of the scheme as an enterprise zone (Sched. 32, para. 5(1), (2)).[3] The order *must* (Sched. 32, para. 5(4)):

(1) specify the date of the designation taking effect (the effective date);
(2) specify the period for which the area is to remain an enterprise zone;
(3) define the boundaries of the zone by means of a plan or map; and

[3] See, *e.g.*, The Lower Swansea Valley Enterprise Zone Designation Order 1981 (S.I. 1981 No. 757). This was the first Enterprise Zone Designation Order to be made. It was made on May 18, 1981 and came into operation on June 11, 1981.

(4) designate as the enterprise zone authority the body which was invited to prepare the scheme.

It will be noted that there is nothing in law to prevent an enterprise zone being situated within an urban development area.

It is further to be noted that the order of the Secretary of State designating the enterprise zone *may* provide that the enterprise zone authority shall be the local planning authority for the zone (Sched. 32, para. 5(7)).

If this is done then the enterprise zone authority will take over the planning powers of any other authority which would otherwise have been the local planning authority for the area of the enterprise zone (Sched. 32, para. 20(1)). This is an important statutory enactment because, like the establishment of an urban development corporation for an urban development area, it could constitute a diminishment of the powers of the traditional local government authority (or authorities) previously discharging planning control functions in the area of the enterprise zone.

Publicity about the designation of an enterprise zone is to be given by the scheme-making body by means of an advertisement (Sched. 32, para. 6(1), (3)) which must contain (Sched. 32, para. 6(2)) a statement:

(1) that the enterprise zone has been created; and
(2) that a copy of the scheme from which the enterprise zone derives can be inspected without payment at a stated place and time.

The Secretary of State has made the following enterprise zone designation orders:

S.I. 1981 No.	*Date of coming into operation*	*Location*	*Designated Enterprise Zone Authority*
757	June 11, 1981	Swansea	Swansea City Council
852	July 10, 1981	Dudley	Dudley B.C.
950	July 31, 1981	Longthwaite Grange (Wakefield)	Wakefield B.C.
1024	August 12, 1981	Salford (3 zones)	Salford City Council
1025	August 12, 1981	Trafford (3 zones)	Trafford B.C.
1070	August 25, 1981	Gateshead (3 zones)	Gateshead M.B.C.
1071	August 25, 1981	Newcastle	Newcastle upon Tyne City Council
1072	August 25, 1981	Speke (Liverpool) (2 zones)	Liverpool City Council
1378	October 23, 1981	Hartlepool (3 zones)	Hartlepool B.C.
S.I. 1982 No.			
462	April 26, 1982	Isle of Dogs	London Docklands Development Corporation

S.I. 1983 No.	*Date of coming into operation—cont.*	*Location—cont.*	*Designated Enterprise Zone Authority—cont.*
896	July 21, 1983	Delyn	Delyn Borough Council
907	July 26, 1983	Wellingborough	Wellingborough B.C.
1007	August 16, 1983	Rotherham	Rotherham M.B.C.
1304	September 23, 1983	Scunthorpe (Normanby Ridge and Queensway)	Scunthorpe B.C.
1305	September 23, 1983	Dale Lane (Wakefield) and Kinsley (Wakefield)	City of Wakefield M.D.C.
1331	October 4, 1983	Workington Allerdale (6 zones)	Allerdale D.C.
1452	October 31, 1983	North West Kent (5 zones)	
		Zones 1 and 2	Gravesham B.C.
		Zones 3 and 4	Rochester-upon-Medway C.C.
		Zone 5	Gillingham B.C.
1473	November 8, 1983	Middlesbrough	Middlesbrough B.C.
1639	December 12, 1983	North East Lancashire (7 zones)	
		(Burnley) No. 1	Burnley B.C.
		(Pendle) No. 2	Pendle B.C.
		(Rossendale) No. 3	Rossendale B.C.
		(Hyndburn) No. 4	Hyndburn B.C.
		(Hyndburn) No. 5	Hyndburn B.C.
		(Hyndburn) No. 6	Hyndburn B.C.
		(Pendle) No. 7	Pendle B.C.
S.I. 1984 No.			
1852	January 1, 1984	Telford (5 zones)	District of the Wrekin Council
347	April 13, 1984	Glenford (Flixborough)	Glenford B.C.
443	April 24, 1984	Milford Haven Waterway (North Shore) (6 zones)	South Pembrokeshire D.C.
444	April 24, 1984	Milford Haven Waterway (South Shore) (7 zones)	Preseli D.C.
1403	October 3, 1984	Dudley (Round Oak)	Dudley M.B.C.
S.I. 1985 No.			
137	March 6, 1985	Lower Swansea Valley (No. 2)	Swansea City Council
S.I. 1986 No.			
1557	October 10, 1986	North West Kent	
		Zone 6	Rochester-upon-Medway C.C.
		Zone 7	Gillingham B.C.

In each of the foregoing orders the period for the enterprise zone is limited to 10 years from the date of the coming into operation of the respective designation order.

6. Modification of Enterprise Zone Scheme and of Enterprise Zone

The scheme from which an enterprise zone derives may be modified (and this includes complete replacement (Sched. 32, para. 13) by the enterprise zone authority on the invitation of the Secretary of State (Sched. 32, paras. 9 and 10). The procedure for achieving a modification follows that for the original making and adoption of the scheme (Sched. 32, paras. 11 and 12).

The Secretary of State may, if he thinks it expedient, modify the designation of an enterprise zone (Sched. 32, para. 15(1), (2)). He may wish to do this, for example, when there has been some modification (as above mentioned) of the scheme from which the enterprise zone derives. However, the power of the Secretary of State to modify an enterprise zone does *not* include (Sched. 32, para. 15(3)) power:

(1) to alter the boundaries of the enterprise zone;
(2) to designate a different enterprise zone authority for the zone; or
(3) to reduce the period during which the zone is to be an enterprise zone.

But if the enterprise zone authority happens to be a new town corporation or an urban development corporation being dissolved under, as the case may be, section 41 of the New Towns Act 1981, or section 166 of the Local Government, Planning and Land Act 1980, then in such case a new body *can* be designated as the enterprise zone authority (Sched. 32, para. 16).

Any order of the Secretary of State modifying an enterprise zone can be made only by statutory instrument with Treasury consent and it is liable to annulment by resolution of either House of Parliament (Sched. 32, para. 15(4)).

7. Planning and Development Control in Enterprise Zones

One of the motivating factors behind the whole idea of the enterprise zone was that planning permission for development should be more easily obtainable than is normally the case. Accordingly, it is provided that the order designating an area of land to be an enterprise zone shall of itself (and without more) have the effect of granting automatic planning permission for any development (or class of development) specified in the scheme (including a modified scheme) from which the enterprise zone derives (Sched. 32, para. 17(1), (2)).

Any automatic planning permission so granted will, however, be subject to such conditions or limitations as are specified in *the enterprise zone scheme* (Sched. 32, para. 17(3)). If none is specified in that scheme then the permission will be completely unconditional (*ibid.*).

Again, any automatic planning permission so granted may, nevertheless, need to receive the formal approval of the enterprise zone authority in respect of such matters (relating to the permitted development) as are specified in the enterprise zone scheme (Sched. 32, paras. 17(6) and 25(1)). As already mentioned, the contents of the enterprise zone scheme are crucial—they will repay close reading.

Where planning permission is granted automatically (as abovementioned) by the order which designates the enterprise zone, the enterprise zone authority even so may, with the approval of the Secretary of State, *direct* that the permission shall *not* apply (Sched. 32, paras. 17(4), (5) and 25) in relation to:

(1) a specified development;
(2) a specified class of development; or
(3) a specified class of development in a specified area of the enterprise zone.

Formerly, if development operations were started under an automatic planning permission emanating from the order which designates the enterprise zone (Sched. 32, para. 17(1)), and if the enterprise zone terminated at, say, the end of a 10 year period, then in such case the enterprise zone scheme no longer authorised the carrying out of such operations *even if they were commenced before the termination of the enterprise zone* (Sched. 32, para. 22). Formal application to the local planning authority needed, in such circumstances, to be made in order to continue the uncompleted development. All this is now changed by the Housing and Planning Act 1986 section 54 which inserts a new paragraph 21 and a new paragraph 22 into Schedule 32 of the Local Government, Planning and Land Act 1980. In the result development operations commenced before an enterprise zone terminates, can now continue till all the development covered by the operations is completed.

Modification of an enterprise zone scheme (as distinct from termination of the zone) will not prevent the continued carrying out of operations begun in accordance with the scheme as it stood before modification (Sched. 32, para. 21).

It may be that the aforementioned automatic grant of planning permission is inadequate (for one reason or another) to cover the particular kind of development which some developer seeks to carry out in the enterprise zone. If this is the case, then planning permission for such development may be applied for, and granted, in the normal way under the Town and Country Planning Act 1971 Part III, or it may be granted by a special development order (Sched. 32, para. 17(7)) made under the 1971 Act, section 24(3).

Provision is made for the obligatory consequential amendment of structure plans by county planning authorities in the light of the provisions of the scheme (or the modified scheme) from which an enterprise zone derives (Sched. 32, paras. 23(1)(*a*) and (2)). Similar provision is made with respect to the obligatory amendment of any local plan relating to land in an enterprise zone (Sched. 32, paras. 23(1)(*b*) and (4)).

8. Rates in Enterprise Zones

Exemption from local authority rates (but not from water rates or charges) is given in respect of any hereditament (provided it is an *exempt* hereditament) in an enterprise zone so long as the area remains designated as an enterprise zone (Sched. 32, para. 27(1), (2)). For the purposes of this exemption *any* hereditament is an exempt hereditament *unless* it is (Sched. 32, paras. 27(3) and 32(1))

(1) a dwelling-house, a private garage or private storage premises; or
(2) specified in Schedule 3 to the Local Government Act 1974 (hereditaments of certain public utilities etc.); or
(3) a hereditament which is occupied by a public utility undertaking and of which the value falls to be ascertained on the profits basis.

If a hereditament is, for the time being, not in use it must, even so, be treated as a dwelling-house, a private garage or private storage premises if it appears that, when next in use, the hereditament will be a hereditament of that description (Sched. 32, para. 27(4)).

Provision is made for exemption from rates in the case of a mixed hereditament ((*i.e.*) a hereditament only partially falling within the definition of "exempt hereditament" as above described) situated in an enterprise zone (Sched. 32, para. 28).

The exemption from rates (as here described) of exempt hereditaments situated within an enterprise zone will cause a consequential (and maybe serious) loss of revenue to the local government authority (the local rating authority) for the area in which the enterprise zone is situated. To cover this loss the Secretary of State *must* make a grant with Treasury consent out of money to be provided by Parliament (Sched. 32, para. 29) of such amount as will fully compensate the local government authority for its revenue loss (Sched. 32, para. 30).

On all of this it may be added that the financial memorandum on

Bill 335 dated July 21, 1980 for the Local Government, Planning and Land Act 1980, declared that:

> "The establishment of enterprise zones will entail a loss of rate revenue for which local authorities will be fully compensated by specific Exchequer grant. The cost will depend on the number of zones, where they are sited, their area and the extent to which they attract new industrial and commercial development. On the basis of the Government's current plans the immediate cost will be £5–10 millions per annum; this will rise as development occurs and the final figure will depend on the amount and value of development."

9. Sources for Further Information on Individual Enterprise Zones

Local contact points concerning enterprise zones in England and Wales are as follows:

ENGLAND

Corby
F H McClenaghan
Director of Industry
Corby Industrial Development Centre
Douglas House
Queens Square, Corby
Northants NN17 1PL
Telephone:
Corby (05363) 62571
Dudley
K Duesbury
Industrial Development Unit
Council House
Dudley
West Midlands DY1 1HF
Telephone:
Dudley (0384) 55433
Glanford
A L Lyman
Glanford Borough Council
Council Offices
Station Road
Brigg
South Humberside DN20 8EG
Telephone:
Brigg (0652) 52441
Hartlepool
E Morley
Industrial Development Officer

ENGLAND—*cont.*

Civic Centre
Hartlepool
Cleveland TS24 8AY
Telephone:
Hartlepool (0429) 66522
Isle of Dogs
C Attwood
London Docklands
Development Corporation
West India House
Millwall Dock
London E14 9TJ
Telephone: 01-515 3000
Middlesbrough
D Brydon
Enterprise Zone Office
Vancouver House
Gurney Street
Middlesbrough
Cleveland TS1 1QP
Telephone:
Middlesbrough (0642) 222279
N E Lancashire
I W Brodhurst
North East Lancashire
Development Association
Stephen House
Bethesda Street
Burnley

ENGLAND—*cont.*

Lancashire BB11 1PR
Telephone:
Burnley (0282) 37411
N W Kent
D Homewood
N W Kent EZ Office
Mountbatten House
28 Military Road
Chatham
Kent ME4 4JE
Telephone:
Medway (0634) 826233
Rotherham
P Fairholm
Rotherham Metropolitan
Borough Council
Department of Planning
Norfolk House
Walker Place
Rotherham
S Yorkshire S60 1QT
Telephone:
Rotherham (0709) 372099
Salford
P Henry
Administrative and Industrial
Liaison Officer
City of Salford
Civic Centre, Chorley Road
Swinton
Greater Manchester M27 2AD
Telephone: 061-793 3237
or 794 4711
Scunthorpe
Mrs J Knox
Scunthorpe Borough Council
Civic Centre
Ashby Road
Scunthorpe
S Humberside DN16 1AB
Telephone:
Scunthorpe (0724) 862141
Speke (Liverpool)
G Davey
Planning and Land
Committee Section
Liverpool City Council
Room 214
Municipal Buildings
Dale Street
Liverpool L69 2DH

ENGLAND—*cont.*

Telephone: 051-227 3911
ext. 736
Telford
Mike Morgan
Enterprise Zone Manager
Telford Development
Corporation
Priorslee
Telford
Shropshire TF2 9NT
Telephone:
Telford (0952) 613131
Trafford
R M Dodsworth
Industrial Development Officer
Trafford Metropolitan Borough
Council
Town Hall
Talbot Road, Stretford
Greater Manchester M32 0TH
Telephone: 061-872 2101
Tyneside (Gateshead)
C Smith
Gateshead Metropolitan
Borough Council
Town Hall
Gateshead
Tyne and Wear NE8 1BP
Telephone:
Gateshead (0632) 771011
Tyneside (Newcastle)
C Hammer
City of Newcastle upon Tyne
Central Policy Division
Civic Centre
Newcastle upon Tyne
NE99 2BH
Telephone: Newcastle upon
Tyne (0632) 328520
Wakefield
R Gregory
Planning Department
City of Wakefield Metropolitan
District Council
Newton Bar
Wakefield
West Yorkshire WF1 2TT
Telephone:
Wakefield (0924) 370211
Wellingborough
R H Entwistle

ENGLAND—*cont.*

Director of Development
Wellingborough Borough
Council
Council Offices
Tithe Barn Road
Wellingborough
Northamptonshire NN8 1BN
Telephone:
Wellingborough (0933) 229777
Workington
M Gordon
Enterprise Zone Manager
Allerdale District Council
Holmewood
Cockermouth
Cumbria CA13 0DW
Telephone:
Workington (0900) 65656

WALES

Delyn
M Gibson

WALES—*cont.*

Delyn Borough Council
Enterprise House
Aber Park
Flint
Clwyd CH6 5BD
Telephone: Flint (035 26) 4004
Lower Swansea Valley
Director of Planning
Swansea City Council
The Guildhall
Swansea SA1 4NL
Telephone:
Swansea (0792) 50821
ext. 2701/2723
Milford Haven Waterway
I W R David
Chief Executive
Preseli District Council
Cambria House
PO Box 27
Haverfordwest
Dyfed SA61 1TP
Telephone:
Haverfordwest (0437) 4551

CHAPTER 25

SIMPLIFIED PLANNING ZONES

Note. In this Chapter the expression "1986 Act" means the Housing and Planning Act 1986 and the expression "1971 Act" means the Town and Country Planning Act 1971.

1. Introductory

In the White Paper (Cmnd. 9571) dated July 1985 and entitled "Lifting the Burden"—the Burden being that of various forms of government control (including planning and development control) over enterprise in all its manifestations—the Government declared (para. 3.5):

> "There is therefore always a presumption in favour of development, unless that development would cause demonstrable harm to interests of acknowledged importance."[1]

The White Paper went on (para. 3.6) to declare that:

> "3.6 In line with this approach to the control of development, and in support of the general aim of deregulation, a number of other measures are being taken to simplify the planning system and reduce the burden of control:
>
> (i) It is proposed to introduce new legislation to permit the setting up of *Simplified Planning Zones* (SPZ) which will extend to other areas the type of planning regime already established in Enterprise Zones. This will enable the local planning authority to specify types of development allowed in an area, so that developers can then carry out development that conforms to the scheme without the need for a planning application and the related fee. Planning permission for other types of development can be applied for in the normal way. This type of planning scheme has proved to be effective and successful in Enterprise Zones and can provide a real stimulus to the redevelopment of derelict or unused land and buildings in areas that are badly in need of regeneration. In addition to providing local planning authorities with powers to introduce SPZ's, they will also be required to consider

[1] See pp. 208 *et seq., ante.*

proposals for the establishment of SPZ's initiated by priv te developers. The Secretaries of State would have reserve powers to direct the preparation of proposals for an SPZ, similar to those that they already have to direct the preparation of alterations to development plans."

The Government have fulfilled the forgoing promise by the enactment of the Housing and Planning Act 1986. Part II of this Act relates to Simplified Planning Zones. These will be established by local planning authorities by means of a new system of Simplified Planning Zone Schemes (it is the word "Scheme" which is the really important part of this expression) each of which will specify types of development permitted in a zone. A developer will be able to carry out such development without making an application for planning permission and paying the requisite fee.[2] (If anyone detects in all of this a certain nostalgic throw-back to 1932 (years before the 1947 Silkin legislation was enacted) when the Town and Country Planning Act of 1932 provided for the making of "town planning schemes,"[3] such a one will not, in my view, be at all wide of the mark).

Part II of the 1986 Act secures all of these new planning arrangements (s.25) by the device of writing into the 1971 Act five new sections, namely, sections 24A, 24B, 24C, 24D and 24E and one new Schedule, namely, Schedule 8A. All these new provisions written into the 1971 Act will come into operation on "an appointed day" (1986 Act, s.57(2)), that is to say, a day appointed by the Secretary of State for the Environment. The Secretary of State has not, at the date of this writing (February 1987) appointed such a day.

2. Procedure for Preparation of a Simplified Planning Zone Scheme

Every local planning authority are under an *obligation* to consider the question of whether a simplified planning zone scheme "is desirable" for their area (or any part of their area) (1971 Act, s.24A(4)(*a*)). This question is to be constantly under review by the authority (*ibid.*). If the answer to the question is *yes*, then the authority *must* (they have no discretion) prepare such a scheme (1971 Act, s.24A(4)(*b*)) in which event the provisions of Schedule 8A of the 1971 Act will apply to the making of the scheme and also to any alteration which may later be made to the scheme (1971 Act, s.24A(5)).

[2] See pp. 188 *et seq.*
[3] See pp. 8 and 9.

In a shire county (*i.e.* a non-metropolitan county)[4] the local planning authority for the purpose of the making or the alteration of a simplified planning zone scheme will be the district planning authority (except as to land in a National Park) (1971 Act, s.24A(6)). In a metropolitan county it follows that, after the abolition on April 1, 1986 of the metropolitan county *council* (Local Government Act 1985, s.1), the metropolitan district councils will have the forgoing responsibility.

Once a simplified planning zone scheme is in force the area to which it relates will be called a "simplified planning zone" (1971 Act, s.24A(1)). Thus it is the scheme which is important; it is the *scheme* which makes the *zone*.

As to the detailed procedure for the making or the alteration of a simplified planning zone scheme reference should be made to Schedule 8A of the 1971 Act (1986 Act, s.25(2)). The "highlights" of that Schedule are as follows.

(1) A scheme must consist of a map defining the area of the zone and a written statement along with such diagrams, illustrations and descriptive matter as the local planning authority think appropriate for explaining or illustrating the provisions of the scheme (Sched. 8A, para. 1). In particular the scheme *must* specify—
   (a) the development permitted by the scheme;
   (b) the land in relation to which planning permission is granted;
   (c) the conditions, limitations or exceptions to which the planning permission is granted; and
   (d) such other matters as may be prescribed by regulations made by the Secretary of State (*ibid.*).

(2) The Secretary of State must be informed of what the local planning authority are doing in connection with the making or alteration of a scheme (*ibid.* para. 2).

(3) If the local planning authority show no inclination to make or alter a scheme, a private individual may request them to do so and, if they refuse or, within three months do not decide to do so, that person may *require* the matter to be reported to the Secretary of State who *may* issue to the authority a direction requiring them to make a scheme (*ibid.*, paras. 3 and 4).

(4) Provision is made for publicity and consultation (public participation) with respect to the proposals of the local planning authority for the making or alteration of a scheme (*ibid.* para.

[4] See pp. 40 and following 53.

5) including publicity and consultation in connection with the shortened procedure for certain alterations which are not, in the eye of the local planning authority, of sufficient importance to warrant the full procedure of Schedule 8A, paragraph 5 (*ibid.* para. 6).

(5) If the Secretary of State is not satisfied with the arrangements for the aforementioned publicity and consultation he may take steps to secure adequacy in such matters (*ibid.* para. 7).

(6) If objections by any person are made to the proposals for making or altering a scheme, provision is made for hearing the objections at a public local inquiry or other hearing (*ibid.* para. 8). The local planning authority have a discretion as to whether they will have a local inquiry or other hearing except when the objections are made in accordance with regulations in which case the local inquiry or other hearing is mandatory (*ibid.*).

(7) If there are no objections to the proposals for making or altering a scheme, or if there are such objections duly made and duly considered, if need be, at a public local inquiry or other hearing, then the local planning authority may, by resolution, formally *adopt* the proposals (with or without modification of the proposals as originally prepared) and thereby make (or alter) the simplified planning zone scheme (*ibid.* para. 9). The scheme will take effect on the date of its adoption and will endure for ten years when it will cease to have effect (1971 Act, s.24C(1)) as also will any planning permission under it (1971 Act, s.24C(2)) *except* in so far as development under that permission has been begun (*ibid.*, s.24C(2)(4)). If development which has been begun (as aforesaid) is not thereafter completed without unreasonable delay, the provisions of section 44 of the 1971 Act (relating to the termination of planning permission if completion of development is unreasonably delayed) are applied (*ibid.* s.24C(3)).[5]

(8) Before proposals for making or altering a scheme are adopted by the local planning authority, the Secretary of State may call in such proposals (1971 Act, Sched. 8A, para. 10) for his own *approval*, modification or rejection (*ibid.* para. 11).

(9) Where a local planning authority have been given a direction by the Secretary of State to make or to alter a scheme (see item (3) above), then, if he is satisfied (after a public local inquiry or other hearing) that the authority are not taking the

[5] As to when development is begun, see p. 215, *ante*.

necessary steps, he may himself make the scheme or the alterations (*ibid.* para. 12).

(10) The Secretary of State may make regulations with respect to the form and content of simplified planning zone schemes and the procedure to be followed in their preparation, withdrawal, adoption, submission, approval, making or alteration (*ibid.* para. 13). Under this authority the Secretary of State, at the date of this writing (February 1987), has not yet made any regulations.

3. Effect of a Simplified Planning Zone Scheme when Adopted or Approved

The *adoption* by the local planning authority (under the 1971 Act, Sched. 8A, para. 9) of proposals for a simplified planning zone scheme, or the *approval* of such proposals by the Secretary of State in a case where he has called in the proposals for his own consideration (under the 1971 Act, Sched. 8A, paras. 10 and 11), has the effect *ipso facto* of granting *planning permission for any development which is specified in the scheme* (1971 Act, s.24A(2)).

Planning permission granted under a simplified planning zone scheme may be granted unconditionally or subject to such conditions, limitation or exceptions as may be specified in the scheme (1971 Act, s.24A(3)). These conditions or limitations may apply to all development which is granted planning permission by the scheme or they may apply only to particular descriptions (set out in the scheme) of such development (*ibid.* s.24B(1)(*a*)). Such conditions or limitations may include the need to get the consent, agreement or approval of the local planning authority with respect to particular descriptions (set out in the scheme) of development permitted by the scheme (*ibid.* s.24B(1)(*b*)).

The adoption or approval of *alterations* to a simplified planning zone scheme has effect as follows (1971 Act, s.24D).

If the alterations are to secure the inclusion of more land in the simplified planning zone, planning permission for any development, as specified in the alterations, on that land is automatically granted (*ibid.* s.24D(2)).

If the alterations are related to the grant of planning permission, then such permission is automatically granted for any development specified in the alterations (*ibid.* s.24D(3)).

If the alterations relate to the withdrawal or relaxation of conditions, limitations or restrictions to which planning permission under the scheme is subject, such withdrawal or relaxation takes effect forthwith (*ibid.* s.24D(4)).

If the alterations are to secure the exclusion of land from the simplified planning zone, or to withdraw a planning permission or to impose new or more stringent conditions etc. subject to which planning permission under the scheme is granted, the alterations cannot take effect until 12 months after their adoption or approval (*ibid.* s.24D(5)). This will ensure that development which is going forward on the basis of an existing scheme will not be prejudicially affected by the alterations to the scheme.

Any alterations to a simplified planning zone scheme do not affect any planning permission automatically granted under the scheme in any case where development authorised by it has been begun (*ibid.* s.24D(6)). As to when development may be said to have been begun, reference should be made to the 1971 Act, section 43 and to page 215, *ante*.

4. Keeping of Registers for, and Challenging Validity of, Simplified Planning Zone Schemes

Once a simplified planning zone scheme is in operation, the register of applications for planning permission showing the manner in which they were dealt with (kept by the local planning authority under 1971 Act, s.34), must contain such further information as may be prescribed by the Secretary of State in regulations made by him with respect to all simplified planning zone schemes in their area (1971 Act, s.34(1) as amended by the 1986 Act, Sched. 6, Pt. II, para. 1.

The validity of a simplified planning zone scheme may be questioned (by any person aggrieved by it)[6] under the 1971 Act but not otherwise (1971 Act, s.242(1) as amended by the 1986 Act, Sched. 6, Pt. II, para. 4). The procedure for any such questioning is dealt with in section 244(1) and (2) of the 1971 Act (1971 Act, s.244(7) as amended by the 1986 Act, Sched. 6, Pt. II, para. 5).

5. Exclusion of Certain Kinds of Land and Certain Development from Simplified Planning Zones and Schemes

The following land may *not* be included in a simplified planning zone (s.24E(1)):

(1) land in a National Park;
(2) land in a conservation area;
(3) land in an area of outstanding natural beauty;
(4) land in a greenbelt identified in a development plan; and

[6] See pp. 221–230.

(5) land notified under the Wildlife and Countryside Act 1981, sections 28 or 29 as an area of special scientific interest.

If, however, land in a simplified planning zone *becomes* land in any one of the above descriptions, it does not thereby become excluded from the zone (s.24E(2)).

The Secretary of State may by order provide that no simplified planning zone scheme shall grant automatic planning permission for development—

(a) in any area or areas specified in the order; or

(b) of any description specified in the order (s.24E(3)).

But development already begun when the order of the Secretary of State comes into force is not affected (s.24E(4)).

6. Commentary

Clearly the making of a simplified planning zone scheme is going to be no simple matter and is going to take time—months rather than weeks (or is it years rather than months?). The local planning authority will need to consider very closely the details of their proposals because the wider or more liberal the development automatically granted by the scheme, the less will the authority, on an *ad hoc* individual basis, be able to exercise their own policies relating to development control. Control by planning authorities of details about development permitted by the scheme (*e.g.* the siting of buildings, the materials to be used in their construction, and the dimensions, design and external appearance of buildings) will be beyond control by the local planning authority unless they have been spelt out deliberately and in detail in the scheme itself. Yet if too much detail is put into a scheme there is a chance that more objections to it will be lodged and, accordingly, the more protracted will be any public local inquiry relating to such objections.

On the other hand, a developer will wish to know (by his reading and examination of the scheme) with some certainty whether he may safely go ahead with his development without making any formal application for planning permission[7] and paying the fees currently applicable in such a case,[7] relying on the provisions of the scheme to support his action. After all, if he goes beyond the scope of the scheme (including its conditions, limitations and exceptions) he is in danger of being faced with an enforcement notice[8] on the basis that he has carried out development without planning permission. The developer may decide to take this risk or (if he has time on his

[7] See pp. 180 and 188, *ante*.

[8] See Chap. 15.

hands) he may apply under section 53(1) of the 1971 Act (as amended by the 1986 Act, Sched. 6, Pt. II, para. 3) for a determination by the local planning authority as to whether or not his development falls within the scope of the scheme.

In short, the drafting of a simplified planning zone scheme may well be as big a headache to the local planning authority as the construing of the meaning and scope of the scheme will be to a developer eager to press on with development which happens to be of an expensive and substantial nature. In such a case, and in order to be absolutely sure of his ground, will the developer seek an *ad hoc* grant of planning permission from the local planning authority? Will he think it better to be slow but sure rather than rapid and wrong? But if he *does* apply to the local planning authority for an *ad hoc* grant of planning permission, will the authority accept his application and deal with it in the ordinary way[9] or will they refer the developer to the contents of their simplified planning zone scheme? We shall see. In the fullness of time all will be revealed. . . .

[9] See pp. 202–210.

Appendix I

I have been pressed to include in this edition of the *Outline of Planning Law*, here and there, some personal observations on the passing planning scene. I am not sure that it is wise to do this sort of thing in a book whose main purpose is to explain what the law of town and country planning in England and Wales *says and does*—not what it *should* say and do.

I myself do not agree with certain aspects of the law explained, as dispassionately as I can, in this "Outline." But the reader, when he comes face to face with town planning control, will have to deal with the law as he finds it and *not* as he would have found it had it all been done and enacted in the more efficient and agreeable manner which would have undoubtedly occurred if the doing of it had been left totally in my hands!

In short, the writer of a law book needs to be objective rather than subjective as he approaches his task. This I have, throughout eight editions of the "Outline," endeavoured to be and that is why I (at first) rejected out of hand the suggestion that in the ninth edition there should be some "personalisation"—I think that is today's "in" word—of the work.

However, the years accumulate; they gather around and about all authors "who daily further from the East must travel"; we all change with the passing decades. One becomes better informed though not necessarily any wiser. (Who said that?). I believe I myself am less "sharp" but probably (at least I hope so) more compassionate than I was when I first put together this "Outline" nearly 40 years ago.

"I cannot be what once I was. . . .
A deep distress hath humanised my soul."

(That *I know* is Mr. William Wordsworth—visiting Tintern Abbey).

Accordingly, I decided, upon reflection, to meet the suggestion about personalisation by including in this Edition two Appendices.

This Appendix I carries an article I wrote in 1974 (it is reproduced here by courtesy of the "Kent Messenger" who first published it) in which I traced the story of local government from the Middle Ages to the present day. It shows the development of today's modern units of local government and the progressive decline, as from 1888 when the county councils and county boroughs were invented, of a motley, multifarious group of *ad hoc* local government bodies.

The modern units of local government were at their zenith in 1929 when the last of the *ad hoc* authorities, the Overseers of the Poor (the Poor Law Guardians) ceased to exist. That was the effect of the Poor Law Act 1929. But nothing stands still. The very next year the Road Traffic Act of 1930 established the first of a new breed of *ad hoc* bodies, namely, the Traffic Commissioners whose duty it was to licence the fast growing number of Passenger Road Coaches and to order their comings and goings along such roads as we had half a century ago.

The article, "Local Government 1974—the Changing Scene" now follows. I hope it will be of, at least, historical interest (particularly to the younger readers of this book) in showing the steps whereby democratic local government achieved the height of its powers in 1929 and then began its long downhill débacle finally getting itself into the sorry state which lead to the even sorrier state brought about by the re-organisation enacted in the Local Government Act 1972—a re-organisation which came into force on April 1, 1974.

The 1974 re-organisation was not to everyone's taste (it was certainly not to mine) and it has lasted hardly more than a decade before the government of the day (of the *same* political persuasion, be it noted, as it was in 1972–74) has determined to make changes in the unpopular arrangements of April 1, 1974 all of which seemed to me to be based on the doubtful (and, today, discredited) principle that "big is best."

* * * * * *

LOCAL GOVERNMENT 1974—THE CHANGING SCENE

ONCE again local government is in a state of turmoil. If this is disputed (and only somebody who knows nothing at all about the subject will seek to sustain such a dispute), then it can be said (and this is without any fear of contradiction whatsoever) that it is at least in a state of transition. Indeed, it is—for at the moment (January 1974) there are two sets of local government on the Statute Book at the same time—the old-style, moribund local government (due to pass away for ever at the last moment of March 31, 1974) and the new-style, up-and-coming local government (due to function at the first moment of April 1st, 1974).

"The old order changeth, yielding place to new." To *new*? Oh, Yes! To *better*? Ah, So! *The proof of the pudding is in the eating! Time alone will tell! We shall see!* These bromides could be extended vastly but, quite seriously, they are absolutely true in the present context.

Accordingly, the cry is *Stand aside; stand clear; the Local Government now standing at platform '74 is about to start. Stand away, now, and give the thing a chance!*

In the meantime what does all this shake-up amount to and how has it all come about—this traumatic upheaval—the greatest in the local government world since the Administrative Counties were invented in 1888? Let us look back for a while before we look forward to the new birth, the new beginning on April 1st, 1974.

In the days of the Middle Ages there were two distinct kinds of local government and this bifurcated arrangement has continued down the ages and the centuries to the present day when it just about comes to an end as will be shown later in the commentary.

In the Middle Ages, local government was *either* Borough Government (when it was in the hands of the Chartered Boroughs, with their Mayors and Corporations), *or* it was County Government when it was in the hands of the County Court (not to be confused with the 19th century County Court for small debts), the Hundred Court, or the Manorial Court. All these courts were administrative as well as judicial bodies.

The close of the Middle Ages saw the end of this arrangement at least so far as County Government was concerned. The Chartered Boroughs continued on their way but in the Counties (that is, outside the Boroughs) it was the growing power of the Justices of the Peace (an institution much earlier started by Edward III) which seized upon the reins of local government and hung on pretty tightly for quite a few centuries.

The eighteenth century saw the development of the *ad hoc* local government authority. Instead of one local authority doing (or tending to do) *all* the business of local government in a given area, the new idea was one authority, one job. This was supposed to be more efficient. In so far as *ad hoc* bodies grew in numbers—and they were certainly very fruitful and multiplied greatly until the middle of the nineteenth century—such growth could only be regarded as a reflection upon the efficiency of the existing local government authorities, that is to say, the Borough Councils in the Chartered Boroughs and the Justices of the Peace (functioning through Quarter Sessions) in the Counties.

In 1789 one of the most decisive events in the history of the world occurred—the Bastille fell and the hinge of history turned. What an outpouring followed that famous event! No wonder the mob of Paris was (and is) regarded as the most famous in the world. The wind of change (to coin a phrase!) began to blow quite strongly. In Britain it led to the great Reform Act of 1832 which put the Sovereign Parliament sitting at Westminster through the hoop in a big way. In 1835, the Chartered Boroughs were reformed; many ancient municipal corporations ceased to exist. Those that remained were to function according to a uniform pattern straight across the board.

What, however, of the Counties? Their turn had to wait almost half a century because, in the meantime, the *ad hoc* bodies had been proliferating at a great pace. Indeed, around 1850 or '60 local government presented to the astonished investigator "a chaos of areas, a chaos of franchises, a chaos of authorities and a chaos of rates." It has been calculated that in 1883 there were[1]:

52 counties;
239 municipal (chartered) boroughs;
70 improvement districts;
1006 urban sanitary districts;
577 rural sanitary districts;
41 port sanitary authorities;
2051 school board districts;
649 unions (for the poor law);
194 lighting and watching districts;
14,946 poor law parishes;
5,064 highway parishes;
13,000 ecclesiastical parishes.

This makes some 37,889 different areas for one purpose or another. It is quite a lot of areas and the jig-saw puzzle is complicated by the fact that these areas repeatedly overlapped each other.

In 1871, a Royal Commission came to the conclusion that there were too many areas. That was sufficient for the reformists whereupon simplification started in a big way.

In 1882 the Municipal (Chartered) Boroughs were further reformed and refined while in 1888 local government in the Counties was given the biggest shake-up of all by the creation of brand new County Councils *elected by the people*. To these new County Councils the local government functions of Quarter Sessions (composed of Justices who were not, be it remembered, *elected* by the people at all but *appointed by the Crown*) were transferred.

But the Local Government Act 1888 not only created *County* Councils; it created *County Borough* Councils. The Bill for the Act contained only a handful of County Boroughs but, by the time it became an Act, some 80 Boroughs had got themselves into the exclusive category of County Borough. The Counties never really recovered from the shock of all this. Why is this so? Is it because the County and the County Borough are mutually exclusive beings? The more the County Boroughs grow in number the less the Counties (at

[1] *Hart's Local Government and Administration,* (9th ed.).

least for local government purposes, though not necessarily for cricketing purposes) become in size. What a thorn in the side of any County was a County Borough!

Such a Borough had not only the local government powers of a Borough but also those of a County as well. It was an all purpose authority in that within its own area it did *all that had to be done* by local government. This was a state of affairs with which the Counties never fully came to terms. They had to wait a long time to change all this. Indeed, they have had to wait till April 1, 1974, when the County may be said to have triumphed, at long last, over the County Borough. Is it a pyrrhic victory? We shall see in due course.

After 1888, year by year, the lights of the *ad hoc* authorities went out as more and more existing (and also new) local government functions were transferred by statute to the new County Borough Councils or to the new County Councils as the case might be. (It will be noted that the bifurcation, earlier referred to, in the system of English Local Government still persists in the reformed styling of the 1880's).

In 1894, by a further local government Act, County Local Government was confirmed in the form of a split level activity—in other words, two-tiered local government was to prevail in the Counties. At the *top* level was the County Council with its Chairman, Aldermen and Councillors; at the *lower* (or second level, if the term is preferred) were the County District Councils which came in three different varieties, namely the Non-County Boroughs (with their mayors, aldermen and councillors), the Urban Districts (with their chairmen and councillors), and the Rural Districts (with their chairmen and councillors). The Rural Districts were further subdivided into Rural Parishes.

The Act of 1894 did not affect the County Boroughs. Thus the position was that, after the reforms of 1882, 1888 and 1894, local government was vested either in an all-purpose authority, namely the County Borough, or it was vested in a split-level , two-tiered arrangement in the Counties with the County Council functioning at the top and a set of County District Councils, whether Non-County Borough Council, Urban District Council, or Rural District Council, functioning at a secondary level.

That has been the "set-up" since 1894. It has existed, for better, for worse, for eighty years. It will come to an end on March 31st, 1974, when it can be said that the ever-simmering battle between the idealogy of an all-purpose authority (the County Borough) as against a split-level form of local government (the County and its attendant and subservient County Districts), comes to a full head and erupts in a big way.

We already know the result; it was enacted for all to see in the Local Government Act 1972 which comes into operation on April 1st, 1974.

The victory went to the Counties. The result is that, from April 1st, 1974, all over the face of our country, the split-level (or two-tiered) system of local government will prevail. No one local government authority will ever again be the complete master of its own house. In every corner of the land there will always be *two* local government authorities (top level and lower level—first level and second level) each with a finger in the pie. Which deals with what? That is the question. It will take time to sort it all out.

The proud Cities of York, Manchester, Liverpool, Bristol, Southampton, Norwich (and many others) will become "Districts" all functioning under the overriding (but not, one trusts, overbearing) aegis of a new Administrative County. Thus does organisation and method lead to simplification and efficiency—or does it? Again, we shall see. There used to be (for example) some 144 local planning authorities ultimately responsible for *all* town planning control within their respective areas. Under the new arrangement there will be some 340 such authorities. The division of responsibility between all of these remains, at the moment of writing, to be finally decided upon . . .

All these new arrangements for local government stem from the setting-up in 1966 of a Royal Commission to examine exhaustively the local government set-up which had existed from 1894. The Royal Commission reported in 1969 in favour (generally speaking) of the all-purpose authority as the most efficient instrument of local government administration. When it came to brass tacks (that is, to the enacting of the reforming legislation) the government of the day plumped for the split-level idea as against the all-purpose idea for local government.

Thus, the Royal Commission on Local Government 1966–69 is responsible neither for what works, nor for what doesn't work, in the new set-up.

April 1st, 1974 is awaited with interest and trepidation. Let me repeat what was earlier said in this commentary—"*the Local Government now standing in Platform '74 is about to start.*" In fact it is raring to go—especially the new councillors—(all the aldermen are abolished). Let us wish it all good luck. Well, why not? If it works, that's fine. If it doesn't then that will be very bad luck (make no mistake about this) for the ratepayers!

Appendix II

"THE QUESTION IS . . . WHICH IS TO BE MASTER—THAT'S ALL"

Address by Sir Desmond Heap, LL.M., Hon. LL.D., P.P.R.T.P.I., at the September 1984 Conference organised by the Bar Council, the Law Society and the Royal Institution of Chartered Surveyors at New College, Oxford, and here reprinted, by courtesy, from "The Metropolitan Problem," Occasional Papers No. 11 of the Journal of Planning and Environment Law (Sweet & Maxwell Ltd., London).

I

I am much honoured in being asked to open this year's Planning Law Conference. I have divided my address into three parts (like Caesar's Gaul). Let me start with a few "wise saws and modern instances."

First, the Government are going ahead with the proposals to abolish the GLC and the Metropolitan County Councils. The Government are determined on this change. We should avoid, this weekend, entering into sterile debate about how wrong it all is. Do not worry too much if the new arrangements are, for example, not totally democratic—indeed, don't worry if they are patently *undemocratic*!

Some people today are beginning to think that democracy has its limits and that the smooth, efficient functioning of whatever particular matter is in hand is something which may lie beyond those limits. In short, the question today is, "Can democracy deliver; if so, can it deliver on time?"

I do not accept that, because an authority which is making a decision is democratically elected, then the decision *must* necessarily be good and right. Conversely, it does not follow that decisions made in an undemocratic way *must* inevitably be wrong. That is nonsense. The Mona Lisa was not painted by a committee whereas we can all recall the old adage that a camel *is* a horse designed by a committee, the contours of the animal disclosing the jostling injection of many competing disciplines. Never forget that the best things in life have always been done, or discovered, by an inspired individualist and not by a committee however worthy and dedicated.

So far as local government is concerned we have already seen the twilight of democracy setting in. No longer are gas, water, electricity, hospitals, public transport, sewerage and drainage democratically controlled by elected councillors as they were 50 years ago when I entered the local government service.

Lewis Silkin made his new 1947 planning system democratic. It was party-politically controlled both centrally and locally. Was he right to arrange things in this way? What happens when central government and local government are at loggerheads as now? Mr. Chris Holland,[1] in the paper he will deliver on Sunday morning, touches on this. His paper is entitled, *The Relevance of Strategic Planning*. Mr. Holland observes that:

> "In choosing to delegate administration through elected bodies rather than agencies of central government, Parliament has created secondary centres of power which are only partially controllable."

At the moment there is a spate of spiteful bickering to and fro between central government and local government, the like of which I have never previously seen during my long association with local government extending (as it now does) over 50 years. If a *modus vivendi* cannot be found the Sovereign Parliament will have to turn to other methods to curb recalcitrant local authorities. The answer may have to be the appointed body—the dreaded quango! "The question is," said Humpty Dumpty [to Alice] . . . which is to be master—that's all."[2] There can surely be little doubt today (and Mr. Holland also touches on this) that some metropolitan authorities have not even *sought* to obtain a *modus vivendi* with the Government. On the contrary, they have adopted the stance of defiant, all-out opposition to national policies formally declared by the Government. In doing this, says Mr. Holland, "they have sown the wind." Well, they are now going to reap the whirlwind. The reason is quite simple. No self-respecting central government, of whatever political persuasion, democratically elected on a sufferage of one man one vote will, or indeed can, tolerate such behaviour. *That* is the reason. The duty of *any* government is to govern. As Humpty Dumpty said, "The question is. . . . " And there is this further point. Today a lot of folk are so disenchanted with the behaviour of local authorities up and down the land that my guess is that they are increasingly ready, willing and waiting for the *appointed board*, such as the London Docks Development Corporation, to turn up and replace government by an over-politicised locally *elected authority*.

Let me say again: if the new arrangements now to be enacted by

[1] Chris J. Holland, M.R.T.P.I., M.C.I.T., M.I.C.E., Partner with Travers Morgan Planning.

[2] Lewis Carroll, *Alice Through the Looking Glass*.

the Government turn out to be undemocratic then don't be surprised and don't cry about it. Remember Lewis Silkin himself in 1946 would not trust democracy when it came to his special pets, the New Towns. The present Government have learnt from this. The Urban Development Corporations are not democratic. The idea of Special Development Orders is not democratic. Today, in the estimation of an increasing number of people, democracy is *not* the golden touchstone that it was.

I turn now to my second "wise saw." Another reason for the Government's determination for local government change is that, under the present administration, there is evidence of a new political philosophy. The Government are out of sympathy with the performance of the public sector—it is regarded as expensive and inefficient. They are determined to subjugate it to the more thrusting, speedier, profit-motivated functioning of the private sector. Undoubtedly, under the new systems in the metropolitan areas the public sector will have to come to terms with the private sector and learn to work with it. I am sure that this is the Government's determination. And if this means a further deepening of the twilight of democracy in local government, so be it!

So, I say to you again, avoid sterile debate about how wicked all these new suggestions are. Remember Lord Thorneycroft's comment in the Lords last June: "Almost all local government reform ends in disaster." Nevertheless, it behoves us all to adopt a constructive stance—to try to make the new set-up work to the best of its possibilities and potential.

My third "wise saw" I make in the context of Mr. Kenneth Blessley's[3] comment in his paper at this Conference to the effect that the Government are being too hasty and that this is the time for a new Royal Commission. To this I say, "Look what happened to Redcliffe-Maud and *his* Royal Commission Report of 1968!" *He* never favoured two-tier, split-level local government. He may have wanted a bigger Manchester (too big some said) but he kept it as an all-purpose authority. It had only one head—the Lord Mayor of Manchester. Today, that personage, constitutionally, is simply the Chairman of a District Council with the Greater Manchester Metropolitan County Council breathing down his neck. In short, the living, beating heart of Mancunium has been broken.

Whilst on the subject of Royal Commissions, we also ought not to forget what happened to the Edwin Herbert Royal Commission which reported on London local government in 1960. The Commission

[3] Kenneth Blessley, C.B.E., M.A., F.R.I.C.S., Valuer and Estate Surveyor for the Greater London Council 1964–1977.

recommended that the cut and thrust of local government in Greater London was to be at the borough level—that is why today's London Boroughs are so much bigger than the London Metropolitan Boroughs they replaced—and *not* at county level. But this is not what has occurred. Neither the Redcliffe-Maud nor the Edwin Herbert Royal Commissions fructified as their respective chairmen fondly hoped. Alas, then, for the fate of Royal Commissions!

II

The second part of my address to you this evening is concerned with the history of local government, or how on earth did we get where we are today? I invite you to consider the matter from an historical point of view because a man without a sense of history is in terrible danger of repeating all the mistakes of yesteryear.

If I start at the beginning of the local government story I shall say that, in the beginning, there were the Chartered Boroughs such as Lyme Regis (now 700 years old since its incorporation by charter in 1284) and Barnstaple (with its twelfth century Charter). Leeds received its first charter in 1527 and Liverpool about 300 years ago. By contrast, Manchester was not incorporated until about 1845. All of that is "in the beginning" but, before the beginning began, there was that unique body known as the Corporation of London—a Corporation by prescription, for no-one knows how or when it began!

Outside the Boroughs, that is to say in the geographical counties, there was also a form of local government but here it was discharged by nominated Justices of the Peace established some 500 years ago by Edward III.

There was a pronounced cleavage between Borough local government and County local government. Neither was wholly democratic. Indeed, County local government was wholly undemocratic because the Justices of the Peace were Royal Appointments. The result of all this was the reform of *Borough* local government in 1835 and the reform of *County* local government in 1888. It all had to become more democratic. Why? Because the Bastille fell in 1789. Liberalism, egalitarianism and rationalism all burst out of that infamous Pandora's Box which was the Bastille. Soon thereafter Lord Byron would be dying at Missalonghi demanding democracy for "the Isles of Greece, the Isles of Greece where burning Sappho loved and sang." The day of the common man was drawing nigh. Democracy was to be the touchstone on which all things were to turn.

Parliament went democratic in 1832 when the Reform Bill was passed. The Boroughs went democratic in 1835. The Counties went democratic in 1888 whilst the 29 Metropolitan Boroughs of London (which were not established in 1888) did not need to *go* democratic—they were democratic from their start in 1899.

It is worthwhile digressing for a moment to consider why the metropolitan boroughs were set up at all. Again, we observe the jealous push and pull between central and local government; the metropolitan boroughs were created to fragment the LCC which was thought to be getting too powerful. The population of the LCC area was then some three millions. But the financial resources of the metropolitan boroughs were too small—their rateable value (except for Westminster, Kensington & Chelsea) was such as *not* to allow them to do anything of note. It was against this background that the Herbert Royal Commission in 1959 blew up the LCC population to some eight millions in an area to be called "Greater London" and then divided that enlarged area into 31 London Boroughs plus the City of London. But Sir Edwin Herbert wanted the cut and thrust of local government, as I have said, to be with the Boroughs and not with the top tier authority which came to be known as the "Greater London Council" when the expression "Council for Greater London" would have been more strictly correct. ("What's in a name?"—Answer: absolutely everything!)

It is worth recalling that in 1888 the Counties did not do as well as they hoped. The Local Government Act 1888 introduced *County* local government but it also introduced *County-Borough* local government. The Bill for the Act provided only for some 21 county boroughs—but the succeeding *Act* contained 83. A county borough, it will be recalled, was an all-purpose local government authority. It did everything. Every new County Borough diminished the powers of the County. The Counties also had to put up with split level local government—the two-tier system—the upper tier comprising the County Council and the lower tier comprising the Noncounty Borough Councils, the Urban District Councils and the Rural District Councils, all of which were known collectively as County District Councils.

The battle was thus joined between County local government and County Borough local government. It was a battle which was to rage with increasing vehemence over the years, and ultimately to cause the setting up of the Redcliffe-Maud Royal Commission in 1966. Redcliffe-Maud sought to preserve the idea of the unitary, all-purpose authority—the expanded County Borough. The government of the day (Labour) took a portion of his recommendations but, before any legislation could be enacted, there was a general election, a Conservative Government took office and wrought havoc with the Royal Commission's proposals. The result was the hotch-potch of local government reform known as the Local Government Act 1972. The

County Councils, after 84 years of bickering won the day. The all-purpose, unitary body—the County Borough—completely disappeared and the proud and independent cities of Manchester, Liverpool, Bristol, Birmingham, Kingston-upon-Hull, Cardiff, Plymouth *et al* all ceased in 1974 (on All-Fool's Day) to exist as independent, all-purpose, unitary local government authorities. There was split level—two-tier Local Government throughout the entire land. This was completely contrary to Redcliffe-Maud's proposals. The end result was mind-blowing in its gratuitous complexity. The world has seen nothing like it since the convoluted, intertwined, bureaucratic excesses of the Ottoman Empire at the zenith of its suffocating power! It was a mess of the first water. It has brought us to the point at which we are today and where this Conference begins. It has produced "The Metropolitan Problem" which you, this weekend, are to discuss and (maybe) to solve.

III

I come now to the third part of my address. I have made much reference to local government in London but the principles applicable in London apply also to all the Metropolitan Counties—Greater Manchester, Merseyside, South Yorkshire, Tyne and Wear, West Midlands and West Yorkshire. In London it appears that more power is to be given to the London Boroughs. In the Metropolitan Counties more power is to be given to the Metropolitan Districts. In each case residual powers (and I think these may well relate to, and only to, main roads, drainage and sewerage, public transport, refuse disposal and the fire service) may come to be dealt with by *ad hoc bodies* appointed by the Government for their professional expertise. There will be nothing democratic about them and, as to this, many (and they are an increasing number) will say, "and no bad thing." I repeat, we are about to witness yet a further darkening of the stage in the on-going, agonising saga of the twilight of local government democracy.

And where in all of this stands the matter of planning control and land development? This is, as yet, by no means clear. Apparently in London and in the Metropolitan Counties there are to be some totally new-style development plans. Mr. Chairman, *stand clear*—the *unitary* development plan is a-coming in! Can you believe it? Would I really be wrong if I said that we are on our way back to the old-style development plan blotted out in 1968 by the two-tier development plan system involving a structure plan and a local plan? The pendulum never stops swinging; it seems now to be poised for a swing back to 1968 and before.

One thing is clear—the planning set-up in the Shire Counties will remain as it is today—*at least for the time being*. Mr. Konrad Schiemann[4] touches on this in his paper. The planning set-up in the Metropolitan Counties will be greatly changed.

The Metropolitan District Councils will make one-piece (*i.e.* unitary) development plans and they will also (as now) grant planning permission for development. Variety is the spice of life, but I do not think that Whitehall will like this sort of thing when they see what will happen. The 1972 planning control system was certainly not properly thought through to its logical conclusions. For example, do you realise that, in addition to the Greater London Development Plan (or structure plan) made by the GLC, each London Borough (all 31 of them) also had to make separate structure plans (as well as local plans) for their respective areas? Well, after the long running saga of the GLDP Inquiry all this was hurriedly swept away by the Town and Country Planning (Amendment) Act 1972.

I wish to conclude by referring again to this questionable matter of whether democracy really has any further or useful part to play in resolving today's town planning problems. Clearly the Government doubts this and can one blame them when one reflects on the current state of bad feeling (quite widespread) between *appointed* planning officers (the experts) and *elected* planning councillors (the amateurs)? I am not going into detail on this. I gave it a good run for its money in an address last November to the RTPI. I shall just say two things. First, that local government politicians (the councillors) are today terribly wishful to retain their seats. Some have made their local government duties a total way of life for which they are now ready (maybe even eager) to receive not only compensation for loss of working hours elsewhere but also a payment—a salary—for carrying out local government duties. This is ridiculous. Ratepayers are not going to stand for it. But it makes today's councillor over-keen to keep his seat and therefore over-prone to avoid unpopular decisions whatever the professional and technical advice may be. (Ask your planning officer friends about this!). Again and again the local planning authority refuses planning permission for development on the basis that the applicant can always appeal.

Secondly, today the current democratic set-up for planning control leads to decisions taken on party-political lines and again this is so whatever the professional and technical advice may be.

So, in view of all this the Government have, in effect, said "Our patience is exhausted—a plague on all your houses—away with you

[4] Konrad Schiemann, Q.C., M.A., LL.B., a member of the Parliamentary Bar; now Mr. Justice Schiemann.

and, forward, the *ad hoc* body full of special knowledge and dispassionate professional expertise and judgment."

Is the Government right? You will have to consider all this, but I warn you that, at the moment, local government democracy is in disgrace (just about) in many places. Is a democratic system the right one for solving the planning problems of the metropolitan areas? Never forget that the totality of planning control is to be found in the metropolitan areas—not in the broad, rolling acres of the shire counties. Eighty per cent. of planning problems touch the centres of Manchester, Liverpool, Birmingham and London. Local government did nothing for 40 years for the ruined London Docks, set on fire 40 years ago precisely last Friday night. (Some of us "remember it well.") Five local government authorities had a finger in the pie. Go and see what an undemocratic, appointed, *ad hoc* Board has now done in five years. This is what is impressing the Government today. Is this wrong? What do you think? Maybe there should be *ad hoc* regional boards for true regional planning—special boards for special areas. Well, why not?

If I may quote him again, Mr. Holland says in his paper,

> "The Metropolitan problem is that of adapting to change . . . we no longer require 90,000 hours of working input from the average life time of those wanting work. Failure to deal with this by directly reducing individual working lifetimes is today concentrating unemployment in the young. Technological change is concentrating unemployment on the less skilled."

These are deep, complex problems and it is indeed the function of true regional planning control of development to apply its mind to them. But I ask you: Can this be done—at least to any sound purpose and effect—when the authority that is charged with doing it is a democratically elected bunch of local government councillors—the monstrous regiment of amateurs, however worthy and sincerely dedicated they may be?

Mr. Blessley, after 13 years with the GLC (and still alive) declares in his paper,

> "So for all these reasons I believe the case has been made out for a metropolitan planning authority for Greater London with statutory powers possibly working within the framework of a strengthened Regional Planning Conference."

I agree with all that (and for Manchester too!) but I pose the question as to whether the metropolitan authority *need* be an elected body—a democratic body. Has not the time come to make it an appointed body like the Urban Development Corporations?

This brings us back to the matter of where local government stands today. My observation on this is that I hope that one day local government will be rescued from the miserable mess which party politics over the last 30 years have made of it. Its depoliticisation is, indeed, "a consummation devoutly to be wished" but today it is a long way off and it cannot get nearer so long as we have with us the type of post-war local government politician (born 1945–50 and still growing strong) who is totally involved with party political dogma emanating from the central office of his party and who uses his town council (or his county council) as a stepping stone to Westminster. With him the variegated needs of local government—borne of the variegated circumstances of infinitely differing *local* needs—with him all such needs are lost under a welter of political ideology.

Very well, if I am right in this assessment of where local democracy stands today then we shall have to decide where democratic participation in these deep and intricate planning matters has to stop. I believe the time has come when serious consideration should be given to the question of whether, within the metropolitan counties (and maybe beyond them if we are going to talk about regional planning control), the time has come to consider whether in these areas the planning authority should continue to be composed *solely* of councillors elected on a party political ticket. At least, should there not be some places for "outsiders" having special knowledge but who have no wish to run for election?

Think on these things; the ball is at your feet. Now is the chance to come forward with some good, solid suggestions—and do not be afraid to be undemocratic! The planning and local government situation is in a state of flux. Mr. Yeats, the Irishman, put the Metropolitan Problem better than he knew:

"Things fall apart; the centre cannot hold;
Mere anarchy is loosed upon the world,
The blood-dimmed tide is loosed, and everywhere
The ceremony of innocence is drowned;
The best lack of all conviction, while the worst
Are full of passionate intensity."

I now leave you in peace, or in blazing indignation, as the case may be and as your outraged conscience may dictate. Thank you all.

INDEX